ACCA

P4 ADVANCED FINANCIAL MANAGEMENT

REVISION QUESTION BANK

For Examinations from September 2017 to June 2018

BECKER

PROFESSIONAL EDUCATION®

Acknowledgement

Past ACCA examination questions are the copyright of the Association of Chartered Certified Accountants and have been reproduced by kind permission.

CONTENTS

Question	Name	Page	Answer	Marks
	Tables and formulae			

The current exam format is a 50 mark case study question and a choice of two from three 25 mark questions as shown by the Exams from June 2013 included in this question bank. Questions with different marks are provided for additional syllabus coverage.

ROLE OF FINANCIAL STRATEGY

COST OF CAPITAL, PORTFOLIO THEORY AND CAPM

INVESTMENT APPRAISAL

BUSINESS VALUATION

MERGERS AND ACQUISITIONS

---

[1] Since the introduction of four exam sessions a year ACCA now publishes a sample of questions from the September and December and March and June examinations.

Formulae

Modigliani and Miller Proposition 2 (with tax)

$$k_e = k_e^i + (1 - T)(k_e^i - k_d)\frac{V_d}{V_e}$$

The Capital Asset Pricing Model

$$E(r_i) = R_f + \beta_i[E(r_m) - R_f]$$

The asset beta formula

$$\beta_a = \left[\frac{V_e}{(V_e + V_d(1 - T))}\beta_e\right] + \left[\frac{V_d(1 - T)}{(V_e + V_d(1 - T))}\beta_d\right]$$

The Growth Model

$$P_O = \frac{D_O(1 + g)}{(r_e - g)}$$

Gordon's growth approximation

$$g = br_e$$

The weighted average cost of capital

$$WACC = \left[\frac{V_e}{V_e + V_d}\right]k_e + \left[\frac{V_d}{V_e + V_d}\right]k_d(1 - T)$$

The Fisher formula

$$(1 + i) = (1 + r)(1 + h)$$

Purchasing power parity and interest rate parity

$$S_1 = S_0 \times \frac{(1 + h_c)}{(1 + h_b)} \qquad F_0 = S_0 \times \frac{(1 + i_c)}{(1 + i_b)}$$

Modified Internal Rate of Return

$$\text{MIRR} = \left[\frac{PV_R}{PV_I}\right]^{\frac{1}{n}} (1 + r_e) - 1$$

The Black-Scholes option pricing model

$$c = P_a N(d_1) - P_e N(d_2) e^{-rt}$$

Where:

$$d_1 = \frac{\ln(P_a/P_e) + (r + 0.5s^2)t}{s\sqrt{t}}$$

$$d_2 = d_1 - s\sqrt{t}$$

The Put Call Parity relationship

$$p = c - P_a + P_e e^{-rt}$$

Present value table

Present value of 1 i.e. $(1 + r)^{-n}$

where   r = discount rate

        n = number of periods until payment

Discount rate (r)

Periods (n)	1%	2%	3%	4%	5%	6%	7%	8%	9%	10%	
1	0.990	0.980	0.971	0.962	0.952	0.943	0.935	0.926	0.917	0.909	1
2	0.980	0.961	0.943	0.925	0.907	0.890	0.873	0.857	0.842	0.826	2
3	0.971	0.942	0.915	0.889	0.864	0.840	0.816	0.794	0.772	0.751	3
4	0.961	0.924	0.888	0.855	0.823	0.792	0.763	0.735	0.708	0.683	4
5	0.951	0.906	0.863	0.822	0.784	0.747	0.713	0.681	0.650	0.621	5
6	0.942	0.888	0.837	0.790	0.746	0.705	0.666	0.630	0.596	0.564	6
7	0.933	0.871	0.813	0.760	0.711	0.665	0.623	0.583	0.547	0.513	7
8	0.923	0.853	0.789	0.731	0.677	0.627	0.582	0.540	0.502	0.467	8
9	0.914	0.837	0.766	0.703	0.645	0.592	0.544	0.500	0.460	0.424	9
10	0.905	0.820	0.744	0.676	0.614	0.558	0.508	0.463	0.422	0.386	10
11	0.896	0.804	0.722	0.650	0.585	0.527	0.475	0.429	0.388	0.350	11
12	0.887	0.788	0.701	0.625	0.557	0.497	0.444	0.397	0.356	0.319	12
13	0.879	0.773	0.681	0.601	0.530	0.469	0.415	0.368	0.326	0.290	13
14	0.870	0.758	0.661	0.577	0.505	0.442	0.388	0.340	0.299	0.263	14
15	0.861	0.743	0.642	0.555	0.481	0.417	0.362	0.315	0.275	0.239	15

(n)	11%	12%	13%	14%	15%	16%	17%	18%	19%	20%	
1	0.901	0.893	0.885	0.877	0.870	0.862	0.855	0.847	0.840	0.833	1
2	0.812	0.797	0.783	0.769	0.756	0.743	0.731	0.718	0.706	0.694	2
3	0.731	0.712	0.693	0.675	0.658	0.641	0.624	0.609	0.593	0.579	3
4	0.659	0.636	0.613	0.592	0.572	0.552	0.534	0.516	0.499	0.482	4
5	0.593	0.567	0.543	0.519	0.497	0.476	0.456	0.437	0.419	0.402	5
6	0.535	0.507	0.480	0.456	0.432	0.410	0.390	0.370	0.352	0.335	6
7	0.482	0.452	0.425	0.400	0.376	0.354	0.333	0.314	0.296	0.279	7
8	0.434	0.404	0.376	0.351	0.327	0.305	0.285	0.266	0.249	0.233	8
9	0.391	0.361	0.333	0.308	0.284	0.263	0.243	0.225	0.209	0.194	9
10	0.352	0.322	0.295	0.270	0.247	0.227	0.208	0.191	0.176	0.162	10
11	0.317	0.287	0.261	0.237	0.215	0.195	0.178	0.162	0.148	0.135	11
12	0.286	0.257	0.231	0.208	0.187	0.168	0.152	0.137	0.124	0.112	12
13	0.258	0.229	0.204	0.182	0.163	0.145	0.130	0.116	0.104	0.093	13
14	0.232	0.205	0.181	0.160	0.141	0.125	0.111	0.099	0.088	0.078	14
15	0.209	0.183	0.160	0.140	0.123	0.108	0.095	0.084	0.074	0.065	15

Annuity table

Present value of an annuity of 1 i.e. $\dfrac{1 - (1 + r)^{-n}}{r}$

where   r = discount rate
          n = number of periods

Discount rate (r)

Periods (n)	1%	2%	3%	4%	5%	6%	7%	8%	9%	10%	
1	0.990	0.980	0.971	0.962	0.952	0.943	0.935	0.926	0.917	0.909	1
2	1.970	1.942	1.913	1.886	1.859	1.833	1.808	1.783	1.759	1.736	2
3	2.941	2.884	2.829	2.775	2.723	2.673	2.624	2.577	2.531	2.487	3
4	3.902	3.808	3.717	3.630	3.546	3.465	3.387	3.312	3.240	3.170	4
5	4.853	4.713	4.580	4.452	4.329	4.212	4.100	3.993	3.890	3.791	5
6	5.795	5.601	5.417	5.242	5.076	4.917	4.767	4.623	4.486	4.355	6
7	6.728	6.472	6.230	6.002	5.786	5.582	5.389	5.206	5.033	4.868	7
8	7.652	7.325	7.020	6.733	6.463	6.210	5.971	5.747	5.535	5.335	8
9	8.566	8.162	7.786	7.435	7.108	6.802	6.515	6.247	5.995	5.759	9
10	9.471	8.983	8.530	8.111	7.722	7.360	7.024	6.710	6.418	6.145	10
11	10.37	9.787	9.253	8.760	8.306	7.887	7.499	7.139	6.805	6.495	11
12	11.26	10.58	9.954	9.385	8.863	8.384	7.943	7.536	7.161	6.814	12
13	12.13	11.35	10.63	9.986	9.394	8.853	8.358	7.904	7.487	7.103	13
14	13.00	12.11	11.30	10.56	9.899	9.295	8.745	8.244	7.786	7.367	14
15	13.87	12.85	11.94	11.12	10.38	9.712	9.108	8.559	8.061	7.606	15

(n)	11%	12%	13%	14%	15%	16%	17%	18%	19%	20%	
1	0.901	0.893	0.885	0.877	0.870	0.862	0.855	0.847	0.840	0.833	1
2	1.713	1.690	1.668	1.647	1.626	1.605	1.585	1.566	1.547	1.528	2
3	2.444	2.402	2.361	2.322	2.283	2.246	2.210	2.174	2.140	2.106	3
4	3.102	3.037	2.974	2.914	2.855	2.798	2.743	2.690	2.639	2.589	4
5	3.696	3.605	3.517	3.433	3.352	3.274	3.199	3.127	3.058	2.991	5
6	4.231	4.111	3.998	3.889	3.784	3.685	3.589	3.498	3.410	3.326	6
7	4.712	4.564	4.423	4.288	4.160	4.039	3.922	3.812	3.706	3.605	7
8	5.146	4.968	4.799	4.639	4.487	4.344	4.207	4.078	3.954	3.837	8
9	5.537	5.328	5.132	4.946	4.772	4.607	4.451	4.303	4.163	4.031	9
10	5.889	5.650	5.426	5.216	5.019	4.833	4.659	4.494	4.339	4.192	10
11	6.207	5.938	5.687	5.453	5.234	5.029	4.836	4.656	4.586	4.327	11
12	6.492	6.194	5.918	5.660	5.421	5.197	4.988	4.793	4.611	4.439	12
13	6.750	6.424	6.122	5.842	5.583	5.342	5.118	4.910	4.715	4.533	13
14	6.982	6.628	6.302	6.002	5.724	5.468	5.229	5.008	4.802	4.611	14
15	7.191	6.811	6.462	6.142	5.847	5.575	5.324	5.092	4.876	4.675	15

Standard normal distribution table

	0·00	0·01	0·02	0·03	0·04	0·05	0·06	0·07	0·08	0·09
0·0	0·0000	0·0040	0·0080	0·0120	0·0160	0·0199	0·0239	0·0279	0·0319	0·0359
0·1	0·0398	0·0438	0·0478	0·0517	0·0557	0·0596	0·0636	0·0675	0·0714	0·0753
0·2	0·0793	0·0832	0·0871	0·0910	0·0948	0·0987	0·1026	0·1064	0·1103	0·1141
0·3	0·1179	0·1217	0·1255	0·1293	0·1331	0·1368	0·1406	0·1443	0·1480	0·1517
0·4	0·1554	0·1591	0·1628	0·1664	0·1700	0·1736	0·1772	0·1808	0·1844	0·1879
0·5	0·1915	0·1950	0·1985	0·2019	0·2054	0·2088	0·2123	0·2157	0·2190	0·2224
0·6	0·2257	0·2291	0·2324	0·2357	0·2389	0·2422	0·2454	0·2486	0·2517	0·2549
0·7	0·2580	0·2611	0·2642	0·2673	0·2703	0·2734	0·2764	0·2794	0·2823	0·2852
0·8	0·2881	0·2910	0·2939	0·2967	0·2995	0·3023	0·3051	0·3078	0·3106	0·3133
0·9	0·3159	0·3186	0·3212	0·3238	0·3264	0·3289	0·3315	0·3340	0·3365	0·3389
1·0	0·3413	0·3438	0·3461	0·3485	0·3508	0·3531	0·3554	0·3577	0·3599	0·3621
1·1	0·3643	0·3665	0·3686	0·3708	0·3729	0·3749	0·3770	0·3790	0·3810	0·3830
1·2	0·3849	0·3869	0·3888	0·3907	0·3925	0·3944	0·3962	0·3980	0·3997	0·4015
1·3	0·4032	0·4049	0·4066	0·4082	0·4099	0·4115	0·4131	0·4147	0·4162	0·4177
1·4	0·4192	0·4207	0·4222	0·4236	0·4251	0·4265	0·4279	0·4292	0·4306	0·4319
1·5	0·4332	0·4345	0·4357	0·4370	0·4382	0·4394	0·4406	0·4418	0·4429	0·4441
1·6	0·4452	0·4463	0·4474	0·4484	0·4495	0·4505	0·4515	0·4525	0·4535	0·4545
1·7	0·4554	0·4564	0·4573	0·4582	0·4591	0·4599	0·4608	0·4616	0·4625	0·4633
1·8	0·4641	0·4649	0·4656	0·4664	0·4671	0·4678	0·4686	0·4693	0·4699	0·4706
1·9	0·4713	0·4719	0·4726	0·4732	0·4738	0·4744	0·4750	0·4756	0·4761	0·4767
2·0	0·4772	0·4778	0·4783	0·4788	0·4793	0·4798	0·4803	0·4808	0·4812	0·4817
2·1	0·4821	0·4826	0·4830	0·4834	0·4838	0·4842	0·4846	0·4850	0·4854	0·4857
2·2	0·4861	0·4864	0·4868	0·4871	0·4875	0·4878	0·4881	0·4884	0·4887	0·4890
2·3	0·4893	0·4896	0·4898	0·4901	0·4904	0·4906	0·4909	0·4911	0·4913	0·4916
2·4	0·4918	0·4920	0·4922	0·4925	0·4927	0·4929	0·4931	0·4932	0·4934	0·4936
2·5	0·4938	0·4940	0·4941	0·4943	0·4945	0·4946	0·4948	0·4949	0·4951	0·4952
2·6	0·4953	0·4955	0·4956	0·4957	0·4959	0·4960	0·4961	0·4962	0·4963	0·4964
2·7	0·4965	0·4966	0·4967	0·4968	0·4969	0·4970	0·4971	0·4972	0·4973	0·4974
2·8	0·4974	0·4975	0·4976	0·4977	0·4977	0·4978	0·4979	0·4979	0·4980	0·4981
2·9	0·4981	0·4982	0·4982	0·4983	0·4984	0·4984	0·4985	0·4985	0·4986	0·4986
3·0	0·4987	0·4987	0·4987	0·4988	0·4988	0·4989	0·4989	0·4989	0·4990	0·4990

This table can be used to calculate N(d), the cumulative normal distribution functions needed for the Black-Scholes model of option pricing. If $d_i > 0$, add 0·5 to the relevant number above. If $d_i < 0$, subtract the relevant number above from 0·5.

Question 1 MUCKY MINING CO

Mucky Mining Co is a minerals exploration, development and production company that operates globally and is listed on the London Stock Exchange.

The company is highly successful with a strong statement of financial position, consistently positive cash flow and profitability and production sustainability from its ever increasing minerals reserves.

Mucky Mining recently won the Monetary Times "transparency" award for its financial statements for the most recent year.

Chairman Connie Flikt described this award as "a great honour and a mark of our objectivity and integrity in financial reporting evidenced by our informative and relevant reporting".

On the same day as winning the transparency award a newspaper report in The Daily Moon newspaper ran with the headline "Kids dig gold for pennies" in which it set out use and abuse of children in appalling working conditions in a mine owned by Mucky Mining.

In an interview with an independent TV news channel Connie Flikt is asked to comment on the Daily Moon report and on an article in the magazine "Green is Good" that criticises the company's mining operations that are scarring the landscape and its careless disregard for reinstatement and decommissioning. Connie makes a brief statement "Mucky Mining is committed to high standards in its employment policies and supports environmental improvement and all stakeholders can rest assured that our business is sustainable and successful and a major contributor to economic, social and environmental improvement that delivers long term growth and return for our shareholders".

Required:

(a)   **Explain and assess the concept of sustainability in the conduct of business and ethical behaviour referring to the scenario as necessary.**   (10 marks)

(b)   **Explain what is meant by a stakeholder, contrasting the responsibilities of listed companies towards stakeholders and shareholders.**   (5 marks)

(c)   **Discuss the importance and limitations of ESOPs (executive share option plans) to the achievement of goal congruence within an organisation.**   (5 marks)

(d)   **Provide examples of covenants that might be attached to bonds, and briefly discuss the advantages and disadvantages to companies of covenants.**   (5 marks)

(25 marks)

Question 2 VADENER CO

Vadener, a UK-based company, has instigated a review of the group's recent performance and potential future strategy. The Board of directors has publicly stated that it is pleased with the group's performance and proposes to devote resources equally to its three operating divisions. Two of the divisions are in the UK, and focus on construction and leisure respectively, and one is in the US and manufactures pharmaceuticals.

Recent summarised accounts for the group and data for the individual divisions are shown below:

	Group data £ million		
Statements of profit or loss	*20X3*	*20X4*	*20X5*
Revenue	1,210	1,410	1,490
Operating costs	800	870	930
Operating profit	410	540	560
Net interest	40	56	65
Profit before tax	370	484	495
Tax (30%)	111	145	149
Profit after tax	259	339	346
Equity dividends	146	170	185
Retained earnings	113	169	161

Statements of financial position			
Non-current assets:			
Tangible assets	1,223	1,280	1,410
Intangible assets	100	250	250
Current assets:			
Inventory	340	410	490
Receivables	378	438	510
Cash	10	15	15
Total assets	2,051	2,393	2,675
Equity and liabilities			
Shareholders' equity	1,086	1,255	1,406
Long term liabilities	400	410	470
	1,486	1,665	1,876
Current liabilities:			
Payables	302	401	430
Short term loans	135	170	201
Taxation	55	72	75
Dividends	73	85	93
	565	728	799
Total equity and liabilities	2,051	2,393	2,675

Note:

The 20X5 amount for shareholders' equity includes a £10 million loss on translation from the US division due to the recent weakness of the $US.

Other group data at year end:	*20X3*	*20X4*	*20X5*
Share price	£12.20	£14.17	£15.42
Number of issued shares (million)	300	300	300
Equity beta			1·10

The company's share price has increased by an average of 12% per year over the last five years.

Other data at year end:	20X3	20X4	20X5
FT 100 index	3,700	4,600	4,960
PE ratio of similar companies	15:1	14:1	15:1
Risk free rate (%)			5
Market return (%)			12

Divisional data 20X5	Construction	Leisure	Pharmaceuticals
Revenue (£m)	480	560	450
Operating profit	160	220	180
Estimated after tax return (%)	13	16	14

Data for the sector:	Construction	Leisure	Pharmaceuticals
Average asset beta	0·75	1·10	1·40

Required:

Prepare a report for the Board of Directors of Vadener Co that

(a) **Evaluate and comment on the performance of Vadener Co and each of its divisions. Highlight performance that appears favourable, and any areas of potential concern for the managers of Vadener. Comment upon the likely validity of the company's strategy to devote resources equally to the operating divisions.**

All relevant calculations must be shown. Approximately 20 marks are available for calculations and 10 marks for discussion. (30 marks)

(b) **Discuss what additional information would be useful in order to more accurately assess the performance of Vadener Co and its divisions.** (8 marks)

(c) **Discuss the possible implications for Vadener Co of the £10 million loss on translation, and recommend what action, if any, the company should take as a result of this loss.** (8 marks)

Professional marks for format, structure and presentation of the report. (4 marks)

(50 marks)

Question 3 PHARMACEUTICAL COMPANY

You have been appointed as deputy Chief Financial Officer to a large multinational pharmaceutical company with trading interests in 24 countries in sub-Saharan Africa, South America and the Indian sub-continent. Your company also has important trading links with the United States, Malaysia and Singapore. There have been a number of issues arising in the previous six months which have impacted upon the company's business interests.

(i) Following an investigation you discover that commissions were paid to a senior official in one country to ensure that the local drug licensing agency concerned facilitated the acceptance of one of your principal revenue earning drugs for use within its national health service.

(ii) You have discovered that an agent of your firm, aware that the licensing agreement might be forthcoming, purchased several call option contracts on your company's equity.

(iii)   A senior member of the firm's treasury team has been taking substantial positions in currency futures in order to protect the risk of loss on the translation of dollar assets into the domestic currency. Over the last 12 months significant profits have been made but the trades do not appear to have been properly authorised. You discover that a long position in 50, $250,000 contracts is currently held but over the last four weeks the dollar has depreciated by 10% and all the signs are that it will depreciate considerably more over the next two months.

(iv)   One drug company has managed to copy a novel drug that you have just released for the treatment of various forms of skin cancer. You have patent protection in the country concerned but your company has not been able to initiate proceedings through the local courts. Contacts with the trade officials at your embassy in the country concerned suggest that the government has made sure that the proceedings have not been allowed to proceed.

The company's chief financial officer has asked you to look into these issues and, with respect to (iv), any World Trade Organisation (WTO) agreements that might be relevant, and to advise her on how the company should proceed in each case.

Required:

Prepare a memorandum advising the chief financial officer on the issues involved and recommending how she should, in each case and in the circumstances, proceed.

(25 marks)

Question 4 MEZZA CO

Mezza Co is a large food manufacturing and wholesale company. It imports fruit and vegetables from countries in South America, Africa and Asia, and packages them in steel cans, plastic tubs and as frozen foods, for sale to supermarkets around Europe. Its suppliers range from individual farmers to Government run cooperatives, and farms run by its own subsidiary companies. In the past, Mezza Co has been very successful in its activities, and has an excellent corporate image with its customers, suppliers and employees. Indeed Mezza Co prides itself on how it has supported local farming communities around the world and has consistently highlighted these activities in its annual reports.

However, in spite of buoyant stock markets over the last couple of years, Mezza Co's share price has remained static. It is thought that this is because there is little scope for future growth in its products. As a result the company's directors are considering diversifying into new areas. One possibility is to commercialise a product developed by a recently acquired subsidiary company. The subsidiary company is engaged in researching solutions to carbon emissions and global warming, and has developed a high carbon absorbing variety of plant that can be grown in warm, shallow sea water. The plant would then be harvested into carbon-neutral bio-fuel. This fuel, if widely used, is expected to lower carbon production levels.

Currently there is a lot of interest among the world's governments in finding solutions to climate change. Mezza Co's directors feel that this venture could enhance its reputation and result in a rise in its share price. They believe that the company's expertise would be ideally suited to commercialising the product. On a personal level, they feel that the venture's success would enhance their generous remuneration package which includes share options. It is hoped that the resulting increase in the share price would enable the options to be exercised in the future.

Mezza Co has identified the coast of Maienar, a small country in Asia, as an ideal location, as it has a large area of warm, shallow waters. Mezza Co has been operating in Maienar for many years and as a result, has a well-developed infrastructure to enable it to plant, monitor and harvest the crop. Mezza Co's directors have strong ties with senior government officials in Maienar and the country's politicians are keen to develop new industries, especially ones with a long-term future.

The area identified by Mezza Co is a rich fishing ground for local fishermen, who have been fishing there for many generations. However, the fishermen are poor and have little political influence. The general perception is that the fishermen contribute little to Maienar's economic development. The coastal area, although naturally beautiful, has not been well developed for tourism. It is thought that the high carbon absorbing plant, if grown on a commercial scale, may have a negative impact on fish stocks and other wildlife in the area. The resulting decline in fish stocks may make it impossible for the fishermen to continue with their traditional way of life.

Required:

Discuss the key issues that the directors of Mezza Co should consider when making the decision about whether or not to commercialise the new product, and suggest how these issues may be mitigated or resolved.

(25 marks)

Question 5   NETRA CO

The finance director of Netra Co wishes to estimate what impact the introduction of debt finance is likely to have on the company's overall cost of capital. The company is currently financed only by equity.

Netra – Summarised capital structure

	$000
Ordinary shares ($0.25 per share)	500
Reserves	1,100
	1,600

The company's current share price is $4.20, and up to $4 million of fixed rate five-year debt could be raised at an interest rate of 10% per year. The corporate tax rate is 33%.

Netra's current earnings before interest and tax are $2.5 million. These earnings are not expected to change significantly for the foreseeable future.

The company is considering raising either:

(i) $2 million in debt finance; or
(ii) $4 million in debt finance

In either case the debt finance will be used to repurchase ordinary shares.

Required:

(a)   **Discuss issues that might influence a company's capital structure strategy.**   (12 marks)

(b)   **Using Modigliani and Miller's model in a world with corporate tax, estimate the impact on Netra's weighted average cost of capital of raising:**

   (i)   **$2 million; and**
   (ii)   **$4 million in debt finance.**

   State clearly any assumptions that you make.   (8 marks)

(c)   **Discuss whether or not the estimates produced in part (b) are likely to be accurate.**

(5 marks)

(25 marks)

Question 6 PENSION FUND

(a)   Assume that it is now 1 December. The financial manager of a large corporate pension fund is concerned about the recent loss in value of the fund due to falling share prices. Although he believes that the equity market is probably near to its low point, and that prices could soon start to rise, there is no certainty of this happening.

To protect the fund's portfolio against possible further falls in share prices he is considering the use of financial futures. The portfolio currently comprises the eight investments below.

Share	Number of shares held	Equity Beta	1 December Price (cents)
MNSD	3,000,000	0·74	110
Ponder	1,000,000	1·15	443
Loyter	2,600,000	0·65	126
Wanlon	800,000	1·32	598
RDT Bank	4,200,000	1·56	76
UMFR	1,700,000	0·82	480
Teleike	900,000	1·11	890
Biller	2,000,000	1·43	267

On 1 December, the March S&P 500 Index futures price is $3,850. The nominal value of an S&P 500 Index contract is $10 per index point (the tick size), which implies a current contract value of $38,500.

Required:

(i)   **Illustrate what hedge should be undertaken to protect the portfolio against possible falls in the share prices.**   **(5 marks)**

Assume that on 31 March, the expiry date of the futures contract, the share prices have moved as shown below, and the S&P 500 Index futures price is $3,625.

(The number of shares held in the portfolio has remained unchanged.)

Share	31 March Price (cents)
MNSD	101
Ponder	420
Loyter	93
Wanlon	520
RDT Bank	81
UMFR	390
Teleike	846
Biller	250

(ii)   **With hindsight, calculate the outcome of the hedge that was illustrated in (i) above. Comment upon your findings.**   **(4 marks)**

(iii)   **Briefly discuss why the financial manager might use stock index futures to alter portfolio risk rather than buy or sell actual shares in the stock market.**
                                                                                  (3 marks)

(iv)   **If the financial manager wished to halve the systematic risk of the portfolio by using long-term interest rate futures, explain (but do not calculate) what hedge he might undertake.**   **(3 marks)**

(b)   You have purchased the following data from a merchant bank.

Company	Forecast total equity return	Covariance with market return
Dedton	16%	32%
Paralot	12%	19%
Sunout	14%	24%
Rangon	18%	43%

The market return and market standard deviation are 14.5% and 5% respectively, and the risk free rate is 6%. Returns and all other data relate to a one-year period.

Required:

(i)   Estimate the "alpha" values for each of these companies' shares and explain what use alpha values might be to financial managers.   (6 marks)

(ii)   Briefly discuss reasons for the existence of alpha values, and whether or not the same alpha values would be expected to exist in one year's time.   (4 marks)

(25 marks)

Question 7 STRAYER CO

The managers of Strayer Co are investigating a potential $25 million investment. The investment would be a diversification away from existing mainstream activities and into the printing industry. $6 million of the investment would be financed by internal funds, $10 million by a rights issue and $9 million by long term loans. The investment is expected to generate pre-tax net cash flows of approximately $5 million per year, for a period of ten years. The residual value at the end of year ten is forecast to be $5 million after tax. As the investment is in an area that the government wishes to develop, a subsidised loan of $4 million out of the total $9 million is available. This will cost 2% below the company's normal cost of long-term debt finance, which is 8%.

Strayer's equity beta is 0·85 and its financial gearing is 60% equity, 40% debt by market value. The average equity beta in the printing industry is 1·2, and average gearing 50% equity, 50% debt by market value. The risk free rate is 5·5% per year and the market return 12% per year.

Issue costs are estimated to be 1% for debt financing (excluding the subsidised loan), and 4% for equity financing. Issue costs are not tax allowable.

The corporate tax rate is 30%.

Required:

(a)   Estimate the Adjusted Present Value (APV) of the proposed investment.   (12 marks)

(b)   Comment upon the circumstances under which APV might be a better method of evaluating a capital investment than Net Present Value (NPV).   (5 marks)

(c)   Discuss why conflicts of interest might exist between a firm's shareholders and bondholders.   (8 marks)

(25 marks)

Question 8 JONAS CHEMICAL SYSTEMS

The board of Jonas Chemical Systems Limited has used payback for many years as an initial selection tool to identify projects for subsequent and more detailed analysis by its financial investment team. The firm's capital projects are characterised by relatively long investment periods and even longer recovery phases. Unfortunately, for a variety of reasons, the cash flows towards the end of each project tend to be very low or indeed sometimes negative. As the company's new chief financial officer (CFO), you are concerned about the use of payback in this context and would favour a more thorough pre-evaluation of each capital investment proposal before it is submitted for detailed planning and approval. You recognise that many board members like the provision of a payback figure as this, they argue, gives them a clear idea as to when the project can be expected to recover its initial capital investment.

All capital projects must be submitted to the board for initial approval before the financial investment team begins its detailed review. At the initial stage the board sees the project's summarised cash flows, a supporting business case and an assessment of the project payback and accounting rate of return.

A recent capital investment proposal, which has passed to the implementation stage after much discussion at board level, had summarised cash flows and other information as follows:

Distillation Plant at the Gulf Refining Centre

	Investment phase		Recovery phase	
	Cash flow (tax adjusted, nominal)	Cumulative cash flow	Cash flow (tax adjusted, nominal)	Cumulative cash flow
	$m	$m	$m	$m
01 January 2018	(9.50)	(9.50)		
31 December 2018	(5.75)	(15.25)		
31 December 2019	(3.00)	(18.25)		
31 December 2020			4.5	(13.75)
31 December 2021			6.40	(7.35)
31 December 2022			7.25	(0.10)
31 December 2023			6.50	6.40
31 December 2024			5.50	11.90
31 December 2025			4.00	15.90
31 December 2026			(2.00)	13.90
31 December 2027			(5.00)	8.90

Cost of capital	8%
Expected net present value ($m)	1.964
Net present value volatility ($m)	1.02
Internal rate of return	11.0%
Payback (years)	5.015

The normal financial rules are that a project should only be considered if it has a payback period of less than five years. In this case the project was passed to detail review by the financial investment team who, on your instruction, have undertaken a financial simulation of the project's net present value to generate the expected value and volatility as shown above. The board minute of the discussion relating to the project's preliminary approval was as follows:

New capital projects – preliminary approvals

Outline consideration was given to the construction of a new distillation facility at the Gulf Refining Centre which is regarded as a key strategic component of the company's manufacturing capability. Mrs Chua (chief financial officer) had given approval for the project to come to the board given its strategic importance and the closeness of the payback estimate to the company's barrier for long term capital investment of five years.

8

Mr Lazar (non-executive director) suggested that they would need more information about the impact of risk upon the project's outcome before giving final approval. Mr Bright (operations director) agreed but asked why the board needed to consider capital proposals twice. The chairman requested the CFO to provide a review of the company's capital approval procedures to include better assessment of the firm's financial exposure. The revised guidelines should include procedures for both the preliminary and final approval stages.

Required:

(a)   **Recommend procedures for the assessment of capital investment projects. You should make proposals about the involvement of the board at a preliminary stage and the information that should be provided to inform their decision. You should also provide an assessment of the alternative appraisal methods.**   (10 marks)

(b)   **Using the appraisal methods you have recommended in (a), prepare the case for the acceptance of the project to build a distillation facility at the Gulf plant with an assessment of the company's likely value at risk. You are not required to undertake an assessment of the impact of the project upon the firm's financial accounts.**   (15 marks)

(25 marks)

Question 9 NEPTUNE

Neptune is a listed company in the telecommunications business. You are a senior financial management advisor employed by the company to review its capital investment appraisal procedures and to provide advice on the acceptability of a significant new capital project – the Galileo.

The project is a domestic project entailing immediate capital expenditure of $800 million at 1 July 20167and with projected revenues over five years as follows:

Year ended 30 June	2018	2019	2020	2021	2022
Revenue ($m)	680·00	900·00	900·00	750·00	320·00

Direct costs are 60% of revenues and indirect, activity based costs are $140 million for the first year of operations, growing at 5% per year over the life of the project. In the first two years of operations, acceptance of this project will mean that other work making a net contribution before indirect costs of $150 million for each of the first two years will not be able to proceed. The capital expenditure of $800 million is to be paid immediately and the equipment will have a residual value after five years' operation of $40 million. The company depreciates plant and equipment on a straight-line basis and, in this case, the annual charge will be allocated to the project as a further indirect charge. Preconstruction design and contracting costs incurred over the previous three years total $50 million and will be charged to the project in the first year of operation.

The company pays tax at 30% on its taxable profits and can claim a 50% first year allowance on qualifying capital expenditure followed by tax-allowable depreciation of 40% applied on a reducing balance basis. Tax is paid one year in arrears. The company has sufficient other profits to absorb any tax-allowable depreciation derived from this project.

The company currently has $7,500 million of equity and $2,500 million of debt in issue quoted at current market values. The current cost of its debt finance is $LIBOR plus 180 basis points. $LIBOR is currently 5·40%, which is 40 basis points above the one month Treasury bill rate. The equity risk premium is 3·5% and the company's beta is 1·40. The company wishes to raise the additional finance for this project by a new bond issue. Its advisors do not believe that this will alter the company's bond rating. The new issue will incur transaction costs of 2% of the issue value at the date of issue.

Required:

(a)   Estimate the adjusted present value of the project and justify the use of this technique.

(18 marks)

(b)   Estimate the modified internal rate of return generated by the project.   (7 marks)

(25 marks)

Question 10 SLOW FASHIONS CO

Slow Fashions Co is considering the following series of investments for the current financial year:

Project bid proposals ($000) for immediate investment.

Project	Now	2018	2019	2020	2021	2022	2023	NPV	IRR
P0801	−620	280	400	120				55	16%
P0802	−640	80	120	200	210	420	−30	69	13%
P0803	−240	120	120	60	10			20	15%
P0804	−1000	300	500	250	290			72	13%
P0805	−120	25	55	75	21			19	17%
P0806	−400	245	250					29	15%

There is no real option to delay any of these projects. All except project P0801 can be scaled down but not scaled up. P0801 is a potential fixed three-year contract to supply a supermarket chain and cannot be varied. The company has a limited capital budget of $1·2 million and is concerned about the best way to allocate its capital to the projects listed. The company has a current cost of finance of 10% but it would take a year to establish further funding at that rate. Further funding for a short period could be arranged at a higher rate.

Required:

(a)   Draft a capital investment plan with full supporting calculations justifying those projects which should be adopted giving:

(i)   the priorities for investment;

(ii)   the net present value and internal rate of return of the plan; and

(iii)   the net present value per dollar invested on the plan.   (17 marks)

(b)   Estimate and advise upon the maximum interest rate which the company should be prepared to pay to finance investment in all of the remaining projects available to it.

(8 marks)

(25 marks)

Question 11 SEAL ISLAND

The Seal Island Nuclear Power Company has received initial planning consent for an Advanced Boiling Water Reactor. This project is one of a number that has been commissioned by the Government of Roseland to help solve the energy needs of its expanding population of 60 million and meet its treaty obligations by cutting CO_2 emissions to 50% of their 2017 levels by 2037.

The project proposal is now moving to the detailed planning stage which will include a full investment appraisal within the financial plan. The financial plan so far developed has been based upon experience of this reactor design in Japan, the US and South Korea.

The core macro-economic assumptions are that Roseland GDP will grow at an annual rate of 4% (nominal) and inflation will be maintained at the 2% target set by the Government.

The construction programme is expected to cost $1 billion over three years, with construction commencing in January 2019. These capital expenditures have been projected, including expected future cost increases, as follows:

Year end	2019	2020	2021
Construction costs ($m)	300	600	100

Generation of electricity will commence in 2022 and the annual operating surplus in cash terms is expected to be $100 million per year (at 1 January 2022 price and cost levels). This value has been well validated by preliminary studies and includes the cost of fuel reprocessing, on-going maintenance and systems replacement as well as the continuing operating costs of running the plant. The operating surplus is expected to rise in line with nominal GDP growth. The plant is expected to have an operating life of 30 years.

Decommissioning costs at the end of the project have been estimated at $600 million at 1 January 2019 prices. Decommissioning costs are expected to rise in line with nominal GDP growth.

The company's nominal cost of capital is 10% per year.

Required:

(i)   **An estimate of the net present value for this project as at the commencement of construction in 2019.**   **(10 marks)**

(ii)   **A discussion of the principal uncertainties associated with this project.**   **(6 marks)**

(iii)   **A sensitivity of the project's net present value (in percentage and in $), to changes in the construction cost, the annual operating surplus and the decommissioning cost. (Assume that the increase in construction costs would be proportional to the initial investment for each year.)**   **(5 marks)**

(iv)   **An explanation of how simulations, such as the Monte Carlo simulation, could be used to assess the volatility of the net present value of this project.**   **(4 marks)**

Note: the formula for an annuity discounted at an annual rate (i) and where cash flows are growing at an annual rate (g) is as follows:

$$A_n = \left[\frac{1 - \left(\frac{1+g}{1+i} \right)^n}{i-g} \right] (1+g)$$

(25 marks)

Question 12 ALLEGRO TECHNOLOGIES

Allegro Technologies Co (ATC), a listed company based in Europe, has been involved in manufacturing motor vehicle parts for many years. Although not involved in the production of complicated engine components previously, ATC recently purchased the patent rights for $2m to produce an innovative energy saving engine component which would cut carbon-based emissions from motor vehicles substantially.

ATC has spent $5m developing prototypes of the component and undertaking investigative research studies. The research studies came to the conclusion that the component will have a significant commercial potential for a period of five years, after which, newer components would come into the market and the sales revenue from this component would fall to virtually nil. The research studies have also found that in the first two years (the development phase) there will be considerable training and development costs and fewer components will be produced and sold. However, sales revenue is expected to grow rapidly in the following three years (the commercial phase).

It is estimated that in the first year, the selling price would be $1,000 per component, the variable costs would be $400 per component and the total direct fixed costs would be $1,500,000. Thereafter, while the selling price is expected to increase by 8% per year, the variable and fixed costs are expected to increase by 5% per year, for the next four years. Training and development costs are expected to be 120% of the variable costs in the first year, 40% in the second year and 10% in each of the following three years.

The estimated average number of engine components produced and sold per year is given in Table 1.

Year	1	2	3	4	5
Units produced and sold	7,500	20,000	50,000	60,000	95,000

There is considerable uncertainty as to the exact quantity that could be produced and sold and the estimated standard deviation of units produced and sold is expected to be as much as 30%.

Machinery costing $120,000,000 will need to be installed prior to commencement of the component production. ATC has enough space in its factory to manufacture the components and therefore will incur no additional rental costs. Tax allowable depreciation is available on the machinery at 10% straight line basis. It can be assumed that, depending on the written down value, a balancing adjustment will be made at the end of the project, when the machinery is expected to be sold for $40,000,000. ATC makes sufficient profits from its other activities to take advantage of any tax loss relief available from this project.

Initially, ATC will require additional working capital for the project of 20% of the first year's sales revenue. Thereafter every $1 increase in sales revenue will require a 10% increase in working capital.

Although this would be a major undertaking for ATC, it is confident that it can raise the finance required for the machinery and the first year's working capital. The financing will be through a mixture of a rights issue and a bank loan, in the same proportion as the market values of its current equity and debt capital. Any annual increase in working capital after the first year will be financed by internally generated funds.

Largo Co, a company based in South-East Asia, has approached ATC with a proposal to produce some of the parts required for the component at highly competitive rates. In exchange, Largo Co would expect ATC to sign a five-year contract giving Largo Co the exclusive production rights for the parts.

Staccato Innovations Co (SIC) is a listed company involved in the manufacture of innovative engine components and engines for many years. As the worldwide demand for energy saving products has increased, it has successfully developed and sold products designed to reduce carbon emissions. SIC has offered to buy the production rights of the component and the machinery from ATC for $113,000,000 after the development phase has been completed in two years' time.

Additional data

ATC, Extracts from its latest statement of financial position

	$m
Non-current assets	336
Current assets less current liabilities	74
6% Bank loan	156
Share capital	52
Reserves	202

ATC shares have a nominal value of $0.50 per share and are currently trading at $3.50 per share. ATC's beta has been quoted at approximately 1.3 over the past year.

SIC, Extracts from its latest statement of financial position

	$m
Non-current assets	417
Current assets less current liabilities	157
5% Loan notes (2022–2024)	92
Share capital	125
Reserves	357

SIC shares have a nominal value of $1 per share and are currently trading at $3.00 per share. Its loan notes are trading at $102 per $100. SIC's beta has been quoted at approximately 1.8 over the past year.

Other data

Tax rate applicable to ATC and SIC	20%

It can be assumed that tax is payable in the same year as the profits on which it is charged.

Estimated risk-free rate of return	3%
Historic equity market risk premium	6%

Required:

Prepare a report to the board of directors of ATC that:

(i) **Assesses whether ATC should undertake the project of developing and commercialising the innovative engine component before taking SIC's offer into consideration. Show all relevant calculations.** (15 marks)

(ii) **Assesses the value of the above project if ATC takes SIC's offer into consideration. Show all relevant calculations.** (10 marks)

(iii) **Discusses the approach taken and the assumptions made for parts (i) and (ii) above.** (8 marks)

(iv) **Discusses possible implications of ATC entering into a contractual agreement with Largo Co. Include in the discussion suggestions of how any negative impact may be reduced.** (5 marks)

(v) Although not mandatory for external reporting purposes, one of the members of the board suggested that adopting an integrated reporting approach when monitoring the project after its implementation, would provide a better assessment of how successful it has been.

Discuss how adopting aspects of integrated reporting may provide a better assessment of the success of the project. (8 marks)

Professional marks for format, structure and presentation of the report. (4 marks)

(50 marks)

Question 13 FUBUKI CO

Fubuki Co, an unlisted company based in Megaera, has been manufacturing electrical parts used in mobility vehicles for people with disabilities and the elderly, for many years. These parts are exported to various manufacturers worldwide but at present there are no local manufacturers of mobility vehicles in Megaera. Retailers in Megaera normally import mobility vehicles and sell them at an average price of $4,000 each. Fubuki Co wants to manufacture mobility vehicles locally and believes that it can sell vehicles of equivalent quality locally at a discount of 37·5% to the current average retail price.

Although this is a completely new venture for Fubuki Co, it will be in addition to the company's core business. Fubuki Co's directors expect to develop the project for a period of four years and then sell it for $16 million to a private equity firm. Megaera's government has been positive about the venture and has offered Fubuki Co a subsidised loan of up to 80% of the investment funds required, at a rate of 200 basis points below Fubuki Co's borrowing rate. Currently Fubuki Co can borrow at 300 basis points above the five-year government debt yield rate.

A feasibility study commissioned by the directors, at a cost of $250,000, has produced the following information.

(1)   Initial cost of acquiring suitable premises will be $11 million, and plant and machinery used in the manufacture will cost $3 million. Acquiring the premises and installing the machinery is a quick process and manufacturing can commence almost immediately.

(2)   It is expected that in the first year 1,300 units will be manufactured and sold. Unit sales will grow by 40% in each of the next two years before falling to an annual growth rate of 5% for the final year. After the first year the selling price per unit is expected to increase by 3% per year.

(3)   In the first year, it is estimated that the total direct material, labour and variable overheads costs will be $1,200 per unit produced. After the first year, the direct costs are expected to increase by an annual inflation rate of 8%.

(4)   Annual fixed overhead costs would be $2·5 million of which 60% are centrally allocated overheads. The fixed overhead costs will increase by 5% per year after the first year.

(5)   Fubuki Co will need to make working capital available of 15% of the anticipated sales revenue for the year, at the beginning of each year. The working capital is expected to be released at the end of the fourth year when the project is sold.

Fubuki Co's tax rate is 25% per year. Tax is payable in the same year as when the profits are earned. Tax allowable depreciation is available on the plant and machinery on a straight-line basis. It is anticipated that the value attributable to the plant and machinery after four years is $400,000 of the price at which the project is sold. No tax allowable depreciation is available on the premises.

Fubuki Co uses 8% as its discount rate for new projects but feels that this rate may not be appropriate for this new type of investment. It intends to raise the full amount of funds through debt finance and take advantage of the government's offer of a subsidised loan. Issue costs are 4% of the gross finance required. It can be assumed that the debt capacity available to the company is equivalent to the actual amount of debt finance raised for the project.

Although no other companies produce mobility vehicles in Megaera, Haizum Co, a listed company, produces electrical-powered vehicles using similar technology to that required for the mobility vehicles. Haizum Co's cost of equity is estimated to be 14% and it pays tax at 28%. Haizum Co has 15 million shares in issue trading at $2·53 each and $40 million bonds trading at $94·88 per $100. The four-year government debt yield is currently estimated at 4·5% and the market risk premium at 4%.

Required:

(a)   **Evaluate, on financial grounds, whether Fubuki Co should proceed with the project.**

(17 marks)

(b)   **Discuss the appropriateness of the evaluation method used and explain any assumptions made in part (a) above.**   (8 marks)

(25 marks)

Question 14 TISA CO

Tisa Co is considering an opportunity to produce an innovative component which, when fitted into motor vehicle engines, will enable them to utilise fuel more efficiently. The component can be manufactured using either process Omega or process Zeta. Although this is an entirely new line of business for Tisa Co, it is of the opinion that developing either process over a period of four years and then selling the productions rights at the end of four years to another company may prove lucrative.

The annual after-tax cash flows for each process are as follows:

Process Omega

Year	0	1	2	3	4
After-tax cash flows ($000)	(3,800)	1,220	1,153	1,386	3,829

Process Zeta

Year	0	1	2	3	4
After-tax cash flows ($000)	(3,800)	643	546	1,055	5,990

Tisa Co has 10 million $0.50 shares trading at $1.80 each. Its loans have a current value of $3·6 million and an average after-tax cost of debt of 4·50%. Tisa Co's capital structure is unlikely to change significantly following the investment in either process.

Elfu Co manufactures electronic parts for cars including the production of a component similar to the one being considered by Tisa Co. Elfu Co's equity beta is 1·40, and it is estimated that the equivalent equity beta for its other activities, excluding the component production, is 1·25. Elfu Co has 400 million $0.25 shares in issue trading at $1.20 each. Its debt finance consists of variable rate loans redeemable in seven years. The loans paying interest at base rate plus 120 basis points have a current value of $96 million. It can be assumed that 80% of Elfu Co's debt finance and 75% of Elfu Co's equity finance can be attributed to other activities excluding the component production.

Both companies pay annual corporation tax at a rate of 25%. The current base rate is 3·5% and the market risk premium is estimated at 5·8%.

Required:

(a)   **Provide a reasoned estimate of the cost of capital that Tisa Co should use to calculate the net present value of the two processes. Include all relevant calculations.**   (10 marks)

(b)   **Calculate the internal rate of return (IRR) and the modified internal rate of return (MIRR) for Process Omega. Given that the IRR and MIRR of Process Zeta are 26·6% and 23·3% respectively, recommend which process, if any, Tisa Co should proceed with and explain your recommendation.**   (9 marks)

(c)   Elfu Co has estimated an annual standard deviation of $800,000 on one of its other projects, based on a normal distribution of returns. The average annual return on this project is $2,200,000.

Required:

Estimate the project's Value at Risk (VaR) at a 99% confidence level for one year and over the project's life of five years. Explain what is meant by the answers obtained.

(6 marks)

(25 marks)

Question 15 ARBORE CO

Arbore Co is a large listed company with many autonomous departments operating as investment centres. It sets investment limits for each department based on a three-year cycle. Projects selected by departments would have to fall within the investment limits set for each of the three years. All departments would be required to maintain a capital investment monitoring system, and report on their findings annually to Arbore Co's board of directors.

The Durvo department is considering the following five investment projects with three years of initial investment expenditure, followed by several years of positive cash inflows. The department's initial investment expenditure limits are $9,000,000, $6,000,000 and $5,000,000 for years one, two and three respectively. None of the projects can be deferred and all projects can be scaled down but not scaled up.

Investment required at start of year

Project	Year one (Immediately)	Year two	Year three	Project net present value
PDur01	$4,000,000	$1,100,000	$2,400,000	$464,000
PDur02	$800,000	$2,800,000	$3,200,000	$244,000
PDur03	$3,200,000	$3,562,000	$0	$352,000
PDur04	$3,900,000	$0	$200,000	$320,000
PDur05	$2,500,000	$1,200,000	$1,400,000	Not provided

PDur05 project's annual operating cash flows commence at the end of year four and last for a period of 15 years. The project generates annual sales of 300,000 units at a selling price of $14 per unit and incurs total annual relevant costs of $3,230,000. Although the costs and units sold of the project can be predicted with a fair degree of certainty, there is considerable uncertainty about the unit selling price. The department uses a required rate of return of 11% for its projects, and inflation can be ignored.

The Durvo department's managing director is of the opinion that all projects which return a positive net present value should be accepted and does not understand the reason(s) why Arbore Co imposes capital rationing on its departments. Furthermore, she is not sure why maintaining a capital investment monitoring system would be beneficial to the company.

Required:

(a)   **Calculate the net present value of project PDur05. Calculate and comment on what percentage fall in the selling price would need to occur before the net present value falls to zero.**

(6 marks)

(b)   **Formulate an appropriate capital rationing model, based on the above investment limits, that maximises the net present value for department Durvo. Finding a solution for the model is not required.**

(4 marks)

(c) Assume the following output is produced when the capital rationing model in part (b) above is solved:

Category 1: Total final value
$1,184,409

Category 2: Adjustable final values

Project PDur01: 0·958	Project PDur03: 0·732	Project PDur05: 1·000
Project PDur02: 0·407	Project PDur04: 0·000	

Category 3:

Constraints Utilised	Slack
Year one: $9,000,000	Year one: $0
Year two: $6,000,000	Year two: $0
Year three: $5,000,000	Year three: $0

Required:

Explain the figures produced in each of the three output categories. (6 marks)

(d) Provide a brief response to the managing director's opinions by explaining:

(i) Why Arbore Co may want to impose capital rationing on its departments; (4 marks)

(ii) The features of a capital investment monitoring system and discussing the benefits of maintaining such a system. (5 marks)

(25 marks)

Question 16 KODIAK COMPANY

Kodiak Company is a small software design business established four years ago. The company is owned by three directors who have relied upon external accounting services in the past. The company has grown quickly and the directors have appointed you as a financial consultant to advise on the value of the company's equity.

The directors have limited liability and the bank loan is secured against the general assets of the business. The directors have no outstanding guarantees on the company's debt.

The company's latest statement of profit or loss and the extracted balances from the latest statement of financial position are as follows:

Profit or loss	$000	Financial position	$000
Revenue	5,000	Opening non-current assets	1,200
Cost of sales	3,000	Additions	66
Gross profit	2,000	Non-current assets (cost)	1,266
Other operating costs	1,877	Accumulated depreciation	367
Operating profit	123	Carrying amount	899
Interest on loan	74	Net current assets	270
Profit before tax	49	Loan	(990)
Income tax expense	15	Net assets employed	179
Profit for the period	34		

During the current year:

(1)   Depreciation is charged at 10% per year on the year-end non-current asset balance before accumulated depreciation and is included in other operating costs in the statement of profit or loss.

(2)   The investment in net working capital is expected to increase in line with the growth in gross profit.

(3)   Other operating costs consisted of:

	$000
Variable component at 15% of sales	750
Fixed costs	1,000
Depreciation on non-current assets	127

(4)   Revenue and variable costs are projected to grow at 9% per year and fixed costs are projected to grow at 6% per year.

(5)   The company pays interest on its outstanding loan of 7·5% per year and incurs tax on its profits at 30%, payable in the following year. The company does not pay dividends.

(6)   The net current assets reported in the statement of financial position contain $50,000 of cash.

One of your first tasks is to prepare for the directors a forward cash flow projection for three years and to value the firm on the basis of its expected free cash flow to equity. In discussion with them you note the following:

■   The company will not dispose of any of its non-current assets but will increase its investment in new non-current assets by 20% per year. The company's depreciation policy matches the write off allowable for tax purposes. This straight-line write off policy is not likely to change.

■   The directors will not take a dividend for the next three years but will then review the position taking into account the company's sustainable cash flow at that time.

■   The level of the loan will be maintained at $990,000 and, on the basis of the forward yield curve, interest rates are not expected to change.

■   The directors have set a target rate of return on their equity of 10% per year which they believe fairly represents the opportunity cost of their invested funds.

Required:

(a)   **Prepare a three-year cash flow forecast on the basis described above highlighting the free cash flow to equity in each year.**   (12 marks)

(b)   **Estimate the value of the equity based upon the expected free cash flow to equity and a terminal value based upon a sustainable growth rate of 3% per year thereafter.**
                                                                                         (4 marks)

(c)   **Advise the directors on the assumptions and the uncertainties within your valuation.**
                                                                                         (5 marks)

(d)   **With reference to option pricing theory, advise the directors how limited liability may give a different value to the business from the value estimated in part (b) above.**
                                                                                         (4 marks)

(25 marks)

Question 17 MLIMA CO

Mlima Co is a private company involved in aluminium mining. About eight years ago, the company was bought out by its management and employees through a leveraged buyout (LBO). Due to high metal prices worldwide, the company has been growing successfully since the LBO. However, because the company has significant debt borrowings with strict restrictive covenants and high interest levels, it has had to reject a number of profitable projects. The company has currently two bonds in issue, as follows:

A 16% secured bond with a nominal value of $80m, which is redeemable at nominal value in five years. An early redemption option is available on this bond, giving Mlima Co the option to redeem the bond at nominal value immediately if it wants to; and A 13% unsecured bond with a nominal value of $40m, which is redeemable at nominal value in ten years.

Mlima Co's Board of Directors (BoD) has been exploring the idea of redeeming both bonds to provide it with more flexibility when making future investment decisions. To do so, the BoD has decided to consider a public listing of the company on a major stock exchange. It is intended that a total of 100 million shares will be issued in the newly-listed company. From the total shares, 20% will be sold to the public, 10% will be offered to the holders of the unsecured bond in exchange for redeeming the bond through an equity-for-debt swap, and the remaining 70% of the equity will remain in the hands of the current owners. The secured bond would be paid out of the funds raised from the listing.

The details of the possible listing and the distribution of equity were published in national newspapers recently. As a result, potential investors suggested that due to the small proportion of shares offered to the public and for other reasons, the shares should be offered at a substantial discount of as much as 20% below the expected share price on the day of the listing.

Mlima Co, financial information

It is expected that after the listing, deployment of new strategies and greater financial flexibility will boost Mlima Co's future sales revenue and, for the next four years, the annual growth rate will be 120% of the previous two years' average growth rate. After the four years, the annual growth rate of the free cash flows to the company will be 3·5%, for the foreseeable future. Operating profit margins are expected to be maintained in the future. Although it can be assumed that the current tax-allowable depreciation is equivalent to the amount of investment needed to maintain the current level of operations, the company will require an additional investment in assets of $0.30 per $1 increase in sales revenue for the next four years.

Extracts from Mlima Co's past three years' statement of profit or loss

Year ended 31 May	2017 $m	2016 $m	2015 $m
Sales revenue	389·1	366·3	344·7
Operating profit	58·4	54·9	51·7
Net interest costs	17·5	17·7	18·0
Profit before tax	40·9	37·2	33·7
Taxation	10·2	9·3	8·4
Profit after tax	30·7	27·9	25·3

Once listed, Mlima Co will be able to borrow future debt at an interest rate of 7%, which is only 3% higher than the risk-free rate of return. It has no plans to raise any new debt after listing, but any future debt will carry considerably fewer restrictive covenants. However, these plans do not take into consideration the Bahari project (see below).

Bahari Project

Bahari is a small country with agriculture as its main economic activity. A recent geological survey concluded that there may be a rich deposit of copper available to be mined in the north-east of the country. This area is currently occupied by subsistence farmers, who would have to be relocated to other parts of the country. When the results of the survey were announced, some farmers protested that the proposed new farmland where they would be moved to was less fertile and that their communities were being broken up. However, the protesters were intimidated and violently put down by the government, and the state-controlled media stopped reporting about them. Soon afterwards, their protests were ignored and forgotten.

In a meeting between the Bahari government and Mlima Co's BoD, the Bahari government offered Mlima Co exclusive rights to mine the copper. It is expected that there are enough deposits to last at least 15 years. Initial estimates suggest that the project will generate free cash flows of $4 million in the first year, rising by 100% per year in each of the next two years, and then by 15% in each of the two years after that. The free cash flows are then expected to stabilise at the year-five level for the remaining 10 years.

The cost of the project, payable at the start, is expected to be $150 million, comprising machinery, working capital and the mining rights fee payable to the Bahari government. None of these costs is expected to be recoverable at the end of the project's 15-year life.

The Bahari government has offered Mlima Co a subsidised loan over 15 years for the full $150 million at an interest rate of 3% instead of Mlima Co's normal borrowing rate of 7%. The interest payable is allowable for taxation purposes.

It can be assumed that Mlima Co's business risk is not expected to change as a result of undertaking the Bahari project.

At the conclusion of the meeting between the Bahari government and Mlima Co's BoD, the president of Bahari commented that working together would be like old times when he and Mlima Co's chief executive officer (CEO) used to run a business together.

Other information

Mlima Co's closest competitor is Ziwa Co, a listed company which mines metals worldwide. Mlima Co's directors are of the opinion that after listing Mlima Co's cost of capital should be based on Ziwa Co's ungeared cost of equity. Ziwa Co's cost of capital is estimated at 9·4%, its geared cost of equity is estimated at 16·83% and its pre-tax cost of debt is estimated at 4·76%. These costs are based on a capital structure comprising of 200 million shares, trading at $7 each, and $1,700 million 5% irredeemable bonds, trading at $105 per $100. Both Ziwa Co and Mlima Co pay tax at an annual rate of 25% on their taxable profits.

It can be assumed that all cash flows will be in $ instead of the Bahari currency and therefore Mlima Co does not have to take account of any foreign exchange exposure from this venture.

Required:

(a)   **Prepare a report for the Board of Directors (BoD) of Mlima Co that:**

   (i)   **Explains why Mlima Co's directors are of the opinion that Mlima Co's cost of capital should be based on Ziwa Co's ungeared cost of equity and, showing relevant calculations, estimate an appropriate cost of capital for Mlima Co;**

(7 marks)

(ii)   Estimates Mlima Co's value without undertaking the Bahari project and then with the Bahari project. The valuations should use the free cash flow methodology and the cost of capital calculated in part (i). Include relevant calculations; (14 marks)

(iii) Advises the BoD whether or not the unsecured bond holders are likely to accept the equity-for-debt swap offer. Include relevant calculations; (5 marks)

(iv)   Advises the board of directors on the listing and the possible share price range, if a total of 100 million shares are issued. The advice should also include:

–   A discussion of the assumptions made in estimating the share price range;

–   In addition to the reasons mentioned in the scenario above, a brief explanation of other possible reasons for changing its status from a private company to a listed one; and

–   An assessment of the possible reasons for issuing the share price at a discount for the initial listing; (12 marks)

Professional marks will be awarded in part (a) for the format, structure and presentation of the report. (4 marks)

(b)   Discuss the possible impact on, and response of, Mlima Co to the following ethical issues, with respect to the Bahari project:

(i)   The relocation of the farmers; and

(ii)   The relationship between the Bahari president and Mlima Co's chief executive officer.

Note: The total marks will be split equally between each part. (8 marks)

(50 marks)

Question 18 INTERGRAND CO

(a)   Discuss the advantages to a company of establishing an overseas operating subsidiary by either:

(i)   Organic growth; or
(ii)   Acquisition. (10 marks)

(b)   The board of directors of Intergrand Co wishes to establish an operating subsidiary in Germany through the acquisition of an existing German company. Intergrand has undertaken research into a number of German quoted companies, and has decided to attempt to purchase Oberberg AG. Initial discussions suggest that the directors of Oberberg AG may be willing to recommend the sale of 100% of the company's equity to Intergrand for a total cash price of 115 million Euro (€), payable in full on acquisition.

Oberberg has provided the managers of Intergrand with internal management information regarding accounting/cash flow projections for the next four years. The projections are in money/nominal terms.

Oberberg AG, Financial projections (€ million)

Year	2017	2018	2019	2020
Sales	38·2	41·2	44·0	49·0
Labour	11·0	12·1	13·0	14·1
Materials	8·3	8·7	9·0	9·4
Overheads	3·2	3·2	3·3	3·4
Interest	2·5	3·0	3·5	3·8
Tax allowable depreciation	6·3	5·8	5·6	5·2
	31·3	32·8	34·4	35·9
Taxable Profit	6·9	8·4	9·6	13·1
Taxation (25%)	1·7	2·1	2·4	3·3
Incremental operating working capital	0·7	0·9	1·0	2·0
Replacement investment	4·2	4·2	4·2	4·2
Investment for expansion	–	–	9·0	–

Summarised statement of profit or loss for the year ending 31 December 2016

		€m
Sales		35·8
Operating expenses	21·1	
Interest expense	3·4	
Depreciation	6·2	
		30·7
Taxable profit		5·1
Taxation (25%)		1·3
Profit after tax		3·8

Statement of financial position as at 31 December 2016

Assets	€m
Non-current assets	73·2
Current assets	58·1
	131·3

Equity and liabilities	
Ordinary shares (€100 per share)	15·0
Reserves	28·0
Medium and long term bank loans	30·0
8% Bond 2023 (€1,000 nominal value)	18·0
Current liabilities	40·3
	131·3

Notes:

(i) The spot exchange rate is 1·625 Euro per $.

(ii) Inflation is at 4% per year in Intergrand's home country and 2% per year in the euro bloc. This differential is expected to continue.

(iii) The market return is 11% and the risk free rate is 4%.

(iv) Oberberg's equity beta is estimated to be 1·4.

(v) Oberberg's 8% bond is currently priced at €1,230 and its share price €300.

(vi) Post-merger rationalisation will involve the sale of some non-current assets of Oberberg in 2017 with an expected after tax market value of €8 million.

(vii) Synergies in production and distribution are expected to yield €2 million per year before tax from 2018 onwards.

(viii) $175,000 has already been spent researching into possible acquisition targets.

(ix) The purchase of Oberberg will provide publicity and exposure in Germany for the Intergrand name and brand. This extra publicity is believed to be the equivalent of Intergrand spending €1 million per year on advertising in Germany.

(x) The weighted average cost of capital of Intergrand is 10%.

(xi) After tax cash flows of Oberberg after 2020 are expected to grow at approximately 2% per year.

(xii) Oberberg does not plan to issue or redeem any equity or debt prior to 2020.

(xiii) After tax redundancy costs as a result of the acquisition are expected to be €5 million, payable almost immediately.

(xiv) Operating working capital comprises receivables and inventory less payables. It excludes short-term loans.

(xv) Current liabilities include negligible amounts of short-term loans.

(xvi) The corporate tax rate is 25% in Germany, and 30% in Intergrand's home country. A bilateral tax treaty exists between the two countries whereby tax paid in one country may be credited against any tax liability in the other country.

(xvii) If Intergrand acquires Oberberg existing exports to Germany yielding a pre-tax cash flow of $800,000 per year will be lost. It is hoped that about half of these exports can be diverted to the French market.

Required:

Intergrand has suggested that Oberberg should be valued based upon the expected present value (to infinity) of the operating free cash flows of Oberberg. These would be discounted at an all-equity rate, and adjusted by the present value of all other relevant cash flows, discounted at an appropriate rate(s).

Acting as a consultant to Intergrand Co, prepare a report evaluating whether or not Intergrand should offer the €115 million required to acquire Oberberg AG. Include in your report discussion of other commercial and business factors that Intergrand should consider prior to making a final decision.

Assume that it is now mid-December 2016.

State clearly any other assumptions that you make. (36 marks)

Approximately 26 marks are available for calculations and 10 for discussion.

Professional marks for format, structure and presentation of the report for part (b). (4 marks)

(50 marks)

Question 19 FLIHI

You are the chief financial officer of Fly4000 a large company in the airline and travel business whose principal market base is in Europe and the Middle East. Its principal hub is a major Northern European airport and Fly4000 has a small holiday business through its partnership with a number of independent tour operators. It has a good reputation as a business carrier within its European market, earned through very high standards of punctuality and service. Following the recent disinvestment of associated interests and a joint venture, it has cash reserves of $860 million.

FliHi is a smaller airline which also has its centre of operations at the same airport as Fly4000. It has, since it was founded in 1988, developed a strong transatlantic business as well as a substantial position in the long and medium haul holiday market. In the year to 31 December 2016 its reported revenue was in $1.7 billion and its profit after tax for the financial year was $50 million. The company's net assets are $120 million and it has $150 million of long term loans. It has recently expanded its fleet of wide bodied jets suitable for its expanding holiday business and has orders placed for the Airbus 380 super-Jumbo to supplement its long haul fleet. FliHi has route licenses to New York and six other major US cities.

FliHi's statement of cash flows for the current and preceding year is as follows:

	31 December 2016		31 December 2015	
	$m	$m	$m	$m
Net cash inflow from operating activities		210.0		95.0
Return on investment and servicing of finance				
Interest received	12.0		6.0	
Interest paid	(4.0)		(3.0)	
Interest element on finance leases	(6.5)		(4.0)	
		1.5		(1.0)
Taxation		(4.1)		(0.2)
Capital expenditure		(120.2)		(75.0)
Acquisitions and disposals				
Proceeds from the sale of interest in joint ventures		10.0		15.0
Cash inflow before management of liquid resources and financing		97.2		33.8
Management of liquid resources				
Decrease/(increase) in short term deposits		35.5		(32.2)
Financing: Repayment of secured loans		(31.0)		(25.0)
Increase/(decrease) in cash for the year		101.7		(23.4)

There is no other airline of comparable size and business mix to FliHi although analysts regard Rover Airways as a useful comparator. The statement below contains market data relating to Rover Airways:

Key fundamentals

Forward P/E	11.00	Dividend Yield	0.00
Price to Book value of equity	1.25	1Yr Total Return (%)	25.07
Price To Cash Flow	3.00	Beta	2.00
1Yr Sales Growth	-1.67	1Yr EPS Growth	80.50
Equity Market Cap $3bn			

The current risk-free rate is 4.5% and the equity risk premium is estimated at 3.5%. The prevailing share price for Rover Airways is $2.90 per share and its P/E ratio is 10. The corporation tax rate for both companies is 30%.

The gearing ratio for Rover Airways, expressed as total debt to total capital (debt plus equity), is 60% and as total debt to equity is 150%.

You may assume that:

(1)   FliHi has undertaken a consistent programme of reinvestment
(2)   The debt in both companies is not expected to be sensitive to market risk.

There has been considerable consolidation in the airline industry and you are advising your board of directors of Fly4000 on the value of FliHi as a potential target for acquisition. It is anticipated that over the longer term the domestic airline industry will settle down to a rate of growth in line with GDP growth in the European economy which stands at 4% per year (nominal).

However, the current rates of growth for this company are likely to be sustained for the next five years before reverting to the GDP growth rate from the sixth year forward.

Required:

(a)   **Estimate the current cost of equity capital for FliHi using the Capital Asset Pricing Model, making notes on any assumptions that you have made.**   (7 marks)

(b)   **Estimate the expected growth rate of FliHi for the next five years using the current rate of retention of free cash flow and your estimate of the required rate of return on equity. Make notes on any assumptions you have made.**   (6 marks)

(c)   **Estimate the value of FliHi on the basis of its expected free cash flow to equity, explaining the limitations of the methods you have used.**   (6 marks)

(d)   **Outline the considerations your colleagues on the board of Fly4000 might bear in mind when contemplating this acquisition**.   (6 marks)

(25 marks)

Question 20 BURCOLENE

Burcolene is a large European-based petrochemical manufacturer, with a wide range of basic bulk chemicals in its product range and with strong markets in Europe and the Pacific region. In recent years, margins have fallen as a result of competition from China and, more importantly, Eastern European countries that have favourable access to the Russian petrochemical industry. However, the company has managed to sustain a 5% growth rate in earnings through aggressive management of its cost base, the management of its risk and careful attention to its value base.

As part of its strategic development, Burcolene is considering a leveraged (debt-financed) acquisition of PetroFrancais, a large petrochemical business that has engaged in a number of high quality alliances with oil drilling and extraction companies in the newly opened Russian Arctic fields. However, the growth of the company has not been particularly strong in recent years, although Burcolene believes that an expected long term growth of 4% per year is realistic under its current management.

Preliminary discussions with its banks have led Burcolene to the conclusion that an acquisition of 100% of the equity of PetroFrancais, financed via a bond issue, would not have a significant impact upon the company's existing credit rating. The key issues, according to the company's advisors, are the terms of the deal and the likely effect of the acquisition on the company's value and its financial leverage.

Both companies are quoted on an international stock exchange and below are relevant data relating to each company:

Financial data as at 30 November 2016

	Burcolene	PetroFrancais
Market value of debt in issue ($bn)	3·30	5·80
Market value of equity in issue ($bn)	9·90	6·70
Number of shares in issue (million)	340·00	440·00
Share options outstanding (million)	25·40	–
Exercise price of options ($ per share)	22·00	–
Company tax rate (%)	30·00	25·00
Equity beta	1·85	0·95
Default risk premium	1·6%	3·0%
Net operating profit after tax and net reinvestment ($m)	450·00	205·00
Current EPS ($ per share)	1·19	0·44

The global equity risk premium is 4·0% and the most appropriate risk free rate derived from the returns on government stock is 3·0%.

Burcolene has a share option scheme as part of its executive remuneration package. In accordance with the accounting standards, the company has expensed its share options at fair value. The share options held by the employees of Burcolene were granted on 1 January 2013. The vesting date is 30 November 2018 and the exercise date is 30 November 2019. Currently, the company has a 5% attrition rate as members leave the company and, of those remaining at the vesting date, 20% are expected not to have achieved the standard of performance required. Your estimate is that the options have a time value of $7·31.

PetroFrancais operates a defined benefits pension scheme which, at its current actuarial valuation, shows a deficit of $430 million.

You have been appointed to advise the senior management team of Burcolene on the validity of the Free Cash Flow to the Firm (FCFF) model as a basis for valuing both firms and on the financial implications of this acquisition for Burcolene. Following your initial discussions with management, you decide that the following points are relevant:

(1)   The free cash flow to all classes of capital can be reliably approximated as net operating profit after tax (NOPAT) less net reinvestment.

(2)   Given the rumours in the market concerning a potential acquisition, the existing market valuations may not fully reflect each company's value.

(3)   The acquisition would be financed by a new debt issue by Burcolene.

Required:

(a)   **Estimate the weighted average cost of capital and the current entity value for each business, taking into account the impact of the share option scheme and the pension fund deficit on the respective value of each company.**   (16 marks)

(b)   **Write a briefing paper for management, advising them on:**

      (i)   **The validity of the free cash flow model, given the growth rate assumptions made by management for both firms;**

      (ii)   **The most appropriate method of deriving a bid price; and**

      (iii)   **The implications of an acquisition such as this for Burcolene's gearing and cost of capital.**   (14 marks)

Professional marks for format, structure and presentation of the briefing paper for part (b). (4 marks)

(c) The Chairman and the Chief Executive Officer (CEO) of Burcolene Co are discussing whether or not the company should adopt a triple bottom line (TBL) reporting system in order to demonstrate Burcolene Co's level of sustainable development. Burcolene Co's competitors are increasingly adopting TBL reporting and the Chairman feels that it would be beneficial for Burcolene to do the same. The CEO, on the other hand, feels that pursuing TBL reporting would be expensive and is not necessary.

Required:

(i) **Explain what TBL reporting involves and how it would help demonstrate Burcolene Co's sustainable development. Support your explanation by including examples of proxies that can be used to indicate the impact of the factors that would be included in a TBL report.** (8 marks)

(ii) **Discuss how producing a TBL report may help Burcolene Co's management focus on improving the financial position of the company. Illustrate the discussion with examples where appropriate.** (8 marks)

(50 marks)

Question 21 PURSUIT CO

Pursuit Co, a listed company which manufactures electronic components, is interested in acquiring Fodder Co, an unlisted company involved in the development of sophisticated but high risk electronic products. The owners of Fodder Co are a consortium of private equity investors who have been looking for a suitable buyer for their company for some time. Pursuit Co estimates that a payment of the equity value plus a 25% premium would be sufficient to secure the purchase of Fodder Co. Pursuit Co would also pay off any outstanding debt that Fodder Co owed. Pursuit Co wishes to acquire Fodder Co using a combination of debt finance and its cash reserves of $20 million, such that the capital structure of the combined company remains at Pursuit Co's current capital structure level.

Information on Pursuit Co and Fodder Co

Pursuit Co

Pursuit Co has a market value debt to equity ratio of 50:50 and an equity beta of $1 \cdot 18$. Currently Pursuit Co has a total firm value (market value of debt plus equity) of $140 million.

Fodder Co Statement of Profit or Loss Extracts

Year ended 31 May All amounts are in $000	2017	2016	2015	2014
Sales revenue	16,146	15,229	14,491	13,559
Operating profit (after tax allowable depreciation)	5,169	5,074	4,243	4,530
Net interest expense	489	473	462	458
Profit before tax	4,680	4,601	3,781	4,072
Taxation (28%)	1,310	1,288	1,059	1,140
Profit after tax	3,370	3,313	2,722	2,932
Dividends	123	115	108	101
Retained profit	3,247	3,198	2,614	2,831

Fodder Co has a market value debt to equity ratio of 10:90 and an estimated equity beta of 1·53. It can be assumed that its tax allowable depreciation is equivalent to the amount of investment needed to maintain current operational levels. However, Fodder Co will require an additional investment in assets of $0.22 per $1 increase in sales revenue, for the next four years. It is anticipated that Fodder Co will pay interest at 9% on its future borrowings.

For the next four years, Fodder Co's sales revenue will grow at the same average rate as the previous years. After the forecasted four-year period, the growth rate of its free cash flows will be half the initial forecast sales revenue growth rate for the foreseeable future.

Information about the combined company

Following the acquisition, it is expected that the combined company's sales revenue will be $51,952,000 in the first year, and its operating profit margin will be 30% for the foreseeable future. After the first year the growth rate in sales revenue will be 5·8% per year for the following three years. Following the acquisition, it is expected that the combined company will pay annual interest at 6·4% on future borrowings.

The combined company will require additional investment in assets of $513,000 in the first year and then $0.18 per $1 increase in sales revenue for the next three years. It is anticipated that after the forecasted four-year period, its free cash flow growth rate will be half of the initial sales revenue growth rate.

It can be assumed that the asset beta of the combined company is the weighted average of the individual companies' asset betas, weighted in proportion of the individual companies' market value.

Other information

The current annual government base rate is 4·5% and the market risk premium is estimated at 6% per year. The relevant annual tax rate applicable to all the companies is 28%.

SGF Co's interest in Pursuit Co

There have been rumours of a potential bid by SGF Co to acquire Pursuit Co. Some financial press reports have suggested that this is because Pursuit Co's share price has fallen recently. SGF Co is in a similar line of business as Pursuit Co and, until a couple of years ago, SGF Co was the smaller company. However, a successful performance has resulted in its share price rising, and SGF Co is now the larger company.

The rumours of SGF Co's interest have raised doubts about Pursuit Co's ability to acquire Fodder Co. Although SGF Co has made no formal bid yet, Pursuit Co's board is keen to reduce the possibility of such a bid. The Chief Financial Officer has suggested that the most effective way to reduce the possibility of a takeover would be to distribute the $20 million in its cash reserves to its shareholders in the form of a special dividend. Fodder Co would then be purchased using debt finance. He conceded that this would increase Pursuit Co's gearing level but suggested it may increase the company's share price and make Pursuit Co less appealing to SGF Co.

Required:

Prepare a report to the Board of Directors of Pursuit Co that:

(i)   **Evaluates whether the acquisition of Fodder Co would be beneficial to Pursuit Co and its shareholders. The free cash flow to firm method should be used to estimate the values of Fodder Co and the combined company assuming that the combined company's capital structure stays the same as that of Pursuit Co's current capital structure. Include all relevant calculations;**   (24 marks)

(ii)   **Discusses the limitations of the estimated valuations in part (i) above;**   (6 marks)

(iii)   **Estimates the amount of debt finance needed, in addition to the cash reserves, to acquire Fodder Co and concludes whether Pursuit Co's current capital structure can be maintained;**   (4 marks)

(iv)   **Explains the implications of a change in the capital structure of the combined company, to the valuation method used in part (i) and how the issue can be resolved;**   (6 marks)

(v)   **Assesses whether the Chief Financial Officer's recommendation would provide a suitable defence against a bid from SGF Co and would be a viable option for Pursuit Co.**   (6 marks)

Professional marks will be awarded for the format, structure and presentation of the report.   (4 marks)

(50 marks)

Question 22 NENTE CO

Nente Co, an unlisted company, designs and develops tools and parts for specialist machinery. The company was formed four years ago by three friends, who own 20% of the equity capital in total, and a consortium of five business angel organisations, who own the remaining 80%, in roughly equal proportions. Nente Co also has a large amount of debt finance in the form of variable rate loans. Initially the amount of annual interest payable on these loans was low and allowed Nente Co to invest internally generated funds to expand its business. Recently though, due to a rapid increase in interest rates, there has been limited scope for future expansion and no new product development.

The Board of Directors, consisting of the three friends and a representative from each business angel organisation, met recently to discuss how to secure the company's future prospects. Two proposals were put forward, as follows:

Proposal 1

To accept a takeover offer from Mije Co, a listed company, which develops and manufactures specialist machinery tools and parts. The takeover offer is for $2·95 cash per share or a share-for-share exchange where two Mije Co shares would be offered for three Nente Co shares. Mije Co would need to get the final approval from its shareholders if either offer is accepted;

Proposal 2

To pursue an opportunity to develop a small prototype product that just breaks even financially, but gives the company exclusive rights to produce a follow-on product within two years.

The meeting concluded without agreement on which proposal to pursue.

After the meeting, Mije Co was consulted about the exclusive rights. Mije Co's directors indicated that they had not considered the rights in their computations and were willing to continue with the takeover offer on the same terms without them.

Currently, Mije Co has 10 million shares in issue and these are trading for $4·80 each. Mije Co's price to earnings (P/E) ratio is 15. It has sufficient cash to pay for Nente Co's equity and a substantial proportion of its debt, and believes that this will enable Nente Co to operate on a P/E level of 15 as well. In addition to this, Mije Co believes that it can find cost-based synergies of $150,000 after tax per year for the foreseeable future. Mije Co's current profit after tax is $3,200,000.

The following financial information relates to Nente Co and to the development of the new product.

Nente Co financial information

Extract from the most recent statement of profit or loss

	$000
Sales revenue	8,780
Profit before interest and tax	1,230
Interest	(455)
Tax	(155)
Profit after tax	620
Dividends	Nil

Extract from the most recent statement of financial position

	$000
Non-current assets	10,060
Current assets	690
Total assets	10,750
Share capital ($0.40 per share)	960
Reserves	1,400
Non-current liabilities: Variable rate loans	6,500
Current liabilities	1,890
Total equity and liabilities	10,750

In arriving at the profit after tax amount, Nente Co deducted tax allowable depreciation and other non-cash expenses totalling $1,206,000. It requires an annual cash investment of $1,010,000 in non-current assets and working capital to continue its operations.

Nente Co's profits before interest and tax in its first year of operation were $970,000 and have been growing steadily in each of the following three years, to their current level. Nente Co's cash flows grew at the same rate as well, but it is likely that this growth rate will reduce to 25% of the original rate for the foreseeable future.

Nente Co currently pays interest of 7% per year on its loans, which is 380 basis points over the government base rate, and corporation tax of 20% on profits after interest. It is estimated that an overall cost of capital of 11% is reasonable compensation for the risk undertaken on an investment of this nature.

New product development (Proposal 2)

Developing the new follow-on product will require an investment of $2,500,000 initially. The total expected cash flows and present values of the product over its five-year life, with a volatility of 42% standard deviation, are as follows:

Year(s)	Now	1	2	3 to 7 (in total)
Cash flows ($000)	–	–	(2,500)	3,950
Present values ($000)	–	–	(2,029)	2,434

Required:

(i)   **Estimate the current value of a Nente Co share, using the free cash flow to firm methodology;**   (6 marks)

(ii)   **Estimate the percentage gain in value of a Nente Co share and a Mije Co share under each payment offer;**   (8 marks)

(iii)   **Estimate the percentage gain in the value of a Nente share due to the follow-on product;**   (6 marks)

(iv)   **Discuss the likely reaction of Nente Co and Mije Co shareholders to the takeover offer, including the assumptions made in the estimates above and how the follow-on product's value can be utilised by Nente Co.**   (5 marks)

(25 marks)

Question 23 SIGRA CO

Sigra Co is a listed company producing confectionary products which it sells around the world. It wants to acquire Dentro Co, an unlisted company producing high quality, luxury chocolates. Sigra Co proposes to pay for the acquisition using one of the following three methods:

Method 1

A cash offer of $5·00 per Dentro Co share; or

Method 2

An offer of three of its shares for two of Dentro Co's shares; or

Method 3

An offer of a 2% coupon bond in exchange for 16 Dentro Co's shares. The bond will be redeemed in three years at nominal value of $100.

Extracts from the latest financial statements of both companies are as follows:

	Sigra Co	Dentro Co
	$000	$000
Sales revenue	44,210	4,680
Profit before tax	6,190	780
Taxation	(1,240)	(155)
Profit after tax	4,950	625
Dividends	(2,700)	(275)
Retained earnings for the year	2,250	350
Non-current assets	22,450	3,350
Current assets	3,450	247
Non-current liabilities	9,700	873
Current liabilities	3,600	436
Share capital ($0.40 per share)	4,400	500
Reserves	8,200	1,788

Sigra Co's current share price is $3·60 per share and it has estimated that Dentro Co's price to earnings ratio is 12·5% higher than Sigra Co's current price to earnings ratio. Sigra Co's non-current liabilities include a 6% bond redeemable in three years at nominal value which is currently trading at $104 per $100 nominal value.

Sigra Co estimates that it could achieve synergy savings of 30% of Dentro Co's estimated equity value by eliminating duplicated administrative functions, selling excess non-current assets and through reducing the workforce numbers, if the acquisition were successful.

Required:

(a) **Estimate the percentage gain on a Dentro Co share under each of the above three payment methods. Comment on the answers obtained.** (19 marks)

(b) In relation to the acquisition, the board of directors of Sigra Co are considering the following two proposals:

Proposal 1

Once Sigra Co has obtained agreement from a significant majority of the shareholders, it will enforce the remaining minority shareholders to sell their shares; and

Proposal 2

Sigra Co will offer an extra $0.03 per share, in addition to the bid price, to 30% of the shareholders of Dentro Co on a first-come, first-serve basis, as an added incentive to make the acquisition proceed more quickly.

Required:

With reference to the key aspects of the global regulatory framework for mergers and acquisitions, briefly discuss the above proposals. (6 marks)

(25 marks)

Question 24 HAV CO

Hav Co is a publicly listed company involved in the production of highly technical and sophisticated electronic components for complex machinery. It has a number of diverse and popular products, an active research and development department, significant cash reserves and a highly talented management who are very good in getting products to market quickly.

A new industry that Hav Co is looking to venture into is biotechnology, which has been expanding rapidly and there are strong indications that this recent growth is set to continue. However, Hav Co has limited experience in this industry. Therefore it believes that the best and quickest way to expand would be through acquiring a company already operating in this industry sector.

Strand Co is a private company operating in the biotechnology industry and is owned by a consortium of business angels and company managers. The owner-managers are highly skilled scientists who have developed a number of technically complex products, but have found it difficult to commercialise them. They have also been increasingly constrained by the lack of funds to develop their innovative products further.

Discussions have taken place about the possibility of Strand Co being acquired by Hav Co. Strand Co's managers have indicated that the consortium of owners is happy for the negotiations to proceed. If Strand Co is acquired, it is expected that its managers would continue to run the Strand Co part of the larger combined company.

Strand Co is of the opinion that most of its value is in its intangible assets, comprising intellectual capital. Therefore, the premium payable on acquisition should be based on the present value to infinity of the after tax excess earnings the company has generated in the past three years, over the average return on capital employed of the biotechnological industry. However, Hav Co is of the opinion that the premium should be assessed on synergy benefits created by the acquisition and the changes in value, due to the changes in the price-to-earnings (PE) ratio before and after the acquisition.

Given below are extracts of financial information for Hav Co for 2016 and Strand Co for 2014, 2015 and 2016:

	Hav Co	Strand Co		
Year ended 30 April	2016	2016	2015	2014
	$m	$m	$m	$m
Earnings before tax	1,980	397	370	352
Non-current assets	3,965	882	838	801
Current assets	968	210	208	198
Share capital ($0.25 per share)	600	300	300	300
Reserves	2,479	183	166	159
Non-current liabilities	1,500	400	400	400
Current liabilities	354	209	180	140

The current average PE ratio of the biotechnology industry is 16·4 times and it has been estimated that Strand Co's PE ratio is 10% higher than this. However, it is thought that the PE ratio of the combined company would fall to 14·5 times after the acquisition. The annual after tax earnings will increase by $140 million due to synergy benefits resulting from combining the two companies.

Both companies pay tax at 20% per annum and Strand Co's annual cost of capital is estimated at 7%. Hav Co's current share price is $9·24 per share. The biotechnology industry's pre-tax return on capital employed is currently estimated to be 20% per annum.

Hav Co has proposed to pay for the acquisition using one of the following three methods:

(i)   A cash offer of $5·72 for each Strand Co share; or

(ii)   A cash offer of $1·33 for each Strand Co share plus one Hav Co share for every two Strand Co shares; or

(iii)   A cash offer of $1·25 for each Strand Co share plus one $100 3% convertible bond for every $5 nominal value of Strand Co shares. In six years, the bond can be converted into 12 Hav Co shares or redeemed at par.

Required:

(a)   Distinguish between the different types of synergy and discuss possible sources of synergy based on the above scenario. (9 marks)

(b)   Based on the two different opinions expressed by Hav Co and Strand Co, calculate the maximum acquisition premium payable in each case. (6 marks)

(c)   Calculate the percentage premium per share that Strand Co's shareholders will receive under each acquisition payment method and justify, with explanations, which payment method would be most acceptable to them. (10 marks)

(25 marks)

Question 25 MAKONIS CO

Makonis Co, a listed company producing motor cars, wants to acquire Nuvola Co, an engineering company involved in producing innovative devices for cars. Makonis Co is keen to incorporate some of Nuvola Co's innovative devices into its cars and thereby boosting sales revenue.

The following financial information is provided for the two companies:

	Makonis Co	Nuvola Co
Current share price	$5·80	$2·40
Number of issued shares	210 million	200 million
Equity beta	1·2	1·2
Asset beta	0·9	1·2

It is thought that combining the two companies will result in several benefits. Free cash flows to firm of the combined company will be $216 million in current value terms, but these will increase by an annual growth rate of 5% for the next four years, before reverting to an annual growth rate of 2·25% in perpetuity. In addition to this, combining the companies will result in cash synergy benefits of $20 million per year, for the next four years. These synergy benefits are not subject to any inflationary increase and no synergy benefits will occur after the fourth year. The debt-to-equity ratio of the combined company will be 40:60 in market value terms and it is expected that the combined company's cost of debt will be 4·55%.

The corporation tax rate is 20%, the current risk free rate of return is 2% and the market risk premium is 7%. It can be assumed that the combined company's asset beta is the weighted average of Makonis Co's and Nuvola Co's asset betas, weighted by their current market values.

Makonis Co has offered to acquire Nuvola Co through a mixed offer of one of its shares for two Nuvola Co shares plus a cash payment, such that a 30% premium is paid for the acquisition. Nuvola Co's equity holders feel that a 50% premium would be more acceptable. Makonis Co has sufficient cash reserves if the premium is 30%, but not if it is 50%.

Required:

(a)   **Estimate the additional equity value created by combining Nuvola Co and Makonis Co, based on the free cash flows to firm method. Comment on the results obtained and briefly discuss the assumptions made.**   (13 marks)

(b)   **Estimate the impact on Makonis Co's equity holders if the premium paid is increased to 50% from 30%.**   (5 marks)

(c)   **Estimate the additional funds required if a premium of 50% is paid instead of 30% and discuss how this premium could be financed.**   (7 marks)

(25 marks)

Question 26 EVERTALK CO

Evertalk Co manufactures mobile phones and operates a network. In order to offer the latest phone technology the company has borrowed extensively on the international bond market. Unfortunately the new technology has proved to be unpopular with consumers, and sales of new handsets and network subscriptions have been less than forecast. As a result the company's share price has fallen to only $0.10, from a high two years ago of $1.80. Capital investment of approximately $100 million per year is required for the company to continue operating at current levels – $20 million for the manufacturing division and $80 million for the network division. Approximately 25% of the sales of the manufacturing division are to the network division.

Statements of profit or loss for the years ending 31 March 2015 and 2016

	2015	2016
	\$m	
Inflows:		
Manufacturing division	280	320
Network division	410	470
	690	790
Outflows:		
Manufacturing division	190	230
Network division	490	560
Tax allowable depreciation	50	60
	730	850
Pre-tax losses	(40)	(60)

Statement of financial position as at 31 March 2016

		\$m
Land and buildings		120
Other non-current assets		175
		295
Current assets		
Inventory	260	
Receivables	85	
Cash	5	
		350
Total assets		645
Ordinary shares (\$0.10 per share)		50
Reserves		46
		96
Non-current liabilities		
12% unsecured bonds 2022		300
Current liabilities		
Floating rate bank loans[1]	40	
Payables	209	
		249
Total equity and liabilities		645

Evertalk's board of directors has arranged a crisis meeting and is considering three proposals:

(i) A corporate restructuring, in which bonds are converted to equity, and which gives control of the company to the current bond holders.

(ii) Sale of the company's shares to Globtalk Co, which operates a successful rival mobile phone network, for the sum of \$50 million. This deal would be conditional upon Globtalk not taking over the liability for any of Evertalk's loans.

(iii) Cease trading and close the company.

---

[1] Currently 8% interest

The restructuring has the following proposed conditions:

(i) Existing ordinary shares will be cancelled and replaced by 100 million new ordinary shares with a nominal value of $0.50 each. 95 million of these will be given to the existing bondholders in exchange for the cancellation of all existing bonds. The bondholders will also make available $100 million of new 10% fixed rate loans.

(ii) Existing shareholders will be offered one 5% convertible bond ($100 nominal value) free of charge in exchange for every 1,000 shares they now own. Conversion into new ordinary shares is available at any time during the next five years at a conversion rate of 50 shares for every $100 convertible bond held.

(iii) 5 million new shares will be given to existing participants in the company's share option scheme in exchange for cancellation of their existing options to purchase 10 million old shares.

Other information:

(i) All existing liabilities have equal claims for repayment against the company's assets.

(ii) No dividends have been paid on ordinary shares for the last three years.

(iii) Losses may not be carried forward for tax purposes.

(iv) Surplus land and buildings could be disposed of for $40 million in order to repay the bank loan.

(v) The value of receivables, cash, non-current assets and payables represented by the two divisions is approximately equal. 90% of the inventory is represented by the manufacturing division.

(vi) The $300 million bond has been borrowed by the network division and the $40 million bank loan by the manufacturing division.

(vii) If the restructuring and new investment does not take place, earnings before tax (after interest payments) are expected to stay at approximately the 2016 level. If new investment takes place, forecast earnings before interest and tax are expected to increase by $30 million as a result of some rationalisation of the network division.

(viii) The current market price of ordinary shares is $0.10 per share, and of bonds $121 per $100 nominal value. The bonds are redeemable at nominal value.

(ix) Corporate tax is at the rate of 30%. The risk free rate is 5% and the market return 14%. The equity beta of the company is 1·15, with the manufacturing division equity beta approximately 0·9, and the network division equity beta approximately 1·35.

 Evertalk's analysts believe that market weighted gearing of about 60% equity, 40% debt is appropriate for the entire sector, but currently this cannot be achieved due to the low share price.

(x) Realisable values of assets if not sold as part of a going concern are estimated to be:

	$m
Land and buildings	140 (including the surplus $40 million)
Other non-current assets	50
Inventory	100
Receivables	70

(xi) Redundancy and closure costs of approximately $100 million would be payable if the company was closed, all payable before any other liabilities. These costs relate equally to the two divisions. All realisable values and closure values are after tax.

36

Required:

Consider the advantages and disadvantages of each of the three proposals, from the viewpoint of each group of existing stakeholders in the company. It should also identify any other strategy(ies) which might be possible for Evertalk Co.

State clearly any assumptions that you make. **(25 marks)**

Question 27 REFLATOR CO

(a)   A division of Reflator Co has recently experienced severe financial difficulties. The management of the division is keen to undertake a buy-out, but in order for the buyout to succeed it needs to attract substantial finance from a venture capital organisation. Reflator is willing to sell the division for $2·1 million and the managers believe that an additional $1 million of capital would need to be invested in the division to create a viable going concern.

Possible financing sources:

Equity from management $500,000, in $0.50 ordinary shares.

Funds from the venture capital organisation:

Equity $300,000, in $0.50 ordinary shares
Debt: 8·5% fixed rate loan $2,000,000
9% subordinated loan with warrants attached $300,000.

The warrants are exercisable any time after four years from now at the rate of 100 ordinary shares at the price of $1.50s per share for every $100 of subordinated loan.

The principal on the 8·5% fixed rate loan is repayable as a bullet payment at the end of eight years. The subordinated loan is repayable by equal annual payments, comprising both interest and principal, over a period of six years.

The division's managers propose to keep dividends to no more than 15% of profits for the first four years.

Independently produced forecasts of earnings before tax and interest after the buy-out are shown below:

Year	1	2	3	4
EBIT ($000)	320	410	500	540

Corporate tax is at the rate of 30% per year.

The managers involved in the buy-out have stated that the book value of equity is likely to increase by about 20% per year during the first four years, making the investment very attractive to the venture capital organisation. The venture capital organisation has stated that it is interested in investing, but has doubts about the forecast growth rate of equity value, and would require warrants for 150 shares per $100 of subordinated loan stock rather than 100 shares.

Required:

(i)   **Discuss the potential advantages of management buy-outs.** (4 marks)

(ii)   **On the basis of the above data, estimate whether or not the book value of equity is likely to grow by 20% per year.** (8 marks)

(iii) **Evaluate the possible implication of the managers agreeing to offer warrants for 150 ordinary shares per $100 of loan stock.** (3 marks)

(b) The MandM Company, a large listed company, has two divisions. The first, the MoneyMint division produces coins and notes for the national bank and generates 80% of the company's revenues. The second, the LunarMint division, manufactures a brand of sweets which are very popular with traders in the financial markets. The company is considering disposing of its LunarMint division. The LunarMint business is no longer viewed as part of the core business of the MandM Company. The chief executive officer commented that he could never understand why the company entered into sweet-making in the first place. The LunarMint business is profitable and low risk, but has not been a high priority for investment.

Required:

Outline the issues that should be considered when disposing of the LunarMint division noting the risks that might be involved. (10 marks)

(25 marks)

Question 28 BBS STORES

BBS Stores, a publicly quoted limited company, is considering unbundling a section of its property portfolio. The company believes that it should use the proceeds to reduce the company's medium-term borrowing and to reinvest the balance in the business (option 1). However, the company's investors have argued strongly that a sale and rental scheme would release substantial cash to investors (option 2).

Attached is the summarised statement of financial position. The company owns all its stores.

	At year end 2016 $m	At year end 2015 $m
Assets		
Non-current assets		
Intangible assets	190	160
Property, plant and equipment	4,050	3,600
Other assets	500	530
	4,740	4,290
Current assets	840	1,160
Total assets	5,580	5,450
Equity and liabilities		
Share capital ($0.25 per share)	425	420
Retained earnings	1,535	980
Total equity	1,960	1,400
Non-current liabilities		
Medium-term loan notes	1,130	1,130
Other non-financial liabilities	890	900
	2,020	2,030
Current liabilities	1,600	2,020
Total liabilities	3,620	4,050
Total equity and liabilities	5,580	5,450

Earnings for 2016 were $670 million (2015: $540 million).

The company's property, plant and equipment within non-current assets for 2016 are as follows:

	Land and buildings	Fixtures, fittings & equipment	Assets under construction	Total
	$m	$m	$m	$m
At revaluation	2,297	4,038	165	6,500
Accumulated depreciation		(2,450)		(2,450)
Carrying amount	2,297	1,588	165	4,050

The property portfolio was revalued at the year end 2016. The assets under construction are valued at a market value of $165 million and relate to new building.

In recent years commercial property values have risen in real terms by 4% per year. Current inflation is 2·5% per year. Property rentals currently earn an 8% return.

The proposal is that 50% of the property portfolio (land and buildings) and 50% of the assets under construction would be sold to a newly established property holding company called RPH that would issue bonds backed by the assured rental income stream from BBS Stores. BBS Stores would not hold any equity interest in the newly formed company nor would they take any part in its management.

BBS Stores is currently financed by equity in the form of $0.25 equity shares with a current market value of $4 per share. The capital debt for the company consists of medium-term loan notes of which $360 million are repayable at the end of two years and $770 million are repayable at the end of six years. Both issues of medium term notes carry a floating rate of LIBOR plus 70 basis points. The interest liability on the six year notes has been swapped at a fixed rate of 5·5% in exchange for LIBOR which is also currently 5·5%. The reduction in the firm's gearing implied by option 1 would improve the firm's credit rating and reduce its current credit spread by 30 basis points. The change in gearing resulting from the second option is not expected to have any impact upon the firm's credit rating. There has been no alteration in the rating of the company since the earliest debt was issued.

The BBS Stores equity beta is currently 1·824. A representative portfolio of commercial property companies has an equity beta of 1·25 and an average market gearing (adjusted for tax) of 50%. The risk free rate of return is 5% and the equity risk premium is 3%. The company's current accounting rate of return on new investment is 13% before tax. You may assume that debt betas are zero throughout.

The effective rate of company tax is 35%.

Required:

On the assumption that the property unbundling proceeds, prepare:

(a)   **A comparative statement showing the impact upon the statement of financial position and on the earnings per share on the assumption that the cash proceeds of the property sale are used:**

      (i)   **To repay the debt, repayable in two years, in full and for reinvestment in non-current assets;**

      (ii)   **To repay the debt, repayable in two years, in full and to finance a share repurchase at the current share price with the balance of the proceeds.**

(12 marks)

(b)   An estimate of the weighted average cost of capital for the remaining business under both options on the assumption that the share price remains unchanged.   (8 marks)

(c)   An evaluation of the potential impact of each alternative on the market value of the firm (you are not required to calculate a revised market value for the firm).   (5 marks)

(25 marks)

Question 29 DORIC CO

Doric Co, a listed company, has two manufacturing divisions: parts and fridges. It has been manufacturing parts for domestic refrigeration and air conditioning systems for a number of years, which it sells to producers of fridges and air conditioners worldwide. It also sells around 30% of the parts it manufactures to its fridge production division. It started producing and selling its own brand of fridges a few years ago. After limited initial success, competition in the fridge market became very tough and revenue and profits have been declining. Without further investment there are currently few growth prospects in either the parts or the fridge divisions. Doric Co borrowed heavily to finance the development and launch of its fridges, and has now reached its maximum overdraft limit. The markets have taken a pessimistic view of the company and its share price has declined to $0.50 per share from a high of $2·83 per share around three years ago.

Extracts from the most recent financial statements

Financial position as at 30 November 2016

Assets	$m	$m
Non-current assets		
Land and buildings		70
Machinery and equipment		50
		120
Current assets		
Inventory	180	
Receivables	40	
		220
Total assets		340
Equity and liabilities		
Share capital ($0.40)		40
Reserves		20
		60
Non-current liabilities		
7% Unsecured bonds 2025	120	
Other unsecured loans (currently 5.33% interest)	30	
		150
Current liabilities		
Payables	70	
Bank overdraft (currently 10% interest)	60	
		130
Total liabilities and capital		340

Statement of profit or loss for the year ended 30 November 2016

			$m
Sales revenue:	Parts division		170
	Fridge division		340
Costs prior to depreciation, interest payments and tax:		Parts division	(120)
		Fridge division	(370)
Tax allowable depreciation			(18)
Finance cost (interest)			(16)
Tax			Nil
Loss			(14)

A survey from the refrigeration and air conditioning parts market has indicated that there is potential for Doric Co to manufacture parts for mobile refrigeration units used in cargo planes and containers. If this venture goes ahead then the parts division before-tax profits are expected to grow by 5% per year. The proposed venture would need an initial one-off investment of $50 million.

Suggested proposals

The board of directors has arranged for a meeting to discuss how to proceed and is considering each of the following proposals:

(1)   To cease trading and close down the company entirely.

(2)   To undertake corporate restructuring in order to reduce the level of debt and obtain the additional capital investment required to continue current operations.

(3)   To close the fridge division and continue the parts division through a leveraged management buy-out, involving some executive directors and managers from the parts division. The new company will then pursue its original parts business as well as the development of the parts for mobile refrigeration business, described above. The proceeds from the sale of the fridge division will be used to pay off existing liabilities. The finance raised from the management buy-out will be used (i) to pay for any remaining liabilities, (ii) to make the capital investment required and (iii) to purchase Doric at a 20% premium above its current market capitalisation.

The following information has been provided for each proposal:

Cease trading

Estimated realisable values of assets not sold as going concern are:

	$m
Land and buildings	60
Machinery and equipment	40
Inventory	90
Receivables	20

Corporate restructuring

The existing ordinary shares will be cancelled and ordinary shareholders will be issued with 40 million new $1 ordinary shares in exchange for a cash payment at par. The existing unsecured bonds will be cancelled and replaced with 270 million of $1 ordinary shares. The bond holders will also contribute $90 million in cash. All the shares will be listed and traded. The bank overdraft will be converted into a secured ten-year loan with a fixed annual interest rate of 7%. The other unsecured loans will be repaid. In addition to this, the directors of the restructured company will get 4 million $1 share options for an exercise price of $1·10, which will expire in four years.

An additional one-off capital investment of $80 million in machinery and equipment is necessary to increase sales revenue for both divisions by 7%, with no change to the costs. After the one-off 7% growth, sales will continue at the new level for the foreseeable future.

It is expected that the Doric's cost of capital rate will reduce by 550 basis points following the restructuring from the current rate.

Management buy-out

The parts division is half the size of the fridge division in terms of the assets and liabilities attributable to it. If the management buy-out proposal is chosen, a pro rata capital investment will be made to machinery and equipment on a one-off basis to increase sales revenue of the parts division by 7%.

It is expected that Doric's cost of capital rate will decrease by 100 basis points following the management buy-out from the current rate.

The following additional information has been provided:

Redundancy and other costs will be approximately $54 million if the whole company is closed, and pro rata for individual divisions that are closed. These costs have priority for payment before any other liabilities in case of closure. The taxation effects relating to this may be ignored.

All other liabilities categories have equal claim for repayment against the company's assets

Corporation tax on profits is 20% and losses cannot be carried forward for tax purposes. Assume that tax is payable in the year incurred.

All the non-current assets, including land and buildings, are eligible for tax allowable depreciation of 15% annually on the book values. The annual reinvestment needed to keep operations at their current levels is roughly equivalent to the tax allowable depreciation. The $50 million investment in the mobile refrigeration business is not eligible for any tax allowable depreciation.

Doric's current cost of capital is 12%.

Required:

(i)   **An estimate of the return the debt holders and shareholders would receive in the event that Doric Co ceases trading and is closed down.** (3 marks)

(ii)   **An estimate of the income position and the value of Doric Co in the event that the restructuring proposal is selected. State any assumptions made.** (7 marks)

(iii)   **An estimate of the amount of additional finance needed and the value of Doric Co if the management buy-out proposal is selected. State any assumptions made.** (7 marks)

(iv)   **A discussion of the impact of each proposal on the existing shareholders, the unsecured bond holders, and the executive directors and managers involved in the management buy-out. Suggest which proposal is likely to be selected.** (8 marks)

(25 marks)

Question 30 PROTEUS CO

Proteus Co, a large listed company, has a number of subsidiaries in different industries but its main line of business is developing surveillance systems and intruder alarms. It has decided to sell a number of companies that it considers are peripheral to its core activities. One of these subsidiary companies is Tyche Co, a company involved in managing the congestion monitoring and charging systems that have been developed by Proteus Co. Tyche Co is a profitable business and it is anticipated that its revenues and costs will continue to increase at their current rate of 8% per year for the foreseeable future.

Tyche Co's managers and some employees want to buy the company through a leveraged management buy-out. An independent assessment estimates Tyche Co's market value at $81 million if Proteus Co agrees to cancel its current loan to Tyche Co. The managers and employees involved in the buy-out will invest $12 million for 75% of the equity in the company, with another $4 million coming from a venture capitalist for the remaining 25% equity.

Palaemon Bank has agreed to lend the balance of the required funds in the form of a 9% loan. The interest is payable at the end of the year, on the loan amount outstanding at the start of each year. A covenant on the loan states that the following debt-equity ratios (using book values) should not be exceeded at the end of each year for the next five years:

Year	1	2	3	4	5
Debt/Equity (%)	350%	250%	200%	150%	125%

Shown below is an extract of the latest annual statement of profit or loss for Tyche Co:

	$000
Sales revenue	60,000
Materials and consumables	12,000
Labour costs	22,000
Other costs	4,000
Allocated overhead charge payable to Proteus Co	14,000
Interest paid	2,000
Taxable profit	6,000
Taxation	1,500
Retained earnings	4,500

As part of the management buy-out agreement, it is expected that Proteus Co will provide management services costing $12 million for the first year of the management buy-out, increasing by 8% per year thereafter.

The current tax rate is 25% on profits and it is expected that 25% of the after-tax profits will be payable as dividends every year. The remaining profits will be allocated to reserves. It is expected that Tyche Co will repay $3 million of the outstanding loan at the end of each of the next five years from the cash flows generated from its business activity.

Required:

(a)   **Briefly discuss the possible benefits to Proteus Co of disposing Tyche Co through a management buy-out.**   (6 marks)

(b)   **Calculate whether the debt-equity covenant imposed by Palaemon Bank on Tyche Co will be breached over the five-year period.**   (12 marks)

(c)   **Discuss briefly the implications of the results obtained in part (b) and outline two possible actions Tyche Co may take if the covenant is in danger of being breached.**   (7 marks)

(25 marks)

Question 31 COEDEN CO

Coeden Co is a listed company operating in the hospitality and leisure industry. Coeden Co's board of directors met recently to discuss a new strategy for the business. The proposal put forward was to sell all the hotel properties that Coeden Co owns and rent them back on a long-term rental agreement. Coeden Co would then focus solely on the provision of hotel services at these properties under its popular brand name. The proposal stated that the funds raised from the sale of the hotel properties would be used to pay off 70% of the outstanding non-current liabilities and the remaining funds would be retained for future investments.

The board of directors are of the opinion that reducing the level of debt in Coeden Co will reduce the company's risk and therefore its cost of capital. If the proposal is undertaken and Coeden Co focuses exclusively on the provision of hotel services, it can be assumed that the current market value of equity will remain unchanged after implementing the proposal.

Coeden Co financial information

Extract from the most recent statement of financial position

	$000
Non-current assets (re-valued recently)	42,560
Current assets	26,840
Total assets	69,400
Share capital ($0.25 per share)	3,250
Reserves	21,780
Non-current liabilities (5·2% redeemable bonds)	42,000
Current liabilities	2,370
Total equity and liabilities	69,400

Coeden Co's latest free cash flow to equity of $2,600,000 was estimated after taking into account taxation, interest and reinvestment in assets to continue with the current level of business. It can be assumed that the annual reinvestment in assets required to continue with the current level of business is equivalent to the annual amount of depreciation. Over the past few years, Coeden Co has consistently used 40% of its free cash flow to equity on new investments while distributing the remaining 60%. The market value of equity calculated on the basis of the free cash flow to equity model provides a reasonable estimate of the current market value of Coeden Co.

The bonds are redeemable at nominal value in three years and pay the coupon on an annual basis. Although the bonds are not traded, it is estimated that Coeden Co's current debt credit rating is BBB but would improve to A+ if the non-current liabilities are reduced by 70%.

Other information

Coeden Co's current equity beta is 1·1 and it can be assumed that debt beta is 0. The risk free rate is estimated to be 4% and the market risk premium is estimated to be 6%.

There is no beta available for companies offering just hotel services, since most companies own their own buildings. The average asset beta for property companies has been estimated at 0·4. It has been estimated that the hotel services business accounts for approximately 60% of the current value of Coeden Co and the property company business accounts for the remaining 40%.

Coeden Co's corporation tax rate is 20%. The three-year borrowing credit spread on A+ rated bonds is 60 basis points and 90 basis points on BBB rated bonds, over the risk free rate of interest.

Required:

(a) **Calculate, and comment on, Coeden Co's cost of equity and weighted average cost of capital before and after implementing the proposal. Briefly explain any assumptions made.** (16 marks)

(b) **Discuss the validity of the assumption that the market value of equity will remain unchanged after the implementation of the proposal.** (4 marks)

(c) As an alternative to selling the hotel properties, the board of directors is considering a demerger of the hotel services and a separate property company which would own the hotel properties. The property company would take over 70% of Coeden Co's long-term debt and pay Coeden Co cash for the balance of the property value.

Required:

Explain what a demerger is, and the possible benefits and drawbacks of pursuing the demerger option as opposed to selling the hotel properties. (5 marks)

(25 marks)

Question 32 NUBO CO

Nubo Co has divisions operating in two diverse sectors: production of aircraft parts and supermarkets. Whereas the aircraft parts production division has been growing rapidly, the supermarkets division's growth has been slower. The company is considering selling the supermarkets division and focusing solely on the aircraft parts production division.

Extracts from the Nubo Co's most recent financial statements are as follows:

Year ended 30 November	2016
	$m
Profit after tax	166
Non-current assets	550
Current assets	122
Non-current liabilities	387
Current liabilities	95

About 70% of Nubo Co's non-current assets and current assets are attributable to the supermarkets division and the remainder to the aircraft parts production division. Each of the two divisions generates roughly half of the total profit after tax. The market value of the two divisions is thought to be equivalent to the price-to-earnings (PE) ratios of the two divisions' industries. The supermarket industry's PE ratio is 7 and the aircraft parts production industry's PE ratio is 12.

Nubo Co can either sell the supermarkets division as a going concern or sell the assets of the supermarkets division separately. If the assets are sold separately, Nubo Co believes that it can sell the non-current assets for 115% of the book value and the current assets for 80% of the book value. The funds raised from the sale of the supermarkets division will be used to pay for all the company's current and non-current liabilities.

Following the sale of the supermarkets division and paying off the liabilities, Nubo Co will raise additional finance for new projects in the form of debt. It will be able to borrow up to a maximum of 100% of the total asset value of the new downsized company.

One of the new projects which Nubo Co is considering is a joint venture with Pilvi Co to produce an innovative type of machinery which will be used in the production of light aircraft and private jets. Both companies will provide the expertise and funding required for the project equally. Representatives from both companies will make up the senior management team and decisions will be made jointly. Legal contracts will be drawn up once profit-sharing and other areas have been discussed by the companies and agreed on.

Pilvi Co has approached Ulap Bank for the finance it requires for the venture, based on Islamic finance principles. Ulap Bank has agreed to consider the request from Pilvi Co, but because the financing requirement will be for a long period of time and because of uncertainties surrounding the project, Ulap Bank wants to provide the finance based on the principles of a Musharaka contract, with Ulap Bank requiring representation on the venture's senior management team. Normally Ulap Bank provides funds based on the principles of a Mudaraba contract, which the bank provides for short-term, low-risk projects, where the responsibility for running a project rests solely with the borrower.

Required:

(a) **Advise Nubo Co whether it should sell the supermarkets division as a going concern or sell the assets separately and estimate the additional cash and debt funds which could be available to the new, downsized company. Show all relevant calculations.** (7 marks)

(b) An alternative to selling the supermarkets division would be to demerge both the divisions. In this case, all of Nubo Co's liabilities would be taken over by the demerged supermarkets division. Also, either of the demerged companies can borrow up to 100% of their respective total asset values.

Required:

Discuss whether a demerger of the supermarkets division may be more appropriate than a sale. (6 marks)

(c) **Discuss why Ulap Bank may want to consider providing the finance based on a Musharaka contract instead of a Mudaraba contract, and the key concerns Nubo Co may have from the arrangement between Pilvi Co and Ulap Bank.** (12 marks)

(25 marks)

Question 33 ASTON CO

Aston Co, a medium-sized internet trading company, has conducted a review of its monthly operating cash flow. Its monthly average operating cash flow has been $14,400 with an observed monthly volatility over the previous five years of trading of 13%. There has been no growth in the trend of operating cash flow over the last 12 months and there is great concern among the small group of shareholders about the credit risk to which the company is exposed. The company has $1·5 million of borrowing repayable in five years and pays an effective interest rate of 8% per year on the debt. Interest is paid monthly. The company has $8,500 of cash in hand or on deposit. The bank has first call upon the assets of the firm. The company estimates the proportion of its loan that would be recoverable in the event of default to be 90% of the outstanding debt value including accrued interest. The inter-bank offered rate is 5·5% per year and the bank normally seeks to recover a risk adjustment of 34 basis points above the spread required to compensate for the expected loss on the loan.

Required:

(a)   On the basis of the annualised operating cash flow after interest and its volatility, estimate the probability of default within 12 months on the assumption that the company has no other lines of credit available.   (12 marks)

(b)   Using the probability of default estimated in (a) discuss the issues that the bank would consider when making a loan of this type and demonstrate how an annual charge of 8% on this loan would be justified.   (13 marks)

(25 marks)

Question 34 GOSLO

The finance division of GoSlo Motor Corporation has made a number of loans to customers with a current pool value of $200 million. The loans have an average term to maturity of four years. The loans generate a steady income to the business of 10·5% per year. The company will use 95% of the loan's pool as collateral for a collateralised loan obligation structured as follows:

■   80% of the collateral value to support a tranche of A-rated floating rate loan notes offering investors LIBOR plus 140 basis points.

■   10% of the collateral value to support a tranche of B-rated fixed rate loan notes offering investors 11%.

■   10% of the collateral value to support a tranche as subordinated certificates (unrated).

In order to minimise interest rate risk, the company has decided to enter into a fixed for variable rate swap on the A-rated floating rate notes, exchanging LIBOR for 8·5%.

Service charges of $240,000 per year will be deducted for administering the income receivable from the underlying pool of loans.

You may ignore prepayment risk.

Required:

(a)   Calculate the expected returns of the investments in each of the three tranches described above. Estimate the sensitivity of the subordinated certificates to a reduction of 1% in the returns generated by the pool.   (12 marks)

(b)   Explain the purpose and the methods of credit enhancement that can be employed on a securitisation such as this scheme.   (6 marks)

(c)   Discuss the risks inherent to the investors in a scheme such as this.   (7 marks)

(25 marks)

Question 35 LEVANTE CO

Levante Co has identified a new project for which it will need to increase its long-term borrowings from $250 million to $400 million. This amount will cover a significant proportion of the total cost of the project and the rest of the funds will come from cash held by the company.

The current $250 million borrowing is in the form of a 4% coupon bond which is trading at $98·71 per $100 and is due to be redeemed at nominal value in three years. This bond has a credit rating of AA. The new borrowing will also be raised in the form of a traded bond with a nominal value of $100 per unit. It is anticipated that the new project will generate sufficient cash flows to be able to redeem the new bond at nominal value after five years. It can be assumed that coupons on both bonds are paid annually.

Both bonds would be ranked equally for payment in the event of default and the directors expect that as a result of the new issue, the credit rating for both bonds will fall to A. The directors are considering the following two alternative options when issuing the new bond:

(i)   Issue the new bond at a fixed coupon of 5% but at a premium or discount, whichever is appropriate to ensure full take up of the bond; or

(ii)   Issue the new bond at a coupon rate where the issue price of the new bond will equal its $100 nominal value.

The following extracts are provided on the government bond spot yield curve and yield spreads for the sector in which Levante operates:

Government bond spot yield curve

Years	1	2	3	4	5
	3·2%	3·7%	4·2%	4·8%	5·0%

Yield spreads (in basis points)

Bond rating	1 year	2 years	3 years	4 years	5 years
AAA	5	9	14	19	25
AA	16	22	30	40	47
A	65	76	87	100	112
BBB	102	121	142	167	193

Required:

(a)   **Calculate the expected percentage fall in the market value of the existing bond if Levante Co's bond credit rating falls from AA to A.**   (5 marks)

(b)   **Advise the directors on the financial implications of choosing each of the two options when issuing the new bond. Support the advice with appropriate calculations.** (6 marks)

(c)   **Advise on the advantages, drawbacks and methods of raising equity finance on overseas stock markets.**   (8 marks)

(d)   **Advise on the advantages, drawbacks and methods of raising debt in the Euromarkets.**
                                                                                    (6 marks)

                                                                                (25 marks)

Question 36 ENNEA CO

Three proposals were put forward for further consideration after a meeting of the executive directors of Ennea Co to discuss the future investment and financing strategy of the business. Ennea Co is a listed company operating in the haulage and shipping industry.

Proposal 1

To increase the company's level of debt by borrowing a further $20 million and use the funds raised to buy back share capital.

Proposal 2

To increase the company's level of debt by borrowing a further $20 million and use these funds to invest in additional non-current assets in the haulage strategic business unit.

Proposal 3

To sell excess non-current haulage assets with a carrying amount of $25 million for $27 million and focus on offering more services to the shipping strategic business unit. This business unit will require no additional investment in non-current assets. All the funds raised from the sale of the non-current assets will be used to reduce the company's debt.

Ennea Co financial information

Extracts from the forecast financial position for the coming year

	$m
Non-current assets	282
Current assets	66
Total assets	348
Equity and liabilities	
Share capital ($0.40 per share)	48
Retained earnings	123
Total equity	171
Non-current liabilities	140
Current liabilities	37
Total liabilities	177
Total liabilities and capital	348

Ennea Co's forecast after tax profit for the coming year is expected to be $26 million and its current share price is $3·20 per share. The non-current liabilities consist solely of a 6% medium term loan redeemable within seven years. The terms of the loan contract stipulates that an increase in borrowing will result in an increase in the coupon payable of 25 basis points on the total amount borrowed, while a reduction in borrowing will lower the coupon payable by 15 basis points on the total amount borrowed.

Ennea Co's effective tax rate is 20%. The company's estimated after tax rate of return on investment is expected to be 15% on any new investment. It is expected that any reduction in investment would suffer the same rate of return.

Required:

(a)   **Estimate and discuss the impact of each of the three proposals on the forecast statement of financial position, the earnings and earnings per share, and gearing of Ennea Co.**

(20 marks)

(b)   An alternative suggestion to proposal three was made where the non-current assets could be leased to other companies instead of being sold. The lease receipts would then be converted into an asset through securitisation. The proceeds from the sale of the securitised lease receipts asset would be used to reduce the outstanding loan borrowings.

Required:

Explain what the securitisation process would involve and what would be the key barriers to Ennea Co undertaking the process.   (5 marks)

(25 marks)

Question 37 BOXLESS CO

(a)   **Discuss the main features of:**

       (i)   **corporate share repurchases (buy-backs); and**
       (ii)   **share (stock) splits;**

       and why companies might use them. Include in your discussion comment on the possible effects on share price of share repurchases and share (inventory) splits in comparison to the payment of dividends. (10 marks)

(b)   Boxless Co has subsidiaries in three overseas countries, Annovia, Cardenda and Sporoon. Corporate taxes for the three countries are shown below:

	Corporate income tax rate	Withholding tax on dividends	% of after tax income remitted to the UK
Annovia	40%	10%	70
Cardenda	25%	–	40
Sporoon	20%	5%	80

The UK corporate tax rate is 30%, and bilateral tax treaties exist between the UK and each of the three countries. Under the treaties, any corporate tax paid overseas on income remitted to the UK may be credited against UK tax liability. Boxless currently remits income from its overseas subsidiaries direct to the UK parent company.

The UK government currently only taxes income from multinational companies' overseas subsidiaries when such income is remitted to the UK. UK tax liability is based upon the grossed up dividend distributions to the UK (grossed up at the local tax rate and before deduction of any withholding tax).

The UK government is now considering taxing the gross income earned by overseas subsidiaries. If such gross income were to be taxed, credit against UK tax liability would be available for all corporate tax paid overseas.

Required:

       (i)   **Estimate the impact on the cash flows of Boxless if the UK government alters the tax rules as detailed above. Assume that the taxable income in each of the subsidiaries is the equivalent of £100,000.** (9 marks)

       (ii)   **For each of the current and possible new tax rules, evaluate what benefit, if any, Boxless would experience if it were to transfer income from its overseas subsidiaries to the parent company via a tax haven holding company. Assume that the UK tax authorities would then treat all income from overseas subsidiaries as coming from a single source, the tax haven holding company. Comment upon your results.** (6 marks)

(25 marks)

Question 38 LAMRI CO

Lamri Co (Lamri), a listed company, is expecting sales revenue to grow to $80 million next year, which is an increase of 20% from the current year. The operating profit margin for next year is forecast to be the same as this year at 30% of sales revenue. In addition to these profits, Lamri receives 75% of the after-tax profits from one of its wholly owned foreign subsidiaries – Magnolia Co (Magnolia), as dividends. However, its second wholly owned foreign subsidiary – Strymon Co (Strymon) does not pay dividends.

Lamri is due to pay dividends of $7·5 million shortly and has maintained a steady 8% annual growth rate in dividends over the past few years. The company has grown rapidly in the last few years as a result of investment in key projects and this is likely to continue.

For the coming year it is expected that Lamri will require the following capital investment.

(1)   An investment equivalent to the amount of depreciation to keep its non-current asset base at the present productive capacity. Lamri charges depreciation of 25% on a straight-line basis on its non-current assets of $15 million. This charge has been included when calculating the operating profit amount.

(2)   A 25% investment in additional non-current assets for every $1 increase in sales revenue.

(3) $4·5 million additional investment in non-current assets for a new project.

Lamri also requires a 15% investment in working capital for every $1 increase in sales revenue.

Strymon produces specialist components solely for Magnolia to assemble into finished goods. Strymon will produce 300,000 specialist components at $12 variable cost per unit and will incur fixed costs of $2·1 million for the coming year. It will then transfer the components to Magnolia at full cost price, where they will be assembled at a cost of $8 per unit and sold for $50 per unit. Magnolia will incur additional fixed costs of $1·5 million in the assembly process.

Tax-Ethic (TE) is a charitable organisation devoted to reducing tax avoidance schemes by companies operating in poor countries around the world. TE has petitioned Lamri's Board of Directors to reconsider Strymon's policy of transferring goods at full cost. TE suggests that the policy could be changed to cost plus 40% mark-up. If Lamri changes Strymon's policy, it is expected that Strymon would be asked to remit 75% of its after-tax profits as dividends to Lamri.

Other information

(1)   Lamri's outstanding non-current liabilities of $35 million, on which it pays interest of 8% per year, and its 30 million $1 issued equity capital will not change for the coming year.

(2)   Lamri's, Magnolia's and Strymon's profits are taxed at 28%, 22% and 42% respectively. A withholding tax of 10% is deducted from any dividends remitted from Strymon.

(3)   The tax authorities where Lamri is based charge tax on profits made by subsidiary companies but give full credit for tax already paid by overseas subsidiaries.

(4)   All costs and revenues are in $ equivalent amounts and exchange rate fluctuations can be ignored.

Required:

(a)   Calculate Lamri's dividend capacity for the coming year prior to implementing TE's proposal and after implementing the proposal.   (14 marks)

(b)   Comment on the impact of implementing TE's proposal and suggest possible actions Lamri may take as a result.   (6 marks)

(c)   Briefly discuss possible advantages to a multinational company from using a holding company based in a tax haven.   (5 marks)

(25 marks)

Question 39 LIMNI CO

Limni Co is a large company manufacturing hand-held electronic devices such as mobile phones and tablet computers. The company has been growing rapidly over the last few years, but it also has high research and development expenditure. It is involved in a number of projects worldwide, developing new and innovative products and systems in a rapidly changing industry. Due to the nature of the industry, this significant growth in earnings has never been stable, but has depended largely on the success of the new innovations and competitor actions. However, in the last two years it seems that the rapid period of growth is slowing, with fewer products coming to market compared to previous years.

Limni Co has never paid dividends and has financed projects through internally generated funds and with occasional rights issues of new share capital. It currently has insignificant levels of debt. The retained cash reserves have recently grown because of a drop in the level of investment in new projects.

The company has an active treasury division which invests spare funds in traded equities, bonds and other financial instruments; and releases the funds when required for new projects. The division also manages cash flow risk using money and derivative markets. The treasury division is currently considering investing in three companies with the following profit after tax (PAT) and dividend history:

Year	Company Theta		Company Omega		Company Kappa	
	PAT	Dividends	PAT	Dividends	PAT	Dividends
	$000	$000	$000	$000	$000	$000
2016	57,100	22,840	93,300	60,560	162,400	44,100
2015	54,400	21,760	90,600	57,680	141,500	34,200
2014	52,800	21,120	88,000	54,840	108,900	26,300
2013	48,200	19,280	85,400	52,230	105,700	20,250
2012	45,500	18,200	82,900	49,740	78,300	15,700

All of the three companies' share capital has remained largely unchanged since 2012.

Recently, Limni Co's Board of Directors (BoD) came under pressure from the company's larger shareholders to start returning some of the funds, currently retained by the company, back to the shareholders. The BoD thinks that the shareholders have a strong case to ask for repayments. However, it is unsure whether to pay a special, one-off large dividend from its dividend capacity and retained funds, followed by small annual dividend payments; or to undertake a periodic share buyback scheme over the next few years.

Limni Co is due to prepare its statement of profit or loss shortly and estimates that the annual sales revenue will be $600 million, on which its profit before tax is expected to be 23% of sales revenue. It charges depreciation of 25% on a straight-line basis on its non-current assets of $220 million. It estimates that $67 million investment in current and non-current assets was spent during the year. It is due to receive $15 million in dividends from its subsidiary companies, on which annual tax of 20% on average has been paid. Limni Co itself pays annual tax at 26%, and the tax authorities where Limni Co is based charge tax on dividend remittances made by overseas subsidiary companies, but give full credit on tax already paid on those remittances. In order to fund the new policy of returning funds to shareholders, Limni Co's BoD wants to increase the current estimated dividend capacity by 10%, by asking the overseas subsidiary companies for higher repatriations.

Required:

(a)   **Discuss Limni Co's current dividend, financing and risk management policies, and suggest how the decision to return retained funds back to the shareholders will affect these policies.**   (8 marks)

(b)   **Evaluate the dividend policies of each of the three companies that Limni Co is considering investing in, and discuss which company Limni Co might select.**   (8 marks)

(c)   **Calculate, and briefly comment on, how much the dividends from overseas companies need to increase by, to increase Limni Co's dividend capacity by 10%.**   (6 marks)

(d)   **Discuss the benefits to Limni Co's shareholders of receiving repayments through a share buyback scheme as opposed to the dividend scheme described above.**   (3 marks)

(25 marks)

Question 40 AVT CO

(a)   **Discuss how a decrease in the value of each of the determinants of the option price in the Black-Scholes option-pricing model is likely to change the price of a call option.** (5 marks)

(b)   AVT Co is considering the introduction of an executive share option scheme.

The scheme would be offered to all middle managers of the company. It would replace the existing scheme of performance bonuses linked to the post-tax earnings per share of the company. Such bonuses in the last year ranged between $5,000 and $7,000. If the option scheme is introduced new options are expected to be offered to the managers each year.

It is proposed for the first year that all middle managers are offered options to purchase 5,000 shares at a price of $5 per share after the options have been held for one year. Assume that the tax authorities allow the exercise of such options after they have been held for one year. If the options are not exercised at that time they will lapse.

The company's shares have just become ex-div and have a current market price of $6.10 per share. The dividend paid was $0.25 per share, a level that has remained constant for the last three years. Assume that dividends are only paid annually.

The company's share price has experienced a standard deviation of 38% during the last year.

The short-term risk free interest rate is 6% per year.

Required:

(i)   **Discuss the relative merits for the company of the existing bonus scheme and the proposed share option scheme.**   (6 marks)

(ii)   **Evaluate whether or not the proposed share option scheme is likely to be attractive to middle managers of AVT Co.**   (7 marks)

(iii)   When told of the scheme one manager stated that he would rather receive put options than call options, as they would be more valuable to him.

(1)   **Discuss whether or not AVT should agree to offer him put options.**   (3 marks)

(2)   **Calculate whether or not he is correct in his statement that put options would be more valuable to him.**   (4 marks)

(25 marks)

Question 41 FOLTER CO

(a)   Folter Co has short-term equity holdings in several companies that may be future take-over targets. The equity market has recently been very volatile, and the finance director is considering how to protect the equity portfolio from adverse market movements, in case some of the holdings need to be sold, at short notice, by the end of October.

The finance director is particularly concerned about 2 million shares that are currently held in Magterdoor Co. The shares are trading at 535 cents.

Assume that it is now 1 June and that option contracts mature at the month end.

Traded options on 1,000 Megterdoor shares:

	CALLS			PUTS		
	July	October	January	July	October	January
500	37·5	52·5	60·5	2·0	24·5	35·0
550	6·5	24·0	34·0	21·0	51·0	60·0

Required:

(i)   **Illustrate how Folter Co might use traded options to protect against a fall in the share price of Magterdoor Co. Assuming that Folter has to sell the shares at the end of October at a price of 485 cents, evaluate the outcome of the hedge(s).** (4 marks)

(ii)   **Assume that the call option delta of Magterdoor is 0·47. Illustrate how a delta neutral hedge might be used to protect against price movements of the shares of Magterdoor. Comment upon any practical problems of using a delta hedge for this purpose.** (4 marks)

(iii)   **Discuss the reasons why the January 550 call option premium is not the same as the intrinsic value of the option.** (2 marks)

(iv)   The managing director of Folter suggests that Folter's holding in Magterdoor be increased from 2% to 6% of Magterdoor's issued shares.

Discuss briefly the advantages and disadvantages of this strategy. (3 marks)

(b)   A firm has $1000m nominal value of bonds in issue, paying 6% coupon and redeemable at nominal value after five years. The fair value of the bonds is $1079.68m and their credit spread is 120bps.

The fair value of the firm's assets is $1100m and Monte Carlo simulation has estimated the annual standard deviation of this asset value at 35%.

The yield to maturity on five-year treasuries is 3%.

Required:

Use option pricing methodology to value the firm's equity, applying the following approaches to recalibrating the firm's debt:

(i)   **restating as the redemption price of an equivalent zero-coupon bond;**
(ii)   **using Macaulay duration.**

Comment on your results. (12 marks)

(25 marks)

Question 42 DIGUNDER

Digunder, a property development company, has gained planning permission for the development of a housing complex at Newtown which will be developed over a three year period. The project has an expected net present value of $4 million at a cost of capital of 10% per year. Digunder has an option to acquire the land in Newtown, at an agreed price of $24 million, which must be exercised within the next two years. Immediate building of the housing complex would be risky as the project has a volatility attached to its future cash flows of 25%.

One source of risk is the potential for development of Newtown as a regional commercial centre for the large number of firms leaving the capital, Bigcity. Within the next two years, an announcement by the government will be made about the development of transport links into Newtown from outlying districts including the area where Digunder hold the land option concerned. The risk free rate is 5%.

Required:

(a)   **Estimate the value of the option to delay the start of the project for two years using the Black Scholes model and comment. Assume that the government will make its announcement about the potential transport link at the end of the two-year period.**

(12 marks)

(b)   **On the basis of your valuation of the option to delay, estimate the overall value of the project, giving a concise rationale for the valuation method you have used.**   (6 marks)

(c)   **Describe the limitations of the valuation method you used in (a) above and describe how you would value the option if the government were to make the announcement at ANY time over the next two years.**   (7 marks)

(25 marks)

Question 43 ALASKA SALVAGE

Alaska Salvage is in discussion with potential lenders about financing an ambitious five-year project searching for lost gold in the central Atlantic. The company has had great success in the past with its various salvage operations and is now quoted on the London Alternative Investment Market. The company is currently financed by 120,000 equity shares trading at $85 per share. It needs to borrow $1·6 million and is concerned about the level of the fixed rates being suggested by the lenders. After lengthy discussions the lenders are prepared to offer finance against a mezzanine issue of fixed rate five-year notes with warrants attached. Each $10,000 note, repayable at par, would carry a warrant for 100 equity shares at an exercise price of $90 per share. The estimated volatility of the returns on the company's equity is 20% and the risk free rate of interest is 5%. The company does not pay dividends to its equity investors.

You may assume that the issue of these loan notes will not influence the current value of the firm's equity. The issue will be made at par.

Required:

(a)   **Estimate, using Black-Scholes Option Pricing Model as appropriate, the current value of each warrant to the lender noting the assumptions that you have made in your valuation.**   (10 marks)

(b)   **Estimate the coupon rate that would be required by the lenders if they wanted a 13% rate of return on their investment.**   (5 marks)

(c) **Discuss the advantages and disadvantages of issuing mezzanine debt in the situation outlined in the case.** (10 marks)

(25 marks)

Question 44 MARENGO CO

The treasury division of Marengo Co, a large quoted company, holds equity investments in various companies around the world. One of the investments is in Arion Co, in which Marengo holds 200,000 shares, which is around 2% of the total number of Arion Co's shares traded on the stock market. Over the past year, due to the general strength in the equity markets following optimistic predictions of the performance of world economies, Marengo's investments have performed well. However, there is some concern that the share price of Arion Co may fall in the coming two months due to uncertainty in its markets. It is expected that any fall in share prices will be reversed following this period of uncertainty.

The treasury division managers in Marengo, Wenyu, Lola and Sam, held a meeting to discuss what to do with the investment in Arion Co and they each made a different suggestion as follows:

(1)   Wenyu was of the opinion that Marengo's shareholders would benefit most if no action were taken. He argued that the courses of action proposed by Lola and Sam, below, would result in extra costs and possibly increase the risk to Marengo Co.

(2)   Lola proposed that Arion Co's shares should be sold in order to eliminate the risk of a fall in the share price.

(3)   Sam suggested that the investment should be hedged using an appropriate derivative product.

Although no exchange-traded derivative products exist on Arion Co's shares, a bank has offered over-the-counter (OTC) option contracts at an exercise price of $3.50 per share in a contract size of 1,000 shares each, for the appropriate time period. Arion Co's current share price is $3.40 per share, although the volatility of the share prices could be as high as 40%.

It can be assumed that Arion Co will not pay any dividends in the coming few months and that the appropriate inter-bank lending rate will be 4% over that period.

Required:

(a) **(i)** **Estimate the number of OTC put option contracts that Marengo Co will need to construct a delta hedge against any adverse movement in Arion Co's share price. Provide a brief explanation of your answer.** (6 marks)

(ii) **Discuss possible reasons for the suggestions made by each of the three managers.** (9 marks)

(b) MesmerMagic Co (MMC) is considering whether to undertake the development of a new computer game based on an adventure film due to be released in 22 months. It is expected that the game will be available to buy two months after the film's release, by which time it will be possible to judge the popularity of the film with a high degree of certainty. However, at present, there is considerable uncertainty about whether the film, and therefore the game, is likely to be successful. Although MMC would pay for the exclusive rights to develop and sell the game now, the directors are of the opinion that they should delay the decision to produce and market the game until the film has been released and the game is available for sale.

MMC has forecast the following end of year operating cash flows for the four-year sales period of the game:

Year	1	2	3	4
Cash flows ($m)	25	18	10	5

MMC will spend $7 million at the start of each of the next two years to develop the game, the gaming platform, and to pay for the exclusive rights to develop and sell the game. Following this, the company will require $35 million for production, distribution and marketing costs at the start of the four-year sales period of the game.

It can be assumed that all the costs and revenues include inflation. The relevant cost of capital for this project is 11% and the risk free rate is 3·5%. MMC has estimated the likely volatility of the operating cash flows at a standard deviation of 30%.

Required:

Estimate the financial impact of the directors' decision to delay the production and marketing of the game. The Black-Scholes Option Pricing model may be used, where appropriate. All relevant calculations should be shown. (10 marks)

(25 marks)

Question 45 KYT CO

Assume that it is now 30 June. KYT Co is a company located in the US that has a contract to purchase goods from Japan in two months' time on 1 September. The payment is to be made in yen and will total 140 million yen.

The managing director of KYT Co wishes to protect the contract against adverse movements in foreign exchange rates, and is considering the use of currency futures. The following data are available.

Spot foreign exchange rate:

      Yen per $ 128·15

Yen currency futures contracts on SIMEX (Singapore Monetary Exchange):

Contract size 12,500,000 yen, contract prices are in $US per yen.

      Contract prices:
      September   0·007985
      December   0·008250

Assume that futures contracts mature at the end of the month.

Required:

(a)   Illustrate how KYT might hedge its foreign exchange risk using currency futures.
                                  (5 marks)

(b)   Show what basis is involved in the proposed hedge. (2 marks)

(c)   Assuming the spot exchange rate is 120 yen per $ on 1 September and that basis decreases steadily in a linear manner, calculate what the result of the hedge is expected to be. Briefly discuss why this result might not occur. Margin requirements and taxation may be ignored. (7 marks)

(d)   Tertial is a UK-based company that has recently commenced exports to Blundonia, a developing country. A payment of 100 million pesos is due from a customer in Blundonia in three months' time. The Blundonian government sometimes restricts the movement of funds from the country, but has indicated that payment to Tertial has a good chance of receiving approval. No forward market or derivatives markets exist for the Blundonian peso.

The Blundonian peso is currently linked to the US dollar.

Exchange rates:	*pesos per £*	*$ per £*
Spot rate	126·4 – 128·2	1·775 – 1·782
3 month forward rate	Not available	1·781 – 1·789

Tertial can borrow at 6% per year or invest at 4% per year in the UK, can borrow at 7% and invest at 4·5% in the US, and at 14% and 10% respectively in Blundonia.

Tertial currently has a £800,000 overdraft in the UK.

Inflation rates:

UK	3%
US	4%
Blundonia	14%

Required:

(i) **Discuss the advantages and disadvantages of the alternative currency hedges (including relevant cross-hedges) that are available to Tertial. Calculate the expected outcome of each hedge, and recommend which hedge should be selected.** (8 marks)

(ii) **Suggest possible action that Tertial might take if the government decides not to allow the transfer of money out of Blundonia.** (3 marks)

(25 marks)

Question 46 GALEPLUS CO

(a) **From the perspective of a corporate financial manager, discuss the advantages and potential problems of using currency swaps.** (5 marks)

(b) Galeplus Co has been invited to purchase and operate a new telecommunications centre in the republic of Perdia. The purchase price is 2,000 million rubbits. The Perdian government has built the centre in order to improve the country's infrastructure, but has currently not got enough funds to pay money owed to the local constructors. Galeplus would purchase the centre for a period of three years, after which it would be sold back to the Perdian government for an agreed price of 4,000 million rubbits. Galeplus would supply three years of technical expertise and training for local staff, for an annual fee of 40 million rubbits, after Perdian taxation. Other after tax net cash flows from the investment in Perdia are expected to be negligible during the three year period.

Perdia has only recently become a democracy, and in the last five years has experienced inflation rates of between 25% and 500%. The managers of Galeplus are concerned about the foreign exchange risk of the investment. Perdia has recently adopted economic stability measures suggested by the IMF, and inflation during the next three years is expected to be between 15% per year and 50% per year.

Galeplus's bankers have suggested using a currency swap for the purchase price of the factory, with a swap of principal immediately and in three years' time, both swaps at today's spot rate. The bank would charge a fee of 0·75% per year (in dollars) for arranging the swap. Galeplus would take 75% of any net arbitrage benefit from the swap, after deducting bank fees.

Relevant borrowing rates are:

	Home country	Perdia
Galeplus	6·25%	PIBOR + 2·0%
Perdian counterparty	8·3%	PIBOR + 1·5%

Note: PIBOR is the Perdian interbank offered rate, which has tended to be set at approximately the current inflation level. Inflation in the home country is expected to be negligible.

	Exchange rates
Spot	85·4 rubbits per $
3 year forward rate	Not available

Required:

(i)   **Estimate the potential annual percentage interest saving that Galeplus might make from using a currency swap relative to borrowing directly in Perdia.**

(6 marks)

(ii)   **Assuming the swap takes place as described, provide a reasoned analysis, including relevant calculations, as to whether or not Galeplus should purchase the communications centre. The relevant risk adjusted discount rate may be assumed to be 15% per year.** (8 marks)

(c)   As alternatives to the currency swap the bank has suggested:

(i)   A swaption with the same terms as the currency swap, and an upfront premium of $300,000.

(ii)   A European style three year currency put option on the total expected net cash flow in year 3 at an exercise price of 160 rubbits per $ and an upfront premium of $1·7 million.

Required:

Discuss and evaluate the relative merits of these suggestions for Galeplus. (6 marks)

(25 marks)

Question 47 LAMMER CO

(a)   Lammer Co is a UK-based company that regularly trades with companies in the US. Several large transactions are due in five months' time. These are shown below. The transactions are in "000" units of the currencies shown. Assume that it is now 1 June and that futures and options contracts mature at the relevant month end.

	Exports to:	Imports from:
Company 1	$490	£150
Company 2	–	$890
Company 3	£110	$750

Exchange rates:	*$US per £*
Spot	1·9156 – 1·9210
3 months forward	1·9066 – 1·9120
1-year forward	1·8901 – 1·8945

Annual interest rates available to Lammer:

	Borrowing	Investing
Sterling up to 6 months	5·5%	4·2%
Dollar up to 6 months	4·0%	2·0%

CME $/£ Currency futures (£62,500)

September	1·9045
December	1·8986

CME currency options prices, $/£ options £31,250 (cents per pound)

	CALLS		PUTS	
	Sept	*Dec*	*Sept*	*Dec*
1·8800	4·76	5·95	1·60	2·96
1·9000	3·53	4·70	2·36	4·34
1·9200	2·28	3·56	3·40	6·55

Required:

Advise on alternative strategies for hedging the five-month currency risk.

Include all relevant calculations relating to the alternative types of hedge. (15 marks)

(b) In a typical financial year Lammer has net dollar imports of $4·2 million. This is expected to continue for five years.

The company's cost of capital is estimated to be 11% per year. Taxation may be ignored, and cash flows may be assumed to occur at the year end.

Required:

Assuming that there is no change in the physical volume or dollar price of imports, estimate the effect on the expected market value of Lammer Co if the market expects the dollar to strengthen by 3% per year against the pound. (5 marks)

(c) **Briefly discuss how Lammer Co might manage the economic exposure of any foreign subsidiaries in the US.** (5 marks)

(25 marks)

Question 48 ASTEROID SYSTEMS

Asteroid Systems is a German-based company with a subsidiary in Switzerland. The company's financial manager expects the Swiss business will remit the equivalent of 1·5 million Euro (€) in two months. Her expectations of the future remittance are based upon the current forward rate.

The current spot and forward rates for Swiss francs against the Euro are extracted from the Financial Times and are shown in the table below.

	Closing mid-point	Change on day	Bid/offer spread	Day high	low	One month Rate	annual %	Three month Rate	annual %
SFr per €	1·6242	0·0107	239–244	1·6261	1·6147	1·6223	1·4	1·6176	1·6

In the euro money market the company can make fixed interest deposits at LIBOR and can borrow at LIBOR plus 20 basis points for terms of greater than one month but up to six months. The company can borrow at fixed rates in the Swiss money market.

LIBOR rates, as quoted in the Financial Times, are as follows:

	€	CHF
spot	3·56688	2·06000
1 week	3·57300	2·06000
2 week	3·58438	2·07000
1 month	3·60900	2·08000
2 month	3·72538	2·17000
3 month	3·78238	2·20000

The company's financial manager is keen to eliminate transaction risk. However, because of the margin requirements and their impact upon the firm's cash flow, she would prefer not to use exchange traded derivatives. Swiss franc borrowing or lending rates would need to be negotiated with the bank.

Required:

(a)   (i)   **Estimate the lowest acceptable Swiss borrowing or lending rate for a money market hedge maturing in two months.** (7 marks)

     (ii)   **Discuss the relative advantages and disadvantages of the use of a money market hedge compared with using exchange traded derivatives for hedging a foreign exchange exposure.** (6 marks)

(b)   You are an importer of stone chippings for building purposes and you have entered into a fixed price contract for the delivery of 10,000 metric tonnes per month for the next six months.

     The first delivery is due in one month's time.

     Each tonne costs €220 under the fixed price contract and will be paid in euros at the end of the month in question. Your domestic currency is the dollar and your supplier is in the euro area. The current rate of exchange is 0·8333 (Euro per dollar). The quoted forward rates and the risk free interest rates in the dollar zone are as follows:

Month	1	2	3	4	5	6
Forward rates (€ per $)	0·8326	0·8314	0·8302	0·8289	0·8278	0·8267
$ zero coupon yield curve	3·25%	3·45%	3·50%	3·52%	3·52%	3·52%

Required:

(i)   **Estimate the forward exchange rate that would be fixed for a six month currency swap with monthly deliveries against the current order of 10,000 metric tonnes per month.** (6 marks)

(ii)   **Outline the advantages and disadvantages of using a plain vanilla currency swap with monthly delivery compared with a series of forward contracts.** (6 marks)

(25 marks)

Question 49 CASASOPHIA CO

Casasophia Co, based in a European country that uses the Euro (€), constructs and maintains advanced energy efficient commercial properties around the world. It has just completed a major project in the USA and is due to receive the final payment of US$20 million in four months.

Casasophia Co is planning to commence a major construction and maintenance project for the government of Mazabia, a small African country, in six months' time. Mazabia's government requires Casasophia Co to deposit the MShs2·64 billion it needs for the project, with Mazabia's central bank, at the commencement of the project. In return, Casasophia Co will receive a fixed sum of MShs1·5 billion after tax, at the end of each year for a period of three years. Neither of these amounts is subject to inflationary increases. The relevant risk adjusted discount rate for the project is assumed to be 12%.

Financial information

Exchange rates available to Casasophia

	Per €1	Per €1
Spot	US$1·3585–US$1·3618	MShs116–MShs128
4-month forward	US$1·3588–US$1·3623	Not available

Currency Futures (Contract size €125,000, Quotation: US$ per €1)

2-month expiry	1·3633
5-month expiry	1·3698

Currency Options (Contract size €125,000, Exercise price quotation: US$ per €1, Premium quotation: cents per euro)

	Calls		Puts	
Exercise price	*2-month expiry*	*5-month expiry*	*2-month expiry*	*5-month expiry*
1·36	2·35	2·80	2·47	2·98
1·38	1·88	2·23	4·23	4·64

Casasophia Co Local Government Base Rate	2·20%
Mazabia Government Base Rate	10·80%

Mazabia's current annual inflation rate is 9·7% and is expected to remain at this level for the next six months. However, after that, there is considerable uncertainty about the future and the annual level of inflation could be anywhere between 5% and 15% for the next few years. The country where Casasophia Co is based is expected to have a stable level of inflation at 1·2% per year for the foreseeable future. A local bank in Mazabia has offered Casasophia Co the opportunity to swap the MShs1.5 billion receivable at the end of each of the project's three years for euros, at the estimated annual MShs/€ forward rates based on the current government base rates.

Required:

(a) **Advise Casasophia Co on, and recommend, an appropriate hedging strategy for the US$ income it is due to receive in four months. Include all relevant calculations.**   (15 marks)

(b) **Given that Casasophia Co agrees to the local bank's offer of the swap, calculate the net present value of the project, in six months' time, in €. Discuss whether the swap would be beneficial to Casasophia Co.**   (10 marks)

(25 marks)

Question 50 LIGNUM CO

Lignum Co, a large listed company, manufactures agricultural machines and equipment for different markets around the world. Although its main manufacturing base is in France and it uses the Euro (€) as its base currency, it also has a few subsidiary companies around the world. Lignum Co's treasury division is considering how to approach the following three cases of foreign exchange exposure that it faces.

Case One

Lignum Co regularly trades with companies based in Zuhait, a small country in South America whose currency is the Zupesos (ZP). It recently sold machinery for ZP140 million, which it is about to deliver to a company based there. It is expecting full payment for the machinery in four months. Although there are no exchange traded derivative products available for the Zupesos, Medes Bank has offered Lignum Co a choice of two over-the-counter derivative products.

The first derivative product is an over-the-counter forward rate determined on the basis of the Zuhait base rate of 8·5% plus 25 basis points and the French base rate of 2·2% less 30 basis points.

Alternatively, with the second derivative product Lignum Co can purchase either Euro call or put options from Medes Bank at an exercise price equivalent to the current spot exchange rate of ZP142 per €1. The option premiums offered are: ZP7 per €1 for the call option or ZP5 per €1 for the put option.

The premium cost is payable in full at the commencement of the option contract. Lignum Co can borrow money at the base rate plus 150 basis points and invest money at the base rate minus 100 basis points in France.

Case Two

Namel Co is Lignum Co's subsidiary company based in Maram, a small country in Asia, whose currency is the Maram Ringit (MR). The current pegged exchange rate between the Maram Ringit and the Euro is MR35 per €1. Due to economic difficulties in Maram over the last couple of years, it is very likely that the Maram Ringit will devalue by 20% imminently. Namel Co is concerned about the impact of the devaluation on its Statement of Financial Position.

Given below is an extract from the current Statement of Financial Position of Namel Co.

	MR 000
Non-current assets	179,574
Current assets	146,622
Total assets	326,196
Share capital and reserves	102,788
Non-current liabilities	132,237
Current liabilities	91,171
Total equity and liabilities	326,196

The current assets consist of inventories, receivables and cash. Receivables account for 40% of the current assets. All the receivables relate to sales made to Lignum Co in Euro. About 70% of the current liabilities consist of payables relating to raw material inventory purchased from Lignum Co and payable in Euro. 80% of the non-current liabilities consist of a Euro loan and the balance are borrowings sourced from financial institutions in Maram.

Case Three

Lignum Co manufactures a range of farming vehicles in France which it sells within the European Union to countries which use the Euro. Over the previous few years, it has found that its sales revenue from these products has been declining and the sales director is of the opinion that this is entirely due to the strength of the Euro. Lignum Co's biggest competitor in these products is based in the USA and US$ rate has changed from almost parity with the Euro three years ago, to the current value of US$1·47 for €1. The agreed opinion is that the US$ will probably continue to depreciate against the Euro, but possibly at a slower rate, for the foreseeable future.

Required:

(i)   **Briefly explains the type of currency exposure Lignum Co faces for each of the above cases;**   (6 marks)

(ii)   **Recommends which of the two derivative products Lignum Co should use to manage its exposure in case one and advises on alternative hedging strategies that could be used. Show all relevant calculations;**   (8 marks)

(iii)   **Computes the gain or loss on Namel Co's Statement of Financial Position, due to the devaluation of the Maram Ringit in case two, and discusses whether and how this exposure should be managed;**   (8 marks)

(iv)   **Discusses how the exposure in case three can be managed.**   (3 marks)

(25 marks)

Question 51 KENDURI CO

Kenduri Co is a large multinational company based in the UK with a number of subsidiary companies around the world. Currently, foreign exchange exposure as a result of transactions between Kenduri Co and its subsidiary companies is managed by each company individually. Kenduri Co is considering whether or not to manage the foreign exchange exposure using multilateral netting from the UK, with the Sterling Pound (£) as the base currency. If multilateral netting is undertaken, spot mid-rates would be used.

The following cash flows are due in three months between Kenduri Co and three of its subsidiary companies. The subsidiary companies are Lakama Co, based in the United States (currency US$), Jaia Co, based in Canada (currency CAD) and Gochiso Co, based in Japan (currency JPY).

Owed by	Owed to	Amount
Kenduri Co	Lakama Co	US$ 4·5 million
Kenduri Co	Jaia Co	CAD 1·1 million
Gochiso Co	Jaia Co	CAD 3·2 million
Gochiso Co	Lakama Co	US$ 1·4 million
Jaia Co	Lakama Co	US$ 1·5 million
Jaia Co	Kenduri Co	CAD 3·4 million
Lakama Co	Gochiso Co	JPY 320 million
Lakama Co	Kenduri Co	US$ 2·1 million

Exchange rates available to Kenduri Co

	US$/£1	CAD/£1	JPY/£1
Spot	1·5938–1·5962	1·5690–1·5710	131·91–133·59
3-month forward	1·5996–1·6037	1·5652–1·5678	129·15–131·05

Currency options available to Kenduri Co

Contract size £62,500, Exercise price quotation: US$/£1, Premium: cents per £1

	Call Options		Put Options	
Exercise price	3-month expiry	6-month expiry	3-month expiry	6-month expiry
1·60	1·55	2·25	2·08	2·23
1·62	0·98	1·58	3·42	3·73

It can be assumed that option contracts expire at the end of the relevant month

Annual interest rates available to Kenduri Co and subsidiaries

	Borrowing rate	Investing rate
UK	4·0%	2·8%
United States	4·8%	3·1%
Canada	3·4%	2·1%
Japan	2·2%	0·5%

Required:

(a) **Advise Kenduri Co on, and recommend, an appropriate hedging strategy for the US$ cash flows it is due to receive or pay in three months, from Lakama Co. Show all relevant calculations to support the advice given.** (12 marks)

(b) **Calculate, using a tabular format (transactions matrix), the impact of undertaking multilateral netting by Kenduri Co and its three subsidiary companies for the cash flows due in three months. Briefly discuss why some governments allow companies to undertake multilateral netting, while others do not.** (10 marks)

(c) **When examining different currency options and their risk factors, it was noticed that a long call option had a high gamma value. Explain the possible characteristics of a long call option with a high gamma value.** (3 marks)

(25 marks)

Question 52 INTEREST RATE MATHS

(a) A $100 nominal value one-year treasury note with 7% annual coupon is trading at $103.
A two year treasury note with 6% coupon is trading at $102.
A three year treasury note with 5% coupon is trading at $98.

Required:

Use "bootstrapping" to find the treasury spot yield curve (4 marks)

(b) A $100 three-year 5% coupon corporate bond has the following spread above treasury spot rates:

1 year	2 year	3 year
29bps	41bps	55bps

Required:

(i) **Value the bond using the corporate spot yield curve, based on the treasury spot rates from (a)** (4 marks)

(ii) **Estimate the bond's yield to maturity.** (3 marks)

(c) **Use the treasury spot rates from (a) to imply the forward interest rates from one year to year two, and from year two to year three.** (4 marks)

(d) **Use the forward rates from (c) to find the theoretical fixed rate leg in a plain vanilla interest rate swap.** (4 marks)

(e) The following five-year loan interest rates are available to Stentor, an AA credit rated company, and to Evnor, a BB+ rated company:

	Fixed rate	*Floating rate*
Stentor	8·75%	LIBOR + 0·50%
Evnor	9·50%	LIBOR + 0·90%

A bank is willing to act as an intermediary to facilitate a five-year swap, for an upfront fee of $20,000 and an annual fee of 0·05% of the swap value. Both of these fees are payable by EACH of the companies. Taxation may be ignored.

Required:

Evaluate, using an illustrative swap, whether or not an interest rate swap may be arranged that is beneficial to both companies. (6 marks)

(25 marks)

Question 53 SHAWTER CO

Assume that it is now mid-December.

The finance director of Shawter, a UK-based company, has recently reviewed the company's monthly cash budgets for the next year. As a result of buying new machinery in three months' time, the company is expected to require short-term financing of £30 million for a period of two months until the proceeds from a factory disposal become available. The finance director is concerned that, as a result of increasing wage settlements, the Bank of England will increase interest rates in the near future.

LIBOR is currently 6% per year and Shawter can borrow at LIBOR + 0·9%.

Derivative contracts may be assumed to mature at the end of the relevant month.

Three types of hedge are available:

- Three-month sterling futures (£500,000 contract size, tick size 0.01%)

December	93·870
March	93·790
June	93·680

- Options on three-month sterling futures (£500,000 contract size, premium cost in annual %)

	Calls			Puts		
	December	March	June	December	March	June
93750	0·120	0·195	0·270	0·020	0·085	0·180
94000	0·015	0·075	0·155	0·165	0·255	0·335
94250	0	0·030	0·085	0·400	0·480	0·555

- FRA prices:

3 v 6	6·11 – 6·01
3 v 5	6·18 – 6·10
3 v 8	6·38 – 6·30

Required:

(a)   (i)   Briefly discuss the relative advantages and disadvantages of the three types of hedge.

(ii)   Illustrate how the short-term interest rate risk might be hedged, and the possible results of the alternative hedges, if interest rates increase by 0·5%.

All relevant calculations must be shown.   (20 marks)

(b)   Explain the possible benefits to a company of undertaking an interest rate swap.

(5 marks)

(25 marks)

Question 54 TRODER CO

(a)   Discuss the advantages of hedging with interest rate caps and collars.   (4 marks)

(b)   Current futures prices suggest that sterling interest rates are expected to fall during the next few months. Troder, a UK-based company, expects to have £400 million available for short-term investment for a period of 5 months commencing late October. The company wishes to protect this short-term investment from a fall in interest rates, but is concerned about the premium levels of interest rate options. It would also like to benefit if interest rates were to increase rather than fall. The company's advisers have suggested the use of a collar option.

LIFFE short sterling options (£500,000), points of 100%

	Calls		Puts	
Strike price	*Sept*	*Dec*	*Sept*	*Dec*
95250	0·040	0·445	0·040	0·085
95500	0	0·280	0·250	0·170
95750	0	0·165	0·500	0·305

LIBOR is currently 5% and Troder can invest short-term at LIBOR minus 25 basis points.

Required:

(i)   Assume that it is now early September. The company wishes to receive more than £6,750,000 in interest from its investment after paying any option premium. Illustrate how a collar hedge may be used to achieve this. **Note:** It is not necessary to estimate the number of contracts for this illustration.   (6 marks)

(ii)   Estimate the maximum interest that could be received with your selected hedge.   (2 marks)

(c)   Arnbrook Co is considering a $50 million three year interest rate swap. The company wishes to have use of floating rate funds, but because of its AA credit rating has a comparative advantage over lower rated companies when borrowing in the domestic fixed rate market. Arnbrook can borrow fixed rate at 6·25% or floating rate at LIBOR plus 0·75%.

LIBOR is currently 5·25%, but parliamentary elections are due in six months' time and future interest rates are uncertain. A swap could be arranged using a bank as an intermediary. The bank would offset the swap risk with a counterparty BBB rated company that could borrow fixed rate at 7·25% and floating rate at LIBOR plus 1·25%. The bank would charge a fee of $120,000 per year to each party in the swap. Arnbrook would require 60% of any arbitrage savings (before the payment of fees) from the swap because of its higher credit rating.

Any fees paid to the bank are tax allowable. The corporate tax rate is 30%.

Required:

(i)   **Discuss the risks that Arnbrook and a participating bank might face when undertaking an interest rate swap.**   (3 marks)

(ii)   **Evaluate whether or not the proposed swap might be beneficial to all parties.**   (4 marks)

(iii)   **If LIBOR was to increase immediately after the forthcoming election to 5·75% and then stay constant for the period of the swap, estimate the present value of the savings from the swap for Arnbrook Co. Interest payments are made semi-annually in arrears. Comment upon whether the swap would have been beneficial to Arnbrook Co.**

The money market may be assumed to be an efficient market.   (6 marks)

(25 marks)

Question 55 PHOBOS CO

Following a collapse in credit confidence in the banking sector globally, there have been high levels of volatility in the financial markets around the world. Phobos Co is a UK listed company and has a borrowing requirement of £30 million arising in two months' time on 1 March and expects to be able to make repayment of the full amount six months from now. The governor of the central bank has suggested that interest rates are now at their peak and could fall over the next quarter. However, the chairman of the Federal Reserve in the United States has suggested that monetary conditions may need to be tightened, which could lead to interest rate rises throughout the major economies. In your judgement there is now an equal likelihood that rates will rise or fall by as much as 100 basis points depending upon economic conditions over the next quarter.

LIBOR is currently 6·00% and Phobos can borrow at a fixed rate of LIBOR plus 50 basis points on the short term money market but the company treasurer would like to keep the maximum borrowing rate at or below 6·6%.

Short term sterling index futures have a contract size of £500,000 and a tick size of £12·50. The open and settlement prices on 1 January are shown below:

	Open	Settlement
March	93·800	93·880
June	93·870	93·940
September	93·890	93·970

You may assume that contracts mature at the end of the relevant month and that basis diminishes in a linear manner.

Options on short sterling futures have a contract size of £500,000 and the premiums (shown as an annual percentage) available against a range of exercise prices are as follows:

Exercise	calls			puts		
	March	June	September	March	June	September
93750	0·155	0·260	0·320	0·045	0·070	0·100
94000	0·038	0·110	0·175	0·168	0·170	0·205
94250	0·010	0·040	0·080	0·300	0·350	0·360

Required:

(a)   Estimate the effective interest rate cost if the anticipated interest rate exposure is hedged:

      (i)   using the sterling interest rate futures; and

      (ii)   the options on short sterling futures.   (17 marks)

(b)   Outline the benefits and dangers to Phobos of using derivative agreements in the management of interest rate risk.   (8 marks)

(25 marks)

Question 56 KATMAI COMPANY

To finance capital investment in its domestic market, the Katmai Company raised $150 million through the issue of 12-year floating rate notes at 120 basis points over LIBOR, interest payable at six month intervals. Following a review of the current yield curve, the company's Chief Financial Officer has become concerned about the potential impact of rising LIBOR on the firm's future cash flows. The loan now has 10 years to maturity. The CFO asks you, his deputy, to examine the choices that are now available to the firm and to recommend the best course of action. She comments that a swap is an obvious choice but that she would appreciate a briefing on the advantages and disadvantages of the alternative approaches to managing the company's interest rate risk and an estimate of the six-monthly Value at Risk (VaR) if nothing is done. As part of your investigation you note that 10-year swap rates are quoted at 5·25–5·40.

In estimating the VaR you note that the firm has a policy of 95% confidence level on its exposure to non-core risk and that the annual volatility of LIBOR is currently 150 basis points.

Required:

(a)   Evaluate the alternative choices the company has for managing its interest rate exposure and recommend, with justification, the course of action the company should follow.

      (12 marks)

(b)   Estimate the six-monthly interest rate and the effective annual rate payable if a vanilla interest rate swap is agreed.   (5 marks)

(c)   Estimate the six monthly Value at Risk on the interest rate exposure associated with this borrowing and comment upon the interpretation of the result.   (8 marks)

(25 marks)

Question 57 SEMBILAN CO

Sembilan Co, a listed company, recently issued debt finance to acquire assets in order to increase its activity levels. This debt finance is in the form of a floating rate bond, with a nominal value of $320 million, redeemable in four years. The bond interest, payable annually, is based on the spot yield curve plus 60 basis points. The next annual payment is due at the end of year one.

Sembilan Co is concerned that the expected rise in interest rates over the coming few years would make it increasingly difficult to pay the interest due. It is therefore proposing to either swap the floating rate interest payment to a fixed rate payment, or to raise new equity capital and use that to pay off the floating rate bond. The new equity capital would either be issued as rights to the existing shareholders or as shares to new shareholders.

Ratus Bank has offered Sembilan Co an interest rate swap, whereby Sembilan Co would pay Ratus Bank interest based on an equivalent fixed annual rate of 3·76¼% in exchange for receiving a variable amount based on the current yield curve rate. Payments and receipts will be made at the end of each year, for the next four years. Ratus Bank will charge an annual fee of 20 basis points if the swap is agreed.

The current annual spot yield curve rates are as follows:

Year	One	Two	Three	Four
Rate	2·5%	3·1%	3·5%	3·8%

The current annual forward rates for years two, three and four are as follows:

Year	Two	Three	Four
Rate	3·7%	4·3%	4·7%

Required:

(a)   **Based on the above information, calculate the amounts Sembilan Co expects to pay or receive every year on the swap (excluding the fee of 20 basis points). Explain why the fixed annual rate of interest of 3·76¼% is less than the four-year yield curve rate of 3·8%.** (8 marks)

(b)   **Demonstrate that Sembilan Co's interest payment liability does not change, after it has undertaken the swap, whether the interest rates increase or decrease.** (6 marks)

(c)   **Discuss the factors that Sembilan Co should consider when deciding whether it should raise equity capital to pay off the floating rate debt.** (11 marks)

(25 marks)

Question 58 AWAN CO

Awan Co is expecting to receive $48,000,000 on 1 February 2018, which will be invested until it is required for a large project on 1 June 2018. Due to uncertainty in the markets, the company is of the opinion that it is likely that interest rates will fluctuate significantly over the coming months, although it is difficult to predict whether they will increase or decrease.

Awan Co's treasury team want to hedge the company against adverse movements in interest rates using one of the following derivative products:

Forward rate agreements (FRAs);
Interest rate futures; or
Options on interest rate futures.

Awan Co can invest funds at the relevant inter-bank rate less 20 basis points. The current inter-bank rate is 4·09%. However, Awan Co is of the opinion that interest rates could increase or decrease by as much as 0·9% over the coming months.

The following information and quotes are provided from an appropriate exchange on $ futures and options. Margin requirements can be ignored.

Three-month $ futures, $2,000,000 contract size
Prices are quoted in basis points at 100 – annual % yield

December 2017:	94·80
March 2018:	94·76
June 2018:	94·69

Options on three-month $ futures, $2,000,000 contract size, option premiums are in annual %

	Calls		Strike	Puts		
December	March	June		December	March	June
0·342	0·432	0·523	94·50	0·090	0·119	0·271
0·097	0·121	0·289	95·00	0·312	0·417	0·520

Voblaka Bank has offered the following FRA rates to Awan Co:

1–7:	4·37%
3–4:	4·78%
3–7:	4·82%
4–7:	4·87%

It can be assumed that settlement for the futures and options contracts is at the end of the month and that basis diminishes to zero at contract maturity at a constant rate, based on monthly time intervals. Assume that it is 1 November 2017 now and that there is no basis risk.

Required:

(a) **Based on the three hedging choices Awan Co is considering, recommend a hedging strategy for the $48,000,000 investment, if interest rates increase or decrease by 0·9%. Support your answer with appropriate calculations and discussion.** (19 marks)

(b) A member of Awan Co's treasury team has suggested that if option contracts are purchased to hedge against the interest rate movements, then the number of contracts purchased should be determined by a hedge ratio based on the delta value of the option.

Required:

Discuss how the delta value of an option could be used in determining the number of contracts purchased. (6 marks)

(25 marks)

Question 59 GLOBAL FINANCIAL CRISIS

Discuss the causes and impacts of the global financial crisis that began in 2007, making specific reference to the role of Collateralised Debt Obligations (CDOs).

(15 marks)

Question 60 MOBILITY OF CAPITAL AND MONEY LAUNDERING

(a) **Discuss the global trend for mobility of capital and state how a multinational firm could manage any remaining barriers to such mobility** (9 marks)

(b) **Discuss the international regulations on money laundering and their implications for a firm's finance director.** (6 marks)

(15 marks)

Question 61 IMF AND WTO

(a)   Discuss how a government might try to reduce a large, persistent, current account deficit on the balance of payments, and illustrate what impact such government action might have on a multinational company operating in the country concerned. Explain the possible role and impact of the International Monetary Fund (IMF) in this process.

(10 marks)

(b)   Provide examples of how countries might impose protectionist measures to control the volume of imports.   (5 marks)

(c)   Discuss the role and main objectives of the World Trade Organisation (WTO), and its potential effect on protectionist measures.   (6 marks)

(d)   Briefly discuss the possible effects of the activities of the WTO for a multinational company with foreign direct investment in a developing country that has recently joined the WTO.   (4 marks)

(25 marks)

Question 62 EXCHANGE RATE SYSTEMS

(a)   Discuss the possible foreign exchange risk and economic implications of each of the following types of exchange rate system for multinational companies with subsidiaries located in countries with these systems:

   (i)   a managed floating exchange rate;
   (ii)   a fixed exchange rate linked to a basket of currencies; and
   (iii)   a fixed exchange rate backed by a currency board system.   (12 marks)

(b)   Your managing director has received forecasts of euro exchange rates in two years' time from three leading banks.

   Euro per £ two year forecasts
   Lottobank   1·452
   Kadbank   1·514
   Grossbank   1·782

   The current spot mid-rate is 1·667 Euro per £.

   A non-executive director of your company has suggested that in order to forecast future exchange rates, the interest rate differential between countries should be used. She states that "as short term interest rates are currently 6% in the UK, and 3·5% in the euro bloc, the exchange rate in two years' time will be 1·747 Euro per £".

   Required:

   (i)   Prepare a brief report discussing the likely validity of the non-executive director's estimate.   (4 marks)

   (ii)   Explain briefly whether or not forecasts of future exchange rates using current interest rate differentials are likely to be accurate.   (3 marks)

(c)   You have also been asked to give advice to the managing director about a tender by the company's Italian subsidiary for an order in Kuwait. The tender conditions state that payment will be made in Kuwait dinars 18 months from now. The subsidiary is unsure as to what price to tender. The marginal cost of producing the goods at that time is estimated to be €340,000 and a 25% mark-up is normal for the company.

Exchange rates
Spot Euro per dinar 0·256 – 0·260
No forward rate exists for 18 months' time.

	Italy	*Kuwait*
Annual inflation rates	3%	9%
Annual interest rates available to the Italian subsidiary:		
Borrowing	6%	11%
Lending	2·5%	8%

Required:

Discuss how the Italian subsidiary might protect itself against foreign exchange rate changes, and recommend what tender price should be used.

All relevant calculations must be shown. (6 marks)

(25 marks)

Question 63 MOOSE CO

You are the Chief Financial Officer of Moose Co, a manufacturing firm which places a strong emphasis on innovation and design with patent protection across all its product range.

The company has two principal manufacturing centres, one in Europe which has been reduced in size in recent years because of high labour costs and the other in South America. However, Moose Co's development has relied upon ready access to the debt market both in Europe and in South America and the company is planning significant expansion with a new manufacturing and distribution centre in South East Asia, with Malaysia being the likely location. The company is highly profitable with strong cash flows although in the last two quarters there has been a downturn in sales in all markets as the global recession has begun to take effect.

Since August 2007, credit conditions have deteriorated across all of the major economies as banks have curtailed their lending following the downgrading of US asset-backed securities. In 2008 and 2009 many banks recorded significant multibillion dollar losses as they attempted to sell off what had become known as "toxic debt", leading to a further collapse in their value. In response many banks also attempted to repair their statements of financial position by rights and other equity issues.

The founder and executive chairman of Moose Co, Alan Bison, is planning a round of meetings with a number of investment banks in leading financial centres around the world to explore raising a $350 million dollar loan for the new development. It has already been suggested that a loan of this size would need to be syndicated or raised through a bond issue. Mr Bison has also heard about the rise in Islamic finance and wonders if this could be an alternative route for Moose Co.

In preparation for those meetings he has asked you to provide him with some briefing notes.

Required:

(a) **Given conditions in the global debt market, as described above, advise on the main factors banks will consider in offering a loan of this size.** (5 marks)

(b) **Assess the relative advantages of loan syndication versus a bond issue for Moose Co.** (4 marks)

(c) **Assess the relative advantages and disadvantages of entering into a capital investment of this scale at this stage of the global economic cycle.** (4 marks)

(d) **Discuss the potential benefits and drawbacks for Moose Co of using "sukuk" bonds to raise the required finance.** (6 marks)

(e) **Identify and discuss four other types of Islamic finance.** (6 marks)

(25 marks)

Question 64 STROM CO

Strom Co is a clothing retailer, with stores selling mid-price clothes and clothing accessories throughout Europe. It sells its own-brand items, which are produced by small manufacturers located in Africa, who work solely for Strom Co. The European sovereign debt crisis has affected a number of countries in the European Union (EU). Consequently, Strom Co has found trading conditions to be extremely difficult, putting pressure on profits and sales revenue.

The sovereign debt crisis in Europe resulted in countries finding it increasingly difficult and expensive to issue government bonds to raise funds. Two main reasons have been put forward to explain why the crisis took place: firstly, a number of countries continued to borrow excessive funds, because their expenditure exceeded taxation revenues; and secondly, a number of countries allocated significant sums of money to support their banks following the "credit crunch" and the banking crisis.

In order to prevent countries defaulting on their debt obligations and being downgraded, the countries in the EU and the International Monetary Fund (IMF) established a fund to provide financial support to member states threatened by the risk of default, credit downgrades and excessive borrowing yields. Strict economic conditions known as austerity measures were imposed on these countries in exchange for receiving financial support.

The austerity measures have affected Strom Co negatively, and the years 2015 and 2016 have been particularly bad, with sales revenue declining by 15% and profits by 25% in 2015, and remaining at 2015 levels in 2016. On investigation, Strom Co noted that clothing retailers selling clothes at low prices and at high prices were not affected as badly as Strom Co or other mid-price retailers. Indeed, the retailers selling low-priced clothes had increased their profits, and retailers selling luxury, expensive clothes had maintained their profits over the last two to three years.

In order to improve profitability, Strom Co's board of directors expects to cut costs where possible. A significant fixed cost relates to quality control, which includes monitoring the working conditions of employees of Strom Co's clothing manufacturers, as part of its ethical commitment.

Required:

(a) **Explain the role and aims of the International Monetary Fund (IMF) and discuss possible reasons why the austerity measures imposed on European Union (EU) countries might have affected Strom Co negatively.** (12 marks)

(b) **Suggest, giving reasons, why the austerity measures might not have affected clothing retailers at the high and low price range, as much as the mid-price range retailers like Strom Co.** (5 marks)

(c) **Discuss the risks to Strom Co of reducing the costs relating to quality control and how the detrimental impact of such reductions in costs could be decreased.** (8 marks)

(25 marks)

Question 65 NOVOROAST CO

Novoroast Co manufactures microwave ovens which it exports to several countries, as well as supplying the home market. One of Novoroast's export markets is a South American country, which has recently imposed a 40% tariff on imports of microwaves in order to protect its local "infant" microwave industry. The imposition of this tariff means that Novoroast's products are no longer competitive in the South American country's market but the government there is, however, willing to assist companies wishing to undertake direct investment locally. The government offers a 10% grant towards the purchase of plant and equipment, and a three-year tax holiday on earnings. Corporate tax after the three-year period would be paid at the rate of 25% in the year that the taxable cash flow arises.

Novoroast wishes to evaluate whether to invest in a manufacturing subsidiary in South America, or to pull out of the market altogether.

The total cost of an investment in South America is 155 million pesos (at current exchange rates), comprising:

- 50 million pesos for land and buildings;
- 60 million pesos for plant and machinery (all of which would be required almost immediately);
- 45 million pesos for working capital.

20 million pesos of the working capital will be required immediately and 25 million pesos at the end of the first year of operation. Working capital needs are expected to increase in line with local inflation.

The company's planning horizon is five years.

Plant and machinery is expected to be depreciated (tax allowable) on a straight-line basis over five years, and is expected to have negligible realisable value at the end of five years. Land and buildings are expected to appreciate in value in line with the level of inflation in the South American country.

Production and sales of microwaves are expected to be 8,000 units in the first year at an initial price of 1,450 pesos per unit, 60,000 units in the second year, and 120,000 units per year for the remainder of the planning horizon.

In order to control the level of inflation, legislation exists in the South American country to restrict retail price rises of manufactured goods to 10% per year.

Fixed costs and local variable costs, which for the first year of operation are 12 million pesos and 600 pesos per unit respectively, are expected to increase by the previous year's rate of inflation.

All components will be produced or purchased locally except for essential microchips which will be imported from the parent company at a cost of $8 per unit, yielding a contribution to the profit of the parent company of $3 per unit. It is hoped to keep this sterling cost constant over the planning horizon.

Corporate tax in the home country is at the rate of 30% per year, payable in the year the liability arises. A bi-lateral tax treaty exists between the home country and the South American country, which permits the offset of overseas tax against any domestic tax liability on overseas earnings. In periods of tax holiday assume that no home country tax would be payable on South American cash flows.

Summarised group data:

Summarised statement of financial position

	$m
Non-current assets	440
Current assets	370
Total assets	810
Financed by:	
Ordinary shares ($1)	200
Reserves	230
	430
6% bonds, eight years until maturity	180
Current liabilities	200
Total equity and liabilities	810

Novoroast's current share price is $4.10 per share, and current bond price is $800 per bond ($1,000 nominal and redemption value).

Forecast inflation rates:

	Home country	South American country
Present	4%	20%
Year 1	3%	20%
Year 2	4%	15%
Year 3	4%	15%
Year 4	4%	15%
Year 5	4%	15%

Foreign exchange rates:

	pesos per $
Spot	13·421
1-year forward	15·636

Novoroast believes that if the investment is undertaken the overall risk to investors in the company will remain unchanged. The company's beta coefficients have been estimated as equity 1·25, debt 0·225. The market return is 14% per year and the risk free rate is 6% per year.

Required:

(a)   **Prepare a report advising whether or not Novoroast Co should invest in the South American country. Include a discussion of the limitations of your analysis.**

State what other information would be useful to assist the decision process.

All relevant calculations must be shown in your report or as an appendix to it. State clearly any assumptions that you make.

(Approximately 20 marks are available for calculations and 10 for discussion.)   (30 marks)

(b)   **If, once the investment had taken place, the government of the South American country imposed a block on the remittance of dividends to the home country, discuss how Novoroast might try to avoid such a block on remittances.**   (5 marks)

(c) Briefly discuss ethical issues that might need to be considered as part of a multinational company's investment decision process. (5 marks)

(d) Advise on the investment's impact on Novoroast's stakeholders, from an integrated reporting perspective. (6 marks)

Professional marks for format, structure and presentation of the report. (4 marks)

(50 marks)

Question 66 HGT CO

HGT Co is a multinational company with two overseas subsidiaries. The company wishes to minimise its global tax bill, and part of its tax strategy is to try to take advantage of opportunities provided by transfer pricing.

HGT has subsidiaries in Glinland and Rytora:

Taxation	Home country	Glinland	Rytora
Tax on overseas profits	30%	40%	25%
Withholding tax on dividends	–	10%	–
Import tariffs on all goods (not tax allowable)	–	–	10%

The subsidiary in Glinland produces 150,000 graphite golf club shafts per year which are then sent to Rytora for the metal heads to be added and the clubs finished off. The shafts have a variable cost in Glinland of $6 each, and annual fixed costs are $140,000. The shafts are sold to the Rytoran subsidiary at variable cost plus 75%.

The Rytoran subsidiary incurs additional unit variable costs of $9, annual fixed costs of $166,000, and sells the finished clubs at $30 each in Rytora.

Bi-lateral tax agreements exist which allow foreign tax paid to be credited against domestic tax liability.

The Rytoran subsidiary remits all profit after tax to the parent company each year, and the Glinland subsidiary remits 50% of its profit after tax.

Required:

(a) The parent company is considering instructing the Glinland subsidiary to sell the shafts to the Rytoran subsidiary at full cost. Evaluate the possible effect of this on tax and tariff payments, and discuss briefly any possible problems with this strategy. (13 marks)

(b) Touten Co is a UK registered multinational company with subsidiaries in 14 countries in Europe, Asia and Africa. The subsidiaries have traditionally been allowed a large amount of autonomy, but Touten is now proposing to centralise most of group treasury management operations.

Required:

(i) Explain the potential benefits of treasury centralisation; and

(ii) Suggest how to minimise any potential problems for the subsidiaries that might arise as a result of treasury centralisation. (12 marks)

(25 marks)

Question 67 BLIPTON

Today is 1 January 2009. Blipton International Entertainment Group is evaluating a proposal from its hotel division to build a 400 bedroom hotel in the East End of London. This area has developed rapidly over the last 15 years and the prospects have been further enhanced by the announcement that London is to host the 2012 Olympics. Blipton is based in Dubai and both reports and accounts for all its transactions in dollars. The current spot rate is $1·4925 per £. The operating costs for the hotel are expected to be £30 per occupied room per day (variable) and a fixed cost of £1·7 million per year expressed in current prices. The proportion of bedrooms occupied, on the basis of opening for 365 days a year, is expected to be as follows:

Year ended 31 December	Occupancy
2009	construction
2010	40%
2011	50%
2012	90%
2013	60%
2014	60%

UK inflation is currently projected by the Bank of England as 2·5% per year and inflation in the United States is 4·8% per year. These rates are expected to be constant over the term of the project. Blipton's real cost of capital is 4·2%. UK hotel property values within the London area are expected to rise in real terms by 8% per year.

The construction cost for this hotel is estimated to be £6·2 million and it will be built over the 12 months to 31 December 2009. As part of the UK's Olympic Development Plan, a 50% first year allowance is available for tax purposes on building projects related to the Games. The balance of the capital expenditure can be claimed in equal instalments over the following three years. UK profit tax is 30% and is levied and paid on profits in the year they arise. There is no additional tax liability on remittance to or from Dubai. The company has sufficient UK profits on its other activities to absorb the tax-allowable depreciation on this project.

In making investment decisions of this type the company operates the following procedure:

(1)   All cash flows including construction costs are assumed to arise at the end of the year concerned and are to be projected in nominal (money) terms over the six year period.

(2)   The residual value of the investment at the end of six years is assumed to be the open market value of the property less a charge for repairs and renewals.

(3)   The charge for repairs and renewals is expected to be £1·2 million in current prices payable on disposal.

(4)   The net present value of the project should be based upon a 100% remittance of net cash flows to Dubai and should be calculated in dollars.

(5)   Average room rates are set at the level required to recover variable cost plus 100%.

Required:

(a)   Prepare a six year nominal dollar projection of the after tax cash flow for this project distinguishing between cash flows arising from its investment phase and those arising from its return phase.   (12 marks)

(b)   Estimate the project's dollar net present value and the modified internal rate of return.
                                                                                             (7 marks)

(c)   **Assess the viability of the project with a summary of the relative advantages and disadvantages of the net present value and modified internal rate of return methods in investment appraisal.** (6 marks)

(25 marks)

Question 68 MULTIDROP

You are the financial manager of Multidrop (Group) a European based company which has subsidiary businesses in North America, Europe, and Singapore. It also has foreign currency balances outstanding with two non-group companies in the UK and Malaysia. Last year the transaction costs of *ad-hoc* settlements both within the group and with non-group companies were significant and this year you have reached agreement with the non-group companies to enter into a netting agreement to clear indebtedness with the minimum of currency flows. It has been agreed that Multidrop (Europe) will be the principal in the netting arrangement and that all settlements will be made in euros at the prevailing spot rate.

The summarised list of year end indebtedness is as follows:

Owed by:	*Owed to:*	
Multidrop (Europe)	Multidrop (US)	US$6·4 million
Multidrop (Singapore)	Multidrop (Europe)	S$16 million
Alposong (Malaysia)	Multidrop (US)	US$5·4 million
Multidrop (US)	Multidrop (Europe)	€8·2 million
Multidrop (Singapore)	Multidrop (US)	US$5·0 million
Multidrop (Singapore)	Alposong (Malaysia)	Rm25 million
Alposong (Malaysia)	NewRing (UK)	£2·2 million
NewRing (UK)	Multidrop (Singapore)	S$4·0 million
Multidrop (Europe)	Alposong (Malaysia)	Rm8·3 million

Currency cross rates (mid-market) are as follows:

Currency	UK £	US $	Euro	Sing $	Rm
1 UK £ =	1·0000	1·4601	1·0653	2·1956	5·3128
1 US $ =	0·6849	1·0000	0·7296	1·5088	3·6435
1 Euro =	0·9387	1·3706	1·0000	2·0649	4·9901
1 Sing $=	0·4555	0·6628	0·4843	1·0000	2·4150
1 Rm =	0·1882	0·2745	0·2004	0·4141	1·0000

You may assume settlement will be at the mid-market rates quoted.

Required:

(a)   **Calculate the inter group and inter-company currency transfers that will be required for settlement by Multidrop (Europe).** (15 marks)

(b)   **Discuss the advantages and disadvantages of netting arrangements with both group and non-group companies.** (10 marks)

(25 marks)

Question 69 PROSPICE MENTIS UNIVERSITY

Prospice Mentis University (PMU) is a prestigious private institution and a member of the Holly League, which is made up of universities based in Rosinante and renowned worldwide as being of the highest quality. Universities in Rosinante have benefited particularly from students coming from Kantaka, and PMU has been no exception. However, PMU has recognised that Kantaka has a large population of able students who cannot afford to study overseas. Therefore it wants to investigate how it can offer some of its most popular degree programmes in Kantaka, where students will be able to study at a significantly lower cost. It is considering whether to enter into a joint venture with a local institution or to independently set up its own university site in Kantaka.

Offering courses overseas would be a first from a Holly League institution and indeed from any academic institution based in Rosinante. However, there have been less renowned academic institutions from other countries which have formed joint ventures with small private institutions in Kantaka to deliver degree programmes. These have been of low quality and are not held in high regard by the population or the government of Kantaka.

In Kantaka, government run universities and a handful of large private academic institutions, none of which have entered into joint ventures, are held in high regard. However, the demand for places in these institutions far outstrips the supply of places and many students are forced to go to the smaller private institutions or to study overseas if they can afford it.

After an initial investigation the following points have come to light:

(1)   The Kantaka government is keen to attract foreign direct investment (FDI) and offer tax concessions to businesses which bring investment funds into the country. It is likely that PMU would need to borrow a substantial amount of money if it were to set up independently. However, the investment funds required would be considerably smaller if it went into a joint venture.

(2)   Given the past experiences of poor quality education offered by joint ventures between small local private institutions and overseas institutions, the Kantaka government has been reluctant to approve degrees from such institutions. Also the government has not allowed graduates from these institutions to work in national or local government, or in nationalised organisations.

(3)   Over the past two years the Kantaka currency has depreciated against other currencies, but economic commentators believe that this may not continue for much longer.

(4)   A large proportion of PMU's academic success is due to innovative teaching and learning methods, and high quality research. The teaching and learning methods used in Kantaka's educational institutions are very different. Apart from the larger private and government run universities, little academic research is undertaken elsewhere in Kantaka's education sector.

Required:

Discuss the benefits and disadvantages of PMU entering into a joint venture instead of setting up independently in Kantaka. As part of your discussion, consider how the disadvantages can be mitigated and the additional information PMU needs in order to make its decision.

(25 marks)

Question 70 KILENC CO

Kilenc Co, a large listed company based in the UK, produces pharmaceutical products which are exported around the world. It is reviewing a proposal to set up a subsidiary company to manufacture a range of body and facial creams in Lanosia. These products will be sold to local retailers and to retailers in nearby countries.

Lanosia has a small but growing manufacturing industry in pharmaceutical products, although it remains largely reliant on imports. The Lanosian government has been keen to promote the pharmaceutical manufacturing industry through purchasing local pharmaceutical products, providing government grants and reducing the industry's corporate tax rate. It also imposes large duties on imported pharmaceutical products which compete with the ones produced locally.

Although politically stable, the recent worldwide financial crisis has had a significant negative impact on Lanosia. The country's national debt has grown substantially following a bailout of its banks and it has had to introduce economic measures which are hampering the country's ability to recover from a deep recession. Growth in real wages has been negative over the past three years, the economy has shrunk in the past year and inflation has remained higher than normal during this time.

On the other hand, corporate investment in capital assets, research and development, and education and training, has grown recently and interest rates remain low. This has led some economists to suggest that the economy should start to recover soon. Employment levels remain high in spite of low nominal wage growth.

Lanosian corporate governance regulations stipulate that at least 40% of equity share capital must be held by the local population. In addition at least 50% of members on the Board of Directors, including the Chairman, must be from Lanosia. Kilenc Co wants to finance the subsidiary company using a mixture of debt and equity. It wants to raise additional equity and debt finance in Lanosia in order to minimise exchange rate exposure. The small size of the subsidiary will have minimal impact on Kilenc Co's capital structure. Kilenc Co intends to raise the 40% equity through an initial public offering (IPO) in Lanosia and provide the remaining 60% of the equity funds from its own cash funds.

Required:

(a)   **Discuss the key risks and issues that Kilenc Co should consider when setting up a subsidiary company in Lanosia, and suggest how these may be mitigated.**   (18 marks)

(b)   The directors of Kilenc Co have learnt that a sizeable number of equity trades in Lanosia are conducted using dark pool trading systems.

      Required:

      Explain what dark pool trading systems are and how Kilenc Co's proposed Initial Public Offering (IPO) may be affected by these.   (7 marks)

(25 marks)

Question 71 CHMURA

Since becoming independent just over 20 years ago, the country of Mehgam has adopted protectionist measures which have made it difficult for multinational companies to trade there. However, recently, after discussions with the World Trade Organisation (WTO), it seems likely that Mehgam will reduce its protectionist measures significantly.

Encouraged by these discussions, Chmura Co, a company producing packaged foods, is considering a project to set up a manufacturing base in Mehgam to sell its goods there and in other regional countries nearby. An initial investigation costing $500,000 established that Mehgam had appropriate manufacturing facilities, adequate transport links and a reasonably skilled but cheap work force. The investigation concluded that, if the protectionist measures were reduced, then the demand potential for Chmura Co's products looked promising. It is also felt that an early entry into Mehgam would give Chmura Co an advantage over its competitors for a period of five years, after which the current project will cease, due to the development of new advanced manufacturing processes.

Mehgam's currency, the Peso (MP), is currently trading at MP72 per $1. Setting up the manufacturing base in Mehgam will require an initial investment of MP2,500 million immediately, to cover the cost of land and buildings (MP1,250 million) and machinery (MP1,250 million). Tax allowable depreciation is available on the machinery at an annual rate of 10% on cost on a straight-line basis. A balancing adjustment will be required at the end of year five, when it is expected that the machinery will be sold for MP500 million (after inflation). The market value of the land and buildings in five years' time is estimated to be 80% of the current value. These amounts are inclusive of any tax impact.

Chmura Co will require MP200 million for working capital immediately. It is not expected that any further injections of working capital will be required for the five years. When the project ceases at the end of the fifth year, the working capital will be released back to Chmura Co.

Production of the packaged foods will take place in batches of product mixes. These batches will then be sold to supermarket chains, wholesalers and distributors in Mehgam and its neighbouring countries, who will repackage them to their individual requirements. All sales will be in MP. The estimated average number of batches produced and sold each year is given below:

Year	1	2	3	4	5
Batches produced and sold	10,000	15,000	30,000	26,000	15,000

The current selling price for each batch is estimated to be MP115,200. The costs related to producing and selling each batch are currently estimated to be MP46,500. In addition to these costs, a number of products will need a special packaging material which Chmura Co will send to Mehgam. Currently the cost of the special packaging material is $200 per batch. Training and development costs, related to the production of the batches, are estimated to be 80% of the production and selling costs (excluding the cost of the special packaging) in the first year, before falling to 20% of these costs (excluding the cost of the special packaging) in the second year, and then nil for the remaining years. It is expected that the costs relating to the production and sale of each batch will increase annually by 10% but the selling price and the special packaging costs will only increase by 5% every year.

The current annual corporation tax rate in Mehgam is 25% and Chmura Co pays annual corporation tax at a rate of 20% in the country where it is based. Both countries' taxes are payable in the year that the tax liability arises. A bi-lateral tax treaty exists between the two countries which permits offset of overseas tax against any tax liabilities Chmura Co incurs on overseas earnings.

The risk-adjusted cost of capital applicable to the project on $-based cash flows is 12%, which is considerably higher than the return on short-dated $ treasury bills of 4%. The current rate of inflation in Mehgam is 8%, and in the country where Chmura Co is based, it is 2%. It can be assumed that these inflation rates will not change for the foreseeable future. All net cash flows from the project will be remitted back to Chmura Co at the end of each year.

Chmura Co's finance director is of the opinion that there are many uncertainties surrounding the project and has assessed that the cash flows can vary by a standard deviation of as much as 35% because of these uncertainties.

Recently Bulud Co offered Chmura Co the option to sell the entire project to Bulud Co for $28 million at the start of year three. Chmura Co will make the decision of whether or not to sell the project at the end of year two.

Required:

(a) **Discuss the role of the World Trade Organisation (WTO) and the possible benefits and drawbacks to Mehgam of reducing protectionist measures.** (9 marks)

(b) **Prepare an evaluative report for the Board of Directors of Chmura Co which addresses the following parts and recommends an appropriate course of action:**

   (i) **An estimate of the value of the project before considering Bulud Co's offer. Show all relevant calculations;** (14 marks)

   (ii) **An estimate of the value of the project taking into account Bulud Co's offer. Show all relevant calculations;** (9 marks)

   (iii) **A discussion of the assumptions made in parts (i) and (ii) above and the additional business risks which Chmura Co should consider before it makes the final decision whether or not to undertake the project.** (14 marks)

   Professional marks will be awarded in part (b) for the format, structure and presentation of the report. (4 marks)

(50 marks)

PILOT PAPER

Question 1 TRAMONT CO

Tramont Co is a listed company based in the USA and manufactures electronic devices. One of its devices, the X-IT, is produced exclusively for the American market. Tramont Co is considering ceasing the production of the X-IT gradually over a period of four years because it needs the manufacturing facilities used to make the X-IT for other products.

The government of Gamala, a country based in south-east Asia, is keen to develop its manufacturing industry and has offered Tramont Co first rights to produce the X-IT in Gamala and sell it to the USA market for a period of four years. At the end of the four-year period, the full production rights will be sold to a government backed company for Gamalan Rupiahs (GR) 450 million after tax (this amount is not subject to inflationary increases). Tramont Co has to decide whether to continue production of the X-IT in the USA for the next four years or to move the production to Gamala immediately.

Currently each X-IT unit sold makes a unit contribution of $20. This unit contribution is not expected to be subject to any inflationary increase in the next four years. Next year's production and sales estimated at 40,000 units will fall by 20% each year for the following three years. It is anticipated that after four years the production of X-IT will stop. It is expected that the financial impact of the gradual closure over the four years will be cost neutral (the revenue from sale of assets will equal the closure costs). If production is stopped immediately, the excess assets would be sold for $2.3 million and the costs of closure, including redundancy costs of excess labour, would be $1.7 million.

The following information relates to the production of the X-IT moving to Gamala. The Gamalan project will require an initial investment of GR 230 million, to pay for the cost of land and buildings (GR 150 million) and machinery (GR 80 million). The cost of machinery is tax allowable and will be depreciated on a straight line basis over the next four years, at the end of which it will have a negligible value.

Tramont Co will also need GR 40 million for working capital immediately. It is expected that the working capital requirement will increase in line with the annual inflation rate in Gamala. When the project is sold, the working capital will not form part of the sale price and will be released back to Tramont Co.

Production and sales of the device are expected to be 12,000 units in the first year, rising to 22,000 units, 47,000 units and 60,000 units in the next three years respectively.

The following revenues and costs apply to the first year of operation:

Each unit will be sold for $70;

The variable cost per unit comprising of locally sourced materials and labour will be GR 1,350, and;

In addition to the variable cost above, each unit will require a component bought from Tramont Co for $7, on which Tramont Co makes $4 contribution per unit;

Total fixed costs for the first year will be GR 30 million.

The costs are expected to increase by their countries' respective rates of inflation, but the selling price will remain fixed at $70 per unit for the four-year period.

The annual corporation tax rate in Gamala is 20% and Tramont Co currently pays corporation tax at a rate of 30% per year. Both countries' corporation taxes are payable in the year that the tax liability arises. A bi-lateral tax treaty exists between the USA and Gamala, which permits offset of overseas tax against any US tax liability on overseas earnings. The USA and Gamalan tax authorities allow losses to be carried forward and written off against future profits for taxation purposes.

Tramont Co has decided to finance the project by borrowing the funds required in Gamala. The commercial borrowing rate is 13% but the Gamalan government has offered Tramont Co a 6% subsidised loan for the entire amount of the initial funds required. The Gamalan government has agreed that it will not ask for the loan to be repaid as long as Tramont Co fulfils its contract to undertake the project for the four years. Tramont Co can borrow dollar funds at an interest rate of 5%.

Tramont Co's financing consists of 25 million shares currently trading at $2.40 each and $40 million 7% bonds trading at $1,428 per $1,000. Tramont Co's quoted beta is 1.17. The current risk free rate of return is estimated at 3% and the market risk premium is 6%. Due to the nature of the project, it is estimated that the beta applicable to the project if it is all-equity financed will be 0.4 more than the current all-equity financed beta of Tramont Co. If the Gamalan project is undertaken, the cost of capital applicable to the cash flows in the USA is expected to be 7%.

The spot exchange rate between the dollar and the Gamalan Rupiah is GR 55 per $1. The annual inflation rates are currently 3% in the USA and 9% in Gamala. It can be assumed that these inflation rates will not change for the foreseeable future. All net cash flows arising from the project will be remitted back to Tramont Co at the end of each year.

There are two main political parties in Gamala: the Gamala Liberal (GL) Party and the Gamala Republican (GR) Party. Gamala is currently governed by the GL Party but general elections are due to be held soon. If the GR Party wins the election, it promises to increase taxes of international companies operating in Gamala and review any commercial benefits given to these businesses by the previous government.

Required:

(a)   **Prepare a report for the Board of Directors (BoD) of Tramont Co that:**

     (i)   **Evaluates whether or not Tramont Co should undertake the project to produce the X-IT in Gamala and cease its production in the USA immediately. In the evaluation, include all relevant calculations in the form of a financial assessment and explain any assumptions made.**

         It is suggested that the financial assessment should be based on present value of the operating cash flows from the Gamalan project, discounted by an appropriate all-equity rate, and adjusted by the present value of all other relevant cash flows. (27 marks)

     (ii)   **Discusses the potential change in government and other business factors that Tramont Co should consider before making a final decision.** (8 marks)

     Professional marks for format, structure and presentation of the report for part (a). (4 marks)

(b)   Although not mandatory for external reporting purposes, one of the members of the BoD suggested that adopting a triple bottom line approach when monitoring the X-IT investment after its implementation, would provide a better assessment of how successful it has been.

     Discuss how adopting aspects of triple bottom line reporting may provide a better assessment of the success of the X-IT. (6 marks)

(c)   Another member of the BoD felt that, despite Tramont Co having a wide range of shareholders holding well diversified portfolios of investments, moving the production of the X-IT to Gamala would result in further risk diversification benefits.

Discuss whether moving the production of the X-IT to Gamala may result in further risk diversification for the shareholders already holding well diversified portfolios.

(5 marks)

(50 marks)

Question 2 ALECTO CO

Alecto Co, a large listed company based in Europe, is expecting to borrow €22,000,000 in four months' time on 1 May 2018. It expects to make a full repayment of the borrowed amount nine months from now. Assume it is 1 January 2018 now. Currently there is some uncertainty in the markets, with higher than normal rates of inflation, but an expectation that the inflation level may soon come down. This has led some economists to predict a rise in interest rates and others suggesting an unchanged outlook or maybe even a small fall in interest rates over the next six months.

Although Alecto Co is of the opinion that it is equally likely that interest rates could increase or fall by 0.5% in four months, it wishes to protect itself from interest rate fluctuations by using derivatives. The company can borrow at LIBOR plus 80 basis points and LIBOR is currently 3.3%. The company is considering using interest rate futures, options on interest rate futures or interest rate collars as possible hedging choices.

The following information and quotes from an appropriate exchange are provided on Euro futures and options. Margin requirements may be ignored.

Three month Euro futures, €1,000,000 contract, tick size 0.01% and tick value €25
March 96.27
June 96.16
September 95.90

Options on three month Euro futures, €1,000,000 contract, tick size 0.01% and tick value €25. Option premiums are in annual %.

	Calls		Strike		Puts	
March	June	September		March	June	September
0.279	0.391	0.446	96.00	0.006	0.163	0.276
0.012	0.090	0.263	96.50	0.196	0.581	0.754

It can be assumed that settlement for both the futures and options contracts is at the end of the month. It can also be assumed that basis diminishes to zero at contract maturity at a constant rate and that time intervals can be counted in months.

Required:

(a)   **Briefly discuss the main advantage and disadvantage of hedging interest rate risk using an interest rate collar instead of options.** (4 marks)

(b)   **Based on the three hedging choices Alecto Co is considering and assuming that the company does not face any basis risk, recommend a hedging strategy for the €22,000,000 loan. Support the recommendation with appropriate comments and relevant calculations in €.** (17 marks)

(c)   **Explain what is meant by basis risk and how it would affect the recommendation made in part (b) above.** (4 marks)

(25 marks)

Question 3 DORIC CO

Doric Co has two manufacturing divisions: parts and fridges. Although the parts division is profitable, the fridges division is not, and as a result its share price has declined to $0.50 per share from a high of $2.83 per share around three years ago. Assume it is now 1 January 2018.

The board of directors are considering two proposals:

(i)   To cease trading and close down the company entirely, or;

(ii)   To close the fridges division and continue the parts division through a leveraged management buyout. The new company will continue with manufacturing parts only, but will make an additional investment of $50 million in order to grow the parts division after-tax cash flows by 3.5% in perpetuity. The proceeds from the sale of the fridges division will be used to pay the outstanding liabilities. The finance raised from the management buy-out will pay for any remaining liabilities, the funds required for the additional investment, and to purchase the current equity shares at a premium of 20%. The fridges division is twice the size of the parts division in terms of its assets attributable to it.

Extracts from the most recent financial statements:
Financial position as at 31 December 2017

	$m
Non-current assets	110
Current assets	220
Share capital ($0.40)	40
Reserves	10
Liabilities (Non-current and current)	280

Statement of profit or loss for the year ended 31 December 2017 $m

		$m
Sales revenue: Parts division		170
Fridges division		340
Costs prior to depreciation, interest payments and tax: Parts division		(120)
	Fridges division	(370)
Depreciation, tax and interest		(34)
Loss		(14)

If the entire company's assets are sold, the estimated realisable values of assets are as follows:

	$m
Non-current assets	100
Current assets	110

The following additional information has been provided:

Redundancy and other costs will be approximately $54 million if the whole company is closed, and pro rata for individual divisions that are closed. These costs have priority for payment before any other liabilities in case of closure. The taxation effects relating to this may be ignored.

Corporation tax on profits is 20% and it can be assumed that tax is payable in the year incurred. Annual depreciation on non-current assets is 10% and this is the amount of investment needed to maintain the current level of activity. The new company's cost of capital is expected to be 11%.

Required:

(a) Briefly discuss the possible benefits of Doric Co's parts division being divested through a management buy-out. (4 marks)

(b) Estimate the return the liability holders and the shareholders would receive in the event that Doric Co is closed and all its assets sold. (3 marks)

(c) Estimate the additional amount of finance needed and the value of the new company, if only the assets of fridges division are sold and the parts division is divested through a management buy-out. Briefly discuss whether or not the management buy-out would be beneficial. (10 marks)

(d) Doric Co's directors are of the opinion that they could receive a better price if the fridges division is sold as a going concern instead of its assets sold separately. They have been told that they need to consider two aspects when selling a company or part of a company: (i) seeking potential buyers and negotiating the sale price; and, (ii) due diligence.

Discuss the issues that should be taken into consideration with each aspect. (8 marks)

(25 marks)

Question 4 GNT CO

GNT Co is considering an investment in one of two corporate bonds. Both bonds have a nominal value of $1,000 and pay coupon interest on an annual basis. The market price of the first bond is $1,079.68. Its coupon rate is 6% and it is due to be redeemed at nominal value in five years. The second bond is about to be issued with a coupon rate of 4% and will also be redeemable at nominal value in five years. Both bonds are expected to have the same gross redemption yields (yields to maturity). The yield to maturity of a company's bond is determined by its credit rating.

GNT Co considers duration of the bond to be a key factor when making decisions on which bond to invest.

Required:

(a) Estimate the Macaulay duration of the two bonds GNT Co is considering for investment. (9 marks)

(b) Discuss how useful duration is as a measure of the sensitivity of a bond price to changes in interest rates. (8 marks)

(c) Among the criteria used by credit agencies for establishing a company's credit rating are the following: industry risk, earnings protection, financial flexibility and evaluation of the company's management.

Briefly explain each criterion and suggest factors that could be used to assess it. (8 marks)

(25 marks)

JUNE 2014

Question 1 COCOA-MOCHA-CHAI

Cocoa-Mocha-Chai (CMC) Co is a large listed company based in Switzerland and uses Swiss Francs as its currency. It imports tea, coffee and cocoa from countries around the world, and sells its blended products to supermarkets and large retailers worldwide. The company has production facilities located in two European ports where raw materials are brought for processing, and from where finished products are shipped out. All raw material purchases are paid for in US dollars (US$), while all sales are invoiced in Swiss Francs (CHF).

Until recently CMC Co had no intention of hedging its foreign currency exposures, interest rate exposures or commodity price fluctuations, and stated this intent in its annual report. However, after consultations with senior and middle managers, the company's new Board of Directors (BoD) has been reviewing its risk management and operations strategies.

The following two proposals have been put forward by the BoD for further consideration:

Proposal one

Setting up a treasury function to manage the foreign currency and interest rate exposures (but not commodity price fluctuations) using derivative products. The treasury function would be headed by the finance director. The purchasing director, who initiated the idea of having a treasury function, was of the opinion that this would enable her management team to make better decisions. The finance director also supported the idea as he felt this would increase his influence on the BoD and strengthen his case for an increase in his remuneration.

In order to assist in the further consideration of this proposal, the BoD wants you to use the following upcoming foreign currency and interest rate exposures to demonstrate how they would be managed by the treasury function:

(i)   a payment of US$5,060,000 which is due in four months' time; and

(ii)   a four-year CHF60,000,000 loan taken out to part-fund the setting up of four branches (see proposal two below).

Interest will be payable on the loan at a fixed annual rate of 2·2% or a floating annual rate based on the yield curve rate plus 0·40%. The loan's principal amount will be repayable in full at the end of the fourth year.

Proposal two

This proposal suggested setting up four new branches in four different countries. Each branch would have its own production facilities and sales teams. As a consequence of this, one of the two European-based production facilities will be closed. Initial cost-benefit analysis indicated that this would reduce costs related to production, distribution and logistics, as these branches would be closer to the sources of raw materials and also to the customers. The operations and sales directors supported the proposal, as in addition to above, this would enable sales and marketing teams in the branches to respond to any changes in nearby markets more quickly. The branches would be controlled and staffed by the local population in those countries. However, some members of the BoD expressed concern that such a move would create agency issues between CMC Co's central management and the management controlling the branches. They suggested mitigation strategies would need to be established to minimise these issues.

Response from the non-executive directors

When the proposals were put to the non-executive directors, they indicated that they were broadly supportive of the second proposal if the financial benefits outweigh the costs of setting up and running the four branches. However, they felt that they could not support the first proposal, as this would reduce shareholder value because the costs related to undertaking the proposal are likely to outweigh the benefits.

Additional information relating to proposal one

The current spot rate is US$1·0635 per CHF1. The current annual inflation rate in the USA is three times higher than Switzerland.

The following derivative products are available to CMC Co to manage the exposures of the US$ payment and the interest on the loan:

Exchange-traded currency futures

Contract size CHF125,000 price quotation: US$ per CHF1

3-month expiry	1·0647
6-month expiry	1·0659

Exchange-traded currency options

Contract size CHF125,000, exercise price quotation: US$ per CHF1, premium: cents per CHF1

	Call Options		Put Options	
Exercise price	3-month expiry	6-month expiry	3-month expiry	6-month expiry
1·06	1·87	2·75	1·41	2·16
1·07	1·34	2·22	1·88	2·63

It can be assumed that futures and option contracts expire at the end of the month and transaction costs related to these can be ignored.

Over-the-counter products

In addition to the exchange-traded products, Pecunia Bank is willing to offer the following over-the-counter derivative products to CMC Co:

(i)   A forward rate between the US$ and the CHF of US$ 1·0677 per CHF1.

(ii)   An interest rate swap contract with a counterparty, where the counterparty can borrow at an annual floating rate based on the yield curve rate plus 0·8% or an annual fixed rate of 3·8%. Pecunia Bank would charge a fee of 20 basis points each to act as the intermediary of the swap. Both parties will benefit equally from the swap contract.

Required:

(a)   **Advise CMC Co on an appropriate hedging strategy to manage the foreign exchange exposure of the US$ payment in four months' time. Show all relevant calculations, including the number of contracts bought or sold in the exchange-traded derivative markets.**   (15 marks)

(b)   **Demonstrate how CMC Co could benefit from the swap offered by Pecunia Bank.**
                                                                                                       (6 marks)

(c) As an alternative to paying the principal on the loan as one lump sum at the end of the fourth year, CMC Co could pay off the loan in equal annual amounts over the four years similar to an annuity. In this case, an annual interest rate of 2% would be payable, which is the same as the loan's gross redemption yield (yield to maturity).

Required:

Calculate the modified duration of the loan if it is repaid in equal amounts and explain how duration can be used to measure the sensitivity of the loan to changes in interest rates. (7 marks)

(d) **Prepare a memorandum for the Board of Directors (BoD) of CMC Co which:**

(i) **Discusses proposal one in light of the concerns raised by the non-executive directors; and** (9 marks)

(ii) **Discusses the agency issues related to proposal two and how these can be mitigated.** (9 marks)

Professional marks will be awarded in part (d) for the presentation, structure, logical flow and clarity of the memorandum. (4 marks)

(50 marks)

Question 2 BURUNG CO

You have recently commenced working for Burung Co and are reviewing a four-year project which the company is considering for investment. The project is in a business activity which is very different from Burung Co's current line of business.

The following net present value estimate has been made for the project:

Year	0	1	2	3	4
	$m	$m	$m	$m	$m
Sales revenue		23·03	36·60	49·07	27·14
Direct project costs		(13·82)	(21·96)	(29·44)	(16·28)
Interest		(1·20)	(1·20)	(1·20)	(1·20)
Profit		8·01	13·44	18·43	9·66
Tax (20%)		(1·60)	(2·69)	(3·69)	(1·93)
Investment/sale	(38·00)				4·00
Cash flows	(38·00)	6·41	10·75	14·74	11·73
Discount factors (7%)	1	0·935	0·873	0·816	0·763
Present values	(38·00)	5·99	9·38	12·03	8·95

Net present value is negative $1·65 million, and therefore the recommendation is that the project should not be accepted.

In calculating the net present value of the project, the following notes were made:

(i)   Since the real cost of capital is used to discount cash flows, neither the sales revenue nor the direct project costs have been inflated. It is estimated that the inflation rate applicable to sales revenue is 8% per year and to the direct project costs is 4% per year.

(ii)   The project will require an initial investment of $38 million. Of this, $16 million relates to plant and machinery, which is expected to be sold for $4 million when the project ceases, after taking any inflation impact into account.

(iii)   Tax allowable depreciation is available on the plant and machinery at 50% in the first year, followed by 25% per year thereafter on a reducing balance basis. A balancing adjustment is available in the year the plant and machinery is sold. Burung Co pays 20% tax on its annual taxable profits. No tax allowable depreciation is available on the remaining investment assets and they will have a nil value at the end of the project.

(iv)   Burung Co uses either a nominal cost of capital of 11% or a real cost of capital of 7% to discount all projects, given that the rate of inflation has been stable at 4% for a number of years.

(v)   Interest is based on Burung Co's normal borrowing rate of 150 basis points over the 10-year government yield rate.

(vi)   At the beginning of each year, Burung Co will need to provide working capital of 20% of the anticipated sales revenue for the year. Any remaining working capital will be released at the end of the project.

(vii)   Working capital and depreciation have not been taken into account in the net present value calculation above, since depreciation is not a cash flow and all the working capital is returned at the end of the project.

It is anticipated that the project will be financed entirely by debt, 60% of which will be obtained from a subsidised loan scheme run by the government, which lends money at a rate of 100 basis points below the 10-year government debt yield rate of 2·5%. The remaining 40% will be funded from Burung Co's normal borrowing sources. Issue costs on both loans are 2% of the gross finance required. It can be assumed that the debt capacity available to Burung Co is equal to the actual amount of debt finance raised for the project.

Burung Co has identified a company, Lintu Co, which operates in the same line of business as that of the project it is considering. Lintu Co is financed by 40 million shares trading at $3·20 each and $34 million debt trading at $94 per $100. Lintu Co's equity beta is estimated at 1·5. The current yield on government treasury bills is 2% and it is estimated that the market risk premium is 8%. Lintu Co pays tax at an annual rate of 20%.

Both Burung Co and Lintu Co pay tax in the same year as when profits are earned.

Required:

(a)   **Calculate the adjusted present value (APV) for the project, correcting any errors made in the net present value estimate above, and conclude whether the project should be accepted or not. Show all relevant calculations.**   (15 marks)

(b)   **Comment on the corrections made to the original net present value estimate and explain the APV approach taken in part (a), including any assumptions made.**   (10 marks)

                                                                                          (25 marks)

Question 3 VOGEL CO

Vogel Co, a listed engineering company, manufactures large scale plant and machinery for industrial companies. Until ten years ago, Vogel Co pursued a strategy of organic growth. Since then, it has followed an aggressive policy of acquiring smaller engineering companies, which it feels have developed new technologies and methods, which could be used in its manufacturing processes. However, it is estimated that only between 30% and 40% of the acquisitions made in the last ten years have successfully increased the company's shareholder value.

Vogel Co is currently considering acquiring Tori Co, an unlisted company, which has three departments. Department A manufactures machinery for industrial companies, Department B produces electrical goods for the retail market, and the smaller Department C operates in the construction industry. Upon acquisition, Department A will become part of Vogel Co, as it contains the new technologies which Vogel Co is seeking, but Departments B and C will be unbundled, with the assets attached to Department C sold and Department B being spun off into a new company called Ndege Co.

Given below are extracts of financial information for the two companies for the year ended 30 April 2017.

	Vogel Co $m	Tori Co $m
Sales revenue	790·2	124·6
Profit before depreciation, interest and tax (PBDIT)	244·4	37·4
Interest	13·8	4·3
Depreciation	72·4	10·1
Pre-tax profit	158·2	23·0

	Vogel Co $m	Tori Co $m
Non-current assets	723·9	98·2
Current assets	142·6	46·5
7% unsecured bond	–	40·0
Other non-current and current liabilities	212·4	20·2
Share capital ($0.50 per share)	190·0	20·0
Reserves	464·1	64·5

Share of current and non-current assets and profit of Tori Co's three departments:

	Department A	Department B	Department C
Share of current and non-current assets	40%	40%	20%
Share of PBDIT and pre-tax profit	50%	40%	10%

Other information

(i) It is estimated that for Department C, the realisable value of its non-current assets is 100% of their book value, but its current assets' realisable value is only 90% of their book value. The costs related to closing Department C are estimated to be $3 million.

(ii) The funds raised from the disposal of Department C will be used to pay off Tori Co's other non-current and current liabilities.

(iii) The 7% unsecured bond will be taken over by Ndege Co. It can be assumed that the current market value of the bond is equal to its book value.

(iv)   At present, around 10% of Department B's PBDIT come from sales made to Department C.

(v)   Ndege Co's cost of capital is estimated to be 10%. It is estimated that in the first year of operation Ndege Co's free cash flows to firm will grow by 20%, and then by 5·2% annually thereafter.

(vi)   The tax rate applicable to all the companies is 20%, and Ndege Co can claim 10% tax allowable depreciation on its non-current assets. It can be assumed that the amount of tax allowable depreciation is the same as the investment needed to maintain Ndege Co's operations.

(vii)   Vogel Co's current share price is $3 per share and it is estimated that Tori Co's price-to-earnings (PE) ratio is 25% higher than Vogel Co's PE ratio. After the acquisition, when Department A becomes part of Vogel Co, it is estimated that Vogel Co's PE ratio will increase by 15%.

(viii)   It is estimated that the combined company's annual after-tax earnings will increase by $7 million due to the synergy benefits resulting from combining Vogel Co and Department A.

Required:

(a)   **Discuss the possible reasons why Vogel Co may have switched its strategy of organic growth to one of growing by acquiring companies.**   (4 marks)

(b)   **Discuss the possible actions Vogel Co could take to reduce the risk that the acquisition of Tori Co fails to increase shareholder value.**   (7 marks)

(c)   **Estimate, showing all relevant calculations, the maximum premium Vogel Co could pay to acquire Tori Co, explaining the approach taken and any assumptions made.**
                                                                             (14 marks)

                                                                             (25 marks)

Question 4 FAOILEAN CO

The chief executive officer (CEO) of Faoilean Co has just returned from a discussion at a leading university on the "application of options to investment decisions and corporate value". She wants to understand how some of the ideas which were discussed can be applied to decisions made at Faoilean Co. She is still a little unclear about some of the discussion on options and their application, and wants further clarification on the following:

(i)   Faoilean Co is involved in the exploration and extraction of oil and gas. Recently there have been indications that there could be significant deposits of oil and gas just off the shores of Ireland. The government of Ireland has invited companies to submit bids for the rights to commence the initial exploration of the area to assess the likelihood and amount of oil and gas deposits, with further extraction rights to follow. Faoilean Co is considering putting in a bid for the rights. The speaker leading the discussion suggested that using options as an investment assessment tool would be particularly useful to Faoilean Co in this respect.

(ii)   The speaker further suggested that options were useful in determining the value of equity and default risk, and suggested that this was why companies facing severe financial distress could still have a positive equity value.

(iii)   Towards the end of the discussion, the speaker suggested that changes in the values of options can be measured in terms of a number of risk factors known as the "greeks", such as the "vega". The CEO is unclear why option values are affected by so many different risk factors.

Required:

(a)   With regard to (i) above, discuss how Faoilean Co may use the idea of options to help with the investment decision in bidding for the exploration rights, and explain the assumptions made when using the idea of options in making investment decisions.

(11 marks)

(b)   With regard to (ii) above, discuss how options could be useful in determining the value of equity and default risk, and why companies facing severe financial distress still have positive equity values.   (9 marks)

(c)   With regard to (iii) above, explain why changes in option values are determined by numerous different risk factors and what "vega" determines.   (5 marks)

(25 marks)

DECEMBER 2014

Question 1 NAHARA CO

Nahara Co is a private holding company owned by the government of a wealthy oil-rich country to invest its sovereign funds. Nahara Co has followed a strategy of risk diversification for a number of years by acquiring companies from around the world in many different sectors.

One of Nahara Co's acquisition strategies is to identify and purchase undervalued companies in the airline industry in Europe. A recent acquisition was Fugae Co, a company based in a country which is part of the European Union (EU). Fugae Co repairs and maintains aircraft engines.

A few weeks ago, Nahara Co stated its intention to pursue the acquisition of an airline company based in the same country as Fugae Co. The EU, concerned about this, asked Nahara Co to sell Fugae Co before pursuing any further acquisitions in the airline industry.

Avem Co's acquisition interest in Fugae Co

Avem Co, a UK-based company specialising in producing and servicing business jets, has approached Nahara Co with a proposal to acquire Fugae Co for $1,200 million. Nahara Co expects to receive a premium of at least 30% on the estimated equity value of Fugae Co, if it is sold.

Extracts from the most recent statements of financial position of Avem Co and Fugae Co are as follows:

	Avem Co $m	Fugae Co $m
Share capital ($0.50 per share)	800	100
Reserves	3,550	160
Non-current liabilities	2,200	380
Current liabilities	130	30
Total capital and liabilities	6,680	670

Each Avem Co share is currently trading at $7·50, which is a multiple of 7·2 of its free cash flow to equity. Avem Co expects that the total free cash flows to equity of the combined company will increase by $40 million due to synergy benefits. After adding the synergy benefits of $40 million, Avem Co then expects the multiple of the total free cash flow of the combined company to increase to 7·5.

Fugae Co's free cash flow to equity is currently estimated at $76·5 million and it is expected to generate a return on equity of 11%. Over the past few years, Fugae Co has returned 77·3% of its annual free cash flow to equity back to Nahara Co, while retaining the balance for new investments.

Fugae Co's non-current liabilities consist entirely of $100 nominal value bonds which are redeemable in four years at the nominal value, on which the company pays a coupon of 5·4%. The debt is rated at B+ and the credit spread on B+ rated debt is 80 basis points above the risk-free rate of return.

Proposed luxury transport investment project by Fugae Co

In recent years, the country in which Fugae Co is based has been expanding its tourism industry and hopes that this industry will grow significantly in the near future. At present tourists normally travel using public transport and taxis, but there is a growing market for luxury travel. If the tourist industry does expand, then the demand for luxury travel is expected to grow rapidly. Fugae Co is considering entering this market through a four-year project. The project will cease after four years because of increasing competition.

The initial cost of the project is expected to be $42,000,000 and it is expected to generate the following after-tax cash flows over its four-year life:

Year	1	2	3	4
Cash flows ($000s)	3,277.6	16,134.3	36,504.7	35,683.6

The above figures are based on the tourism industry expanding as expected. However, it is estimated that there is a 25% probability that the tourism industry will not grow as expected in the first year. If this happens, then the present value of the project's cash flows will be 50% of the original estimates over its four-year life.

It is also estimated that if the tourism industry grows as expected in the first year, there is still a 20% probability that the expected growth will slow down in the second and subsequent years, and the present value of the project's cash flows would then be 40% of the original estimates in each of these years.

Lumi Co, a leisure travel company, has offered $50 million to buy the project from Fugae Co at the start of the second year. Fugae Co is considering whether having this choice would add to the value of the project.

If Fugae Co is bought by Avem Co after the project has begun, it is thought that the project will not result in any additional synergy benefits and will not generate any additional value for the combined company, above any value the project has already generated for Fugae Co.

Although there is no beta for companies offering luxury forms of travel in the tourist industry, Reka Co, a listed company, offers passenger transportation services on coaches, trains and luxury vehicles. About 15% of its business is in the luxury transport market and Reka Co's equity beta is 1·6. It is estimated that the asset beta of the non-luxury transport industry is 0·80. Reka Co's shares are currently trading at $4·50 per share and its debt is currently trading at $105 per $100. It has 80 million shares in issue and the book value of its debt is $340 million. The debt beta is estimated to be zero.

General information

The corporation tax rate applicable to all companies is 20%. The risk-free rate is estimated to be 4% and the market risk premium is estimated to be 6%.

Required:

(a) **Discuss whether or not Nahara Co's acquisition strategies, of pursuing risk diversification and of purchasing undervalued companies, can be valid.** (7 marks)

(b) **Discuss why the European Union (EU) may be concerned about Nahara Co's stated intention and how selling Fugae Co could reduce this concern.** (4 marks)

(c) **Prepare a report for the Board of Directors of Avem Co, which:**

   (i) **Estimates the additional value created for Avem Co, if it acquires Fugae Co without considering the luxury transport project;** (10 marks)

   (ii) **Estimates the additional value of the luxury transport project to Fugae Co, both with and without the offer from Lumi Co;** (18 marks)

   (iii) **Evaluates the benefit attributable to Avem Co and Fugae Co from combining the two companies with and without the project, and concludes whether or not the acquisition is beneficial. The evaluation should include any assumptions made.** (7 marks)

   Professional marks will be awarded in part (c) for the format, structure and presentation of the report. (4 marks)

(50 marks)

Question 2 KESHI CO

Keshi Co is a large multinational company with a number of international subsidiary companies. A centralised treasury department manages Keshi Co and its subsidiaries' borrowing requirements, cash surplus investment and financial risk management. Financial risk is normally managed using conventional derivative products such as forwards, futures, options and swaps.

Assume it is 1 December 2017 today and Keshi Co is expecting to borrow $18,000,000 on 1 February 2018 for a period of seven months. It can either borrow the funds at a variable rate of LIBOR plus 40 basis points or a fixed rate of 5·5%. LIBOR is currently 3·8% but Keshi Co feels that this could increase or decrease by 0·5% over the coming months due to increasing uncertainty in the markets.

The treasury department is considering whether or not to hedge the $18,000,000, using either exchange-traded March options or over-the-counter swaps offered by Rozu Bank.

The following information and quotes for $ March options are provided from an appropriate exchange. The options are based on three-month $ futures, $1,000,000 contract size and option premiums are in annual %.

March calls	Strike price	March puts
0·882	95·50	0·662
0·648	96·00	0·902

Option strike prices are quoted in basis points at 100 minus the annual % yield and settlement of the options contracts is at the end of March 2018. The current basis on the March futures price is 44 points; and it is expected to be 33 points on 1 January 2018, 22 points on 1 February 2018 and 11 points on 1 March 2018.

Rozu Bank has offered Keshi Co a swap with a counterparty that can borrow at a variable rate of LIBOR plus 30 basis points or a fixed rate of 4·6%, where Keshi Co receives 70% of any benefits accruing from undertaking the swap, prior to any bank charges. Rozu Bank will charge Keshi Co 10 basis points for the swap.

Keshi Co's chief executive officer believes that a centralised treasury department is necessary in order to increase shareholder value, but Keshi Co's new chief financial officer (CFO) thinks that having decentralised treasury departments operating across the subsidiary companies could be more beneficial. The CFO thinks that this is particularly relevant to the situation which Suisen Co, a company owned by Keshi Co, is facing.

Suisen Co operates in a country where most companies conduct business activities based on Islamic finance principles. It produces confectionery products including chocolates. It wants to use Salam contracts instead of commodity futures contracts to hedge its exposure to price fluctuations of cocoa. Salam contracts involve a commodity which is sold in advance based on an agreed price, quantity and quality. Full payment is received by the seller immediately, for an agreed delivery to be made in the future.

Required:

(a)   **Based on the two hedging choices Keshi Co is considering, recommend a hedging strategy for the $18,000,000 borrowing. Support your answer with appropriate calculations and discussion.** (15 marks)

(b)   **Discuss how a centralised treasury department may increase value for Keshi Co and the possible reasons for decentralising the treasury department.** (6 marks)

(c)   **Discuss the key differences between a Salam contract, under Islamic finance principles, and futures contracts.** (4 marks)

(25 marks)

Question 3 RIVIERE CO

Riviere Co is a small company based in the European Union (EU). It produces high quality frozen food which it exports to a small number of supermarket chains located within the EU as well. The EU is a free trade area for trade between its member countries.

Riviere Co finds it difficult to obtain bank finance and relies on a long-term strategy of using internally generated funds for new investment projects. This constraint means that it cannot accept every profitable project and often has to choose between them.

Riviere Co is currently considering investment in one of two mutually exclusive food production projects: Privi and Drugi. Privi will produce and sell a new range of frozen desserts exclusively within the EU. Drugi will produce and sell a new range of frozen desserts and savoury foods to supermarket chains based in countries outside the EU. Each project will last for five years and the following financial information refers to both projects.

Project Drugi, annual after-tax cash flows expected at the end of each year (€000s)

Year	Current	1	2	3	4	5
Cash flows (€000s)	(11,840)	1,230	1,680	4,350	10,240	2,200

	Privi	Drugi
Net present value	€2,054,000	€2,293,000
Internal rate of return	17·6%	Not provided
Modified internal rate of return	13·4%	Not provided
Value at risk (over the project's life)		
95% confidence level	€1,103,500	Not provided
90% confidence level	€860,000	Not provided

Both projects' net present value has been calculated based on Riviere Co's nominal cost of capital of 10%. It can be assumed that both projects' cash flow returns are normally distributed and the annual standard deviation of project Drugi's present value of after-tax cash flows is estimated to be €400,000. It can also be assumed that all sales are made in € (Euro) and therefore the company is not exposed to any foreign exchange exposure.

Notwithstanding how profitable project Drugi may appear to be, Riviere Co's board of directors is concerned about the possible legal risks if it invests in the project because they have never dealt with companies outside the EU before.

Required:

(a)   **Discuss the aims of a free trade area, such as the European Union (EU), and the possible benefits to Riviere Co of operating within the EU.**   (5 marks)

(b)   **Calculate the figures which have not been provided for project Drugi and recommend which project should be accepted. Provide a justification for the recommendation and explain what the value at risk measures.**   (13 marks)

(c)   **Discuss the possible legal risks of investing in project Drugi which Riviere Co may be concerned about and how these may be mitigated.**   (7 marks)

(25 marks)

JUNE 2015

Question 1 IMONI CO

Yilandwe, whose currency is the Yilandwe Rand (YR), has faced extremely difficult economic challenges in the past 25 years because of some questionable economic policies and political decisions made by its previous governments. Although Yilandwe's population is generally poor, its people are well-educated and ambitious. Just over three years ago, a new government took office and since then it has imposed a number of strict monetary and fiscal controls, including an annual corporation tax rate of 40%, in an attempt to bring Yilandwe out of its difficulties. As a result, the annual rate of inflation has fallen rapidly from a high of 65% to its current level of 33%. These strict monetary and fiscal controls have made Yilandwe's government popular in the larger cities and towns, but less popular in the rural areas which seem to have suffered disproportionately from the strict monetary and fiscal controls.

It is expected that Yilandwe's annual inflation rate will continue to fall in the coming few years as follows:

Year	Inflation rate
1	22·0%
2	14·7%
3 onwards	19·8%

Yilandwe's government has decided to continue the progress made so far, by encouraging foreign direct investment into the country. Recently, government representatives held trade shows internationally and offered businesses a number of concessions, including:

(i)   zero corporation tax payable in the first two years of operation; and

(ii)   an opportunity to carry forward tax losses and write them off against future profits made after the first two years.

The government representatives also promised international companies investing in Yilandwe prime locations in towns and cities with good transport links.

Imoni Co

Imoni Co, a large listed company based in the USA with the US dollar ($) as its currency, manufactures high tech diagnostic components for machinery, which it exports worldwide. After attending one of the trade shows, Imoni Co is considering setting up an assembly plant in Yilandwe where parts would be sent and assembled into a specific type of component. Once assembled, the component will be exported to companies based in the European Union (EU). These exports will be invoiced in euros (€).

Assembly plant in Yilandwe: financial and other data projections

It is initially assumed that the project will last for four years. The four-year project will require immediate investments of YR21,000 million for land and buildings, YR18,000 million for machinery and YR9,600 million for working capital. The working capital will need to be increased annually at the start of each of the next three years by Yilandwe's inflation rate and it is assumed that working capital will be released at the end of the project's life.

It can be assumed that the assembly plant can be built very quickly and production started almost immediately. This is because the basic facilities and infrastructure are already in place as the plant will be built on the premises and grounds of a school. The school is ideally located, near the main highway and railway lines. As a result, the school will close and the children currently studying there will be relocated to other schools in the city. The government has agreed to provide free buses to take the children to these schools for a period of six months to give parents time to arrange appropriate transport in the future for their children.

The current selling price of each component is €700 and this price is likely to increase by the average EU rate of inflation from year 1 onwards.

The number of components expected to be sold each year are as follows:

Year	1	2	3	4
Sales component units (000s)	150	480	730	360

The parts needed to assemble into the components in Yilandwe will be sent from the USA by Imoni Co at a cost of $200 per component unit, from which Imoni Co would currently earn a pre-tax contribution of $40 for each component unit. However, Imoni Co feels that it can negotiate with Yilandwe's government and increase the transfer price to $280 per component unit. The variable costs related to assembling the components in Yilandwe are currently YR15,960 per component unit. The current annual fixed costs of the assembly plant are YR4,600 million. All these costs, wherever incurred, are expected to increase by the respective country's annual inflation every year from year 1 onwards.

Imoni Co pays corporation tax on profits at an annual rate of 20% in the USA. The tax in both the USA and Yilandwe is payable in the year that the tax liability arises. A bilateral tax treaty exists between Yilandwe and the USA. Tax allowable depreciation is available at 25% per year on the machinery on a straight-line basis.

Imoni Co will expect to receive annual royalties from the assembly plant. The normal annual royalty fee is currently $20 million, but Imoni Co feels that it can negotiate this with Yilandwe's government and increase the royalty fee by 80%. Once agreed, this fee will not be subject to any inflationary increase in the project's four-year period.

If Imoni Co does decide to invest in an assembly plant in Yilandwe, its exports from the USA to the EU will fall slightly and it will incur redundancy costs. As a result, Imoni Co's after-tax cash flows will reduce by the following amounts:

Year	1	2	3	4
Redundancy and lost contribution	$20,000	$55,697	$57,368	$59,089

Imoni Co normally uses its cost of capital of 9% to assess new projects. However, the finance director suggests that Imoni Co should use a project specific discount rate of 12% instead.

Other financial information

Current spot rates

Euro per dollar	€0·714/$1
YR per euro	YR142/€1
YR per dollar	YR101·4/$1

Forecast future rates based on expected inflation rate differentials

Year	1	2	3	4
YR/$1	120·1	133·7	142·5	151·9

Year	1	2	3	4
YR/€1	165·0	180·2	190·2	200·8

Expected inflation rates

EU expected inflation rate: Next two years	5%
EU expected inflation rate: Year 3 onwards	4%
USA expected inflation rate: Year 1 onwards	3%

Required:

(a) Discuss the possible benefits and drawbacks to Imoni Co of setting up its own assembly plant in Yilandwe, compared to licensing a company based in Yilandwe to undertake the assembly on its behalf. (5 marks)

(b) Prepare a report which:

    (i) Evaluates the financial acceptability of the investment in the assembly plant in Yilandwe; (21 marks)

    (ii) Discusses the assumptions made in producing the estimates, and the other risks and issues which Imoni Co should consider before making the final decision; (17 marks)

    (iii) Provides a reasoned recommendation on whether or not Imoni Co should invest in the assembly plant in Yilandwe. (3 marks)

    Professional marks will be awarded in part (b) for the format, structure and presentation of the report. (4 marks)

(50 marks)

Question 2 CHAWAN CO

The treasury department of Chawan Co, a listed company, aims to maintain a portfolio of around $360 million consisting of equity shares, corporate bonds and government bonds, which it can turn into cash quickly for investment projects. Chawan Co is considering disposing 27 million shares, valued at $2·15 each, which it has invested in Oden Co. The head of Chawan Co's treasury department is of the opinion that, should the decision be made to dispose of its equity stake in Oden Co, this should be sold through a dark pool network and not sold on the stock exchange where Oden Co's shares are listed. In the last few weeks, there have also been rumours that Oden Co may become subject to a takeover bid.

Oden Co operates in the travel and leisure (T&L) sector, and the poor weather conditions in recent years, coupled with a continuing recession, has meant that the T&L sector is under-performing. Over the past three years, sales revenue fell by an average of 8% per year in the T&L sector. However, there are signs that the economy is starting to recover, but this is by no means certain.

Given below are extracts from the recent financial statements and other financial information for Oden Co and the T&L sector.

Statement of financial position at 31 May (all amounts in $m)

	2015	2016	2017
Total non-current assets	972	990	980
Total current assets	128	142	126
Total assets	1,100	1,132	1,106
Equity			
Ordinary shares ($0·50)	300	300	300
Reserves	305	329	311
Total equity	605	629	611
Non-current liabilities			
Bank loans	115	118	100
Bonds	250	250	260
Total non-current liabilities	365	368	360
Current liabilities			
Trade and other payables	42	45	37
Bank overdraft	88	90	98
Total current liabilities	130	135	135
Total equity and liabilities	1,100	1,132	1,106

Statement of profit or loss for the year ending 31 May (all amounts in $m)

	2015	2016	2017
Sales revenue	1,342	1,335	1,185
Operating profit	218	203	123
Finance costs	(23)	(27)	(35)
Profit before tax	195	176	88
Taxation	(35)	(32)	(16)
Profit for the year	160	144	72

Other financial information (Based on annual figures to 31 May of each year)

	2014	2015	2016	2017
Oden Co average share price ($)	2·10	2·50	2·40	2·20
Oden Co dividend per share ($)	0·15	0·18	0·20	0·15
T&L sector average share price ($)	3·80	4·40	4·30	4·82
T&L sector average earnings per share ($)	0·32	0·36	0·33	0·35
T&L sector average dividend per share ($)	0·25	0·29	0·29	0·31
Oden Co's equity beta	1·5	1·5	1·6	2·0
T&L sector average equity beta	1·5	1·4	1·5	1·6

The risk-free rate and the market return have remained fairly constant over the last ten years at 4% and 10% respectively.

Required:

(a)   **Explain what a dark pool network is and why Chawan Co may want to dispose of its equity stake in Oden Co through one, instead of through the stock exchange where Oden Co's shares are listed.**   (5 marks)

(b)   **Discuss whether or not Chawan Co should dispose of its equity stake in Oden Co. Provide relevant calculations to support the discussion.**   (20 marks)

   Note: Up to 10 marks are available for the calculations.

                                                                                          (25 marks)

Question 3 OKAZU CO

In order to raise funds for future projects, the management of Bento Co, a large manufacturing company, is considering disposing of one of its subsidiary companies, Okazu Co, which is involved in manufacturing rubber tubing. They are considering undertaking the disposal through a management buy-out (MBO) or a management buy-in (MBI). Bento Co wants $60 million from the sale of Okazu Co.

Given below are extracts from the most recent financial statements for Okazu Co:

Year ending 30 April (all amounts in $000)

	2017
Total non-current assets	40,800
Total current assets	12,300
Total assets	53,100
Equity	24,600
Non-current liabilities	16,600
Current liabilities	
Trade and other payables	7,900
Bank overdraft	4,000
Total current liabilities	11,900
Total equity and liabilities	53,100

Year ending 30 April (all amounts in $000)

	2017
Sales revenue	54,900
Operating profit	12,200
Finance costs	1,600
Profit before tax	10,600
Taxation	2,120
Profit for the year	8,480

Notes relating to the financial statements above:

(i)   Current assets, non-current assets and the trade and other payables will be transferred to the new owner when Okazu Co is sold. The bank overdraft will be repaid by Bento Co prior to the sale of Okazu Co.

(ii)   With the exception of the bank overdraft, Bento Co has provided all the financing to Okazu Co. No liabilities, except the trade and other payables specified above, will be transferred to the new owner when Okazu Co is sold.

(iii)   It is estimated that the market value of the non-current assets is 30% higher than the book value and the market value of the current assets is equivalent to the book value.

(iv)   The group finance costs and taxation are allocated by Bento Co to all its subsidiaries in pre-agreed proportions.

Okazu Co's senior management team has approached Dofu Co, a venture capital company, about the proposed MBO. A new company would be formed to undertake the MBO and Dofu Co has agreed to provide finance for the new company on the following basis:

(i) $30 million loan in the form of an 8% bond on which interest is payable annually, based on the loan amount outstanding at the start of each year. The bond will be repaid on the basis of fixed equal annual payments (constituting of interest and principal) over the next four years;

(ii) $20 million loan in the form of a 6% convertible bond on which interest is payable annually. Conversion may be undertaken from the beginning of year five onwards on the basis of 50 equity shares for every $100;

(iii)   5,000,000 $1 equity shares for $5,000,000.

Okazu Co's senior management will contribute $5,000,000 for 5,000,000 $1 equity shares and own the remaining 50% of the equity stake in the new company.

As a condition for providing the finance, Dofu Co will impose a restrictive covenant that the new company's gearing ratio will be no higher than 75% at the end of its first year of operations, and then fall to no higher than 60%, 50% and 40% at the end of year two to year four respectively. The gearing ratio is determined by the book value of debt divided by the combined book values of debt and equity.

After the MBO, it is expected that Okazu Co's earnings before interest and tax will increase by 11% per year and annual dividends of 25% on the available earnings will be paid for the next four years. It is expected that the annual growth rate of dividends will reduce by 60% from year five onwards. The new company will pay tax at a rate of 20% per year. The new company's cost of equity has been estimated at 12%.

Required:

(a)   **Distinguish between a management buy-out (MBO) and a management buy-in (MBI). Discuss the relative benefits and drawbacks to Okazu Co if it is disposed through a MBO instead of a MBI.** (5 marks)

(b)   **Estimate, showing all relevant calculations, whether the restrictive covenant imposed by Dofu Co is likely to be met.** (12 marks)

(c)   **Discuss, with supporting calculations, whether or not an MBO would be beneficial for Dofu Co and Okazu Co's senior management team.** (8 marks)

(25 marks)

Question 4 DAIKON CO

For a number of years Daikon Co has been using forward rate agreements to manage its exposure to interest rate fluctuations. Recently its chief executive officer (CEO) attended a talk on using exchange-traded derivative products to manage risks. She wants to find out by how much the extra cost of the borrowing detailed below can be reduced, when using interest rate futures, options on interest rate futures, and a collar on the options, to manage the interest rate risk. She asks that detailed calculations for each of the three derivative products be provided and a reasoned recommendation to be made.

Daikon Co is expecting to borrow $34,000,000 in five months' time. It expects to make a full repayment of the borrowed amount in 11 months' time. Assume it is 1 June 2017 today. Daikon Co can borrow funds at LIBOR plus 70 basis points. LIBOR is currently 3·6%, but Daikon Co expects that interest rates may increase by as much as 80 basis points in five months' time.

The following information and quotes from an appropriate exchange are provided on LIBOR-based $ futures and options.

Three-month $ December futures are currently quoted at 95·84. The contract size is $1,000,000, the tick size is 0·01% and the tick value is $25.

Options on three-month $ futures, $1,000,000 contract, tick size 0·01% and tick value $25. Option premiums are in annual %.

December calls	Strike price	December puts
0·541	95·50	0·304
0·223	96·00	0·508

Initial assumptions

It can be assumed that maturity for both the futures and options contracts is at the end of the relevant month; that basis diminishes to zero at a constant rate until the contract matures and time intervals can be counted in months; that margin requirements may be ignored; and that if the options are in-the-money, they will be exercised at the end of the hedge instead of being sold.

Further issues

In the talk, the CEO was informed of the following issues:

(i)   Futures contracts will be marked-to-market daily. The CEO wondered what the impact of this would be if 50 futures contracts were bought at 95·84 on 1 June and 30 futures contracts were sold at 95·61 on 3 June, based on the $ December futures contract given above. The closing settlement prices are given below for four days:

Date	Settlement price
1 June	95·84
2 June	95·76
3 June	95·66
4 June	95·74

(ii)   Daikon Co will need to deposit funds into a margin account with a broker for each contract they have opened, and this margin will need to be adjusted when the contracts are marked-to-market daily.

(iii)   It is unlikely that option contracts will be exercised at the end of the hedge period unless they have reached expiry. Instead, they more likely to be sold and the positions closed.

Required:

(a)   Based on the three hedging choices available to Daikon Co and the initial assumptions given above, draft a response to the chief executive officer's (CEO) request made in the first paragraph of the question.   (15 marks)

(b)   Discuss the impact on Daikon Co of each of the three further issues given above. As part of the discussion, include the calculations of the daily impact of the mark-to-market closing prices on the transactions specified by the CEO.   (10 marks)

(25 marks)

SEPTEMBER/DECEMBER 2015

Question 1 CIGNO CO

Cigno Co is a large pharmaceutical company, involved in the research and development (R&D) of medicines and other healthcare products. Over the past few years, Cigno Co has been finding it increasingly difficult to develop new medical products. In response to this, it has followed a strategy of acquiring smaller pharmaceutical companies which already have successful products in the market and/or have products in development which look very promising for the future. It has mainly done this without having to resort to major cost-cutting and has therefore avoided large-scale redundancies. This has meant that not only has Cigno Co performed reasonably well on the stock market, but it has also maintained a high level of corporate reputation.

Anatra Co is involved in two business areas: the first area involves the R&D of medical products, and the second area involves the manufacture of medical and dental equipment. Until recently, Anatra Co's financial performance was falling, but about three years ago a new chief executive officer (CEO) was appointed and she started to turn the company around. Recently, the company has developed and marketed a range of new medical products, and is in the process of developing a range of cancer-fighting medicines. This has resulted in good performance on the stock market, but many analysts believe that its shares are still trading below their true value. Anatra Co's CEO is of the opinion that the turnaround in the company's fortunes makes it particularly vulnerable to a takeover threat, and she is thinking of defence strategies that the company could undertake to prevent such a threat. In particular, she was thinking of disposing of some of the company's assets and focussing on its core business.

Cigno Co is of the opinion that Anatra Co is being held back from achieving its true potential by its equipment manufacturing business and that by separating the two business areas, corporate value can be increased. As a result, it is considering the possibility of acquiring Anatra Co, unbundling the manufacturing business, and then absorbing Anatra Co's R&D business. Cigno Co estimates that it would need to pay a premium of 35% to Anatra Co's shareholders to buy the company.

Financial information: Anatra Co

Given below are extracts from Anatra Co's latest statement of profit or loss and statement of financial position for the year ended 30 November 2017:

	$m
Sales revenue	21,400
Profit before interest and tax (PBIT)	3,210
Interest	720
Pre-tax profit	2,490

	$m
Non-current liabilities	9,000
Share capital ($0.50)	3,500
Reserves	4,520

Anatra Co's share of revenue and profits between the two business areas are as follows:

	Medical products R&D	Equipment manufacturing
Share of revenue and profit	70%	30%

Post-acquisition benefits from acquiring Anatra Co

Cigno Co estimates that following the acquisition and unbundling of the manufacturing business, Anatra Co's future sales revenue and profitability of the medical R&D business will be boosted. The annual sales growth rate is expected to be 5% and the profit margin before interest and tax is expected to be 17·25% of sales revenue, for the next four years. It can be assumed that the current tax allowable depreciation will remain equivalent to the amount of investment needed to maintain the current level of operations, but that the company will require an additional investment in assets of $0·40 for every $1 increase in sales revenue.

After the four years, the annual growth rate of the company's free cash flows is expected to be 3% for the foreseeable future.

Anatra Co's unbundled equipment manufacturing business is expected to be divested through a sell-off, although other options such as a management buy-in were also considered. The value of the sell-off will be based on the medical and dental equipment manufacturing industry. Cigno Co has estimated that Anatra Co's manufacturing business should be valued at a factor of 1·2 times higher than the industry's average price-to-earnings ratio. Currently the industry's average earnings-per-share is $0·30 and the average share price is $2·40.

Possible additional post-acquisition benefits

Cigno Co estimates that it could achieve further cash flow benefits following the acquisition of Anatra Co, if it undertakes a limited business re-organisation. There is some duplication of the R&D work conducted by Cigno Co and Anatra Co, and the costs related to this duplication could be saved if Cigno Co closes some of its own operations. However, it would mean that many redundancies would have to be made including employees who have worked in Cigno Co for many years. Anatra Co's employees are considered to be better qualified in these areas of duplication, and would therefore not be made redundant.

Cigno Co could also move its headquarters to the country where Anatra Co is based and thereby potentially save a significant amount of tax, other than corporation tax. However, this would mean a loss of revenue for the government where Cigno Co is based.

The company is concerned about how the government and the people of the country where it is based might react to these issues. It has had a long and beneficial relationship with the country and with the country's people.

Cigno Co has estimated that it would save $1,600 million in after-tax free cash flows to the firm at the end of the first year as a result of these post-acquisition benefits. These cash flows would increase by 4% per annum for the next three years.

Estimating the combined company's weighted average cost of capital

Cigno Co is of the opinion that as a result of acquiring Anatra Co, the cost of capital will be based on the equity beta and the cost of debt of the combined company. The asset beta of the combined company is the individual companies' asset betas weighted in proportion of the individual companies' market value of equity. Cigno Co has a market value debt to equity ratio of 40:60 and an equity beta of 1·10.

It can be assumed that the combined companies will also have a market value debt to equity ratio of 40:60.

Currently, Cigno Co's total firm value (market values of debt and equity) is $60,000 million and Anatra Co's asset beta is 0·68.

Additional information

- The estimate of the risk free rate of return is 4·3% and of the market risk premium is 7%.
- The corporation tax rate applicable to all companies is 22%.
- Anatra Co's current share price is $3 per share, and it can be assumed that the book value and the market value of its debt are equivalent.
- The pre-tax cost of debt of the combined company is expected to be 6.0%.

Important note

Cigno Co's board of directors (BoD) does not require any discussion or computations of currency movements or exposure in this report. All calculations are to be presented in $ millions. The BoD also does not expect any discussion or computations relating to the financing of the acquisition in this report, other than the information provided above on the estimation of the cost of capital.

Required:

(a)   **Distinguish between a divestment through a sell-off and a management buy-in as forms of unbundling.**   (4 marks)

(b)   **Prepare a report for the board of directors (BoD) of Cigno Co which:**

    (i)   **Estimates the value attributable to Cigno Co's shareholders from the acquisition of Anatra Co before taking into account the cash benefits of potential tax savings and redundancies, and then after taking these into account;**   (18 marks)

    (ii)   **Assesses the value created from (b)(i) above, including a discussion of the estimations made and methods used;**   (8 marks)

    (iii)   **Advises the BoD on the key factors it should consider in relation to the redundancies and potential tax savings.**   (4 marks)

    Professional marks will be awarded in part (b) for the format, structure and presentation of the report.   (4 marks)

(c)   **Discuss whether the defence strategy suggested by Anatra Co's CEO of disposing assets is feasible.**   **(6 marks)**

(d)   Takeover regulation, where Anatra Co is based, offers the following conditions aimed at protecting shareholders: the mandatory-bid condition through sell out rights, the principle of equal treatment, and squeeze-out rights.

    Required:

    Explain the main purpose of each of the three conditions.   (6 marks)

                                                                                                                        (50 marks)

Question 2 ARMSTRONG GROUP

The Armstrong Group is a multinational group of companies. Today is 1 September. The treasury manager at Massie Co, one of Armstrong Group's subsidiaries based in Europe, has just received notification from the group's head office that it intends to introduce a system of netting to settle balances owed within the group every six months. Previously inter-group indebtedness was settled between the two companies concerned.

The predicted balances owing to, and owed by, the group companies at the end of February are as follows:

Owed by	Owed to	Local currency million (m)
Armstrong (USA)	Horan (South Africa)	US $12·17
Horan (South Africa)	Massie (Europe)	SA R42·65
Giffen (Denmark)	Armstrong (USA)	D Kr21·29
Massie (Europe)	Armstrong (USA)	US $19·78
Armstrong (USA)	Massie (Europe)	€1·57
Horan (South Africa)	Giffen (Denmark)	D Kr16·35
Giffen (Denmark)	Massie (Europe)	€1·55

The predicted exchange rates, used in the calculations of the balances to be settled, are as follows:

	D Kr	US$	SA R	€
1 D Kr =	1·0000	0·1823	1·9554	0·1341
1 US $ =	5·4855	1·0000	10·7296	0·7358
1 SA R =	0·5114	0·0932	1·0000	0·0686
1 € =	7·4571	1·3591	14·5773	1·0000

Settlement will be made in dollars, the currency of Armstrong Group, the parent company. Settlement will be made in the order that the company owing the largest net amount in dollars will first settle with the company owed the smallest net amount in dollars.

Note: *D Kr is Danish Krone, SA R is South African Rand, US $ is United States dollar and € is Euro.*

Required:

(a) **(i)** **Calculate the inter-group transfers which are forecast to occur for the next period.** (8 marks)

(ii) **Discuss the problems which may arise with the new arrangement.** (3 marks)

(b) Massie Co is due to receive €25 million from Bardsley Co, a company outside the Armstrong Group, on 30 November. Massie Co's treasury manager intends to invest this money for the six months until 31 May, when it will be used to fund some major capital expenditure. However, the treasury manager is concerned about changes in interest rates. Predictions in the media range from a 0·5% rise in interest rates to a 0·5% fall.

Because of the uncertainty, the treasury manager has decided to protect Massie Co by using derivatives. The treasury manager wishes to take advantage of favourable interest rate movements. Therefore she is considering options on interest rate futures or interest rate collars as possible methods of hedging, but not interest rate futures. Massie Co can invest at LIBOR minus 40 basis points and LIBOR is currently 3·6%.

The treasury manager has obtained the following information on Euro futures and options. She is ignoring margin requirements.

Three-month Euro futures, €1,000,000 contract, tick size 0·01% and tick value €25.

September	95·94
December	95·76
March	95·44

Options on three-month Euro futures, €1,000,000 contract, tick size 0·01% and tick value €25. Option premiums are in annual %.

	Calls		Strike		Puts	
September	December	March		September	December	March
0·113	0·182	0·245	96·50	0·002	0·123	0·198
0·017	0·032	0·141	97·00	0·139	0·347	0·481

It can be assumed that settlement for the contracts is at the end of the month. It can also be assumed that basis diminishes to zero at contract maturity at a constant rate and that time intervals can be counted in months.

Required:

Based on the choice of options on futures or collars which Massie Co is considering and assuming the company does not face any basis risk, recommend a hedging strategy for the €25 million receipt. Support your recommendations with appropriate comments and relevant calculations. (14 marks)

(25 marks)

Question 3 FLUFFTORT CO

Five years ago the Patel family invested in a new business, Flufftort Co, which manufactures furniture. Some family members became directors of Flufftort Co, others have not been actively involved in management. A venture capital firm, Gupte VC, also made a 20% investment in Flufftort Co. A representative of Gupte VC was appointed to Flufftort Co's board. Flufftort Co also took out a long-term 8·5% bank loan.

Sales have generally been disappointing. As a result, members of the Patel family have been reluctant to invest further in Flufftort Co. Over the last year Gupte VC has taken a tougher attitude towards Flufftort Co. Gupte VC pressurised Flufftort Co to pay a dividend of $2 million for the year ended 30 June 2017. Gupte VC has also said that if Flufftort Co's financial results do not improve, Gupte VC may exercise its right to compel Flufftort Co to buy back its shares at par on 30 June 2018.

However, Flufftort Co's most recent product, the Easicushion chair, has been a much bigger success than expected. In order to produce enough Easicushion chairs to affect its results substantially, Flufftort Co will need to make significant expenditure on manufacturing facilities and additional working capital.

Extracts from statement of profit or loss for year ended 30 June 2017 and forecast statement of profit or loss for year ended 30 June 2018

	2017	2018 Forecast
	$m	$m
Operating profit	8·0	6·0
Finance cost	(3·0)	(3·0)
Profit before tax	5·0	3·0
Tax on profits (20%)	(1·0)	(0·6)
Profit for the period	4·0	2·4
Dividends	(2·0)	–
Retained earnings	2·0	2·4

Note

The forecast statement of profit or loss for the year ended 30 June 2018 is not affected by the proposed investment. This can be assumed only to affect results after 30 June 2018. The figure shown for retained earnings in the 2018 forecast can be assumed to be the net increase in cash for the year ended 30 June 2018.

Summarised statement of financial position as at 30 June 2017

Assets	$m
Non-current assets	69·0
Current assets excluding cash	18·0
Cash	7·6
Total assets	94·6
Equity and liabilities	
Share capital ($1 shares)	50·0
Retained earnings	2·6
Total equity	52·6
Long-term liabilities	
8·5% Bank loan	30·0
9% Loan note	5·0
Total long-term liabilities	35·0
Current liabilities	7·0
Total liabilities	42·0
Total equity and liabilities	94·6

Notes

1. 55% of shares are owned by the members of the Patel family who are directors, 25% by other members of the Patel family and 20% by Gupte VC.

2. The bank loan is secured on the non-current assets of Flufftort and is due for repayment on 31 December 2021. The loan is subject to a covenant that the ratio of equity to non-current liabilities should be greater than 1·3 on a book value basis. Flufftort has also been granted an overdraft facility of up to $5 million by its bank.

3. The loan note is held by Rajiv Patel, a member of the Patel family who is not a director. The loan note is unsecured, is subordinated to the bank loan and has no fixed date for repayment.

4. If no finance is available for investment in manufacturing facilities, non-current assets, current assets excluding cash, the bank loan, loan note and current liabilities can be assumed to be the same at 30 June 2018 as at 30 June 2017.

However, the chief executive and finance director of Flufftort Co intend to propose that the company should be refinanced to fund the expanded production of the Easicushion chair. They have not yet consulted anyone else about their proposals.

Details of the proposed refinancing are as follows:

1. The members of the Patel family who are directors would subscribe to an additional 15 million $1 shares at par.

2. Gupte VC would subscribe to an additional 20 million $1 shares at par.

3. The 8·5% bank loan would be renegotiated with the bank and the borrowing increased to $65 million, to be repaid on 30 June 2024. The expected finance cost of the loan would be 10% per annum.

4. Rajiv Patel's loan note would be replaced by 5 million $1 shares.

5. The refinancing would mean non-current assets would increase to $125 million, current assets other than cash would increase to $42 million and current liabilities would increase to $12 million.

6. Operating profits would be expected to increase to $20 million in the first full year after the facilities are constructed (year ended 30 June 2019) and $25 million in the second year (year ended 30 June 2020). No dividends would be paid for these two years, as cash surpluses would be used for further investment as required. Tax on company profits can be assumed to remain at 20%.

Required:

(a) **(i)** **Prepare a projected statement of financial position as at 30 June 2018, on the assumption that Gupte VC exercises its rights and Gupte VC's shares are repurchased and cancelled by Flufftort Co.** (4 marks)

(ii) **Prepare a projected statement of financial position as at 30 June 2018 on the assumption that the proposed refinancing and investment take place.** (4 marks)

(iii) **Prepare projected statements of profit or loss for the years ended 30 June 2019 and 30 June 2020 on the basis that the profit forecasts are correct.** (4 marks)

(b) **Evaluate whether the suggested refinancing scheme is likely to be agreed by all finance providers. State clearly any assumptions which you make.** (13 marks)

(25 marks)

Question 4 MOONSTAR CO

Moonstar Co is a property development company which is planning to undertake a $200 million commercial property development. Moonstar Co has had some difficulties over the last few years, with some developments not generating the expected returns and the company has at times struggled to pay its finance costs. As a result Moonstar Co's credit rating has been lowered, affecting the terms it can obtain for bank finance. Although Moonstar Co is listed on its local stock exchange, 75% of the share capital is held by members of the family who founded the company. The family members who are shareholders do not wish to subscribe for a rights issue and are unwilling to dilute their control over the company by authorising a new issue of equity shares. Moonstar Co's board is therefore considering other methods of financing the development, which the directors believe will generate higher returns than other recent investments, as the country where Moonstar Co is based appears to be emerging from recession.

Securitisation proposals

One of the non-executive directors of Moonstar Co has proposed that it should raise funds by means of a securitisation process, transferring the rights to the rental income from the commercial property development to a special purpose vehicle. Her proposals assume that the leases will generate an income of 11% per annum over a ten-year period. She proposes that Moonstar Co should use 90% of the value of the investment for a collateralised loan obligation which should be structured as follows:

- 60% of the collateral value to support a tranche of A-rated floating rate loan notes offering investors LIBOR plus 150 basis points

- 15% of the collateral value to support a tranche of B-rated fixed rate loan notes offering investors 12%

- 15% of the collateral value to support a tranche of C-rated fixed rate loan notes offering investors 13%

- 10% of the collateral value to support a tranche as subordinated certificates, with the return being the excess of receipts over payments from the securitisation process

The non-executive director believes that there will be sufficient demand from investors for all tranches of the loan notes. Investors will expect that the income stream from the development to be low risk, as they will expect the property market to improve with the recession coming to an end and enough potential lessees to be attracted by the new development.

The non-executive director predicts that there would be annual costs of $200,000 in administering the loan. She acknowledges that there would be interest rate risks associated with the proposal, and proposes a fixed for variable interest rate swap on the A-rated floating rate notes, exchanging LIBOR for 9·5%.

However the finance director believes that the prediction of the income from the development that the non-executive director has made is over-optimistic. He believes that it is most likely that the total value of the rental income will be 5% lower than the non-executive director has forecast. He believes that there is some risk that the returns could be so low as to jeopardise the income for the C-rated fixed rate loan note holders.

Islamic finance

Moonstar Co's chief executive has wondered whether Sukuk finance would be a better way of funding the development than the securitisation.

Moonstar Co's chairman has pointed out that a major bank in the country where Moonstar Co is located has begun to offer a range of Islamic financial products. The chairman has suggested that a Mudaraba contract would be the most appropriate method of providing the funds required for the investment.

Required:

(a) **Calculate the amounts in $ which each of the tranches can expect to receive from the securitisation arrangement proposed by the non-executive director and discuss how the variability in rental income affects the returns from the securitisation.** (11 marks)

(b) **Discuss the benefits and risks for Moonstar Co associated with the securitisation arrangement that the non-executive director has proposed.** (6 marks)

(c) (i) **Discuss the suitability of Sukuk finance to fund the investment, including an assessment of its appeal to potential investors.** (4 marks)

(ii) **Discuss whether a Mudaraba contract would be an appropriate method of financing the investment and discuss why the bank may have concerns about providing finance by this method.** (4 marks)

(25 marks)

MARCH/JUNE 2016

Question 1 LIRIO CO

Lirio Co is an engineering company which is involved in projects around the world. It has been growing steadily for several years and has maintained a stable dividend growth policy for a number of years. The board of directors (BoD) is considering bidding for a large project which requires a substantial investment of $40 million. It can be assumed that the date today is 1 March 2018.

The BoD is proposing that Lirio Co should not raise the finance for the project through additional debt or equity. Instead, it proposes that the required finance is obtained from a combination of funds received from the sale of its equity investment in a European company and from cash flows generated from its normal business activity in the coming two years. As a result, Lirio Co's current capital structure of 80 million $1 equity shares and $70 million 5% loan notes is not expected to change in the foreseeable future.

The BoD has asked the company's treasury department to prepare a discussion paper on the implications of this proposal. The following information on Lirio Co has been provided to assist in the preparation of the discussion paper.

Expected income and cash flow commitments (prior to undertaking the large project) for the year to the end of February 2019

Lirio Co's sales revenue is forecast to grow by 8% next year from its current level of $300 million, and the operating profit margin on this is expected to be 15%. It is expected that Lirio Co will have the following capital investment requirements for the coming year, before the impact of the large project is considered:

1.	A $0·10 investment in working capital for every $1 increase in sales revenue;

2.	An investment equivalent to the amount of depreciation to keep its non-current asset base at the present productive capacity. The current depreciation charge, already included in the operating profit margin, is 25% of the non-current assets of $50 million;

3.	A $0·20 investment in additional non-current assets for every $1 increase in sales revenue;

4.	$8 million additional investment in other small projects.

In addition to the above sales revenue and profits, Lirio Co has one overseas subsidiary – Pontac Co, from which it receives dividends of 80% of profits. Pontac Co produces a specialist tool which it sells locally for $60 each. It is expected that it will produce and sell 400,000 units of this specialist tool next year. Each tool will incur variable costs of $36 per unit and total annual fixed costs will be $4 million.

Lirio Co pays corporation tax at 25% and Pontac Co pays corporation tax at 20%. In addition to this, a withholding tax of 8% is deducted from any dividends remitted from Pontac Co. A bi-lateral tax treaty exists between the countries where Lirio Co is based and where Pontac Co is based. Therefore corporation tax is payable on profits made by subsidiary companies, but full credit is given for corporation tax already paid overseas.

It can be assumed that receipts from Pontac Co are in $ amounts and exchange rate fluctuations on these can be ignored.

Sale of equity investment in the European country

It is expected that Lirio Co will receive Euro (€) 20 million in three months' time from the sale of its investment. The € has continued to remain weak, while the $ has continued to remain strong through 2017 and the start of 2018. The financial press has also reported that there may be a permanent shift in the €/$ exchange rate, with firms facing economic exposure. Lirio Co has decided to hedge the € receipt using one of currency forward contracts, currency futures contracts or currency options contracts.

Contracts and rates are available to Lirio Co

	Per €1
Spot rates	$1·1585–$1·1618
Three-month forward rates	$1·1559–$1·1601

Currency futures (contract size $125,000, quotation: € per $1)

March futures	€0·8638
June futures	€0·8656

Currency options (contract size $125,000, exercise price quotation € per $1, premium € per $1)

	Calls		Puts	
Exercise price	*March*	*June*	*March*	*June*
0·8600	0·0255	0·0290	0·0267	0·0319

It can be assumed that futures and options contracts expire at the end of their respective months.

Dividend history, expected dividends and cost of capital, Lirio Co

Year to end of February	*2015*	*2016*	*2017*	*2018*
Number of $1 equity shares in issue (000)	60,000	60,000	80,000	80,000
Total dividends paid ($ 000)	12,832	13,602	19,224	20,377

It is expected that dividends per share will grow at the historic rate, if the large project is not undertaken.

Expected dividends and dividend growth rates if the large project is undertaken

Year to end of February 2019	Remaining cash flows, after the investment in the $40 million project and the sale of the equity investment, will be paid as dividends.
Year to end of February 2020	The dividends paid will be the same amount as the year to the end of February 2019.
Year to end of February 2021	Dividends paid will be $0·31 per share.
In following years	Dividends will grow at an annual rate of 7%.

Lirio Co's cost of equity capital is estimated to be 12%.

Required:

(a) **With reference to purchasing power parity, explain how exchange rate fluctuations may lead to economic exposure.** (6 marks)

(b) **Prepare a discussion paper, including all relevant calculations, for the board of directors (BoD) of Lirio Co which:**

    (i)   **Estimates Lirio Co's dividend capacity for the year to the end of February 2019, prior to investing in the large project or disposing of the equity investment;**   (9 marks)

    (ii)   **Advises Lirio Co on, and recommends, an appropriate hedging strategy for the Euro (€) receipt it is due to receive in three months' time from the sale of the equity investment;**   (14 marks)

    (iii)   **Using the information on dividends provided in the question, and from (b) (i) and (b) (ii) above, assesses whether or not the project would add value to Lirio Co;**   (8 marks)

    (iv)   **Discusses issues surrounding the proposed methods of financing the project which need to be considered further.**   (9 marks)

Professional marks will be awarded in part (b) for the format, structure and presentation of the discussion paper.   (4 marks)

    (50 marks)

Question 2 LOUIEED CO

Louieed Co, a listed company, is a major supplier of educational material, selling its products in many countries. It supplies schools and colleges and also produces learning material for business and professional exams. Louieed Co has exclusive contracts to produce material for some examining bodies. Louieed Co has a well-defined management structure with formal processes for making major decisions.

Although Louieed Co produces online learning material, most of its profits are still derived from sales of traditional textbooks. Louieed Co's growth in profits over the last few years has been slow and its directors are currently reviewing its long-term strategy. One area in which they feel that Louieed Co must become much more involved is the production of online testing materials for exams and to validate course and textbook learning.

Bid for Tidded Co

Louieed Co has recently made a bid for Tidded Co, a smaller listed company. Tidded Co also supplies a range of educational material, but has been one of the leaders in the development of online testing and has shown strong profit growth over recent years. All of Tidded Co's initial five founders remain on its board and still hold 45% of its issued share capital between them. From the start, Tidded Co's directors have been used to making quick decisions in their areas of responsibility. Although listing has imposed some formalities, Tidded Co has remained focused on acting quickly to gain competitive advantage, with the five founders continuing to give strong leadership.

Louieed Co's initial bid of five shares in Louieed Co for three shares in Tidded Co was rejected by Tidded Co's board. There has been further discussion between the two boards since the initial offer was rejected and Louieed Co's board is now considering a proposal to offer Tidded Co's shareholders two shares in Louieed Co for one share in Tidded Co or a cash alternative of $22·75 per Tidded Co share. It is expected that Tidded Co's shareholders will choose one of the following options:

(i)   To accept the two-shares-for-one-share offer for all the Tidded Co shares; or

(ii)   To accept the cash offer for all the Tidded Co shares; or,

(iii)   60% of the shareholders will take up the two-shares-for-one-share offer and the remaining 40% will take the cash offer.

In case of the third option being accepted, it is thought that three of the company's founders, holding 20% of the share capital in total, will take the cash offer and not join the combined company. The remaining two founders will probably continue to be involved in the business and be members of the combined company's board.

Louieed Co's finance director has estimated that the merger will produce annual post-tax synergies of $20 million. He expects Louieed Co's current price-earnings (PE) ratio to remain unchanged after the acquisition.

Extracts from the two companies' most recent accounts are shown below:

	Louieed $m	Tidded $m
Profit before finance cost and tax	446	182
Finance costs	(74)	(24)
Profit before tax	372	158
Tax	(76)	(30)
Profit after tax	296	128
Issued $1 nominal shares	340 million	90 million
PE ratios, based on most recent accounts	14	15·9
Long-term liabilities (market value) ($m)	540	193
Cash and cash equivalents ($m)	220	64

The tax rate applicable to both companies is 20%.

Assume that Louieed Co can obtain further debt funding at a pre-tax cost of 7·5% and that the return on cash surpluses is 5% pre-tax.

Assume also that any debt funding needed to complete the acquisition will be reduced instantly by the balances of cash and cash equivalents held by Louieed Co and Tidded Co.

Required:

(a)   **Discuss the advantages and disadvantages of the acquisition of Tidded Co from the viewpoint of Louieed Co.**   (6 marks)

(b)   **Calculate the PE ratios of Tidded Co implied by the terms of Louieed Co's initial and proposed offers, for all three of the above options.**   (5 marks)

(c)   **Calculate, and comment on, the funding required for the acquisition of Tidded Co and the impact on Louieed Co's earnings per share and gearing, for each of the three options given above.**

   Note: Up to 10 marks are available for the calculations.   (14 marks)

                                                                                         (25 marks)

Question 3 STAPLE GROUP

Staple Group is one of Barland's biggest media groups. It consists of four divisions, organised as follows:

- **Staple National** – the national newspaper, the Daily Staple. This division's revenues and operating profits have decreased for the last two years.

- **Staple Local** – a portfolio of 18 local and regional newspapers. This division's operating profits have fallen for the last five years and operating profits and cash flows are forecast to be negative in the next financial year. Other newspaper groups with local titles have also reported significant falls in profitability recently.

- **Staple View** – a package of digital channels showing sporting events and programmes for a family audience. Staple Group's board has been pleased with this division's recent performance, but it believes that the division will only be able to sustain a growth rate of 4% in operating profits and cash flows unless it can buy the rights to show more major sporting events. Over the last year, Staple View's biggest competitor in this sector has acquired two smaller digital broadcasters.

- **Staple Investor** – established from a business which was acquired three years ago, this division offers services for investors including research, publications, training events and conferences. The division gained a number of new clients over the last year and has thus shown good growth in revenues and operating profits.

Some of Staple Group's institutional investors have expressed concern about the fall in profitability of the two newspaper divisions.

The following summarised data relates to the group's last accounting year. The % changes in pre-tax profits and revenues are changes in the most recent figures compared with the previous year.

			Division		
	Total	National	Local	View	Investor
Revenues ($m)	1,371·7	602·4	151·7	496·5	121·1
Increase/(decrease) in revenues (%)		(5·1)	(14·7)	8·2	16·5
Pre-tax profits ($m)	177·3	75·6	4·5	73·3	23·9
Increase/(decrease) in pre-tax profits (%)		(4·1)	(12·6)	7·4	19·1
Post-tax cash flows ($m)	120·2	50·7	0·3	53·5	15·7
Share of group net assets ($m)	635·8	267·0	66·6	251·2	51·0
Share of group long-term liabilities ($m)	230·9	104·4	23·1	93·4	10·0

Staple Group's board regards the Daily Staple as a central element of the group's future. The directors are currently considering a number of investment plans, including the development of digital platforms for the Daily Staple. The finance director has costed the investment programme at $150 million. The board would prefer to fund the investment programme by disposing parts or all of one of the other divisions. The following information is available to help assess the value of each division:

- One of Staple Group's competitors, Postway Co, has contacted Staple Group's directors asking if they would be interested in selling 15 of the local and regional newspapers for $60 million. Staple Group's finance director believes this offer is low and wishes to use the net assets valuation method to evaluate a minimum price for the Staple Local division.

- Staple Group's finance director believes that a valuation using free cash flows would provide a fair estimate of the value of the Staple View division. Over the last year, investment in additional non-current assets for the Staple View division has been $12·5 million and the incremental working capital investment has been $6·2 million. These investment levels will have to increase at 4% annually in order to support the expected sustainable increases in operating profit and cash flow.

- Staple Group's finance director believes that the valuation of the Staple Investor division needs to reflect the potential it derives from the expertise and experience of its staff. The finance director has calculated a value of $118·5 million for this division, based on the earnings made last year but also allowing for the additional earnings which he believes that the expert staff in the division will be able to generate in future years.

Assume a risk-adjusted, all-equity financed, cost of capital of 12% and a tax rate of 30%. Goodwill should be ignored in any calculations.

Staple Group's finance and human resources directors are looking at the staffing of the two newspaper divisions. The finance director proposes dismissing most staff who have worked for the group for less than two years, two years' employment being when staff would be entitled to enhanced statutory employment protection. The finance director also proposes a redundancy programme for longer-serving staff, selecting for redundancy employees who have complained particularly strongly about recent changes in working conditions. There is a commitment in Staple Group's annual report to treat employees fairly, communicate with them regularly and enhance employees' performance by structured development.

Required:

(a) **Evaluate the options for disposing of parts of Staple Group, using the financial information to assess possible disposal prices. The evaluation should include a discussion of the benefits and drawbacks to Staple Group from disposing of parts of the Staple Group.** (19 marks)

(b) **Discuss the significance of the finance director's proposals for reduction in staff costs for Staple Group's relationships with its shareholders and employees and discuss the ethical implications of the proposals.** (6 marks)

(25 marks)

Question 4 FURLION CO

Furlion Co manufactures heavy agricultural equipment and machinery which can be used in difficult farming conditions. Furlion Co's chief executive has been investigating a significant opportunity in the country of Naswa, where Furlion Co has not previously sold any products. The government of Naswa has been undertaking a major land reclamation programme and Furlion Co's equipment is particularly suitable for use on the reclaimed land. Because of the costs and other problems involved in transporting its products, Furlion Co's chief executive proposes that Furlion Co should establish a plant for manufacturing machinery in Naswa. He knows that the Naswan government is keen to encourage the development of sustainable businesses within the country.

Initial calculations suggest that the proposed investment in Naswa would have a negative net present value of $1·01 million. However, Furlion Co's chief executive believes that there may be opportunities for greater cash flows in future if the Naswan government expands its land reclamation programme. The government at present is struggling to fund expansion of the programme out of its own resources and is looking for other funding. If the Naswan government obtains this funding, the chief executive has forecast that the increased demand for Furlion Co's products would justify $15 million additional expenditure at the site of the factory in three years' time. The net present value for this expansion is estimated to be $0.

It can be assumed that all costs and revenues include inflation. The relevant cost of capital is 12% and the risk free rate is 4%. The chief executive has estimated the annual volatility of operating cash flows at a standard deviation of 30%.

One of Furlion Co's non-executive directors has read about possible changes in interest rates and wonders how these might affect the investment appraisal.

Required:

(a)   **Assess, showing all relevant calculations, whether Furlion Co should proceed with the significant opportunity. Discuss the assumptions made and other factors which will affect the decision of whether to establish a plant in Naswa. The Black Scholes pricing model should be used, where appropriate.**   (16 marks)

(b)   **Explain what is meant by an option's rho and discuss the impact of changes in interest rates on the appraisal of the investment.**   (5 marks)

(c)   **Discuss the possibility of the Naswan government obtaining funding for further land reclamation from the World Bank, referring specifically to the International Development Association.**   (4 marks)

(25 marks)

Answer 1 MUCKY MINING CO

(a) Sustainability

Sustainability is a term with several meanings, even in this context.

A sustainable business could mean a successful business with tangible and intangible assets and future cash flows that in the current environment or any predicted changes or foreseeable uncertainties is able to continue to operate successfully in business in the long term.

A sustainable business may also be seen as one that recognises ethical obligations towards society through it social and environmental policies. It could be regarded as a business that recognises and balances economic, social and environmental objectives. In this context the business is sustainable in the long-run because it meets the requirement of a very broad range of stakeholders both now and in the future. Sustainability implies that it protects society and environment by not compromising future generations in its activities and use of resources.

Sustainability may also be seen as doing those things economic, social and environmental that supports the long-run maximisation of profit or shareholder value. This is the so called "ethics pays" view.

The term ethics used in the question is concerned with what is right and wrong in terms of business decision-making, behaviour and activity. An ethical business being an honest and transparent business that meets the moral requirements of society and operates in a socially and environmentally acceptable way.

There are inevitably some potential conflicts between achieving objectives in terms of return, growth and risk and achieving social and environmental objectives. Focus on economic objectives may be a short-term view that is not sustainable in the long run. Shareholders, customers and other stakeholders may not be supportive of pure profit maximising if they have "ethical", social and environmental concerns. This could lead to a falling or static share price or revenues.

In the scenario it is clear that Mucky Mining is economically successful. The company does however have social and environmental issues with its potentially immoral labour practices and potential disregard for the environment in its mining operations.

The media reports are however unconfirmed.

As a listed company shareholders may express their dissatisfaction orally, in writing, at votes or by walking away and selling their shares.

The scenario does not give information regarding the legality of the social and environmental issues but putting the morals to one side both issues could give rise to economic cost for the company beyond reputation damage in terms of potential fines and damages.

Ultimately a sustainable business contributes to the economic and social success of a nation in a way that does not compromise future generations.

(b)   **Stakeholders**

A stakeholder is a person, organisation, individual or group who has a legitimate interest in, is impacted by or impacts upon an entity or its activities or operations. Some stakeholders have legal interests, some have contractual interests and some impose their interest upon the entity. Stakeholders may be within the entity or even be running it, some may merely be connected (e.g. shareholders, suppliers and customers) whilst some may be external (e.g. government, lobby groups and society or communities). Stakeholders have varying power to influence and interests that connect them to an entity.

Listed companies can be regarded as firms with a purely economic purpose or entities with economic, social and environmental purposes.

Listed companies have a particular issue in that ownership and control are largely separated. The directors who run or control the business do not usually have significant shareholdings that give them ownership or effective legal entity voting control. Although directors can be removed, shareholders rarely take such action and directors are generally promoted from within or selected from outside by the board.

When the question refers to responsibilities of listed companies this could be seen as the responsibilities of the board.

Legally directors must act in good faith in what they believe are the interests of the company. UK law requires consideration of social and environmental matters but leaves it up to directors to determine what they wish to do to promote the success of the company.

Shareholders are particularly important to listed company directors since the directors will actively operate to deliver shareholder value in terms of return and growth at an acceptable risk to the shareholders. They will to some extent be judged on the share price performance.

Delivering these objectives may however require social and environmental concern to create a sustainable business. Ethic does tend to pay.

Some shareholders may also be "ethical" members who are willing to pay a premium for high standards of social and environmental performance.

Stakeholders other than shareholders may therefore be seen as a key to maximising long-term shareholder value. Satisfied customers, suppliers, employees and society may support this.

Listed companies are likely to put shareholders at the top of their stakeholder priority list. This is due to the fundamentals of traditional and legal company purpose.

Other stakeholders' legitimacy may be judged by their power, or influence, and interest or willingness to engage.

(c)   **ESOPs and goal congruence**

Goal congruence refers to the situation where the goals of different groups coincide. In many companies there are potential conflicts of objectives between the owners of the company, the shareholders, and their agents, the managers of the company. Other interest groups such as liabilities, the government, employees, and the local community might also have conflicting objectives to the company's shareholders.

One way by which managers, and sometimes employees in general, might be motivated to take decisions/engage in actions which are consistent with the goals of the shareholders is through ESOPs. ESOPs will not, however, assist in encouraging goal congruence between other interest groups and the shareholders and managers.

ESOPs allow managers to purchase a company's shares at a fixed price during a specified period of time in the future, usually a period of years. They are aimed at encouraging managers to take decisions which will result in high NPV projects, which will lead to an increase in share price and shareholder wealth. The managers are believed to seek high NPV investments as they, as shareholders, will participate in the benefits as share prices increase.

There is, however, little evidence of a positive correlation between share option schemes and the creation of extra share value. There is no guarantee that ESOPs will achieve goal congruence. Share options will only be part of the total remuneration package and may not be the major influence on managerial decisions. If share prices fall managers do not have to purchase the shares, and the value of the option to buy shares becomes worthless or very small. This means that managers face less risk than shareholders as they have an option which may be exercised if things go well, but may be ignored if things go badly. Shareholders have to face both circumstances. Managers may be rewarded when share prices increase due to factors that have nothing to do with their managerial skills. Additionally ESOP schemes often base reward in part upon earnings per share, an accounting ratio which, at least in the short term, is subject to manipulation by managers to their advantage. Although ESOPs may assist in the achievement of goal congruence, they are by no means a perfect solution.

(d)   **Examples of bond covenants**

- An asset covenant. This would govern the company's acquisition, use and disposal of assets. This could be for specified types of assets, or assets in general.

- Financing covenant. This covenant often defines the type and amount of additional debt that the company can issue, and its ranking and potential claim on assets in case of future default.

- Dividend covenant. A dividend covenant restricts the amount of dividend that the company is able to pay. Such covenants might also be extended to share repurchases.

- Financial ratio covenants, fixing the limit of key ratios such as the gearing level, interest cover, net working capital, or a minimum ratio of tangible assets to total debt.

- Merger covenant, restricting future merger activity of the company.

- Investment covenant, concerned with the company's future investment policy.

- Sinking fund covenant whereby the company makes payments, typically to the bond trustees, who might gradually repurchase bonds in the open market, or build up a fund to redeem bonds.

There will often also be a "bonding covenant" that describes the mechanisms by which the above covenants are to be monitored and enforced. This often includes an independent audit and the appointment of a trustee representing the interests of the bondholders

From the company's perspective the major disadvantage of covenants is that they restrict the freedom of action of the managers, and could prevent viable investments, or mergers from occurring. They also necessitate monitoring and other costs. However, covenants are also of value to companies. Without covenants the company might not be able to raise as much funds in the form of debt, as lenders would not be prepared to take the risk. Even if lenders were to take the risk they would require a higher default premium (higher interest rates) in order to compensate for the risk. The existence of covenants therefore reduces the cost of borrowing for a company.

Answer 2 VADENER CO

Report to the board of directors of Vadener Co

(a)   Performance evaluation

Group performance may be analysed by using financial ratios, growth trends and comparative market data. Alternative definitions exist for some ratios, and other ratios are equally valid.

Operating and profitability ratios

		20X3	20X4	20X5
Return on capital:	$\dfrac{\text{EBIT}}{\text{M \& LT capital}}$	$\dfrac{410}{1,486} = 27{\cdot}6\%$	$\dfrac{540}{1,665} = 32{\cdot}4\%$	$\dfrac{560}{1,876} = 29{\cdot}9\%$
Asset turnover:	$\dfrac{\text{Sales}}{\text{Capital employed}}$	$\dfrac{1,210}{1,486} = 0{\cdot}81$	$\dfrac{1,410}{1,665} = 0{\cdot}85$	$\dfrac{1,490}{1,876} = 0{\cdot}79$
Profit margin:	$\dfrac{\text{EBIT}}{\text{Sales}}$	$\dfrac{410}{1,210} = 33{\cdot}9\%$	$\dfrac{540}{1,410} = 38{\cdot}3\%$	$\dfrac{560}{1,490} = 37{\cdot}6\%$

Liquidity ratios

		20X3	20X4	20X5
Current ratio:	$\dfrac{\text{Current assets}}{\text{Current liabilities}}$	$\dfrac{728}{565} = 1{\cdot}29$	$\dfrac{863}{728} = 1{\cdot}19$	$\dfrac{1,015}{799} = 1{\cdot}27$
Acid test:	$\dfrac{\text{Current assets - inventory}}{\text{Current liabilities}}$	$\dfrac{388}{565} = 0{\cdot}69$	$\dfrac{453}{728} = 0{\cdot}62$	$\dfrac{525}{799} = 0{\cdot}66$

Market ratios

		20X3	20X4	20X5
Dividend yield:	$\dfrac{\text{Dividend per share}}{\text{Market price}}$	$\dfrac{48.7}{1,220} = 4{\cdot}0\%$	$\dfrac{56.7}{1,717} = 4{\cdot}0\%$	$\dfrac{61.7}{1,542} = 4{\cdot}0\%$
Earnings per share:	$\dfrac{\text{Earnings after tax}}{\text{Number of shares}}$	$\dfrac{259}{300} = 86{\cdot}3$	$\dfrac{339}{300} = 113{\cdot}0$	$\dfrac{346}{300} = 115{\cdot}3$
PE ratio:	$\dfrac{\text{Market price}}{\text{Earnings per share}}$	$\dfrac{1,220}{86.3} = 14{\cdot}1$	$\dfrac{1,417}{113} = 12{\cdot}5$	$\dfrac{1,542}{115.3} = 13{\cdot}4$
Gearing:	$\dfrac{\text{Total borrowing}}{\text{Borrowing + equity}}$	$\dfrac{535}{1,621} = 33\%$	$\dfrac{580}{1,835} = 32\%$	$\dfrac{671}{2,077} = 32\%$

It is difficult to reach conclusions about the performance of Vadener without more comparative data from similar companies.

Return on capital at around 30% is dominated by the effect of high profit margins, but the split between divisions is not provided. Asset utilisation is well below 1, which implies relatively inefficient utilisation of assets. Vadener might investigate whether this could be improved.

Liquidity has improved during the last year, and although below some commonly used benchmarks might be satisfactory for the sectors that Vadener is involved with. However, some aspects of working capital require attention. Inventory levels have increased from 28% of revenue in 20X3 to 33% in 20X5, and the collection period for receivables has similarly increased from 114 days to 125 days.

Payables have also increased more than proportionately to revenue. Vadener should take action to improve the efficiency of its working capital management.

In contrast operating costs have fallen over the three years from 66% to 62% of revenue, indicating greater efficiency. Gearing appears to be relatively low at around 32%, but comparative data is needed, and interest cover is high at more than eight times in 20X5.

Investors do not appear to be entirely satisfied with group performance. The FT market index has increased by 34% between 20X3 and 20X5, whereas Vadener's share price has only increased by 26%. With an equity beta of 1·1 Vadener's share price would be expected to increase by more than the market index. Vadener's PE ratios are also lower than those of similar companies, suggesting that investors do not value the company's future prospects as highly as those of its competitors.

The required return from Vadener's shares may be estimated using the capital asset pricing model (CAPM).

Required return = 5% + (12% – 5%) 1·1 = 12·7%

An approximation of the actual return from Vadener's shares is the 12% average annual increase in share price plus 4% annual dividend yield, or 16%. The total return is higher than expected for the systematic risk. Given this, Vadener should investigate the reasons why its share price has performed relatively poorly. One possibility is the company's dividend policy.

Dividends have consistently been more than 50% of available after tax earnings, which might not be popular with investors.

Divisional performance

The information on the individual divisions is very sparse. All divisions are profitable, but the return from the pharmaceutical division is relatively low for its systematic risk.

Using CAPM to approximate required returns:

	Required return	*Actual return*
Construction	5% + (12% – 5%) 0·75 = 10·25%	13%
Leisure	5% + (12% – 5%) 1·1 = 12·7%	16%
Pharmaceuticals	5% + (12% – 5%) 1·40 = 14·8%[1]	14%

---

[1] It is assumed that the same market parameters are valid for the US based division.

The construction and leisure divisions appear to have greater than expected returns (a positive alpha) and the pharmaceutical division slightly less than expected for the risk of the division. The pharmaceutical division has recently suffered a translation loss due to the weakness of the US dollar, and the potential economic exposure from changes in the value of the dollar should be investigated.

From a financial perspective it would appear that the company should not devote equal resources to the divisions, and should focus its efforts on construction and leisure. However, the future prospects of the sectors are not known, nor the long term strategy of Vadener, which might be to expand international operations in the US or elsewhere.

The strategic use of resources should not be decided on the basis of the limited financial information that is available.

(b) **Other information that would be useful**

- Cash flow forecasts for the group and the individual divisions.

- Full product and market information for each of the divisions.

- Details of recent investments in each of the divisions and the expected impact of such investment on future performance.

- Detailed historic performance data of the divisions over at least three years, and similar data for companies in the relevant sectors.

- Competitors and potential growth rates in each of the sectors.

- The economic exposure of the US division

- The future strategic plans of Vadener. Are there any other proposed initiatives?

- How the company's equal resource strategy will be viewed by investors. The company has performed worse than the market in recent years despite having a higher beta than the market.

(c) **Implications of translation loss**

A translation loss of £10 million is not necessarily a problem for Vadener.

Translation exposure, sometimes known as accounting exposure, often does not reflect any real cash flow changes. It is changes in cash flow that, in an efficient market, will impact on the share price and value of a company. For example, a translation loss might in part reflect a lower home currency value of an overseas factory, but the factory will still be the same and will still be producing goods. It is the impact on the home currency cash flows from the continuing operations of the factory that will affect share price.

However, if the market is not efficient, investors might not understand that there are no real cash flow implications from the exposure, and might be worried about the effect of the translation loss on Vadener, and possibly sell their shares. If this is the case Vadener might consider internal hedges to reduce translation exposure. In most cases this would not be recommended, and companies must also be careful that hedges to manage translation exposure do not adversely affect the efficient operations of the business, or be contrary to hedges that are being undertaken to protect against other forms of currency exposure such as transaction exposure.

Answer 3 PHARMACEUTICAL COMPANY

To: **Chief Financial Officer**
From: **Deputy Financial Officer**

Four issues of concern

The four issues you have raised with me touch upon our ethical and commercial responsibilities.

(i)   The payment of a commission to an official in any country can be justified if it was in recognition of a service performed that (a) she or he was legitimately entitled to perform for payment, (b) that the payment was duly authorised within this company and (c) a service was received for which the payment was fair and reasonable. Clearly, such a payment should not have been made if it contravened the ruling law in either this or the official's country. Given this, a payment for consultancy, legal or lobbying services to an independent consultant would be legitimate. However, given that the individual concerned was an official of the agency concerned then the payment should not have been authorised. As the payment was for a substantial amount the matter should be taken up with the company's chief executive officer with a view to an internal investigation being mounted. Disciplinary action should be considered when a more detailed understanding of the circumstances is known. It may also be appropriate to raise this with the health department in the government of the country concerned with a view to full public disclosure of the facts once the situation has been clarified.

(ii)   The actions of the agent in using price sensitive information for personal gain would be classed as insider dealing irrespective of whether the transactions took place on the shares, or on options on the shares of our company. Much depends on what could be established in the circumstances. Did the agent know that the licensing agreement would be forthcoming or was it a speculative trade on the anticipation that it would be granted? If it were the former then it would be classed as insider trading. The more difficult issue relates to speculative trading in that if the attempt to gain the licence was in the public domain then the dealing would not be an issue. If however, the agent was only aware of the possibility through his or her relationship with this company then it would be insider dealing.

(iii)   This problem raises a number of issues. First, hedging is not an efficient means of reducing translation risk. Translation risk arises because of the conversion of assets and liabilities held in dollars into the domestic currency for accounting purposes. Translation risk will impact upon the residual earnings of the business but does not impact upon the firm's cash flow as no transaction has occurred. There would appear to be an absence of risk management policy in this area and even though a senior member of the treasury team has been making the trades, policy of this type should be set at board level through a risk management committee. Second, substantial trades of this type should be authorised and again, it would appear, that there is an absence of policy in this area. Disciplinary action against the treasury manager concerned would only be appropriate if trading of this type lay outside his or her role description or if there was an explicit policy in place requiring authorisation for trades of greater than a given size. In deciding what action to take, making a gain or a loss is irrelevant. Third the current position suggests a $1·25 million loss is likely against a dollar position of $12·5 million. This may not be material from the point of view of the company's overall financial position but the potential for further loss on an uncovered position such as this should be immediately reversed by shortening the contract concerned. If the loss is deemed material then a brief statement to shareholders should be made specifying the magnitude of the loss and the action taken.

(iv)   This problem appears to be an abuse of copyright and as such is against the WTO's Trade Related Aspects of Intellectual Property Rights "TRIPS" agreement. However, to gain protection under TRIPS we have to make sure that we have made supply available of the drugs concerned. If a member country takes the view that we have abused our patent position then they can issue a "compulsory licence" which would allow a competitor to produce the product under licence. At the Doha ministerial conference in 2001 it was agreed that TRIPS should not prevent a country adopting measures for the protection of its population's health. In this case it would appear that the dispute is one of piracy and gaining protection through the local courts. Although this could in principle be resolved through the WTO and the dispute resolution procedure, this may be an issue which would be most satisfactorily resolved through intergovernmental mediation. Any bilateral concession would need to be multi-lateralised through the WTO in light of the member's most favoured-nation obligations. It would be worthwhile attempting to discover exactly why the government concerned has blocked access to the courts to ensure that there are no public health policy issues involved and from there attempting to secure the involvement of our own government in helping to resolve the issue.

Answer 4 MEZZA CO

Tutorial note: *This question can be answered in a variety of ways and the suggested answer below is indicative. Credit would be given for reasonable answers considering alternatives or additions to the two issues discussed below.*

Key issues the directors should consider

The directors' overarching aim should be to maximise Mezza's long-term value and thereby maximise the value to its shareholders. Hence, any decision should be made with this aim as the primary objective. However, the directors should also try to minimise the negative consequences resulting from the implementation of the project, taking into account the company's responsibility to its stakeholders.

The first key issue to consider is whether commercialising the new product would add value to the company. Initially it would appear that the investment in the new venture may be beneficial to the company. The product would be meeting market needs for a substantial period of time, as a tool in tackling climate change. It would possibly enhance the company's corporate reputation in helping to tackle the negative impact of climate change. Furthermore, it may enable the research subsidiary company to undertake future research and development projects in similar products.

However, whether the positive factors described above lead to an increase in the value of the company warrants further discussion and investigation. The company needs to assess the likely income the investment will generate and take account of the inherent risk of the venture. Presumably this is a new product and therefore it is likely that the uncertainty and risk to income flows will be significant. The directors should also take account of the fact that their remuneration package contains share options and these may induce them to act in an overly risky manner, where they would benefit from increasing share prices but not lose if the share price falls. This may not be beneficial to the shareholders or other stakeholders who do not hold such options.

Due diligence procedures for the project need to be undertaken before the decision is made. The company's directors need to undertake a full assessment of how realistic the estimates of revenues and income are likely to be. They would also need to assess the likelihood of competitors and alternative products which may affect the future sales of the product. A full investigation of the uncertainties and risks needs to be undertaken, possibly using techniques such as sensitivity, probability and project duration analysis. Risks need to be accounted for in the assessment of the likely value added. This would be of particular importance if the directors are to convince the shareholders and other stakeholders that they are not taking unacceptable levels of risk. Realistic time scales need to be determined of how long it would take to commercialise the product, perhaps by considering how other companies undertook similar projects. The adequacy of the expertise and infrastructure required by the company needs to be assessed.

The second key issue for the directors to consider is the location of the plant product. There are a number of factors which would make the location ideal for Mezza. The location provides the ideal conditions for the plant to grow in the quantity required for commercialisation. The relationship with the government is strong and the government wants to develop new industries, hence the project is likely to be seen in a positive light. It is possible therefore that many legal and administrative barriers would be reduced to enable production to commence quickly. Finally, Mezza has the infrastructure it needs in place and therefore set-up costs are likely to be significantly lower. These factors would provide financial benefits for Mezza and may make the investment viable.

However, there are ethical and environmental concerns in using this area for the project. It may be perceived that the relationship with the government is too close and this will prevent proper scrutiny by the government. The livelihood of the affected fishermen needs to be considered, as well as the impact on the wildlife and the environment. Going ahead with the project may result in a significant negative impact on Mezza's reputation and possibly contradicts with the company's (and the directors') values.

Therefore, the dilemma that the directors face is that the project would be perceived as helping the global environment but damaging the local environment.

How issues may be mitigated or resolved

The directors could take a number of steps to reduce or eliminate this negative impact. Given that the fishermen do not have a significant "voice" or power, Mezza's board could try to hide the issue, but it is unlikely that their personal values would allow such a situation. The directors could speak with the leaders of the fishermen's community to explain the benefits and consequences on the fishermen, possibly offering the fishermen priority to the new jobs that the project would create. They could influence and work with the government to part-develop the area for tourists and also leave areas for the fishermen to continue their activity. This may be possible if the whole area is not needed for plant cultivation at once. These additional wealth enhancing opportunities may convince the fishermen of the merits of the project. The company could continue looking for alternative areas to cultivate the crop and possibly engage in research and development to create crops which are not harmful to the fish stock and the wildlife. However, these steps would cost money and Mezza needs to balance revenues it is likely to receive against the additional costs.

In terms of the relationship with the government, Mezza may be able to demonstrate that it worked with the government to improve the livelihood of the fishermen. It could also ensure that it follows due process in terms of legal and administrative requirements, even though this would possibly delay the product's launch.

Mezza needs to consider the likely positive benefits against the costs, both direct and to the wider community, before taking on the project. It needs to consider the effect on long-term value creation and corporate reputation would be a major factor in determining this. Although Maienar's government may try to approve the project quickly, Mezza should consider the full impact of the proposed project, alternatives and consequences, and try to manage the entire process to ensure that there is not an overall negative impact on the company's reputation.

Answer 5 NETRA CO

(a)   Capital structure strategy

From a corporate perspective there are two vital questions:

(1)   Can the value of a company, and hence shareholder wealth, be increased by varying the capital structure?

(2)   What effect will capital structure have on risk?

If value can be created by a sensible choice of capital structure then companies should try to achieve an optimal, or almost optimal, capital mix, as long as this mix does not have detrimental effects on other aspects of the company's activities.

Evidence on the importance of capital structure to a company's value is not conclusive. There is general agreement that, as long as a company is in a tax paying position, the use of debt can reduce the overall cost of capital due to the interest on debt being a tax allowable expense in almost all countries. This was suggested by two Nobel Prize winning economists, Miller and Modigliani. However, high levels of debt also bring problems, and companies with very high gearing are susceptible to various forms of risk, sometimes known as the costs of financial distress. This might include the loss of cash flows because customers and suppliers are worried about the financial stability and viability of the company and move business elsewhere or impose less favourable trading terms, or even extra costs that would exist (payments to receivers etc.) if the company was to go out of business.

A common perception about capital structure is that as capital gearing is increased the weighted average cost of capital (WACC) falls at first. However, beyond a certain level of gearing the risk to both providers of debt and equity finance increases, and the return demanded by them to compensate for this risk also increases, leading to an increase in the WACC. There is a trade-off between the value created by additional tax relief on debt and the costs of financial distress. Overall, there is therefore an optimal capital structure, which will vary between companies and will depend upon factors such as the nature of the company's activities, realisable value of assets, business risk, etc. According to the theory, companies with many tangible assets should have relatively high gearing, companies with high growth or that are dependent on R&D or advertising would have relatively low gearing.

Impact of personal tax on the capital structure decision is less clear, although investors are undoubtedly interested in after tax returns. If personal tax treatment differs on different types of capital, then investors may have a preference for the most tax efficient type of capital.

Not all companies behave as if there is an optimal capital structure, and on average, in countries such as the UK and US, the average capital gearing is lower than might be expected if companies were trying to achieve an optimal structure. It must however be remembered that moving from one capital structure to another cannot take place overnight.

The cost of debt, via interest rates, and the cost of equity, can change quite quickly. It is therefore not surprising that companies do not appear to be at an optimal level.

Where no optimal level appears to be sought by a company, there are several suggested strategies with respect to capital structure. Among the most popular is the pecking order theory, which is based on information asymmetry, the fact that managers have better information about their company than the company's shareholders. This leads to a company preferring internal finance to external finance, and only using external finance in order to undertake wealth creating (positive NPV) investments. Companies use the safest sources of finance first:

(1)   Internal funds (including selling marketable securities);
(2)   Debt;
(3)   Equity.

The amount of external finance used depends upon the amount of investment compared with the amount of internal funds, and the resultant capital structure reflects the relative balance of investment and available internal funds.

Another view is that capital structure is strongly influenced by managerial behaviour. There are potential conflicts of objectives between owners and managers (agency problems). Capital structure will be influenced by senior managers' personal objectives, attitudes to risk, compensation schemes and availability of alternative employment. A risk averse manager seeking security may use relatively little debt. Free cash flow (cash flow available after replacement investment) is sometimes perceived to be used by managers for unwise acquisitions/investments which satisfy their personal objectives, rather than returning it to shareholders. Many such managerial/agency aspects may influence capital structure, and this does not give clear guidance as to capital structure strategy.

No matter what the conclusion about the impact of capital structure on cash flows it is likely that some financing packages may be more highly regarded by investors than others. For example, securities designed to meet the needs of certain types of investor (zero coupon bonds, etc.), securities that are more liquid, securities with lower transactions costs, and securities which reduce conflict between parties concerned with the company, especially shareholders, managers and the providers of debt.

Conclusion

It is likely that the choice of capital structure can directly affect cash flows and shareholder wealth, but too high a level of gearing will increase risk. The impact on cash flows and corporate value of the capital structure decision is far less than the impact of capital investment decisions.

(b)   **Modigliani and Miller with tax**

Tutorial note: To answer the question the cost of equity must be estimated. CAPM is considered to be a reasonably accurate theory but no data is provided to allow its use here. This leaves the DVM but no dividend information is provided. Therefore the only way to produce an answer is to assume a dividend policy. The model answer below assumes the company distributes all post-tax profits as dividend. Different assumptions will produce completely different answers. In the exam you must be prepared to make (and clearly state) bold assumptions in order to answer questions.

Assuming that all earnings are paid out as dividends, the current cost of equity (and overall cost of capital) is:

	$000
EBIT	2,500
Taxation	825
Dividends	1,675

$$K_e = \frac{1,675}{8,400} = 19.94\%$$

(The market value of equity is two million shares × $4.20 per share = $8.4 million.)

Miller and Modigliani state that if equity is replaced by debt the total value of the company will increase. This is because interest on debt is tax allowable, the company pays less tax which benefits shareholders who therefore value the company more highly. Mathematically:

Value geared = Value ungeared + Dt (Amount of debt × tax rate)
With $2 million debt, V geared = 8,400 + 660 = 9,060
V equity = V overall – V debt, 9,060 – 2,000 = 7,060

With $4 million debt, V geared = 8,400 + 1,320 = 9,720
V equity = V overall – V debt, 9,720 – 4,000 = 5,720

$2 million debt	$000	*$4 million debt*	$000
EBIT	2,500		2,500
Interest	200		400
	2,300		2,100
Taxation	759		693
	1,541		1,407

$$K_e = \qquad \frac{1,541}{7,060} = 21.83\% \qquad \frac{1,407}{5,720} = 24.60\%$$

WACC

$$21.83 \times \frac{7,060}{9,060} + 10\,(1 - 0.33)\,\frac{2,000}{9,060} = 18.49\%$$

$$24.60 \times \frac{5,720}{9,720} + 10(1 - .33)\,\frac{4,000}{9,720} = 17.23\%$$

Alternatively using $WACC = K_{e(u)}\left(1 - \dfrac{Dt}{E + D}\right)$

$$19.94\left(1 - \frac{2,000 \times .33}{7,060 + 2,000}\right) = 18.49\% \qquad 19.94\left(1 - \frac{4,000 \times .33}{5,720 + 4,000}\right) = 17.23\%$$

The higher the level of gearing the lower the cost of capital becomes, due to the benefit from tax relief on interest payments.

(c) **Accuracy of estimates**

As debt is introduced into the capital structure it is likely that the cost of capital will initially fall. However, the estimates produced in (a) may not be accurate because:

- They rely on the assumptions of the Miller and Modigliani model, many of which are unrealistic. The assumptions are that the capital market is perfectly efficient, debt is risk free, information is costless and readily available, there are no transactions costs, investors are rational and make the same forecasts about the performance of companies, and investors and companies can borrow at the risk free rate.

- Only corporate taxation is considered and not the impact of other forms of taxation including personal taxation.

- MM assumed that debt is permanent. Netra's debt has a five year time horizon.

- The estimates ignore possible costs that might be incurred as gearing increases, which would reduce share price and increase the cost of equity (and possibly debt). These include bankruptcy costs, agency costs, and tax exhaustion.

- Inaccuracies exist in the measurement of the data required for the model.

Answer 6 PENSION FUND

(a) *(i)* *Hedge to protect the portfolio*

In order to hedge against possible future falls in share prices stock index futures should be sold. If share prices do actually fall then the loss would be offset by a gain on such futures contracts, although in most cases the gain will not exactly match the cash market loss. As stock index futures relate to a portfolio with a beta of approximately 1 (the market portfolio), the size of any hedge will need to be adjusted for the relative systematic risks of the portfolio held and the market portfolio.

The 1 December market value of the portfolio is $40·492 million.

The market weighted beta of the eight share portfolio is:

$3·3\ (0·74) + 4·43\ (1·15) + 3·276\ (0·65) + 4·784\ (1·32) + 3·192\ (1·56) + 8·16\ (0·82) + 8·01\ (1·11) + 5·34\ (1·43) = 44·18$, which divided by the portfolio's market value of $40·492 gives a beta of 1·091.

As the portfolio beta is higher than one, in order to protect against a fall in share price the number of contracts used should be increased to reflect this difference in beta.

The suggested hedge is to sell $\dfrac{\$40,492,000}{\$38,500} \times 1·091$ March futures contracts or 1,147 contracts.

(ii) *Outcome of the hedge*

On 31 March the new portfolio value based on the prices given is $36,454,000, a loss of $4,038,000.

The gain on the futures contracts is $(3,850 – 3,625)\ 1,147 \times \$10 = \$2,580,750$

The hedge efficiency is $\dfrac{\$2,580,750}{\$4,038,000}$ or 63·9%

The hedge has not made sufficient profit to offset the cash market loss. Possible reasons for this are:

■ The actual share prices of the portfolio have fallen by more than would be expected for a portfolio with a beta of 1·091.

■ The portfolio could not be hedged by an exact number of contracts. However, for a portfolio of this size the effect of an inexact hedge is likely to be insignificant.

(iii) *Using stock index futures to alter portfolio risk*

Stock index futures have three major advantages over buying and selling of actual shares:

■ Transactions costs of futures contracts are much less than those associated with buying and selling shares. The futures hedge would have to be undertaken on many occasions before the cost was equivalent.

■ The pension fund manager may not wish to sell the actual shares, especially as he expects their prices to start to rise.

■ Even in well-developed markets the sale of several million shares might cause a price reduction, and the manager might not receive the desired price for the shares.

(iv)   Halving systematic risk

Halving the systematic risk could be achieved in a number of ways, but the simplest is probably to buy long term interest rate futures to the same value as the existing portfolio. The underlying government bonds related to the long term interest rate futures may reasonably be assumed to be almost risk free (i.e. have a beta of approximately zero_. The combined beta of these futures contracts and the share portfolio will therefore be approximately half of the current portfolio beta ($0.5 \times 1.091 + 0.5 \times 0 = 0.5455$).

(b)   *(i)   Alpha values*

The alpha value is any abnormal return that exists relative to the required return from an investment, as estimated by using the capital asset pricing model (CAPM). The beta of the companies' shares may be estimated from:

$$\text{Beta} = \frac{\text{Covariance } R_1, R_M}{\text{Variance } R_M}$$

The beta estimates are:

Dedton $\dfrac{32}{25} = 1.28$ Paralot $\dfrac{19}{25} = 0.76$

Sunout $\dfrac{24}{25} = 0.96$ Rangon $\dfrac{43}{35} = 1.72$

Tutorial note: *Variance of the market's returns is the square of the market's standard deviation (i.e. $5 \times 5 = 25$).*

Required returns	Forecast returns	Alpha
Dedton 6% + (14.5% – 6%) 1.28 = 16.88%	16%	–0.88%
Paralot 6% + (14.5% – 6%) 0.76 = 12.46%	12%	–0.46%
Sunout 6% + (14.5% – 6%) 0.96 = 14.16%	14%	–0.16%
Rangon 6% + (14.5% – 6%) 1.72 = 20.62%	18%	–2.62%

A positive alpha value implies that it is possible to make higher than normal return, for the systematic risk taken. A negative alpha implies a lower than normal return.

A financial manager wishing to invest in shares might favour those with a positive alpha, subject to the shares satisfying other selection criteria such as the desired level of risk.

If a positive or negative alpha exists for the shares of the company of the financial manager, and the market is at least semi-strong form efficient, the alpha would be expected to move to zero as the company's share price changes due to arbitrage profit taking. For example in theory a company with a positive alpha would expect relatively high demand for its shares, increasing share price and thereby decreasing return until the alpha is zero.

(ii)   Existence of alpha values

Positive or negative alpha values exist for shares most of the time. If CAPM is a realistic model alpha values should only be temporary and the same alpha values would not be expected to exist in a year's time. Alphas may exist due to inaccuracies and/or limitations of the CAPM model including:

- CAPM tends to overstate the required return of high beta securities and to understate the required return of low beta securities. The returns of small companies, returns on certain days of the week or months of the year are observed to differ from those expected from CAPM.

- Data input into the model may be inaccurate. For example it is impossible to accurately calculate the market risk and return.

- Other factors in addition to systematic risk might influence required return. The arbitrage pricing theory (APT) suggests that a multi-factor model is necessary.

- CAPM is based on a number of unrealistic assumptions.

Answer 7 STRAYER CO

Tutorial note: *There is some debate about exactly how APV should be calculated. The current examiner's answers show that:*

- *the amount of debt should be grossed up to cover its issue costs (unless otherwise stated);*
- *the tax shield should be discounted at the firm's pre-tax cost of debt (unless the question suggests the debt is risk-free).*

(a) **Adjusted Present Value (APV)**

Assuming the risk of companies in the printing industry is similar to that of Strayer's new investment, the beta of the printing industry will be used to estimate the discount rate for the base case NPV. Ungearing the beta of the printing industry:

$$\text{Asset beta} = \text{equity beta} \times \frac{E}{E + D(1-t)} = 1 \cdot 2 \times \frac{50}{50 + 50(1 - 0 \cdot 30)} = 0 \cdot 706$$

Using CAPM

K_e ungeared $= 5 \cdot 5\% + (12\% - 5 \cdot 5\%)\ 0 \cdot 706 = 10 \cdot 09\%$ or approximately 10%

Annual after tax cash flows $= \$5$ million $(1 - 0 \cdot 3) = \$3,500,000$

		$
From annuity tables with a 10% discount rate:		
Present value of annual cash flows	$3,500,000 \times 6 \cdot 145 =$	21,507,500
Present value of the residual value	$5,000,000 \times 0 \cdot 386 =$	1,930,000
		23,437,500
Less initial investment		25,000,000
Base case NPV		(1,562,500)

Financing side effects relate to the tax shield on interest payments, the subsidised loan, and issue costs associated with external financing.

Issue costs	$
Debt $5 million $\times \ ^1/_{99} =$	50,505
Equity $10 million $\times \ ^4/_{96} =$	416,667
	467,172

Tax relief

$5,050,505 8% loan. Interest payable is $404,040 per year, tax relief is $404,040 × 0·3 = $121,212 per year.

$4 million subsidised loan. Interest is $240,000 per year, tax relief $72,000 per year.

Total annual tax relief $193,212 per year.

The present value of this tax relief, discounted at the usual pre-tax cost of debt of 8% is: $193,212 × 6.71 = $1,296,452

The company saves 2% per year on $4,000,000 = $80,000 but loses tax shield of $24,000. Net saving = $56,000

This will be discounted at the firm's pre-tax cost of debt, 8%: $56,000 × 6.71 = $375,760

The adjusted present value is estimated to be:
($1,562,500) – $467,172 + $1,296,452 + $375,760 = $(357,460)

Based on these estimates the project is not worthwhile.

(b)   When APV may be a better technique to use than NPV

■   There is a significant change in capital structure as a result of the investment.

■   The investment involves complex tax payments and tax allowances, and/or has periods when taxation is not paid.

■   Subsidised loans, grants or issue costs exist.

■   Financing side effects exist (e.g. the subsidised loan) which require discounting at a different rate than that applied to the mainstream project.

(c)   Conflicts between shareholders and bondholders

Bondholders are concerned that payments of interest and repayments of principal are made on time and without problems. The willingness of bondholders to provide funds to companies depends upon the risks and returns that they face, including the companies' expected cash flows, assets (including available security on assets), and credit ratings. Shareholders, in theory, seek to maximise the value of their shares. This is not necessarily consistent with the interests of bondholders, or the incentive to maximise the total value of the company (the value of equity plus debt). Shareholders seeking to maximise their wealth might take actions that are detrimental to bondholders. For example, shareholders, normally through their agents, managers, might use the finance provide by bondholders to invest in very risky projects, which change the character of the risk that the bondholders face. If the risky projects are successful, then the rewards flow primarily to the shareholders. If the projects fail then much of the cost of failure will fall on the bondholders. If there are no constraints on shareholders, the shareholders might have a natural incentive to take such risks. Management, acting on behalf of shareholders, might also reduce the wealth, and/or increase the risk of bondholders by:

(i)   Selling off assets of the company;
(ii)   Paying large dividends;
(iii)   Borrowing additional funds that rank above existing bonds in terms of prior payment upon liquidation.

The incentive for shareholders to take on risks at bondholders' expense is especially strong when the company is in financial difficulties and in danger of failing. In such circumstances the shareholders may believe that they have little to lose by undertaking risky projects. In the case of corporate failure significant "bankruptcy costs" normally exist. Direct costs of bankruptcy include receivers and lawyers' fees, whilst indirect costs might include loss of cash flow prior to failure through loss of sales, worse credit terms, etc. When corporate failure occurs most of the firm's value will be transferred to its debt holders who ultimately bear most of the bankruptcy costs.

Answer 8 JONAS CHEMICAL SYSTEMS

(a)   **Proposed procedures for large CAPEX**

This paper proposes revised guidelines for the Board approval of large (in excess of $10,000) capital investment projects. The current two stage process of preliminary and final approval serves an important role in ensuring that any initial concerns of the Board in terms of strategic fit and risk are brought to the attention of the Financial Appraisal Team. The two stage process would consider:

Stage 1

Business proposal including assessment of strategic requirement, business fit and identified risks.

Outline financial appraisal to include capital requirement, mode of financing, expected net present value (NPV), modified internal rate of return (MIRR) and project duration.

It is recommended that conventional payback is dropped because it ignores the cost of finance and the magnitude of post-payback cash flows. Duration is recommended as this measures the time required to recover half of the project value.

Stage 2

A proposed business plan must be presented giving the business case with an assessment of strategic benefits, risks, finalised capital spend and capital source.

A value impact assessment giving an NPV calculation supported by a calculation of the project value at risk. The NPV of the project represents our best estimate of the likely impact of the investment on the value of the firm. This is the key statistic from the capital market perspective in that, unless we are assured that the project NPV is positive, the investment will reduce and not enhance the value of the firm. This NPV calculation should be supported by a MIRR which measures the additional economic return of the project over the firm's cost of capital where intermediate cash flows are reinvested at that cost of capital. In a highly competitive business the reinvestment assumption implicit in the MIRR is more realistic that that assumed with IRR where intermediate cash flows are assumed to be reinvested at the IRR. This may be satisfactory for near-the-money projects but is far less satisfactory for projects which offer high levels of value addition to the firm.

An accounting impact assessment including the differential rate of return on capital employed and a short term liquidity assessment. Although positive NPV projects are value enhancing they may not do so in ways that are readily apparent in the financial reports. To manage investor expectations effectively the firm needs to be aware of the impact of the project on the firm's reported profitability and this is most accurately reflected by the differential rate of return measure. Accounting rate of return as normally calculated does not examine the impact of the project on the financial position of the firm but is restricted to the rate of return the investment offers on the average capital employed.

An assessment of the project duration. This project, for example, reveals a duration of 4.46 years which is the mean time over which half of the project value is recovered. This is more useful than the other liquidity based measures especially when used as a relative as opposed to an absolute measure of the cash recovery. Cash recovery assumes that the future project cash flows are achieved at a constant rate over the life of the project.

(b)   **Case for acceptance**

The proposed business case concludes that this is a key strategic investment for the firm to maintain operating capacity at the Gulf Plant. The financial assessment is as detailed above (excluding an assessment of the impact of the project on the financial reports of the firm).

(i)   NPV

The NPV of this project is calculated using a discount rate of 8% and gives a value of $1.964 million. The volatility attaching to the NPV of $1.02 million indicates that there is (z) standard deviations between the expected NPV and zero as follows:

$$z = \frac{1.964 - 0}{1.02} = 1.9255$$

This suggests that this project has a 97.3% probability that it will have a positive NPV or conversely a 2.7% probability of a negative NPV (these probabilities are taken from the normal density function tables supplied).

Tutorial note: *What is being looked for here is the probability that the project's NPV could fall to zero from its expected level of $1.964m. This fall would represent 1.964 ÷ 1.02 = 1.92 standard deviations below the mean. From the normal distribution tables (1.9 on the left column and 0.02 (second decimal) on the top row) gives the probability of 0.4726. Adding 0.5 (the other half of the normal distribution) = 0.9726 (i.e. 97.3%). There is therefore a 97.3% chance that the actual NPV will not fall below zero (i.e. there is a 2.7% chance that it will fall below zero).*

The project Value at Risk relies upon an assessment of the number of years that the project cash flow is at risk (10), the annual volatility and the confidence level required by the firm. The formula for project VaR is:

Project VaR = $N(0.95) \times s \times \sqrt{T}$
Project VaR = $1.645 \times 1.02 \times 3.162 = \$5.3$ million

This assumes a 95% confidence level, at 99% the project VaR is $7.51 million. This value reflects the fact that the capital invested is at risk for 10 years and assumes that the volatility of the project is fairly represented by the volatility of its NPV.

Tutorial note: *95% and 99% are the standard confidence levels used in Value at Risk analysis. VaR is calculated as the related z-score multiplied by the standard deviation multiplied by the square root of the number of years that the investment is at risk.*

(ii)   Project return

Tutorial note: *There are two methods of calculating MIRR; compounding the project returns forwards to future values or using the published formula which inputs the present value of returns (PV of returns = PV of investment + NPV).*

MIRR assumes that project returns are reinvested at the WACC rather than at the IRR (i.e. a conservative reinvestment assumption to estimate a realistic economic return from the project).

The IRR is shown as 11.01%. MIRR is calculated by (i) projecting forward the cash flows in the recovery stage of the project at 8% to future value of $41.798 million and (ii) discounting back the investment phase cash flows to give a present value of the investment of $17.396 million.

$$\text{MIRR} = \sqrt[10]{\frac{41.798}{17.396}} - 1 = 9.16\%$$

Alternatively the published formula can be used:

$$\text{MIRR} = \left[\frac{PV_R}{PV_I}\right]^{\frac{1}{n}} (1 + r_e) - 1$$

$$= \left[\frac{1.964 + 17.396}{17.396}\right]^{\frac{1}{10}} (1 + 0.08) - 1 = 9.16\%$$

This rate suggests that the margin on the cost of capital is rather small with only a 1.16% premium for the strategic and competitive advantage implied by this project.

(iii)   Project liquidity

With a present value of the recovery phase of $19.361 million and of the investment phase of $17.396 million this suggests that the project will have a recovery period of:

$$recovery = 2 + \frac{17.396}{19.361} \times 8 = 9.188 \; years$$

Tutorial note: *Project recovery is the time taken to payback the cost of investment, assuming that the present value of returns is generated at a constant rate. Arguably, discounted payback is a better liquidity measure as it does not assume constant generation of returns.*

In practice the actual recovery is shorter than this because the expected cash inflows occur earlier rather than later during the recovery phase of the project.

The project duration is calculated by multiplying the proportion of cash recovered in each year (discounted recovery cash flow/present value of the recovery phase) by the relevant year number from project commencement. The sum of the weighted years gives the project duration.

Year	3	4	5	6	7	8	9	10
Discounted cash flow (recovery) ($m)	3.5722	4.7042	4.9342	4.0961	3.2092	2.1611	-1.0005	-2.316
Present value of recovery phase 19.3606								
Duration of recovery phase proportion of CF recovered	0.1845	0.2430	0.2549	0.2116	0.1658	0.1116	-0.0517	-0.1196
Weighted years	0.5535	0.9719	1.2743	1.2694	1.1603	0.8930	-0.4651	-1.1962
Project duration (years) 4.46								

Tutorial notes: *4.46 is the Macaulay duration of the project's returns. This is calculated in the same way as a bond's duration (i.e. the weighted average period of the returns; the weighting being the proportion of returns generated in each period). When estimating project duration the discounting could be done at the IRR rather than at the WACC.*

The project duration reveals that the project is more highly cash generative in the early years notwithstanding the two year investment phase.

In summary, the analysis confirms that this project if financially viable, it will be value adding to the firm although there is substantial value at risk given the volatility of the NPV quoted. In terms of return the premium over the firm's hurdle rate is small at 1.16% and any significant deterioration in the firms cost of capital would be very damaging to the value of this project. The liquidity statistics reveal that the bulk of the project's cash returns are promised in the early part of the recovery phase and that half the value invested in the project should be recovered by year five. Taking this into account acceptance is recommended to the board.

Answer 9 NEPTUNE

(a) **Adjusted present value**

The adjusted present value technique separates the value created by the Galileo project into two components: (a) the value of the project cash flows at the firm's pure rate of equity (i.e., the unlevered WACC), and (b) the gain or loss of value associated with the costs and benefits of the new finance.

The adjusted present value method is only appropriate where the project does not affect the firm's exposure to business risk. With the Galileo project we can estimate the alteration to the firm's cash flows as a whole if the project were to proceed. This adjustment entails a substantial tax benefit because of tax-allowable depreciation but also a tax charge attributable to the increase in the firm's taxable earnings generated by the project.

The project cash flows exclude all non-relevant costs but include the opportunity costs associated with the redeployment of labour. The projected relevant cash flows and the calculation on the eventual profit on the sale of the capital equipment are as follows:

	0	1	2	3	4	5
Sales revenue		680·00	900·00	900·00	750·00	320·00
Direct costs		−408·00	−540·00	−540·00	−450·00	−192·00
Redeployment of labour		−150·00	−150·00			
Operating cash flow		122·00	210·00	360·00	300·00	128·00

	0	1	2	3	4	5	6
Operating cash flow		122·00	210·00	360·00	300·00	128·00	
Tax on operating cash flows			−36·60	−63·00	−108·00	−90·00	−38·40
		122·00	173·40	297·00	192·00	38·00	−38·40
Capital expenditure	−800·00					40·00	
Tax saved:							
On allowable depreciation			120·00	48·00	28·80	17·28	
On balancing allowance							13.92
Nominal project cash flow	−800·00	122·00	293·40	345·00	220·80	95·28	−24·48

The valuation of this future cash flow involves the firm's cost of capital on the basis that it is ungeared (the pure equity rate). The calculation of the ungeared rate is shown in Note 1.

Using the ungeared rate of approximately 9% to discount the project cash flows and LIBOR plus the firm's credit spread (7·2%) to discount the tax benefit associated with the project an adjusted present value is estimated as follows:

	0	1	2	3	4	5	6
Nominal project cash flow	−800·00	122·00	293·40	345·00	220·80	95·28	−24·48
Discount at 9%	−800·00	112	247	266	156	62	−15
Base case NPV	28						
Gross debt raised (800 ÷ 0.98)	816.32						
Annual interest		58.78	58.78	58.78	58.78	58.78	
Tax saving			17·63	17·63	17·63	17·63	17·63
Discount at 7.2%			15	14	13	12	12
Present value of tax shield	66						
Issue costs (816.32 – 800)	−16						
APV = 28 + 66 – 16 =	78						

Tutorial note: *It is assumed that issue costs are not tax deductible.*

This suggests that the new project will add substantial value to the firm although $50 million is attributable to the tax benefit associated with the new financing less 2% transaction cost associated with the new debt finance. With this project the clear advice on the basis of the financial analysis is to proceed although it is worth bearing in mind that more marginal projects may be solely justified through the financing effect.

(b) **Modified internal rate of return (MIRR)**

One procedure for calculating the MIRR is to calculate the terminal value of the cash flows from the recovery phase of the project using the company's cost of capital of 8·97%.

	1	2	3	4	5	6
Nominal project cash flow	122·00	293·40	345·00	220·80	95·28	−24·48
Compound factor using 8·97%	1·5365	1·4100	1·2940	1·1874	1·0897	1·0000
Terminal cash flow	187·45	413·70	446·43	262·18	103·83	−24·48
Future value of recovery cash flows	1,389					

MIRR is found by calculating the IRR of the modified project cash flow:

$$-800 + \frac{1,389}{(1 + MIRR)^6} = 0$$

Therefore:

$$MIRR = \sqrt[6]{\frac{1,389}{800}} - 1 = 9.6\%$$

An alternative approach is to use the published formula:

$$MIRR = \left[\frac{PV_R}{PV_I}\right]^{\frac{1}{n}} (1 + r_e) - 1$$

In this case, because we are concerned solely with the project's nominal cash flow excluding financing costs we use the ungeared cost of equity as the appropriate discount and reinvestment rate.

$$\text{MIRR} = \left[\frac{800 + 28}{800} \right]^{\frac{1}{6}} (1 + 0.0897) - 1 = 9.6\%$$

Tutorial note: *The examiner's answer uses n=6 when calculating MIRR. However, as the useful economic life of the asset is actually five years it would be acceptable to set n = 5.*

It is to be expected that in a highly competitive business new business opportunities with significant net present values are hard to find. This project, if successful, will add to the value of the firm and offers a rate of return just 0.6% higher than the current reinvestment rate.

Note 1

Assuming the beta of debt is zero:

$$\beta a = \frac{V_d (1 - T)}{V_e + V_d (1 - T)} \beta e$$

$$\beta a = \frac{2,500}{(7,500 + 2,500(1 - 0.30))} \times 1.4$$

$$\beta a = 1 \cdot 1351$$

Cost of equity capital (ungeared), $r_e = 0 \cdot 05 + 1 \cdot 1351 \times 0 \cdot 035 = 0 \cdot 0897$ (8·97%)

Answer 10 SLOW FASHIONS CO

(a)   **Capital investment plan**

NPV is not a sufficient criterion for choosing between projects when capital is in short supply. On the assumption that the priority of the firm is to maximise NPV overall then the optimal ranking of projects is achieved through the profitability index as measured by the NPV per $ of invested capital at year zero. The ranking of the projects using the NPV index is as follows:

	Investment	NPV	IRR	PI	Cumulative investment
P0805	−120	19	17%	0·1573	120
P0802	−640	69	13%	0·1085	760
P0801	−620	55	16%	0·0892	1,380
P0803	−240	20	15%	0·0841	1,620
P0806	−400	29	15%	0·0733	2,020
P0804	−1,000	72	13%	0·0719	3,020

Tutorial notes: *It appears that the PI for P0805 = $^{19}/_{120}$ = 0.1583. This is slightly different from the examiner's answer above which may have been produced using a spread sheet without rounding the NPV figure.*

Ranking the projects by their PI gives preference for P0805, P0802 then P0801. However this would require total finance of 120 + 640 + 620 = 1,380 when only 1,200 is available. The complication is that P0801 is "indivisible" (i.e. the project cannot be scaled down; it must be done 100% or not at all).

In this situation the only way to find the optimal investment plan is to schedule the overall NPV created by either "promoting" P0801 (to 100%) or "demoting" it (to 0%).

If promoted the choice should be P0805 (always the best project) and then P0801. This would leave capital remaining of 1,200 – 120 – 620 = 460. P0802 is the next best but only 72% of its full scale (460 ÷ 640) can be undertaken.

If P0801 is demoted the choice should be P0805, then P0802, then P0803. This leaves capital of 1,200 – 120 – 640 – 240 = 200 to invest in 50% (200 ÷ 400) of P0806.

Overall is it slightly better to promote P0801 than to demote it.

Acceptance of PO801 ahead of PO802 (which can be scaled):

	Investment	NPV	IRR	PI	Cum inv	proportion	NPV
P0805	–120	19	17%	0·1573	120	1	19
P0801	–620	55	16%	0·0892	740	1	55
P0802	–640	69	13%	0·1085	1,380	0·71875	50
P0803	–240	20	15%	0·0841	1,620		
P0806	–400	29	15%	0·0733	2,020		
P0804	–1,000	72	13%	0·0719	3,020		

Plan NPV   124

Removal of PO801 from the plan:

	Investment	NPV	IRR	PI	Cum inv	proportion	NPV
P0805	–120	19	17%	0·1573	120	1	19
P0802	–640	69	13%	0·1085	760	1	69
P0803	–240	20	15%	0·0841	1,000	1	20
P0806	–400	29	15%	0·0733	1,400	0·5	15
P0804	–1,000	72	13%	0·0719	2,400		
P0801	–620	55	16%	0·0892	740		

Plan NPV   123

(i)   The revised plan should be to produce all of PO805, PO801 and a reduced scale of production on PO802.

(ii)   The NPV of the optimal plan is $124 million.

The IRR cannot be calculated using the proportions of projects invested because of scale effects but must be calculated for the overall plan. Using the interpolation method and calculating the NPV of the optimum plan at 14% and 18% the IRR can be estimated by interpolation:

Discount	NPV
14%	12
18%	–85

$$IRR = 14\% \; \frac{12}{12 + 85} \times 4\% = 14.5\%$$

(iii)   The profitability index for the plan = 124 ÷ 1,200 = $0·1033 per dollar invested.

(b) **Maximum interest rate**

When calculating the rate for short-term financing the maximum rate which should be offered is that which generates a zero NPV on those projects which do not qualify for the current plan. The IRR is not appropriate as that is the rate that would be the maximum rate for investment over the life of the projects concerned. This is however, a short-term capital rationing problem. The profitability index gives the NPV of each pound invested.

Project	Now	2018	2019	2020	2021	2022	2023
PO802 (balance of the marginal project)	−180	23	34	56	59	118	−8
P0803	−240	120	120	60	10		
P0806	−400	245	250				
P0804	−1,000	300	500	250	290		
Cash flows of rejected projects	−1,820	688	904	366	359	118	−8
Discount at 10%	−1,820	625	747	275	245	73	−5
NPV of rejected projects	141						
Profitability index	0·07742						

Given that 10% is the rate assuming no short-term market failure for finance for this company, the maximum rate for the one year over which capital rationing is expected to hold is 17·74%.

Tutorial note: *From (a) 72% of P0802 should be undertaken. Therefore, if more capital was available the remaining 28% of this project should be completed and this is how the cash flows have been forecast above for P0802 (i.e. 28% of the full scale). If we add the remaining projects and find the PI it is 7.74% (i.e. if we could find additional finance at our normal cost of capital of 10% it would generate 7.74 cents of surplus value per dollar invested). Hence, the maximum interest rate acceptable to obtain extra finance is 17.74% (10% + 7.74%).*

Answer 11 SEAL ISLAND

Tutorial note: *The standard financial appraisal is supplemented by a sensitivity analysis. A discussion of the principal uncertainties and recommendation of a further process of evaluation to assess the volatility of the project is presented.*

(i) **Estimation of NPV of the project**

Estimated Project NPV (all values quoted in $ million):

30-year annuity factor, growth rate 4% and discount rate 10%

Tutorial note: *The formula for the present value of a growing annuity is provided in the question. This is used to value the annual operating cash flow which grows with nominal GDP at 4%.*

$$A_n = \left[\frac{1 - \left(\frac{1+g}{1+i} \right)^n}{i - g} \right] (1+g) = \left[\frac{1 - \left(\frac{1.04}{1.1} \right)^{30}}{0.1 - 0.04} \right] 1.04 = 14.11$$

Year/Type	Cash flows ($m)	DF (10%)	Present value ($m)
2019 Construction	(300)	$1 \cdot 1^{-1}$	(272·7)
2020 Construction	(600)	$1 \cdot 1^{-2}$	(495·9)
2021 Construction	(100)	$1 \cdot 1^{-3}$	(75·1)
2022–2051 Annual operating surplus	100	$14 \cdot 11 \times 1 \cdot 1^{-3} = 10 \cdot 601$	1060·1
2052 Decommissioning	600	$1 \cdot 04^{33} \times 1 \cdot 1^{-33} = 0 \cdot 1571$	(94·3)
NPV			122·1

Tutorial notes: *The construction costs were stated in the scenario in nominal terms and can be simply discounted at the nominal discount rate.*

The operating surplus can be valued using the annuity formula above but this would give the present value as if the cash flow starts after one year, whereas it actually starts after four years. Therefore, the annuity value must be discounted back by three years.

The decommissioning costs were stated to be at current cost levels and so must be inflated at 4% for 33 years before being discounted.

On the basis of the above, the net present value of the project as at 1 January 2019 is $122·1 million which indicates that the project will add value to the business.

(ii) **Analysis of principal uncertainties associated with this project**

Uncertainty in capital investment projects can be categorised as mis-estimation of:

(i)   the timing and level of capital expenditure over the investment phase of the project;
(ii)   the operating surpluses from the project and their timing;
(iii)   the timing and amount of closure costs; and
(iv)   the discount rate.

Capital expenditure: with large scale investment projects uncertainty will attach to the timing and costs of the capital construction. Where building is undertaken by external contractors there may be legal issues in forming a complete contract and in monitoring performance against it. In addition to engineering difficulties causing delay in construction, problems can also occur on the costs of labour, raw material supplies and other costs.

Operating surplus: This will depend upon a number of capacity estimates (theoretical and actual), market costs for labour, materials and operating overheads. In addition, the supply of electricity is subject to national demand and unit prices will depend upon alternative capacity, alternative energy supplies (fossil and renewable) and whether they can contribute to marginal or to base load.

Closure costs: These can be high in this industry although their remoteness diminishes their significance in present value terms. The timing and estimates of the magnitude of such costs will have a small impact upon the viability of the project as a capital investment.

Discount rate: This can be difficult to estimate for a project of this scale. In practice such rates are taken from a mixture of models and sources, all of which have uncertainties attached. The gearing of the business will determine the importance of uncertainty attaching to each capital source. There is also likely to be significant social externalities with a project of this type affecting its valuation and hence the discount rate which should be applied. Such social externalities range from the reduction in dependence upon fossil fuels and associated carbon emissions, the relatively low pollution costs compared with fossil fuels, and the stability and security of supply.

In addition there may be a range of real options attaching to a project of this type:

(i)   the option to delay;
(ii)   the option to expand or contract capacity;
(iii)   the option to withdraw early or extend the operating life of the project.

Each of these will add value to the firm by helping to eliminate the downside exposure and focusing the expected value calculation on the upside of the possible distribution of outcomes.

(iii)   Project sensitivity

In order for the NPV to reduce to nil it must fall by $122·1m.

Construction cost

Cost increase per $100m × $(3 \times 1 \cdot 1^{-1} + 6 \times 1 \cdot 1^{-2} + 1 \times 1 \cdot 1^{-3}) = \$122 \cdot 1m$
Cost increase per $100m × $(3 \times 0 \cdot 9091 + 6 \times 0 \cdot 8264 + 1 \times 0 \cdot 7513) = \$122 \cdot 1m$

Cost increase per $100m = $122·1m ÷ 8·4370 = $14·47m
Year 1 cost will increase to $343·41m ($300m + $14·47m × 3), Year 2 cost will increase to $686·82m and year 3 cost will increase to $114·47m. An increase of 14·47% in each year before NPV becomes zero.

Annual operating surplus

$122·1m ÷ 10·601 = $11·52m
Surplus needs to reduce to $88·48m (11·52%) before NPV becomes zero.

Decommissioning costs

$122·1m ÷ 0·1571 = $777·2m
Decommissioning costs need to increase by $777·2m (129·5%) in 1 January 2019 value before NPV becomes zero.

The annual operating surplus is the most sensitive to changes.

(iv)   Volatility assessment

The assessment of the volatility (or standard deviation) of the NPV of a project entails the simulation of the financial model using estimates of the distributions of the key input parameters and an assessment of the correlations between variables. Some of these variables are normally distributed but some (such as the decommissioning cost) are assumed to have limit values and a most likely value. Given the shape of the input distributions, simulation employs random numbers to select specimen value for each variable in order to estimate a "trial value" for the project NPV. This is repeated a large number of times until a distribution of NPVs emerge. By the central limit theorem the resulting distribution will approximate normality and from which project volatility can be estimated.

In its simplest form, Monte Carlo simulation assumes that the input variables are uncorrelated. However, more sophisticated modelling can incorporate estimates of the correlation between variables. Other refinements such as the Latin Hypercube technique can reduce the likelihood of spurious results occurring through chance in the random number generation process. The output from a simulation will give the expected NPV for the project and a range of other statistics including the standard deviation of the output distribution. In addition, the model can rank order the significance of each variable in determining the project NPV.

Answer 12 ALLEGRO TECHNOLOGIES

Report to the ATC Board of Directors

Assessment of the investment in the engine component project

This report recommends whether or not ATC would benefit by investing in the engine component project by considering the following alternatives open to it, and explains the approach taken in each case and the assumptions made:

■ The value of the project without the SIC offer to buy the project on completion of the two-year development phase.

■ The value of the project after taking into account SIC's offer.

The report also considers the possible implications of the offer made by Largo on the project.

Approach taken

The approach taken is to estimate the NPV) of the project based on the given estimates of costs and revenues without the SIC offer (see appendices one and three).

This is followed by a revised estimate of the value of the project, after taking into consideration SIC's offer. This is based on viewing the project as a real option to abandon (put option) the project and using Black-Scholes Option Pricing (BSOP) model to give an estimate of this value (see Appendix 2).

Assumptions made and initial assessment

In calculating the value of the project, the following assumptions have been made:

Since this is a new venture for ATC but an on-going business for SIC, an estimate of the project's risk, as measured by the project's risk-adjusted beta, is made (Appendix 3, W4) using SIC's business risk (SIC's asset beta) but ATC's financial risk (project equity beta). This risk-adjusted beta is used to calculate the cost of equity and then the cost of capital (discount rate) for the project (Appendix 3, W4).

■ As part of the W4 calculation in Appendix 3, it is assumed that debt is riskless and has a beta of zero.

■ Unless indicated otherwise, it is assumed that all cash flows occur at the end of the year.

■ The patent purchase cost and the investigative research costs are past costs, and therefore not part of the calculation of the value of the project, which is based on future cash flows.

■ The option for ATC is the opportunity to "sell" the project to SIC after two years if the cash flows do not appear to be favourable, hence this is a put option to abandon a project. Since the option is exercised after two years, it can be considered to be a "European" type option and the BSOP model can be applied, together with the put-call parity relationship.

Based on the calculations in the appendices, from the cost and revenue estimates provided, the NPV before considering the SIC option is negative at $9,359,000 approximately (Appendix 1). However after taking into account the value of the put option, the NPV is positive at $8,087,000 approximately (Appendix 2). Therefore, it would be beneficial for ATC to undertake the project, if it can decide whether to continue with the project or sell it to SIC for $133 million after a period of two years. However, without this option it should not proceed with the project.

ATC will not actually obtain the value of the option, however the option value takes into account the volatility or uncertainty of the project. In this case, it indicates that the project is worth pursuing because the volatility may result in increases in future cash flows and the project becomes profitable. On the other hand, the project can be abandoned for $113 million in two years if the likelihood of sufficient future cash flows remains doubtful. The value attached to this choice is $17,446,000 approximately (Appendix 2). In the meantime, ATC can put into place mechanisms to make the production and sales targets more certain and profitable. Therefore, the time ATC has before it needs to make a decision is reflected in the value of the project by considering real options using the BSOP model.

The BSOP model makes several assumptions such as perfect markets, constant interest rates and lognormal distribution of asset prices. It also assumes that volatility can be assessed and stays constant throughout the life of the project, and that the underlying asset can be traded. Neither of these assumptions would necessarily apply to real options. Therefore, the Board needs to treat the value obtained as indicative rather than definitive, and take the assumptions and limitations into consideration before making a final decision.

Implications of the Largo offer on the value of the project

From the above discussion, it is evident that the project has a negative NPV if it is not considered in conjunction with an option to abandon. The abandonment option makes the project viable. However, if ATC enters into a five-year contractual agreement with Largo then this may make the two-year offer by SIC to buy the project redundant. There is no guarantee that SIC would continue to ask Largo to produce the parts and ATC would not be able to honour the contract and keep the SIC's offer open at the same time. ATC would need to consider the impact of the cost savings from the agreement with Largo against the possible loss of the option. The Board may also wish to consider how binding the contract would be legally, and also consider the negative impact to ATC's reputation and additional costs if it breaches the contract in future.

In order to mitigate the impact of the issue, the Board may wish to approach Largo to discuss the terms of the contract and the provision of possible exclusion clauses. The Board may also want to investigate the reasons behind Largo's insistence of a five-year contract and offer alternatives such as asking Largo to produce components for other ATC products if this venture should cease. Alternatively the Board may initiate discussions with SIC to consider whether it would be willing to honour the contract should the project be sold to them in two years.

In summary, the initial recommendation is that, based on the projected revenue and cost estimates, the project should be pursued if it taken together with SIC's offer to buy the project after two years. However, on its own it is not worthwhile. The offer by Largo may make SIC's offer invalid initially but the Board should consider alternatives, some of which are suggested above.

Integrated reporting

The integrated reporting framework was launched by the International Integrated Reporting Council (IIRC) in December 2013. The IIRC is a global coalition of regulators, investors, companies, standard setters, the accounting profession and non-government organisations. It has a vision of a business environment in which integrated thinking becomes standard business practice. This would be facilitated by integrated reporting (<IR>).

A primary motivation behind <IR> is that financial information alone is insufficient as an indicator of the long-term *sustainability* of a business. <IR> combines *financial* and *non-financial* information in one report with the goal of maximising the value of information provided to stakeholders with a variety of interests in an organisation. Accounting for the long-term sustainability of an organisation is important for both the organisation and those who provide financial capital to an organisation.

In the context of the proposed project the financial impact is captured through the NPV which, including the value of the embedded put option, suggests a potential increase in shareholder wealth of around $8 million. Although the shareholders are clearly the key stakeholder in a quoted company such as ATC the board need to be accountable to other stakeholders.

When thinking of how value may be created for others, management of ATC could assess how making the investment in the development and commercialization of the innovative engine component and accepting the proposals by Largo and SIC:

■ improve customer satisfaction;
■ affect suppliers' willingness to trade with ATC and the terms and conditions of that trade;
■ affect ATC's reputation; and
■ affect the local communities in which manufacturing takes place.

For example <IR> could capture the potentially favourable environmental impacts of the project – the innovative component is designed to reduce carbon emissions. Environmental performance is relevant to wider society as a stakeholder.

On the other hand if production is outsourced to Largo then there could be job losses within ATC, albeit potentially offset at the global level by jobs created in Largo. Ultimately the board of ATC are primarily accountable to ATC's employees and any redundancies need to be handled with sensitivity.

Appendix 1 – NPV calculation (ignoring SIC offer)

Year	0	1	2	3	4	5
$000						
Sales revenue (W1)		7,500	21,600	58,300	75,540	129,200
Less:						
Variable costs (W2)		3,000	8,400	22,050	27,780	46,170
Fixed costs		1,500	1,575	1,654	1,736	1,823
Training and development		3,600	3,360	2,205	2,778	4,617
Cash flows before tax		(600)	8,265	32,391	43,246	75,590
Taxation (W3)		2,520	747	(4,078)	(6,249)	(8,718)
Working capital	(1,500)	(1,410)	(3,670)	(1,724)	(5,366)	13,670
Machinery	(120,000)					40,000
Net cash flows	(121,500)	510	5,342	26,589	31,631	120,542
Present values @12% (W4)	(121,500)	455	4,259	18,926	20,102	68,399

NPV is approximately $(9,359,000)

Appendix 2 – Value of put option (incorporating the offer from SIC)

Present value of underlying asset (Pa) = \$107,427,000 (approximately)
(This is the sum of the present values of the cash flows foregone in years 3, 4 and 5)
Price offered by Largo (Pe) = \$113 million
Risk-free rate of interest (r) = 3%
Time to expiry of option (t) = 2 years
Volatility of underlying asset (s) = 30%

Tutorial note: *The volatility of project cash flows would technically be higher than 30% due to the impact of operational gearing (i.e. fixed costs magnify volatility).*

$d_1 = [\ln(107,427,000 \div 113,000,000) + (0.03 + 0.5 \times 0.32) \times 2] \div [0.3 \times \sqrt{2}] = 0.234$
$d_2 = 0.234 - 0.3 \times \sqrt{2} = -0.190$

$N(d_1) = 0.5 + 0.0925 = 0.5925$
$N(d_2) = 0.5 - 0.0753 = 0.4247$

Call value = $\$107,427,000 \times 0.5925 - \$113,000,000 \times 0.4247xe^{-0.03\times2}$ = approx \$18,454,000
Put value = $\$18,454,000 - \$107,427,000 + \$113,000,000xe^{-0.03\times2}$ = approx \$17,446,000

NPV with put option = \$17,446,000 – \$9,359,000 = approx \$8,087,000

Appendix 3

WORKINGS to support NPV calculation (Appendix 1)

(1)	Year	1	2	3	4	5
	Units produced and sold	7,500	20,000	50,000	60,000	95,000
	Unit price ($)	1,000	1,080	1,166	1,259	1,360
	Sales revenue ($000)	7,500	21,600	58,300	75,540	129,200

(2)	Year	1	2	3	4	5
	Units produced and sold	7,500	20,000	50,000	60,000	95,000
	Unit variable costs ($)	400	420	441	463	486
	Variable costs ($'000)	3,000	8,400	22,050	27,780	46,170

(3)	Year	1	2	3	4	5
	Cash flows before tax ($000)	(600)	8,265	32,391	43,246	75,590
	Tax allowable depreciation ($000)	(12,000)	(12,000)	(12,000)	(12,000)	(32,000)
	Tax able flows ($000)	(12,600)	(3,735)	20,391	31,246	43,590
	Taxation (20%) ($000)	(2,520)	(747)	4,078	6,249	8,718

(4)   Asset beta of project = $1.8 \times (3 \times 125) \div (3 \times 125 + 92 \times 1.02 \times 0.8) = 1.50$

Equity beta: project beta adjusted for financial risk of ATC
     = $1.5 \times (3.5 \times 104 + 156 \times 0.8) \div (3.5 \times 104) = 2.014$

Cost of equity = $3\% + 2.014 \times 6\% = 15.08\%$

WACC (discount rate) = $(15.08\% \times 364 + 6\% \times 0.8 \times 156) \div 520 = 11.996\%$ approx 12%.

Answer 13 FUBUKI CO

(a)   Adjusted Present Value

Tutorial note: *The requirement does not specify which method of project appraisal should be used. However it is reasonable to assume that an estimate of the absolute change in shareholder wealth from the project (i.e. using NPV or APV) is required.*

Although any sensible attempt at NPV would gain some marks this approach would not be appropriate as the existing WACC of 8% does not capture the project's level of business risk or the impact of the project's finance on the firm's capital structure. Although a proxy can be used to model the project's business risk there is no way to estimate the firm's post-project capital structure as the existing values of equity and debt are unknown.

The recommended approach is therefore APV which can deal both with the project's level of business risk and the effects of the financing package, including subsidies and issue costs.

Base case

	Unit price/cost	Inflation	Now	Year 1	Year 2	Year 3	Year 4
Units Produced and sold				1,300	1,820	2,548	2,675
$000							
Sales revenue	2·5	3%		3,250	4,687	6,758	7,308
Direct costs	1·2	8%		(1,560)	(2,359)	(3,566)	(4,044)
Attributable fixed costs 1,000		5%		(1,000)	(1,050)	(1,103)	(1,158)
Profits				690	1,278	2,089	2,106
Working capital	15%		(488)	(215)	(311)	(82)	1,096
Taxation (W1)				(10)	(157)	(360)	(364)
Incremental cash flows							
Investment/sale			(14,000)				16,000
Net cash flows			(14,488)	465	810	1,647	18,838
Present value (at 10% (W2))			(14,488)	422	670	1,237	12,867
Base case NPV			708				

WORKINGS

(1)   Taxation

	Year 1	Year 2	Year 3	Year 4
Profits	690	1,278	2,089	2,106
Less: allowances	650	650	650	650
Taxable profits	40	628	1,439	1,456
Tax	10	157	360	364

Tutorial note: *Full credit would be given for the assumption that allowances are 750 in the first three years and 350 in the final year.*

(2) Discount rate

Discount rate (Haizum's ungeared K_e)

$k_{e(g)} = k_{e(u)} + (1-t)(k_{e(u)} - k_d)V_d \div V_e$

$V_e = 2 \cdot 53 \times 15 = 37 \cdot 95$

$V_d = 40 \times 0 \cdot 9488 = 37 \cdot 952$

Assume $V_d \div V_e = 1$

$14 = k_{e(u)} + 0 \cdot 72 \times (k_{e(u)} - 4 \cdot 5) \times 1$

$14 = 1 \cdot 72 k_{e(u)} - 3 \cdot 24$

$k_{e(u)} = 10 \cdot 02$ assume 10%

Tutorial note: *The ungeared cost of equity has been found using Modigliani and Miller's Proposition 2 (exam formula). An alternative approach would be to imply Haizum's equity beta using CAPM and then degear to the asset beta.*

The base case NPV is calculated as approximately $708,000. This is positive but marginal.

Financing side effects

		$000
Issue costs ($^4/_{96} \times$ \$14,488)		(604)
Tax shield:		
Annual tax relief	$= (14,488 \times 80\% \times 0 \cdot 055 \times 25\%)$	
	$+ (14,488 \times 20\% \times 0 \cdot 075 \times 25\%)$	
	$= 159 \cdot 4 + 54 \cdot 3 = 213 \cdot 7$	
	$213 \cdot 7 \times 3 \cdot 588$	766
Subsidy benefit: $(14,488 \times 80\% \times 0 \cdot 02 \times 75\% \times 3 \cdot 588)$		624
Total benefit of financing side effects		786
Adjusted present value (708 + 786)		1,494

Tutorial note: *Finance is required for both the capital expenditure and the initial working capital. The scenario states that issue costs are 4% of the **gross** finance required (i.e. $^4/_{96} \times$ 14,488 rather than 4% × 14,488). To be consistent there is an argument that issue costs should be added to the level of debt (i.e. gross debt would be 14,488 + 604 = 15,092). Any candidate that took this view would be awarded full marks.*

The annuity factor used in calculating the present values of the tax shield and subsidy benefits is based on 4·5% government yield. It could be argued that 7·5% may also be used as this reflects the firm's normal borrowing rate and reflects its default risk. Full marks would be awarded for either approach.

The addition of the financing side effects gives an increased present value and probably the project would not be considered marginal. Once these are taken into account Fubuki would probably undertake the project.

(b) Appropriateness of APV and assumptions made

The adjusted present value can be used where the impact of using debt financing is significant. Here the impact of each of the financing side effects from debt is shown separately rather than being imputed into the weighted average cost of capital. The project is initially evaluated by only taking into account the business risk element of the new venture. This shows that although the project results in a positive NPV, it is fairly marginal and volatility in the input factors could turn the project. Sensitivity analysis can be used to examine the sensitivity of the factors. The financing side effects show that almost 110% value is added when the positive impact of the tax shields and subsidy benefits are taken into account even after the issue costs.

Assumptions

Tutorial note: *Credit given for alternative, valid assumptions.*

1.   Haizum's ungeared cost of equity is used because it is assumed that this represents the business risk attributable to the new line of business.

2.   The ungeared cost of equity is calculated on the assumption that Modigliani and Miller's (MM) proposition 2 applies.

3.   It is assumed that initial working capital requirement will form part of the funds borrowed but the subsequent requirements will be available from the funds generated from the project.

4.   The feasibility study is ignored as a past cost.

5.   It is assumed that the five-year debt yield is equivalent to the risk-free rate.

6.   It is assumed that the annual reinvestment needed on plant and machinery is equivalent to the tax allowable depreciation.

7.   It is assumed that all cash flows occur at the end of the year unless specified otherwise.

8.   All amounts are given in $000 to the nearest $000. When calculating the units produced and sold, the nearest approximation for each year is taken.

Assumptions 4, 5, 6, 7 and 8 are standard assumptions made for a question of this nature. Assumptions 1, 2 and 3 warrant further discussion. Taking assumption 3 first, it is reasonable to assume that before the project starts, the company would need to borrow the initial working capital as it may not have access to the working capital needed. In subsequent years, the cash flows generated from the operation of the project may be sufficient to fund the extra working capital required. In the case of Fubuki, because of an expected rapid growth in sales in years 2 and 3, the working capital requirement remains high and the management need to assess how to make sufficient funds available.

Considering assumptions 1 and 2, the adjusted present values methodology assumes that MM proposition 2 applies and the equivalent ungeared cost of equity does not take into account the cost of financial distress. This may be an unreasonable assumption. The ungeared cost of equity is based on another company which is in a similar line of business to the new project, but it is not exactly the same. It can be difficult to determine an accurate ungeared cost of equity in practice. However, generally the discount rate (cost of funds) tends to be the least sensitive factor in investment appraisal and therefore some latitude can be allowed.

Answer 14 TISA CO

(a)   **Cost of capital estimate**

Use Elfu's information to estimate the component project's asset beta. Then based on Tisa's capital structure, estimate the component project's equity beta and weighted average cost of capital. Assume that the beta of debt is zero.

Elfu: MV_e = $1·20 × 400m shares = $480m
Elfu: MV_d = $96m

Elfu: Portfolio asset beta =
$1·40 × $480m ÷ ($480m + $96m × (1 − 0·25)) = 1·217$
Elfu: Asset beta of other activities =
$1·25 × $360m ÷ ($360m + $76·8m × (1 − 0·25)) = 1·078$

$1·217$ = component asset beta × $0·25$ + $1·078$ × $0·75$
Component asset beta = $[1·217 − (1·078 × 0·75)] ÷ 0·25 = 1·634$

Component equity beta based on Tisa's capital structure =
$1·634 × [($18m + $3·6m × 0·75) ÷ $18m] = 1·879$
Using CAPM, component $Ke = 3·5\% + 1·879 × 5·8\% = 14·40\%$
Component WACC = $(14·40\% × $18m + 4·5\% × $3·6m) ÷ ($18m + $3·6m) = 12·75\%$

(b)   **IRR and MIRR**

Process Omega

Year	0	1	2	3	4
Net cash flows ($000)	(3,800)	1,220	1,153	1,386	3,829
PV 12·75% ($000)	(3,800)	1,082	907	967	2,369
NPV ($000)	1,525				
PV 30%	(3,800)	938	682	631	1,341
NPV ($000)	(208)				

IRR is approximately 27·3%

MIRR is approximately 22·7%
$([(5,325 ÷ 3,800)^{1/4} × (1·1275)] − 1)$

Alternatively

MIRR can be calculated as follows:

Year	Cash flows ($000)	Multiplier	Re-invested amount ($000)
1	1,220	$1·1275^3$	1,749
2	1,153	$1·1275^2$	1,466
3	1,386	$1·1275$	1,563
4	3,829	1	3,829

Total re-invested amount ($000) = 8,607
MIRR = $(8,607 ÷ 3,800)^{1/4} − 1 = 22·7\%$

The IRR assumes that positive cash flows in earlier years are reinvested at the IRR and therefore process Omega, which has higher initial cash flows when compared to process Zeta, gives a slightly higher IRR. The MIRR assumes that positive cash flows are reinvested at the cost of capital. This is a more reasonable assumption and produces a result consistent with the NPV. Therefore, process Zeta should be adopted, although the difference is not significant.

Tutorial note: *Using 13% instead of 12·75% as the cost of capital would be acceptable.*

(c) **Value At Risk**

99% confidence level requires the value at risk (VaR) to be within 2·33 standard deviations from the mean, based on a single tail measure.

Annual VaR = 2·33 × $800,000 = $1,864,000
Five year VaR = $1,864,000 × √5 approx = $4,168,000

The figures mean that Elfu can be 99% confident that the cash flows will not fall by more than $1,864,000 in any one year and $4,168,000 in total over five years from the average returns. Therefore the company can be 99% certain that the returns will be $336,000 or more every year [$2,200,000 – $1,864,000]. And it can be 99% certain that the returns will be $6,832,000 or more in total over the five-year period [$11,000,000 – $4,168,000]. There is a 1% chance that the returns will be less than $336,000 each year or $6,832,000 over the five-year period.

Answer 15 ARBORE CO

(a) **NPV and sensitivity analysis**

PDur05
Annual sales revenue = $14 × 300,000 units = $4,200,000
Annual costs = $3,230,000
Annual cash flows = $970,000

NPV of PDur05 =
($2,500,000) + ($1,200,000 × $1·11^{-1}$) + ($1,400,000 × $1·11^{-2}$) + $970,000 × 7·191 × $1·11^{-3}$
= ($2,500,000) + ($1,081,000) + ($1,136,000) + $5,100,000
= $383,000

In order for the NPV to fall to nil, the PV of the project's annual cash flows needs to equal to:
$2,500,000 + $1,081,000 + $1,136,000 = $4,717,000

Annual cash flows need to reduce to: $4,717,000 ÷ (7·191 × $1·11^{-3}$) = $897,110
Sales revenue would reduce to: $897,110 + $3,230,000 = $4,127,110
Selling price would fall to: $4,127,110 ÷ 300,000 units = $13·76
Percentage fall = ($14·00 – $13·76) ÷ $14 × 100% = 1·7%

Tutorial note: *The estimate of the annual cash flows will differ if tables are used rather than a calculator. This is acceptable and would be allowed for when marking.*

Comment: The NPV of the project is very sensitive to changes in the selling price of the product. A small fall in the selling price would reduce the NPV to nil or negative and make the project not worthwhile.

(b)   **Formulation of linear programming model**

A multi-period capital rationing model would use linear programming and is formulated as follows:

If:
Y1 = investment in project PDur01; Y2 = investment in project PDur02; Y3 = investment in project PDur03; Y4 = investment in project PDur04; and Y5 = investment in project PDur05

Then the objective is to maximise
464Y1 + 244Y2 + 352Y3 + 320Y4 + 383Y5

Given the following constraints
Constraint year 1: 4,000Y1 + 800Y2 + 3,200Y3 + 3,900Y4 + 2,500Y5 ≤ 9,000
Constraint year 2: 1,100Y1 + 2,800Y2 + 3,562Y3 + 0Y4 + 1,200Y5 ≤ 6,000
Constraint year 3: 2,400Y1 + 3,200Y2 + 0Y3 + 200Y4 + 1,400Y5 ≤ 5,000

And where Y1, Y2, Y3, Y4, Y5 ≥ 0

(c)   **Interpretation of output**

Category 1: Total Final Value. This is the maximum NPV that can be earned within the three-year constraints of capital expenditure, by undertaking whole, part or none of the five projects. This amount is less than the total NPV of all five projects if there were no constraints.

Category 2: Adjustable Final Values. These are the proportions of projects undertaken within the constraints to maximise the NPV. In this case, all of project PDur05, 95·8% of project PDur01, 73·2% of project PDur03 and 40·7% of project PDur02 will be undertaken.

Category 3: Constraints utilised, slack. This indicates to what extent the constraint limits are used and whether any investment funds will remain unused. The figures indicate that, in order to achieve maximum NPV, all the funds in all three years are used up and no funds remain unused.

(d)   **Director's opinions**

(i)   Soft capital rationing

Normally, positive NPV projects should be accepted as they add to the value of the company by generating returns in excess of the required rate of return (the discount rate). However, in this case, Arbore seems to be employing soft capital rationing by setting internal limits on capital available for each department, possibly due to capital budget limits placed by the company on the amounts it wants to borrow or can borrow. In the latter case, the company faces limited access to capital from external sources, for example, because of restrictions in bank lending, costs related to the issue of new capital and lending to the company being perceived as too risky. This is known as hard capital rationing and can lead to soft capital rationing.

(ii)   Capital investment monitoring

A capital investment monitoring system (CIMS) monitors how an investment project is progressing once it has been implemented. Initially the CIMS will set a plan and budget of how the project is to proceed. It sets milestones for what needs to be achieved and by when. It also considers the possible risks, both internal and external, which may affect the project. CIMS then ensures that the project is progressing according to the plan and budget. It also sets up contingency plans for dealing with the identified risks.

The benefits, to Arbore, of CIMS are that it tries to ensure, as much as possible, that the project meets what is expected of it in terms of revenues and expenses. Also that the project is completed on time and risk factors that are identified remain valid. A critical path of linked activities which make up the project will be identified. The departments undertaking the projects will be proactive, rather than reactive, towards the management of risk, and therefore possibly be able to reduce costs by having a better plan. CIMS can also be used as a communication device between managers charged with managing the project and the monitoring team. Finally CIMS would be able to re-assess and change the assumptions made of the project, if changes in the external environment warrant it.

Answer 16 KODIAK COMPANY

(a)   Three-year cash flow forecast

Given the details supplied, a forward forecast of the statement of profit or loss and of the statement of financial position is a precursor to the cash flow forecast. On the assumptions (as stated in the question but not reproduced here) the following projection is obtained (all figures in $000):

Projected statement of profit or loss	*Year 1*	*Year 2*	*Year 3*
Revenue (9% growth)	5,450	5,941	6,475
Cost of sales (9% growth)	3,270	3,564	3,885
Gross profit	2,180	2,377	2,590
Operating costs (W1)	2,012	2,159	2,317
Operating profit	168	218	273
Projected cash flows			
Operating profit	168	218	273
Add depreciation (W2)	134	144	155
Less incremental working capital (W3)	(20)	(21)	(24)
Less taxation (W4)	(15)	(28)	(43)
Less interest	(74)	(74)	(74)
Free cash flow to equity	193	239	287
Less investment in non-current assets (W2)	(79)	(95)	(114)
Free cash flow to equity	114	144	173

WORKINGS

(1)   Operating costs

Variable costs (9% growth)	818	891	971
Fixed costs (6% growth)	1,060	1,124	1,191
Depreciation (W2)	134	144	155
Total operating costs	2,012	2,159	2,317

(2)   Non-current assets and depreciation

Non-current assets at beginning	1,266	1,345	1,440
Additions (20% growth)	79	95	114
Non-current assets	1,345	1,440	1,554
Depreciation (10%)	134	144	155

(3)   Working capital

Working capital (9% growth)	240	261	285
Incremental WC	240−220=20	261−240=21	285−261=24

Initial working capital equals net current assets less cash. Alternatively, the full 270 can be used as working capital as well. Credit will be given for either assumption.

(4)   Taxation

One year in arrears (30%)	15 (given)	30%×(168−74)	30%×(218−74)
		= 28	= 43

(b)   Value of the equity

Our estimate of the value of this firm's equity on a going concern basis assumes that cash will be generated and reinvestment made according to the above projection. The free cash flow after reinvestment which is potentially distributable and the terminal value of the business assuming a constant rate of reinvestment of 3% forward is as follows:

	0	1	2	3
Free cash flow after reinvestment		114	144	173
Terminal value				2,546
Required rate of return	10%			
Present value of cash flows (discounted at 10%)		104	119	2,043
Value of equity	2,266			

The terminal value is calculated as follows:

$$Value_3 = \frac{FCFE_3(1.03)}{R_e - 3\%} = \frac{173 \times (1.03)}{10\% - 3\%} = 2,546 \ (\$000)$$

Where Re is the required rate of return of 10% per year.

The value of equity on the basis of the above projections, is $2,266,000.

(c)   Assumptions and uncertainties

This valuation is based on a number of assumptions which you should consider when reviewing this analysis. We have taken your judgement that 10% fairly reflects the market rate of return required for an investment of this type. This rate should compensate you for the business risk to which your firm is exposed. For an investment held within the context of a widely diversified portfolio the rate of return you should expect will only be conditioned by your exposure to market risk. However, in the context of a sole equity investment then the rate of return you may require could be more than that which would be available from the market for an investment of this type.

In generating our projections we have assumed the estimates are certain and that the firm is a going concern. In considering this investment further you may wish to explicitly consider the variability attaching to the underlying variables in the projection and the possible range of values that may result. Of particular importance is the assumption of a three-year forecast. In practice the period chosen does depend upon the nature of the business and in particular the uncertainties to which it is exposed.

Finally we have assumed a terminal value based on future cash flows from year three forward growing at a compound rate of 3% into the indefinite future. The resulting value will be particularly sensitive to this figure and it may be that you may wish to consider a different rate depending on what you regard as sustainable in the long term for a business of this type.

(d) **Option pricing theory**

In considering the value of this business you should note that the company has a very high level of gearing and that this imparts additional value to you through your possession of limited liability. The value quoted above is a fair value of the business in your hands based on the expected value of the future cash flows of the enterprise accruing to you. This is the equivalent of the fair value of the firm's assets less its outstanding liabilities including its debt.

However, the possession of limited liability gives you an effective call option on the value of the business against the lenders in that *in extremis*, if the value of your equity fell to zero, you could liquidate and the lenders would bear any loss. As shareholders you have the potential of "upside" gains but are not exposed to downside losses. This advantage on the upside means that your limited liability represents an asymmetric claim on the business and this is a valuable right which is particularly important during the growth stage of a business.

This additional value is termed its "structural value" and it is at its maximum when the value of the assets of the firm approximate to the value of the outstanding debt but it diminishes as that differential widens. A structural valuation of your firm could be undertaken but would need estimates of the volatility of the returns generated by the firm's assets and the length of time which the debt will be held to maturity.

Answer 17 MLIMA CO

(a) **Report to the Board of Directors, Mlima Co**

Initial public listing: price range and implications

This report considers a range of values of Mlima and possible share price, based on 100 million issued shares in preparation of the initial public listing. The assumptions made in determining the value range and the likelihood of the unsecured bond holders accepting the 10% equity-for-debt swap offer are discussed. Alternative reasons for the listing and reasons for issuing the share at a discount are evaluated.

Cost of capital explanation

Ziwa's ungeared cost of equity represents the return Ziwa's shareholders would require if Ziwa was financed entirely by equity and had no debt. The return would compensate them for the business risk undertaken by the company.

This required rate of return would compensate Mlima's shareholders as well because, since both companies are in the same industry, they face the same business risk. This rate is then used as Mlima's cost of capital because of the assumption that Mlima will not issue any debt and faces no financial risk. Therefore its cost of equity (ungeared) is its cost of capital.

Estimated value

Based on a cost of capital of 11% (Appendix 1), the value of Mlima is estimated at $564·3m (Appendix 2), prior to considering the impact of the Bahari project. The value of the Bahari project, without taking into account the benefits of the tax shield and the subsidies, does not exceed the initial investment. With the benefits of the tax shield and subsidies, it is estimated that the project will generate a positive NPV of $21·5m (Appendix 3). Taking the Bahari project into account gives a value for Mlima at just under $586m.

Possible share price (100m shares)	*Without the Bahari project*	*With the Bahari project*
At full value	$5·64 per share	$5·86 per share
With 20% discount	$4·51 per share	$4·69 per share

Unsecured bond holders (equity-for-debt swap)

The current value of the unsecured bond is estimated at $56·8m (Appendix 4) and if the unsecured bond holders are to be offered a 10% equity stake in Mlima post-listing, then only the share price at $5·86 would be acceptable to them. If the listing is made at the lowest price of $4·51 per share, then they would need to be offered around a 12·6% equity stake ($56·8m ÷ $4·51 = 12·594m).

The value of the bond is based on a flat yield curve (or yield to maturity) of 7%, which is the rate at which Mlima can borrow funds and therefore its current yield. A more accurate method would be to assess the yield curve based on future risk-free rates and credit spreads for the company.

Assumptions

The main assumptions made are around the accuracy of the information used in estimating the values of the company and the project. For example, the value of the company is based on assumptions of future growth rates, profit margins, future tax rates and capital investment. The basis for estimating the future growth rates and profit margins may not be accurate. With the Bahari project projections of future cash flows are made for 15 years and the variability of these has been estimated. The reasonableness of these estimates needs to be assessed. Are they based on past experience and/or have professional experts judged the values?

The cost of capital is estimated based on a competitor's ungeared cost of equity, on the basis that Mlima is in a similar line of business and therefore faces similar business risk. The financial risk element has been removed since it has been stated that Mlima is not looking to raise extra debt finance. However, it is possible that the business risks faced by Mlima and that faced by Ziwa, the competitor, are not the same. Accepting the Bahari project would also change the risk profile of Mlima and therefore its discount rate.

The values are based on the Bahari government fulfilling the subsidised loan concession it has offered. Mlima needs to consider the likelihood of this concession continuing for the entire 15 years and whether a change of government may jeopardise the agreement. The political and other risks need to be assessed and their impact assessed.

It has been assumed that the underwriting and other costs involved with the new listing are not significant or have been catered for, before the assessment of the cash flows. This assumption needs to be reviewed and its accuracy assessed.

Reasons for the public listing

The main reason given for the public listing is to use the funds raised to eliminate the debt in the company. There are other reasons why a company may undertake a public listing. These include: gaining a higher reputation by being listed and therefore reducing the costs of contracting with stakeholders; being able to raise funds more easily in the future; the listing will provide the current owners with a value for their equity stake; and the listing may enable the current owners to sell their equity stakes and gain from the value in the organisation.

Issuing shares at a discount

Issuing only 20% of the share capital to the public at the initial listing would make them minority shareholders effectively. As such, their ability to influence the decision-making process in the company would be severely curtailed, since even if all the new investors voted as a bloc against a decision, they would not be able to overturn it. The discounted share price would reflect the additional risk of investing in a company as a minority shareholder. In this case, the position of the unsecured bond holders is important. If the unsecured bond holders, holding between 10% and 12·6% of the share capital in an equity-for-debt swap, are included with the new investors, then the equity stake rises to 30%–32·6%. In such a case, shareholders, as a bloc, would have a significant influence on the company's decisions. The question that should be asked is whether the current unsecured bond holders are more closely aligned to the interests of the current owners or to the interests of the new investors.

The second reason for issuing shares at a discount is to ensure that they do all get sold and as a reward for the underwriters. Research suggests that, normally, for new listings, shares are issued at a discount and the price of such shares rises immediately after launch.

Conclusion

The report and the calculations in the appendices suggest a price range for the listing of between $4·51 and $5·86 per share, depending on whether or not the Bahari project is undertaken, the discount at which the shares are issued and the assumptions made. It is recommended that Mlima should consult its underwriters and potential investors about the possible price they would be willing to pay before making a final decision (known as book-building).

If 20 million shares are offered to the public for $4·51 each, this will result in total funds raised of just over $90 million. If $80 million is then spent in paying for the secured bond, just over $10 million liquid funds remain. Therefore, Mlima needs to consider whether issuing the shares at a discount would ensure sufficient liquid funds are available for it to continue its normal business. In addition to this, the Bahari investment may result in a change in the desired capital structure of the company and have an impact on the cost of capital. Finally, being listed will result in additional listing costs and annual costs related to additional reporting requirements.

These factors should be balanced against the benefits of undertaking the new listing before a final decision is made.

Report compiled by:

Date:

APPENDICES

Appendix 1 – Cost of capital

Ziwa
MV debt = $1,700m × 1·05 = $1,785m
MV equity = 200m × $7 = $1,400m

Ziwa, ungeared Ke
$K_{e(g)} = K_{e(u)} + (1 - t) (K_{e(u)} - K_d)$ Debt/Equity
$16·83\% = K_{e(u)} + 0·75 × (K_{e(u)} - 4·76\%) × 1,785 ÷ 1,400$
$16·83\% + 4·55\% = 1·9563 × K_{e(u)}$
$K_{e(u)} = 10·93\%$ (say 11%)

Appendix 2 – Estimate of value prior to Bahari project

Value based on future free cash flows

Historic mean sales revenue growth = $\sqrt{(389·1 ÷ 344·7)} - 1 = 0·625$ or 6·25%
Next four years annual growth rate of sales revenue = 120% of 6·25% = 7·5%
Thereafter 3·5% of cash flows per annum
Operating profit margin (approx) = 15%
(58·4 ÷ 389·1, 54·9 ÷ 366·3 and 51·7 ÷ 344·7 all approximately 15%)

Year (in $ millions)	1	2	3	4
Sales revenue	418·3	449·7	483·4	519·7
Operating profit	62·7	67·5	72·5	78·0
Less taxation (25%)	(15·7)	(16·9)	(18·1)	(19·5)
Less additional capital investment (30c per $1 change in sales revenue)	(8·8)	(9·4)	(10·1)	(10·9)
Free cash flows	38·2	41·2	44·3	47·6
PV of free cash flows (11%)	34·4	33·4	32·4	31·4

PV first four years — $131·6m
PV after four years $(47·6 × 1·035) ÷ (0·11 - 0·035) × 1·11^{-4}$ — $432·7m

Value of company — $564·3m

Appendix 3 – Value of the Bahari project

Base case present value

Year	Free Cash flows (in $ millions)	PV (11%) (in $ millions)
1	4·0	3·6
2	8·0	6·5
3	16·0	11·7
4	18·4	12·1
5	21·2	12·6
6 to 15	21·2	**74·0
Total		120·5

** The free cash flows in years 6 to 15 are an annuity for 10 years at 11%, then discounted back for five years: $21 \cdot 2 \times 5 \cdot 889 \times 0 \cdot 593 = 74 \cdot 0$

PV of the tax shield and subsidy
Annuity factor (7%, 15 years) = $9 \cdot 108$
Annual tax shield benefit interest paid = $3\% \times \$150m \times 25\% = \$1 \cdot 1m$
Subsidy benefit = $4\% \times \$150m \times (1 - 25\%) = \$4 \cdot 5m$
PV of tax shield and subsidy benefit = $5 \cdot 6 \times 9 \cdot 108 = \$51 \cdot 0m$
Adjusted present value = $\$120 \cdot 5m + \$51 \cdot 0m - \$150 \cdot 0m = \$21 \cdot 5m$

Appendix 4 – Estimated value of the unsecured bond

Assume a flat yield or yield to maturity of 7%
Annual coupon interest = $\$5 \cdot 2m$ ($13\% \times \$40m$)
10-year annuity at 7% = $7 \cdot 024$; Discount factor (10 years, 7%) = $0 \cdot 508$
Bond value = $\$5 \cdot 2m \times 7 \cdot 024 + \$40m \times 0 \cdot 508 = \$56 \cdot 8m$

(b)   Ethical issues

It is likely that Mlima's actions will be scrutinised more closely in the run up to the listing and once it has been listed. In both the situations, the company should consider the action it should take based on its ethical and accountability code. Most major corporations now publicise such codes of behaviour and would consult these in cases of ethical and/or accountability difficulties.

With the first situation concerning the relocation of the farmers, Mlima would consult its ethical code to judge how far its responsibility lay. It may take the view that the matter is between the farmers and the government, and it is not directly or indirectly responsible for the situation. In any case, it is likely that the mining rights will be assigned to another company, should Mlima decide to walk away from the deal. It is unlikely that, even if Mlima did not agree to the offer, the plight of the farmers would cease.

Instead, Mlima may decide to try to influence the government with respect to the farmers by urging the government to keep the community together and offer the farmers better land. Mlima may also decide to offer jobs and training to farmers who decide not to leave.

With the second situation concerning the Bahari president and Mlima's CEO, although it would make good business sense to forge strong relationships as a means of competitive advantage, Mlima should ensure that the negotiation was transparent and did not involve any bribery or illegal practice. If both the company and Bahari government can demonstrate that they acted in the best interests of the company and the country respectively, and individuals did not benefit as a result, then this should not be seen in a negative light.

Mlima needs to establish a clear strategy of how it would respond to public scrutiny of either issue. This may include actions such as demonstrating that it is acting according to its ethical code, pre-empting media scrutiny by releasing press statements, and using its influence to ensure the best and correct outcome in each case for the stakeholders concerned.

Tutorial note: *Credit will be given for alternative, relevant approaches to the calculations, comments and suggestions/recommendations.*

Answer 18 INTERGRAND CO

(a)   **Establishing an overseas operating subsidiary**

(i)   Advantages of organic growth

Organic growth is internal growth, achieved by expansion of existing business or investment in new projects. One advantage is that any investment can be planned exactly to the needs of the organisation. A further advantage is that organic growth tends by definition to be in a related area, thus overcoming the problems which arise from diversification into non-core areas, which might substantially increase the risk of failure. Organic growth also avoids the payment of a considerable premium over the existing market price that is often required in an acquisition. This premium is not always justified by expected savings/synergies.

(ii)   Advantages of acquisition

- Growth, market penetration, access to new markets or productive capacity may be achieved at a much quicker rate by buying existing operations.

- High start-up costs are avoided.

- Barriers to entry in an industry or country may be avoided.

- The acquisition may remove an actual or potential competitor from the market.

- The bidder acquires an instant market share, probable expertise of local markets, and an existing "reputation" of the acquired company. In a foreign country with different language, culture, business practices and accounting, tax and legal systems such expertise is essential.

- They may offer advantages that do not exist with organic growth. These include possible synergy, asset stripping, acquisition of skilled managers or labour, brands, patents and trademarks, acquisition of "surplus" cash or tax losses.

The relative risk of acquisitions and organic growth is important. This is not always easy to quantify, but an acquisition in a foreign country would normally be less risky than an organic start-up situation.

(b)   **Report on the possible acquisition of Oberberg AG**

In financial terms, Oberberg should be purchased if the expected adjusted present value (APV) of the acquisition is positive, in other words the incremental cash flows exceed the price to be paid. However, it is important that the acquisition fits well with the strategic plans of Intergrand, and strategic issues or other non-financial considerations might outweigh the financial findings.

Expected operating cash flows of Oberberg

Year	2016 €m	20174 €m	2018 €m	2019 €m
Sales	38·2	41·2	44·0	49·0
Savings from synergies	–	2·0	2·0	2·0
	38·2	43·2	46·0	51·0
Labour	11·0	12·1	13·0	14·1
Materials	8·3	8·7	9·0	9·4
Overheads	3·2	3·2	3·3	3·4
Tax allowable depreciation	6·3	5·8	5·6	5·2
	28·8	29·8	30·9	32·1
Taxable profit	9·4	13·4	15·1	18·9
Taxation (25%)	(2·4)	(3·4)	(3·8)	(4·7)
	7·0	10·0	11·3	14·2
Add back depreciation	6·3	5·8	5·6	5·2
Incremental operating working capital	(0·7)	(0·9)	(1·0)	(2·0)
Replacement investment	(4·2)	(4·2)	(4·2)	(4·2)
Operating free cash flows	8·4	10·7	11·7	13·2
Discount factors (9%)	0·917	0·842	0·772	0·708
Present values	7·7	9·0	9·0	9·3

Cash flows after 2019 are expected to grow at 2% per year. Based on the present value to infinity such cash flows are valued at $\dfrac{13 \cdot 2(1 \cdot 02)}{0 \cdot 09 - 0 \cdot 02} = 192 \cdot 3$

$192 \cdot 3 \times 0 \cdot 708 = 136 \cdot 2$

The present value of operating free cash flows is €171·2 million.

Notes

The free cash flows of Oberberg should be discounted at a rate reflecting the risk of Oberberg. Assuming corporate debt to be virtually risk free, the ungeared beta of Oberberg may be estimated using:

$$\text{Beta asset} = \text{Beta equity} \times \frac{E}{E + D(1 - t)}$$

E, the market value of equity is 150,000 shares × €300 per share = €45 million
D, the market value of debt is (18 million × 1.230) + 30 million = €52.14 million

$$\text{Beta asset} = 1 \cdot 4 \times \frac{45}{45 + 52 \cdot 14(1 - 0 \cdot 25)} = 0 \cdot 75$$

Using CAPM, the cost of equity for Oberberg without gearing is:

$4\% + (11\% - 4\%) \, 0 \cdot 75 = 9 \cdot 25\%$

9% will be used as the discount rate for operating cash flows.

Present values of other relevant cash flows

	€m
Additional home country tax	(10·5)
Publicity benefit	7·0
Lost exports	(4·3)
Sale of assets	8·0
Redundancy	(5·0)
Investment for expansion	(6·8)
Tax relief benefits from debt	13·0
	————
	1·4
	————

Notes

(i)   Extra taxation. As the tax rate in the home country is 5% higher than in Germany, an extra tax liability would arise after acquisition.

Year	2016	2017	2018	2019
	€m	€m	€m	€m
Taxable	9·4	13·4	15·1	18·9
Extra tax (5%)	(0·47)	(0·67)	(0·76)	(0·95)
Discount factors (10%)	0·909	0·826	0·751	0·683
Present values	(0·43)	(0·55)	(0·57)	(0·65)

Extra tax after 2019 is assumed to grow at 2% per year. Based on the present value to infinity such cash flows are valued at $\dfrac{0·95(1·02)}{0·10-0·02} = (12·11) \times 0·683 = (8·27)$

Total present value of extra tax is €10·47 million.

The cost of capital of Intergrand has been used as the discount rate.

(ii)   The benefit of extra publicity is €1 million per year, less tax relief (as the cost of advertising to Intergrand would have been net of tax relief).The present value to infinity of this is $\dfrac{0·7}{0·10} = 7·0$ million, using Intergrand's discount rate of 10%.

(iii)   The investment should be charged with the lost export cash flows. After tax these are $\$800,000 \times 0·5 \times (1 - 0·3) = \$280,000$ per year. However, using the purchasing power parity theory the dollar is expected to fall in value by $\dfrac{1·04}{1·02} = 1·0196$ or 1·96% per year.

Expected exchange rates are:

Year	2016	2017	2018	2019
€ per $	1·594	1·563	1·533	1·504
$280,000 in €	446·3	437·6	429·2	421·1
Discount factors at 10%	0·909	0·826	0·751	0·683
Present value	405·7	361·5	322·3	287·6

Loss after 2019 is approximately $\dfrac{421·1}{0·10} = 4,211 \times 0·683$ or $= 2,876$

Tutorial note: *The 2019 loss is extrapolated to perpetuity by dividing the 2019 cash flow into the discount rate and then multiplying by a 4-year discount factor (as the perpetuity starts at T_5 not T_1).*

A quicker way to find the present value of this perpetuity is to take the present value of 2019 cash flow and divide by the discount rate (i.e. 287.6 ÷ 10% = 2876).

This assumes a constant rate between € and $.

The total expected PV from lost exports is 4,253 or €4·3 million

(iv)   Investment for expansion of €9 million in 2018 is included as its effects have been included in the subsequent cash flows.

The present value of this investment, using Intergrand's discount rate, is:

$9 \times 0·751 = 6·8$ million.

(v)   Tax relief from the use of debt

Tax shield	=	$kd \times D \times t$
where kd	=	required return of debt holders ÷ pre-tax cost of debt
D	=	current market value of the debt
t	=	tax rate

If we assume the debt will be refinanced into perpetuity: .

$$\text{PV of tax shield} = \frac{Kd \times D \times t}{kd} = D \times t$$

Market value of bond $= 18 \times 1.23 = 22.14$

Assume market value of loans = book value = 30

Total value of debt $= 52.14$

Present value of tax shield $= 52.14 \times 0.25 = 13$

(vi)   Cash spent on researching acquisition targets is a sunk cost, and therefore irrelevant to the decision.

The expected adjusted present value (APV) is:

	€m
Operating cash flows	171·2
Other incremental cash flows	1·4
Value of the firm	172·6

However, in order to estimate the price to be paid for Oberberg's shares the market value of any outstanding debt should be subtracted. For Oberberg these total €52.14 million.

The maximum price to offer for Oberberg's shares based on estimated cash flows to infinity is $172·6 – 52.14 = €120.46$ million.

This is only slightly above the asking price of €115 million, and is subject to a considerable margin of error.

Factors that Intergrand should consider prior to making a final decision include:

(i)   Cash flows to infinity are used. The present value of cash flows beyond 2019 constitutes the majority of Oberberg's value. If a shorter time horizon were used the present values would be much less.

(ii)   The results are based on forecasts by the managers of Oberberg. The assumptions behind these forecasts need to be examined to assess the likely validity of the forecasts.

(iii)   A single estimate of the APV is of limited value. Sensitivity analysis or simulation analysis should be undertaken to examine the impact of cash flows differing from those projected.

(iv)   The data does not take into account any future embedded options that might arise from the purchase of Oberberg. Such options could increase the expected APV.

(v)   The risk of the investment might be inaccurately estimated, and this risk could change over time.

(vi)   Tax rates and tax allowance rules might alter.

(vii)   If the Euro continues to appreciate in value the dollar economic value of the investment might increase, although economic exposure such as this is difficult to quantify.

(viii) There is no certainty that the lost exports can be diverted to an alternative market.

(ix)   There is no information on the size of Intergrand, and how important the acquisition is relative to the total activities of Intergrand. If it is of major importance much more research needs to be undertaken into the proposed acquisition in terms of how integration would occur, including organisational structures, cultures and human resource policies.

(x)   Do alternative investments exist that would be a better strategic fit for Intergrand, or have a higher expected NPV/APV?

(xi)   Will the two organisations integrate successfully? Are there significant differences in organisational cultures?

(xii)   Will key staff of Oberberg stay on after the acquisition?

(xiii) What will be the effect on morale within Oberberg of the redundancies and asset disposals?

(xiv)   Would Intergrand need to make any additional investment in Oberberg?

Answer 19 FLIHI

(a)   **Current cost of equity capital**

The cost of equity capital is derived from the CAPM but given that FliHi is an unquoted company a proxy must be used to estimate the company's equity beta, adjusted to reflect the financial risk exposure of FliHi.

Rover Airways appears to be a suitable proxy. First degear Rover's equity beta to an asset beta, assuming the debt of debt is zero:

$$\beta_a = \frac{V_d(1-T)}{V_e + V_d(1-T)} \beta e = \frac{3}{(3 + 4.5(1 - 0.30))} \times 2 = 0.9756$$

Now regear to FliHi's gearing level, using book values of equity and debt in the absence of market values:

Calculate the tax adjusted gearing ratio for FliHi.

$$\beta_a = \frac{V_d(1-T)}{V_e + V_d(1-T)} \beta e$$

$$0.9756 = \frac{120}{(120 + 150(1 - 0.3))} \beta e$$

$$\beta_e = 1.8294$$

This is the estimated equity beta for FliHi which, when applied to the CAPM, gives an expected rate of return as follows:

$$0.045 + (1.8294 \times 0.035) = 10.9\%$$

The equity cost of capital for FliHi is therefore approximately 10.9%.

The modelling of the equity cost of capital has embedded within it the assumptions implicit in the CAPM that:

- Investors are mean variance efficient;
- Markets are frictionless;
- Expectations are homogenous; and
- There is a risk free asset.

However, of more practical significance we have also assumed that:

- The underlying exposure to market risk is the same for both companies (this is questionable given the differences in the markets in which they operate).

- That the book gearing ratio is a reasonable approximation to the market gearing ratio. The use of book values, can seriously distort the cost of capital that is calculated converting it into a measure of the average cost of capital in the firm's historical gearing ratio rather than in the ratio of the current capitalised values of the firm's equity and debt.

- That FliHi does not carry a size and default premium on its cost of capital. Default and size premiums can be included through the use of such variants on the standard CAPM as the Fama and French 3 factor model which incorporates these elements of risk.

(b)   **Expected growth rate**

Gordon's approximation requires a retention ratio which can be derived from the cash flow statement. The free cash flow to equity (before reinvestment) is defined as operating cash flow less interest and tax:

For 2016 the FCFE is as follows:

FCFE = operating cash flow – net interest paid – tax
FCFE ($m) = 210 + 1.5 – 4.1 = $207.4 million

In the current year $120.2m was reinvested. This implies a retention ratio (b) of:

$$b = \frac{reinvestment}{FCFE} = \frac{120.2}{207.4} = 0.58$$

Tutorial note: *It could be argued that reinvestment during the year = CAPEX less disposal proceeds (120.2 – 10 = 110.2). The examiner would accept this approach but does not make the adjustment as (i) it is not known whether management disposed of the JV in order to finance investment or to increase dividends, and (ii) proceeds from disposal in JV is a non-recurring item.*

Gordon's approximation was originally developed to measure the growth in earnings assuming a given retention ratio and rate of return. We can apply the same logic to the free cash flow model but here we are looking at the rate of cash generation by the business on new capital investment. The current rate of return is, in principle, the internal rate of return (IRR) on the current business portfolio. Assuming that the business is highly competitive then the IRR will be close to the company's equity cost of capital. Growth is therefore expected to be:

$$g = b \times r_e = 0.58 \times 0.1090 = 0.06322 \ (= 6.322\%)$$

Tutorial note: *There is a problem in using Gordon's model in this way. Although the retention ratio has been estimated as 58%, not all of this would be growth expenditure; some would be for routine replacement of existing assets. No data is given about the split. The depreciation expense, if known, could arguably be used as a proxy for replacement expenditure. Even better would be an estimate of "economic depreciation" which estimates the cash required to maintain existing assets. As always, in an exam of this level, candidates are advised to do the best they can with the information given, explain their method, write their assumptions and state what additional data would be required to improve their analysis.*

Using the company's current rate of return on equity from the accounts gives:

$$ROE = \frac{Net\,profit}{Equity\,employed\,(net\,assets)} = \frac{50}{120} = 42\%$$

This would suggest a rate of growth of 24.2% which is unlikely in this industry.

On the basis of a growth rate of 6.322% and given that the year six growth rate and forward will be 4%, the pattern of growth we anticipate is therefore:

Year	1	2	3	4	5	6
Growth rate	6.322%	6.322%	6.322%	6.322%	6.322%	4.00%

The assumptions here are embedded within the method of measuring growth. Gordon's growth approximation will give the next year value for the FCFE for the business on the assumption that the cost of capital is achieved and no more.

We have also assumed that the current figures for cash generation and reinvestment are typical and likely to be replicated over the near term. In this context we would note the significant increase in operating cash flow from 2015 and question whether this was sustainable.

(c)   **Expected free cash flow to equity**

Using the free cash flow to equity net of reinvestment we have the free cash flow which is, in principle, distributable. We build a valuation model expanding this free cash flow through the next five years. From year six forward the rate of growth is a perpetuity and we use the free cash flow analogue of the dividend growth model to estimate the value at year six.

Step 1: take the growth rates as projected and estimate the future free cash flow to equity taking ($207.4m – $120.2m=$87.2m) as the starting point.

Step 2: discount these projected values at the cost of equity capital (10.9%) to give a present value of $384.89 million.

Step 3: using the formula: $V_e = \dfrac{FCFE_0(1+g)}{re - g}$

Calculate the value of the growing perpetuity at the end of year 6 (note the timing of the year is important) using the expected FCFE in year 5. This gives a value at year 5 of $1,785.73.

Step 4: discount this at 10.9% to give a present value of the residual term of $1,064.53

Step 5: add the two present values to give a valuation of the firm's equity at $1,449.42.

Year	2017	2018	2019	2020	2021	2022
Growth	6.32%	6.32%	6.32%	6.32%	6.32%	4.00%
FCFE (2016) = $87.2m	92.71	98.57	104.81	111.43	118.48	
Discount at 10.9%	83.60	80.15	76.84	73.67	70.63	
PV of year 1–6	$384.89					
PV of perpetuity at 2022					$1,785.73	
PV of perpetuity at 2016	$1,064.53					
PV of the firm's equity	$1,449.42					

The limitations of the method are that it assumes:

- the current operating cash flows are sustainable;
- the constant patterns of growth of operating cash flow will be achieved as specified;
- the rate of return required by investors is constant throughout the life of the business;
- the business has an indefinite life beyond 2022.

These assumptions are unlikely to hold in practice and it should be noted that where the rate of growth (4%) is relatively low compared with the cost of equity that we would not expect the perpetuity to be a good approximation of residual value. It might be better to seek a likely break-up value from the accounts as the residual value of the business. If we take the company's net asset figure and extrapolate forward at the rate of growth as shown above we obtain a figure of $169.55 million in 2022 which has a present value of $91.14 million. This would put a value on the business of $476.03 million.

This incidentally gives a closer approximation to the market valuation if we apply the Rover Airlines PE ratio to FliHi's net profit figure:

Value   = benchmark PE × FliHi Earnings
                 = 11.0 × $50 million = $550 million

(d)   **Considerations when contemplating this acquisition**

The proposed acquisition of FliHi represents a substantial capital investment for your airline. However, there are a number of issues which you might wish to consider before making a bid. These issues I have separated into synergies, risk exposure, future options, financing and valuation.

Synergies: From the perspective of your respective markets there would appear to be considerable advantage in integration.   From the synergistic perspective these can be categorised as:

- **Revenue** synergies: is there likely to be an enhancement in your ability to capture market share in a way that will add shareholder value. Simply acquiring the business as it stands will not be sufficient as investors can achieve the same at lower cost by diversification. Synergies only arise if a market opportunity presents itself which would not exist if both firms remain independent. One example would be where the domestic and European service can be used as a feeder system for an expanded long haul business from your principal airport and centre of operations.

- **Cost** synergies: are there opportunities to save cost through more efficient operations? Economies of scale and scope are available in the airline business in the areas of in-flight catering, fuel supplies, maintenance and ticketing. The larger fleet size would also present operational opportunities.

- **Financial** synergies: would the company have greater opportunities in the domestic and international capital market to acquire finance at more favourable rates and under better conditions.

Risk exposure: the larger operation would not necessarily improve the firm's exposure to market risk and indeed is likely to leave it unchanged as we would expect the underlying asset beta of both firms to be the same.   There are a number of other risk areas that could be improved: operational risk may be mitigated by the firm's increased ability to hedge its operations (see the notes on the real options available below).   Other risk effects include: economic, political, transactions and translation.   Some of these are minimised (transactions) largely because your business is principally in the domestic market.

Future options: an acquisition of this type can create real options to expand, redeploy and exchange resources which add value to the proposition not easily captured with conventional valuation procedures. A real option is a claim upon some future course of action which can be exercised at your discretion. The availability of the new Airbus 380 offers potential both within the long haul business but also to medium haul holiday destinations at peak seasons. Access to your fleet of short to medium range aircraft offers the possibility of opening the European market to your long haul business. When and how you exercise these real options depends on circumstances at the time but paradoxically the more uncertain the underlying business the greater the value that attaches to this flexibility.

Financing: an acquisition of this type would require substantial extra financing. FliHi would appear to have a high level of off balance sheet value partly because of the scale of their operational leasing of aircraft but more significantly because of their business name and the quality of their operations.   A substantial sum is likely to be paid for the goodwill of this business which suggests that this may not be a proposition that would be attractive to the debt market. Your own substantial cash reserves and the level of retained earnings suggest that this may be the route to financing this acquisition through a cash offer plus shares.

Valuation: we estimate the value of FliHi based on its current cash flow generation to be of the order of $1.450 billion. Using market multiples a lower figure of $550 million is obtained. The key point of this valuation process is to determine the lowest likely figure that the owners of FliHi would be prepared to accept. Our judgement is that the figure is likely to be closer to the upper end of this range. The free cash flow model relies upon our best forecast of future cash flow and reinvestment within the business. We believe that the owners of FliHi would have access to similar advice. The key question now to resolve is what would be the value of FliHi to your company. This has most of the characteristics of a type 2 acquisition where the financial risk of the business is likely to be disturbed. For this reason we would need to value your current business using available market data and revalue it on the basis that the bid goes ahead using your preferred financing package. The potential increase in the value of your firm will reveal the potential control premium at any proposed offer price that may be decided upon.

Answer 20 BURCOLENE

(a)   **Weighted average cost of capital and the current entity value**

The first step in the valuation is to calculate each company's WACC. The cost of capital is calculated post-tax and using the relevant market values to calculate the market gearing ratio.

	Burcolene	PetroFrancais
Cost of equity (using the CAPM, 3% risk free and 4% equity risk premium)	$03 + 1·85 × 0·04$ = 0·104	$03 + 0·95 × 0·04$ = 0·068
Market gearing	$3·3 ÷ (3·3 + 9·9) = 0·25$	$5·8 ÷ (5·8 + 6·7) = 0·464$
Cost of debt	$0·03 + 0·016 = 0·046$	$0·03 + 0·03 = 0·06$
WACC	$0·75 × 104 + 25 × 046 × 0·7$ = 0·0861	$0·536 ×·068 + 464 × 06 × 0·75$ = 0·0573

The core valuation formula is: $V_0 = \dfrac{FCF_1}{WACC - g}$

As free cash flow is NOPAT – net reinvestment then:

$$V_0 = \frac{FCF_1}{WACC - g} = \frac{(NOPAT - \text{net reinvestment})_1}{WACC - g}$$

The figures quoted are for NOPAT – reinvestment for the current year. For the two companies the value before either pension or share option scheme adjustments is therefore (in $):

$$V_B = \frac{450 × (1·05)}{0·0861\ 0·05} = \$13·107bn \quad \text{and} \quad V_P = \frac{205 × (1·04)}{0·0573\ 0·04} = \$12·303bn$$

However, the respective company values will need to be reduced by the relevant charge for the outstanding options and the pension deficit. Using the fair value approach the value of each option outstanding is given by:

Option value = intrinsic value + time value
Option value = (actual price – exercise price) + time value
Option value = 29·12 – 22·00 + 7·31 = $14·43

Tutorial note: *The actual price is given by the total value of equity $9·9bn ÷ 340m = $29·12 per share.*

The number of options likely to be exercised= $25·4m × (1 – 0·05)^3 × 0·8 = 17·42$ million

Tutorial note: *The model answer uses three years' attrition in the number of options. An alternative would be to show two years' attrition (i.e. between now and the vesting date).*

Which gives a value of options outstanding = $251·4m.

And an estimated market valuation of Burcolene of:

$V_B = \$13\cdot107bn - \$251\cdot35m = \$12\cdot855bn$

The value of PetroFrancais is much more straightforward being:

$V_P = \$12\cdot303bn - \$430m = \$11\cdot873bn$

(b)   **Report to management**

Subject: Valuation and Financial Implications of an Acquisition of PetroFrancais

This is potentially a type III acquisition where both the firm's exposure to business risk and financial risk change. The value of the combined entity will depend upon the post-acquisition values of the component cash streams: (i) the cash flow from the existing business; (ii) the cash flow from the acquired business and (iii) any synergistic cash flows less the cost of acquisition.

However, estimating the value of these cash flows relies upon an estimate of the post-acquisition required rate of return – which cannot be estimated until we know the value of the component cash flows. This problem requires an iterative solution and which can be solved using a spreadsheet package.

Validity of the Free Cash Flow to the Firm Model

Our estimates of the value using NOPAT as a proxy for free cash flow produces values that are reasonably close to the current market valuation of both companies. The models value Burcolene at $12·855 billion and PetroFrancais at $11·873 billion compared with current market valuations of $13·1 billion and $12·5 billion respectively. The estimation error is 1·9% and 5·3% respectively.

Tutorial note: *$13.1bn is the quoted entity value of Burcolene (i.e. market value of equity plus market value of debt (9.9 + 3.3)).*

Although minor the differences can be explained by any of the following:

- The model used may mis-specify the market valuation process. In either case NOPAT may not be a sufficiently close approximation to each firm's free cash flow.

- The underpinning models in the cost of capital calculations may not be valid. The capital asset pricing model, for example, does not capture fully all the risk elements that are priced in competitive markets.

- The estimates of growth may be overoptimistic (both valuations are highly sensitive to variation in the implied level of growth).

- The markets may have reacted positively to rumours of an acquisition.

- The capital markets may be inefficient.

However, on the basis of this preliminary analysis, the low levels of modelling error suggest that the NOPAT based model should form the basis for valuing a combined business.

Deriving a bid price

In preparation of an offer, a due diligence process should, as part of its brief, consider the likely growth of each cash stream within the context of the combined business and the variability associated with the future growth rates of each cash stream. This information could then be used to estimate the firm's future cash flows (i) to (iii) above using a cost of capital derived from the current required rates of return and market values.

An iterative procedure can then be used to bring the derived values into agreement with those used to estimate the firm's cost of capital. This valuation less the cost of acquisition and the firm's current debt gives the post-acquisition equity value. The maximum price that should be paid for PetroFrancais is that which leaves the equity value of Burcolene unchanged.

This estimation process, although procedurally complex, does reinforce a key point with type III acquisitions that the sum of the equity valuation of both parties is not a good indication of the value of the combined business.

Providing the management of Burcolene can come to a reliable valuation of the combined business then, providing they remain within the bid-price parameters, the acquisition should increase shareholder value. Good valuation methods should capture the benefits and the consequential costs of combined operation. In this case, improving equity value for the Burcolene investors depends upon a number of factors. A simulation of the most important parameters in the valuation model: forward growth, the cost of equity, default premiums and the cost of debt should allow Burcolene to estimate the likely equity value at risk given any chosen bid price. A simulation would also provide an estimate of the probability of a loss of equity value for Burcolene's investors at the chosen bid price.

Implications for gearing and cost of capital

Financing an acquisition of this magnitude through debt will raise the book gearing of the business although its impact upon the market gearing of the firm is less easy to predict. Much depends on the magnitude of any surplus shareholder value generated by the combination and how it is distributed. An acquisition such as this will increase market gearing if the benefits accrue to the target shareholders. The reverse may occur if the bulk of the acquisition value accrues to the Burcolene investors. Similarly the impact upon the firm's overall cost of capital, the impact of the tax shield and the exposure to default risk again all depend upon the agreed bid price and the distribution of acquisition value between the two groups of investors.

(c) **Triple Bottom Line**

Tutorial note: *This question could be answered in a variety of ways and the suggested answer below is indicative. Credit would be given for reasonable answers considering alternatives or additions to the explanations and discussion below.*

(i) *TBL reporting and demonstrating sustainable development*

A triple bottom line (TBL) report provides a quantitative summary of a corporation's performance in terms of its economic or financial impact, its impact on environmental quality and its impact on social performance. The principle of TBL reporting is that a corporation's true performance must be measured in terms of a balance between economic (profits), environmental (planet) and social (people) factors; with no one factor growing at the expense of the others.

A corporation's sustainable development is about how these three factors can grow and be combined so that a corporation is building a reputation as being a good citizen. The contention is that a corporation that accommodates the pressures of all the three factors will enhance shareholder value by addressing the needs of its stakeholders.

Whereas TBL reporting is a quantitative summary of the corporation performance in the three factors over a previous time period, say a year, sustainable development tends to be forward looking and qualitative. Therefore TBL provides the measurement tool to assess a corporation's performance against its stated aims.

Each factor can be assessed or measured using a number of proxies. The economic impact can be measured by considering proxies such as operating profits, dependence on imports and the extent to which the local economy is supported by purchasing locally produced goods and services. Social impact can be measured by considering proxies such as working conditions, fair pay, using appropriate labour force (not child labour), ethical investments, and maintenance of appropriate food standards. Environmental impact can be measured by considering proxies such as ecological footprint, emissions to air, water and soil, use of energy and water, investments in renewable resources.

(ii) *How TBL reporting may improve financial position*

An assessment by the management of a corporation's performance in the three factors – economic, environmental and social, that make up the TBL report will result in an improvement in the financial position, if long-term shareholder value is increased as a result of the report being produced. In this case, the benefits that accrue from the assessment and production of a TBL report must exceed the costs of undertaking the report. It is likely to be the case that the costs of producing the report are relatively easy to measure but the financial benefits may be more difficult to measure and may take place over a longer time period. Some examples of the ways in which Burcolene may benefit financially are explained below.

Focusing on and reporting the company's environmental and social impact may build and enhance its reputation. Increasing reputation may increase the long-term revenue of Burcolene. On the other hand, if Burcolene does not follow (or even try to lead) its competitors in this area then the loss of reputation may damage its revenues stream and lower its corporate value.

Consideration and improvement of working standards and consulting employees as part of this process, when assessing social factors, may help in retaining and attracting high performing, high calibre employees. This will benefit Burcolene in the long term because of increased employee motivation and performance. Employee involvement may also help reduce the costs related to the company's risk management activity and thus have a direct cost reduction impact.

Improvement of due diligence procedures as part of the economic factor assessment may help limit direct legal costs and indirect costs incurred in maintaining stakeholder relationships. Communication with stakeholders and thus improving the quality of reporting may result in improvements in governance procedures. This in turn would lead to a reduction of the costs related to risk management.

Assessing and improving the environmental factor impact in the TBL report may result in Burcolene making efforts to reduce its carbon footprint by placing less reliance on exports and developing local expertise in producing the inputs it needs. This may reduce the risk of supplier related problems and alleviate problems related to possible inventory shortfalls. It may also improve Burcolene's reputation, leading to long-term financial benefits.

Monitoring and reporting on the performance of employees and managers as part of the assessment of economic and social factors may help identify areas where work can be done more effectively and efficiently. It may help managers reconsider business processes and question areas where improvements can be made.

In all the above examples, the result of the assessment required in producing the TBL report and comparing the corporation's progress in relation to its aim of becoming a sustainable organisation will create opportunities which senior managers can develop into financial benefits. The extent to which these opportunities are successfully developed depends on the quality of assessment and the organisation's ability to enable change to happen.

Answer 21 PURSUIT CO

Tutorial note: *Up to 4 professional marks were available for the layout, presentation and structure of an answer in the style of a report.*

Report to the Board of Directors of Pursuit Co

(i) **Evaluation of potential acquisition of Fodder Co**

Calculations for this part are given in the Appendix. To assess whether or not the acquisition would be beneficial to Pursuit's shareholders, the additional synergy benefits after the acquisition has been paid for need to be ascertained.

The estimated synergy benefit from the acquisition is approximately $9,074,000 (see Appendix), which is the post-acquisition value of the combined company less the values of the individual companies. However, once Fodder's shareholders have been paid, the benefit to Pursuit's own shareholders reduces to approximately $52,000 (see Appendix), which is minimal. Even a small change in the variables and assumptions could negate this. It is therefore doubtful that Pursuit's shareholders would view the acquisition as beneficial to themselves or the company.

(ii) **Limitations of the estimated valuations**

The limitations of the estimates stem from the fact that although the valuation model used is theoretically sound, it is difficult to apply it in practice for the following reasons.

The calculations in part (i) are based on a number of assumptions such as the growth rate in the next four years, the perpetual growth rate after the four years, additional investment in assets, stable tax rates, discount rates and profit margins and the assumption that debt is risk free when computing the asset beta. All these assumptions would be subject to varying margins of error.

It may be difficult for Pursuit to assess the performance of the combined company to any degree of accuracy and therefore the synergy benefits may be hard to predict.

No information is provided about transaction costs associated with the acquisition.

Although it may be possible to estimate the equity beta of Pursuit, being a listed company, to a high level of accuracy, estimating Fodder's equity beta may be more problematic, because it is a private company.

Given the above, it is probably more accurate to present a range of possible values for the combined company depending on different scenarios and the likelihood of their occurrence, before a decision is made.

(iii) **Evaluation of whether Pursuit's existing capital structure can be maintained**

The current value of Pursuit is $140,000,000, of which the market value of equity and debt are $70,000,000 each. The value of the combined company before paying Fodder's shareholders is approximately $189,169,000 and, if the capital structure is maintained, the market values of debt and equity would be approximately $94,584,500 each. This would be an increase in debt of approximately $24,584,500.

The actual amount payable for Fodder's debt and to its shareholders including the premium is approximately $49,116,500 [4,009 + 36,086 × 1·25]. If $20,000,000 is financed using cash reserves, then additional debt of approximately $29,116,500 will actually need to be raised. Hence, if only debt finance and cash reserves are used, the capital structure cannot be maintained.

(iv) **Implications of change in capital structure**

If Pursuit aims to acquire Fodder using debt finance and cash reserves, then the capital structure of the combined company will change. It will also change if they adopt the Chief Financial Officer's recommendation and acquire Fodder using only debt finance.

Both these options will cause the cost of capital of the combined company to change. This in turn will cause the value of the company to change. This will cause the proportion of market value of equity to market value of debt to change and thus change the cost of capital. Therefore the changes in the market value of the company and the cost of capital are interrelated (i.e. there is a recursive or circular loop between the cost of capital and valuations).

To resolve this problem, an iterative procedure needs to be adopted where the combined equity beta factor and the weighted average cost of capital (WACC) are recalculated to take account of the changes in the capital structure and then the combined company is re-valued. This procedure is repeated until the equity and debt values input into the WACC reconcile to the valuations found by using that WACC to discount the forecast cash flows. This process is normally done using a spreadsheet package such as Excel. This method is used when both the business risk and the financial risk of the acquiring company change as a result of an acquisition (referred to as a type III acquisition).

Alternatively an adjusted present value approach may be undertaken.

(v) **Defending Fodder from a hostile bid**

The Chief Financial Officer's suggestion appears to be a disposal of "crown jewels". Without the cash reserves, Pursuit may become less valuable to SGF. Also, the reason for the depressed share price may be because Pursuit's shareholders do not agree with the policy to retain large cash reserves. Therefore returning the cash reserves to the shareholders may lead to an increase in the share price and make a bid from SGF more unlikely. This would not initially contravene the regulatory framework as no formal bid has been made. However, Pursuit must investigate further whether the reason for a possible bid from SGF might be to gain access to the large amount of cash or it might have other reasons. Pursuit should also try to establish whether remitting the cash to the shareholders would be viewed positively by them.

Whether this is a viable option for Pursuit also depends on the bid for Fodder. In part (iii) it was established that significant debt would be needed even if the cash reserves are used to pay for some of the acquisition cost. If the cash is remitted as a special dividend, a further $20,000,000 of debt would be needed. The increased gearing may have significant implications on Pursuit's future investment plans and may result in increased restrictive covenants. Ultimately gearing might have to increase to such a level that this method of financing might not be possible. Pursuit should investigate the full implications further and assess whether the acquisition is worthwhile given the marginal value it provides for the shareholders (see part (i)).

Appendix

Interest is ignored as its impact is included in the companies' discount rates.

Fodder cost of capital

$Ke = 4 \cdot 5\% + (1 \cdot 53 \times 6\%) = 13 \cdot 68\%$
$WACC = 13 \cdot 68\% \times 0 \cdot 9 + 9\% \times (1 - 0 \cdot 28) \times 0 \cdot 1 = 12 \cdot 96\%$ assume 13%

Fodder

Sales revenue growth rate $= (16,146 \div 13,559)^{1/3} - 1 \times 100\% = 5 \cdot 99\%$ assume 6%
Operating profit margin = approx 32% of sales revenue

Fodder cash flow and value computation ($000)

Year	1	2	3	4
Sales revenue	17,115	18,142	19,231	20,385
Operating profit	5,477	5,805	6,154	6,523
Less tax (28%)	(1,534)	(1,625)	(1,723)	(1,826)
Less additional investment				
(22c/$1 revenue increase)	(213)	(226)	(240)	(254)
Free cash flows	3,730	3,954	4,191	4,443
PV (13%)	3,301	3,097	2,905	2,725

	$(000)
PV (first 4 years)	12,028
PV (after 4 years) $[2,725 \times 1 \cdot 03 \div (0 \cdot 13 - 0 \cdot 03)]$	28,067
Firm value	40,095

Combined company cost of capital calculation

Asset beta (Pursuit) $= 1 \cdot 18 \times 0 \cdot 5 \div (0 \cdot 5 + 0 \cdot 5 \times 0 \cdot 72) = 0 \cdot 686$
Asset beta (Fodder) $= 1 \cdot 53 \times 0 \cdot 9 \div (0 \cdot 9 + 0 \cdot 1 \times 0 \cdot 72) = 1 \cdot 417$
Asset beta of combined company $= (0 \cdot 686 \times 140,000 + 1 \cdot 417 \times 40,095) \div (140,000 + 40,095) = 0 \cdot 849$
Equity beta of combined company $= 0 \cdot 849 \times (0 \cdot 5 + 0 \cdot 5 \times 0 \cdot 72) \div 0 \cdot 5 = 1 \cdot 46$

$Ke = 4 \cdot 5\% + (1 \cdot 46 \times 6\%) = 13 \cdot 26\%$
$WACC = 13 \cdot 26\% \times 0 \cdot 5 + 6 \cdot 4\% \times 0 \cdot 5 \times 0 \cdot 72 = 8 \cdot 93\%$, assume 9%

Combined company cash flow and value computation ($000)

Sales revenue growth rate $= 5 \cdot 8\%$, operating profit margin = 30% of sales revenue

Year	1	2	3	4
Sales revenue	51,952	54,965	58,153	61,526
Operating profit	15,586	16,490	17,446	18,458
Less tax (28%)	(4,364)	(4,617)	(4,885)	(5,168)
Less additional investment				
(18c/$1 revenue increase)	(513)	(542)	(574)	(607)
Free cash flows	10,709	11,331	11,987	12,683
PV (9%)	9,825	9,537	9,256	8,985

PV (first 4 years)	37,603
PV (after 4 years) $[8,985 \times 1 \cdot 029 \div (0 \cdot 09 - 0 \cdot 029)]$	151,566
Firm value	189,169

Synergy benefits $= 189,169,000 - (140,000,000 + 40,095,000) = \$9,074,000$
Estimated premium required to acquire Fodder $= 0 \cdot 25 \times 36,086,000 = \$9,022,000$
Net benefit to Pursuit's shareholders $= \$52,000$

Answer 22 NENTE CO

(i)   **Estimate of Nente Co equity value based on Free Cash Flows**

Company value = Free cash flows (FCF) × (1 + growth rate (g)) ÷ (cost of capital (k) – g)

$k = 11\%$

Past g = (latest profit before interest and tax (PBIT) ÷ earliest PBIT)$^{1/\text{no. of years of growth}}$ – 1

Past g = $(1{,}230 \div 970)^{1/3} - 1 = 0{\cdot}0824$

Future g = ¼ × 0·0824 = 0·0206

FCF calculation

FCF = PBIT + non cash flows – cash investment – tax
FCF = $1,230,000 + $1,206,000 – $1,010,000 – ($1,230,000 × 20%) = $1,180,000

Company value = $1,180,000 × 1·0206 ÷ (0·11 – 0·0206) = $13,471,000
Equity value = $13,471,000 – $6,500,000 = $6,971,000
Per share = $6,971,000 ÷ 2,400,000 shares = $2·90

(ii)   **Estimated returns to Nente Co and Mije Co Shareholders**

Cash offer

Gain in value to a Nente share = ($2·95 – $2·90) ÷ $2·90 = 1·7%

Additional earnings after acquisition = $620,000 + $150,000 = $770,000
Additional EPS created from acquisition = $770,000 ÷ 10,000,000 = 7·7c per share
Increase in share price based on PE of 15 = 7·7c × 15 = $1·16

Additional value created = $1·16 × 10,000,000 =	$11,600,000
Less: paid for Nente acquisition = ($2·95 × 2,400,000 shares)	$(7,080,000)
Value added for Mije shareholders =	$4,520,000

Gain in value to a Mije share ($4,520,000 ÷ 10,000,000)	45·2c
or 45·2c ÷ 480c =	9·4%

Share-for-share offer

Earnings combined company = $620,000 + $150,000 + $3,200,000 = $3,970,000
Shares in combined company = 10,000,000 + 2,400,000 × ²/₃ = 11,600,000
EPS = 34·2c per share ($3,970,000 ÷ 11,600,000)
Expected share price = 34·2c × 15 = 513c or $5·13 per share

Three Nente shares = $2·90 × 3 = $8·70	
Gain in value to a Mije share ($5·13 – $4·80) ÷ $4·80	6·9%

Gain in value to a Nente share ($10·26 – $8·70) ÷ $8·70	17·9%

(iii) **Value of follow-on product**

Present value of the positive cash flows =	$2,434,000
Present value of the cash outflow =	$(2,029,000)
NPV of the new product	$405,000

Based on conventional NPV, without considering the value of the option to delay the decision, the project would increase the value of the company by $405,000.

Considering the value of the option to delay the decision:

Price of asset (PV of future positive cash flows) =	$2,434,000
Exercise price (initial cost of project, not discounted) =	$2,500,000
Time to expiry of option =	2 years
Risk free rate (estimate) =	3·2%
Volatility =	42%

$d_1 = [\ln(2,434 \div 2,500) + (0·032 + 0·5 \times 0·42^2) \times 2] \div (0·42 \times \sqrt{2}) = 0·359$
$d_2 = 0·359 - (0·42 \times \sqrt{2}) = -0·235$

$N(d_1) = 0·5 + (0·1368 + 0·9 \times (0·1406 - 0·1368)) = 0·6402$
$N(d_2) = 0·5 - (0·0910 + 0·5 \times (0·0948 - 0·0910)) = 0·4071$
Value of option to delay the decision = $2,434,000 \times 0·6402 - 2,500,000 \times 0·4071 \times e^{-(0·032 \times 2)}$
= $1,558,247 - $954,655 = $603,592$
The project increases the value of the company by $603,592 or 25·1c per share ($603,592 ÷ 2,400,000 shares). In percentage terms this is an increase of about 8·7% (25·1c ÷ 290c).

(iv) **Comment**

The results of the calculation are summarised below:

Estimated price of a Nente share before the takeover offer and follow-on product		$2·90 per share (i)

Estimated increase in share price	Nente	Mije
Cash offer (ii)	1·7%	9·4%
Share-for-share offer (ii)	17·9%	6·9%
Estimate of the value per share of the follow-on product to Nente		8·7% (iii)

It is unlikely that Nente shareholders would accept the cash offer because it is little more than the estimated price of a Nente share before the takeover offer. However, the share-for-share offer gives a larger increase in value of a share of 17·9%. Given that the normal premium on acquisitions ranges from 20% to 40%, this is closer to what Nente shareholders would find acceptable. It is also greater than the additional value from the follow-on product. Therefore, based on the financial figures, Nente's shareholders would find the offer of a takeover on a share-for-share exchange basis the most attractive option. The other options considered here yield lower expected percentage increase in share price.

Mije shareholders would prefer the cash offer so that they can maximise the price of their shares and also not dilute their shareholding, but they would probably accept either option because the price of their shares increases. However, Mije shareholders would probably assess whether or not to accept the acquisition proposal by comparing it with other opportunities that the company has available to it and whether this is the best way to utilise its spare cash flows.

The calculations and analysis in each case is made on a number of assumptions. For example, in order to calculate the estimated price of a Nente share, the free cash flow valuation model is used. For this, the growth rate, the cost of capital and effective time period when the growth rate will occur (perpetuity in this instance) are all estimates or based on assumptions. For the takeover offer, the synergy savings and PE ratio value are both assumptions. For the value of the follow-on product and the related option, the option variables are estimates and it is assumed that they would not change during the period before the decision. The value of the option is based on the possibility that the option will only be exercised at the end of the two years, although it seems that the decision can be made any time within the two years.

The follow-on product is initially treated separately from the takeover, but Nente may ask Mije to take the value of the follow-on product into consideration in its offer. The value of the rights that allow Nente to delay making a decision are themselves worth $603,592 (see (iii)) and add just over 25c or 8·7% to the value of a Nente share. If Mije can be convinced to increase their offer to match this or the rights could be sold before the takeover, then the return for Nente's shareholders would be much higher at 26·6% (17·9% + 8·7%).

In conclusion, the most favourable outcome for Nente shareholders would be to accept the share-for-share offer, and try to convince Mije to take the value of the follow-on product into consideration. Prior to accepting the offer Nente shareholders would need to be assured of the accuracy of the results produced by the computations in the appendices.

Tutorial note: *Credit would be given for alternative relevant discussion and suggestions.*

Answer 23 SIGRA CO

(a) **Percentage gain for each payment method**

Number of Sigra shares = 4,400,000 ÷ 0·4 = 11,000,000 shares
Sigra earnings per share (EPS) = $4,950,000 ÷ 11,000,000 shares = 45c per share
Sigra price to earnings (PE) ratio = $3·6 ÷ $0·45 = 8

Dentro PE ratio = 8 × 1·125 = 9
Dentro shares = $500,000 ÷ 0·4 = 1,250,000 shares
Dentro EPS = $625,000 ÷ 1,250,000 = 50c per share
Estimate of Dentro value per share = $0·5 × 9 = $4·50 per share

Cash offer

Dentro share percentage gain under cash offer
$0·50 ÷ $4·50 × 100% = 11·1%

Share-for-share exchange

Equity value of Sigra = 11,000,000 × $3·60 =	$39,600,000
Equity value of Dentro = 1,250,000 × $4·50 =	$5,625,000
Synergy savings = 30% × $5,625,000 =	$1,688,000
Total equity value of combined company	$46,913,000
Number of shares for share-for-share exchange	
11,000,000 + [1,250,000 × ³/₂] =	12,875,000
Expected share price of combined company	$3·644 per share

Dentro share percentage gain under share-for-share offer
[½($3·644 × 3 − $4·50 × 2)] ÷ $4·50 × 100% = 21·5%

Bond offer

Rate of return

$$\$104 = \$6 \times (1 + r)^{-1} + \$6 \times (1 + r)^{-2} + \$106 \times (1 + r)^{-3}$$

If r is 5%, price is $102·72
If r is 4%, price is $105·55

r is approximately = 4% + (105·55 − 104) ÷ (105·55 − 102·72) × 1% = 4·55%

Price of new bond =
$2 × 1·0455^{-1} + $2 × 1·0455^{-2} + $102 × 1·0455^{-3} = $93·00

Value per share = $93·00 ÷ 16 = $5·81 per share

Dentro share percentage gain under bond offer
Bond offer: ($5·81 − $4·50) ÷ $4·50 × 100% = 29·1%

Comments

An initial comparison is made between the cash and the share-for-share offers. Although the share-for-share exchange gives a higher return compared to the cash offer, Dentro's shareholders may prefer the cash offer as the gains in the share price are dependent on the synergy gains being achieved. However, purchase for cash may mean that the shareholders face an immediate tax burden. Sigra's shareholders would probably prefer the cash option because the premium would only take $625,000 of the synergy benefits ($0·50 × 1,250,000 shares), whereas a share-for-share exchange would result in approximately $1,209,000 of the synergy benefits being given to the Dentro shareholders (21·5% × $4·50 × 1,250,000 shares).

The bond offer provides an alternative which may be acceptable to both sets of shareholders. Dentro's shareholders receive the highest return for this and Sigra's shareholders may be pleased that a large proportion of the payment is deferred for three years. In present value terms, however, a very high proportion of the projected synergy benefits are given to Dentro's shareholders (29·1% × $4·50 × $1,250,000 = $1,637,000).

(b) **Regulatory framework**

The regulatory framework within the European Union, the EU takeovers directive, will be used to discuss the proposals. However it is acceptable for candidates to refer to other directives and discuss the proposals on that basis.

Proposal 1

With regards to the first proposal, the directive gives the bidder squeeze-out rights, where the bidder can force minority shareholders to sell their shares. However, the limits set for squeeze-out rights are generally high (UK: 90%; Belgium, France, Germany and the Netherlands: 95%; Ireland 80%). It is likely therefore that Sigra will need a very large proportion of Dentro's shareholders to agree to the acquisition before they can force the rest of Dentro's shareholders to sell their shares. Dentro's minority shareholders may also require Sigra to purchase their shares, known as sell-out rights.

Proposal 2

With regards to the second proposal, the principle of equal treatment in the directive requires that all shareholders should be treated equally. In general terms, the bidder must offer to minority shareholders the same terms as those offered to other shareholders. It could be argued here that the principle of equal treatment is contravened because later shareholders are not offered the extra 3 cents per share, even though the 30% is less than a majority shareholding. It is highly unlikely that Sigra will be allowed to offer these terms.

Answer 24 HAV CO

(a) **Types of synergy**

An acquisition creates synergy benefits when the value of the combined entity is more than the sum of the two companies' values. Synergies can be separated into three types: revenue synergies which result in higher revenues for the combined entity, higher return on equity and a longer period when the company is able to maintain competitive advantage; cost synergies which result mainly from reducing duplication of functions and related costs, and from taking advantage of economies of scale; financial synergies which result from financing aspects such as the transfer of funds between group companies to where it can be utilised best, or from increasing debt capacity.

In this scenario, the following synergy benefits may arise from the two companies coming together. Financial synergies may be available because Strand does not have the funds to innovate new products. On the other hand, Hav has cash reserves available. It may be possible to identify and quantify this synergy based on the projects that can be undertaken after the acquisition, but would have been rejected before, and their corresponding NPV. Furthermore, as the company increases in size, the debt capacity of the combined company may increase, giving it additional access to finance. Finally, the acquisition may result in a decrease in the cost of capital of the combined company.

Cost synergies may arise from the larger company being able to negotiate better terms and lower costs from their suppliers. And there may be duplication of functional areas such as in research and development and head office which could be reduced and costs saved. These types of synergies are easier to identify and quantify but would be more short-lived. Therefore, if the markets are going to be positive about the acquisition, Hav will need to show where more long-term synergies are coming from as well as these.

Revenue synergies are perhaps where the greatest potential for growth comes from but are also more difficult to identify, quantify and enact. Good post-acquisition planning is essential for these synergies to be realised but they can be substantial and long-lasting. In this case, Hav's management can help market Strand's products more effectively by using their sales and marketing talents resulting in higher revenues and longer competitive advantage. Research and development activity can be combined to create new products using the technologies in place in both companies, and possibly bringing innovative products to market quicker. The services of the scientists from Strand will be retained to drive innovation forward, but these need to be nurtured with care since they had complete autonomy when they were the owners of Strand.

The main challenge in ensuring long-lasting benefits is not only ensuring accurate identification of potential synergies but putting into place integration processes and systems to gain full benefit from them. This is probably the greater challenge for management, and, when poorly done, can result in failure to realise the full value of the acquisition. Hav needs to be aware of this and make adequate provisions for it.

Tutorial note: *Credit would be given for alternative relevant comments and suggestions.*

(b) **Maximum premium**

Based on excess earnings method

Average pre-tax earnings: $(397 + 370 + 352) \div 3 = \$373 \cdot 0m$
Average capital employed: $[(882 + 210 - 209) + (838 + 208 - 180) + (801 + 198 - 140)] \div 3 = \$869 \cdot 3m$
Excess annual value/annual premium $= 373m - (20\% \times \$869 \cdot 3m) = \$199 \cdot 1m$
After-tax annual premium $= \$199 \cdot 1m \times 0 \cdot 8 = \$159 \cdot 3m$
PV of annual premium (assume perpetuity) $= \$159 \cdot 3m \div 0 \cdot 07 = \$2,275 \cdot 7m$

According to this method, the maximum premium payable is $\$2,275 \cdot 7m$ in total.

Based on price-to-earnings (PE) ratio method

Strand estimated PE ratio $= 16 \cdot 4 \times 1 \cdot 10 = 18 \cdot 0$
Strand profit after tax: $\$397m \times 0 \cdot 8 = \$317 \cdot 6m$
Hav profit after tax $= \$1,980m \times 0 \cdot 8 = \$1,584 \cdot 0m$

Hav, current value $= \$9 \cdot 24 \times 2,400$ shares $= \$22,176 \cdot 0m$
Strand, current value $= \$317 \cdot 6m \times 18 \cdot 0 = \$5,716 \cdot 8m$

Combined company value $= (\$1,584m + \$317 \cdot 6m + \$140 \cdot 0m) \times 14 \cdot 5 = \$29,603 \cdot 2m$

Maximum premium $= \$29,603 \cdot 2m - (\$22,176 \cdot 0m + \$5,716 \cdot 8) = \$1,710 \cdot 4m$

(c) **Percentage premium for each payment method**

Strand, current value per share $= \$5,716 \cdot 8m \div 1,200m$ shares $= \$4 \cdot 76$ per share

Maximum premium % based on PE ratio $= \$1,710 \cdot 4m \div \$5,716 \cdot 8m \times 100\% = 29 \cdot 9\%$
Maximum premium % based on excess earnings $= \$2,275 \cdot 7m \div \$5,716 \cdot 8m \times 100\% = 39 \cdot 8\%$

Cash offer: premium (%)
$(\$5 \cdot 72 - \$4 \cdot 76) \div \$4 \cdot 76 \times 100\% = 20 \cdot 2\%$

Cash and share offer: premium (%)
1 Hav share for 2 Strand shares
Hav share price $= \$9 \cdot 24$
Per Strand share $= \$4 \cdot 62$
Cash payment per share$= \$1 \cdot 33$
Total return $= \$1 \cdot 33 + \$4 \cdot 62 = \$5 \cdot 95$
Premium percentage $= (\$5 \cdot 95 - \$4 \cdot 76) \div \$4 \cdot 76 \times 100\% = 25 \cdot 0\%$

Cash and bond offer: premium (%)
Each share has a nominal value of $\$0 \cdot 25$, therefore $\$5$ is $\$5 \div \$0 \cdot 25 = 20$ shares
Bond value $= \$100 \div 20$ shares $= \$5$ per share
Cash payment $= \$1 \cdot 25$ per share
Total $= \$6 \cdot 25$ per share
Premium percentage $= (\$6 \cdot 25 - \$4 \cdot 76) \div \$4 \cdot 76 = 31 \cdot 3\%$

On the basis of the calculations, the cash together with bond offer yields the highest return; in addition to the value calculated above, the bonds can be converted to 12 Hav shares, giving them a price per share of $\$8 \cdot 33$ ($\$100 \div 12$). This price is below Hav's current share price of $\$9 \cdot 24$, and therefore the conversion option is already in-the-money.

It is probable that the share price will increase in the 10-year period and therefore the value of the convertible bond should increase. A bond also earns a small coupon interest of $3 per $100 a year. The 31·3% return is the closest to the maximum premium based on the excess earnings method and more than the maximum premium based on the PE ratio method. It would seem that this payment option transfers more value to the owners of Strand than the value created based on the PE ratio method.

However, with this option Strand shareholders only receive an initial cash payment of $1·25 per share compared to $1·33 per share and $5·72 per share for the other methods. This may make it the more attractive option for the Hav shareholders as well, and although their shareholding will be diluted most under this option, it will not happen for some time.

The cash and share offer gives a return in between the pure cash and the cash and bonds offers. Although the return is lower, Strand's shareholders become owners of Hav and have the option to sell their equity immediately. However, the share price may fall between now and when the payment for the acquisition is made. If this happens, then the return to Strand's shareholders will be lower.

The pure cash offer gives an immediate and definite return to Strand's shareholders, but is also the lowest offer and may also put a significant burden on Hav having to fund so much cash, possibly through increased debt.

It is likely that Strand's shareholder/managers, who will continue to work within Hav, will accept the mixed cash and bond offer. They, therefore, get to maximise their current return and also potentially gain when the bonds are converted into shares. Different impacts on shareholders' personal taxation situations due to the different payment methods might also influence the choice of method.

Answer 25 MAKONIS CO

(a)   Additional equity value created

Combined company, cost of capital

Asset beta $(1·2 \times 480 + 0·9 \times 1,218) \div (480 + 1,218) = 0·985$
Equity beta $(0·985 \times (60 + 40 \times 0·8) \div 60) = 1·51$
Cost of equity
$2\% + 1·51 \times 7\% = 12·57\%$

Cost of capital
$12·57\% \times 0·6 + 4·55\% \times 0·8 \times 0·4 = 9·00\%$

Combined company equity value ($ millions)

Year	1	2	3	4
Free cash flows before synergy (growing at 5%)	226·80	238·14	250·05	262·55
Synergies	20·00	20·00	20·00	20·00
Free cash flows	246·80	258·14	270·05	282·55
PV of free cash flows at 9%	226·42	217·27	208·53	200·17

Tutorial note: *The PV figures are slightly different if discount table factors are used, instead of formulae. Full credit would be given if discount tables were used instead.*

Total PV of cash flows (years 1 to 4) = $852·39 million
Total PV of cash flows (years 5 to perpetuity) = $262·55 \times 1·0225 \div (0·09 - 0·0225) \times 1·09^{-4}$
= $2,817·51 million

Total value to firm = $3,669·90 million

Value attributable to equity holders = $3,669·90 million $\times$ 0·6 = $2,201·94 million

Additional value created from the combined company = $2,201·94 million – ($1,218 million + $480 million) = $2,201·94 million – $1,698·00 million = $503·94 million (or 29·7%)

Although the equity beta and therefore the risk of the combined company is more than Makonis on its own, probably due to Nuvola's higher business risk (reflected by the higher asset beta), overall the benefits from growth in excess of the risk free rate and additional synergies have led to an increase in the value of combined company of just under 30% when compared to the individual companies' values.

However, a number of assumptions have been made in obtaining the valuation, for example:

■ The assumption of growth of cash flows in perpetuity and whether this is realistic or not;

■ Whether the calculation of the combined company's asset beta when based on the weighted average of market values is based on good evidence or not;

■ It has been assumed that the figures such as growth rates, tax rates, free cash flows, risk free rate of return, risk premium, and so on are accurate and do not change in the future.

In all these circumstances, it may be appropriate to undertake sensitivity analysis to determine how changes in the variables would impact on the value of the combined company, and whether the large increase in value is justified.

(b)   **Impact of increase in control premium**

Value of Nuvola equity = $2·40 $\times$ 200m shares = $480m
30% premium: 1·3 $\times$ $480m = $624m
50% premium: 1·5 $\times$ $480m = $720m

New number of shares = 210m + ½ $\times$ 200m = 310m

Loss in value per share of combined company, if 50% premium paid instead of 30% premium = ($720m – $624m) $\div$ 310m shares = $0·31 per share.

This represents a drop in value of approx 5·3% on original value of a Makonis share ($0·31 $\div$ $5·80).

(c)   **Additional finance required**

The amount of cash required will increase substantially, by about $96 million, if Makonis agrees to the demands made by Nuvola's equity holders and pays the 50% premium. Makonis needs to determine how it is going to acquire the additional funds and the implications from this. For example, it could borrow the money required for the additional funds, but taking on more debt may affect the cost of capital and therefore the value of the company. It could raise the funds by issuing more equity shares, but this may not be viewed in a positive light by the current equity holders.

Makonis may decide to offer a higher proportion of its shares in the share-for-share exchange instead of paying cash for the additional premium. However, this will affect its equity holders and dilute their equity holding further. Even the current proposal to issue 100 million new shares will mean that Nuvola's equity holders will own just under $^1/_3$ of the combined company and Makonis' shareholders would own just over $^2/_3$ of the combined company.

Makonis should also consider what Nuvola's equity holders would prefer. They may prefer less cash and more equity due to their personal tax circumstances, but, in most cases, cash is preferred by the target firm's equity holders.

Answer 26 EVERTALK CO

(i) Corporate restructuring

For a restructuring to be successful it must treat all stakeholders fairly in accordance with their respective rights, and, if possible, offer each group a more favourable outcome than would occur if the company were to be liquidated. The company should also expect to be viable as a going concern as a result of the restructuring.

Estimated liquidation value:

	$m
Land and buildings	140 (including the surplus $40 million)
Other non-current assets	50
Inventory	100
Receivables	70
Cash	5
Less redundancy and closure costs	(100)
	265
Liabilities	
Bank loan	40
Bond	300
Other liabilities	209
	549

If the company were liquidated, on average liabilities would receive approximately 48% of cash due to them. Ordinary shareholders would receive nothing.

Examining each of the individual stakeholder's positions:

Bondholders

The bondholders are to be offered 95 million shares in exchange for existing bonds of $300 million, effectively pricing each share at $3.16. They give up their rights to repayment of $300 million, of which about $145 million could be expected if the company is liquidated (equivalent to a value of $1.53 per share). On the other hand they have to subscribe an additional $100 million in order to allow rationalisation of the network division, and to improve the cash flow of the company. The bondholders would gain control of the company, but this is only of value if the company is expected to survive.

Tutorial note: *Existing bondholders are owed $300m. If they agree to cancel their debt in exchange for 95m shares they are effectively paying 300 ÷ 95 = $3.16 per share. If they chose to liquidate the company they would receive $145m, which is effectively 145 ÷ 95 = $1.53 per share.*

The effect on the company is that interest of $300m × 12% would be saved, and the $40 million bank loan would be repaid from the disposal of surplus assets, saving a further $40m × 8% = $3·2 million interest.

Projected free cash flow of the company

	$m	
Current income from operations (after interest)	(60)	
Add		
Interest savings	39	($300m × 12% + $40m × 8%)
Rationalisation gains	30	
Add back depreciation	46	(assumed to reduce pro-rata to $40m disposal)
Replacement investment	(100)	
Free cash flow	(45)	

Tutorial note: *Other items such as working capital are assumed to be constant.*

On this basis, even without discounting, the company as a whole is not likely to be financially viable after the proposed restructuring. In this situation the bondholders would be better not to accept the proposed reconstruction as they could potentially lose more of their investment if the company were subsequently forced into liquidation. However, if the bondholders accepted the offer and then closed the network division their position might be improved. The implications of closing the network division are discussed below.

Existing shareholders

If the company fails, existing shareholders would receive nothing. The proposal gives them at least some possibility of future value, and might be acceptable. Shareholders could of course currently sell their shares for $0.10 per share; however, if many of the shareholders were to sell the price would fall from this level. The convertible offer would then need to be judged against the revenue from the sale of shares. The initial conversion price of $2.00 per share does not look favourable; on current evidence the share price is unlikely to reach $2.00 during the next five years.

Participants in the share option schemes

It is likely that currently the share options have little or no value as the current share price is so low. This offer appears to be generous to this group who are existing managers/directors of the company, and probably unfair to other stakeholders.

Other liabilities

The scheme does not offer any change in legal status to such liabilities. It could, however, slightly improve the future financial viability of the company, or, as the amount of loans outstanding is reduced, probably improve the proportion of funds repaid in the event of liquidation. If, however, the new loans are secured, this could have an adverse effect on other liabilities. The proposed restructuring does not offer a viable financial solution to the company's current problems.

Other possible strategies: Closure of the network division

Given that the manufacturing division is performing much better than the network division, consideration should be given to closing the network division. The subscriber base of the network division could possibly be sold. Future activities, and any restructuring, could then be focussed on the manufacturing division that is currently profitable.

(ii)   **Sale of company to Globtalk**

Globtalk would probably close the network division as it is loss-making and a direct competitor to its own network. If the network division is closed receipts are expected to be:

	$m	
Land and buildings	50	($100m × 0·5. Other $40m assumed used to repay bank loan)
Other non-current assets	25	($50m × 0·5)
Inventory	10	($100m × 0·1)
Receivables	35	($70m × 0·5)
Cash	2·5	
Less:		
Other liabilities	(104·5)	($209m × 0·5)
Bonds	(300)	
Closure costs	(50)	($100m × 0·5)
Net liabilities	(332)	

Tutorial note: *Note (v) of the scenario states that half (0.5) of all assets are attributable to each division, except for inventory where only 10% (0.1) is regarding the network division. The model answer suggests Globtalk would close the loss-making network division and attempts to value the remaining business on this basis.*

If the $300 million remaining bond liability is excluded from the closure, the outcome is an expected deficit on disposal of only $32 million.

The projected free cash flow of the manufacturing division is:

	$m	
Current income from operations (after interest)	90	
Add back interest if bank loan is repaid	3	
	93	
Tax (30%)	(28)	(tax would be payable in future)
Add depreciation	12	(assumed to relate to 20% of current annual depreciation as manufacturing division only undertakes 20% of replacement expenditure)
Less replacement investment	(20)	
Free cash flow	57	

If the network division is closed and none of the lost sales (25%) are replaced, then free cash flow would reduce to approximately $41 million. This is not an exact estimate, and in reality sales could increase rather than decrease, as Globtalk would be likely to use the division as a supplier of phones to its own network customers. Without any sales reduction the present value of the free cash flow to infinity at a 10% discount rate (see Appendix below) is $570 million. If a shorter and more conservative time horizon of 10 years is used the present value of a free cash flow of $57m per year for 10 years is: $57m × 6·145 = $350 million.

With a sales reduction the values are $410 million and $252 million.
Both of these estimates are well in excess of the $50 million price offered.

If Globtalk acquires Evertalk, there is potential also to access Evertalk's existing network subscribers (or at least part of them), and there could be vertical synergies with the manufacturing division.

Even if Globtalk were to take full responsibility for existing loans, at a total cost of $382 million ($332m net liabilities plus $50m purchase cost), its offer could still be below the expected value of Evertalk with the network division closed.

Given the above data it is recommended that any acquisition by Globtalk should be conditional upon the company accepting liability for Evertalk's existing loans.

(iii)   **Closure of the company**

Closure of the entire company is not recommended. Given the poor performance of the network division it is recommended that this division is closed. The manufacturing division is viable, and could either continue to be operated by Evertalk, or sold to Globtalk. Closure of the network division would lead to a deficit of approximately $332 million (see above), which could not easily be paid by the manufacturing division.

Conclusion

Unless an alternative restructuring scheme can be agreed, which would reduce the burden of the closure of the network division to the company, sale to Globtalk might be the best alternative, conditional upon Globtalk accepting the liability for all existing loans.

Appendix – WACC for the manufacturing division

Cost of equity for the manufacturing division:

$R_f + (R_m - R_f)$ beta, or $5\% + (14\% - 5\%)\ 0{\cdot}9 = 13{\cdot}1\%$

The cost of debt may be estimated by using the current bank loan rate of 8%, or from the current bond price, by trial and error.

$$\$121 = \frac{12}{1+Kd} + \frac{12}{(1+Kd)^2} + \dots \frac{12}{(1+Kd)^7} + \frac{100}{(1+Kd)^7}$$

		$
At 8%	$12 \times 5{\cdot}206 =$	62·47
	$100 \times 0{\cdot}583 =$	58·30
		120·77

The cost of debt (before tax) is approximately 8%.

WACC for the manufacturing division, using target gearing of 60% equity, 40% debt is:

$13{\cdot}1\%\ (0{\cdot}6) + 8\%\ (1 - 0{\cdot}3)\ (0{\cdot}4) = 10{\cdot}1\%$

10% will be used as the discount rate.

Tutorial note: *The after tax cost of debt is used as the manufacturing division is expected to pay tax in the future.*

Answer 27 REFLATOR CO

(a)   *(i)*   *Potential advantages of a management buy-out*

The advantages of a buy-out may be viewed from the perspectives of each of the parties involved.

The selling company may regard a buy-out as preferable to the liquidation of a loss making division.   A buy-out might result in a higher disposal price, and has the social effect of protecting jobs. Selling part of the organisation might allow the company to focus on its core competence.

The current managers, with their existing expertise of the markets, relationships with clients, etc. may have a better chance of successfully operating the company. They are also likely to be highly motivated through their significant equity holdings, and by the potential for large capital gains if the company succeeds.

A venture capitalist or other type of investor normally takes a high risk, in the hope of high returns mainly through capital gains. Most investors would seek some form of exit route for their investment after several years, possible through a listing on the AIM or other relevant market. In some countries investing in buy-outs may offer tax advantages.

(ii)   *Likelihood of book value of equity growing by 20% per year*

The increase in the value of equity may be estimated from the expected retained earnings over the four year period. The maximum 15% dividend payment is assumed.

Year	0	1	2	3	4
Earnings before interest and tax		320,000	410,000	500,000	540,000
Interest 8·5%		170,000	170,000	170,000	170,000
Interest 9% loan (Note)		27,000	23,411	19,499	15,236
Earnings before tax		123,000	216,589	310,501	354,764
Taxation (30%)		36,900	64,977	93,150	106,429
Earnings after tax		86,100	151,612	217,351	248,335
Dividend (15%)		12,915	22,742	32,603	37,250
Retained earnings		73,185	128,870	184,748	211,085
Book value of equity	800,000	873,185	1,002,055	1,186,803	1,397,888

Growth in the book value of equity from 800,000 to 1,397,888 over four years is a compound growth rate of 14·97%. This is considerably less than the 20% growth rate claimed by the managers.

It should be noted that this is a book value of equity. The market value of equity is much more relevant to a potential investor, and is likely to be very different from this book value.

Note: Interest on the 9% loan

The equal annual payment comprising interest and capital that is necessary to pay off a $300,000 loan over six years is:

$$\frac{300,000}{4\cdot486} = \$66,875 \text{ (4·486 is the PV annuity factor for six years at 9\%)}$$

Year	Remaining value	Interest	Repayment of capital
1	300,000	27,000	39,875
2	260,125	23,411	43,464
3	216,661	19,499	47,376
4	169,285	15,236	51,639

(iii)   Possible implication of offering warrants

At the start of the buy-out, the equity holding would be 1,000,000 shares by the managers, and 600,000 by the venture capital organisation. The initial warrant proposal would allow the venture capital organisation to purchase 300,000 new shares after four years, a total of 900,000. The revised suggestion would allow 450,000 new shares to be purchased which would give majority ownership and control of the company to the venture capital organisation. This is likely to be unacceptable to the managers, unless they also will have further opportunities to increase their share ownership (e.g. through other forms of option).

(b)   MandM

Corporate disposal of this type raises a number of issues. In deciding whether disposal is the appropriate course of action MandM should follow, the company needs to clarify its motives for disposal. The question suggests that there is no business case for retaining the LunarMint operation. However, the concept of what is core business and what is not, is a matter of judgement – and where that business is profitable, senior management need to be very careful in making that judgement. The question arises why did they diversify into this rather odd line of business for a money mint manufacturing company in the first place? Was it because printing money was not generating the returns required for the level of risk being carried?

The steps involved in the procedure for preparing a business such as this for sale are as follows:

(1)   A decision would need to be made about the nature of the assets being transferred and the process for resolving whether and how any joint assets might be sold. Fair value for all of the assets to be disposed of should be established on the basis of a going concern.

(2)   Checking the status of all intellectual property, that all patents are established and where necessary further valuable corporate knowledge, brand symbols and proprietary processes should be patented or protected by copyright.

(3)   Identification and valuation of the LunarMint contribution to the business. This may involve improving the business by a thorough operating and business process review, implementing any changes that might improve reported profitability and removing any impediments to a sale. It may be that the whole business is to be sold as a going concern or that only elements of the business will be disposed of. The valuation must assess the impact of the disposal upon the shareholder value in MandM both before and after a potential sale to identify a threshold value which will lead to no loss of shareholder value. Where the impact upon the firm's exposure to systematic risk is significant the valuation process will be recursive entailing sophisticated modelling of the potential loss of cash-flow to the group and the impact of the uncoupling on the firm's asset beta.

(4)   Any regulatory issues need to be clarified. Would sale to any of the potential purchasers conflict with the public interest and present problems gaining approval for the acquisition?

(5)   Potential buyers will need to be sought through open tender or through an intermediary. Depending on the nature of the assets being sold a single bidder may be sought or preparations made for an auction of the business as a going concern. Members of the LunarMint supply chain and distribution channels may be interested, as may be competitors in the confectionary business. High levels of discretion are required in the search process to protect the value of the business from adverse competitive action. An interested and dominant competitor may open a price war in order to force down prices and hence the value of LunarMint prior to a bid.

(6)   Once a potential buyer has been found, access should be given so that they can conduct their own due diligence. Up-to-date accounts should be made available and all legal documentation relating to assets to be transferred made available.

(7)   The company should undertake its own due diligence to check the ability of the potential purchaser to complete a transaction of this size. Before proceeding it would be necessary to establish how the purchaser intends to finance the purchase, the timescale involved in their raising the necessary finance and any other issues that may impede a clean sale.

(8)   If not already involved the firm's legal team will need to assess any contractual issues on sale, the transfer of employment rights, the transfer of intellectual property and any residual rights and responsibilities to MandM. Normally, a clean separation should be sought unless an agreement is required concerning the use of joint assets.

(9)   In the light of the above and (3) in particular a sale price will be negotiated which will increase the shareholder value of LunarMint. The negotiation process should be conducted by professional negotiators who have been thoroughly briefed on the terms of the sale, the conditions attached and all of the legal requirements. The consideration for the sale, the deeds for the assignment of assets and terms for the transfer of staff and their accrued pension rights will also all be subject to agreement.

(10)   Once the sale has been agreed in principle it is important to address all of the employment issues which will include communicating with staff the reasons for the sale, the protection of their rights on transfer, the handling of any incentive payments including share options and the transfer of their pension rights. This step may involve discussion with unions and other employee representatives.

(11)   Given the size of the business being sold shareholder agreement may also be required and if so the process should be put in place to gain their approval.

(12)   Finally the contracts for sale and the completion documents can be exchanged and the sale completed.

Answer 28 BBS STORES

(a)   **Impact of property unbundling on statement of financial position and reported EPS**

The unbundling of the buildings component entails a sale value of 50% of the land and buildings and 50% of the assets under construction to yield a sale value of $1,231 million. Under option 1 $360 million would be used to repay the outstanding medium-term loan notes and the balance as reinvestment within the business of $871 million. Option 2 would entail repayment of the loan and a share buyback. The value released would buy back $871 million ÷ $4 = 217·75 million shares with a nominal value of $54·44 million and a charge to reserves of $817 million.

The comparative statements of financial position under each option are as follows:

	As at year end 2017 $m	Sale proceeds $m	Reinvestment option 1 $m	$m	Share buyback option 2 $m	$m	As at year end 2016 $m
Assets							
Non-current assets							
Intangible assets	190			190		190	160
Property, plant and equipment	4,050	–1,231	871	3,690	–1,231	2,819	3,600
Other assets	500			500		500	530
	4,740			4,380		3,509	4,290
Current assets	840	1,231	–1,231	840		840	1,160
Total assets	5,580			5,220		4,349	5,450
Equity and liabilities							
Share capital	425			425	–54	371	420
Retained earnings	1,535			1,535	–817	718	980
Total equity	1,960			1,960		1,089	1,400
Non-current liabilities							
Borrowings and other financial liabilities	1,130		–360	770	–360	770	1,130
Other liabilities	890			890		890	900
	2,020			1,660		1,660	2,030
Current liabilities	1,600			1,600		1,600	2,020
Total liabilities	3,620			3,260		3,260	4,050
Total equity and liabilities	5,580			5,220		4,349	5,450

The first option has the effect of reducing the company's book gearing from 36·6% (borrowing and other financial liabilities to total capital employed) to 28·2% with option 1 or increasing it to 41·4% with option 2.

Tutorial note: *The model answer calculates gearing as per its stated definition (i.e. debt ÷ (debt + equity) using book values). So current gearing is 36.6% (1,130 ÷ (1,130 + 1,960)).*

The net impact upon the earnings of the business is less straightforward. Under options 1 and 2 the company would benefit from a reduction in interest payable but would be required to pay an open market rent at 8% per year on the property released. In addition, under option 1, the reduction in gearing would lead to a 30 basis points saving in interest on the variable component of the swap. Under option 1 the company would be able to earn a rate of return of 13% on the funds reinvested.

The adjustment to the current earnings to show these effects is as follows:

	Current $m	Option 1 $m	Option 2 $m
Earnings for the year	670·00	670·00	670·00
Add back interest saved (net of tax)			
$360 million × 6·2% × 0·65		14·51	14·51
Reduction in credit spread on six-year debt			
$770 million × 0·003 × 0·65		1·50	
Deduct additional property rent (net of tax)			
$1,231 × 8% × 0·65		–64·01	–64·01
Add additional return on equity			
$871 million × 13% × 0·65		74·00	
Revised earnings	670·00	696·00	620·50
Number of shares in issue	1,700	1,700	1,484
Revised EPS (cents per share)	39·41	40·94	41·81

Given that the company has swapped out its variable rate liability there will be no change in the interest charge to earnings for the six-year debt from the current 5·5% per year unless the lender has the ability to vary the variable rate on current borrowing for changes in credit rating. Because the fixed rate and the floating rate are the same at 6·2% (given the current credit spread is 70 basis points over LIBOR, or in addition to the swap rate of 5·5%) the nominal value of the company's debt is equal to its current market value.

(b)   **Impact of unbundling on the firm's overall cost of finance**

The current equity cost of capital is calculated as follows:

5% + 1.82 × 3% = 10.47%

The current weighted average cost of capital is:

$$WACC = \frac{6,800}{6,800 + 1,130} \times 10.47\% + \frac{1,130}{6,800 + 1,130} \times 6.2\% \times 0.65 = 9.56\%$$

Tutorial note: *The key to forecasting the cost of equity post-unbundling is to find the asset beta of retail and the asset beta of property. Steps:*

■   *Degear the firm's existing equity beta to asset beta. The firm's asset beta is a weighted average of the asset beta of property (1.25 × 50% = 0.625) and the asset beta of retail.*

■   *The asset beta of retail is not known but the weightings of the existing firm between property and retail are known. Total value of equity is 6,800 (425 × $^{100}/_{25}$ × 4). Value of property is 2,462 (2,297 + 165). So value of retail is 4,338 (6,800 – 2,462).*

■   *Imply the asset beta of retail and hence all required data to build up the cost of capital estimates following disposal of half of the property.*

To calculate the unbundled cost of equity first ungear the firm's existing beta. Assuming the beta of debt is zero:

$$\beta_a = \frac{V_d(1-T)}{V_e + V_d(1-T)} \beta e$$

$$\beta_a = \frac{6,800}{6,800 + 1,130 \times (1 - 0.35)} \times 1.824 = 1.646$$

The retail asset beta is then calculated from the weighted average of the component betas:

$$\beta_A = \frac{V_R}{V_T} \beta_R + \frac{V_P}{V_T} \beta_P$$

$$1.646 = \frac{4,338}{6,800} \times \beta_R + \frac{2,462}{6,800} \times 0.625$$

$$\beta_R = \left[1.646 - \frac{2,462}{6,800} \times 0.625 \right] \times \frac{6,800}{4,338} = 2.225$$

However, the beta of the continuing firm will be a combination of this retail beta and the property beta of the remaining firm. On the assumption that the share price does not change under either option the cost of equity capital is estimated as follows:

	Option 1	*Option 2*
Value of the equity	= 425 × 4 × 4 = $6,800 million	= 371 × 4 × 4 = $5,936 million

Asset beta of

reconstructed firm $\beta_A = \dfrac{V_R}{V_T} \beta_R + \dfrac{V_P}{V_T} \beta_P$ $\qquad\qquad \beta_A = \dfrac{V_R}{V_T} \beta_R + \dfrac{V_P}{V_T} \beta_P$

$$\beta_A = \frac{5,569}{6,800} \times 2.225 + \frac{1,231}{6,800} \times 0.625 \qquad \beta_A = \frac{4,705}{5,936} \times 2.225 + \frac{1,231}{5,936} \times 0.625 =$$

$$= 1.935 \qquad\qquad\qquad\qquad = 1.893$$

Tutorial note: *When unbundling/reconstructing the firm's asset beta the examiner has used the relative equity values of the firm's business segments. A technically superior and acceptable alternative would be to use the relative **asset** values for the weightings.*

Equity beta of reconstructed firm:

$$1.935 = \frac{6,800}{6,800 + 770(1 - 0.35)} \beta_e \qquad 1.893 = \frac{5,936}{5,936 + 770(1 - 0.35)} \beta_e$$

$$\beta_e = 2.0775 \qquad\qquad\qquad \beta_e = 2.053$$

Cost of equity $\qquad = 5\% + 2 \cdot 0775 \times 3\% = 11 \cdot 23\% \qquad = 5\% + 2 \cdot 053 \times 3\% = 11 \cdot 16\%$

$$WACC\,(1) = \frac{6,800}{(6,800 + 770)} \times 11.23\% + \frac{770}{(6,800 + 770)} \times 5.9\% \times 0.65 = 10.48\%$$

And

$$WACC\,(2) = \frac{5,936}{(5,936 + 770)} \times 11.16\% + \frac{770}{(5,936 + 770)} \times 6.2\% \times 0.65 = 10.34\%$$

Note that under option 1, the variable component of the swap would be reduced by 30 basis points. However, the market value of the debt would remain unchanged because given LIBOR and the fixed component of the swap are the same at 5·5%, the reduction in basis points will reduce the effective coupon and the yield to 5·9%.

Both options will significantly increase the cost of capital for the company from 9·56% to 10·48% in the case of option 1 and 10·34% in the case of option 2.

(c) **Potential impact on value of the firm**

The value of the firm for a low geared business such as this is represented by the present value of the firm's future earnings discounted at the company's cost of capital. The ownership of property does not add value to the business providing that the company can enjoy a continuing and unencumbered use of the asset concerned.

On the assumption that an independent property company can be established and an arm's length rental agreement concluded then it is possible that the ownership of the property assets could be taken "off balance sheet". However, the ease with which this can be done depends upon the local accounting regulations and accounting standards.

As it stands option 1 appears to increase the potential earnings more than currently or than option 2. However option 2 offers the highest EPS. With an unbundling exercise such as this it is difficult to predict with precision the likely impact upon the value of the firm. The removal of part of the firm's property portfolio will increase the equity beta but this will be offset by the reduction in the firm's gearing. Much also depends upon the ability of the business to generate a return of 13% on the reinvested proceeds of the property sale. If this is not achieved then a significant loss in shareholder value would result. For this reason the shareholders might prefer the lower risk option of a repurchase of their equity at 400c leaving the firm's EPS largely unchanged.

The analysis of the impact upon the firm's equity cost of capital assumes that the value of the firm's equity at 400c per share will remain unchanged. In practice that is unrealistic and a model of the firm's value would have to be constructed to test the full impact of either option on shareholder value. Given the problem is recursive in that the output value determines the estimation of the equity beta, which is also an input variable in the calculation, computer modelling would be required.

Answer 29 DORIC CO

The decision should be taken in the best interests of the shareholders and other stakeholders of the company.

Obviously all the input numbers should be considered on basis of their reasonableness and accuracy.

Hence the positions of the interested parties will be considered on this basis.

(1) **Cease trading and liquidate the Company**

This is probably not in the best interest of any party. Debt holders only receive 55·7c for every $1 invested and the shareholders receive nothing (see Appendix, Proposal 1). Furthermore, the parts division is continuing to make a profit and should possibly continue.

The board of directors may want to consider closing just the fridge division, and focusing on the parts manufacturing division, with the possibility of pursuing the option of the mobile refrigeration business. However, in this case, the problem of the lack of funding might continue.

(2) **Corporate restructuring and management buy-out**

Shareholders

The shareholders would benefit from either proposal two or three, as opposed to the first proposal, as they stand to gain some funds. The restructuring proposal requires them to pay $40 million cash for new shares but lose their control of the company (the shareholding falls to just under 13%). On the other hand the statement of financial position looks robust with a $20 million cash float and bank overdraft facilities probably available at previous levels (see Appendix, Proposal 2). This may make the company more successful in the future, as directors are less restricted by covenants. The value at $256·3 million currently only gives existing shareholders a share (or stake) of about $33·3 million (13% × $256·3m), which is less than the amount they would inject.

The shareholders would benefit immediately if the management buy-out option is taken because they will receive a premium on the share price, although this may still be lower than when the company's share price was at its height.

Therefore the shareholders need to weigh up whether they would like to possibly benefit from future company prospects (not evident at the moment) or whether they would like to sell their shares for 60c per share. They would probably opt for the management buy-out.

Unsecured bond holders

The unsecured bond holders' position is not dissimilar to the shareholders' position in that with the restructuring, their financial position depends on the future success of the company, but with the management buy-out they benefit from receiving the full repayment of their initial investment. However, their preferred proposal is probably more difficult to judge.

With the restructuring option they would become the majority shareholder with just over 87% of the company for a total investment of $210 million. They would be able to play a major part in influencing the management's decision possibly with representation on the Board. However, they would be exposed to additional risk as equity holders, as opposed to being debt holders.

The value attributable to them based on perpetuity cash flows is $223 million ($256·3 × 87%) approximately, which is more than their investment. Like the shareholders they would benefit from any future projects that the re-structured business undertakes.

They would also receive the shares at a significant discount, 270 million shares for $210 million which is 77·7c per $1 par value. The ability to influence the Board and the possibility of obtaining a higher return than their investment from almost the start may sway them to accept the restructuring option. On the other hand, the management buy-out pays them what is due immediately, but they cannot participate in future benefits.

Bond holders may therefore be more tempted to opt for the restructuring when compared to shareholders.

Directors and management participating in the management buy-out

If the restructuring is considered as opposed to liquidation then clearly a significant benefit to the management and directors is that they would retain their employment, unless the new shareholder owners decide to terminate some of their contracts.

The possibility of the offer of the share options is interesting. At first the $1·10 exercise price may seem generous as the directors would be able to exercise when the price of shares increase by just 10%. However, it is unlikely that the share price will start at $1 per share. If the estimate of the value to perpetuity of $256·3 million is taken against the total number of shares of 310 million; giving a theoretical share price of 82·7c per share. This means that the share price needs to increase by over 33% before the option will become in-the-money. The option is currently well out-of-money and would have a low value. Given the asymmetric payoff of the option and the need to increase the price dramatically, directors and managers may be tempted to act in an excessively risky manner, to the detriment of the shareholders and other stakeholders. Indeed research has shown that the presence of share options in individual pay structure do make option holders behave in a more risky manner compared to pay structures which do not contain options.

The management buy-out may influence different classes of managers and directors very differently. For those who participate in the management buy-out, the calculations seem to indicate a clear benefit (see Appendix, Proposal 3) of a gain net of the cost of the buy-out. It would seem that by having a 5% growth, the value has increased to more than 50% of the initial cost of the buy-out, although some unreasonable assumptions have been made. For managers and directors not participating in the buy-out, it is likely that they will lose their employment once the fridge division is sold.

Conclusion

Given that the shareholders will probably prefer the management buy-out, and as it appears to have a significant advantage for the participating managers, it is likely that this will be the option that is preferred. Although some parties may not approve of the option, it is unlikely that their "voice" will be strong enough to alter the decision.

Appendix – Calculations for each option

Proposal 1: Cease trading

Estimated break-up values of assets	$m
Land and Buildings	60
Machinery and Equipment	40
Inventory	90
Receivables	20
	___
Total	210
Less redundancy and other costs	(54)
	___
	156
	___
Current and non-current liabilities	
Payables	70
Bank overdraft	60
Unsecured bonds	120
Other unsecured loans	30
	___
	280
	___

The current and non-current liabilities will receive 55·7c per $1 owing to them (156 ÷ 280). Shareholders will receive nothing.

Proposal 2: Restructure

Financial position	$m
Non-current assets	
Land and buildings	70
Machinery and equipment (assuming all new investment is here)	130
	———
	200
	———
Current assets	
Inventory	180
Receivables	40
Cash ($40m + $90m – $80m – $30m)	20
	———
	240
	———
Total assets	440
	———
Current liabilities	
Payables	70
Non-current liabilities	
Bank loan (7% interest)	60
Share capital ($1 per share par value, 40m + 270m)	310
	———
Total Liabilities and capital	440
	———

Income position	$m
Sales revenue (510 × 1·07)	545·7
Costs prior to depreciation, interest payments and tax	(490)
Tax allowable depreciation (15% × 200)	(30)
Finance cost (interest) (7% × 60)	(4·2)
Tax	(4·3)
	———
Profit	17·2
	———

Tutorial note: *Even after the 7% growth, the fridge division is still loss-making. Revenue = $340 × 1·07 = $363·8m, costs (unchanged) = $370m.*

Cash position	$m
Profit before interest and tax	25·7
Tax (20%)	(5·14)
	———
Net cash flow	20·56
	———

Tutorial note: *Depreciation is not added back because it is the same amount as needed to maintain operations.*

Value of company after re-structuring

Cost of capital = 6·5%

Estimated value based on cash flows to perpetuity
$20·56m ÷ 0·065 = $316·3m

Value attributable to shareholders (net of bank loan) = $316·3 – $60m = $256·3m

Proposal 3: Management buy-out

	$m
Value of selling fridge division ($^2/_3 \times 210$ (proposal 1))	140
Redundancy and other costs ($^2/_3 \times 54$)	(36)
Funds available from sale of division	104
Amount of current and non-current liabilities (proposal 1)	280
Amount of management buy-out funds needed to pay current and non-current liabilities	176
Amount of management buy-out funds needed to pay shareholders	60
Equipment needed to increase sales by 7% ($^1/_3$ of 80m)	26.7
Investment needed for new venture	50
Total funds needed for management buy-out	312·7

Estimating value of new company after buy-out	$m
Sales revenue (70%* $\times$ 170m $\times$ 1·07)	127·3
Costs (70%* $\times$ 120)	(84·0)
Profits before depreciation	43·3
Growth in profits due to new venture (5%)	2·2
Depreciation ($^1/_3 \times 200 \times 15\%$)	(10)
Tax (20%)	(7·1)
Cash flows before interest payment	28·4

Tutorial note: *It is assumed that, as before, the depreciation and the amount of capital investment needed are roughly equal. It is assumed that no additional investment in non-current assets or working capital is needed, even though sales revenue is increasing. It is assumed that additional initial working capital requirement is part of the new venture investment of $50m.*

*It is assumed that 30% of the sales revenue lost due to the closure of the fridge division is not recovered.

Cost of capital = 11%

Estimated value based on cash flows to perpetuity = $28·4 \div (0·11 - 0·05) = \$473·3m$

This is over 50% in excess of the funds invested in the new venture.

Answer 30 PROTEUS CO

(a) **Possible benefits of divesting Tyche through a management buy-out**

Management buy-out costs may be less for Proteus compared with other forms of disposal such as selling the assets of the company or selling the company to a third party.

It may be the quickest method in raising funds for Proteus compared to the other methods.

There would be less resistance from the managers and employees, making the process smoother and easier to accomplish.

Proteus may retain a better relationship and beneficial links with Tyche and may be able to purchase or sell goods and services to it, as seems to have happened with the management service.

It may be able to get a better price for the company. The current management and employees possibly have the best knowledge of the company and are able to make it successful. Therefore they may be willing to pay more for it.

It may increase Proteus's reputation among its internal stakeholders such as the management and employees. It may also increase its reputation with external stakeholders and the markets if it manages the disposal successfully and efficiently.

Tutorial note: *Credit would be given for alternative relevant comments.*

(b) **Potential breach of debt covenant**

In order to forecast whether or not the covenant is likely to be breached, the proportion of debt to equity needs to be calculated each year. The debt will reduce by $3 million every year and the equity will increase by reserves every year. In order to calculate the increase in reserves every year, the forecast statements of profit or loss need to be determined.

Forecast statements of profit or loss ($000s)

Years	1	2	3	4	5
Operating income before management fee (W1)	23,760	25,661	27,714	29,931	32,325
Management service fee	12,000	12,960	13,997	15,116	16,326
Interest payable (W2)	5,850	5,580	5,310	5,040	4,770
Profit before tax	5,910	7,121	8,407	9,775	11,229
Tax payable (25%)	1,478	1,780	2,102	2,444	2,807
Profit after tax	4,432	5,341	6,305	7,331	8,422
Dividend payable (25%)	1,108	1,335	1,576	1,833	2,106
Balance transferred to reserves	3,324	4,006	4,729	5,498	6,316

Book value of equity

Years	1	2	3	4	5
Opening equity	16,000	19,324	23,330	28,059	33,557
Reserves	3,324	4,006	4,729	5,498	6,316
Closing equity	19,324	23,330	28,059	33,557	39,873

Debt/Equity computations

Years	1	2	3	4	5
Debt at year end	62,000	59,000	56,000	53,000	50,000
Equity value at year end	19,324	23,330	28,059	33,557	39,873
Debt ÷ Equity	321%	253%	200%	158%	125%
Restrictive condition	350%	250%	200%	150%	125%
Restriction breached?	No	Yes	No	Yes	No

WORKINGS

(1) Operating income before management fee

Current operating profit before management service charge = $60,000,000 – ($12,000,000 + 22,000,000 + 4,000,000) = $22,000,000. This amount will grow by 8% every year.

(2) Interest payable ($000s)

Years	1	2	3	4	5
Outstanding loan at the start of the year	65,000	62,000	59,000	56,000	53,000
Interest	5,850	5,580	5,310	5,040	4,770

(c) Implications

Based on the calculations in part (b) above, the restrictive covenant is due to be breached in years two and four. In years three and five, it has just been met, and only in year one will Tyche be operating well within the conditions of the restrictive covenant. This raises two main issues:

(1) Tyche needs to establish how the bank will react to the conditions not being met and will it put Tyche's business in jeopardy?

(2) Because the conditions are nearly breached in years three and five, Tyche needs to determine the likelihood of the revenues and costs figures being achieved. A very small deviation from the figures may cause the conditions to be breached.

Sensitivity analysis and other forms of risk analysis may need to be undertaken and provisions put into place to deal with unexpected breaches in the covenant.

Possible actions

Tyche can consider the following possible actions in the years where it is likely that the covenant may be breached:

- The directors may decide to award themselves and the other shareholders lower or no dividends. This would probably need to be negotiated and agreed.

- The directors may want to ask the venture capitalist to take a higher equity stake for more funds at the outset. Both parties would need to agree to this.

- Tyche may want to try and negotiate less onerous terms with the bank or ask it for more flexibility when applying the restrictive covenant. Given that the restrictive covenant is not likely to be breached by a significant amount, the bank will probably not want to undertake legal proceedings to close Tyche and would probably be open to negotiations.

- Tyche may decide to pay off more of the loan each year from its cash reserves, if it has enough funds, in order to reduce the year-end outstanding debt.

Tutorial note: *Only two actions were required.*

Answer 31 COEDEN CO

(a)   **Impact of unbundling on cost of capital**

Before implementing the proposal

Cost of equity = 4% + 1·1 × 6% = 10·6%
Cost of debt = 4% + 0·9% = 4·9%

Market value of debt (MV$_d$):

Per $100: $5·2 × 1·049^{-1} + $5·2 × 1·049^{-2} + $105·2 × 1·049^{-3} = $100·82
Total value = $42,000,000 × $100·82 ÷ $100 = $42,344,400

Market value of equity (MV$_e$):

As share price is not given, use the free cash flow growth model to estimate this. The question states that the free cash flow to equity model provides a reasonable estimate of the current market value of the company.

Assumption 1: *Estimate growth rate using the rb model. The assumption here is that free cash flows to equity (FCFE) which are retained will be invested to yield at least at the rate of return required by the company's shareholders. This is the estimate of how much the free cash flows to equity will grow by each year.*

r = 10·6% and b = 0·4, therefore g is estimated at 10·6% × 0·4 = 4·24%

MV$_e$ = 2,600 × 1·0424 ÷ (0·106 – 0·0424) approximately = $42,614,000

Tutorial note: *The examiner's answer values equity based on the gross FCFE of 2,600 which is before deducting growth expenditure. There is a strong argument that the equity valuation should in fact be based upon the net FCFE (i.e. 2,600 × 60% × 1·0424 ÷ (0·106 – 0·0424) = $25,568,000). This approach would be accepted by the marking team.*

The proportion of MV$_e$ to MV$_d$ is approximately 50:50

Therefore, cost of capital:
10·6% × 0·5 + 4·9% × 0·5 × 0·8 = 7·3%

After implementing the proposal

Coeden, asset beta estimate
1·1 × 0·5 ÷ (0·5 + 0·5 × 0·8) = 0·61

Asset beta, hotel services only

Assumption 2: *The question does not provide an asset beta for hotel services only, which is the approximate measure of Coeden's business risk once the properties are sold. Assume that Coeden's asset beta is a weighted average of the property companies' average beta and hotel services beta.*

Asset beta of hotel services only:
0·61 = Asset beta (hotel services) × 60% + 0·4 × 40%
Asset beta (hotel services only) approximately = 0·75

Coeden, hotel services only, estimate of equity beta

MV_e = $42,614,000 (Based on the assumption stated in the question)

MV_d = Per $100: $5·2 × 1·046^{-1} + $5·2 × 1·046^{-2} + $105·2 × 1·046^{-3} = $101·65
Total value = $12,600,000 × $101·65 ÷ $100 = $12,807,900 say $12,808,000

0·75 = equity beta × 42,614 ÷ (42,614 + 12,808 × 0·8)
0·75 = equity beta × 0·806
Equity beta = 0·93

Coeden, hotel services only, WACC

Cost of equity = 4% + 0·93 × 6% = 9·6%
Cost of capital = 9·6% × 0·769 + 4·6% × 0·231 × 0·8 = 8·2%

Comment

	Before proposal implementation	*After proposal implementation*
Cost of equity	10·6%	9·6%
WACC	7·3%	8·2%

Implementing the proposal would increase the asset beta of Coeden because the hotel services industry on its own has a higher business risk than a business which owns its own hotels as well. However, the equity beta and cost of equity both decrease because of the fall in the level of debt and the consequent reduction in the company's financial risk. The company's cost of capital increases because the lower debt level reduces the extent to which the weighted average cost of capital can be reduced due to the lower cost of debt. Hence the board of directors is not correct in assuming that the lower level of debt will reduce the company's cost of capital.

(b) **Potential change in market value of equity**

It is unlikely that the market value of equity would remain unchanged because of the change in the growth rate of free cash flows and sales revenue, and the change in the risk situation due to the changes in the business and financial risks of the new business.

In estimating the asset beta of Coeden as offering hotel services only, no account is taken of the changes in business risk due to renting rather than owning the hotels. A revised asset beta may need to be estimated due to changes in the business risk.

The market value of equity is used to estimate the equity beta and the cost of equity of the business after the implementation of the proposal. But the market value of equity is dependent on the cost of equity, which is, in turn, dependent on the equity beta. Therefore, neither the cost of equity nor the market value of equity is independent of each other and they both will change as a result of the change in business strategy.

(c) **Demerger**

A demerger would involve the company splitting into two (or more) parts, with each part becoming a separate, independent company. The shareholders would then hold shares in each separate, independent company.

Each company would most probably have its own separate management team. On the other hand, selling the hotel properties outright would be termed as a divestment, where a company would sell part of its assets.

Benefits

There are a number of possible benefits in pursuing a demerger option for Coeden and its shareholders. The management teams would be able to focus on creating value for each company separately, and create a unique financial structure that is suitable for each company. The full value of each company would become apparent as a result. Coeden's shareholders may have invested in the company specifically for its risk profile and selling the properties may imbalance their portfolios. With a demerger, the portfolio diversification remains unchanged. Communication may be stronger between the two management teams with a demerger. Since Coeden trades heavily on its brand name, the quality and maintenance of the hotel properties is critical, and good communication links will help ensure that these are safeguarded. However, responsibility for maintenance of the properties will need to be negotiated. Selling a lot of properties all at once may flood the market and lower the value that can be obtained for each hotel property.

Drawbacks

A number of possible drawbacks for Coeden and its shareholders may occur if it pursues the option to demerge. The demerger may be an expensive process to undertake and may result in a decline in the value of the companies overall. The bond holders may not agree to 70% of the long-term loans to be transferred to a property company and may ask for the terms of the loans to be re-negotiated. The new property company would need to raise the extra finance to pay the cash for the remaining property values. Coeden may not have the expertise amongst its management staff to manage a property company or to recruit an appropriate management team. Overall, the main drawbacks revolve around the additional costs that would probably need to be incurred if the demerger option is pursued.

Tutorial note: *Credit would be given for alternative, valid points.*

Answer 32 NUBO CO

(a)   **Sale as going concern or separate assets**

Current and non-current liabilities = $387m + $95m = $482m

Sale of assets of supermarkets division
Proportion of assets to supermarkets division
Non-current assets = 70% × $550m = $385m; Current assets = 70% × $122m = $85·4m

Sale of assets = $385m × 1·15 + $85·4m × 0·80 = $511·07m

Sale of supermarkets division as a going concern
Profit after tax attributable to the supermarkets division: ½ × $166m = $83m

Estimate of value of supermarkets division based on the PE ratio of supermarket industry: $83 × 7 = $581m.

Tutorial note: *Multiplying profit after tax by the PE ratio actually gives the value of equity (assets minus liabilities) rather than the value of assets as suggested by the model answer.*

Although both options generate sufficient funds to pay for the liabilities, the sale of the supermarkets division as a going concern would generate higher cash flows and the spare cash of $99m [$581m – $482m] can be used by Nubo for future investments. This is based on the assumption that the value based on the industries' PE ratios is accurate.

Proportion of assets remaining within Nubo
30% × ($550m + $122m) = $201·6m

Add extra cash generated from the sale of $99m

Maximum debt capacity = $300·6m

Total additional funds available to Nubo for new investments = $300·6m + $99m = $399·6m

(b)   Demerger

A demerger would involve splitting Nubo into two separate companies which would then operate independently of each other. The equity holders in Nubo would continue to have an equity stake in both companies.

Normally demergers are undertaken to ensure that each company's equity values are fair. For example, the value of the aircraft parts production division based on the PE ratio gives a value of $996m (12 × $83m) and the value of the supermarkets division as $581m. If the current company's value is less than the combined values of $1,577m, then a demerger may be beneficial. However, the management and shareholders of the new supermarkets company may not be keen to take over all the debt.

Nubo's equity holders may view the demerger more favourably than the sale of the supermarkets division. At present their equity investment is diversified between the aircraft parts production and supermarkets. If the supermarkets division is sold, then the level of their diversification may be affected. With the demerger, since the equity holders will retain an equity stake in both companies, the benefit of diversification is retained.

However, the extra $99m cash generated from the sale will be lost in the case of a demerger. Furthermore, if the new aircraft parts production company can only borrow 100% of its asset value, then its borrowing capacity and additional funds available to it for new investments will be limited to $201·6m instead of $399·6m.

(c)   Mudaraba vs musharaka

With a Mudaraba contract, the profits which Pilvi makes from the joint venture would be shared according to a pre-agreed arrangement when the contract is constructed between Pilvi and Ulap Bank. Losses, however, would be borne solely by Ulap Bank as the provider of the finance, although provisions can be made where losses can be written off against future profits. Ulap Bank would not be involved in the executive decision-making process. In effect, Ulap Bank's role in the relationship would be similar to an equity holder, holding a small number of shares in a large organisation.

With a Musharaka contract, the profits which Pilvi makes from the joint venture would still be shared according to a pre-agreed arrangement similar to a Mudaraba contract, but losses would also be shared according to the capital or other assets and services contributed by both the parties involved in the arrangement. Therefore a value could be put to the contribution-in-kind made by Pilvi and any losses would be shared by Ulap Bank and Pilvi accordingly. Within a Musharaka contract, Ulap Bank can also take the role of an active partner and participate in the executive decision-making process. In effect, the role adopted by Ulap Bank would be similar to that of a venture capitalist.

With the Mudaraba contract, Pilvi would essentially be an agent to Ulap Bank, and many of the agency issues facing corporations would apply to the arrangement, where Pilvi can maximise its own benefit at the expense of Ulap Bank. Pilvi may also have a propensity to undertake excessive risk because it is essentially holding a long call option with an unlimited upside and a limited downside.

1088

Ulap Bank may prefer the Musharaka contract in this case, because it may be of the opinion that it needs to be involved with the project and monitor performance closely due to the inherent risk and uncertainty of the venture, and also to ensure that the revenues, expenditure and time schedules are maintained within initially agreed parameters. In this way, it may be able to monitor and control agency related issues more effectively and control Pilvi's risky actions and decisions. Being closely involved with the venture would change both Pilvi's and Ulap Bank's roles and make them more like stakeholders rather than principals and agents, with a more equitable distribution of power between the two parties.

Nubo's concerns would mainly revolve around whether it can work with Ulap Bank and the extra time and cost which would need to be incurred before the joint venture can start. If Pilvi had not approached Ulap Bank for funding, the relationship between Nubo and Pilvi would be less complex within the joint venture. Although difficulties may arise about percentage ownership and profit sharing, these may be resolved through negotiation and having tight specific contracts. The day-to-day running, management and decision-making process could be resolved through negotiation and consensus. Therefore having a third party involved in all aspects of the joint venture complicates matters.

Nubo may feel that it was not properly consulted about the arrangements between Pilvi and Ulap Bank, and Pilvi would need to discuss the involvement of Ulap Bank with Nubo and gets its agreement prior to formalising any arrangements. This is to ensure a high level of trust continues to exist between the parties, otherwise the venture may fail.

Nubo may want clear agreements on ownership and profit-sharing. They would want to ensure that the contract clearly distinguishes them as not being part of the Musharaka arrangement which exists between Pilvi and Ulap Bank. Hence negotiation and construction of the contracts may need more time and may become more expensive.

Nubo may have felt that it could work with Pilvi on a day-to-day basis and could resolve tough decisions in a reasonable manner. It may not feel the same about Ulap Bank initially. Clear parameters would need to be set up on how executive decision making will be conducted by the three parties. Therefore, the integration process of bringing a third partner into the joint venture needs to be handled with care and may take time and cost more money.

The above issues would indicate that the relationship between the three parties is closer to that of stakeholders, with different levels of power and influence, at different times, as opposed to a principal–agent relationship. This would create an environment which would need ongoing negotiation and a need for consensus, which may make the joint venture hard work. Additionally, it would possibly be more difficult and time consuming to accomplish the aims of the joint venture.

Tutorial note: *Credit would be given for alternative relevant comments and suggestions for parts (b) and (c).*

Answer 33 ASTON CO

(a)   **Probability of default**

Default is defined as that point at which the firm is unable to meet its interest and/or principal payments when they fall due. From the monthly average cash flow we deduct the monthly interest payment. The monthly payment is based on the effective monthly rate as follows:

$$i_m = \sqrt[1/12]{(1 + i_a)} - 1 = \sqrt[1/12]{1.08} - 1 = 0.6434\%$$

The expected monthly cash flow will then be:

$c_m = \$14,400 - (0 \cdot 006434 \times \$1,500,000) = \$4,748 \cdot 4.$

To give an annual expected cash flow after interest of $56,987·4.

We now need to determine the probability over the course of 12 months that this figure will fall below zero. For this we need to calculate the annual volatility of cash flows. Given that the monthly volatility before interest is 13%, we must translate this to volatility after fixed interest in two stages. First, calculate the proportion of fixed interest to monthly cash flow (G):

$$G = \frac{(0.006434 \times \$1,500,000)}{14,400} = 0.6702$$

And second, calculate the monthly volatility after interest (σ_m) as follows:

$$\sigma_m = \frac{\sigma'_m}{1 - G} = \frac{13\%}{1 - 0.6702} = 39.42\%$$

The annualised volatility is as follows:

Annualised volatility $= 0.3942 \times \sqrt{12} = 136 \cdot 55\%$

Standard deviation of annual cash flows $= 136 \cdot 55\% \times \$56,987 = \$77,818$

Tutorial note: *The volatility of cash flows can be calculated more simply because the dollar volatility of pre-interest cash flow is by definition the same as the dollar volatility of the post-interest cash flow. Hence dollar volatility $= \$14,400 \times 12 \times 13\% \times \sqrt{12} = \$77,818$.*

Given a critical cash value of zero (i.e. if the cash flow less interest falls below zero) then the expected cash difference to default including the $8,500 of cash in hand is $65,487. This figure represents 0·842 standard deviations.

Using the standard normal tables this shows a value of 0·3 or a cumulative probability that the cash flow plus reserve will be above the default probability of 0·8. This tells us that there is a 20% chance of failure within 12 months.

(b)   **Issues to be considered by the bank**

Making a loan of this type resolves down to an estimate of the probability of default, the potential default loss, the rate the lender needs to recover to cover the cost of finance in the inter-bank market plus an additional charge for bearing the risk attaching to the loan.

The probability of default on interest payments is determined by the expected annual cash flow after interest payments and the volatility of that residual cash flow. If, on an annual basis, that cash flow falls below zero then default is deemed to occur.

The next most important issue for a lender is the potential recoverability of its borrowing. This will be governed by a number of factors: the percentage of the loan covered by the firm's net assets excluding the loan, the liquidity of those assets under forced sale, the market demand for these assets (and hence their price) and any director's or other guarantees that may be in place. If the net assets exceed the value of the outstanding loan then default will not occur as it would be possible for the firm to liquidate some of the surplus asset value to service the debt.

In this case the probability of recovery is 90% which implies a loss of 10% of the loan in the event of default. When estimating its potential loss the bank will calculate the present value of the outcomes over a year of each \$1 invested discounting at the risk free rate plus the additional rate of return it requires as compensation for bearing the risk of default. Using the following decision tree:

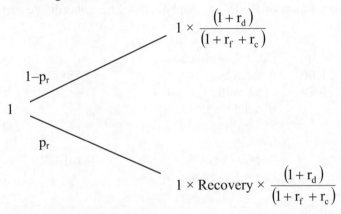

Where: p_r is the probability of default, r_d is the rate of return required to compensate for the loss on default, r_f is the risk free rate and r_c is the additional return required by the bank for bearing the risk attaching to this loan.

The logic of this calculation is that the bank has put at risk, over 12 months, the value of its original loan (\$1) and the rate of interest it decides to charge (r_d). If the bank was indifferent to the outcomes (i.e. it is risk neutral with respect to those outcomes) then it would discount each of the possibilities at the risk free rate (r_f). However, it is not risk neutral and r_c is the premium it requires to offset its risk aversion.

Putting the information provided into an equation and solving:

$$1 = (1 - p_r) \times \frac{(1 + r_d)}{(1 + r_f + r_c)} + p_r \times \text{Recovery} \times \frac{(1 + r_d)}{(1 + r_f + r_c)}$$

$$r_d = \frac{1 + r_f + 0.034}{(1 - p_r) + p_r \times \text{Recovery}} - 1 = \frac{1.0584}{(1 - 0.2) + 0.2 \times 0.9} - 1 = 8.00\%$$

To summarise, the bank requires 5·5% to cover its own cost of finance on the money market, 2·16% to cover the expected loss on the loan given the probability of default and the potential for recovery and 0·34% as compensation for carrying the risk attaching to the loan.

In practice the estimation of default probability and recoverability will depend upon a number of judgements about the credit-worthiness of the business, an assessment of its business plan and the willingness of the lender to finance a high risk business of this type.

Answer 34 GOSLO

(a) **Expected return on each tranche**

Tutorial note: *This scenario is about the process of securitisation (i.e. the transformation of illiquid assets (in this case loans made to customers) into liquid assets (i.e. cash) which could then be used to make another cycle of loans). The underlying loans are used as security for the Collateralised Loan Obligation (CLO) issue (in fact the CLO will be slightly over-collateralised as its face value will be only 95% of the underlying loans). The CLO is known as a structured finance product as it is split into three tranches (i) the top or senior tranche (ii) the middle or "mezzanine" tranche (iii) the bottom or "equity" tranche. As income is received from the underlying pool of loans it is used to progressively service the tranches in the CLO like a cascade.*

In order to estimate the returns an annual cash account should be created showing the cash flow receivable from the pool of assets and the cash payments against the various liabilities created by the securitisation process. In this securitisation a degree of leverage has been introduced by the swap giving a return of 19·05% to the holders of the subordinate certificates but carrying a high degree of risk.

Cash flow receivable	$m	*Cash flow payable*		$m
$200 million × 10·5%	21·00	A-rated bonds	LIBOR	
less service charge	0·24	$152 million at 1·4%		2·13
		B-rated bonds		
		$19 million at 11%		2·09
		SWAP		
		Receive LIBOR	–LIBOR	
		Pay 8·5% on $152m		12·92
	20·76			17·14
		Balance to the subordinated certificates		3·62

Tutorial note: *The face value of the A-rated bonds has been calculated as $200m × 95% × 80% = $152m.*

The return to the holders of the certificates is $3·62 million on $19 million or 19·05%. A reduction of 1% in the cash flow receivable brings about a fall in the annual receivable to $20·79 million, reducing the balance available for the subordinated certificates to $3·41 million. A reduction of 1% in the cash flow receivable, results in a fall of 5·80% ((3·62 – 3·41) ÷ 3·62) in revenue of the subordinated certificates.

(b) **Credit enhancement**

After the securitisation of mortgages, car loan securitisation is the most important source of refinancing in the US and in Europe. Structured finance arrangements such as this are also used in a variety of other industries from banking to entertainment.

The process of credit enhancement is the process whereby a relatively high risk cash flow (car loans) can be converted into a range of collateralised loan obligations satisfying the varying risk appetites of different investors. In the securitisation process a rating agency would normally advise on the structure of the liabilities created such that the AAA tranche will attract investors such as banks and other financial institutions who demand a low level of risk exposure. This reduction in risk for the senior and intermediate level notes is balanced by a significant transfer of risk to the subordinated certificate holders. Tranching the issue rather than creating a single issue of an asset backed security is the most important mechanism for credit enhancement.

Other approaches can entail insuring the risk of the issue through the use of credit default swaps or by transferring a greater asset pool than is securitised (over collateralisation).

Tutorial note: *The process of securitisation is usually achieved through the formation of an offshore Special Purpose Vehicle (SPV). The underlying pool of loans (and their future income stream) would be transferred into the SPV which would be "ring-fenced" (i.e. could not be touched if the company itself become insolvent). The SPV will therefore achieve an enhanced credit rating upon which it can issue the CLOs.*

(c) **Risks for investors in structured finance products**

Correlation risk: it is often assumed that defaults on the asset side of the securitisation process are uncorrelated. However, if a degree of positive correlation is present (such as defaulting car loans being positively associated with rising unemployment) then this can create higher than anticipated volatility in the receivables.

Timing and liquidity risk: the question only refers to average returns which presumably consist of a mixture of repayments, interest and possibly the anticipated recovery from repossessions. Modelling the cash flow "waterfall" is a difficult issue where the timing of the cash receipts is crucial in fulfilling the commitments to the various tranches.

Default and collateral risk: the success of the securitisation will be dependent upon the assessment of the quality of the loans made to car purchasers. Dealers selling cars are responsible for the primary credit assessment and tight controls are necessary for ensuring that the loans are properly negotiated. Risk arises both in terms of default but also in the value of the vehicle on repossession.

From GoSlo's perspective the risks attaching to the process are more straightforward and to a certain extent depend on the motivation for the securitisation. If it is simply to refinance activity then the risk is that the issues will be undersubscribed. If it is also to remove the assets from the statement of financial position then much will depend on whether loans of this type can be transferred to a special purpose vehicle such that full legal ownership passes.

Tutorial note: *An example of the risks associated with structured finance products is the role of CMOs (Collateralised Mortgage Obligations) in the financial crisis of 2007. US mortgage banks had made significant amounts of high risk home loans to sub-prime borrowers. Fearing default on these loans the banks transferred them into offshore SPVs, paid the fees of credit ratings agencies, and securitised the loans into CMO issues. As quality financial journals such as The Economist had warned for many years "risk can be packaged, repackaged and endlessly transferred – but it will not have disappeared".*

Answer 35 LEVANTE CO

(a) **Impact on existing bond of cut in credit rating**

Tutorial note: *A "spot" interest rate refers to the required return on a specific future cash flow. Rather than discounting every cash flow at a bond's overall yield to maturity (which is itself an average of spot rates) it is more accurate to separately value each constituent cash flow at the specific spot rate for that period.*

Spot yield rates applicable to Levante (based on A credit rating)

1 year	3·85%
2 year	4·46%
3 year	5·07%
4 year	5·80%
5 year	6·12%

Bond value based on A rating =
$$\$4 \times 1\cdot0385^{-1} + \$4 \times 1\cdot0446^{-2} + \$104 \times 1\cdot0507^{-3} = \$97\cdot18 \text{ per } \$100$$

Current price based on AA rating = $98·71

Fall in value = $(97\cdot18 - 98\cdot71) \div 98\cdot71 \times 100\% = 1\cdot55\%$

(b)   **New bond issue**

Spot rates applicable to Levante (based on A credit rating) [from above]:

1 year	3·85%
2 year	4·46%
3 year	5·07%
4 year	5·80%
5 year	6·12%

(i)   *Value of 5% coupon bond*

$$\$5 \times 1\cdot0385^{-1} + \$5 \times 1\cdot0446^{-2} + \$5 \times 1\cdot0507^{-3} + \$5 \times 1\cdot0580^{-4} + \$105 \times 1\cdot0612^{-5} = \$95\cdot72$$
Hence the bond will need to be issued at a discount if only a 5% coupon is offered.

(ii)   *Coupon rate to allow issue at $100 par value*

Since the 5% coupon bond is only valued at $95·72, a higher coupon needs to be offered. The required coupon equals the yield to maturity (YTM) of the 5% coupon bond above. YTM is the internal rate of return (IRR) of the bond (i.e. the annualised rate that discounts the future cash flows to the market price).

$$\$5 \times (1 + YTM)^{-1} + \$5 \times (1 + YTM)^{-2} + \$5 \times (1 + YTM)^{-3} + \$5 \times (1 + YTM)^{-4} + \$105 \times (1 + YTM)^{-5} = \$95\cdot72$$

Trial and error estimates YTM at approximately 6%; this gives the bond value as $95·78, which is close enough to $95·72
$$\$5 \times (1\cdot06)^{-1} + \$5 \times (1\cdot06)^{-2} + \$5 \times (1\cdot06)^{-3} + \$5 \times (1\cdot06)^{-4} + \$105 \times (1\cdot06)^{-5} = \$95\cdot78$$

Hence if the coupon payment is 6% or $6 per $100 bond unit then the bond market value will equal the par value at $100.

$$\$6 \times (1\cdot06)^{-1} + \$6 \times (1\cdot06)^{-2} + \$6 \times (1\cdot06)^{-3} + \$6 \times (1\cdot06)^{-4} + \$106 \times (1\cdot06)^{-5} = \$100$$

Alternatively

Take R as the coupon rate, such that:

$$(R \times 1\cdot0385^{-1}) + (R \times 1\cdot0446^{-2}) + (R \times 1\cdot0507^{-3}) + (R \times 1\cdot0580^{-4}) + (R \times 1\cdot0612^{-5}) + (100 \times 1\cdot0612^{-5}) = \$100$$

$4\cdot2826R + 74\cdot30 = \$100$
$R = 6\%$ or $6 per $100

Advice

If only a 5% coupon is offered, the bonds will have to be issued at just under a 4·3% discount. To raise the full $150 million, if the bonds are issued at a 4·3% discount, then 1,567,398 $100 bond units need to be issued (1,500,000 × 100 ÷ (100 – 4.3)) This is an extra 67,398 bond units for which Levante will need to pay an extra $6,739,800 when the bonds are redeemed in five years.

On the other hand, paying a higher coupon every year of 6% instead of 5% will mean that an additional annual interest payment of $1,500,000 is needed for each of the next five years.

If the directors feel that the drain in resources of $1,500,000 every year is substantial and that the project's profits will cover the extra $6,739,800 in five years' time, then they should issue the bond at a discount and at a lower coupon rate. On the other hand, if the directors feel that they would like to spread the amount payable then they should opt for the higher coupon alternative.

(c)   **International equity finance**

The key advantages of accessing overseas equity markets include:

- Potentially larger amounts of finance could be raised than in domestic markets – this is particularly relevant to firms in emerging markets where the local stock exchange may not be well developed, or even non-existent.

- Increased reputation of the firm – particularly if the overseas stock exchange requires high levels of corporate governance.

- Creating a wider shareholder base – potentially reducing the risk of conflicts between individual investors.

If the firm is able to meet the regulatory requirements for directly listing its shares on an overseas market then, in terms on boosting its reputation and increasing its international exposure, this may be the preferred route. However the costs of the initial listing, followed by annual compliance costs, may be prohibitive, particularly for a relatively small firm.

The listing rules of major global stock markets are provided below.

Tutorial note: *Candidates would be expected to have an overall appreciation of regulatory requirements rather than detailed knowledge.*

Key: NYSE = New York Stock Exchange, NASDAQ = New York based market for technology firms LSE = London Stock Exchange (main market), Euronext = a pan-European stock exchange based in Amsterdam and with subsidiaries in Belgium, France, Portugal and the United Kingdom. Euronext is part of the NYSE group.

"Free float" refers to the value, number, or proportion, of shares available to the general public.

	NYSE	NASDAQ	Tokyo	LSE	Euronext
Minimum free float	$40m	1.25m shares	30%	25%	25%
Minimum market capitalization	$150m	$160m	2bn yen	£700,000	none
Minimum years of audited accounts	1 year	1 year	3 years	3 years	3 years

In addition the authorities of the firm's home country may prohibit the listing of its shares on overseas markets or insist that it simultaneously makes on issue in the domestic market. Such restrictions are particularly common for firms in emerging markets. In this case it may be preferable to indirectly access overseas markets through the issue of depository receipts.

A depositary receipt (DR) is a negotiable (transferable) instrument that is traded on a major stock exchange and represents a share that has been issued by a foreign company on its local market. One of the most common types of DRs is the American depositary receipt (ADR) but DRs have spread to other parts of the globe in the form of global depositary receipts (GDRs). ADRs are typically traded on the New York Stock Exchange (NYSE) and GDRs are commonly listed on the London Stock Exchange. Both ADRs and GDRs are usually denominated in US dollars, but can also be denominated in Euros.

In the US "Level I" ADRs are traded in the Over the Counter (OTC) market and "level II ADRs" are traded on the NYSE. An Initial Public Offerings (IPOs) to raise new finance would require a "level III ADR" which carries higher regulatory requirements.

(d)   **International debt finance**

Euromarkets refer to investing or borrowing currency outside of its country of issue. In this context "Euro" does not refer to the European single currency but to the offshore nature of the Euromarkets.

Euromarkets are attractive to potential investors as interest is paid gross, without the deduction of withholding tax. Investors also enjoy the privacy of the Euromarkets, either via the light regulation of offshore banks or the "bearer form" characteristic of Eurobonds (i.e. possession of the certificate is bone fide evidence of ownership and no register of investors is maintained).

For the above reasons firms can raise large amounts of finance at relatively low cost in the Euromarkets.

If Euromarkets are used the main choices for a firm are:

(i)   Eurocurrency or Eurocredit loans from the international banking system;
(ii)   The issue of securities direct to the market.

The Eurocurrency market specialises in short to medium-term loans. Large loans can be raised quickly with issue costs, often through syndicates of banks. Eurocredits are medium-long term international bank loans, which may be arranged by individual banks or syndicates. Interest on both of these types of loan is normally at a floating rate benchmarked to LIBOR. Draw-down dates are often flexible, but additional fees may be payable if the full amount of the loan is not taken immediately, and early redemption penalties are common.

There are various options if issuing securities on the Euromarket:

■   The Euronote market involves short to medium-term issues of high quality commercial paper;

■   Euro-medium term notes, usually underwritten by a bank;

■   Eurobonds, medium to long-term foreign currency bonds.

Both the Eurobond and Euronote market provide the opportunity to borrow either fixed or floating rate finance. Eurobonds may be convertible or have warrants attached which can offer attractions to both issuers and investors.

A disadvantage of the Eurobond market is that issue costs are higher than the Eurocurrency market, and it takes longer to arrange Eurobond issues.

Answer 36 ENNEA CO

(a)   Impact of proposals

Forecast financial position

Amounts in $000	Current	Proposal 1	Proposal 2	Proposal 3
Non-current assets	282,000	282,000	302,000	257,000
Current assets	66,000	64,720	67,720	63,682
Total assets	348,000	346,720	369,720	320,682
Current liabilities	37,000	37,000	37,000	37,000
Non-current liabilities	140,000	160,000	160,000	113,000
Total liabilities	177,000	197,000	197,000	150,000
Share capital (40c per share)	48,000	45,500	48,000	48,000
Retained earnings	123,000	104,220	124,720	122,682
Total equity	171,000	149,720	172,720	170,682
Total liabilities and capital	348,000	346,720	369,720	320,682

Adjustments to forecast earnings

Amounts in $000	Current	Proposal 1	Proposal 2	Proposal 3
Initial profit after tax	26,000	26,000	26,000	26,000
Interest on additional borrowing ($20m $\times$ 6% $\times$ (1 $-$ 0·2))		(960)	(960)	
Additional interest on extra coupon ($160m $\times$ 0·25% $\times$ (1 $-$ 0·2))		(320)	(320)	
Interest saved on less borrowing ($27m $\times$ 6% $\times$ (1 $-$ 0·2))				1,296
Interest saved on lower coupon ($113m $\times$ 0·15% $\times$ (1 $-$ 0·2))				136
Return on additional investment ($20m $\times$ 15%)			3,000	
Return lost on less investment ($25m $\times$ 15%)				(3,750)
Profit on sale of non-current assets				2,000
Adjusted profit after tax	26,000	24,720	27,720	25,682
Gearing % (non-current liabilities/equity)	81·9%	106·9%	92·6%	66·2%
Number of shares (000)	120,000	113,750	120,000	120,000
EPS (adjusted profit after tax ÷ number of shares)	21·67c	21·73c	23·10c	21·40c

Tutorial note: *Gearing defined as non-current liabilities ÷ (non-current liabilities + equity) and/or using market value of equity is acceptable as well.*

The profit from the sale of the assets for proposal 3, of $2,000,000, is assumed to be after tax. Answers which consider the profit to be before tax, and therefore only take into account $1,600,000 as the net profit, will receive full credit.

The following explanations are not required for the answer but are included to explain the approach taken:

Explanations of the financial position based on the three proposals

Proposal 1

Debt is increased by $20m and share capital reduced by the same amount as follows: from par value = $20m × 40c ÷ 320c = $2·5m; from retained earnings = $20m × 280c ÷ 320c = $17·5m.

Additional interest payable totalling $1,280,000 ($960,000 + $320,000) is taken off retained earnings due to reduction in profit after tax and taken off current assets because presumably it is paid from cash. Note that an alternative answer would be to add the additional interest payable to current liabilities.

Proposal 2

Debt and non-current assets are increased by $20m.

Additional interest payable as above, plus the additional investment of $20 million will generate a rate of return of 15%, which is $3,000,000 income. Net impact is $1,720,000 income which is added to retained earnings as an addition to profit after tax and added to current assets as a cash income (presumably).

Proposal 3

Net non-current assets are reduced by the $25 million, their value at disposal. Since they were sold for $27 million, this is how much the non-current liabilities are reduced by and the profit of $2 million is included in the retained earnings.

Interest saved totals $1,432,000 ($1,296,000 + $136,000). The reduction in investment of $25 million will lose $3,750,000, at a rate of return of 15%. Net impact is $2,318,000 loss which is subtracted from earnings as a reduction from profit after tax and deducted from current assets as a cash expense (presumably). Overall therefore the profit is reduced by $318,000 [$2,000,000 – $2,318,000].

If the profit from the sale of the asset is assumed to be $1,600,000 ($2,000,000 less tax), then the statement of financial position, EPS and gearing figures will all change to reflect this.

Discussion

Proposals 1 and 3 appear to produce opposite results to each other. Proposal 1 would lead to a small increase in the earnings per share (EPS) due to a reduction in the number of shares although profits would decrease by approximately 5%, due to the increase in the amount of interest payable as a result of increased borrowings. However, the level of gearing would increase substantially (by about 30%).

With proposal 3, although the overall profits would fall, because of the lost earnings due to downsizing being larger than the gain in interest saved and profit made on the sale of assets, this is less than proposal 1 (1·2%). Gearing would reduce substantially (19·2%).

Proposal 2 would give a significant boost in the EPS from 21·67c per share to 23·10c per share, which the other two proposals do not. This is mainly due to increase in earnings through extra investment. However, the amount of gearing would increase by more than 13%.

Overall proposal 1 appears to be the least attractive option. The choice between proposals 2 and 3 would be between whether the company would prefer larger EPS or less gearing. This would depend on factors such as the capital structure of the competitors, the reaction of the equity market to the proposals, the implications of the change in the risk profile of the company and the resultant impact on the cost of capital. Ennea should also bear in mind that the above are estimates and the actual results will probably differ from the forecasts.

Tutorial note: *Credit would be given for alternative relevant comments and suggestions.*

(b)   **Securitisation**

Asset securitisation in this case would involve taking the future incomes from the leases that Ennea makes and converting them into assets. These assets are sold as bonds now and the future income from lease interest will be used to pay coupons on the bonds. Effectively Ennea foregoes the future lease income and receives money from sale of the assets today.

The income from the various leases would be aggregated and pooled, and new securities (bonds) issued based on these. The tangible benefit from securitisation occurs when the pooled assets are divided into tranches and tranches are credit rated. The higher rated tranches would carry less risk and have less return, compared to lower rated tranches. If default occurs, the income of the lower tranches is reduced first, before the impact of increasing defaults move to the higher rated tranches. This allows an asset of low liquidity to be converted into securities which carry higher liquidity.

Ennea would face a number of barriers in undertaking such a process. Securitisation is an expensive process due to management costs, legal fees and ongoing administrative costs. The value of assets that Ennea wants to sell is small and therefore these costs would take up a significant proportion of the income. High cost implications mean that securitisation is not feasible for small asset pools.

Normally asset pools would not offer the full value of the asset as securities. For example, only 90% of the asset value would be converted into securities, leaving the remaining 10% as a buffer against possible default. This method of credit enhancement would help to credit-rate the tranches at higher levels and help their marketability. However, Ennea would not be able to take advantage of the full asset value if it proceeds with the asset securitisation.

Tutorial note: *Credit would be given for alternative relevant comments and suggestions.*

Answer 37 BOXLESS

(a)   **Share repurchases and stock splits**

   (i)   *Share repurchases*

Share repurchases are a way for companies to distribute earnings to shareholders other than by a cash dividend. They are also a means of altering a target capital structure; supporting the share price during periods of weakness; and deterring unwelcome take-over bids. Companies typically repurchase shares either by making a tender offer for a block of shares, or by buying the shares in the open market.

In the absence of taxation and transactions costs share repurchase and the payment of dividends should have the same effect on share value. However, the different treatment of taxation on dividends and capital gains in many countries may lead to a preference for share repurchases by investors.

If the repurchase of shares is by means of a tender offer, this will often be at a price in excess of the current market value, and may have a different effect on overall company value.

An important question for share value is what information a share repurchase conveys to the market about the company and its futures prospects.

Managers should take decisions that maximise the intrinsic value of the firm. This, in theory, involves undertaking the optimum amount of positive NPV investments. The use of share repurchases, and the payment of dividends, will therefore be influenced by the amount of investment that the company undertakes. When a company does not have sufficient investments to fully utilise available cash flow, the payment of dividends or share repurchases are more likely.

Analysts are believed to normally consider an increase in dividends or share repurchases as good news, as they suggest that the company has more cash, and possibly greater earnings potential, than previously believed. However, if this subsequently proves not to be so, share prices will adjust downwards.

Share repurchases in themselves do not create value for the company, but the market may see the information or signals that they provide as significant new information that will affect the share price.

(ii)   Share splits

Share splits are the issue of additional shares at no cost to existing shareholders in proportion to their current holdings, but with lower par value. Share splits have no effect on corporate cash flows and, in theory, should not affect the value of the company. The share price, in theory, should reduce proportionately to the number of new shares that are issued.

Motives for share splits

(i)   A company wishes to keep its share price within a given trading range (e.g. below £10 per share). It is sometimes argued that investors might be deterred by a high share price, and that lower share prices would ensure a broader spread of share ownership. Shareholders could actually lose from lower prices, as the bid-offer spread (the difference between buying and selling prices) is often higher as a percentage of share price for lower priced shares.

(ii)   Companies hope that the market will regard a share split as good news, and that the share price will increase (relative to the expected price) as a result of the announcement. Evidence suggests that even if such reaction occurs it is short-lived unless the company improves cash flows, increases dividends, etc. in subsequent periods.

(b) **Impact of changing tax rules**

(i)   *Impact on cash flows of alteration*

	Annovia £000	Cardenda £000	Sporoon £000
Taxable income	100	100	100
Local corporate income tax	40	25	20
Available for distribution	60	75	80
Amount paid as dividend to UK before withholding tax	42	30	64
Withholding tax on dividend	4·2	–	3·2
Distribution to UK gross of withholding tax	42	30	64
Grossed up for UK tax ($\times 100 \div (100 - \text{local tax rate})$)	70	40	80
UK tax liability (30%)	21	12	24
Foreign tax credit	21	10	19·2
UK tax payable	–	2	4·8

Overseas taxation is 92·4 (40 + 25 + 20 +4·2 +3·2). Total taxation is 99·2 (overseas tax plus UK tax).

If the UK government taxes gross income:

	Annovia £000	Cardenda £000	Sporoon £000
Income	100	100	100
Local corporate income tax	40	25	20
Available for distribution	60	75	80
Amount paid as dividend to UK before withholding tax	42	30	64
Withholding tax on dividend	4·2	–	3·2
Income for UK tax purposes	100	100	100
UK tax liability (30%)	30	30	30
Foreign tax credit	30	25	23·2
UK tax payable	–	5	6·8

Total taxation is 104·2, an increase of 5·0.

(ii)   *Using a tax haven holding company*

	Current situation £000	Proposed new tax £000
Gross distribution to UK from holding company (net of overseas corporate tax)	136	
Grossed up for UK tax	190	300
UK tax liability	57	90
Foreign tax credit	57	90
UK tax payable	–	–
Total taxation	92·4	92·4

In both cases using what is sometimes known as a dividend mixer company in a tax haven will reduce the total tax payable, by reducing the UK tax payable. This is because Boxless can make more use of the credits available in the UK from foreign tax that has been paid, especially in the relatively high tax country of Annovia. In the case of the proposed new tax rule, Boxless has paid sufficient foreign tax to save 11·8 in UK tax relative to not using the tax haven holding company.

Answer 38 LAMRI CO

(a)   Dividend capacity prior to TE proposal implementation

	$000
Operating profit (30% × $80,000,000)	24,000
Less interest (8% × $35,000,000)	(2,800)
Less taxation (28% × (24,000 – 2,800))	(5,936)
Less investment in working capital (15% × ($^{20}/_{120}$ × 80,000))	(2,000)
Less investment in additional non-current assets (25% × ($^{20}/_{120}$ × 80,000))	(3,333)
Less investment in project	(4,500)
Cash flows from domestic operations	5,431
Cash flows from overseas subsidiary dividend remittances (W1)	3,159
Additional tax payable on Magnolia profits (6% × 5,400)	(324)
Dividend capacity	8,266

Dividend Capacity After TE Proposal Implementation	
Cash flows from domestic operations (as above)	5,431
Cash flows from overseas subsidiaries dividend remittances (W2)	2,718
Additional tax payable on Magnolia profits (6% × 3,120)	(187)
Dividend capacity	7,962
Estimate of actual dividend for coming year (7,500 × 1·08)	8,100

Tutorial note: *The impact of depreciation is neutral, as this amount will be spent to retain assets at their current productive capability.*

WORKINGS

(1)   Prior to implementation of TE proposal

	Strymon $000	*Magnolia* $000
Sales revenue	5,700	15,000
Cost		
Variable	(3,600)	(2,400)
Fixed	(2,100)	(1,500)
Transfer		(5,700)
Profit before tax	Nil	5,400
Tax	Nil	1,188
Profit after tax	Nil	4,212
Remitted	Nil	3,159
Retained	Nil	1,053

(2)   **After implementation of TE proposal**

	Strymon	Magnolia
	$000	$000
Sales revenue	7,980	15,000
Cost		
Variable	(3,600)	(2,400)
Fixed	(2,100)	(1,500)
Transfer		(7,980)
Profit before tax	2,280	3,120
Tax (42%, 22%)	958	686
Profit after tax	1,322	2,434
Remitted (75% × 1,322 × 90%)	892	
Remitted		1,826
Retained	331	608
Total remitted	2,718	

(b)   **Impact of implementing TE proposal**

Lamri's dividend capacity before implementing TE's proposal ($8,266,000) is more than the dividend required for next year ($8,100,000). If the recommendation from TE is implemented as policy for next year then there is a possibility that Lamri will not have sufficient dividend capacity to make the required dividend payments. It requires $8,100,000 but will have $7,962,000 available. The reason is due to the additional tax that will be paid in the country in which Strymon operates, for which credit cannot be obtained. Effectively 14% additional tax and 10% withholding tax will be paid. Some of this amount is recovered because lower additional tax is paid on Magnolia's profits but not enough.

The difference between what is required and available is small and possible ways of making up the shortfall are as follows. Lamri could lower its growth rate in dividends to approximately 6·2% ((7,962 ÷ 7,500) – 1 × 100%) and have enough capacity to make the payment. However, if the reasons for the lower growth rate are not explained to the shareholders and accepted by them, the share price may fall.

An alternative could be to borrow the small amount needed possibly through increased overdraft facilities. However, Lamri may not want to increase its borrowings and may be reluctant to take this option. In addition to this, there is a possibility that because of the change of policy this shortfall may occur more often than just once, and Lamri may not want to increase borrowing regularly.

Lamri may consider postponing the project or part of the project, if that option were available. However, this must be considered in the context of the business. From the question narrative, the suggestion is that Lamri have a number of projects in the pipeline for the future. The option to delay may not be possible or feasible.

Perhaps the most obvious way to get the extra funds required is to ask the subsidiary companies (most probably Strymon) to remit a higher proportion of their profits as dividends. In the past Strymon did not make profits and none were retained hence there may be a case for a higher level of remittance from there. However, this may have a negative impact on the possible benefits, especially manager morale.

Tutorial note: *Credit would be given for alternative relevant suggestions (e.g. the use of a "dividend mixer company" positioned between the overseas subsidiaries and the ultimate parent company. The dividend mixer company (usually established in an offshore tax haven) would collect dividends from the subsidiaries and then pay a single dividend up to the parent company. If this scheme is carefully, legally and ethically designed it can maximise claims for double tax relief (i.e. reduce the group's overall tax burden).*

(c)   Possible advantages of basing a holding company in a tax haven

- Reducing the total tax paid by a multinational company by allowing better use to be made of credits from foreign tax payments by overseas subsidiaries against a domestic tax liability. This is typically due to the taxable income from overseas subsidiaries, if channelled via a tax haven holding company, being treated as coming from one source rather than several separate sources. This may allow more overseas tax credits to be fully utilised.

- Reduction of capital gains tax when taxable gains are made in foreign subsidiaries. Such gains may escape tax if they are deemed to accrue in the tax haven.

- A reduction in withholding tax. Diverting income through tax havens may reduce the withholding tax liability relative to making distributions direct from a subsidiary to a parent company.

- Holding companies may be tax efficient refinancing centres, which allow the efficient redistribution within the group of cash generated by overseas subsidiaries, without the cash being distributed via the parent company.

Answer 39 LIMNI CO

(a)   Dividend. financing and risk management policies

As a high growth company, Limni probably requires the cash flows it generates annually for investing in new projects and has therefore not paid any dividends. This is a common practice amongst high-growth companies, many of which declare that they have no intention of paying any dividends. The shareholder clientele in such companies expects to be rewarded by growth in equity value as a result of the investment policy of the company.

Capital structure theory would suggest that because of the benefit of the tax shield on interest payments, companies should have a mix of equity and debt in their capital structure. Furthermore, the pecking order proposition would suggest that companies tend to use internally generated funds before going to markets to raise debt capital initially and finally equity capital. The agency effects of having to provide extra information to the markets and where one investor group benefits at the expense of another have been cited as the main deterrents to companies seeking external sources of finance. To a certain extent, this seems to be the case with Limni in using internal finance first, but the pecking order proposition seems to be contradicted in that it seeks to go straight to the equity market and undertake rights issues thereafter. Perhaps the explanation for this can be gained from looking at the balance of business and financial risk. Since Limni operates in a rapidly changing industry, it probably faces significant business risk and therefore cannot afford to undertake high financial risk, which a capital structure containing significant levels of debt would entail. This, together with agency costs related to restrictive covenants, may have determined Limni's financing policy.

Risk management theory suggests that managing the volatility of cash flows enables a company to plan its investment strategy better. Since Limni uses internally generated funds to finance its projects, it needs to be certain that funds will be available when needed for the future projects, and therefore managing its cash flows will enable this. Moreover, because Limni faces high business risk, managing the risk that the company's managers cannot control through their actions, may be even more necessary.

The change to making dividend payments or undertaking share buybacks will affect all three policies. The company's clientele may change and this may cause share price fluctuations. However, since the recommendation for the change is being led by the shareholders, significant share price fluctuations may not happen. Limni's financing policy may change because having reduced internal funds means it may have to access debt markets and therefore have to look at its balance between business and financial risk. The change to Limni's financial structure may result in a change in its risk management policy, because it may be necessary to manage interest rate risk as well.

Tutorial note: *Credit would be given for alternative relevant comments.*

(b)   **Evaluation of dividend policies**

In the case of company Theta, dividends are growing but not at a stable rate. In fact company Theta is paying out $0·40 in dividends for every $1 in earnings, and has a fixed dividend cover ratio of 2·50. This would be confusing for the shareholders, as they would not know how much dividend they would receive from year to year.

Although profits have risen over the past five years, if profits do fall, company Theta may reduce dividends and therefore send the wrong signals to shareholders and investors. This may cause unnecessary fluctuations of the share price or result in a depressed share price.

In the case of company Omega, annual dividends are growing at a stable rate of approximately 5% per year, while the company's earnings are growing steadily at around 3% per year, resulting in an increasing payout ratio. Also a high proportion of earnings are paid out as dividends, increasing from 60% in 2012 to almost 65% in 2016. This would indicate a company operating in a mature industry, signalling that there are few new projects to invest in and therefore reducing the retention rate. Such an investment would be attractive to investors requiring high levels of dividend returns from their investments.

In the case of company Kappa, although a lower proportion of earnings is paid out as dividends (from about 20% in 2012 to about 27% in 2016), they are growing at a higher but stable rate of 29%–30% per year. The company's earnings are growing rapidly but erratically, ranging between 3% and 35% between 2012 and 2016. This probably indicates a growing company, possibly similar to Limni itself, where perhaps returns to investors having been coming from share price growth, but one where dividends are becoming more prominent. Such an investment would be attractive to investors requiring lower levels of dividend returns, but higher capital returns from their investments.

Due to company Theta's confusing dividend policy, which may lead to erratic dividend payouts and a depressed share price, Limni would probably not want to invest in that company. The choice between company Omega and company Kappa would depend on how Limni wants to receive its return from the investment, maybe taking into account factors such as taxation implications, and the period of time it wishes to invest for, in terms of when the returns from an investment will be maximised and when it will need the funds for future projects.

Tutorial note: *Credit would be given for alternative relevant comments.*

(c) **Increase in dividend capacity**

Current dividend capacity

	$000
Profit before tax (23% × $600,000,000)	138,000
Tax (26% × $138,000,000)	(35,880)
Profit after tax	102,120
Add back depreciation (25% × $220,000,000)	55,000
Less investment in assets	(67,000)
Remittances from overseas subsidiaries	15,000
Additional tax on remittances (6% × $15,000,000)	(900)
Dividend capacity	104,220

Increase in dividend capacity = 10% × $104,220,000 = $10,422,000

Gross up for tax = $10,422,000 ÷ 0·94 = $11,087,234

% increase in remittances from overseas subsidiaries = 73·9% [$11,087,234 ÷ $15,000,000]

Dividend repatriations need to increase by 73·9% from Limni's international subsidiaries in order to increase the dividend capacity by 10%. Limni would need to consider whether or not it is feasible for its subsidiaries to increase their repatriations to such an extent, and the impact this will have on the motivation of the subsidiaries' managers and on the subsidiaries' ability to operate as normal.

(d) **Share buyback**

The main benefit of a share buyback scheme to investors is that it helps to control transaction costs and manage tax liabilities. With the share buyback scheme, the shareholders can choose whether or not to sell their shares back to the company. In this way they can manage the amount of cash they receive. On the other hand, with dividend payments, and especially large special dividends, this choice is lost, and may result in a high tax bill. If the shareholder chooses to re-invest the funds, it will result in transaction costs. An added benefit is that, as the share capital is reduced, the earnings per share and the share price may increase. Finally, share buybacks are normally viewed as positive signals by markets and may result in an even higher share price.

Answer 40 AVT CO

(a) **Effect on price of a call option**

Option prices in the basic Black-Scholes model relating to European options are determined by the following five factors:

(1)   The spot price of the underlying security;

(2)   The exercise price of the option;

(3)   The time until expiry of the option;

(4)   The risk of the option, as normally measured by the historic volatility of the return on the underlying security;

(5)   The risk free rate of interest within the economy.

A decrease in the value of each of these factors will have the following effect:

- **The spot price.** As the spot price falls the call option will become less valuable as the exercise of the option will result in the purchase of a security of lower value than previously.

- **The exercise price.** The lower the exercise price, the greater the value of a call option as there is more potential for profit upon exercising the option.

- **The time until expiry of the option.** A reduction in the time to expiry of the option will reduce the value of the option, as the time value element of the option price is reduced.

- **The risk of the option.** A reduction in risk will reduce the value of a call option. This is because the decrease in variance reduces the chance that the security price will lie within the tail of the distribution (i.e. above the exercise price) of the share price when the option expires.

- **The risk free rate.** A reduction in the risk free rate will decrease the value of the call option because the money saved by purchasing the call option rather than the underlying security is reduced. If an option is purchased the cash saved could be invested at the risk free rate. A reduction in the risk free rate makes purchasing the call option relatively unattractive and reduces the option price.

(b)   **Executive share option scheme**

(i)   *Relative merits of existing bonus scheme and proposed share option scheme*

The existing bonus scheme, based on earnings per share, has the advantage that such earnings are easily measured. However, this scheme suffers from the problems of all accounting based measures in that it may be influenced by the accounting policies selected, and is not based on the economic cash flows of the company, which are likely to influence the share price. Maximisation of earnings per share is not the same as maximisation of share price and shareholder wealth.

The advantage of the share option scheme is that, in theory, it will motivate managers to improve the share price as they will directly benefit from this. This should achieve goal congruence with shareholders who are also seeking to maximise the share price. However, the extent to which their total remuneration is influenced by the incentive scheme may influence managers' decisions and their motivation to maximise share price.

It is also debatable how much middle managers can directly influence share price, and whether or not they are aware of which of their decisions will have the desired influence. A further problem of share option schemes is that share prices frequently move for reasons that are nothing to do with the actions of managers, (e.g. lower interest rates). Ideally managers should be rewarded for their contribution to share price increases, but this is very difficult to measure.

(ii)   *Attractiveness of proposed share option scheme to middle management*

Using the Black-Scholes model for European options:

As there is a dividend payment due during the option period, the share price, Pa, should be reduced by the present value of the expected dividend.

Dividend per share has remained constant for three years. It is assumed that it will be constant next year. The present value of the dividend (discounted at the risk free rate) is:

$$\frac{25}{1.06} = 23 \cdot 585 \text{ cents}$$

Pa is estimated to be $610 - 23 \cdot 585 = 586 \cdot 42$ cents

$$d_1 = \frac{\ln(P_a/P_e) + (r + 0.5s^2)t}{s\sqrt{t}}$$

$$d_1 = \frac{\ln\left(\dfrac{586.42}{500}\right) + (0.06 + 0.5 \times 0.38^2) \times 1}{0.38 \times \sqrt{1}} = 0 \cdot 7674$$

$$d_2 = d_1 - s\sqrt{t}$$

$$d_2 = 0.7674 - 0.38\sqrt{1} = 0.3874$$

From normal distribution tables:

$N(d_1) = 0 \cdot 5 + 0 \cdot 2786 = 0 \cdot 7786$
$N(d_2) = 0 \cdot 5 + 0 \cdot 1507 = 0 \cdot 6507$

$$c = P_a N(d_1) - P_e N(d_2)e^{-rt}$$

Call price $= (586 \cdot 42 \times 0 \cdot 7786) - (500 \times 0.6507 \times e^{-0.06 \times 1}) = 456 \cdot 59 - 306 \cdot 41 = 150 \cdot 18$ cents

The expected option call price is $150 \cdot 18$ cents per share, giving a current option value of $5,000 \times 150 \cdot 18$ cents $= \$7,509$

The options are currently in the money and are likely to be attractive to managers as they have an expected value in excess of the bonuses that are currently paid. However, the risk to managers of the two schemes differs and this might influence managerial preferences, depending on individual managers attitudes to risk. The Black-Scholes model assumes that the volatility of the share price over the past year will continue for the coming year. This is very unlikely. A different volatility will greatly influence the value of the option at the expiry date.

(iii)   Put options

(1)   AVT should not agree to grant the manager put options. The holder of a put option, which allows a share to be sold at a fixed price, would benefit more the further the price of the share fell below the exercise price of the option. As far as the options are concerned it would be in the manager's interest to take decisions that reduced the company's share price, rather than increased it.

(2)   The put option price may be found from the put-call parity equation:

$$p = c - P_a + P_e e^{-rt} = 150 \cdot 18 - 586 \cdot 42 + 470 \cdot 90 = 34 \cdot 66 \text{ cents}$$

The manager is incorrect. Put options are not more valuable than call options in this situation.

Answer 41 FOLTER CO

(a)   *(i)*   *Hedging with options*

Folter can protect against possible falls in the share price by buying put options in Magterdoor's shares. Ideally a put option would be purchased at the money (i.e. at the current market price of the shares). This opportunity is not available. If an in the money price of 550 cents is selected, the outcome with a market price at the end of October of 485 cents would be:

550 (exercise price) – 51 (option premium) = 499 cents × 2 million shares = $9·98m.

If the exercise price of 500 cents is used the outcome would be:
500 – 24·5 = 475·5 × 2m = $9·51m

If no hedge were undertaken the shares would be worth $9·70m.

The success of the hedge would depend upon the exercise price selected.

However, if the price at the end of October was not 485, but was in excess of the relevant exercise price of the option, then the option would be allowed to lapse.

(ii)   *Delta neutral hedge*

The purpose of a delta neutral hedge is to set up a risk-free portfolio. Any adverse movement in a share price would be offset by a similar favourable movement in the option price. A delta of 0·47 means that for every share held $1/0·47$ call options would need to be sold to establish the delta neutral hedge.

$$\frac{2,000,000}{1,000 \times 0·47} = 4,255 \text{ call options would need to be sold}$$

Delta hedges are only valid for small movements in the share price. As the share price changes, so will the relevant delta, and the hedge would need to be frequently rebalanced in order to maintain the delta neutral position.

(iii)   *Why call option premium is not the same as intrinsic value*

The intrinsic value of the January 550 call option is zero, as the exercise price exceeds the current market price. The option premium of 34 cents is the time value of the option. The time value depends upon the remaining time to the expiration of the option, the volatility of the option and the level of interest rates. As these variables increase, so will the time value of the option.

(iv)   *Increasing holding*

Apart from the obvious cost and risk associated with increasing the holding, an increase to 6% means that Folter would have to publicly declare its holding in Magterdoor, which might reveal that a take-over is being considered. Under the City Code on Take-overs and Mergers any holding over 3% must be disclosed to the target company.

The main advantage of increasing the percentage holding is that it makes achieving the ownership of more than 50% of the shares easier. It might be argued that if Folter has to reveal its holding to Magterdoor, a larger holding than 6% should be considered.

(b)   **Valuing equity as an option**

Tutorial note: *Robert Merton views shareholders as effectively having a call option over the firm's assets, the exercise price being the amount required to pay off the firm's debts and the time to expiry being the maturity of the debt. Complications arise as the exercise price needs to be stated as a single sum, whereas the firm's actual debt will be serviced by coupon payments as well as redemption price. Hence, prior to input into the Black Scholes model, the firm's debt needs to be "recalibrated" using the alternative methods suggested in the requirement.*

(i)   Redemption price of an equivalent zero-coupon bond

The bondholders could today sell their bonds on the secondary market for $1,079.68m. If they agreed to hold their bonds until redemption date, but receive zero coupon, they would expect a single sum which, when discounted to present value at the bond's yield to maturity, would equal $1,079.68m

YTM = risk-free rate + credit spread = 3% + 1.2% = 4.2%

The equivalent single sum after 5 years = $1,079.68 \times 1.042^5$ = $1,326.28m

Exercise price = 1,326.28
Time to expiry = 5

Price of underlying assets = 1,100

Volatility of underlying assets = 0.35
Risk free rate = 0.03

$$d_1 = \frac{\ln\left(\frac{1,100}{1,326.28}\right) + \left(0.03 + 0.5 \times 0.35^2\right) \times 5}{0.35 \times \sqrt{5}} = 0.34$$

$$d_2 = 0.34 - (0.35 \times \sqrt{5}) = -0.44$$

The areas under the normal curves for these two values are $N(d_1) = 0.6331$ and $N(d_2) = 0.33$.

The value of the call option on the firm's assets:

$$c = 1100 \times 0.6331 - 1326.28 \times 0.33 \times e^{-0.03 \times 5} = \$320m$$

The Black Scholes model values the firm's equity at $320m, significantly above today's net asset value of $30m ($1,100m – $1,079.68m)

The extra value derives from the protection of limited liability status. If the value of assets falls below the value of liabilities then shareholders can simply walk away (i.e. they have limited exposure to downside risk). On the other hand if the value of assets significantly rises then shareholders will make large gains (i.e. they have unlimited upside potential).

(ii)   The duration approach

Tutorial note: *Macaulay duration is the weighted average period of a bond's future cash flows, the weighting being the relative proportion of returns generated in each period. The first step is to discount the future cash flows at the bond's yield to maturity (note that the total PV equals the bond's market price, albeit with a small rounding difference). Then each PV is divided into the bond price to find the proportion received each year. Each proportion is then multiplied by the relevant year and then summed to find the duration.*

Year	1	2	3	4	5	Total
Cash flow	60	60	60	60	1,060	1,300
Present value at YTM	57.58	55.26	53.01	50.89	862.91	1079.65
Proportion	0.05	0.05	0.05	0.05	0.8	1
Proportion × year	0.05	0.10	0.15	0.20	4	4.5

The bond's Macaulay duration is 4.5 years.

If the time to expiry of the call option is set at the debt's duration (as opposed to its redemption date) then the exercise price should be set at the debt's face value plus cumulative coupons (i.e. 1,300).

Exercise price = 1,300
Time to expiry = 4.5

Price of underlying assets = 1,100

Volatility of underlying assets = 0.35
Risk free rate = 0.03

$$d_1 = \frac{\ln\left(\dfrac{1,100}{1,300}\right) + \left(0.03 + 0.5 \times 0.35^2\right) \times 4.5}{0.35 \times \sqrt{4.5}} = 0.33$$

$$d_2 = 0.33 - (0.35 \times \sqrt{4.5}) = -0.41$$

The areas under the normal curves for these two values are $N(d_1) = 0\cdot6293$ and $N(d_2) = 0\cdot3409$.

The value of the call option on the firm's assets:

$$c = 1,100 \times 0\cdot6293 - 1,300 \times 0\cdot3409 \times e^{-0.03 \times 4.5} = \$305m$$

This slightly lower than the valuation using the zero-coupon approach and technically less accurate. However the duration approach is often used in practice as it can deal with firms that have several types of debt in issue of varying maturities (i.e. the weighted average duration can be used to set the time to expiry).

Answer 42 DIGUNDER

(a)   **Value of the option to delay start of project for two years**

Tutorial note: *This is a straightforward application of the Black and Scholes option pricing model. Each of the input components is stated in the question.*

Current price = Present Value of the Project = $28 million
Exercise price = capital expenditure = $24 million
Exercise date = 2 years (or 500 trading days)
Risk free rate = 5%
Volatility = 25%

Using the formula as specified:

$$d_1 = \frac{\ln\left(\frac{28}{24}\right) + \left(0.05 + 0.5 \times 0.25^2\right) \times 2}{0.25 \times \sqrt{2}}$$

$$d_2 = 0.8956 - 0.25 \times \sqrt{2} = 0.5421$$

The areas under the normal curves for these two values are $N(d_1) = 0.8147$ and $N(d_2) = 0.7061$.

Using the derived values for $N(d_1)$ and $N(d_2)$ the value of the call option on the value represented by this project is:

$$c = 0.8147 \times 28 - 0.7061 \times 24 \times e^{-.05 \times 2} = \$7.48 \text{ million}$$

This implies that at the current time the project has a value equal to its NPV plus the value of the call option to delay (i.e. $11.48 million). The additional value arises because the delay option allows the company to avoid the downside element of risk.

Tutorial note: *The error in adding the project NPV to the value of the call option (which already includes the NPV) demonstrates the risk of double-counting when using Real Options Pricing Theory.*

(b)   **Overall value of project**

This project has NPV of $4 million on a capital expenditure of $24 million which is significant, but has a volatility estimate of 25% of the present value per year. This volatility is brought about by uncertainties about Government's intentions with respect to the Bigcity-Newtown transport link and the consequential impact upon property values.

Currently, the project presents substantial value at risk and there is a high likelihood that the project will not be value generating. To surmount this, an estimate is provided of the value of the option to delay construction for two years until the Government's transport plans will be made known.

Option to delay

The option to delay construction is particularly valuable in this case. It eliminates much of the downside risk that the project does not generate the cash flows expected and it gives us the ability to proceed at a point in time most favourable to us. The nature of the delay option is that it is more valuable the greater the volatility of the underlying cash flows and the greater the time period before we are required to exercise.

The valuation of the option to delay has been undertaken using the Black and Scholes model which members have been briefed about with respect to fair value accounting practices under IFRS. The model has some limiting assumptions relating to the underlying nature of the cash flows and our ability to adjust our exposure to risk as time passes. In reality, the use of this type of modelling is more appropriate for financial securities that are actively traded. Our use of the model is an approximation of the value of the flexibility inherent in this project and although the model will not have the precision found in its security market applications it does indicate the order of magnitude of the real option available. A positive value of $11·5 million is suggested by the model underlying the considerable benefit in delay.

In interpreting this valuation it is important to note that the actual project present value at commencement could be significantly larger than currently estimated and will certainly not be less than zero (otherwise the option to build will not be exercised). The additional value reflects the fact that downside risk is eliminated by the ability to delay the decision to proceed.

On the basis of our valuation the option to delay commencement of the project should be taken and investment delayed until the Government's intention with respect to transport links becomes clearer. On this basis we would place a value of $11·5 million on the project including the delay option.

(c) **Limitations on valuation method**

The Black and Scholes model makes a **number of assumptions** about the underlying nature of the pricing and return distributions which may not be valid with this type of project. More problematically it assumes that continuous adjustment of the hedged position is possible and that the option is European style. Where the option to delay can be exercised over any set period of time up to the exercise date the Black and Scholes model will cease to be accurate. For a call option, such as the option to delay, then the level of inaccuracy is likely to be quite low especially for options that are close to the money.

Given that an option always has time value it will invariably be in the option holder's interest to wait until exercise date before exercising his or her option. However, in those situations where the level of accuracy is particularly important, or where it is suspected that the Black and Scholes assumptions do not hold, then the binomial option pricing approach is necessary.

Answer 43 ALASKA SALVAGE

(a) **Current value of warrants**

A warrant is an option attached to another financial instrument on issue which can be detached and negotiated independently of the underlying issue. Warrants are usually exercised over a longer term than traded options but can be valued in exactly the same way using the Black Scholes Option Pricing Model by inserting into the standard formula.

The calculation has been performed as follows:

$$c = 85_a N(d_1) - 90N(d_2)e^{+0.05 \times 5}$$

Where:

$$d_1 = \frac{\ln(85/90) + (0.05 + 0.5 \times 0.2^2) \times 5}{0.2 \times \sqrt{5}} = 0.6548$$

$$d_2 = d_1 - 0.2 \times \sqrt{5} = 0.2076$$

From normal distribution tables calculate the area under the curve represented by d_1 and d_2:

$$c = (85 \times 0.7437) - (90 \times 0.5822 \times e^{-0.05 \times 5}) = 22.41$$

As each warrant represents an option on 100 equity shares the value of each warrant is \$2,241.

The Black Scholes model makes a number of restrictive assumptions:

(1)   The warrant is a "European" style option.
(2)   The share price follows a log-normal distribution and is continuously traded.
(3)   Unrestricted short selling of the underlying security is permitted.
(4)   There are no market frictions such as taxes or transaction costs.
(5)   No dividends are paid during the life of the warrant.

These assumptions are less realistic with a company such as Alaska Salvage than with a large enterprise with a full listing. It is unlikely, for example, that the company's shares will be actively traded or that the share market is efficient in its pricing of the equity.

(b)   **Coupon rate**

The coupon rate is derived from the cash flow to the lender as follows:

Step 1: Lay out the cash flow to the lender showing the value of the warrant as a benefit accruing immediately to the lender.

	0	1	2	3	4	5
Issue price	(10,000)					
Coupon		10,000 × c%	10,000 × c%	10,000 × c%	10,000 × c%	10,000 × c%
Repayment						10,000
Call value	2,241					

The present value of future cash flows to the lender, discounted at 13%, must equal the issue price of the bond less the value of warrants (i.e. $10,000 - 2,241 = 7,759$).

Step 2: Solve the following equation where c% is the coupon rate and A and V are the five-year annuity and discount factors at 13% respectively:

$$7,759 = (10,000 \times c\% \times A) + (10,000 \times V)$$

Therefore: $7,759 = (10,000 \times c\% \times 3.517) + (10,000 \times 0.543)$

By rearrangement: $c\% = \dfrac{7,759 - 10,000 \times 0.543}{10,000 \times 3.517} = 6.62\%$

Therefore a 6.62% coupon rate will give an effective rate of return on the investment to the lender of 13%.

(c) **Advantages and disadvantages of issuing mezzanine debt**

Mezzanine debt such as this is one mechanism by which a small, high growth firm such as Alaska Salvage can raise debt finance where the risk of default is high and/or there is a low level of asset coverage for the loan. In this case raising a loan of $1·6 million would raise the market gearing of the firm from zero (assuming there is no current outstanding debt) to 13·6% (debt to total capitalisation). This increase in borrowing against what might be presumed to be specialised salvaging equipment and the forward cost of operation may not be attractive to the commercial banking sector and may need specialised venture finance. The issue of warrants gives the lender the opportunity to participate in the success of the venture but with a reasonable level of coupon assured. However, the disadvantage for the current equity investors is that the value of their investment will be reduced by the value of the warrants issued. The extent to which this will be worthwhile depends upon the value of the firm on the assumption that the project proceeds and is financed in the way described. This should ultimately decide the maximum value that they would be prepared to pay to finance the new project.

Answer 44 MARENGO CO

(a)   *(i)*   *Delta hedge*

Tutorial note: *Delta hedging is a dynamic hedging technique which attempts to perfectly neutralise the risk on an underlying position. If the price of the shares falls there will be a loss on the shareholding. However, if put options on the share have also been bought these will rise in value. This raises the question of how many puts should be bought to ensure any loss on the shares is perfectly offset by a gain on the puts? The answer comes from delta as this statistic estimates the change in value of an option compared to a change in value of the underlying share. Delta is therefore also known as "the hedge ratio".*

The number of put contracts to purchase depends on the hedge ratio, which in turn depends on the delta of the option. This measures the change in the option price over the change in the price of the share, and therefore helps determine how many option contracts are needed to protect against a fall in the share price. For put options an estimate of delta is given by $N(-d_1)$.

$$d_1 = [\ln(P_a/P_e) + (r + 0·5s^2)t] \div (st^{1/2})$$

$$d_1 = [\ln(340 \div 350) + ((0·04 + 0·5 \times 0·4^2) \times {}^1/_6)] \div (0·4 \times {}^1/_6{}^{0·5}) = -0·055$$

$$-d_1 = 0·055$$

$$N(-d_1) = 0·5 + (0·0199 + \tfrac{1}{2}(0·0239 - 0·0199)) = 0·5219$$

Tutorial note: *The delta of a put option = delta of a call option – 1 = $N(d_1) - 1$*

Put contracts to be bought for a delta hedge = $200,000 \div (0·5219 \times 1,000) = 383·2$ rounding to 383 contracts.

(ii)   *Attitudes to risk management*

Wenyu's position is based on the theoretical case put forward for not managing corporate risk. In a situation of market efficiency where information is known and securities are priced correctly, holding well diversified portfolios will eliminate (or at least significantly reduce) unsystematic risk. The position against hedging states that in such cases companies would not increase shareholder value by hedging or eliminating risk because there will be no further reduction in unsystematic risk. In a situation of perfect markets, the cost of reducing any systematic risk will exactly equal the benefit derived from such a reduction. Shareholders would not gain from risk management or hedging, in fact if the costs exceed the benefits due to transactional costs then hedging may result in a reduction in shareholder value.

However, hedging or the management of risk may result in increasing corporate (and therefore shareholder) value if market imperfections exist, and in these situations reducing the volatility of a company's earnings will result in higher cash inflows. Proponents of hedging cite three main situations where reduction in volatility may increase cash flows – in situations: where the rate of tax is increasing; where a firm could face significant financial distress costs due to high volatility in earnings; and where stable earnings increases certainty and the ability to plan for the future and therefore resulting in stable investment policies by the firm.

It would appear that none of the reasons for hedging explains the situation described in the scenario. Given that Marengo is a large company with a variety of investments, it is unlikely that reducing the volatility of one investment will significantly alter the cash flows of the company. There could be other reasons for reducing risk through hedging and these are explored further on.

Lola's proposal of selling Arion shares is based on the fact that such a move would eliminate the risk of a reduction in price altogether. This proposal has a number of limitations which the managers need to consider carefully. Presumably the purpose of Marengo's strategy of investing in companies is to generate value from such activity. It is likely that it generates higher value than the risk-free rate of return (which would be obtained if funds were invested in "no-risk" investments). The funds generated from selling Arion shares will need to be invested elsewhere to generate the target returns. Unless investments are available which seem to be better than Arion, there may not be a case for selling Arion shares. In addition to this, selling such a large quantity of shares can potentially make the share price reduce significantly and the managers would need to investigate whether there is sufficient liquidity in the markets for such a large sale. Finally, the sale may unbalance the investment portfolio.

Sam's proposal would entail purchasing OTC put options from the bank. This can be an expensive alternative as purchasing a right would entail having to pay premiums on the options, which can be substantial. If the option is not exercised then the cost will be the full amount of the premium. On the other hand, options will allow Marengo to be protected against downside movements, whilst still benefiting from positive movements in the share price. However, options bring additional risks with them. For example, delta is not stable and the rate of change in an option is measured by the gamma. The option value also changes as time to expiry reduces (measured by theta) and as volatility of the underlying asset changes (measured by vega).

Active hedging may reduce agency costs. For example, unlike shareholders, managers and employees of the company may not be diversified. Hedging allows the risks exposed to them to be reduced. Additionally hedging may allow managers to not be concerned about market movements which are not within their control and instead allow them to focus on business issues on which they can exercise control. A consistent hedging strategy or policy may be used as a signalling tool to reduce the conflict of interest between bondholders and shareholders, and thus reduce restrictive covenants. Although a single transaction, like this scenario, may have little impact on this, it should be part of the overall risk management policy of the company.

The case for hedging or not is not clear cut and should not be taken on an individual or piecemeal basis. Instead the company should consider its overall risk management strategy and the resultant value creation opportunities. Subsequent hedging decisions should be based on the overall strategy.

(b) **Financial impact of delaying production**

NPV ignoring the option to delay the decision

Year	Current	1	2	3	4	5	6
Cash flows ($)	–7m	–7m	–35m	25m	18m	10m	5m
PV (11%) ($)	–7m	–6·31m	–28·42m	18·28m	11·86m	5·93m	2·68m

Net present value = $(2·98 million)
On this basis the project would be rejected.

Value of option to delay the decision until the film is released and its popularity established:

Present value of project's operating cash flows (from above) =

$18·28m + $11·86m + $5·93m + $2·68m = $38·75m

Inputs to Black Scholes model:
Today's value of the underlying asset (P_a) = $38·75m
Exercise price (P_e) = $35m
Exercise date = 2 years
Risk free rate = 3·5% = 0.035
Volatility = 30% = 0.30

$d_1 = [\ln(38·75 \div 35) + (0·035 + 0·5 \times 0·30^2) \times 2] \div (0·30 \times \sqrt{2}) = 0·617$
$d_2 = 0·6170 - (0·30 \times \sqrt{2}) = 0·1927 = 0.193$

Using the published normal distribution table:
$N(d_1) = 0·5 + 0·2291 + 0·7 \times (0·2324 - 0·2291) = 0·7314$
$N(d_2) = 0·5 + 0·0753 + 0·3 \times (0·0793 - 0·0753) = 0·5765$

Value of option to delay the decision = $38·75 \times 0·7314 - 35 \times 0·5765 \times e^{-0·035 \times 2}$
= 28·34 – 18·81 = $9·53m

Overall value of the project = $9·53m – $2·98m = $6·55m

Hence by taking into account the option to delay the decision, the project should be accepted for investment.

The option to delay the decision has given MMC's managers the opportunity to monitor and respond to changing circumstances before committing to the project, such as a rise in popularity of this type of genre of films in the next two years or increased competition from similar new releases or a sustained marketing campaign launched by the film's producers before its launch. Although the project looks unattractive at present, it may not be the case if the film on which it is based is successful.

The option pricing formula requires numerous assumptions to be made about the variables, the primary one being the assumption of volatility. It therefore does not provide a correct value but an indication of the value of the option to delay the decision. Hence it indicates that the management should consider the project further and not dismiss it, even though current conventional net present value is negative.

The option to delay the decision may not be the only option within the project. For example, the gaming platform that the company needs to develop for this game may have general programmes which may be used in future projects and MMC should take account of these.

Or if the film is successful, it may lead to follow-on projects involving games based on film sequels.

Tutorial note: *Credit would be given for alternative relevant comments.*

Answer 45 KYT CO

(a)   *(i)*   *Establishing the hedge using currency futures*

KYT needs to purchase yen on the spot market in two months' time. To protect against the risk of the yen strengthening against the $US, KYT should *buy* yen futures contracts, hoping to sell them at a higher price if the yen strengthens. This is intended to offset any loss relative to the current spot rate when the yen are purchased in the spot market in two months' time.

The most suitable contract will be the contract that matures at the nearest date after 1 September, the September contract. To protect 140 million yen, 11 contracts will need to be bought. This will leave 2·5 million yen unhedged.

(ii)   *Basis involved*

Basis is the difference between the current spot price and the futures price, in this case Y128·15 – Y125·23 or 2.92 yen. (September futures in terms of yen per $ = 1 ÷ 0.007985 = 125.23)

(iii)   *Expected result of hedge*

Basis will be zero at the maturity date of the futures contract, 30 September. If it reduces in a linear manner, the expected basis on 1 September is $\dfrac{2.92 \times 1}{3} = 0{\cdot}973$ yen

The expected futures price is 0·973 yen below the spot price of 120 yen 120 – 0.973 = 119·027 yen per $. 1 ÷ 119.027 = 0·008401 $ per yen

Expected result:

Spot market	Futures market
30 June	30 June
Yen 140m = $1,092,470	Buy 11 September yen contracts at 0·007985 (Contracts are for a total of 137,500,000 yen)
1 September	1 September
Yen 140m = $1,166,667	Sell 11 September yen contracts at 0·008401
Loss on the spot market = $74,197	Futures gain is 137,500,000 (0·008401 – 0·007985) = $57,200

Tutorial note: *11 yen futures contract, each with a notional face value of 12, 500,000 yen were traded. Hence the total face value = 11 × 12, 500,000 = 137,500,000 yen.*

Hedge efficiency is $\dfrac{57,200}{74,197} = 77\%$

This result may not occur as basis is unlikely to decrease in a linear manner. Depending on the movement in basis the hedge efficiency might be higher or lower than 77%.

(b) *(i)* *Alternative currency hedges*

Money market hedges are available, either directly in the Blundonian peso or as a cross hedge in $US. A forward market cross hedge is also possible.

Money market hedges lock in the expected cash flow from a foreign exchange transaction by utilising both interest rates and exchange rates. They do not however allow the hedger to benefit from favourable movements in the spot rate. The peso hedge also runs the risk that the government will block the outflow of funds from Blundonia.

Money market hedge

Immediately, borrow B pesos 96,618,357 at 14% per year (100m ÷ 1·035)
Convert at the spot rate of P128·2/£ into £753,653
Use the funds to reduce the UK overdraft at 6% per year, £753,653 × 1·015 = £764,958.

This is the effective £ receipt in three months' time.

Assuming the funds are not needed for other purposes it is better for them to be used to repay some of the overdraft rather than invest in the UK money market.

Cross hedges via the dollar are risky. Although the peso is fixed against the $US, the much higher inflation rate in Blundonia suggests that there will be pressure on the Blundonian government to devalue the peso from its current fixed rate. If a devaluation was to occur during the next three months cross hedges would not be effective. Additionally funds still have to be remitted from Blundonia to the US in order to fulfil the hedges.

The spot cross rates between the B peso and the $ are P70·93 – 72·23/$

$$\frac{100\text{m pesos}}{72\cdot23} = \$1,384,466$$

Cross forward hedge

Sell $1,384,466 3 months forward at $1·789/£ = £773,877

(The $1,384,466 would be bought using the 100 million pesos at the spot rate of P72·23/$, assuming the fixed rate between the peso and dollar does not change.)

Forward hedges are easy to arrange via banks, lock in the expected future cash flow, but, in common with money market hedges, do not allow the hedger to take advantage of favourable currency movements.

Cross money market hedge

Immediately borrow $1,360,655 at 7% per year ($1,384,466 ÷ 1·0175)
Convert at the spot rate of $1·782 into £763,555.
Use the £ to reduce the overdraft, £763,555 × 1·015 = £775,008.

The cross money market hedge provides better expected receipts but is more risky than the direct money market hedge. The cross hedge is recommended, as long as Tertial is willing to risk the devaluation of the peso against the $US.

(ii)   Possible action if transfer of money is not allowed

Tertial could use the 100m pesos to invest in Blundonia, but as the company has only just commenced exports this is unlikely to be a favoured alternative.

A counter-trade deal is possible, where the 100m pesos are used to purchase goods in Blundonia. The goods might be sold to a third party outside Blundonia. The third party would pay Tertial an agreed equivalent sum in sterling or another acceptable "hard" currency. This form of transaction should be acceptable to the Blundonian government as it does not involve cash leaving the country.

Answer 46 GALEPLUS CO

(a)   Advantages of currency swaps

- They allow companies to undertake foreign currency hedging, often for longer periods than is possible with forwards.

- They are usually cheaper than long term forwards, where such products exist.

- Finance may be obtained at a cheaper rate than would be possible by borrowing directly in the relevant market. This occurs by taking advantage of arbitrage if a company has a relative funding advantage in one country.

- They may provide access to finance in currencies that could not be borrowed directly (e.g. due to government restrictions or lack of a credit rating in the overseas market).

- Currency swaps offer the opportunity to restructure the company's debt profile without physically redeeming debt or issuing new debt.

- Currency swaps might be used to avoid a country's exchange control restrictions.

Potential problems

- If the swap is directly with a corporate counterparty the potential default risk of the counterparty must be considered. Swaps arranged with a bank as the direct counterparty tend to be much less risky.

- Political or sovereign risk, the possibility that a government will introduce restrictions that interfere with the performance of the swap.

- Basis risk. With a floating to floating swap basis risk might exist if the two floating rates are not pegged to the same index.

- Exchange rate risk. The swap may result in a worse outcome than would have occurred if no swap had been arranged.

(b) **Currency swap**

(i) *Potential annual percentage interest saving*

Interest rate differentials:

	Fixed rate	Floating rate
Galeplus	6·25%	PIBOR + 2%
Counterparty	8·30%	PIBOR + 1·5%
	(2·05%)	0·5%

The overall arbitrage opportunity from using a currency swap is 2·55% per year. Banks fees are 0·75% per year leaving 1·8%. 75% of 1·8% is 1·35% that would be the benefit per year to Galeplus in terms of interest saving from using a currency swap.

(ii) *Purchase decision*

Assuming inflation rates in Perdia are between 15% and 50% per year, the best and worse-case exchange rates are:

	Rubbits per $	
	Best case	Worst case
Spot	85·40	85·40
Year 1	98·21	128·10
Year 2	112·94	192·15
Year 3	129·88	288·23

Cash flows (million rubbits)

Year	0	1	2	3
Purchase cost	(2,000)			
Fees		40	40	40
Sale price				4,000
	(2,000)	40	40	4,040
Discount factors (15%)	1	0·870	0·756	0·658
Present values	(2,000)	34·8	30·24	2,658·32

With a currency swap 2,000 million of the year 3 cash flows will be at the current spot rate of 85·40 rubbits per $, with the remainder at the end of year 3 spot rate.

Discounted cash flows ($ million)

Worst case rates	(23·42)	0·27	0·16	20·07
Estimated NPV	($2·92)			
Best case rates	(23·42)	0·35	0·27	25·75
Estimated NPV	$2·95			

Tutorial note: *Year 3 at worst case rates = 2,000 ÷ 85.4 (swap rate) + 2,040 ÷ 288.23 = 30.50. PV = 30.5 × 0.658 = 20.07.*

The financial viability of the investment depends upon exchange rate movements. The greater the depreciation in the value of the rubbit relative to the pound, the worse the outcome of the investment. This is due to the year 3 price of the telecommunications centre remaining constant no matter what the exchange rate is at the time.

These estimates assume that exchange rates remain in the above range. In reality they could be better or worse. Additionally non-financial factors such as political risk would influence the decision. For example given the government's current cash flow position how likely is the payment of 4,000 million rubbits to be made in three years' time? Other factors such as taxation in the home country would also need to be considered.

Unless there are strong strategic reasons for buying the centre (e.g. possible future cash flow benefits beyond year 3) the investment is not recommended. In order for the investment to take place a better hedge against currency risk would need to be found, or the price to be received in year 3 renegotiated to reflect the impact of adverse exchange rate changes.

(c) **Alternatives to currency swap**

(i) *Swaption*

A swaption is an option on a swap. It allows the buyer to choose whether or not to undertake the swap, depending on exchange rates in three years' time. The swap rate in this example is the current spot rate of 85.40 rubbits per $. A swaption at this exercise price would offer no benefit to Galeplus relative to the straight swap unless the rubbit were to strengthen relative to 85·40 per $, in which case the swap would not be used as the end of year 3 spot rate would be more favourable to Galeplus. Given the relative inflation rates in the home country and Perdia, according to the purchasing power parity theory it is very unlikely that the rubbit will strengthen relative to the dollar. The use of a swaption is not recommended.

(ii) *European style three year currency put option*

The currency put option will limit the downside risk of the year 3 cash flows whilst allowing Galeplus to take advantage of favourable exchange rate movements. Using the worst case exchange rate forecasts, the option would be exercised at the end of year 3.

Discounted cash flows (million rubbits)

Year	0	1	2	3
Present values	(2,000)	34·8	30·24	2,658·32

Discounted cash flows ($ million)

	0	1	2	3
Worst case rates	(23·42)	0·27	0·16	16·61
Less option premium	$1·7			
Estimated NPV	($8·08)			

Tutorial note: *The put option would be exercised if the spot rate moves to worst case scenario. In this case PV of year 3 = 4,040 ÷ 160 × 0.658 = 16.61.*

Using the best case exchange rate forecasts, the option would not be exercised at the end of year three as the expected spot exchange rate at that time is more favourable.

Discounted cash flows (million rubbits)

Year	0	1	2	3
Present values	(2,000)	34·8	30·24	2,658·32

Discounted cash flows ($ million)

Best case rates	(23·42)	0·35	0·27	20·47
Less option premium	$1·7			
Estimated NPV	($4·03)			

In both cases the outcome from the put option is very poor. The end of year 3 exchange rate of the rubbit would have to be much stronger than 160 per $ in order for the option to be the preferred hedge. The rate would have to move to approximately 108 rubbits per $, which is unlikely. Unless Galeplus is prepared to take the risk of this happening the use of currency options is not recommended.

Tutorial note: *108 rubbits per $ is the breakeven spot rate at which the project produces zero NPV after paying the option premium.*

Answer 47 LAMMER CO

(a) **Hedging strategies for foreign exchange exposure in five months' time**

Only relevant net dollar exposures should be hedged. Net dollar imports in five months' time are $1,150,000. This is the amount to be hedged. The transactions in sterling are not exposed and should not be hedged. The exposure may be hedged using the forward foreign exchange market, a money market hedge, currency futures hedge or currency options hedge. A combination of these hedges is also possible, or alternatively a partial hedge may be selected that protects only part of the exposure.

Forward market hedge

No five month forward rate is given. The rate may be interpolated from the three month and one year rates for buying dollars.

Estimated five month forward rate is: $(1·9066 \times {}^{7}/_{9}) + (1·8901 \times {}^{2}/_{9}) = 1·9029$

Tutorial note: *An alternative way to find the 5-month forward rate is as follows:*

3 month forward rate = 1.9066
12 month forward rate = 1.8901
9 month difference = 1.9066 – 1.8901 = 0.0165
5 month rate by interpolation = 1.9066 – (${}^{2}/_{9}$ × 0.0165) = 1.9029

Hedging with a forward contact will fix the £ payment at: $\dfrac{\$1,150,000}{1·9029} = £604,341$

Money market hedge

In order to protect against any future strengthening of the dollar, Lammer could borrow £ now and convert £ into dollars to ensure that the company is not exposed if there are changes in the $/£ exchange rate.

Borrow £595,373 at 5·5% per year for five months, total cost £609,017
Convert into $ at the spot rate of $1·9156/£ to yield $1,140,496
Invest in the US at 2·0% per year to yield a total of $1,150,000 which will be used to make payment for the imports ($1,140,496 × 1·008333 = $1,150,000).

A money market hedge is more expensive than the forward hedge.

Currency futures hedge

The currency exposure is in five months' time. To protect against the risk of the dollar strengthening December futures should be sold.

Basis is $1·9156 - 1·8986 = 1·7$ cents. This relates to a futures contract maturing in seven months' time.

Expected basis in five months' time is $1·7 \times {}^2/_7 = 0·486$ cents

Expected lock-in futures rate may be estimated by: $1·8986 + 0·00486 = 1·9035$

This is slightly more favourable than the forward market rate, but there are a number of possible disadvantages of using currency futures:

(i) Basis risk might exist. The actual basis at the close out date in five months' time might be different from the expected basis of 0·486 cents.

(ii) Currency futures will involve either under-hedging or over-hedging as an exact number of contracts for the risk is not available.

$$\frac{\$1,150,000}{1·9035} = £604,150, \quad \frac{£604,150}{£62,500} = 9·67 \text{ contracts}$$

(iii) Currency futures involve the upfront payment of a margin (security deposit). If daily losses are made on the futures contracts additional margin will need to be provided to keep the futures contracts open.

Currency options hedge

As $ need to be purchased, Lammer will need to buy December put options on £.

Exercise price	$	£	no. of contracts
1·8800	1,150,000	611,702	19·57
1·9000	1,150,000	605,263	19·37
1·9200	1,150,000	598,958	19·17

It is assumed that Lammer will under-hedge using 19 contracts and will purchase the remaining dollars in the forward market (in reality it would probably wait and use the spot market in five months' time). 19 contracts is £593,750.

Exercise price	$	Premium $	Premium £ at spot	Under-hedge $
1·8800	1,116,250	17,575	9,175	33,750
1·9000	1,128,125	25,769	13,452	21,875
1·9200	1,140,000	38,891	20,302	10,000

Worst case outcomes if the options are exercised:

Exercise price	Basic cost (£)	Premium	Under-hedged £ at forward	Total
1·8800	593,750	9,175	17,736	620,661
1·9000	593,750	13,452	11,496	618,698
1·9200	593,750	20,302	5,255	619,307

As is normal, the currency options worst case outcomes are much more expensive than alternative hedges. However, if the dollar weakens relative to the pound, option contracts allow the company to purchase the required dollars in five months' time in the spot market and let the options lapse (or alternatively sell the options to take advantage of any remaining time value). In this situation the dollar would have to weaken to about 1·98/£ before the currency options became more favourable than the forward contract or futures hedge. Forward contracts or futures contracts appear to be the best form of hedge.

(b) **Estimated effect on expected market value**

	$ per £	£ equivalent of $4·2m	£ difference to spot	DF (11%)	PV
Spot	1·9156	2,192,525			
1 year	1·8581	2,260,374	67,849	0·901	61,132
2 years	1·8024	2,330,226	137,701	0·812	111,813
3 years	1·7483	2,402,334	209,809	0·731	153,370
4 years	1·6959	2,476,561	284,036	0·659	187,180
5 years	1·6450	2,553,191	360,666	0·593	213,875
					727,370

Tutorial note: *The current spot rate for buying dollars is 1.9156 dollars per pound. If the dollar appreciates by 3% then after one year each pound will buy 1.9156 × 0.97 = 1.8581 dollars. The rise in the dollar increases the cost of Lammer's imports and damages the value of the firm – this is economic risk (i.e. exposure of the value of cash flows to long term exchange rate changes). A currency swap would be one way of hedging this risk.*

The strengthening of the dollar is expected to reduce the present value of cash flows, and, if the market is efficient, the market value of Lammer, by £727,370.

(c) **Managing economic exposure of any foreign subsidiaries**

Economic exposure relates to the change in the value of a company as a result of unexpected changes in exchange rates. Unless there are known contractual future cash flows it is difficult to hedge economic exposure using options, swaps, or other financial hedges as the amount of the exposure is unknown.

Economic exposure is normally managed by internationally diversifying activities, and organising activities to allow flexibility to vary the location of production, the supply sources of raw materials and components, and international financing, in response to changes in exchange rates.

To some extent multinational companies may offset economic exposure by arranging natural hedges (e.g. by borrowing funds in the US and then servicing the interest payments and the repayment of principal on the borrowing with cash flows generated by subsidiaries in the US).

Marketing strategies may also be used to offset the effects of economic exposure. For example if UK products were to become relatively expensive in the US due to a fall in the value of the dollar, a UK company might adopt an intensive marketing campaign to create a better brand or quality image for its products.

Answer 48 ASTEROID SYSTEMS

Tutorial note: *The objective is to fix (€/SFr) currency exchange rates for two months for an expected remittance of SFr 2·4299 million. This is achieved with a money market hedge for the two month exposure.*

(a)   *(i)   Hedging the two month Swiss franc exposure*

Forward contracts in the money market are the most straightforward way of eliminating transaction risk. The exposure to movements in the Swiss Franc can be eliminated by entering into a forward contract to purchase the currency at SFr 1·6199 per Euro (Note 1). Alternatively, given access to fixed rate finance in the Swiss market a reverse money market hedge can be established by borrowing in SFr and depositing in Euros. Given that the interest rates can be locked in this would offer a better forward rate at two months at any borrowing rate less than SFr LIBOR + 7 (Note 2).

Note (1)

The current expectation of remittances is based on an estimate of the two-month forward rate of ½ (1·6223 + 1·6176) = 1·6199 for the Swiss Franc.

Swiss Francs = 1·6199 × 1·5m = SFr 2·4299m in two months using the forward rate above.

Note (2)

The money market hedge is based on interest rate parity and using the IRP formula we can calculate the maximum rate of interest that can be borne for the money market hedge to be worthwhile.

The technique for a reverse money market hedge is identical to that for a conventional hedge except that the counter currency is borrowed in the foreign market, converted at spot and deposited in the domestic market. However, for a money market hedge to work, the company must be able to secure short term money market finance in both the base and the counter currency area. With the SFr exposure it is possible to borrow at fixed in the Swiss market. Using the no arbitrage condition of the interest rate parity formula we can determine the maximum rate of interest the company should agree in creating a money market hedge. The interest rate in the base currency to use is the best rate for depositing in the Euromarkets:

$$1.6199 = 1.6244 \times \frac{\left(1 + i_c \times \dfrac{2}{12}\right)}{\left(1 + 0.03725 \times \dfrac{2}{12}\right)}$$

i_c = 2.056%

If the company can borrow at less than spot Swiss 2·056% in the Swiss market then the money market hedge will be preferred to a forward sale of SFr 1·5 million.

(ii)   Money market hedge vs exchange-traded derivatives

A money market hedge is a mechanism for the delivery of foreign currency, at a future date, at a specified rate without recourse to the forward forex market. If a company is able to achieve preferential access to the short term money markets in the base and counter currency zones then it can be a cost effective substitute for a forward agreement. However, it is difficult to reverse quickly and is cumbersome to establish as it requires borrowing/lending agreements to be established denominated in the two currencies.

Exchange traded derivatives such as futures and foreign exchange options offer a rapid way of creating a hedge and are easily closed out. For example, currency futures are normally closed out and the profit/loss on the derivative position used to offset the gain or loss in the underlying. The fixed contract sizes for exchange traded products mean that it is often impossible to achieve a perfect hedge and some gain or loss on the unhedged element of the underlying or the derivative will be carried. Also, given that exchange traded derivatives are priced in a separate market to the underlying there may be discrepancies in the movements of each and the observed delta may not equal one. This basis risk is minimised by choosing short maturity derivatives but cannot be completely eliminated unless maturity coincides exactly with the end of the exposure. Furthermore less than perfectly hedged positions require disclosure under IFRS 9. Currency hedging using the derivatives market may also involve significant cash flows in meeting and maintaining the margin requirements of the exchange. Unlike futures, currency options will entail the payment of a premium which may be an expensive way of eliminating the risk of an adverse currency movement.

With relatively small amounts, the OTC market represents the most convenient means of locking in exchange rates. Where cross border flows are common and business is well diversified across different currency areas then currency hedging is of questionable benefit. Where, as in this case, relatively infrequent flows occur then the simplest solution is to engage in the forward market for hedging risk. The use of a money market hedge as described may generate a more favourable forward rate than direct recourse to the forex market. However the administrative and management costs in setting up the necessary loans and deposits are a significant consideration.

(b)   *(i)*   *Forward exchange rate for a six month currency swap*

Tutorial note: *The requirement is to discover the fixed exchange rate for an agreed monthly delivery of euros over six months to settle a contract for 10,000 tonnes of aggregate at an agreed price of €220 per tonne.*

The calculation required is to equate the present value of a single agreed forward rate with the present value of the six forward rates specified in the question.

The procedure is to calculate the present value of the variable forward rates using discount rates derived from the yield curve data. The sum of the discounted forward prices is then divided by the sum of the discount rates to obtain an equivalent fixed forward rate on the swap. The calculations are as follows:

	1	*2*	*3*	*4*	*5*	*6*
Forward rates (€ per $)	0·8326	0·8314	0·8302	0·8289	0·8278	0·8267
$ zero coupon yield curve	3·25%	3·45%	3·50%	3·52%	3·52%	3·52%
Discount factor	0·9973	0·9943	0·9913	0·9883	0·9854	0·9826
Prepaid forward price	0·8303	0·8267	0·8229	0·8192	0·8157	0·8123
PV of prepaid forward prices	4·9272					
Sum of discount factors	5·9392					
Fixed forward rate on swap	0·8296					

As rates change continuously, the monthly discount factor should be calculated on a continuous time basis:

$$\text{Discount factor}_1 = e^{-yxt} = e^{-0.0325\frac{1}{12}} = 0.9973$$

Tutorial note: *Discrete time discounting, although less accurate, would be accepted.*

Tutorial note: *Although the examiner's methodology is technically correct, the final answer can be found more quickly as a simple average of the forward rates (i.e. (0·8326 + 0·8314 + 0·8302 + 0·8289 + 0·8278 + 0·8267) ÷ 6 = 0.8296).*

(ii)   Plain vanilla currency swap

Currency swaps can be for the exchange of different currencies at an agreed rate, or for the swap of interest rate liabilities on borrowing in different currencies. This currency swap entails an agreement to swap a constant dollar sum in exchange for a sequence of currency payments in Euros at the agreed amount each month. The attraction of a currency swap such as this is that it avoids having to enter into a sequence of forward contracts (a forward strip) with a currency dealer with the associated charges and budget variability entailed. The two rates quoted assume a zero arbitrage swap rate and no commission on the swap. Inevitably, a higher rate will be quoted on the swap to cover the required commission. A disadvantage of swap agreements is the relatively complex contract procedure which must be pursued to ensure that the counter-parties to the swap are in agreement as to the terms. Forward contracts tend to be less cumbersome to both negotiate and contract with the currency dealer.

Answer 49 CASASOPHIA CO

(a)   Hedging the $20m receivable after four months

The information provided enables Casasophia to hedge its US$ income using forward contracts, future contracts or option contracts.

Forward contracts

Since it is a dollar receipt, the 1·3623 rate will be used.
Locked in receipt = US$20m ÷ 1·3623 = €14,681,054

The hedge fixes the rate at 1·3623 and is legally binding.

Futures contracts

This futures position needs to produce a gain if the dollar depreciates against the Euro, in order to cover potential losses on the spot market.

However each futures contract is referenced against a block of the Euro (€125,000). As the hedge needs to produce a gain if the Euro rises against the dollar it should be set up through initially buying Euro futures. A "long position" is taken to make gains on a rising underlying asset, in this case the Euro.

The five-month futures contracts should be used as they will still be trading after four months when the hedge would be closed out by then selling Euro futures.

It is assumed that the basis will fall in a linear manner over the life of the futures contract. However, as the contract will be closed out before its expiry date, this may not be the case due to basis risk, and a better or worse outcome than expected may result.

The expected outcome of the hedge can be found through interpolating between today's prices of the two-month and five-month futures contracts (i.e. to find the theoretical price of a four-month contract). Expected "lock-in" rate = $1·3698 - (^1/_3 \times (1·3698 - 1·3633)) = 1·3676$

Expected receipt = US$20m ÷ 1·3676 = €14,624,159

Number of contracts needed = €14,624,159 ÷ €125,000 = 117 contracts

Tutorial note: *Alternatively, the futures lock-in rate may be estimated by interpolating between today's spot rate and the price of five-month futures (i.e. $1\cdot3698 - (^1/_5 \times (1\cdot3698 - 1\cdot3618)) = 1\cdot3682$).*

This produces a lower Euro receipt than using a forward contract. Furthermore futures contracts require margin payments and are marked-to-market on a daily basis, whereas any gain is not realised until the contracts are closed out.

Like the forward contracts, futures contracts fix the rate (ignoring basis risk) and are legally binding.

Option contracts

Options have an advantage over forwards and futures because the holder of an option can later choose whether to exercise or lapse the option. However, a premium is payable for this flexibility.

Casasophia would like the right but not the obligation to buy Euros. Therefore it should today acquire call options on the Euro.

Exercise Price: $1·36/€1

$20,000,000 ÷ 1·36 = €14,705,882. Number of options required = €14,705,882 ÷ €125,000 = 117·6 contracts. 117 call options would be purchased.

Tutorial note: *It would be acceptable to round up to 118 options.*

€ receipts = 117 × 125,000 = €14,625,000
Premium paid = 117 × 0·0280 × 125,000 = US$409,500
Premium in € = 409,500 ÷ 1·3585 = €301,435
Amount not hedged = US$20m – (117 × €125,000 × 1·36) = US$110,000
Use forwards to cover amount not hedged = US$110,000 ÷ 1·3623 = €80,746

Total receipts = 14,625,000 – 301,435 + 80,746 = €14,404,311

Exercise Price: $1·38/€1

$20,000,000 ÷ 1·38 = €14,492,754 or 115·9 contracts
115 call options purchased

€ receipts = 115 × 125,000 = €14,375,000
Premium paid = 115 × 0·0223 × 125,000 = US$320,563
Premium in € = 320,563 ÷ 1·3585 = €235,968
Amount not hedged = US$20m – (115 × €125,000 × 1·38) = US$162,500
Use forwards to cover amount not hedged = US$162,500 ÷ 1·3623 = €119,284

Total receipts = 14,375,000 – 235,968 + 119,284 = €14,258,316

Both these hedges are significantly worse than the forward or futures contracts hedges. This is due to the high premiums payable to let the option lapse if the prices move in Casasophia's favour. With futures and forwards, Casasophia cannot take advantage of the dollar strengthening against the Euro. However, this needs to be significant before the cost of the option premium can be justified.

Conclusion

It is recommended that Casasophia use the forward markets to hedge against the dollar depreciating in four months' time against the Euro. However, Casasophia needs to be aware that forward contracts are not traded on a formal exchange and therefore default risk exists. Furthermore, the exchange rate is fixed once the forward contract is agreed.

(b)   **Project NPV**

Use interest rate parity theory to set the forward rates within the currency swap:

½ year	$128 \times 1 \cdot 108 \div 1 \cdot 022 = 138 \cdot 77$
	$128 + ½ (138 \cdot 77 – 128) = 133 \cdot 4$
1½ years	$133 \cdot 4 \times 1 \cdot 108 \div 1 \cdot 022 = 144 \cdot 6$
2½ years	$144 \cdot 6 \times 1 \cdot 108 \div 1 \cdot 022 = 156 \cdot 8$
3½ years	$156 \cdot 8 \times 1 \cdot 108 \div 1 \cdot 022 = 170 \cdot 0$

Present value calculations (with time zero being six months from today):

	Year 1	*Year 2*	*Year 3*	*Total*
Income (MShs, million)	1,500	1,500	1,500	
Income (€ million, based on forward rates)	10·37	9·57	8·82	
Discounted Income (€ million at 12%)	9·26	7·63	6·28	23·17

Expected spot rate in 12 months (using purchasing power parity) =
$116 \times 1 \cdot 097 \div 1 \cdot 012 = 125 \cdot 7$
Expected spot rate in 6 months
$116 + ½ (125 \cdot 7 – 116) = 120 \cdot 9$ MShs per €1

Expected cost of investment = MShs 2,640,000,000 ÷ 120·9 = €21·84m

Net present value = €23·17m – €21·84m = €1·33m

The calculation of the forward rates based on the interest rate parity indicates that the MShs rates are depreciating against the Euro because the Mazabia base rate at 10·8% is higher than the European country's local base rate at 2·2%. However, even where the forward rates are fixed, based on interest rate parity, the project is worthwhile for Casasophia.

According to the purchasing power parity, future spot currency rates will change in proportion to the inflation level differentials between two countries. Hence if Mazabia's inflation level is higher than the European Union, its currency will depreciate against the Euro.

Given that the inflation level in Mazabia is expected to range from 5% to 15% over the next few years, there is uncertainty over the NPV of the project in euros if the swap is not accepted. The swap fixes the future exchange rates, although Casasophia will lose out if the inflation rate is lower than 9·7%, since the future spot rate will depreciate by less than what is predicted by the forward rates. The situation will be opposite if the level of inflation is higher than 9·7%.

Casasophia will also need to consider the risk of default by the local bank. Casasophia may ask Mazabia's government to act as guarantor to reduce this risk. Overall, if such an agreement could be reached, it would probably be beneficial to agree to the swap to ensure a certain level of income.

Casasophia may also want to explore whether it is possible for the grant funding from the European Union being paid to it directly, to reduce its exposure to the likely depreciation of MShs.

Tutorial note: *It could be argued that the main risk on this project is the uncertain cost in euros terms of the MShs 2,640,000,000 investment required in six months. If candidates notice a relevant issue not addressed by the requirement then they should make brief reference to this.*

Answer 50 LIGNUM CO

(i)   **Types of currency exposure**

With case one, Lignum faces a possible exposure due to the receipt it is expecting in four months in a foreign currency, and the possibility that the exchange rates may move against it between now and in four months' time. This is known as transactions exposure. With case two, the exposure is in the form of translation exposure, where a subsidiary's assets are being translated from the subsidiary's local currency into Euro. The local currency is facing an imminent depreciation of 20%. Finally in the third case, the present value of future sales of a locally produced and sold good is being eroded because of overseas products being sold for a relatively cheaper price. The case seems to indicate that because the US$ has depreciated against the Euro, it is possible to sell the goods at the same dollar price but at a lower Euro price. This is known as economic exposure.

(ii)   **Transaction exposure**

Using forward rate

Forward rate = $142 \times (1 + (0{\cdot}085 + 0{\cdot}0025) \div 3) \div (1 + (0{\cdot}022 - 0{\cdot}0030) \div 3) = 145{\cdot}23$
Income in Euro fixed at ZP145·23 = ZP140m ÷ 145·23 = €963,988

Using OTC options

Purchase call options to cover for the ZP rate depreciating
Gross income from option = ZP140m ÷ 142 = €985,915

Cost

€985,915 × ZP7 = ZP6,901,405
In € = ZP6,901,405 ÷ 142 = €48,601
€48,601 × (1 + 0·037 ÷ 3) = €49,200

Tutorial note: *Use borrowing rate on the assumption that extra funds to pay costs need to borrowed initially; investing rate can be used if that is the stated preference.*

Net income = €985,915 – €49,200 = €936,715

Transactions exposure, as faced by Lignum in situation one, lasts for a short while and is easier to manage by means of derivative products or more conventional means. Here Lignum has access to two derivative products: an OTC forward rate and OTC option. Using the forward rate gives a higher return of €963,988, compared to options where the return is €936,715. However, with the forward rate, Lignum is locked into a fixed rate (ZP145·23 per €1) whether the foreign exchange rates move in its favour or against it. With the options, the company has a choice and if the rate moves in its favour, that is if the Zupeso appreciates against the Euro, then the option can be allowed to lapse. Lignum needs to decide whether it is happy receiving €963,988, no matter what happens to the exchange rate over the four months or whether it is happy to receive at least €936,715 if the ZP weakens against the €, but with a possibility of higher gains if the Zupeso strengthens.

Lignum should also explore alternative strategies to derivative hedging. For example, money markets, leading and lagging, and maintaining a Zupeso account may be possibilities. If information on the investment rate in Zupesos could be obtained, then a money market hedge could be considered. Maintaining a Zupeso account may enable Lignum to offset any natural hedges and only convert currency periodically to minimise transaction costs.

(iii) **Translation exposure**

MR devalued rate = MR35 × 1·20 = MR42 per €1

	MR000	Exposed?	€000 at current rate MR35 per €1	€000 at devalued rate MR42 per €1
Non-current assets	179,574	Yes	5,131	4,276
Current assets	146,622	60%	2,514	2,095
Non-current liabilities	(132,237)	20%	(756)	(630)
Current liabilities	(91,171)	30%	(781)	(651)
Share capital and reserves	102,788		6,108	5,090

Translation loss = €6,108,000 – €5,090,000 = €1,018,000

Hedging translation risk may not be necessary if the stock market in which Lignum's shares are traded is efficient. Translation of currency is an accounting entry where subsidiary accounts are incorporated into the group accounts. No physical cash flows in or out of the company. In such cases, spending money to hedge such risk means that the group loses money overall, reducing the cash flows attributable to shareholders. However, translation losses may be viewed negatively by the equity holders and may impact some analytical trends and ratios negatively. In these circumstances, Lignum may decide to hedge the risk.

The most efficient way to hedge translation exposure is to match the assets and liabilities. In Namel's case the assets are more exposed to the Maram Ringit compared to the liabilities, hence the weakening of the Maram Ringit from MR35 per €1 to MR42 per €1 would make the assets lose more (accounting) value than the liabilities by €1,018,000. If the exposure for the assets and liabilities were matched more closely, for example by converting non-current liabilities from loans in Euro to loans in MR, translation exposure would be reduced.

(iv) **Economic exposure**

Economic exposure, which is not part of transactions exposure, is long-term in nature and therefore more difficult to manage. There are for example, few derivatives which are offered over a long period, with the possible exception of swaps. A further issue is that economic exposure may cause a substantial negative impact to a company's cash flows and value over the long period of time. In this situation, if the US$ continues to remain weak against the Euro, then Lignum will find it difficult to maintain a sustained advantage against its American competitor. A strategic, long-term viewpoint needs to be undertaken to manage risk of this nature, such as locating production in countries with favourable exchange rates and cheaper raw material and labour inputs or setting up a subsidiary company in the USA to create a natural hedge for the majority of the US$ cash flows.

Answer 51 KENDURI CO

(a)   **Hedging transaction exposure**

Only the transactions resulting in cash flows between Kenduri and Lakama are considered for hedging. Other transactions are not considered.

Net flow in US$: US$4·5m payment – US$2·1m receipt = US$2·4m payment

Hedge the US$ exposure using the forward market, the money market and options.

(i)   Forward market

US$ hedge: 2,400,000 ÷ 1·5996 = £1,500,375 payment

(ii)   Money market

US$ hedge
Invest in US$: 2,400,000 ÷ (1 + (¼ × 0·031)) = US$2,381,543
Convert into £ at spot: US$2,381,543 ÷ 1·5938 = £1,494,255
Borrow in £: £1,494,255 × (1 + (¼ × 0·040)) = £1,509,198

Tutorial note: *Full credit would be given for using the investing rate of 2·8% instead of the borrowing rate of 4%, where this approach is explained and justified.*

The forward market is preferred due to lower payment costs.

(iii)   Options

Kenduri would purchase Sterling three-month put options to protect itself against a strengthening US$ to £.

Exercise price: $1·60/£1
£ payment = 2,400,000 ÷ 1·60 = 1,500,000 or 24 contracts
24 put options purchased

Premium payable = 24 × 0·0208 × 62,500 = US$31,200
Premium in £ = 31,200 ÷ 1·5938 = £19,576
Total payments = £1,500,000 + £19,576 = £1,519,576

Exercise price: $1·62/£1
£ payment = 2,400,000 ÷ 1·62 = 1,481,481 or 23·7 contracts
23 put options purchased

£ payment = 23 × 62,500 = £1,437,500
Premium payable = 23 × 0·0342 × 62,500 = US$49,163
Premium in £ = 49,163 ÷ 1·5938 = £30,846
Amount not hedged = US$2,400,000 – (23 × 62,500 × 1·62) = US$71,250
Use forwards to hedge amount not hedged = US$71,250 ÷ 1·5996 = £44,542
Total payments = 1,437,500 + 30,846 + 44,542 = £1,512,888

Both these hedges are worse than the hedge using forward or money markets. This is due to the premiums payable to let the option lapse if the prices move in Kenduri's favour. Options have an advantage over forwards and money markets because the prices are not fixed and the option buyer can let the option lapse if the rates move favourably. Hence options have an unlimited upside but a limited downside. With forwards and money markets, Kenduri cannot take advantage of the US$ weakening against the £.

Conclusion

The forward market minimises the payment and is therefore recommended over the money market. However, options give Kenduri the choice of an unlimited upside, although the cost is higher. Therefore the choice between the forward market and the option market depends on the risk preference of the company.

(b)   Multilateral netting

Based on spot mid-rates: US$1·5950/£1; CAD1·5,700/£1; JPY132·75/£1

In £000

		Payments from			
		UK	USA	Canada	Japan	Total
Receipts to	UK		1,316·6	2,165·6		3,482·2
	USA	2,821·3		940·4	877·7	4,639·4
	Canada	700·6			2,038·2	2,738·8
	Japan		2,410·5			2,410·5
Total payments		3,521·9	3,727·1	3,106·0	2,915·9	
Total receipts		3,482·2	4,639·4	2,738·8	2,410·5	
Net receipt/(payment)		(39·7)	912·3	(367·2)	(505·4)	

Each of Kenduri, Jaia and Gochiso will make payments of £ equivalent to the amount given above to Lakama.

Multilateral netting involves minimising the number of transactions taking place through each country's banks. This would limit the fees that these banks would receive for undertaking the transactions and therefore governments who do not allow multilateral netting want to maximise the fees their local banks receive. On the other hand, some countries allow multilateral netting in the belief that this would make companies more willing to operate from those countries and any banking fees lost would be more than compensated by the extra business these companies and their subsidiaries bring into the country.

(c)   Long call with high gamma

Gamma measures the rate of change of the delta of an option. Deltas range from near 0 for a long call option which is deep out-of-money, where the price of the option is insensitive to changes in the price of an underlying asset, to near 1 for a long call option which is deep in-the-money, where the price of the option moves in line and largely to the same extent as the price of the underlying asset. When the long call option is at-the-money, the delta is 0·5 but also changes rapidly. Hence, the gamma is highest for a long call option which is at-the-money. The gamma is also higher when the option is closer to expiry. It would seem, therefore, that the option is probably trading near at-the-money and has a relatively short time period before it expires.

Answer 52 INTEREST RATE MATHS

(a)   **Treasury spot rates**

One-year spot rate = $(107 \div 103) - 1 = 3.88\%$

The two-year spot rate can be implied by "stripping" the two-year treasury note into its constituent cash flows and discounting each at the relevant spot rate (where s = two-year spot rate):

$102 = (6 \div 1.0388) + ((106 \div (1 + s)^2)$

$96.22 = ((106 \div (1 + s)^2)$

$s = \sqrt{(106 \div 96.22)} - 1 = 4.96\% =$ two-year spot rate

The process is then repeated to imply the three year spot rate:

$98 = (5 \div 1.0388) + (5 \div 1.0496^2) + ((105 \div (1 + s)^3)$

$88.65 = ((105 \div (1 + s)^3)$

$s = (105 \div 88.65)^{1/3} - 1 = 5.8\% =$ three-year spot rate

(b)   **Corporate bond analysis**

Year	Spread (bps)	Treasury spot	Corporate spot	$		PV $
1	29	388	4.17%	5	$5 \div 1.0417 =$	4.80
2	41	496	5.37%	5	$5 \div 1.0537^2 =$	4.50
3	55	580	6.35%	105	$105 \div 1.0635^3 =$	87.29
						96.59

Tutorial note: *Yield to maturity (YTM) is the equal annual rate that discounts the bond's future cash flows to its market price. YTM is simply the IRR of the bond's cash flows, estimated using linear interpolation.*

Time	$ $	6% DF	PV $	7% DF	PV $
0	(96.59)	1	(96.59)	1	(96.59)
1-3	5	2.673	13.36	2.624	13.12
3	100	0.84	84	0.816	81.60
			0.77		(1.87)

YTM = IRR = $6\% + 0.77 \div (0.77 + 1.87) = 6.29\%$

(c)   **Forward interest rates**

Tutorial note: *Forward interest rates geometrically link spot rates.*

$(1.0388) \times (1 + \text{forward rate}) = 1.0496^2$
Forward rate (year one to two) = 6.05%

$(1.0496^2) \times (1 + \text{forward rate}) = 1.058^3$
Forward rate (year two to three) = 7.50%

(d) **Theoretical fixed rate**

Tutorial note: *The fixed rate leg in the swap would be set to be equivalent in cost to taking a loan today for one year, rolling it over from year one to two and then refinancing it again from year two to three. Taking $100 as national principal the cash flows from such a series of loans would be expected to be:*

Time	$
0	100
1	(3.88)
2	(6.05)
3	(107.5)

For the fixed rate in the swap to be equivalent in cost it would be set as the IRR of the above cash flows:

Time	$	5%DF	PV	6%DF	PV
0	100	1	100	1	100
1	(3.88)	0.952	(3.69)	0.943	(3.66)
2	(6.05)	0.907	(5.49)	0.89	(5.38)
3	(107.5)	0.864	(92.88)	0.84	(90.3)
			(2.06)		0.66

IRR = 5% + (2.06 ÷ (2.06 + 0.66)) = 5.76% = swap fixed rate

(e) **Evaluation of proposed swap**

The differential between fixed rates is 0·75%. The differential between floating rates is 0·40%. The maximum arbitrage gain is therefore 0·35%, or 0·175% to each company if the gain is shared equally. The following swap has been devised so that the gains are shared equally, but alternative swap payments are possible that would achieve the same result.

	Stentor	Evnor
Actual borrowing	(8·75%)	(LIBOR + 0·90%)
Swap payments:		
Stentor pays Evnor	(LIBOR)	LIBOR
Evnor pays Stentor	8·425%	(8·425%)
Total cost	LIBOR + 0·325%	9·325%
Saving relative to direct borrowing	0·175%	0·175%

Whether the swap will be beneficial depends upon the size of the swap. For example a 0·175% annual saving on a swap of $10 million is $17,500. The bank's initial fee is $20,000 and annual fee of 0·05% is $5,000.

A swap could, in theory, be arranged that is beneficial to both companies, although the benefits in this example would only start in year two. In reality, Stentor, the higher credit rated company, is likely to receive the larger share of any arbitrage gain, reducing the benefit of the swap for Evnor.

Answer 53 SHAWTER CO

(a)   **Alternative hedges**

The current cost of borrowing for two months is £30,000,000 × 6·9% × $\dfrac{2}{12}$ = £345,000

Futures

The company may use futures contracts to attempt to make a gain on the futures market that will offset any potential loss in the cash market.

Futures are market-traded instruments that are only available with fixed contract sizes and maturity dates, and only on a limited selection of financial instruments. Hence it might not be possible to exactly hedge the cash market exposure. Futures also require the deposit of a margin, either in cash or approved securities.

The financing is expected to be needed in three months' time, in mid-March. March contracts will be used as they have the closest expiry date after the date the funds are needed (combinations of two contracts are also possible).

As the period at risk is two months, the number of contracts needed may be estimated from:

$\dfrac{£30,000,000}{£500,000} \times \dfrac{2}{3}$ = 40 contracts

To protect against an expected interest rate increase 40 contracts would be sold.

Basis is the current LIBOR rate of 94·00 less the March futures price, 93·79 = 0·21

There are 3½ months until the contract expires. The funds are needed in three months. The expected basis at the time of borrowing is therefore:

0·21 × $^{1}/_{7}$ = 0·03. The change in basis is 0·18

The expected futures price in three months is 93·79 – 0·5 + 0·18 = 93·47 (or using the new LIBOR of 93·50 less the remaining basis of 0·03 = 93·50 – 0·03 or 93·47)

The expected futures gain if futures are closed out in three months is:

40 × £12·50 (93·79 – 93·47) × 100 = £16,000

The overall cost of the loan is expected to be £345,000 + £25,000 (the extra borrowing cost if interest rates increase by 0·5%) – £16,000 = £354,000

Tutorial note: *The futures price at the closeout date might differ from 93·47, as the decline in basis might not be linear.*

Options

The option contracts specified are also market traded, with similar limitations to the futures, but it is also possible to obtain OTC (over the counter) interest rate options which are tailored directly to a company's needs.

The obvious disadvantage of options is that a premium is payable, often upfront. However, if interest rates were to fall rather than rise the option would be allowed to lapse, and the company would take advantage of the lower market interest rates. In the case of a futures contract this would not be possible.

Hedge

Buy 40 March put options

Premium cost:
Strike price

93750	£30 million $\times$ 0·085% $\times$ $^2/_{12}$ =	£4,250
94000	£30 million $\times$ 0·255% $\times$ $^2/_{12}$ =	£12,750
94250	£30 million $\times$ 0·480% $\times$ $^2/_{12}$ =	£24,000

If interest rates increase by 0·5% the options will be exercised (or sold if there is any time value left) and the futures contracts sold at the exercise price.

The profit on options contracts will be the exercise price less the expected futures price multiplied by 100%, the tick value and the number of contracts.

Exercise price		*Profit*
93750	(93·75 – 93·47) $\times$ 100 $\times$ 40 $\times$ £12·5 =	£14,000
94000	(94·00 – 93·47) $\times$ 100 $\times$ 40 $\times$ £12·5 =	£26,500
94250	(94·25 – 93·47) $\times$ 100 $\times$ 40 $\times$ £12·5 =	£39,000

Overall cost
Exercise price		
93750	£345,000 + £25,000 – £14,000 + £4,250 =	£360,250
94000	£345,000 + £25,000 – £26,500 + £12,750 =	£356,250
94250	£345,000 + £25,000 – £39,000 + £24,000 =	£355,000

The 94250 exercise price has an expected total cost of only £1,000 more than the expected futures cost. It might be worth buying this contract in case interest rates fall, which would allow the company to let the option lapse and take advantage of the lower cash market rates.

A collar option which has lower net premium costs, but which restricts the benefits from a fall in interest rates might also be considered.

FRAs

FRAs are OTC instruments, which allow the rate on borrowing at some future period to be fixed today (similar to a forward contract in the foreign exchange market). As with futures, FRAs do not allow the buyer or seller to take advantage of favourable interest rate movements. Unlike futures, FRAs have no margin requirement.

As the company wishes to borrow funds in three months' time for a period of two months, the appropriate FRA would be the 3 v 5 contract.

The company would BUY a FRA covering the amount of £30,000,000.

The contract effectively locks in the rate to the FRA rate of 6·18% + 0.9% = 7.08%

The overall cost is £30,000,000 $\times$ 7·08% $\times$ $^2/_{12}$ = £354,000

The futures hedge and the FRA have the same expected total cost. However, because of basis risk the futures cost is not certain, and the futures contracts require margin payments. For these reasons the FRA might be preferred to futures. If there is believed to be a chance of a fall in interest rates the 94250 option might be selected for the hedge.

(b) **Possible benefits of interest rate swaps**

- The ability to obtain finance at a cheaper cost than would be possible by borrowing directly in the relevant market.

- The opportunity to effectively restructure a company's capital profile without physically redeeming debt.

- Long-term hedging against interest rate movements as swaps may be arranged for periods of several years.

- The ability to access a type of finance which could not be accessed directly (e.g. because the borrower is relatively unknown in the market or has a relatively low credit rating).

Answer 54 TRODER CO

(a) **Interest rate caps and collars**

Interest rate caps and collars are available on the over the counter (OTC) market or may be devised using market based interest rate options. They may be used to hedge current or expected interest receipts or payments. An interest cap places an upper limit on the interest rate to be paid, and is useful to a potential borrower of funds at a future date. The borrower, by purchasing a cap, will limit the interest paid to the agreed cap strike price (less any premium paid). OTC caps are available for periods of up to 10 years and can thus protect against long-term interest rate movements. As with all options, if interest rates were to move in a favourable direction the buyer of the cap could let the option lapse and take advantage of the more favourable rates in the spot market.

The main disadvantage of options is the premium cost. A collar option reduces the premium cost by limiting the possible benefits of favourable movements. It involves the simultaneous purchase and sale of options or, in the case of OTC collars the equivalent net premium to this. The premium paid for the purchase of the options would be partly or wholly offset by the premium received from the sale of options. Where it is wholly offset a zero cost collar exists.

(b) **Collar hedge**

For the company to earn interest of £6,750,000 it would need to earn an annualised interest rate, after premium costs of $\dfrac{£6,750,000}{£400,000,000} \times \dfrac{12}{5} = 4 \cdot 05\%$

The collar needs to produce a minimum of more than $4 \cdot 05\%$ including premium costs.

As Troder is investing, a lending collar will be required whereby the company will simultaneously buy a floor and sell a cap. Buying a call option that will increase in value if interest rates fall will set the floor, or minimum interest rate. The cap, achieved by selling put options, will set the maximum interest, with the company foregoing any higher interest rate than the put option exercise price, but paying a lower overall premium. The overall cost of the collar will be the call option premium paid less the put option premium received.

In order to achieve a return of more than 4·05% (£6,750,000) a collar needs to be arranged with the call strike price higher than the put strike price (in order to set the maximum interest that can be received).

Alternatives

Call strike price	Interest rate	Less call cost	Plus put receipt	Less 0·25%	Total
95750	4·25%	0·165%	0·170% (95500)	0·25%	4·005%
95750	4·25%	0·165%	0·085% (95250)	0·25%	3·92%
95500	4·50%	0·280%	0·085% (95250)	0·25%	4·055%

Only the purchase of a call at 95500 and sale of a put at 95250 will result in a minimum return of £6,750,000. The actual minimum return (ignoring any possible remaining time value that might increase the return) is:

$$£400,000,000 \times \frac{5}{12} \times 4·055\% = £6,758,333$$

If a collar is set with the same put and call price the return will be:

Strike price	Interest rate	Less call cost	Plus put receipt	Less 0·25%	Total
95250	4·75%	0·445%	0·085%	0·25%	4·14%
95500	4·50%	0·280%	0·170%	0·25%	4·14%
95750	4·25%	0·165%	0·305%	0·25%	4·14%

This would achieve the required 4·05%, but would not allow Troder to take advantage of any favourable movement in interest rates.

(ii) Maximum interest received

The maximum return would occur if market interest rates are at least 4·75% and the call option were allowed to lapse. The put option would be exercised by its buyer and the maximum overall return would be:

Strike price	Interest rate (call not exercised)	Less call cost	Plus put receipt	Less 0·25%	Total
95500	4·75%	0·280%	0·085%	0·25%	4·305%

This would yield: $£400,000,000 \times \dfrac{5}{12} \times 4·305\% = £7,175,000$

(c) *(i) Risks in undertaking interest rate swap*

- Default risk by the counterparty to the swap. If the counterparty is a bank this risk will normally be very small. A bank would face larger counterparty default risk, especially from counterparties such as the BBB company with a relatively low credit rating.

- Market or position risk. This is the risk that market interest rate will change such that the company undertaking the swap would have been better off, with hindsight, if it had not undertaken the swap.

- Banks often undertake a "warehousing" function in swap transactions. The size and/or maturity of the transactions desired by each counterparty to the bank often do not match. In such cases the bank faces gap or mismatch risk which it will normally hedge in the futures or other markets.

(ii)   *Evaluation of swap*

	Fixed rate	Floating rate
Arnbrook	6·25%	LIBOR + 0·75%
BBB company	7·25%	LIBOR + 1·25%
Difference	1·00%	0·50%

There is a potential 0·50% arbitrage saving from undertaking the swap. On a $50 million swap this is $250,000 per year.

Arnbrook would require 60% of any saving, or $150,000 annually ($105,000 after tax). The BBB company would receive $100,000 annually ($70,000 after tax).

The bank would charge each party $120,000 per year. After tax this is a cost of $84,000 each. This would leave a net loss of $14,000 for the BBB rated counterparty company.

The swap is not potentially beneficial to all parties, unless the savings are shared equally.

(iii)   *Increase in LIBOR*

Arnbrook will pay floating rate interest as a result of the swap. If Arnbrook receives 60% of the arbitrage savings, it will save 0·5% (0·60) on its interest rates relative to borrowing directly in the floating rate market, and effectively pay LIBOR + 0·45%, or 5·70% at current interest rates. If LIBOR moves to 5·75% in six months' time, Arnbrook will then pay 6·20% floating rate interest for the remaining period of the swap.

Interest savings in each six month periods are $50 million × 0·30% × 0·5 = $75,000

If the money market is efficient, the relevant discount rate will be the prevailing interest rate paid by Arnbrook.

Period:	Savings $	Discount factor	Present value ($)
0–6 months	75,000	0·972 (5·7%)	72,900
6 months–1 year	75,000	0·942 (6·2%)	70,650
1 year–18 months	75,000	0·913 (6·2%)	68,475
18 months–2 years	75,000	0·887 (6·2%)	66,525
2 years–30 months	75,000	0·860 (6·2%)	64,500
30 months–3 years	75,000	0·835 (6·2%)	62,625
Total present values			405,675

The interest rate swap is estimated to produce interest rate savings with a present value of $405,675 relative to borrowing floating rate directly. The swap would be beneficial, even after deducting the fee of $120,000 per year.

With hindsight lower interest costs would have been available by borrowing at 6·25% in the fixed rate market.

Answer 55 PHOBOS CO

(a)   **Effective interest rate cost**

(i)   Sterling interest rate futures

Tutorial note: *This is a straightforward question on hedging interest rate exposure using interest rate futures.*

Step (1) Calculate the current interest:

Current interest   = (LIBOR + 50) × exposure time × principal
                = $6 \cdot 50\% \times {}^4/_{12} \times £30,000,000 = £650,000$

Step (2) Select the first available future with maturity following the commencement of underlying borrowing and choose the appropriate hedging strategy.

Sell March futures at settlement of 93·88.

Step (3) Calculate the number of contracts:

$$\text{Contracts} = \frac{\text{principal}}{\text{contract size}} \times \frac{\text{Exposure period}}{\text{Contract period}} = \frac{£30,000,000}{£500,000} \times \frac{4}{3} = 80$$

Step (4) Calculate the basis:

Basis on 1st January = spot price – futures price = 94·00 – 93·88 = 12 basis points or "ticks"

Assuming linear convergence then basis on 1st March will be four ticks given the contracts will still have one month to run.

Step (5) Estimate close-out price if interest rates (a) increase by 100 basis points (b) decrease by 100 basis points.

(a) Close out will be 93·00 – 0·04 = 92·96
(b) Close out will be 95·00 – 0·04 = 94·96

Step (6) Calculate gain and/or loss in the futures market and the equivalent cost:

	7·00%	5·00%
Interest rate at close out	7·00%	5·00%
Current price	93·88	93·88
Futures price at close out	92·96	94·96
Ticks	92	−108
On 80 contracts at £12·50 per tick	92,000	−108,000
Cost of loan in spot market	750,000	550,000
less profit/(loss) on futures	92,000	−108,000
Net cost of loan	658,000	658,000
Annual equivalent	6·58%	6·58%

(ii)   Options on short sterling futures

Traded options allow the management of this type of risk, but the hedge carries a premium. Given the current LIBOR of 6% and an exposure until 1st March the March puts at 94,000 are best suited for this type of exposure. A put option allows the holder, at exercise, the right to short the futures at the stated price. These options are exercised (or sold back to the market) if the March futures price is less than the stated exercise price.

Step (1) Choose the most effective option strategy to minimise basis risk.

March puts on three month futures at 94000

Step (2) Calculate the required numbers of contracts: as for futures = 80 contracts

Step (3) Calculate premium payable: $80 \times 16 \cdot 8 \times £12 \cdot 50 = £16,800$

Step (4) Calculate basis on 1st March on the underlying (as before) = 4 ticks

Step (5) Test outcomes against expected movements in interest rates:

Interest rate at close out	7·00%	5·00%
Futures price at close out	92·96	94·96
Exercise price	94·00	94·00
Option payoff	104·00	0
Position payoff on 80 contracts at £12·50 per tick	104,000	0
Cost of loan in spot market	750,000	550,000
less option payoff	–104,000	0
less premium	16,800	16,800
Net cost of loan	662,800	566,800
Annual equivalent	6·63%	5·67%
Expected payoff assuming equal likelihoods	6·15%	

This ignores the time value of the option at close out but assumes that it will only be the intrinsic value. With one month before close out with the volatilities implied in this example the time value of the in-the-money options could be significant and should be calculated.

At 6·63% the effective cost is just above the required threshold of 6·6% but with an expected payoff of 6·15% (given equal likelihoods of a rise or a fall in interest rates). Given the absence of a time value estimate on close out, and the possibility of capturing the benefit of a fall in rates, the use of options should be the preferred alternative.

(b)   Benefits and dangers of using derivative agreements to manage interest rate risk

Derivatives offer an opportunity for a firm to vary its exposure to interest rate risk at a given rate of interest on the underlying principal (hedging) or to decrease the rate of interest on its principal at an increased level of risk exposure. For hedging purposes derivatives permit the management of exposure either for the long term (swaps) or for the short term (Forward Rate Agreements (FRAs), Interest Rate Futures (IRFs), Interest Rate Options (IROs) and hybrids). With forward and futures contracts, the mechanism of hedging is the same in that an offsetting position is struck such that both parties forego the possibility of upside in order to eliminate the risk of downside in the underlying rate movements. Where the option to benefit from favourable rate movements is required or in situations where there is uncertainty whether a hedge will be required, then an IRO may be the more appropriate alternative.

Such hedging can be more or less efficient depending on the ability to set up perfectly matched exposures with zero default risk. Matching depends upon the nature of the contract. With OTC agreements the efficiency of the match may be perfect but the risk of default remains. With traded derivatives, the efficiency of the match may be less than perfect either through size effects or because of the lack of a perfect match on the underlying (for example the use of a LIBOR derivative against an underlying reference rate which is not LIBOR). There will also be basis risk where the maturity of the derivative does not coincide exactly with the underlying exposure.

Where a company forms a view that future spot rates will be lower than those specified by the forward yield curve they may decide to alter their exposure to interest rate risk in order to capture the benefit of the reduced rate. This can be achieved through the use of IROs. Alternatively, leveraged swap or leveraged FRA positions can be taken to avoid the upfront cost of an IRO. For example, taking multiples of the variable leg of a swap (i.e. agreeing to swap fixed for variable) where a higher than market fixed rate is swapped for "n" multiples of the variable rate. However, as a number of cases have demonstrated it may be very difficult with these types of arrangement to gauge the degree of risk exposure and to ensure that they are effectively managed by the firm. In the 1990s a number of companies in the US and elsewhere took leveraged positions, without recognising the degree of their exposure and took losses that threatened the survival of the firm.

Answer 56 KATMAI COMPANY

(a)   Alternative choices for managing interest rate exposure

(i)   Do nothing: with this strategy the company is taking a gamble on the yield curve that future interest rates will remain unchanged or indeed may fall. Much would depend on the degree of interest rate diversification the company may have on overseas debt and on the magnitude of any interest payable.

(ii)   Retire and reissue fixed rate debt: with this strategy the company will issue fixed rate bonds and use the proceeds to retire the floating rate notes. This will eliminate any downside risk associated with increasing interest rates but will be an expensive option to pursue as commissions, arrangement fees and underwriting costs can be between 2–3% of the value of the loan.

(iii)   Enter a fixed for variable interest rate swap: Normally this will entail swapping the liability for the LIBOR component of the swap for a fixed rate. The advantage of a swap agreement is that it is easy to establish through the highly organised OTC swap market. The disadvantage is that the company will be committed for the term of the swap which means that the company would have to reverse out of the swap if it found itself in a position to retire the loan notes earlier than planned.

Moving from variable to fixed interest rates is unlikely to have a significant impact upon the company's weighted average cost of capital or its value but it will stabilise the firm's financing flows which should make forward planning and budgeting easier. Therefore, in deciding between the three alternatives the directors should assess whether taking risk of this sort is a part of its core business or whether managing interest rate volatility in the budgeting process is a diversionary activity. Either (ii) or (iii) will reduce managerial and labour risk exposure by reducing the volatility of the surplus from which their remuneration and other compensation is drawn. From an equity investor point of view therefore, given the costs of hedging, (i) may be the preferred strategy. From the perspective of other stakeholders (iii) is likely to be the least costly alternative for achieving stability in future financing flows. From a managerial perspective (iii) is the recommended course of action.

(b) **Vanilla interest rate swap**

Six monthly interest rate

Payments	LIBOR ÷ 2 + 0·6%
Receipt under a vanilla swap	LIBOR ÷ 2
Payment on fixed leg	5·4% ÷ 2 = 2·7%
Net payment	3·30%

The six-monthly rate is therefore 3·30% or an effective annual rate:

EAR = 1·0332 − 1 = 6·71%

(c) **Value at Risk**

Given that the annual interest rate volatility is 1·5%, the standard deviation of six-monthly rates is:

$$\delta_6 = \delta_a \times \sqrt{\frac{1}{2}} = 1.5\% \times 0.7071 = 1.061$$

Value at risk (VaR) = Loan × δ_6 × CL = $150 million × 1·061% × 1·645 = $2·62 million

Where the confidence level of 95% is taken from the normal tables supplied and is, assuming a single tail, 1·645 standard deviations away from the mean.

VaR is defined (Jorion, 2007) as the "worst loss over a target horizon such that there is a low, pre-specified probability that the actual loss will be larger". Currently the six-monthly interest rate is LIBOR plus 120 basis points. Let us assume for the moment that LIBOR is 5% per year. The six-monthly interest on this loan will be 3·1% or $4·65 million. There is a 5% chance that the actual interest paid would be greater than ($4·65 million + $2·.62 million) $7·27 million or, to put it another way, there is a 95% likelihood that the actual interest payable will be less than this figure. A number of assumptions constrain our interpretation of VaR. The first is that interest rates are assumed to follow a "random walk" in that the current rate is the mean of the distribution of future possible rates, second that the volatility of future rates remains unchanged and third, that the distribution of rates is normal.

In practice, although the "normality" assumption may be useful in simplifying the mathematics of VaR, calculation shows that actual rate distributions exhibit significant skew and that the likelihood of extreme outcomes is somewhat higher than would be expected. However, VaR does simplify the representation of risk by placing a monetary value on the exposure arising from different sources.

Answer 57 SEMBILAN CO

(a) **Expected cash flows in swap**

Gross amounts of annual interest receivable by Sembilan from Ratus Bank based on year 1 spot rate and years 2, 3 and 4 forward rates:

Year 1 0·025 × $320m = $8m
Year 2 0·037 × $320m = $11·84m
Year 3 0·043 × $320m = $13·76m
Year 4 0·047 × $320m = $15·04m

Gross amount of annual interest payable by Sembilan to Ratus Bank:

$3.76\frac{1}{4}\% \times \$320m = \$12.04m$

At the start of the swap, Sembilan will expect to receive or (pay) the following net amounts at the end of each of the next four years:

Year 1: $8m – $12·04m = $(4·04m) payment
Year 2: $11·84m – $12·04m = $(0·20m) payment
Year 3: $13·76m – $12·04m = $1·72m receipt
Year 4: $15·04m – $12·04m = $3m receipt

Tutorial note: *At the commencement of the swap contract the NPV of the net annual flows, discounted at the yield curve rates, is zero.*

The reason the equivalent fixed rate of 3·76¼% is less than the 3·8% four-year yield curve rate, is because the 3·8% rate reflects the zero-coupon rate with only one payment made in year four. Here the bond pays coupons at different time periods when the yield curve rates are lower. Therefore the fixed rate is lower.

(b)   Proof that swap fixes interest expense

	% Impact	*Yield Interest 3%*	*Yield Interest 4%*
Borrow at yield interest + 60bp	(Yield+0·6)%	$(11·52m)	$(14·72m)
Receive yield	Yield	$9·6m	$12·8m
Pay fixed 3·76¼%	(3·76¼)%	$(12·04m)	$(12·04m)
Fee 20bp	(0·2)%	$(0·64m)	$(0·64m)
Net cost	(4·56¼)%	$(14·6m)	$(14·6m)

The receipt and payment based on the yield curve cancels out interest rate fluctuations, fixing the rate at 3·76¼% + 0·6% + 0·2% = 4·56¼%

(c)   Issuing equity to repay debt

Reducing the amount of debt by issuing equity and using the cash raised from this to reduce the amount borrowed changes the capital structure of a company and Sembilan needs to consider all the possible implications of this.

As the proportion of debt increases in a company's financial structure, the level of financial distress increases and with it the associated costs. Companies with high levels of financial distress would find it more costly to contract with their stakeholders. For example, they may have to pay higher wages to attract the right calibre of employees, give customers longer credit periods or larger discounts, and may have to accept supplies on more onerous terms. Furthermore, restrictive covenants may make it more difficult to borrow funds (debt and equity) for future projects. On the other hand, because interest is payable before tax, larger amounts of debt will give companies greater taxation benefits, known as the tax shield. Presumably, Sembilan has judged the balance between the levels of equity and debt finance, such that the positive and negative effects of gearing result in minimising the required rate of return and maximising the value of the company.

By replacing debt with equity the balance may no longer be optimal and therefore the value of Sembilan may not be maximised. However, reducing the amount of debt would result in a higher credit rating for the company and reduce the scale of restrictive covenants. Having greater equity would also increase the company's debt capacity. This may enable the company to raise additional finance and undertake future profitable projects more easily. Less financial distress may also reduce the costs of contracting with stakeholders.

The process of changing the financial structure can be expensive. Sembilan needs to determine the costs associated with early redemption of debt. The contractual clauses of the bond should indicate the level and amount of early redemption penalties. Issuing new equity can be expensive especially if the shares are offered to new shareholders, such as costs associated with underwriting the issue and communicating or negotiating the share price. Even raising funds by issuing rights can be expensive.

As well as this, Sembilan needs to determine the extent to which the current shareholders will be able to take up the rights and the amount of discount that needs to be given on the rights issue to ensure 100% take up. The impact on the current share price from the issue of rights needs to be considered as well. Studies on rights issues seem to indicate that the markets view the issue of rights as a positive signal and the share price does not reduce to the expected theoretical ex-rights price. However, this is mainly because the markets expect the funds raised to be used on new, profitable projects. Using funds to reduce the debt amount may not be viewed so positively.

Sembilan may also have to provide information and justification to the market because both the existing shareholders and any new shareholders will need to be assured that the company is not benefiting one group at the expense of the other. If sufficient information is not provided then either shareholder group may discount the share price due to information asymmetry. However, providing too much information may reduce the competitive position of the company.

Tutorial note: *Credit would be given for alternative relevant comments and suggestions.*

Answer 58 AWAN CO

(a)   **Hedging against falling yield on investments**

Using forward rate agreements (FRAs):

FRA rate 4·82% (3–7), since the investment will take place in three months' time for a period of four months.

If interest rates increase by 0·9% to 4·99%

Investment return = 4·79% × $^4/_{12}$ × $48,000,000 =	$766,400
Payment to Voblaka bank = (4·99% – 4·82%) × $48,000,000 × $^4/_{12}$ =	$(27,200)
Net receipt =	$739,200
Effective annual interest rate = 739,200 ÷ 48,000,000 × $^{12}/_4$ =	4·62%

If interest rates decrease by 0·9% to 3·19%

Investment return = 2·99% × $^4/_{12}$ × $48,000,000 =	$478,400
Receipt from Voblaka Bank = (4·82% – 3·19%) × $48,000,000 × $^4/_{12}$ =	$260,800
Net receipt =	$739,200
Effective annual interest rate (as above)	4·62%

Using futures:
Need to hedge against a fall in interest rates, therefore *go long* in the futures market. Awan needs March contracts as the investment will be made on 1 February.

Tutorial note: *The price of interest rate futures is quoted as (100 – implied interest rate). Awan fears a fall in interest rates as this would cut the yield on its investments. If interest rates fall then the price of interest rate futures would rise. To make a potential gain on this price rise Awan should initially **buy** futures, referred to as taking a "long position" (i.e. "go long").*

No. of contracts needed = $\$48,000,000 \div \$2,000,000 \times {}^4/_3 = 32$ contracts.

Basis
Current price (on 1 November) – futures price = total basis
$(100 - 4 \cdot 09) - 94 \cdot 76 = 1 \cdot 15$
Unexpired basis = ${}^2/_5 \times 1 \cdot 15 = 0 \cdot 46$

If interest rates increase by 0·9% to 4·99%

Investment return (from above)	$766,400
Expected futures price $(100 - 4 \cdot 99 - 0 \cdot 46) = 94 \cdot 55$	
Loss on the futures market	
$\quad ((0 \cdot 9455 - 0 \cdot 9476) \times \$2,000,000 \times {}^3/_{12} \times 32)$	$(33,600)
Net return	$732,800
Effective annual interest rate $(\$732,800 \div \$48,000,000 \times {}^{12}/_4)$	4·58%

If interest rates decrease by 0·9% to 3·19%

Investment return (from above)	$478,400
Expected futures price $(100 - 3 \cdot 19 - 0 \cdot 46) = 96 \cdot 35$	
Gain on the futures market	
$\quad ((0 \cdot 9635 - 0 \cdot 9476) \times \$2,000,000 \times {}^3/_{12} \times 32)$	$254,400
Net return	$732,800
Effective annual interest rate (as above)	4·58%

Using options on futures:
Need to hedge against a fall in interest rates, therefore *buy call options*. As before, Awan needs 32 March call option contracts $(\$48,000,000 \div \$2,000,000 \times {}^4/_3)$.

Tutorial note: *As seen earlier a futures hedge would involve initially buying futures. An options hedge requires the right, but not the obligation, to buy futures. Holding call options gives the right to buy the underlying futures contract (i.e. buy call options).*

If interest rates increase by 0·9% to 4·99%

Exercise price	94·50	95·00
Futures price	94·55	94·55
Exercise ?	Yes	No
Gain in basis points	5	0
Underlying investment return (from above)	$766,400	$766,400
Gain on options $(0 \cdot 0005 \times 2,000,000 \times {}^3/_{12} \times 32)$	$8,000	$0
Premium		
$0 \cdot 00432 \times \$2,000,000 \times {}^3/_{12} \times 32$	$(69,120)	
$0 \cdot 00121 \times \$2,000,000 \times {}^3/_{12} \times 32$		$(19,360)
Net return	$705,280	$747,040
Effective interest rate	4·41%	4·67%

If interest rates decrease by 0·9% to 3·19%

Exercise price	94·50	95·00
Futures price	96·35	96·35
Exercise ?	Yes	Yes
Gain in basis points	185	135
Underlying investment return (from above)	$478,400	$478,400
Gain on options		
$(0·0185 \times 2,000,000 \times {}^3/_{12} \times 32)$	$296,000	
$(0·0135 \times 2,000,000 \times {}^3/_{12} \times 32)$		$216,000
Premium		
As above	$(69,120)	
As above		$(19,360)
Net return	$705,280	$675,040
Effective interest rate	4·41%	4·22%

Discussion

The FRA offer from Voblaka Bank gives a slightly higher return compared to the futures market; however, Awan faces a credit risk with over-the-counter products like the FRA, where Voblaka Bank may default on any money owing to Awan if interest rates should fall. The March call option at the exercise price of 94·50 seems to fix the rate of return at 4·41%, which is lower than the return on the futures market and should therefore be rejected. The March call option at the exercise price of 95·00 gives a higher return compared to the FRA and the futures if interest rates increase, but does not perform as well if the interest rates fall. If Awan takes the view that it is more important to be protected against a likely fall in interest rates, then that option should also be rejected. The choice between the FRA and the futures depends on Awan's attitude to risk and return, the FRA gives a small, higher return, but carries a credit risk. If the view is that the credit risk is small and it is unlikely that Voblaka Bank will default on its obligation, then the FRA should be chosen as the hedge instrument.

(b)   Delta hedging

The delta value measures the extent to which the value of a derivative instrument, such as an option, changes as the value of its underlying asset changes. For example, a delta of 0·8 would mean that a company would need to purchase 1·25 call options $({}^1/_{0·8})$ to hedge against a rise in price of an underlying asset of that contract size, known as the hedge ratio. This is because the delta indicates that when the underlying asset increases in value by $1, the value of the equivalent option contract will increase by only $0·80.

The option delta is equal to $N(d_1)$ from the Black-Scholes Option Pricing (BSOP) formula. This means that the delta is constantly changing when the volatility or time to expiry change. Therefore even when the delta and hedge ratio are used to determine the number of option contracts needed, this number needs to be updated periodically to reflect the new delta.

Answer 59 GLOBAL FINANCIAL CRISIS

The root cause of the crisis can be traced back to the 1970s when the Community Reinvestment Act 1977 put pressure on US financial institutions to made credit available to all sectors of society. The main great US mortgage providers, the Federal Home Loan Mortgage Corporation and Federal National Mortgage Association ("Freddie Mac" and "Fannie Mae" respectively) started to grant mortgages to people who, under normal banking criteria, presented a very high risk of default. These were the so called "sub-prime mortgages".

When banks lend through mortgages such loans are an asset on the statement of financial position, representing cash flow to the bank in future years through interest payments and eventual repayment of the principal.

By then "securitising" a mortgage loan, the banks removes the risk attached to its future cash receipts and converts the loan back into immediate cash which it can lend again, and so on, in an expanding cycle of credit formation.

Securitisation is achieved by transferring the lending to specifically created companies called "special purpose vehicles" (SPV). The SPV effectively purchases a bank's mortgage book for cash which is raised through the issue of bonds backed by the income stream flowing from the mortgage holder – these bonds are known as Mortgage Backed Securities (MBS).

In the case of sub-prime mortgages, the high levels of risk called for a different type of securitisation, achieved by the creation of derivative-style instruments known as "collateralised debt obligations" or CDOs.

CDOs are a way of repackaging the risk of a large number of risky assets such as sub-prime mortgages. Unlike a bond issue, where the risk is spread evenly between all the bond holders, CDOs divide the risk into layers or "tranches", so that some investors take proportionately more of the risk for a bigger return and others take little or no risk for a much lower return.

By repackaging home loans into MBS, then "chopping up" the risk into CDOs, the final holder of the risk is very distant from the original home owner and cannot analyse the credit risk for themselves. Hence the holder of a CDO has to put their faith in the ratings agencies and, in the event of default or late payment, has no mechanism for enforcing the underlying loan.

Hence the holder of the CDO would often use a credit default swap (CDS) to transfer the risk yet another step further.

Quality journals (e.g. The Economist) had been warning for many years that this was a dangerous game of "pass the parcel", particularly with a housing bubble ready to burst in the US and UK. Risk can be repackaged, chopped up, transferred – but it does not disappear.

When the property price bubble burst in 2005 many sub-prime borrowers found themselves in "negative equity", where the value of their homes fell below the level of outstanding mortgage. Rising unemployment resulted in a significant increase in the number of defaults and a "drying up" of the liquidity that the CDOs required to satisfy their investors.

Suspicion grew across the financial markets that some banks were holding large amounts of CDOs which were not worth what they appeared to be. Banks are often highly geared with typically less than 10% of their asset value covered by equity. A loss of asset value can soon destroy a bank's equity and it was this risk which led some banks to start selling their holdings of CDOs. However with few buyers available the values of CDOs fell in a "death spiral".

Furthermore the sub-prime debt issued in the US had become distributed across the global markets, leading to "financial contagion". In addition other countries' own banks (e.g. Northern Rock in the UK) had issued asset-backed securities to refinance the issue of further sub-prime mortgages in booming property markets.

Healthy banks began to suspect the credit worthiness of other banks and, as a result, became reluctant to lend on the interbank market. LIBOR, the rate at which banks lend short-term, began to rise, thereby threatening the liquidity of banking operations and so a credit squeeze became a crunch.

The vulnerability of banks to risk soon feeds through into the real economy, as credit begins to dry up and borrowing rates rise. Home buyers cannot raise mortgages and, as a result, property prices continue to fall, further exacerbating the crisis.

A recession in the real economy, with job losses and insolvencies, means that more people default on their home loans. Consumer confidence begins to deteriorate and, as a result, previously strong economies begin to slow down.

Faced with the worst recession in living memory the major central banks (US Federal Reserve Bank, UK Bank of England, European Central Bank) launched huge programmes of "quantitative easing" - buying assets from commercial banks in order to inject cash into the economy and reduce interest rates close to zero in nominal terms (and negative in real terms).

However this flood of cheap cash in the economy had led to another series of asset price bubbles – in 2014 the US and UK stock markets and, more worryingly, property prices reaching or even exceeding their pre-crisis levels.

Answer 60 MOBILITY OF CAPITAL AND MONEY LAUNDERING

(a)   **Capital mobility**

Perfect mobility of capital is when capital is able to move without cost or restriction between countries. If this occurred the interest rate, adjusted for inflation and risk, would be equal in all countries.

Over recent decades many barriers to the international movement of capital across national boundaries have been removed. Financial integration has been greatly enhanced by:

- The removal of capital controls by the US, Germany, Canada, Switzerland, the Netherlands, the UK and Japan in the 1970s;

- Financial integration among EU countries from the 1990s, combined with expansion of the EU;

- Technical innovation that has reduced transaction costs both for exchanging currencies and for international cash transfers.

Despite these developments significant differences in real interest rates between currencies still exist. Perfect capital mobility is prevented partly by some countries still imposing controls on capital movements, and partly by lack of information about foreign countries, which makes the risks of investment or lending abroad appear greater than those for home country activities even if the actual risk is similar.

Barriers to capital mobility tend to be more prevalent in developing countries which are highly concerned with protecting domestic companies and/or the value of the currency.

Common measures include:

- Restrictions on foreign direct investment (FDI), especially into "strategically important" segments of the economy such as defence, natural resources and the banking system;

- Currency controls – restrictions on converting the domestic currency into "hard currency"

- Restrictions on the use of multilateral netting – preventing multinationals from settling intercompany balances on a net basis. Governments sometimes impose this restriction in order to increase fees for their domestic banks.

- Blocks, or at least restrictions on, dividends being paid to overseas shareholders.

Although such policies may reduce "capital flight" they also tend to reduce foreign direct investment and hence access to technology and knowledge.

If FDI is restricted then the potential investor may consider other methods of entering the overseas market, such as licensing production or entering into a joint venture with a local firm. However each of these carries the risk of "industrial espionage" in the form of technology or trade secrets being stolen.

If there are restrictions on the conversion of currency this could potentially be mitigated in advance with political lobbying. If currency restrictions are subsequently imposed then counter-trade may be a solution (i.e. exchanging overseas production for a globally traded commodity).

If restrictions are placed on multilateral netting then the group may have to accept this inconvenience.

Blocks on dividend remittances can potentially be circumvented through the use of transfer pricing or royalty payments/licence fees paid by the overseas subsidiary to the parent. The tax, legal and ethical implications of such schemes would need to be considered. Alternatively the overseas subsidiary could be financed by a loan from the parent company and hence the return made via interest as opposed to dividends.

(b) **Money laundering**

Money laundering regulations apply to businesses that could be at risk to abuse through money laundering and terrorist financing.

At a global level The Financial Action Task Force (FATF) is an inter-governmental body which sets standards and implements legal, regulatory and operational measures for the combating of money laundering and terrorist financing. These global standards are issued through its Recommendations which are agreed by FATF participating countries.

In the European Union (EU) The Third Money Laundering Directive 2005 sets out member state obligations in meeting FATF's Recommendations

In the UK the Money Laundering Regulations 2007 implement, in part, the EU Directive. The Regulations require the financial, accountancy, legal and other business sectors to apply risk-based customer due diligence measures and take other steps to prevent their services being used for money laundering or terrorist financing.

The finance director of any firm must therefore take steps to ensure that customers, and indeed the owners of the business, are not using the firm for money laundering.

Money laundering is defined in the UK as any handling of the proceeds of any crime, including any process by which proceeds of crime are concealed or disguised so that they may be made to appear to be of legitimate origin.

Unlike certain other jurisdictions (notably the US and much of Europe) UK money laundering offences are not limited to the proceeds of serious crimes, nor are there any monetary limits.

A money laundering offence under UK legislation need not involve money, since the legislation covers assets of any description. Therefore any person who commits an acquisitive crime (i.e. one from which he obtains some benefit in the form of money or an asset of any description) in the UK will inevitably also commit a money laundering offence under UK legislation.

Therefore if the finance director believes that illegally-obtained assets of any description are introduced into the business he is required to report his suspicions to the authorities.

Answer 61 IMF AND WTO

(a)   **Current account deficit**

Large current account deficit means that the value of exports of goods, services, investment income and current transfers is much less than the value of imports of these items. If the government believes that the deficit is not a temporary phenomenon, which will be largely self-correcting, it may attempt to reduce the deficit by taking one or more of a selection of economic measures. However, a country with large foreign currency reserves may decide to finance the deficit by running down some of those reserves and may not take significant additional actions for some time.

Economic measures

(1)   Monetary policy. A government will often take deflationary measures to reduce the money supply. This may be through increases in interest rates, or attempting to reduce the money supply through actions such as credit restrictions, wage and/or price controls and reductions in government expenditure. Increased interest rates will tend to reduce local borrowing and demand for imports, and attract overseas funds into the country to take advantage of the higher interest rates (until interest rate and exchange rates are in equilibrium once more)

(2)   Fiscal policy. Governments often reduce consumer spending, including spending on imports, by increasing taxation.

(3)   Devaluation. If the country is part of a fixed exchange rate system the currency may be devalued in order to make imports more expensive and exports more competitive.

(4)   Exchange controls, tariffs, and quotas are all measures, which may be used to reduce imports, and to reduce a current account deficit. However, these may be contrary to World Trade Organisation (WTO) agreements.

(5)   Export stimulation through government subsidies, although these too are often restricted by the WTO.

(6)   Borrowing. The government may finance the deficit by borrowing from international commercial banks or international organisations such as the IMF. Such borrowing, however, may not tackle the underlying symptoms of the deficit.

The IMF may provide loans to help finance a balance of payments deficit. An important feature of most IMF loans is the conditions attached to the loans. Countries receiving IMF loans are required to take strong economic measures to try to improve or eliminate the economic problems that made the loans necessary, and to stimulate medium to long-term economic development. These conditions typically include currency devaluation, controls over inflation via the money supply, public expenditure cuts to reduce government budget deficits and local tax increases. Most loans are for a period of up to five years. The IMF also offers loans under the Extended Fund Facility in order to overcome severe structural balance of payments problems, and special supplementary borrowing facilities, often at concessionary rates of interest, to countries with severe problems.

The actions of the IMF help to reduce volatility in international exchange rates, and to facilitate world trade. This has beneficial effects on the trading activities of multinational companies. However, the strong influence of the IMF on the macroeconomic policies of developing nations often leads to short term deflation and to reductions in the size of markets for multinational companies' products. Conflicts may exist between multinationals, who wish to freely move capital internationally, and governments trying to control the money supply and inflation.

Tax increases often accompany economic austerity measures, import tariff quotas may make operations more difficult and increases in interest rates raise the cost of finance. In the medium to long term the structural adjustments might stimulate economic growth and increase the size of markets for multinational companies, but IMF economic conditions may cause significant short to medium term difficulties for subsidiaries of multinationals in the countries concerned.

Most of the government policies discussed above tend to reduce domestic economic growth and increase unemployment, and are detrimental to a multinational company operating in the country concerned. For example, the impact of higher interest rates usually results in higher borrowing costs for a multinational company.

A possible beneficial effect is when the multinational exports a high proportion of its products, and the incremental demand stimulated by the devaluation/fall in value of the local currency results in an overall increase in the present value of cash flows to the multinational.

(b)   **How countries might impose protectionist measures to control the volume of imports**

Historically, the most important protectionist measures were tariffs, a levy or effectively a tax on imports, and quotas, which restricted either the volume or value of imports. In most recent years import barriers have tended to become more subtle, largely in response to the actions of GATT (General Agreement on Tariffs and Trade) and the WTO, which sought to promote free trade. Such barriers include explicit or "hidden" subsidies favouring local companies, and regulations/red tape that made access to markets by importers difficult. These might include onerous environmental or health regulations, very lengthy bureaucratic process before permission to import is given, and very slow customs procedures which delay the entry of goods into a market. All of these measures are intended to deter overseas companies from exporting to the country.

(c)   **Role and main objectives of WTO**

In 1995 the WTO succeeded GATT as the major world forum for international negotiations and agreement in trade. It now encompasses almost 150 countries, which represent the vast majority of world trade. In contrast to GATT, which focussed on the trade in goods, the WTO also covers trade in services including banks, insurance companies, telecommunications and hotels, intellectual property and agriculture.

The WTO's overriding objectives are to promote freer trade and thereby to help trade flow smoothly, and to reduce or eliminate protectionist barriers. It administers trade agreements, acts as a forum for negotiations and settles trade disputes. Its activities involve:

(i)   Extending trade concessions equally to all members of the WTO.

(ii)   Encouraging lower tariffs and fairer trade around the world, including anti-dumping measures and subsidies.

(iii)   Introducing rules that make trade more predictable.

(iv)   Stimulating competition through cutting subsidies.

(d)   **Possible effect of activities for multinationals**

A developing country that had recently joined the WTO would be expected to gradually reduce any barriers to trade of its goods and services. However, because it is a developing country it would be permitted a much longer time to undertake such measures. The effect on multinational companies could vary. If the multinational currently takes advantage of protectionist barriers that exist in the country, such barriers would be gradually removed exposing the multinational to more competition.

However, freer trade might facilitate the expansion of the multinational's exports into more markets and stimulate demand for its products. In either case the multinational company would normally have a considerable period of time in which to modify its operations in response to the reduction in barriers to trade.

Answer 62 EXCHANGE RATE SYSTEMS

(a) Implications of alternative systems

Managed floating exchange rate

A managed floating exchange rate will be mainly influenced by the market supply and demand for a currency, but is also subject to intervention by the relevant government. The government will buy or sell the currency in order to influence the exchange rate, often to keep it within a desired range against the dollar or other key currency. The government will not normally reveal how or when it will intervene in the foreign exchange market, and floating exchange rates such as this are difficult to forecast as they directly respond to economic events, relevant new information and to government intervention. This could lead to volatility in foreign exchange rates, which might be a deterrent to foreign trade.

In theory, managed exchange rates should gradually adjust to changing economic relationships between nations. For example, as a country moves into a balance of trade deficit, this would normally lead to a fall in the value of the country's currency, which in turn will make the country's exports more attractive, and will reduce the trade deficit. Floating exchange rates should prevent persistent deficits, and result in fewer large speculative international movements of funds. From a multinational company's perspective the difficulty in forecasting such rates makes accurate cash budgeting for international activities more onerous, increases currency risk, and in many cases makes some form of currency hedging essential.

Fixed exchange rate linked to a basket of currencies

An economy that fixes its exchange rate against the dollar or other major currency will inevitably be affected by the state of the economy and the policies of the country to which it has linked. For example, if inflation or the money supply increases in the US, similar effects may be experienced in countries which have their currencies tied to the dollar.

An exchange rate linked to a basket of currencies is less susceptible to economic influences from a single country, although if the basket is weighted by international trade, a dominant trade partner might still have a major influence. In theory, fixed exchange rates offer greater stability, and future rates should be easier to forecast, which reduces risk and aids international pricing and cash budgeting. However, fixed exchange rates do not remain fixed forever; devaluation or revaluation may occur if inflation, interest rates and other economic variables diverge between the relevant countries. The direction of a possible change in rates is quite easy to predict, but not the exact timing of devaluation or revaluation, or the magnitude of any change in currency values. Fixed rates are also more susceptible to currency speculation.

Fixed exchange rates backed by a currency board system

This type of exchange rate regime shares many characteristics of other fixed exchange rate systems, but the currency board means that any domestic currency issues are backed by an equal amount of some "hard" currency, such as the dollar. In theory the domestic currency could be converted at any time into the hard currency at a fixed exchange rate. This backing by a "hard" currency is aimed at achieving greater economic stability, and less exchange rate volatility. A currency board system might result in a fall in the domestic money supply, high interest rates, and thus high "local" financing costs for multinational companies. For some countries, such as Hong Kong, a currency board has proved successful. For others, such as Argentina, it has failed. A multinational company will normally experience lower inflation and more stable economic conditions when a currency board exists.

(b)   **Future exchange rates**

(i)   Validity of non-executive director's estimate

According to the International Fisher Effect (IFE) interest rate differentials between any two countries provide an unbiased predictor of future changes in the spot rate of exchange.

If interest rates are 6% in the UK, and 3·5% in the euro bloc the expected annual change in spot exchange rates is: $\dfrac{0.035 - 0.06}{1.06} \times 100\% = -2·358\%$ with the Euro **strengthening** against the pound.

The expected exchange rate in two years' time is $1.667 \times (1-.02358)^2 = $ Euro $1·589$ per £.

The non-executive director has incorrectly used the relationships between interest rates and exchange rates, implying that sterling is expected to strengthen rather than weaken against the Euro. $(1·667 \times (1·02358)^2 = 1·747/£)$.

(ii)   ·   Using current interest rates

Forecasts of exchange rates using interest rate differentials are not likely to be accurate. Reasons for this include:

■   The interest rate differential may change during the next two years.

■   Even if the interest differential remains constant the IFE is an unbiased, not accurate, predictor of future exchange rates.

■   Exchange rates may not be in equilibrium at the current time. The IFE predicts movements from an equilibrium position.

■   Factors other than interest rates influence exchange rates, including government intervention in foreign exchange markets.

(c)   Protection of Italian subsidiary

The order is not yet definite. If the subsidiary wishes to protect against foreign exchange risk at the tender stage, an over the counter option from a commercial bank is suggested. If the tender is not successful the option would not be exercised, and the total cost would be the option premium. An option to sell Kuwait Dinar (buy a put option on dinar) could be taken for either

(i)   the full 18 month period until payment is due;
(ii)   the period until the result of the tender is known, and then a further hedge taken for the remainder of the period if the tender is successful.

For a short maturity option during the tender period the premium would be relatively low. The further hedge could be another option contract, or a money market hedge involving borrowing Kuwait dinar and converting to Euro at the current spot rate.

The sum to be borrowed, plus interest at 11% per year, would total the amount of the Dinar receipts in 18 months' time. The funds converted to Euro at spot would be immediately available in Italy.

Estimates of future exchange rates may be made using either the purchasing power parity theorem (PPP) or interest rate parity theorem. Using the purchase price of Euro, 0·256 Euro/Dinar, PPP from an Italian viewpoint suggests:

$$\frac{0.09 - 0.03}{1.03} \times 100\% = \text{or } 5\cdot825\% \text{ per year premium on the Euro.}$$

In 18 months' time the premium is expected to be $(1+0\cdot05825)(1+0\cdot05825)^{0\cdot5} = 8\cdot864\%$.

The expected spot is $\dfrac{0.256}{1.0886} = 0\cdot235$ Euro per dinar.

Tutorial note: *This assumes that exchange rates are currently in equilibrium.*

Interest rate differentials between the Euro and Dinar are 5% and 5·5% for borrowing and lending rates respectively. These could be used to estimate future spot rate, but evidence suggests that interest rate parity is not as accurate a predictor as purchasing power parity.

The normal price would be €340,000 × 1·25 = €425,000

At spot (using the purchase price of Euro) this is: $\dfrac{425,000}{0.256} = 1,660,156$ dinars

However, in 18 months' time the dinar is expected to have weakened. Using the forecast spot rate in 18 months' time as the basis for the tender gives:

$$\frac{425,000}{0.235} = 1,808,511 \text{ dinars}$$

If an option hedge is used the tender price could be increased by the amount of the option premium.

The recommended tender price is not less than 1,660,156 dinars, plus the premium cost of an option to buy Euro in 18 months' time at the present spot rate, or 1,808,511 dinars if no foreign exchange hedge is undertaken.

Answer 63 MOOSE CO

(a) **Factors bank will consider**

The "credit crunch" led to an unwillingness by the banks to lend, particularly to one another, resulting in a drain in the liquidity across the capital markets. Interest rates are now low as central banks attempt to stimulate their economies. The business of banks is to earn profits by borrowing short and lending long and they are still willing to lend to high class corporate customers. And probably at competitive interest rates. The banks will be concerned about the following:

The risk of default: although there has been a slackening of demand for the company's product our relatively high credit rating would still make us an attractive prospect for lenders. They will need to undertake a credit risk assessment which will include a thorough examination of our asset strength, existing capitalisation, operating strength and income gearing. An important measure will be the firm's current cash flow/debt obligations ratio.

Recovery: the assessment of our asset strength will form a part of their assessment of the potential recoverability of the debt in the event of default.

(b) **Loan syndication vs bond issue**

Syndication is where a group of banks combine with one bank taking the lead in the arrangement. Syndication allows banks to offer much larger loans in combination than would be feasible singly, and given the range of banks involved can tailor loans (perhaps across different currencies) to more exactly match our requirements. The management of the syndicate lies with the arranging bank but the effective cost will be somewhat higher than with a conventional loan but usually much lower than the cost of raising the necessary finance through a bond issue.

A bond issue is where the debt is securitised and floated onto the capital market normally with a fixed interest coupon and a set redemption date. Initial set up costs can be high especially if the issue is underwritten. A loan of the size envisaged is towards the low end of what would normally be raised through this means. Some bond issues can be syndicated in that a number of borrowers of similar risk are combined by the investment bank chosen to manage the issue.

The advantage of syndication is that it reduces the costs of issue. However, it may be that the best offer would entail accepting a variable rate based on LIBOR which would have to be swapped out if we wished to minimise interest rate risk.

(c) **Relative advantages and disadvantages of capital investment**

In assessing this capital investment we have to make some assumptions about the immediate future in terms of the general economic conditions and to what extent we have a delay option on the project concerned. Where there is a positive delay option then from a financial perspective the best advice may be to delay investment dependent on the likely actions by the competitors and how markets for the product develop. Where there are significant competitive reasons for proceeding we should only proceed if the NPV of the project is worthwhile. Given the magnitudes of the uncertainties involved at this stage of the economic cycle the decision to proceed should only be made when we are sure that we have estimated the potential magnitude of the risks and taken them into account in our analysis.

(d) **Sukuk bonds**

Sukuk are bonds which comply with the principles of Islamic finance. The sukuk holders' return for providing finance would be a share of the income generated by Moose's project in South East Asia.

Potential benefits for Moose

- Although the global financial crisis has restricted the availability of credit in traditional financial centres the growth of Islamic finance has continued unabated – Estimates of the size of the Islamic Finance market in 2016 range from $1.66 trillion to $2.1 trillion with expectations of market size to be $3.4 trillion by end of 2018.

- Moose is considering Malaysia as the location of its manufacturing base in South East Asia. Malaysia is a particularly successful market for Islamic finance and attractive for investors of any religion – 80% of Sharia-compliant assets in Malaysia are held by non-Muslims.

- Moose could use the initial sukuk issue as a learning experience in the world of Islamic finance. If the issue is successful then the firm could use this a platform for further use of Islamic-compliant instruments in future.

Potential limitations

- Moose already has significant levels of debt raised in the traditional financial markets of Europe and South America. The principles of Islamic finance discourage the use of excessive levels of debt, potentially cutting demand for the sukuk issue.

- Sukuk bonds have to be assessed by Islamic scholars to establish their Sharia compliance. However, there are no agreed standards for this assessment and different scholars may reach different opinions, again putting the success of the issue at risk.

- The directors need to be aware that Islamic finance could not be used for projects involving alcohol or pork or anything else that the Sharia considers unlawful or undesirable (haram). Furthermore the project should have a social or moral aspect to comply with Islamic principles.

- Typically, an issuer of the sukuk would acquire property to be leased to tenants to generate income. The issuer collects the income and distributes it to the sukuk holders. The proposed manufacturing project would have to be structured in such a way as to fit the style of sukuk finance.

- As the payment of interest is prohibited on a sukuk bond there is no certainty that the tax authorities will grant Moose a tax shield on the payments made to the sukuk holders.

(e) **Other Islamic instruments (only four need to be discussed)**

- Murabaha – trade credit for asset acquisition that avoids the payment of interest. A bank buys the asset and then sells it to the customer on a deferred basis at a price that includes an agreed mark-up. The mark-up cannot be increased, even if the client does not take the asset within the time agreed in the contract.

- Ijara – lease finance whereby the bank buys an item for a customer and then leases it back over a specific period at an agreed amount. The customer's payments include a contribution to the purchase price, a rent for use of the property and insurance charges. At the end of the finance term the customer can exercise an option to have the property transferred into their name.

- Mudaraba – a form of equity finance. A bank provides all the capital and its customer provides expertise, manages the investment project and may provide labour. Profits generated are distributed according in a predetermined ratio. Any losses are borne by the provider of capital, who has no control over the management of the project.

- Musharaka – joint venture or partnership between two parties who both provide capital towards the financing of new or established projects. Profits are shared on a pre-agreed ratio with losses shared on the basis of the relative amounts of equity invested.

- Salam contracts – where a business sells a commodity to an Islamic bank today but for future delivery. Cash is received immediately by the business and the quantity, quality, and the future date and time of delivery are determined immediately. The sales price would usually be at a discount. In turn, the bank would probably resell the salam contract to receive immediate cash and profit. Salam contracts are prohibited for commodities such as gold, silver and other money-type assets.

■ Istisna contracts – often used for long-term, large construction projects of property and machinery. Here, the Islamic bank funds the construction project for a client that is delivered on completion to that client. The client pays an initial deposit, followed by instalments to the bank, the amount and frequency of which are determined at the start of the contract.

■ Qard hassan/Qardul hassan (good loan/benevolent loan) – a loan extended on a goodwill basis, and the debtor is only required to repay the amount borrowed. However, the debtor may, at his or her discretion, pay an extra amount to the creditor.

Answer 64 STROM CO

Tutorial note: *The following answer is indicative. Credit would be given for alternative, valid points.*

(a)   **IMF**

The role of the IMF is to oversee the global financial systems, in particular to stabilise international exchange rates, help countries to achieve balance of payments and facilitate in the country's development through influencing the economic policies of the country in question. Where necessary, it offers temporary loans, from member states' deposits, to countries facing severe financial and economic difficulties. These temporary loans are often offered with different levels of conditions or austerity measures.

The IMF believes that in order to regain control of the balance of payments, the country should take action to reduce the level of demand for goods and services. To achieve this, the IMF often requires countries to adopt strict austerity measures such as reducing public spending and increased taxation, as conditions of the loan. It believes these conditions will help control the inflationary pressures on the economy, and reduce the demand for goods and services. As a result, this will help the country to move away from a position of a trade deficit and achieve control of its balance of payments.

However, these deflationary pressures may cause standards of living to fall and unemployment to rise. The IMF regards these as short-term hardships necessary to help countries sort out their balance of payment difficulties and international debt problems. The IMF has faced a number of criticisms for the conditions it has imposed, including the accusation that its policies impact more negatively on people with lower or mid-range incomes, hinder long-term development and growth, and possibly result in a continuous downward spiral of economic activity.

Strom trades throughout Europe and economic activity in these countries has been curtailed in the last few years due, initially, to the banking crisis, and then due to the austerity measures that governments have adopted. For retailers, this could pose two possible problems. First, with limited growth and higher taxes, people would have less money to spend. Secondly, increasing levels of unemployment would also limit disposable incomes. It is possible that customers may have curtailed their expenditure on clothes and clothing accessories in order to meet other needs.

Some companies may have to spend proportionally more on marketing and possibly offer more discounts and other customer incentives in order to stay competitive and to maintain market share. This additional cost would hit their profit levels negatively. From the details in the question, it is evident that in 2015 profits have reduced by more than the fall in sales revenue. This could be due to Strom being forced to spend more on activities such as marketing or it could be because it has found it difficult to reduce its cost base. More analysis is needed to determine the exact cause.

It seems that Strom is trying to address the problem of declining profitability by trimming its costs. In circumstances where sales revenues are declining, and it is not possible to stabilise or increase these, then cost structures may need to be altered in order to make reasonable profits.

(b) **Impact of austerity**

The low-price clothing retailers might have benefited from the austerity measures because of a switch by customers from mid-price clothes to low-price clothes. If, due to the austerity measures, people have less money to spend, and if, as stated above, austerity measures impact the mid-income and low-income earners more negatively, then it is possible that their buying preferences change from mid-price to low-price clothes. This would be especially true if there is limited brand loyalty and customers perceive that the low-price items are of a similar quality or provide a better value-for-money.

On the other hand, it is possible that brand loyalty is more significant with high-price clothes, making switching to mid-price clothes difficult. Customers who buy these clothes may prefer not to switch and would rather spend less elsewhere. It is also possible that the austerity measures did not affect the population who buy high-price clothes to the same extent as other groups of the population. Or it may be that this population group is more resilient to the austerity measures imposed by the government, especially if the assertion is true that the IMF conditions affect people who are in the low or mid income categories more than the people in the high income category.

(c) **Reduction in quality control**

The obvious risk in reducing resources allocated to the quality control functions would be that some inspections would be reduced. This may result in defective goods being sold. The costs related to processing returns of defective goods may outweigh the savings made. Reduction in monitoring the working conditions of employees of the clothing suppliers may encourage them to retain their questionable employment practices. This may compromise the company's ethical stance and standards.

The less obvious, but more significant, risk is the impact that unethical labour practices and working conditions may have on the reputation of the company and its products. Potentially, lower quality and defective clothes could seriously harm the company's reputation and result in lower sales revenue over a long period of time. Once damaged, such reputation would be hard to rebuild. The damage in reputation of the company regarding its ethical stance could also be potentially disastrous. Different stakeholder groups could react in negative ways, for example, customers may switch their custom, investors may sell their shares and the press may run negative campaigns against the company. The consequences of such damage could be long term and sometimes permanent.

Strom will need to review where and how resources are allocated in order to decrease or minimise the detrimental impact of a reduction in the quality control costs. For example, savings could be made by eliminating duplicated quality control processes or eliminating processes that are not necessary. Strom should also evaluate whether alternative, less resource intensive processes and procedures can be implemented without compromising the quality control and monitoring of working conditions. Experts should be used to undertake the assessment. Critical processes and procedures should be retained even if they require significant resources. The risk of making errors in the assessment should be evaluated and discussed at a senior level to ensure that Strom is comfortable with undertaking the likely risk.

Answer 65 NOVOROAST CO

(a)   **Report on the proposed investment in the South American country by Novoroast**

Novoroast should assess the expected financial viability of the proposed investment using the NPV of expected dollar cash flows. However, international direct investment is sometimes undertaken for strategic reasons, which, at least in the short term, might outweigh financial considerations.

Estimates of future cash flows require forecasts of exchange rates. Based on purchasing power parity the expected peso exchange rate is:

	Pesos per $	
Spot	13·421	
Year 1	15·636	year 1 $\dfrac{1.20}{1.03} \times 13 \cdot 421 = 15 \cdot 636$
Year 2	17·290	
Year 3	19·119	
Year 4	21·141	other years $\dfrac{1.15}{1.04} \times$ previous rate
Year 5	23·377	

Projected cash flows of the South American subsidiary are:

South American cash flows (million pesos)

Year	0	1	2	3	4	5
Sales		11·6	95·7	210·5	231·6	254·7
Variable costs		4·8	43·2	99·4	114·3	131·4
Fixed costs		12·0	14·4	16·6	19·0	21·9
UK chips		1·0	8·3	18·4	20·3	22·4
Depreciation		12·0	12·0	12·0	12·0	12·0
		29·8	77·9	146·4	165·6	187·7
Taxable net cash flow		(18·2)	17·8	64·1	66·0	67·0
Taxation (25%)			tax holiday		16·5	16·8
		(18·2)	17·8	64·1	49·5	50·2
Add back depreciation		12·0	12·0	12·0	12·0	12·0
		(6·2)	29·8	76·1	61·5	62·2
Land and buildings	(50)					104·9
Plant and machinery	(54)					
Working capital	(20)	(29·0)	(9·8)	(8·8)	(10·2)	77·8
Remittable to parent	(124)	(35·2)	20·0	67·3	51·3	244·9

Home country cash flows ($ million)

Year	0	1	2	3	4	5
Remittable	(9.24)	(2.25)	1.16	3.52	2.43	10.48
Earnings from chips		0.02	0.18	0.36	0.36	0.36
Tax on chips		(0.01)	(0.05)	(0.11)	(0.11)	(0.11)
Additional tax on SA cash flow (5%)		–	–	–	(0.16)	(0.14)
	(9.24)	(2.24)	1.29	3.77	2.52	10.59
Discount factors (14%)	1	0.877	0.769	0.675	0.592	0.519
Present values	(9.24)	(1.96)	0.99	2.54	1.49	5.50

The expected NPV is: ($680,000)

Notes:

(i)   Working capital is assumed to be released at the end of year 5.

Tutorial note: *Working capital investment requires 20 cash outflow at time zero as per scenario. T_1 requires 25 outflow as per scenario plus 20% increase on the initial investment to maintain its value in line with inflation (i.e. incremental investment = 25 + (20 × 20%) = 29). At this point out total investment in working capital = 20 + 29 = 49.*
At T_2 the real value of working capital again needs to be maintained (in line with the previous year's inflation rate as per scenario). Extra investment at T_2 =49× 20% = 9.8.

On the last day of the project the investment in working capital is assumed to be released (i.e. falls to zero). This creates a cash inflow equal to the brought forward cumulative investment in working capital. Cross casting the working capital flows should equal zero (i.e. what goes out comes back in). Of course taking into account the time value of money the working capital adjustments reduce the NPV. Finally note that working capital adjustments have no tax implications.

(ii)   No tax is assumed to be payable on the increase in value of land and buildings.

(iii)   Discount rate

$K_e = 6\% + (14\% – 6\%)\ 1·25 = 16\%$
$K_d = 6\% + (14\% – 6\%)\ 0·225 = 7·8\%$

$$WACC = 16\% \times \frac{820}{964} + 7·8\% \ (1 – 0·3)\ \frac{144}{964} = 14·42\%$$

14% will be used as the discount rate.

The expected NPV of the investment is negative. The investment does not appear to be financially viable.

The financial projections are, however, subject to considerable inaccuracy. This relates in particular to:

■   Estimates of future exchange rates based on forecast inflation levels.
■   Sales forecasts.
■   Price and cost changes may differ from those forecast.
■   Tax rates are subject to change
■   The realisable values in year five are very difficult to estimate.
■   The discount rate may not correctly reflect the systematic risk of the investment.

Sensitivity analysis or simulation analysis should be used in order to ascertain the impact of changes in sales and other key cash flows. It would be better to undertake several financial projections, based on different assumptions of sales, exchange rates, etc. in order to estimate a range of possible NPVs, rather than use a single point value.

A crucial question is what happens to cash flows beyond the company's five-year planning horizon. The year five residual values have been based on the realisable value of assets, not cash flows beyond year five. The latter could produce a much higher expected NPV.

If the investment has the potential to lead to future opportunities/investments, the value of such options should be estimated.

The strategic importance of the venture to Novoroast must also be investigated, as this may heavily influence the final decision.

Any final decision must encompass all relevant non-financial factors of which little detail has been provided. Novoroast must, in particular, be satisfied that there is an acceptable level of political risk, and that there will be no problems with exchange controls and the remittance of funds. The expected period that the import tariff will continue for is important to the decision.

(b)   **Block on remittance of dividends**

This might be avoided by means of:

- Increasing transfer prices paid by the foreign subsidiary to the parent company.

- Lending the equivalent of the dividend to the parent company.

- Making payments to the parent company in the form of royalties, payment for patents, or management fees.

- Charging the subsidiary additional head office overhead

- Parallel loans, whereby the subsidiary in the South American country lends cash to the subsidiary of another a company requiring funds in the South American country. In return the parent company would receive the loan of an equivalent amount of cash from the other subsidiary's parent company.

The government of the South American country might try to prevent many of these measures being used.

(c) **Ethical issues**

Multinational companies may engage in activities which, although not illegal, are questionable ethically, and may have detrimental long-term effects on the company's reputation. Ethical considerations include:

- Would the investment cause pollution or other environmental damage in the South American country?

- Does the investment involve experiments on animals, genetic modifications etc.?

- Should the investment be undertaken if the country has a poor record on human rights?

- If local officials ask for "inducements" to facilitate the investment process, should these be paid?

- Would the investment in any way assist trading in drugs or arms?

- Are wages to be paid in the South American country below subsistence level? Are working conditions of an acceptable standard?

(d) **Integrated reporting**

The integrated reporting framework was launched by the International Integrated Reporting Council (IIRC) in December 2013. The IIRC is a global coalition of regulators, investors, companies, standard setters, the accounting profession and non-government organisations. It has a vision of a business environment in which integrated thinking becomes standard business practice. This would be facilitated by integrated reporting <IR>.

A primary motivation behind <IR> is that financial information alone is insufficient as an indicator of the long-term *sustainability* of a business. <IR> combines *financial* and *non-financial* information in one report with the goal of maximising the value of information provided to stakeholders with a variety of interests in an organisation. Accounting for the long-term sustainability of an organisation is important for both the organisation and those who provide financial capital to an organisation.

The <IR> process also encourages an organisation to consider the use of multiple types of capital including financial capital, manufactured capital, intellectual capital, human capital, social and relationship capital, and natural capital. Novoroast management should not only consider how the investment in South America will affect financial capital (cash flow and use of funds) but the impact of the investment on other forms of capital.

For a listed firm such as Novoroast the key stakeholder is clearly the shareholders and the project's negative NPV suggests a loss in the total value of their equity of $680,000. However integrated reporting could balance this loss against potential gains for other stakeholders such as:

- Creation of new jobs in the South American country, both directly through employment in Novoroast's subsidiary and also in its local suppliers.

- Promotion of sustainable economic growth in the South American country through bringing new technology and expertise.

Answer 66 HGT CO

(a) **Transfer pricing**

Under the current scheme

	Glinland $000	Rytora $000
Sales	1,575	4,500
Variable costs	900	1,350
Cost from Glinland	–	1,575
Fixed costs	140	166
Profit before tax	535	1,409
Corporate tax	214	352
Profit after corporate tax	321	1,057
Withholding tax	16	–
Import tariff	–	157
Retained	161	–
Remitted	144	900
Home country taxation		
Taxable profit	535	1,409
Tax charge	160	423
Less: tax credit[1]	160	352
Tax paid in home country	0	71

[1] Tax credit is allowed up to the UK tax liability

Total taxes and tariffs 214 + 16 + 352 + 157 + 71 = 810

If goods are sold at cost by the Glinland subsidiary

	Glinland	Rytora
Sales	1,040	4,500
Variable costs	900	1,350
Cost from Glinland	–	1,040
Fixed costs	140	166
Profit before tax	–	1,944
Corporate tax	–	486
Profit after corporate tax	–	1,458
Withholding tax	–	–
Import tariff	–	104
Retained	–	–
Remitted	–	1,354
Home country taxation		
Taxable profit	–	1,944
Tax charge	–	583
Less tax credit[1]	–	486
Tax paid in home country	0	97

[1] Tax credit is allowed up to the home country tax liability

Total taxes and tariffs 486 + 104 + 97 = 687

The proposed change would result in an overall saving of 810,000 – 687,000 = $123,000 a year.

However, the proposal might not be acceptable to:

■ The tax authorities in Glinland, where $230,000 in taxation would be lost. The tax authorities might insist on an arm's length price for transfers between Glinland and Rytora.

  Tutorial note: *Existing tax paid to Glinland government = 214 +16 = 230. This would fall to zero if the transfer price was changed as proposed.*

■ The subsidiary in Glinland, which would no longer make a profit, or have retentions available for future investment in Glinland. Depending on how performance in Glinland was evaluated, this might adversely affect rewards and motivation in Glinland.

(b) **Centralised treasury**

Centralisation of group treasury management functions means that decisions regarding currency management, short-term investment and borrowing and financial risk management will be taken centrally rather than at subsidiary level. This will permit significant efficiency improvements and cost savings. The major effects will be that:

■ Decisions will be taken in line with the tactical and strategic objectives of the group as a whole, rather than by individual subsidiaries which might from time to time have different objectives.

■ A central treasury can better appreciate the total foreign exchange exposure position of the group. Netting and matching of receivables and payables in different currencies will be possible, allowing transactions cost savings as only the net amounts need be hedged or transmitted.

■ Better knowledge will exist of total debts and cleared bank balances. This will facilitate interest rate hedging. Surplus cash from one subsidiary will be lent to other subsidiaries at relatively favourable rates, at the very least eliminating a bank lending-borrowing spread.

■ Cash may be aggregated together and invested at better rates, and borrowing may be possible at favourable rates, including from international markets to which individual subsidiaries would not have direct access.

■ It is expensive to establish a high quality specialist treasury management team and supporting technical infrastructure. It is not financially prudent to set up high cost expert teams for each subsidiary.

■ A centralised treasury will collect and analyse relevant economic and financial information, and supply such information to subsidiaries to aid in their decision-making.

■ Transfer prices will be centrally set to try to minimise the group global tax bill.

■ A centralised treasury function, with effective internal controls, will be able to prevent the possibility of major financial losses such as occurred with the collapse of Barings.

The main effect of any form of centralisation is of course that some decision-making will be removed from senior managers of the subsidiaries. The centralisation is intended to increase the efficiency of subsidiaries. Subsidiary management should be encouraged to participate in the implementation process, and should be fully consulted.

From time to time centralised treasury decisions, taken in the interests of the group, might distort reported cash flows and/or profitability of subsidiaries. Any such distortions should be removed from data used for the performance evaluation of the subsidiaries, and managers of subsidiaries will only be evaluated on the results of actions over which they have full control.

It is important that information flows to the central treasury from subsidiaries are quick and accurate. Full computer support and links should be provided. If subsidiaries have specialist knowledge of any local conditions that the central team needs to be aware of this should be communicated as quickly as possible.

Answer 67 BLIPTON

(a) Project cash flow forecast

It is assumed that the benefits of the tax-allowable depreciation will be recovered irrespective of the success of the operating phase of the project. They are therefore considered a credit to the investment phase,

Tutorial note: *Candidates who consider the tax benefits as part of the recovery phase would not be penalised.*

It is assumed that future spot exchange rates will follow purchasing power parity theory

Investment phase (£)

	01 Jan 2009	31 Dec 2009	31 Dec 2010	31 Dec 2011	31 Dec 2012	31 Dec 2013	31 Dec 2014
Nominal project cash flow	–6,200,000						
Tax saving (on allowable depreciation)	930,000	310,000	310,000	310,000			
Nominal project cash flow after tax (investment phase)	–5,270,000	310,000	310,000	310,000			
Rate of exchange	0·6552	0·6409	0·6268	0·6130	0·5996	0·5864	
$value of investment phase	–8,043,346	483,695	494,576	505,710	0	0	

Return phase (£)

	01 Jan 2009	31 Dec 2009	31 Dec 2010	31 Dec 2011	31 Dec 2012	31 Dec 2013	31 Dec 2014
Occupancy rate (OR)	0		0·4	0·5	0·9	0·6	0·6
Residual value of property							8,915,309
Rooms let (400 × OR × 365)			58,400	73,000	131,400	87,600	87,600
Revenue (rooms let × £60)			3,504,000	4,380,000	7,884,000	5,256,000	5,256,000
Variable operating costs (rooms let × £30)			–1,752,000	–2,190,000	–3,942,000	–2,628,000	–2,628,000
Fixed costs			–1,700,000	–1,700,000	–1,700,000	–1,700,000	–1,700,000
Project operating cash flow (real)			52,000	490,000	2,242,000	928,000	928,000
Project operating cash flow (nominal)			54,633	527,676	2,474,749	1,049,947	1,076,195
Tax on operating cash flows (at 30%)			–16,390	–158,303	–742,425	–314,984	–322,859
Nominal project cash flow after tax (return phase)			38,243	369,373	1,732,324	734,963	9,668,646
Rate of exchange			0·6409	0·6268	0·6130	0·5996	0·5864
$ value of return phase			59,670	589,300	2,825,977	1,225,755	16,488,141

Tutorial note: *Although the examiner's answer does not show a working for the residual value it is strongly recommended that candidates do show workings for such detailed calculations, particularly as different approaches or assumptions could be used. For reference the model answer was calculated as follows:*

$$6,200,000 \times 1.08^5 \times 1.025^5 - (1,200,000 \times 1.025^6) = 8,915,309$$

However the model answer has ignored tax on the disposal (there would be a balancing charge as the property has already been written down to zero tax book value) and tax relief on the repairs. A superior answer would show the residual value post-tax (i.e. 8,915,309 × 0.7 = 6,240,716).

(b) **Project NPV and MIRR**

NPV

Given that the Dubai rate of inflation is 4·8% per year and the company's real cost of capital is 4·2% per year the nominal cost of capital is estimated using the Fisher formula:

$i_{nom} = (1 + inf)(1 + i_{real}) - 1$
$i_{nom} = (1·048)(1·042) - 1 = 9·2016\%$

Discounting the project cash flows (investment plus return) at this nominal cost of capital gives a project NPV as follows:

	01 Jan 2009	31 Dec 2009	31 Dec 2010	31 Dec 2011	31 Dec 2012	31 Dec 2013	31 Dec 2014
Nominal project cash flow (investment plus return)	−8,043,346	543,365	1,083,876	3,331,687	1,225,755	16,488,141	
Nominal cost of capital (Dubai)	0·092016						
Discounted cash flow	0	−7,365,593	455,653	832,324	2,342,870	789,330	9,722,942
NPV	6,777,525						

A positive NPV of $6,777,525 strongly suggests that this project is viable and will add to shareholder value.

Modified internal rate of return (MIRR)

Tutorial note: *The model answer shows two methods of estimating MIRR (i) using PV of returns and the published MIRR formula (ii) compounding the returns forwards to **terminal** values, dividing into the PV of investment cost, then finding the geometric average return.*

$$MIRR = \left[\frac{PV_R}{PV_I} \right]^{\frac{1}{n}} (1 + r_e) - 1$$

Where PV_R is the present value of the return phase of the project, PV_I is the present value of the investment phase and re is the firm's cost of capital.

	01 Jan 2009	31 Dec 2009	31 Dec 2010	31 Dec 2011	31 Dec 2012	31 Dec 2013	31 Dec 2014
PV_R	13,002,093		50,038	452,532	1,987,251	789,330	9,722,942
PV_I	−6,224,568	−7,365,593	405,614	379,792	355,619		

$$MIRR = \left[\frac{13,002,093}{6,224,568} \right]^{\frac{1}{6}} (1.092016) - 1 = 23.47\%$$

Alternatively MIRR can be found by compounding forward the return phase cash flows at the firm's cost of capital and then calculating the IRR using the terminal value of the return phase and the present value of the investment phase as follows:

	01 Jan 2009	31 Dec 2009	31 Dec 2010	31 Dec 2011	31 Dec 2012	31 Dec 2013	31 Dec 2014
Year 6 cash flow							16,488,141
Year 5 cash flow							1,338,544
Year 4 cash flow							3,369,975
Year 3 cash flow							767,403
Year 2 cash flow							84,854
Future value of return phase							22,048,918
PV_I	–6,224,568						

MIRR is the discount rate which solves the following equation:

$$6{,}224{,}568 = \frac{22{,}048{,}918}{(1 + MIRR)^6}$$

$$MIRR = \sqrt[6]{\frac{22{,}048{,}918}{6{,}224{,}568}} - 1 = 23.47\%$$

(c) **Recommendation and discussion of methods**

This project is expected to deliver an increase in shareholder value of $6·78 million, at the firm's current cost of finance. NPV focuses on the current equivalent monetary value associated with capital expenditure leading to future cash flows arising from investment. The conversion to present value is achieved by discounting the future cash flows at the firm's cost of capital – a rate designed to reflect the scarcity of capital finance, inflation and risk.

Although the NPV technique is subject to a number of assumptions about the perfection and efficiency of the capital market it does generate an absolute measure of increase in shareholder value and as such avoids scale and other effects associated with percentage performance measures. Given the magnitude of the NPV of the project it is safe to assume that it is value-adding assuming that the underlying cash projections can be relied upon.

However, in certain circumstances it can be useful to have a "headroom" percentage which reliably measures the rate of return on an investment such as this. In this case the MIRR of 23·47% is 14·26% greater than the firm's cost of capital.

MIRR measures the economic yield of the investment (i.e. the discount rate which delivers a zero NPV) under the assumption that any cash surpluses are reinvested at the firm's current cost of capital. The standard IRR assumes that reinvestment will occur at the IRR which may not, in practice, be achievable. MIRR does not suffer from the multiple root problem when calculating IRR on complex cash flows.

Although MIRR, like IRR, cannot replace NPV as the principle evaluation technique it does give a measure of the maximum cost of finance that the firm could sustain and allow the project to remain worthwhile. For this reason it gives a useful insight into the margin of error, or room for negotiation, when considering the financing of particular investment projects.

Answer 68 MULTIDROP

(a)   Determination of the currency transfers required

There are a number of ways this problem can be handled. Two methods are shown here, the first uses a transactions matrix and the second is a route minimisation algorithm.

Given that all balances are to be cleared through the European office, proceed as follows:

Convert all indebtedness between parties to Euros using the specified exchange rates

	Million	€m
US$	6·40	4·67
S$	16·00	7·75
US$	5·40	3·94
Euros	8·20	8·20
US$	5·00	3·65
Rm	25·00	5·01
£	2·20	2·34
S$	4·00	1·94
Rm	8·30	1·66

Transactions Matrix (amounts in € million)

		Owed to					
		Europe	US	Malaysia	Singapore	UK	Owed by
	Europe		4·67	1·66			6·33
	US	8·20					8·20
Owed by	Malaysia		3·94			2·34	6·28
	Singapore	7·75	3·65	5·01			16·41
	UK				1·94		1·94
	Owed to	15·95	12·26	6·67	1·94	2·34	
	Owed by	6·33	8·20	6·28	16·41	1·94	
	Net	9·62	4·06	0·39	−14·47	0·40	

Multidrop (Europe) pays the US, UK and Malaysian business €4·06 million, €0·40 million, and €0·39 million respectively, and receives from Singapore €14·47 million. The net income is €9·62 million to Multidrop (Europe).

Route Minimisation Algorithm

Step 1: Network of Indebtedness

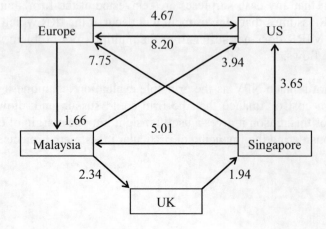

Step 2: Resolve any bilaterals

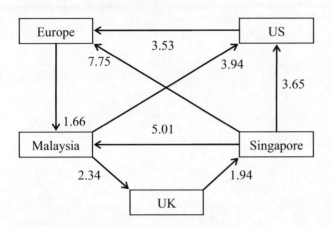

Step 3: Identify and clear circuits

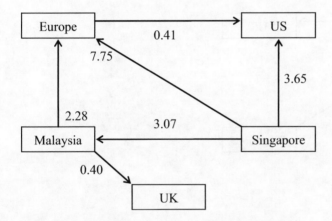

Step 4: Identify and clear cross indebtedness

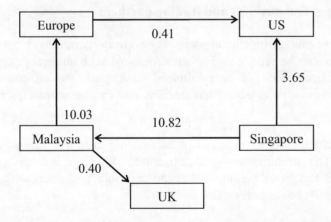

And also:

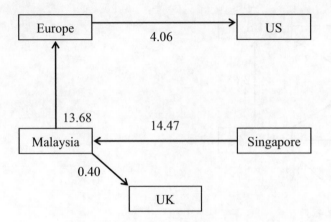

Step 5: Finally resolve all indebtedness in favour of Europe

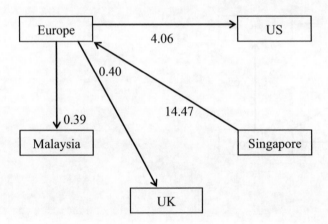

(All amounts are in € million)

(b)   Netting arrangements with the global business and trading partners

Netting is a mechanism whereby mutual indebtedness between group members or between group members and other parties can be reduced. The advantages of such an arrangement is that the number of currency transactions can be minimised, saving transaction costs and focusing the transaction risk onto a smaller set of transactions that can be more effectively hedged.

It may also be the case, if exchange controls are in place limiting currency flows across borders, that balances can be offset, minimising overall exposure. Where group transactions occur with other companies the benefit of netting is that the exposure is limited to the net amount reducing hedging costs and counterparty risk.

The disadvantages: some jurisdictions do not allow netting arrangements, and there may be taxation and other cross border issues to resolve. It also relies upon all liabilities being accepted – and this is particularly important where external parties are involved. There will be costs in establishing the netting agreement and where third parties are involved this may lead to re-invoicing or, in some cases, re-contracting.

Answer 69 PROSPICE MENTIS UNIVERSITY

Tutorial note: *This question can be answered in a variety of ways and the suggested answer below is indicative. Credit will be given for reasonable answers that take a different approach. The question asks for a discussion of whether or not PMU should undertake a joint venture. It does not require candidates to discuss whether or not PMU should venture into Kantaka and credit will not be given for answers which discuss this.*

There are a number of benefits that PMU can potentially take advantage of if it went into a joint venture with a Kantaka academic institution, such as sharing of risks, possible lower running costs and the partner's existing experience of the local market and lower capital investment costs. These are balanced against the potential disadvantages of going into a joint venture such as loss of reputation, product quality and staffing, government restrictions, cultural differences, managerial issues, contractual issues and loss of tax concessions. Each of these issues will be discussed, together with strategies for mitigation of the disadvantages and other information that is required.

PMU does not have the experience of doing business overseas and in particular in Kantaka. Having a partner to guide PMU on the local market and its expectations would be beneficial. It may be able to assist PMU in determining how to market the degree programmes effectively. The partner may also be able to advise PMU on pricing decisions and on how to minimise costs. A well-constructed contract could be instrumental in effective risk sharing in case the demand and revenues do not grow as expected.

The capital investment cost is lower if PMU enters into a joint venture. Presumably PMU would have access to the partner's infrastructure and systems. They may also be able to utilise the expertise of the local academic and administrative staff. Training costs may also be lower as the academic staff may have the required level of expertise.

PMU may have an easier access to the local capital markets. This may be particularly beneficial where revenues are matched with the costs of capital. If the fee income is in the Kantaka currency but interest is payable in the Rosinante currency, then there is a potential for long-term currency exposure. This may be serious if the Kantaka currency continues to weaken. Although some economic data suggests that this may not be the case, it is not very persuasive. It may therefore be beneficial to borrow money using the local currency markets.

Perhaps the most significant disadvantage of progressing with a joint venture is the loss of reputation. It seems that due to historical reasons the Kantaka government may not treat the joint venture favourably by not recognising the degrees issued and not allowing the graduates to seek employment in government controlled organisations. In addition to this, joint ventures have a low reputation with the local population. PMU needs to consider its wider reputation as well. For example, there may be negative publicity if the institution chosen has a poor reputation. In order to mitigate this, PMU needs to choose a partner carefully through detailed due diligence. It may consider linking with an institution with high reputation and perhaps meet with and petition the government to give public and official backing to its degree programmes. However, this may take considerable time and effort.

PMU also needs to consider whether the government will recognise its degrees if it sets up its own site. It is not clear from the question whether this is the case.

Linked to this is the quality of the product. Students would have certain expectations of the institution and the quality of the degrees needs to match this. If PMU enters into a joint venture with the expectation of using its partner's infrastructure, systems and staff, it needs to ensure that these match the expectations of its customers. For example, if it uses local staff to deliver its degrees then these staff must be properly trained to ensure that the correct standards are achieved. It may be the case that training costs make it more expensive than getting staff to come from Rosinante. It may be the case that initially a higher proportion of the staff are from Rosinante and then the numbers are lowered as the local staff gain the required skills.

PMU also needs to consider government restrictions other than the ones described above. For example, would the government issue visas for staff from Rosinante and would the government allow repatriation of funds as easily from a joint venture as from PMU's own investment? PMU would need to meet with government officials or seek legal advice to clarify situations such as these.

PMU needs to ensure that cultural differences between expatriate staff from Rosinante and local staff in Kantaka are minimised and they all share common corporate values. The two organisational cultures may be very different. It would require time and resources to get a common ground between the two organisations and a shared identity. Strategies need to be developed and enacted to ensure that this happens, perhaps through implementation of staff exchange programmes and secondments. Human resources need to develop techniques to help expatriate staff settle into the country. The costs related to all these need to be compared with PMU setting up its own site.

Managers' actions may be restricted in the case of joint ventures because the opinions of both the partners need to be taken into account. Managers of the joint venture may feel that they are not being listened to by the management at PMU. And the managers at PMU may feel that the actions of the managers at the partner are incongruent with aims of PMU. Clear guidelines need to be developed and communicated to limit dysfunctional behaviour between the managers, perhaps asking all the parties concerned to be involved in the development of the joint venture.

There may be difficulties in agreeing to the terms and conditions of the contract between the parties involved. Legal representation and clear communication between the senior management would be needed from both parties to agree: clear terms, conditions and boundaries; the roles and responsibilities of both sides; and, the ownership percentage and profit sharing arrangements.

Finally, if PMU proceeds with financing the joint venture using local funding, it may lose the tax concessions attached to any FDI.

The financial consequences of this need to be assessed.

Additional information

- Financial assessment of both positions to include for example the consequences of loss of tax concessions. Sensitivity analysis of different projections and an assessment of the likelihood of their occurrence.

- Possibility of hiring experts to advise PMU to set up in Kantaka, as opposed to going for a joint venture.

- Outcomes from the government discussions on whether or not PMU degrees will get recognition in Kantaka.

- Assessment of whether the partner's infrastructure and systems meet PMU's requirements.

- Likely movement in the Kantaka currency and instruments such as swaps to hedge currency fluctuations.

- The reputation of a PMU degree with Kantaka's people.

- Quality of local staff, their ability to teach to the methods required and the need for expatriate staff from Rosinante.

- An assessment of government restrictions on for example, issuing visas, repatriation of funds, etc.

Answer 70 KILENC CO

Tutorial note: *The following answer is indicative. Credit would be given for alternative suggestions of risks and issues, and their management or control.*

(a)   Risks and issues of establishing overseas subsidiary

Kilenc needs to consider a number of risks and issues when making the decision about whether or not to set up a subsidiary company in Lanosia. It should then consider how these may be managed or controlled.

Key risks/issues

Kilenc needs to assess the impact on its current exports to Lanosia and the nearby countries if the subsidiary is set up. Presumably, products are currently exported to these countries and if these exports stop, then there may be a negative impact on the employees and facilities currently employed in this area. Related to this may be the risk of loss of reputation if the move results in redundancies. Furthermore, Kilenc should consider how the subsidiary and its products would be seen in Lanosia and the nearby countries. For example, would the locally made products be perceived as being of comparative quality as the imported products?

The recession in Lanosia may have a negative impact on the market for the products. The cost of setting up the subsidiary company needs to be compared with the benefits from extra sales revenue and reduced costs. There is a risk that the perceived benefits may be less than predicted or the establishment of a subsidiary may create opportunities in the future once the country recovers from the recession.

Currently the government offers support for companies involved in the pharmaceutical industry. Kilenc may find it difficult to set up the subsidiary if it is viewed as impeding the development of the local industry by the government. For example, the government may impose restrictions or increase the taxes the subsidiary may have to pay.

On the other hand, the subsidiary may be viewed as supporting the economy and the growth of the pharmaceutical industry, especially since 40% of the shares and 50% of the Board of Directors would be in local hands. The government may even offer the same support as it currently offers the other local companies.

Kilenc wants to finance the subsidiary through a mixture of equity and debt. The implications of raising equity finance are discussed in part (b) of the question. However, the risks surrounding debt finance needs further discussion. Raising debt finance in Lanosia would match the income generated in Lanosia with debt interest payments, but the company needs to consider whether or not it would be possible to borrow the money.

Given that the government has had to finance the banks may mean that the availability of funds to borrow may be limited. Also interest rates are low at the moment but inflation is high, this may result in pressure on the government to raise interest rates in the future. The consequences of this may be that the borrowing costs increase for Kilenc.

The composition of the Board of Directors and the large proportion of the subsidiary's equity held by minority shareholders may create agency issues and risks. Kilenc may find that the subsidiary's Board may make decisions which are not in the interests of the parent company, or that the shareholders attempt to move the subsidiary in a direction which is not in the interests of the parent company. On the other hand, the subsidiary's Board may feel that the parent company is imposing too many restrictions on its ability to operate independently and the minority shareholders may feel that their interests are not being considered by the parent company.

Kilenc needs to consider the cultural issues when setting up a subsidiary in another country. These may range from cultural issues of different nationalities and doing business in the country to cultural issues within the organisation. Communication of how the company is organised and understanding of cultural issues is very important in this case. The balance between independent autonomy and central control needs to be established and agreed.

Risks such as foreign exchange exposure, product health and safety compliance, employee health and safety regulations and physical risks need to be considered and assessed. For example, foreign exchange exposures arising from exporting the products to nearby countries need to be assessed. The legal requirements around product health and safety and employee health and safety need to be understood and complied with. Risks of physical damage such as from floods or fires on the assets of the business need to be established.

Mitigating the risks and issues

A full analysis of the financial costs and benefits should be undertaken to establish the viability of setting up the subsidiary. Sensitivity and probability analysis should be undertaken to assess the impact and possibility of falling revenues and rising costs. Analysis of real options should be undertaken to establish the value of possible follow-on projects.

Effective marketing communication such as media advertising should be conducted on the products produced by the subsidiary to ensure that the customers' perceptions of the new products do not change. This could be supported by retaining the packaging of the products. Internal and external communication should explain the consequences of any negative impact of the move to Lanosia to minimise any reputational damage. Where possible, employees should be redeployed to other divisions, in order to minimise any negative disruption.

Negotiations with the Lanosian government should be undertaken regularly during the process of setting up the subsidiary to minimise any restrictions and to maximise any benefits such as favourable tax rates. Where necessary and possible, these may be augmented with appropriate insurance and legal advice. Continuing lobbying may also be necessary after the subsidiary has been established to reduce the possibility of new rules and regulations which may be detrimental to the subsidiary's business.

An economic analysis may be conducted on the likely movements in inflation and interest rates. Kilenc may also want to look into using fixed rate debt for its long-term financing needs, or use swaps to change from variable rates to fixed rates. The costs of such activity need to be taken into account.

Clear corporate governance mechanisms need to be negotiated and agreed on, to strike a balance between central control and subsidiary autonomy. The negotiations should involve the major parties and legal advice may be sought where necessary. These mechanisms should be clearly communicated to the major parties.

The subsidiary organisation should be set up to take account of cultural differences where possible. Induction sessions for employees and staff handbooks can be used to communicate the culture of the organisation and how to work within the organisation.

Foreign exchange exposure, health and safety regulation and risk of physical loss can be managed by a combination of hedging, insurance and legal advice.

(b) **Dark pools**

Dark pool trading systems allow share orders to be placed and matched without the traders' interests being declared publicly on the normal stock exchange. Therefore the price of these trades is determined anonymously and the trade is only declared publicly after it has been agreed. Large volume trades which use dark pool trading systems prevent signals reaching the markets in order to minimise large fluctuations in the share price or the markets moving against them.

The main argument put forward in support of dark pool trading systems is that by preventing large movements in the share price due to volume sales, the markets' artificial price volatility would be reduced and the markets maintain their efficiency.

The contrary arguments suggest that in fact market efficiency is reduced by dark pool trading systems because such trades do not contribute to the price changes. Furthermore, because most of the individuals who use the markets to trade equity shares are not aware of the trade, transparency is reduced. This, in turn, reduces the liquidity in the markets and therefore may compromise their efficiency. The ultimate danger is that the lack of transparency and liquidity may result in an uncontrolled spread of risks similar to what led to the recent global financial crisis.

It is unlikely that the dark pool trading systems would have an impact on Kilenc's subsidiary company because the subsidiary's share price would be based on Kilenc's share price and would not be affected by the stock market in Lanosia. Market efficiency in general in Lanosia would probably be much more important.

Answer 71 CHMURA

(a) **WTO**

The World Trade Organisation (WTO) was set up to continue to implement the General Agreement on Tariffs and Trade (GATT), and its main aims are to reduce the barriers to international trade. It does this by seeking to prevent protectionist measures such as tariffs, quotas and other import restrictions. It also acts as a forum for negotiation and offering settlement processes to resolve disputes between countries.

The WTO encourages free trade by applying the most favoured nation principle between its members, where reduction in tariffs offered to one country by another should be offered to all members.

Whereas the WTO has had notable success, some protectionist measures between groups of countries are nevertheless allowed and some protectionist measures, especially non-tariff based ones, have been harder to identify and control.

Mehgam could benefit from reducing protectionist measures because its actions would make other nations reduce their protectionist measures against it. Normally countries retaliate against each other when they impose protectionist measures. A reduction in these may allow Mehgam to benefit from increased trade and economic growth. Such a policy may also allow Mehgam to specialise and gain competitive advantage in certain products and services, and compete more effectively globally. Its actions may also gain political capital and more influence worldwide.

Possible drawbacks of reducing protectionist policies mainly revolve around the need to protect certain industries. It may be that these industries are developing and in time would be competitive on a global scale. However, inaction to protect them now would damage their development irreparably.

Protection could also be given to old, declining industries, which, if not protected, would fail too quickly due to international competition, and would create large scale unemployment making such inaction politically unacceptable. Certain protectionist policies are designed to prevent "dumping" of goods at a very cheap price, which hurt local producers.

Tutorial note: *Credit would be given for alternative relevant discussion.*

(b)   **Report to the Board of Directors (BoD), Chmura Co**

This report recommends whether or not Chmura should invest in a food packaging project in Mehgam, following Mehgam reducing its protectionist measures. It initially considers the value of the project without taking into account the offer made by Bulud to purchase the project after two years. Following this, Bulud's offer is considered. The report concludes by recommending a course of action for the BoD to consider further.

Estimated value of the Mehgam project and initial recommendation

The initial NPV of the project is negative at approximately $(451,000) (see Appendix 1). This would suggest that Chmura should not undertake the project.

Bulud's offer is considered to be a real option for Mehgam. Since it is an offer to sell the project as an abandonment option, a put option value is calculated based on the finance director's assessment of the standard deviation and using the Black-Scholes option pricing (BSOP) model. The value of the put option is added to the initial NPV of the project without the option, to give the value of the project. Although Chmura will not actually obtain any immediate cash flow from Bulud's offer, the real option computation indicates that the project is worth pursuing because the volatility may result in increases in future cash flows.

After taking account of Bulud's offer and the finance director's assessment, the NPV of the project is positive at approximately $2,993,000 (see Appendix 2). This would suggest that Chmura should undertake the project.

Assumptions

It is assumed that all the figures relating to variables such as revenues, costs, taxation, initial investments and their recovery, inflation figures and cost of capital are accurate. There is considerable uncertainty surrounding the accuracy of these, and in addition to the assessments of value conducted in appendices one and two, sensitivity analysis and scenario analysis are probably needed to assess the impact of these uncertainties.

It is assumed that future exchange rates will reflect the differential in inflation rates between the two countries. It is, however, unlikely that exchange rates will move fully in line with the inflation rate differentials.

It is assumed that the value of the land and buildings at the end of the project is a relevant benefit, even if the land and buildings are retained by Chmura.

It is assumed that Chmura will be given and will utilise the full benefit of the bi-lateral tax treaty and therefore will not pay any additional tax in the country where it is based.

It is assumed that the short-dated $ treasury bills are equivalent to the risk-free rate of return required for the BSOP model. And it is assumed that the finance director's assessment of the 35% standard deviation of cash flows is accurate.

It is assumed that Bulud will fulfil its offer to buy the project in two years' time and there is no uncertainty surrounding this. Chmura may want to consider making the offer more binding through a legal contract.

The BSOP model makes several assumptions such as perfect markets, constant interest rates and lognormal distribution of asset prices. It also assumes that volatility can be assessed and stays constant throughout the life of the project, and that the underlying asset can be traded. Neither of these assumptions would necessarily apply to real options. Therefore the BoD needs to treat the value obtained as indicative rather than definitive.

Additional business risks

Before taking the final decision on whether or not to proceed with the project, Chmura needs to take into consideration additional risks, including business risks, and where possible mitigate these as much as possible. The main business risks are as follows:

Investing in Mehgam may result in political risks. For example, the current government may be unstable and if there is a change of government, the new government may impose restrictions, such as limiting the amount of remittances which can be made to the parent company. Chmura needs to assess the likelihood of such restrictions being imposed in the future and consider alternative ways of limiting the negative impact of such restrictions.

Chmura will want to gain assurance that the countries to which it will sell the packaged food batches remain economically stable and that the physical infrastructure such as railways, roads and shipping channels are maintained in good repair. Chmura will want to ensure that it will be able to export the special packaging material into Mehgam. Finally, it will need to assess the likelihood of substantial protectionist measures being lifted.

As much as possible, Chmura will want to ensure that fiscal risks such as imposition of new taxes and limits on expenses allowable for taxation purposes do not change. Currently, the taxes paid in Mehgam are higher than in Chmura's host country, and even though the bi-lateral tax treaty exists between the countries, Chmura will be keen to ensure that the tax rate does not change disadvantageously.

Chmura will also want to protect itself, as much as possible, against adverse changes in regulations. It will want to form the best business structure, such as a subsidiary company, joint venture or branch, to undertake the project. Also, it will want to familiarise itself on regulations such as employee health and safety law, employment law and any legal restrictions around land ownership.

Risks related to the differences in cultures between the host country, Mehgam, and the countries where the batches will be exported to would be a major concern to Chmura. For example, the product mix in the batches which are suitable for the home market may not be suitable for Mehgam or where the batches are exported. Chmura will also need to consider the cultural differences and needs of employees and suppliers.

The risk of the loss of reputation through operational errors would need to be assessed and mitigated. For example, in setting up sound internal controls, segregation of duties is necessary. However, personal relationships between employees in Mehgam may mean that what would be acceptable in another country may not be satisfactory in Mehgam. Other areas where Chmura will need to focus on are the quality control procedures to ensure that the quality of the food batches is similar to the quality in the host country.

Recommendation

With Bulud's offer, it is recommended that the BoD proceed with the project, as long as the BoD is satisfied that the offer is reliable, the sensitivity analysis/scenario analysis indicates that any negative impact of uncertainty is acceptable and the business risks have been considered and mitigated as much as possible.

If Bulud's offer is not considered, then the project gives a marginal negative NPV, although the results of the sensitivity analysis need to be considered. It is recommended that, if only these results are taken into consideration, the BoD should not proceed with the project. However, this decision is marginal and there may be other valid reasons for progressing with the project such as possibilities of follow-on projects in Mehgam.

Report compiled by:

Date:

APPENDICES

Appendix 1 – Estimated value of the Mehgam project excluding the Bulud Co offer

Year	1	2	3	4	5
Sales revenue (W2)	1,209·6	1,905·1	4,000·8	3,640·7	2,205·4
Production and selling costs (W3)	(511·5)	(844·0)	(1,856·7)	(1,770·1)	(1,123·3)
Special packaging costs (W4)	(160·1)	(267·0)	(593·7)	(572·0)	(366·9)
Training and development costs	(409·2)	(168·8)	0	0	0
Tax allowable depreciation	(125)	(125)	(125)	(125)	(125)
Balancing allowance					(125)
Taxable profits/(loss)	3·8	500·3	1,425·4	1,173·6	465·2
Taxation (25%)	(1·0)	(125·1)	(356·4)	(293·4)	(116·3)
Add back depreciation	125	125	125	125	250
Cash flows (MP, millions)	127·8	500·2	1,194·0	1,005·2	598·9
Exchange rate (W1)	76·24	80·72	85·47	90·50	95·82
Cash flows ($000s)	1,676·3	6,196·7	13,969·8	11,107·2	6,250·3
Discount factor for 12%	0·893	0·797	0·712	0·636	0·567
Present values ($000s)	1,496·9	4,938·8	9,946·5	7,064·2	3,543·9

Present value of cash flows approx = $26,990,000

PV of value of land, buildings and machinery in year 5 = (80% × MP1,250m + MP500m) ÷ 95·82 × 0·567 approx = $8,876,000

PV of working capital = MP200m ÷ 95·82 × 0·567 approx = $1,183,000
Cost of initial investment in $ = (MP2,500 million + MP200 million) ÷ 72 = $37,500,000
NPV of project = $26,990,000 + $8,876,000 + $1,183,000 – $37,500,000 = $(451,000)

WORKINGS

(1) **Exchange rates**

Year	1	2	3	4	5
MP/$1	$72 \times {}^{1 \cdot 08}/_{1 \cdot 02}$	$76 \cdot 24 \times {}^{1 \cdot 08}/_{1 \cdot 02}$	$80 \cdot 72 \times {}^{1 \cdot 08}/_{1 \cdot 02}$	$85 \cdot 47 \times {}^{1 \cdot 08}/_{1 \cdot 02}$	$90 \cdot 50 \times {}^{1 \cdot 08}/_{1 \cdot 02}$
	$= 76 \cdot 24$	$= 80 \cdot 72$	$= 85 \cdot 47$	$= 90 \cdot 50$	$= 95 \cdot 82$

(2) **Sales revenue (MP million)**

Year	1	2	3	4	5
	$10,000 \times$	$15,000 \times$	$30,000 \times$	$26,000 \times$	$15,000 \times$
	$115,200 \times 1 \cdot 05$	$115,200 \times 1 \cdot 05^2$	$115,200 \times 1 \cdot 05^3$	$115,200 \times 1 \cdot 05^4$	$115,200 \times 1 \cdot 05^5$
	$= 1,209 \cdot 6$	$= 1,905 \cdot 1$	$= 4,000 \cdot 8$	$= 3,640 \cdot 7$	$= 2,205 \cdot 4$

(3) **Production and selling (MP million)**

Year	1	2	3	4	5
	$10,000 \times$	$15,000 \times$	$30,000 \times$	$26,000 \times$	$15,000 \times$
	$46,500 \times 1 \cdot 1$	$46,500 \times 1 \cdot 1^2$	$46,500 \times 1 \cdot 1^3$	$46,500 \times 1 \cdot 1^4$	$46,500 \times 1 \cdot 1^5$
	$= 511 \cdot 5$	$= 844 \cdot 0$	$= 1,856 \cdot 7$	$= 1,770 \cdot 1$	$= 1,123 \cdot 3$

(4) **Special packaging (MP million)**

Year	1	2	3	4	5
	$10,000 \times 200$	$15,000 \times 200$	$30,000 \times 200$	$26,000 \times 200$	$15,000 \times 200$
	$\times 76 \cdot 24 \times 1 \cdot 05$	$\times 80 \cdot 72 \times 1 \cdot 05^2$	$\times 85 \cdot 47 \times 1 \cdot 05^3$	$\times 90 \cdot 50 \times 1 \cdot 05^4$	$\times 95 \cdot 82 \times 1 \cdot 05^5$
	$= 160 \cdot 1$	$= 267 \cdot 0$	$= 593 \cdot 7$	$= 572 \cdot 0$	$= 366 \cdot 9$

Appendix 2 – Estimated value of the Mehgam project including the Bulud Co offer

Present value of underlying asset (Pa) = $30,613,600 (approximately)
(This is the sum of the present values of the cash flows foregone in years 3, 4 and 5)

Price offered by Bulud (Pe) = $28,000,000

Risk free rate of interest (r) = 4% (assume government treasury bills are valid approximation of the risk free rate of return)

Volatility of underlying asset (s) = 35%

Time to expiry of option (t) = 2 years

$d_1 = [\ln(30,613 \cdot 6 \div 28,000) + (0 \cdot 04 + 0 \cdot 5 \times 0 \cdot 35^2) \times 2] \div [0 \cdot 35 \times \sqrt{2}] = 0 \cdot 589$
$d_2 = 0 \cdot 589 - 0 \cdot 35 \times \sqrt{2} = 0 \cdot 094$

$N(d_1) = 0 \cdot 5 + 0 \cdot 2220 = 0 \cdot 7220$
$N(d_2) = 0 \cdot 5 + 0 \cdot 0375 = 0 \cdot 5375$

Call value = $30,613,600 \times 0 \cdot 7220 - $28,000,000 \times 0 \cdot 5375 \times e^{-0 \cdot 04 \times 2}$ = approx $8,210,000
Put value = $8,210,000 - $30,613,600 + $28,000,000 \times e^{-0 \cdot 04 \times 2}$ = approx $3,444,000

NPV of the project with put option = $3,444,000 – $451,000 = approx $2,993,000

Tutorial note: *Credit would be given for relevant discussion and recommendation.*

PILOT PAPER

Answer 1 TRAMONT CO

(a)   **Report to the Board of Directors, Tramont Co**

Evaluation of whether the production of X-IT should move to Gamala

This report evaluates the possibility of moving the production of the X-IT to Gamala from the USA. Following the initial evaluation the report discusses the key assumptions made, the possible impact of a change in the government in Gamala after the elections due to take place shortly and other business factors that should be considered before a final decision is made.

Initially a base case NPV calculation is conducted to assess the impact of the production in Gamala. This is then adjusted to show the impact of cash flows in the USA as a result of the move, the immediate impact of ceasing production and the impact of the subsidy and the tax shield benefits from the loan borrowing.

Based on the calculations presented in the Appendix, the move will result in a positive adjusted present value of just over $2.4 million. On this basis, the initial recommendation is that the production of X-IT should cease in the USA and the production moved to Gamala instead.

Assumptions

It is assumed that the borrowing rate of 5% is used to calculate the benefits from the tax shield. It could be argued that the risk free rate of 3% could be used as the discount rate instead of 5% to calculate the present value of benefits from the tax shields and the subsidies.

In adjusted present value calculations, the tax shield benefit is normally related to the debt capacity of the investment, not the actual amount of debt finance used. Since this is not given, it is assumed that the increase in debt capacity is equal to the debt finance used.

It has been assumed that many of the input variables, such as for example the tax and tax-allowable depreciation rates, the various costs and prices, units produced and sold, the rate of inflation and the prediction of future exchange rates based on the purchasing power parity, are accurate and will change as stated over the four-year period of the project. In reality any of these estimates could be subject to change to a greater or lesser degree and it would appropriate for Tramont to conduct uncertainty assessments like sensitivity analysis to assess the impact of the changes to the initial predictions.

Tutorial note: *Credit would be given for alternative relevant assumptions.*

Government change

From the facts of the case it would seem that a change of government could have a significant impact on whether or not the project is beneficial to Tramont. The threat to raise taxes may not be too significant as the tax rates would need to increase to more than 30% before Tramont would lose money. However, the threat by the opposition party to review "commercial benefits" may be more significant.

Just over 40% of the present value comes from the tax shield and subsidy benefits. If these were reneged then Tramont would lose a significant of the value attached to the project. Also the new government may not allow remittances every year, as is assumed in part (i). However this may not be significant since the largest present value amount comes from the final year of operation.

1184

Other business factors

Tramont should consider the possibility of becoming established in Gamala, and this may lead to follow-on projects. The real options linked to this should be included in the analysis.

Tramont's overall corporate strategy should be considered. Does the project fit within this strategy? Even if the decision is made to close the operation in the USA, there may be other alternatives and these need to be assessed.

The amount of experience Tramont has in international ventures needs to be considered. For example, will it be able to match its systems to the Gamalan culture? It will need to develop strategies to deal with cultural differences. This may include additional costs such as training which may not have been taken into account.

Tramont needs to consider if the project can be delayed at all. From part (i), it can be seen that a large proportion of the opportunity cost relates to lost contribution in years 1 and 2. A delay in the commencement of the project may increase the overall value of the project.

Tramont needs to consider the impact on its reputation due to possible redundancies. Since the production of X-IT is probably going to be stopped in any case, Tramont needs to communicate its strategy to the employees and possibly other stakeholders clearly so as to retain its reputation. This may make the need to consider alternatives even more important.

Tutorial note: *Credit would be given for alternative relevant comments.*

Conclusion

Following from a detailed sensitivity analysis, analysis of a possible change in the government and an evaluation of the financial benefits accruing from the other business factors discussed above, the BoD can make a decision of whether to move the production to Gamala or not. This initial evaluation suggests that moving the production of the X-IT to Gamala would be beneficial.

Report compiled by:

Date:

Appendix – Gamalan Project Operating Cash Flows (all amounts in GR/$ 000s)

Year	Now	1	2	3	4
Sales revenue (W2)		48,888	94,849	214,442	289,716
Local variable costs (W3)		(16,200)	(32,373)	(75,385)	(104,897)
Imported component (W4)		(4,889)	(9,769)	(22,750)	(31,658)
Fixed costs		(30,000)	(32,700)	(35,643)	(38,851)
Profits before tax		(2,201)	20,007	80,664	114,310
Taxation (W5)		0	0	(7,694)	(18,862)
Investment	(230,000)				450,000
Working capital	(40,000)	(3,600)	(3,924)	(4,277)	51,801
Cash flows (GR)	(270,000)	(5,801)	16,083	68,693	597,249
Exchange rate (W1)	55.00	58.20	61.59	65.18	68.98
Cash flows ($)	(4,909)	(100)	261	1,054	8,658
Discount factor for 9.6% (W6)					
(Full credit given if 10% is used as the					
discount rate)		0.912	0.832	0.760	0.693
Present values ($)	(4,909)	(91)	217	801	6,000

NPV of the cash flows from the project is approx $2,018,000.

Adjusted present value (APV)	$000
NPV of cash flows	2,018
Impact of additional tax in USA, opportunity cost (revenues foregone from current operations) and additional contribution from component exported to project (net of tax) (W7)	(1,237)
Closure revenues and costs ($2,300 – $1,700)	600
Tax shield	
Benefit of subsidy (W8)	1,033
Total APV	2,414

WORKINGS

(1)   Exchange rates

Year	1	2	3	4
GR/$1	$55 \times {}^{1.09}/_{1.03}$	$58.20 \times {}^{1.09}/_{1.03}$	$61.59 \times {}^{1.09}/_{1.03}$	$65.18 \times {}^{1.09}/_{1.03}$
	= 58.20	= 61.59	= 65.18	= 68.98

(2)   Sales revenue (GR 000s)

Year	1	2	3	4
Price × units ×	$70 \times 12,000 \times 58.20$	$70 \times 22,000 \times 61.59$	$70 \times 47,000 \times 65.18$	$70 \times 60,000 \times 68.98$
exchange rate	= 48,888	= 94,849	= 214,442	= 289,716

(3)   Local variable costs (GR 000s)

Year	1	2	3	4
Cost × units × inflation after year 1	$1,350 \times 12,000$ = 16,200	$1,350 \times 22,000 \times$ 1.09 = 32,373	$1,350 \times 47,000 \times$ 1.092 = 75,385	$1,350 \times 60,000 \times$ 1.093 = 104,897

(4)   Imported Component (GR000s)

Year	1	2	3	4
Price × units × inflation after year 1 × exchange rate	$7 \times 12,000 \times 58.20$ $= 4,889$	$7 \times 22,000 \times 1.03$ $\times 61.59 = 9,769$	$7 \times 47,000 \times 1.032$ $\times 65.18 = 22,750$	$7 \times 60,000 \times 1.033$ $\times 68.98 = 31,658$

(5)   Taxation

Year	1	2	3	4
Profits before tax	(2,201)	20,007	80,664	114,310
Tax allowable depreciation	(20,000)	(20,000)	(20,000)	(20,000)
Profit/(loss) after depreciation	(22,201)	7	60,664	94,310
Taxable profits	0	0	38,470	94,310
Taxation (20%)	0	0	(7,694)	(18,862)

(6)   Gamala project all-equity financed discount rate

Tramont equity beta = 1.17
$MV_e = \$2.40 \times 25m$ shares = \$60m
$MV_d = \$40m \times \$1,428 \div \$1,000 = \$57.12m$

Tramont asset beta (assuming debt is risk free)
$1.17 \times 60m \div (60m + 57.12m \times 0.7) = 0.70$

Project asset beta = 0.70 + 0.40 = 1.10
Project all-equity financed discount rate = 3% + 6% × 1.1 = 9.6%

(7)   Additional tax, additional contribution and opportunity cost ($000s)

Year	1	2	3	4
Additional tax				
Taxable profits ÷ exchange rate × 10%	0	0	$38,470 \times \frac{1}{65.18} \times$ $10\% = (59)$	$94,310 \times \frac{1}{68.98} \times$ $10\% = (137)$
Opportunity cost				
Units × contribution × (1 − tax)	$40 \times \$20 \times 0.7$ $= (560)$	$32 \times \$20 \times 0.7$ $= (448)$	$25.6 \times \$20 \times 0.7$ $= (358)$	$20.48 \times \$20 \times 0.7$ $= (287)$
Additional contribution				
Units × contribution × inflation × (1 − tax)	$12 \times \$4 \times 0.7$ $= 34$	$22 \times \$4 \times 1.03 \times 0.7$ $= 63$	$47 \times \$4 \times 1.032 \times 0.7$ $= 140$	$60 \times \$4 \times 1.033 \times 0.7$ $= 184$
Total cash flows	(526)	(385)	(277)	(240)
PV of cash flows Discount at 7%	(492)	(336)	(226)	(183)

NPV is approx $(1,237,000)

(8) **Tax shield and subsidy benefits ($/GR000s)**

Year	1	2	3	4
Annual tax shield (GR) Interest × loan × tax rate	6% × 270m × 20% = 3,240	3,240	3,240	3,240
Annual subsidy benefit (GR) Interest gain × loan × (1–tax rate)	7% × 270m × 0.8 = 15,120	15,120	15,120	15,120
Total tax shield + subsidy benefits (GR)	18,360	18,360	18,360	18,360
Exchange rate (GR/$1)	58.20	61.59	65.18	68.98
Cash flows ($)	315	298	282	266
PV of cash flows Discount at 5%	300	270	244	219

NPV of tax shield and subsidy benefit is approx $1,033,000

Tutorial note: *The model answer uses the overseas tax rate of 20% to value the tax shield and the post-tax value of the subsidy. However there is a string argument that the group's effective tax rate of 30% should be used in these calculations.*

(b) **Triple Bottom Line**

A triple bottom line (TBL) report provides a quantitative summary of performance in terms of economic or financial impact, impact on the environment and impact on social performance. TBL provides the measurement tool to assess a corporation's or project's performance against its objectives.

The principle of TBL reporting is that true performance should be measured in terms of a balance between economic (profits), environmental (planet) and social (people) factors; with no one factor growing at the expense of the others. The contention is that a corporation that accommodates the pressures of all the three factors in its strategic investment decisions will enhance shareholder value, as long as the benefits that accrue from producing such a report exceeds the costs of producing it.

For example, in the case of the X-IT, reporting on the impact of moving the production to Gamala, in terms of the impact on the employees and environment in the USA and in Gamala will highlight Tramont as a good corporate citizen, and thereby increase its reputation and enable it to attract and retain high performing, high calibre employees. It can also judge the impact on the other business factors mentioned in the report above.

Tutorial note: *Credit would be given for alternative relevant answers.*

(c) **Corporate diversification**

Shareholders holding well-diversified portfolios will have diversified away unsystematic or company specific risk, and will only face systematic risk (i.e. risk that cannot be diversified away). Therefore a company cannot reduce risk further by undertaking diversification within the same system or market. However, further risk reduction may occur if the diversification is undertaken by the company, on behalf of the shareholders, into a system or market where they themselves do not invest. Some studies indicate that even shareholders holding well-diversified portfolios may benefit from risk diversification where companies invest in emerging markets.

In the case of Tramont and the X-IT, it is not clear whether diversification benefits will result in the investment in Gamala. The benefits are dependent on the size of the investment, and on the nature of the business operations undertaken in Gamala by Tramont. And whether these operations mirror an investment in a significantly different system or market. If the investment is large, the operations are similar to undertaking a Gamalan company. Tramont's shareholders who do not hold similar companies' shares in their portfolios may then gain risk diversification benefits from the Gamalan investment.

Answer 2 ALECTO CO

(a) **Collar vs options**

The main advantage of using a collar instead of options to hedge interest rate risk is lower cost. A collar involves the simultaneous purchase and sale of both call and put options at different exercise prices. The option purchased has a higher premium when compared to the premium of the option sold, but the lower premium income will reduce the higher premium payable. With a normal uncovered option, the full premium is payable.

However the disadvantage of this is that, whereas with a hedge using options the buyer can get full benefit of any upside movement in the price of the underlying asset, with a collar hedge the benefit of the upside movement is limited or capped as well.

Tutorial note: *The requirement is slightly confusing as a collar hedge does itself require the use of options.*

(b) **Interest rate hedging**

Using futures

Need to hedge against a rise in interest rates, therefore *go short* in the futures market. Alecto needs June contracts as the loan will be required on 1 May.

Tutorial note: *The price of interest rate futures is quoted as (100 – implied interest rates). Therefore if interest rates rise, as Alecto fears, the price of interest rate futures would fall (in the same way that bond prices fall when yields rise). Alecto should take a position on futures that would create a gain on falling prices – hence initially **sell** futures (i.e. taking a "short" position).*

No. of contracts needed = €22,000,000 ÷ €1,000,000 × $^{5}/_{3}$ = 36.67 say 37 contracts.

Basis
Current price (on 1 January) – futures price = total basis
$(100 - 3.3) - 96.16 = 0.54$
Unexpired basis = $^{2}/_{6} \times 0.54 = 0.18$

If interest rates increase by 0.5% to 3.8%

Cost of borrowing funds = $4.6\% \times \frac{5}{12} \times €22,000,000 =$ €421,667

Expected futures price = $100 - 3.8 - 0.18 = 96.02$

Gain on the futures market = $(9616 - 9602) \times €25 \times 37 =$ €12,950

Net cost = €408,717

Effective interest rate = $408,717 \div 22,000,000 \times \frac{12}{5} = 4.46\%$

If interest rates decrease by 0.5% to 2.8%

Cost of borrowing funds = $3.6\% \times \frac{5}{12} \times €22,000,000 =$ €330,000

Expected futures price = $100 - 2.8 - 0.18 = 97.02$

Loss on the futures market = $(9,616 - 9,702) \times €25 \times 37 =$ €79,550

Net cost = €409,550

Effective interest rate = $€409,550 \div €22,000,000 \times \frac{12}{5} = 4.47\%$

Tutorial note: *Net cost should be the same. Difference is due to rounding the number of contracts.*

Using options on futures

Need to hedge against a rise in interest rates, therefore buy put options. As before, Alecto needs 37 June put option contracts ($€22,000,000 \div €1,000,000 \times \frac{5}{3}$).

Tutorial note: *From earlier analysis a futures hedge would initially involve selling futures. An options hedge requires holding the right, but not the obligation, to sell futures (i.e. buy puts on futures).*

If interest rates increase by 0.5% to 3.8%

Exercise Price	96.00	96.50
Futures Price	96.02	96.02
Exercise ?	No	Yes
Gain in basis points	0	48
Underlying cost of borrowing (from above)	€421,667	€421,667
Gain on options (0 and €25 × 48 × 37)	€0	€44,400
Premium		
16.3 × €25 × 37	€15,078	
58.1 × €25 × 37		€53,743
Net cost €436,745	€431,010	
Effective interest rate	4.76%	4.70%

If interest rates decrease by 0.5% to 2.8%

Exercise Price	96.00	96.50
Futures Price	97.02	97.02
Exercise ?	No	No
Gain in basis points	0	0
Underlying cost of borrowing (from above)	€330,000	€330,000
Gain on options	€0	€0
Premium		
16.3 × €25 × 37	€15,078	
58.1 × €25 × 37		€53,743
Net cost	€345,078	€383,743
Effective interest rate	3.76%	4.19%

Using a collar

Buy June put at 96.00 for 0.163 and sell June call at 96.50 for 0.090.
Premium payable = 0.073

Tutorial note: *The answer indicates that a collar requires simultaneously buying puts and selling calls but gives no explanation. Earlier analysis showed that buying puts would protect the firm from rising interest rates while allowing participation in falling rates – creating a "cap". To reduce the cost of buying a cap the firm could simultaneously do the exact opposite and sell a "floor" through selling call options to receive premium. Various combinations of strike prices are possible – the model answer suggests buying puts at 96.00 (sets a cap at 4%) and selling calls at 65.50 (sets a floor at 3.5%).*

If interest rates increase by 0.5% to 3.8%

	Buy put	Sell Call
Exercise Price	96.00	96.50
Futures Price	96.02	96.02
Exercise ?	No	No

Underlying cost of borrowing (from above)	€421,667
Premium	
7.3 × €25 × 37	€6,753
Net cost	€428,420
Effective interest rate	4.67%

If interest rates decrease by 0.5% to 2.8%

	Buy put	Sell Call
Exercise Price	96.00	96.50
Futures Price	97.02	97.02
Exercise ?	No	Yes

Underlying cost of borrowing (from above)	€330,000
Premium	
7.3 × €25 × 37	€6,753
Loss on exercise (52 × €25 × 37)	€48,100
Net cost	€384,853
Effective interest rate	4.20%

Hedging using the interest rate futures market fixes the rate at 4.47%, whereas with options on futures or a collar hedge, the net cost changes. If interest rates fall in the future then a hedge using options gives the most favourable rate. However, if interest rates increase then a hedge using futures gives the lowest interest payment cost and hedging with options give the highest cost, with the collar hedge in between the two. If Alecto's aim is to fix its interest rate whatever happens to interest rates then the preferred instrument would be futures.

This recommendation is made without considering margin and other transactional costs, and basis risk, which is discussed below. These need to be taken into account before a final decision is made.

Tutorial note: *Credit would be given for alternative approaches to the calculations in (b).*

(c) **Basis risk**

Basis risk occurs when the basis does not diminish at a constant rate. In this case, if a futures contract is held till it matures then there is no basis risk because at maturity the derivative price will equal the underlying asset's price. However, if a contract is closed out before maturity (here the June futures contracts will be closed two months prior to expiry) there is no guarantee that the price of the futures contract will equal the predicted price based on basis at that date. For example, in part (b) above the predicted futures price in four months assumes that the basis remaining is 0.18, but it could be more or less. Therefore the actual price of the futures contract could be more or less.

This creates a problem in that the effective interest rate for the futures contract above may not be fixed at 4.47%, but may vary and therefore the amount of interest that Alecto pays may not be fixed or predictable. On the other hand it could be argued that the basis risk will probably be smaller than the risk exposure to interest rates without hedging and therefore although some risk will exist, its impact will be smaller.

Answer 3 DORIC CO

(a) **Benefits of divesting via MBO**

Possible benefits of disposing a division through a management buy-out may include:

- Management buy-out costs may be less compared with other forms of disposal such as selling individual assets of the division or selling it to a third party.

- It may be the quickest method in raising funds compared to the other methods.

- There would be less resistance from the managers and employees making the process smoother and easier to accomplish than if both divisions were to be closed down.

- It may offer a better price. The current management and employees possibly have the best knowledge of the division and are able to make it successful. Therefore they may be willing to pay more for it.

Tutorial note: *Credit would be given for alternative relevant benefits.*

(b) **Outcome from liquidation**

Close the company	$m
Sale of all assets	210
Less redundancy and other costs	(54)
Net proceeds from sale of all assets	156
Total liabilities	280

The liability holders will receive $0.56 per $1 owing to them ($156m ÷ $280m). Shareholders will receive nothing.

(c) **Outcome from MBO**

	$m
Value of selling fridges division ($^2/_3 \times 210$)	140
Redundancy and other costs ($^2/_3 \times 54$)	(36)
Funds available from sale of division	104
Amount of current and non-current liabilities	280
Amount of management buy-out funds needed to pay current and non-current liabilities (280 – 104)	176
Amount of management buy-out funds needed to pay shareholders	60
Investment needed for new venture	50
Total funds needed for management buy-out	286

Estimating value of new company after buy-out	$m
Sales revenue	170
Costs	(120)
Profits before depreciation	50
** Depreciation (($^1/_3 \times \$100m + \$50m) \times 10\%$)	(8.3)
Tax (20%)	(8.3)
** Cash flows before interest payment	33.4

** It is assumed that the depreciation is available on the re-valued non-current assets plus the new investment. It is assumed that no additional investment in non-current assets or working capital is needed, even though cash flows are increasing.

Estimate of value based on perpetuity = $33.4 (1.035) \div (0.11 – 0.035) = \$461m$

This is about 61% in excess of the funds invested in the new venture, and therefore the buy-out is probably beneficial. However, the amounts are all estimates and a small change in some variables like the growth rate or the cost of capital can have a large impact on the value. Also the assumption of cash flow growth in perpetuity may not be accurate. It is therefore advisable to undertake a sensitivity analysis.

(d) **Sale of division as a going concern**

Potential buyers will need to be sought through open tender or through an intermediary. Depending on the nature of the business being sold a single bidder may be sought or preparations made for an auction of the business. Doric's suppliers and distributors may be interested, as may be competitors in the same industry. High levels of discretion are required in the search process to protect the value of the business from adverse competitive action. Otherwise, an interested and dominant competitor may open a price war in order to force down prices and hence the value of the fridges division prior to a bid.

Once a potential buyer has been found, access should be given so that they can conduct their own due diligence. Up-to-date accounts should be made available and all legal documentation relating to assets to be transferred made available. Doric should undertake its own due diligence to check the ability of the potential purchaser to complete a transaction of this size. Before proceeding, it would be necessary to establish how the purchaser intends to finance the purchase, the timescale involved in their raising the necessary finance and any other issues that may impede a clean sale. Doric's legal team will need to assess any contractual issues on the sale, the transfer of employment rights, the transfer of intellectual property and any residual rights and responsibilities to Doric.

A sale price will be negotiated which is expected to maximise the return. The negotiation process should be conducted by professional negotiators who have been thoroughly briefed on the terms of the sale, the conditions attached and all of the legal requirements. The consideration for the sale, the deeds for the assignment of assets and terms for the transfer of staff and their accrued pension rights will also all be subject to agreement.

Answer 4 GNT CO

(a)   **Calculation of duration**

In order to calculate the duration of the two bonds, the present value of the annual cash flows and the price or value at which the bonds are trading at need to be determined. To determine the present value of the annual cash flows, they need to be discounted by the gross redemption yield.

Gross Redemption Yield (GRY)

Try 5%
$60 \times 1.05^{-1} + 60 \times 1.05^{-2} + 60 \times 1.05^{-3} + 60 \times 1.05^{-4} + 1,060 \times 1.05^{-5} =$
$60 \times 4.3295 + 1,000 \times 0.7835 = 1,043.27$

Try 4%
$60 \times 4.4518 + 1,000 \times 0.8219 = 1,089.01$

$GRY = 4 + [(1,089.01 - 1,079.68) \div (1,089.01 - 1,043.27)] = 4.2\%$

Bond 1 (PV of cash flows)

$60 \times 1.042^{-1} + 60 \times 1.042^{-2} + 60 \times 1.042^{-3} + 60 \times 1.042^{-4} + 1,060 \times 1.042^{-5}$

PV of cash flows (years 1 to 5) = $57.58 + 55.26 + 53.03 + 50.90 + 862.91 = 1,079.68$

Market price = $1,079.68

$Duration = [57.58 \times 1 + 55.26 \times 2 + 53.03 \times 3 + 50.90 \times 4 + 862.91 \times 5] \div 1,079.68 = 4.49 \text{ years}$

Bond 2 (PV of Coupons and Bond Price)

$Price = 40 \times 1.042^{-1} + 40 \times 1.042^{-2} + 40 \times 1.042^{-3} + 40 \times 1.042^{-4} + 1,040 \times 1.042^{-5}$

PV of cash flows (years 1 to 5) = $38.39 + 36.84 + 35.36 + 33.93 + 846.63 = 991.15$

Market Price = $991.15

$Duration = [38.39 \times 1 + 36.84 \times 2 + 35.36 \times 3 + 33.93 \times 4 + 846.63 \times 5] \div 991.15 = 4.63 \text{ years}$

(b)   **Usefulness of duration**

The sensitivity of bond prices to changes in interest rates is dependent on their redemption dates. Bonds which are due to be redeemed at a later date are more price-sensitive to interest rate changes, and therefore are riskier.

Duration measures the average time it takes for a bond to pay its coupons and principal and therefore measures the redemption period of a bond. It recognises that bonds which pay higher coupons effectively mature "sooner" compared to bonds which pay lower coupons, even if the redemption dates of the bonds are the same. This is because a higher proportion of the higher coupon bonds' income is received sooner. Therefore these bonds are less sensitive to interest rate changes and will have a lower duration

Duration can be used to assess the change in the value of a bond when interest rates change using the following formula:

$\Delta P = [-D \times \Delta i \times P] \div [1 + i]$, where P is the price of the bond, D is the duration and i is the redemption yield.

However, duration is only useful in assessing small changes in interest rates because of convexity. As interest rates increase the price of a bond decreases and vice versa, but this decrease is not proportional for coupon paying bonds, the relationship is non-linear. In fact the relationship between the changes in bond value to changes in interest rates is in the shape of a convex curve to origin, see below.

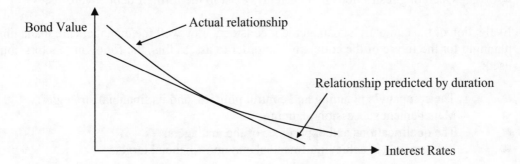

Duration, on the other hand, assumes that the relationship between changes in interest rates and the resultant bond is linear. Therefore duration will predict a lower price than the actual price and for large changes in interest rates this difference can be significant.

Duration can only be applied to measure the approximate change in a bond price due to interest changes, only if changes in interest rates do not lead to a change in the shape of the yield curve. This is because it is an average measure based on the gross redemption yield (yield to maturity). However, if the shape of the yield curve changes, duration can no longer be used to assess the change in bond value due to interest rate changes.

Tutorial note: *Credit would be given for alternative benefits/limitations of duration.*

(c) **Credit ratings**

Industry risk measures the resilience of the company's industrial sector to changes in the economy. In order to measure or assess this, the following factors could be used:

- Impact of economic changes on the industry in terms how successfully the firms in the industry operate under differing economic outcomes;

- How cyclical the industry is and how large the peaks and troughs are;

- How the demand shifts in the industry as the economy changes.

Earnings protection measures how well the company will be able to maintain or protect its earnings in changing circumstances. In order to assess this, the following factors could be used:

- Differing range of sources of earnings growth;
- Diversity of customer base;
- Profit margins and return on capital.

Financial flexibility measures how easily the company is able to raise the finance it needs to pursue its investment goals. In order to assess this, the following factors could be used:

- Evaluation of plans for financing needs and range of alternatives available;
- Relationships with finance providers (e.g. banks);
- Operating restrictions that currently exist in the form of debt covenants.

Evaluation of the company's management considers how well the managers are managing and planning for the future of the company. In order to assess this, the following factors could be used:

- The company's planning and control policies, and its financial strategies;
- Management succession planning;
- The qualifications and experience of the managers;
- Performance in achieving financial and non-financial targets.

JUNE 2014

Answer 1 COCOA-MOCHA-CHAI

(a)   **Foreign exchange hedging strategies**

The foreign exchange exposure of the dollar payment due in four months can be hedged using the following derivative products:

Forward rate offered by Pecunia Bank;
Exchange-traded futures contracts; and
Exchange-traded options contracts.

Using the forward rate

Payment in Swiss Francs = US$5,060,000 ÷ 1·0677 = CHF4,739,159

Using futures contract

Since a dollar payment needs to be made in four months' time, CMC needs to hedge against Swiss Francs weakening. Hence, the company should go short and the six-month futures contract is undertaken.

Tutorial note: *The futures contracts are based upon a standard quantity (125,000) of the Swiss Franc. As CMC wants to protect itself against a fall in the Swiss Franc it should initially **sell** futures, taking a "short" position. It plans to close the hedge in four months' time (when it would buy back the futures contracts) and should therefore establish the hedge using the 6-month contracts.*

It is assumed that the basis differential will narrow in proportion to time.

Predicted futures rate = $1·0647 + [(1·0659 - 1·0647) \times \frac{1}{3}] = 1·0651$

Tutorial note: *The calculation above uses linear interpolation between the price of 3-month and 6-month futures to estimate the outcome of the planned 4-month hedge.*

Alternatively the estimated 4-month "lock-in rate" can be found by interpolating between the spot rate and price of 6-month futures: $1·0635 + [(1·0659 - 1·0635) \times \frac{4}{6}] = 1·0651$

Expected payment = US$5,060,000 ÷ 1·0651 = CHF4,750,728
No. of contracts sold = CHF4,750,728 ÷ CHF125,000 = approx. 38 contracts

Using options contracts

Since a dollar payment needs to be made in four months' time, CMC needs to hedge against Swiss Francs weakening. Hence, the company should purchase six-month put options.

Tutorial note: *Each options contract is on a standard quantity (125,000) of the Swiss Franc. CMC would like the right, but not the obligation, to **sell** Swiss Francs; hence it should buy **put** options on the Swiss Franc.*

Exercise price US$1·06 per CHF1

Payment = US$5,060,000 ÷ 1·06 = CHF4,773,585
Buy 4,773,585 ÷ 125,000 = 38·19 put contracts, say 38 contracts

CHF payment = CHF4,750,000
Premium payable = 38 × 125,000 × 0·0216 = US$102,600
In CHF = 102,600 ÷ 1·0635 = CHF96,474
Amount not hedged = US$5,060,000 – (38 × 125,000 × 1·06) = US$25,000
Use forward contracts to hedge this = US$25,000 ÷ 1·0677 = CHF23,415
Total payment = CHF4,750,000 + CHF96,474 + CHF23,415 = CHF4,869,889

Exercise price US$1·07 per CHF1

Payment = US$5,060,000 ÷ 1·07 = CHF4,728,972
Buy 4,728,972 ÷ 125,000 = 37·83 put contracts, say 38 contracts (but this is an over-hedge)

CHF payment = CHF4,750,000
Premium payable = 38 × 125,000 × 0·0263 = US$124,925
In CHF = 124,925 ÷ 1·0635 = CHF117,466
Amount over-hedged = US$5,060,000 – (38 × 125,000 × 1·07) = US$22,500
Using forward contracts to show benefit of this = US$22,500 ÷ 1·0677 = CHF21,073
Total payment = CHF4,750,000 + CHF117,466 – CHF21,073 = CHF4,846,393

Advice

Forward contracts minimise the payment and option contracts would maximise the payment, with the payment arising from the futures contracts in between these two. With the option contracts, the exercise price of US$1·07 per CHF1 gives the lower cost. Although transaction costs are ignored, it should be noted that with exchange-traded futures contracts, margins are required and the contracts are marked-to-market daily.

It would therefore seem that the futures contracts and the option contract with an exercise price of US$1·06 per CHF1 should be rejected. The choice between forward contracts and the 1·07 options depends on CMC's attitude to risk. The forward rate is binding, whereas option contracts give the company the choice to let the option contract lapse if the CHF strengthens against the US$. Observing the rates of inflation between the two countries and the exchange-traded derivatives this is likely to be the case, but it is not definite. Moreover, the option rates need to move in favour considerably before the option is beneficial to CMC, due to the high premium payable.

It would therefore seem that forward markets should be selected to minimise the amount of payment, but CMC should also bear in mind that the risk of default is higher with forward contracts compared with exchange-traded contracts.

(b)   **Plain vanilla interest rate swap**

	CMC	Counterparty	Interest rate differential
Fixed rate	2·2%	3·8%	1·6%
Floating rate	Yield rate + 0·4%	Yield rate + 0·8%	0·4%

CMC has a comparative advantage in borrowing at the fixed rate and the counterparty has a comparative advantage in borrowing at the floating rate. Total possible benefit before Pecunia Bank's fee is 1·2%, which if shared equally results in a benefit of 0·6% each, for both CMC and the counterparty.

	CMC	*Counterparty*
CMC borrows at	2·2%	
Counterparty borrows at		Yield rate + 0·8%
Advantage	60 basis points	60 basis points
Net result	Yield rate – 0·2%	3·2%
SWAP		
Counterparty receives		Yield rate
CMC pays	Yield rate	
Counterparty pays		2·4%
CMC receives	2·4%	

After paying the 20 basis point fee, CMC will effectively pay interest at the yield curve rate and benefit by 40 basis points or 0·4%, and the counterparty will pay interest at 3·4% and benefit by 40 basis points or 0·4% as well.

Tutorial note: *Full marks would be given where the question is answered by estimating the arbitrage gain of 1·2% and deducting the fees of 0·4%, without constructing the above table.*

(c)   **Modified duration**

Annuity factor, 4 years, 2% = 3·808
Equal annual amounts repayable per year = CHF60 million ÷ 3·808 = CHF15,756,303

Macaulay duration
$(15,756,303 \times 0·980 \times 1 \text{ year} +$
$15,756,303 \times 0·961 \times 2 \text{ years} +$
$15,756,303 \times 0·942 \times 3 \text{ years} +$
$15,756,303 \times 0·924 \times 4 \text{ years}) \div 60 \text{ million}$
$= 2·47 \text{ years}$

Modified duration = 2·47 ÷ 1·02 = 2·42 years

The equation linking modified duration (D), and the relationship between the change in interest rates (Δi) and change in price or value of a bond or loan (ΔP) is given as follows:

$\Delta P = [-D \times \Delta i \times P]$
Where P is the current value of a loan or bond and is a constant.

The size of the modified duration will determine how much the value of a bond or loan will change when there is a change in interest rates. A higher modified duration means that the fluctuations in the value of a bond or loan will be greater, hence the value of 2·42 means that the value of the loan or bond will change by 2·42 times the change in interest rates multiplied by the original value of the bond or loan.

The relationship is only an approximation because duration assumes that the relationship between the change in interest rates and the corresponding change in the value of the bond or loan is linear. In fact, the relationship between interest rates and bond price is in the form of a curve which is convex to the origin (i.e. non-linear). Therefore duration can only provide a reasonable estimation of the change in the value of a bond or loan due to changes in interest rates, when those interest rate changes are small.

(d) **MEMORANDUM**

From: Financial advisor
To: The Board of Directors, CMC Co
Date: 3 June 2018

Subject: Discussion of the proposal to manage foreign exchange and interest rate exposures and the proposal to move operations to four branches and consequential agency issues

This memo discusses the proposal of whether or not CMC should undertake the management of foreign exchange and interest rate exposure, and the agency issues resulting from the proposal to locate branches internationally and how these issues may be mitigated. Each proposal will be considered in turn.

(i)   Proposal One: Management of foreign exchange and interest rate exposure

The non-executive directors are correct if CMC is in a situation where markets are perfect and efficient, where information is freely available and where securities are priced correctly. In this circumstance, risk management or hedging would not add value and if shareholders hold well diversified portfolios, unsystematic risk will be largely eliminated. The position against hedging states that in such cases companies would not increase shareholder value by hedging or eliminating risk because there will be no further reduction in unsystematic risk. Furthermore, the cost of reducing any systematic risk will equal or be greater than the benefit derived from such risk reduction. Shareholders would not gain from risk management or hedging; in fact, if the costs exceed the benefits, then hedging may result in a reduction in shareholder value.

Risk management or hedging may result in increasing corporate (and therefore shareholder) value if market imperfections exist, and in these situations, reducing the volatility of a company's earnings will result in higher cash inflows. Proponents of hedging cite three main situations where reduction in volatility or risk may increase cash flows – in situations: where the rate of tax is increasing; where a firm could face significant financial distress costs due to high volatility in earnings; and where stable earnings increases certainty and the ability to plan for the future, thus resulting in stable investment policies by the firm.

Active hedging may also reduce agency costs. For example, unlike shareholders, managers and employees of the company may not hold diversified portfolios. Hedging allows the risks faced by managers and employees to be reduced. Additionally, hedging may allow managers to be less concerned about market movements which are not within their control and instead allow them to focus on business issues over which they can exercise control. This seems to be what the purchasing director is contending. On the other hand, the finance director seems to be more interested in increasing his personal benefits and not necessarily in increasing the value of CMC.

A consistent hedging strategy or policy may be used as a signalling tool to reduce the conflict of interest between bondholders and shareholders, and thus reduce restrictive covenants.

It is also suggested that until recently CMC had no intention of hedging and communicated this in its annual report. It is likely that shareholders will therefore have created their own risk management policies. A strategic change in the policy may have a negative impact on the shareholders and the clientele impact of this will need to be taken into account.

The case of whether to hedge or not is not clear cut and CMC should consider all the above factors and be clear about why it is intending to change its strategy before coming to a conclusion. Any intended change in policy should be communicated to the shareholders. Shareholders can also benefit from risk management because the risk profile of the company may change, resulting in a reduced cost of capital.

(ii)   Proposal Two: International branches, agency issues and their mitigation

Principal–agent relationships can be observed within an organisation between different stakeholder groups. With the proposed branches located in different countries, the principal–agent relationship will be between the directors and senior management at CMC in Switzerland, and the managers of the individual branches. Agency issues can arise where the motivations of the branch managers, who are interested in the performance of their individual branches, diverge from the management at CMC headquarters, who are interested in the performance of the whole organisation.

These issues may arise because branch managers are not aware of, or appreciate the importance of, the key factors at corporate level. They may also arise because of differences in cultures and divergent backgrounds.

Mitigation mechanisms involve monitoring, compensation and communication policies. All of these mechanisms need to work in a complementary fashion in order to achieve goal congruence, much like the mechanisms in any principal–agent relationship.

Monitoring policies would involve ensuring that key aims and strategies are agreed between all parties before implementation, and results monitored to ensure adherence with the original agreements. Where there are differences (e.g. due to external factors) new targets need to be agreed. Where deviations are noticed, these should be communicated quickly.

Compensation packages should ensure that reward is based on achievement of organisational value and therefore there is every incentive for the branch managers to act in the best interests of the corporation as a whole.

Communication should be two-way, in that branch managers should be made fully aware of the organisational objectives, and any changes to these, and how the branch contributes to these, in order to ensure their acceptance of the objectives. Furthermore, the management at CMC headquarters should be fully aware of cultural and educational differences in the countries where the branches are to be set up and fully plan for how organisational objectives may nevertheless be achieved within these differences.

Tutorial note: *Credit would be given for alternative, relevant approaches to the calculations, comments and suggestions/recommendations.*

Answer 2 BURUNG CO

(a)   Adjusted Present Value

All figures are in $ million

Year	0	1	2	3	4
Sales revenue (inflated, 8% p.a.)		24·87	42·69	61·81	36·92
Direct costs (inflated, 4% p.a.)		(14·37)	(23·75)	(33·12)	(19·05)
EBITDA		10·50	18·94	28·69	17·87
Tax (W1)		(0·50)	(3·39)	(5·44)	(3·47)
Working capital (W2)	(4·97)	(3·57)	(3·82)	4·98	7·38
Investment/sale of machinery	(38·00)				4·00
Cash flows	(42·97)	6·43	11·73	28·23	25·78
Discount factors (12%, W3)	1	0·893	0·797	0·712	0·636
Present values	(42·97)	5·74	9·35	20·10	16·40

Base case net present value is approximately $8·62 million.

WORKINGS

(1)   Taxation

All figures are in $ million

Year	0	1	2	3	4
EBITDA		10·50	18·94	28·69	17·87
Tax-allowable depreciation		8·00	2·00	1·50	0·50
Taxable profit		2·50	16·94	27·19	17·37
Tax (20%)		0·50	3·39	5·44	3·47

Tutorial note: *In the year of disposal a balancing allowance can be claimed based on the difference between the brought forward tax book value of 4.5 (16 – 8 – 2 – 1.5) and the disposal proceeds of 4.*

(2)   Working capital

Year	0	1	2	3	4
Working capital (20% of sales revenue)		4·97	8·54	12·36	7·38
Working capital required/(released)	4·97	3·57	3·82	(4·98)	(7·38)

(3)   Ungeared cost of equity

Lintu asset beta = $1·5 \times \$128m \div (\$128m + \$31·96m \times 0·8) = 1·25$ approx

All-equity financed discount rate = $2\% + 1·25 \times 8\% = 12\%$

Financing side effects

		$000
Issue costs $^2/_{98} \times \$42{,}970{,}000$		(876·94)

Tax shield

Annual tax relief	$= (\$42{,}970{,}000 \times 60\% \times 0{\cdot}015 \times 20\%)$	
	$+ (\$42{,}970{,}000 \times 40\% \times 0{\cdot}04 \times 20\%)$	
	$= 77{\cdot}35 + 137{\cdot}50 = 214{\cdot}85$	

The present value of the tax relief annuity $= 214{\cdot}85 \times 3{\cdot}63$ 779·91

Annual subsidy benefit

$\$42{,}970{,}000 \times 60\% \times 0{\cdot}025 \times 80\% = 515{\cdot}64$

The present value of the subsidy benefit annuity $= 515{\cdot}64 \times 3{\cdot}63$ 1,871·77

Total benefit of financing side effects   1,774·74

Financing the project entirely by debt would add just under $1·78 million to the value of the project, or approximately, an additional 20% to the all-equity financed project.

The adjusted present value (APV) of the project is just under $10·4 million and therefore it should be accepted.

Tutorial notes: *There is a strong argument that the calculations above should be based on the gross amount of finance raised, including issue costs (i.e. 42, 970,000 + 876,940 = 43,846,940).*

In calculating the present values of the tax shield and subsidy benefits, the annuity factor used is based on 4% to reflect the normal borrowing/default risk of the company.

Alternatively, 2% or 2·5% could be used depending on the assumptions made. Credit will be given where these are used to estimate the annuity factor, where the assumption is explained.

(b)   **Corrections made to the original net present value**

The original approach to exclude depreciation from the net present value computation was correct, but tax-allowable depreciation needs to be taken away from profit estimates before tax is calculated, reducing the profits on which tax is payable.

Interest should not be included in net present value calculations. Instead, it is imputed within the discounting process.

Revenues and costs need to be are inflated and then discounted at a nominal rate. Where different cash flows are subject to different rates of inflation, applying a real rate to non-inflated amounts would not give an accurate answer.

The impact of the working capital requirement must be included in the estimate as, although all the working capital is recovered at the end of the project, the flows of working capital are subject to different discount factors when their present values are calculated.

Approach taken

The value of the project is initially assessed considering only the business risk involved in undertaking the project. The discount rate used is based on Lintu's asset beta which measures only the business risk of that company. Since Lintu is in the same line of business as the project, it is deemed appropriate to use its discount rate, instead of 11% that Burung uses normally.

The impact of debt financing and the subsidy benefit are then considered. In this way, Burung can assess the value created from its investment activity and then the additional value created from the manner in which the project is financed.

Assumptions made

It is assumed that all figures used are accurate and any estimates made are reasonable. Burung may want to consider undertaking a sensitivity analysis to assess this.

It is assumed that the initial working capital required will form part of the funds borrowed but that the subsequent working capital requirements will be available from the funds generated by the project. The validity of this assumption needs to be assessed since the working capital requirements at the start of years 2 and 3 are substantial.

It is assumed that Lintu's asset beta and all-equity financed discount rate represent the business risk of the project. The validity of this assumption also needs to be assessed. For example, Lintu's entire business may not be similar to the project, and it may undertake other lines of business. In this case, the asset beta would need to be adjusted so that just the project's business risk is considered.

It is assumed that issue costs are not tax allowable

Tutorial note: *Credit would be given for alternative, relevant explanations.*

Answer 3 VOGEL CO

(a) **Reasons for moving from organic to acquisition-based growth**

Vogel may have switched from a strategy of organic growth to one of growth by acquisition, if it was of the opinion that such a change would result in increasing the value for the shareholders.

Acquiring a company to gain access to new products, markets, technologies and expertise may be quicker and less costly. Horizontal acquisitions may help Vogel eliminate key competitors and enable it to take advantage of economies of scale. Vertical acquisitions may help Vogel to secure the supply chain and maximise returns from its value chain.

Organic growth may take a long time, can be expensive and may result in little competitive advantage being established due to the time taken. Also organic growth, especially into a new area, would need managers to gain knowledge and expertise of an area or function, which they not currently familiar with. Furthermore, in a saturated market, there may be little opportunity for organic growth.

Tutorial note: *Credit would be given for alternative relevant comments.*

(b) **Actions to reduce risk of failure**

Vogel can take the following actions to reduce the risk that the acquisition of Tori fails to increase shareholder value.

Since Vogel has pursued an aggressive policy of acquisitions, it needs to determine whether or not this has been too aggressive and detailed assessments have been undertaken. Vogel should ensure that the valuation is based on reasonable input figures and that proper due diligence of the perceived benefits is undertaken prior to the offer being made. Often it is difficult to get an accurate picture of the target when looking at it from the outside. Vogel needs to ensure that it has sufficient data and information to enable a thorough and sufficient analysis to be undertaken.

The sources of synergy need to be properly assessed to ensure that they are achievable and what actions Vogel needs to undertake to ensure their achievement. This is especially so for the revenue-based synergies. An assessment of the impact of the acquisition on the risk of the combined company needs to be undertaken to ensure that the acquisition is not considered in isolation but as part of the whole company.

The Board of Directors of Vogel needs to ensure that there are good reasons to undertake the acquisition, and that the acquisition should result in an increase in value for the shareholders. Research studies into mergers and acquisitions have found that often companies are acquired not for the shareholders' benefit, but for the benefit or self-interest of the acquiring company's management. The non-executive directors should play a crucial role in ensuring that acquisitions are made to enhance the value for the shareholders. A post-completion audit may help to identify the reasons behind why so many of Vogel's acquisitions have failed to create value. Once these reasons have been identified, strategies need to be put in place to prevent their repetition in future acquisitions.

Procedures need to be established to ensure that the acquisition is not overpaid. Vogel should determine the maximum premium it is willing to pay and not go beyond that figure. Research indicates that often too much is paid to acquire a company and the resultant synergy benefits are not sufficient to cover the premium paid. Often this is the result of the management of the acquiring company wanting to complete the deal at any cost, because not completing the deal may be perceived as damaging to both their own, and their company's reputation. The acquiring company's management may also want to show that the costs related to undertaking due diligence and initial negotiation have not been wasted. Vogel and its management need to guard against this and maybe formal procedures need to be established which allow managers to step back without loss of personal reputation.

Vogel needs to ensure that it has proper procedures in place to integrate the staff and systems of the target company effectively, and also to recognise that such integration takes time. Vogel may decide instead to give the target company a large degree of autonomy and thus make integration less necessary; however, this may result in a reduction in synergy benefits. Vogel should also have strategies which allow it sufficient flexibility when undertaking integration so that it is able to respond to changing circumstances or respond to inaccurate information prior to the acquisition. Vogel should also be mindful that its own and the acquired company's staff and management need to integrate and ensure a good working relationship between them.

Tutorial note: *The above answer covers more areas than would be needed to achieve full marks for the part. Credit would be given for alternative relevant comments.*

(c)   **Estimate of maximum premium to pay**

Approach taken

The maximum premium payable is equal to the maximum additional benefit created from the acquisition of Tori, with no increase in value for the shareholders of Vogel (although the shareholders of Vogel would probably not approve of the acquisition if they do not gain from it).

The additional benefit can be estimated as the sum of the cash gained (or lost) from selling the assets of Department C, spinning off Department B and integrating Department A, less the sum of the values of Vogel and Tori as separate companies.

Estimation

Cash gained from selling the assets of Department C = (20% × $98·2m) + (20% × $46·5m × 0·9) – ($20·2 + $3m) = $19·64m + $8·37m – $23·2m = $4·81m

Value created from spinning off Department B into Ndege Co

	$ million
Free cash flow of Ndege	
Current share of PBDIT (0·4 × $37·4m)	14·96
Less: attributable to Department C (10%)	(1·50)
Less: tax allowable depreciation (0·4 × 98·2 × 0·10)	(3·93)
Profits before tax	9·53
Tax (20%)	(1·91)
Free cash flows	7·62

Value of Ndege =
Present value of cash flow in year 1: $7·62m × 1·2 × 1·1–1 = $8·31m
Add: present value of cash flows from year 2 onwards:
($9·14m × 1·052) ÷ (0·1 – 0·052) × 1·1 – 1 = $182·11m
Less debt = $40m
Value to shareholders of Ndege = $150·42m

Vogel's current value = $3 × 380m = $1,140m
Vogel, profit after tax = $158·2m × 0·8 = $126·56m
Vogel, PE ratio before acquisition = $1,140·0m ÷ $126·56m = 9·01 say 9
Tori, PE ratio before acquisition = 9 × 1·25 = 11·25
Vogel, PE ratio after acquisition = 9 × 1·15 = 10·35

Tori's current value = 11·25 × ($23·0 × 0·8) = $207·0m

Value created from combined company

($126·56m + 0·5 × $23·0m × 0·8 + $7m) × 10·35 = $1,477·57

Maximum premium = ($1,477·57m + $150·42m + $4·81m) – ($1,140m + $207·0m) = $285·80m

Assumptions

Based on the calculations given above, it is estimated that the value created will be $285·80m.

However, Vogel needs to assess whether the numbers it has used in the calculations and the assumptions it has made are reasonable. For example, Ndege's future cash flows seem to be growing without any additional investment in assets and Vogel needs to establish whether or not this is reasonable. It also needs to establish how the increase in its PE ratio was determined after acquisition. Perhaps sensitivity analysis would be useful to show the impact on value changes, if these figures are changed. Given its poor record in generating value previously, Vogel needs to pay particular attention to these figures.

Answer 4 FAOILEAN CO

(a)   **Real options pricing theory**

With conventional investment decisions, it is assumed that once a decision is made, it has to be taken immediately and carried to its conclusion. These decisions are normally made through conventional assessments using methods such as net present value. Assessing projects through option pricing may aid the investment decision making process.

Where there is uncertainty with regard to the investment decision and where a company has flexibility in its decision making, valuing projects using options can be particularly useful. For example, situations may exist where a company does not have to make a decision on a now-or-never basis, or where it can abandon a decision, which has been made, at some future point, or where it has an opportunity for further expansion as a result of the original decision. In such situations, using option pricing formulae, which incorporate the uncertainty surrounding a project and the time before a decision has to be made, can determine a value attached to this flexibility. This value can be added to the conventional net present value computation to give a more accurate assessment of the project's value.

In the situation which Faoilean is considering, the initial exploration rights may give it the opportunity to delay the decision of whether to undertake the extraction of oil and gas to a later date. In that time, using previous knowledge and experience, it can estimate the quantity of oil and gas which is present more accurately. It can also use its knowledge to assess the variability of the likely quantity. Faoilean may be able to negotiate a longer time scale with the government of Ireland for undertaking the initial exploration, before it needs to make a final decision on whether and how much to extract.

Furthermore, Faoilean can explore the possibilities of it exiting the extraction project, once started, if it is proving not to be beneficial, or if world prices of oil and gas have moved against it. It could, for example, negotiate a get-out clause which gives it the right to sell the project back to the government at a later date at a pre-agreed price. Alternatively, it could build facilities in such a way that it can redeploy them to other activities, or scale the production up or down more easily and at less cost.

These options give the company the opportunity to step out of a project at a future date, if uncertainties today become negative outcomes in the future.

Finally, Faoilean can explore whether or not applying for the rights to undertake this exploration project could give it priority in terms of future projects, perhaps due to the new knowledge or technologies it builds during the current project. These opportunities would allow it to gain competitive advantage over rivals, which, in turn, could provide it with greater opportunities in the future, but which are uncertain at present.

Faoilean can incorporate these uncertainties and the time before the various decisions need to be made into the option formulae to determine the additional value of the project, on top of the initial net present value calculation.

The option price formula used with investment decisions is based on the Black-Scholes Option Pricing (BSOP) model. The BSOP model makes a number of assumptions as follows:

- The underlying asset operates in perfect markets and therefore the movement of market prices cannot be predicted;

- The BSOP model uses the risk-free rate of interest. It is assumed that this is known and remains constant, which may not be the case where the time it takes for the option to expire may be long;

- The BSOP model assumes that volatility can be assessed and stays constant throughout the life of the project; again with long-term projects these assumptions may not be valid;

- The BSOP model assumes that the underlying asset can be traded freely. This is probably not accurate where the underlying asset is an investment project.

These assumptions mean that the value based around the BSOP model is indicative and not definitive.

Tutorial note: *Credit would be given for alternative relevant comments.*

(b)   **Merton's structural debt model**

Shareholders can be regarded as conceptually holding a call option on the firm's assets, the exercise price being the amount needed to cancel the firm's debt on its redemption date. For simplicity the author of this model, Robert Merton, assumed the firm's debt is a single zero-coupon bond. In this case, the face value of debt is equivalent to the exercise price, and the repayment term of debt as the time to expiry of the option.

If at expiry, the value of the assets is greater than the face value of debt, then the option is in-the-money. If the value of the assets is less than the face value of debt, then the option is out-of-money and equity is worthless.

For example, say V is the market value of the assets in a company, E is the market value of equity, and F is the face value of debt, then,

If at expiry $V > F$ (option is in-the-money), then the option has intrinsic value to the equity holders and $E = V - F$;

Otherwise if $F > V$ (option is out-of-money), then the option has no intrinsic value and no value for the equity holders, and $E = 0$.

Prior to expiry of the debt, the call option (value to holders of equity) will also have a time value attached to it. The BSOP model can be used to assess the value of the option to the equity holders which can consist of both time value and intrinsic value if the option is in-the-money, or just time value if the option is out-of-money.

Within the BSOP model, $N(d_1)$, the delta value, shows how the value of equity changes when the value of the company's assets change.

$N(d_2)$ depicts the probability that the call option will be in-the-money on the expiry date (i.e. have intrinsic value for the equity holders).

As $N(d_2)$ is the probability that the value of assets will be above the level of debt on its redemption date, then $1 - N(d_2)$ measures the probability that the value of assets will not cover the repayment of debt, in which case the firm would default.

Option pricing can be used to explain why companies facing severe financial distress can still have positive equity values. A company facing severe financial distress would presumably be one where the equity holders' call option is well out-of-money and therefore has no intrinsic value. However, as long as the debt on the option is not at expiry, then that call option will still have a time value attached to it. Therefore, the positive equity value reflects the time value of the option, even where the option is out-of-money, and this will diminish as the debt comes closer to expiry. The time value indicates that even though the option is currently out-of-money, there is a possibility that due to the volatility of asset values, by the time the debt reaches maturity, the company will no longer face financial distress and will be able to meet its debt obligations.

Tutorial note: *Credit would be given for alternative relevant comments.*

(c) **The Greeks**

According to the BSOP model, the value of an option is dependent on five variables: the value of the underlying asset, the exercise price, the risk-free rate of interest, the implied volatility of the underlying asset, and the time to expiry of the option. These five variables are input into the BSOP formula, in order to compute the value of a call option (the value of an equivalent put option can be computed by the BSOP model and put-call parity relationship). The different risk factors determine the impact on the option value of the changes in the five variables.

The "vega" determines the sensitivity of an option's value to a change in the implied volatility of the underlying asset. Implied volatility is what the market is implying the volatility of the underlying asset will be in the future, based on the price changes in an option. The option price may change independently of whether or not the underlying asset's value changes, due to new information being presented to the markets. Implied volatility is the result of this independent movement in the option's value, and this determines the "vega". The "vega" only impacts the time value of an option and as the "vega" increases, so will the value of the option.

Tutorial note: *Credit would be given for alternative relevant comments.*

DECEMBER 2014

Answer 1 NAHARA CO

(a) **Acquisition strategies**

Risk diversification, especially into diverse business sectors, has often been stated as a reason for undertaking mergers and acquisitions (M&As). Like individuals holding well-diversified portfolios, a company with a number of subsidiaries in different sectors could reduce its exposure to unsystematic risk. Another possible benefit of diversification is sometimes argued to be a reduction in the volatility of cash flows, which may lead to a better credit rating and a lower cost of capital.

The argument against this states that since individual investors can undertake this level of risk diversification both quickly and cheaply themselves, there is little reason for companies to do so. Indeed, research suggests that markets do not reward this risk diversification.

Nevertheless, for Nahara, undertaking M&As may have beneficial outcomes, especially if the sovereign fund has its entire investment in the holding company and is not well-diversified itself. In such a situation unsystematic risk reduction can be beneficial. The case study does not state whether or not the sovereign funds are invested elsewhere and therefore a definitive conclusion cannot be reached.

If Nahara is able to identify undervalued companies and after purchasing the company can increase the value for the holding company overall, by increasing the value of the undervalued companies, then such M&As activity would have a beneficial impact on the funds invested. However, for this strategy to work, Nahara must:

■ Possess a superior capability or knowledge in identifying bargain buys ahead of its competitor companies. To achieve this, it must have access to better information, which it can tap into quicker, and/or have superior analytical tools. Nahara should assess whether or not it does possess such capabilities, otherwise its claim is not valid;

■ Ensure that it has quick access to the necessary funds to pursue an undervalued acquisition. Even if Nahara possesses superior knowledge, it is unlikely that this will last for a long time before its competitors find out; therefore it needs to have the funds ready, to move quickly. Given that it has access to sovereign funds from a wealthy source, access to funds is probably not a problem;

■ Set a maximum ceiling for the price it is willing to pay and should not go over this amount, or the potential value created will be reduced.

If, in its assessment, Nahara is able to show that it meets all the above conditions, then the strategy of identifying and pursuing undervalued companies may be valid.

(b) **Regulatory risk**

In a similar manner to the Competition and Markets Authority in the UK, the European Union (EU) will assess significant mergers and acquisitions' (M&As) impact on competition within a country's market. It will, for example, use tests such as worldwide turnover and European turnover of the group after the M&A. It may block the M&A, if it feels that the M&A will give the company monopolistic powers or enable it to carve out a dominant position in the market so as to negatively affect consumer choice and prices.

Sometimes the EU may ask for the company to sell some of its assets to reduce its dominant position rather than not allow an M&A to proceed. It would appear that this may be the case behind the EU's concern and the reason for its suggested action.

(c) **Report to the Board of Directors, Avem Co**

Proposed acquisition of Fugae Co

This report evaluates whether or not it is beneficial for Avem to acquire Fugae. Initially the value of the two companies is determined separately and as a combined entity, to assess the additional value created from bringing the two companies together. Following this, the report considers how much Nahara and Avem will gain from the value created. The assumptions made to arrive at the additional value are also considered. The report concludes by considering whether or not the acquisition will be beneficial to Avem and to Nahara.

Appendix 1 shows that the additional value created from combining the two companies is approximately $451·5 million, of which $276·8 million will go to Nahara, as the owner of Fugae. This represents a premium of about 30% which is the minimum acceptable to Nahara. The balance of the additional value will go to Avem which is about $174·7 million, representing an increase in value of 1·46% [$174·7m ÷ $12,000m].

Appendix 2 shows that accepting the project would increase Fugae's value as the expected net present value is positive.

After taking into account Lumi's offer, the expected net present value is higher. Therefore, it would be beneficial for Fugae to take on the project and accept Lumi's offer, if the tourism industry does not grow as expected, as this will increase Fugae's value.

Assumptions

It is assumed that all the figures relating to synergy benefits, betas, growth rates, multipliers, risk adjusted cost of capital and the probabilities are accurate. There is considerable uncertainty surrounding the accuracy of these, and in addition to the probability analysis conducted in appendix 2 and the assessments of value conducted in appendix 1, a sensitivity analysis is probably needed to assess the impact of these uncertainties.

It is assumed that the rb model provides a reasonably good estimate of the growth rate, and that perpetuity is not an unreasonable assumption when assessing the value of Fugae.

It is assumed that the capital structure would not change substantially when the new project is taken on. Since the project is significantly smaller than the value of Fugae itself, this is not an unreasonable assumption.

When assessing the value of the project, the outcomes are given as occurring with discrete probabilities and the resulting cash flows from the outcomes are given with certainty. There may be more outcomes in practice than the ones given and financial impact of the outcomes may not be known with such certainty. The Black-Scholes Option Pricing model may provide an alternative and more accurate way of assessing the value of the embedded "real option" to abandon the project.

It is assumed that Fugae can rely on Lumi paying the $50m at the beginning of year two with certainty. Fugae may want to assess the reliability of Lumi's offer and whether formal contracts should be drawn up between the two companies.

Furthermore, Lumi may be reluctant to pay the full amount of money once Fugae becomes a part of Avem.

Concluding comments

Although Nahara would gain more than Avem from the acquisition both in percentage terms and in monetary terms, both companies benefit from the acquisition. If Fugae were to take on the project, although it is value-neutral to the acquisition, Nahara could ask for an additional 30% of $12·3 million value to be transferred to it, which is about $3·7 million. Hence the return to Avem would reduce by a small amount, but not significantly.

As long as all the parties are satisfied that the value is reasonable despite the assumptions highlighted above, it would appear that the acquisition should proceed.

Report compiled by:

Date:

APPENDICES

Appendix 1: Additional value created from combining Avem Co and Fugae Co

Avem, current equity value = $7·5 per share × 1,600 million shares = $12,000m
Avem, free cash flow to equity = $12,000 million ÷ 7·2 = $1,666·7m

Fugae growth rate is calculated on the basis of the g = br_e model (Gordon's growth approximation).
Fugae, estimate of growth rate = 0·227 × 0·11 = 0·025 = 2·5%
Fugae, current equity value estimate = $76·5 million × 1·025 ÷ (0·11 – 0·025) = $922·5m

Tutorial note: *The scenario states "over the past few years Fugae has returned 77.3% of its annual FCFE back to Nahara" which implies that the current year FCFE of $76.5m refers to Fugae's gross FCFE (i.e. pre-reinvestment). 22.7% of the gross FCFE will be reinvested to produce an 11% return (and hence a 2.5% sustainable growth rate) and the balance (77.3%) is the post-reinvestment FCFE (i.e. dividend capacity).*

Arguably the correct value of equity = $76.5m × 1.025 × 0.773÷ 0.11 – 0.025 = $713m as FCFE valuation should be performed on the post-reinvestment figure (equivalent to the dividend valuation model which discounts dividends not earnings).

Therefore the model answer potentially over-values Fugae's equity by simultaneously implying growth via reinvestment but then valuing the pre-reinvestment FCFE.

Valuation is an art not a science – any candidate taking a reasoned and well explained approach would be given credit.

Combined company, estimated additional value created =
([$1,666·7m + $76·5m + $40m] × 7·5) – ($12,000m + $922·5m) = $451·5m

Gain to Nahara for selling Fugae, 30% × $922·5m = $276·8m

Avem will gain $174·7 million of the additional value created, $451·5m – $276·8m = $174·7m

APPENDIX 2: Value of project to Fugae Co

Appendix 2.1 – Estimate of risk-adjusted cost of capital for discounting the project's cash flows

The project value is calculated based on its cash flows which are discounted at the project's risk adjusted cost of capital, to reflect the business risk of the project.

Reka Co's overall asset beta

Reka equity value = $4·50 × 80 million shares = $360m
Reka debt value = 1·05 × $340 million = $357m
Asset beta = 1·6 × $360m ÷ ($360m + $357m × 0·8) = 0·89

Project's asset beta (PAB)

0·89 = (PAB × 0·15) + (0·80 × 0·85)
PAB = 1·4

Fugae Co

Market value of equity = $922·5m

Market value of debt:

Yield to maturity (pre-tax cost of debt) = Risk free rate of return plus the credit spread
= 4% + 0·80% = 4·80%

Market value of a $100 bond: $5·4 × $1·048^{-1}$ + $5·4 × $1·048^{-2}$ + $5·4 × $1·048^{-3}$ + $105·4 × $1·048^{-4}$ = $102·14 per $100

Total market value of debt = 1·0214 × $380m = $388·1m

Project's risk adjusted equity beta

1·4 × ($922·5m + $388·1m × 0·8) ÷ $922·5m = 1·87

Project's risk adjusted cost of equity

4% + (1·87 × 6%) = 15·2%

Project's risk adjusted cost of capital

(15·2% × $922·5m) + (4·8% × 0·8 × $388·1m) ÷ ($922·5m + $388·1m) = 11·84%, say 12%

Appendix 2.2 – Estimate of expected value of the project without the offer from Lumi Co

Year	1	2	3	4
Cash flows ($000)	3,277·6	16,134·3	36,504·7	35,683·6
Discount factor for 12%	0·893	0·797	0·712	0·636
Present values ($000)	2,926·9	12,859·0	25,991·3	22,694·8

Probabilities are assigned to possible outcomes based on whether or not the tourism market will grow. The expected net present value (PV) is computed on this basis.

PV year 1: $2,926,900

50% of PV years 1 to 4: $32,236,000

PV years 2 to 4: $61,545,100
40% PV years 2 to 4: $24,618,040

Expected present value of cash flows:

$= [0·75 \times (2,926,900 + (0·8 \times 61,545,100 + 0·2 \times 24,618,040))] + [0·25 \times 32,236,000]$
$= [0·75 \times (2,926,900 + 54,159,688)] + [0·25 \times 32,236,000] = 42,814,941 + 8,059,000 = \$50,873,941$

Expected NPV of project = $50,873,941 – $42,000,000 = $8,873,941

Estimate of expected value of the project with the offer from Lumi Co

PV of $50m = $50,000,000 × 0·893 = $44,650,000

If the tourism industry does not grow as expected in the first year, then it is more beneficial for Fugae to exercise the offer made by Lumi, given that Lumi's offer of $44·65 million (PV of $50 million) is greater than the PV of the years two to four cash flows ($30·8 million approximately) for that outcome. This figure is then incorporated into the expected net present value calculations.

50% of year 1 PV: $1,463,450

Expected present value of project = $[0·75 \times (2,926,900 + 54,159,688)] + [0·25 \times (1,463,450 + 44,650,000)] = 42,814,941 + 11,528,363 = \$54,343,304$

Expected NPV of project = $54,343,304 – $42,000,000 = $12,343,304

Tutorial note: *Credit would be given for alternative, relevant approaches to the calculations, comments and suggestions/recommendations.*

Answer 2 KESHI CO

(a)   Using traded options

Need to hedge against a rise in interest rates, therefore buy put options.

Tutorial note: *The statement "buy put options", being the correct strategy, would be awarded the relevant marks. The reasoning for buying options is that this potentially hedges the whole risk (whereas selling options would only provide protection to the extent of any premium received). Keshi fears rising interest rates, which would lead to a falling price of interest rate futures (as they are priced at 100 - yield). For a flexible hedge Keshi would like the right, but not the obligation, to sell futures and hence it should acquire puts on futures. Buying puts on futures creates an interest rate "cap" protecting the firm from rising interest rates while allowing participation in falling rates.*

To establish the hedge (on 1 December) Keshi needs 42 March put option contracts ($18,000,000 ÷ $1,000,000 × $^7/_3$).

Tutorial note: *When calculating the number of options required both the principal and duration of the physical loan ($18,000,000 for 7 months) must be compared to the notional loan underlying the futures contract ($1,000,000 for 3 months).*

Expected futures price on 1 February if interest rates increase by 0·5% =

$100 – (3·8 + 0·5) – 0·22 = 95·48$

Tutorial note: *The ACCA's convention is that the hedge will be closed (in this case the options exercised or lapsed) on the same date that the physical loan will be taken (in this case 1 February). To determine the outcome of the hedge it is necessary to model the price of March futures on 1 February. The scenario states that the basis will be 22 points (0.22%) on 1 February and the default assumption is that basis is positive (i.e. the futures yield is above prevailing LIBOR). Hence, if LIBOR has risen from 3.8% to 4.3% then the implied yield in the futures contracts would be 4.3% + 0.22% = 4.52% and the quoted price of the futures 100 – 4.52 =95.48.*

Expected futures price on 1 February if interest rates decrease by 0·5% =

$100 – (3·8 – 0·5) – 0·22 = 96·48$

If interest rates increase by 0·5% to 4·3%

Exercise price	95·50	96·00
Futures price	95·48	95·48
Exercise?	Yes	Yes
Gain in basis points	2	52
Underlying cost of borrowing		
4·7% × $^7/_{12}$ × $18,000,000	$493,500	$493,500
Gain on options		
0·0002 × $1,000,000 × $^3/_{12}$ × 42	$2,100	
0·0052 × $1,000,000 × $^3/_{12}$ × 42		$54,600
Premium		
0·00662 × $1,000,000 × $^3/_{12}$ × 42	$69,510	
0·00902 × $1,000,000 × $^3/_{12}$ × 42		$94,710
Net cost	$560,910	$533,610
Effective interest rate	5·34%	5·08%

If interest rates decrease by 0·5% to 3·3%

Exercise price	95·50	96·00
Futures price	96·48	96·48
Exercise?	No	No
Gain in basis points	0	0
Underlying cost of borrowing		
3·7% × $^{7}/_{12}$ × $18,000,000	$388,500	$388,500
Gain on options	$0	$0
Premium	$69,510	$94,710
Net cost	$458,010	$483,210
Effective interest rate	4·36%	4·60%

Using swaps

	Keshi Co	Counterparty	Basis differential
Fixed rate	5·5%	4·6%	0·9%
Floating rate	LIBOR + 0·4%	LIBOR + 0·3%	0·1%

Prior to the swap, Keshi will borrow at LIBOR + 0·4% and swaps this rate to a fixed rate. Total possible benefit is 0·8% before Rozu Bank's charges.

Keshi gets 70% of the benefit	
Net benefit after fees (70% × 0·8) – 0·10	0·46%
Keshi's effective borrowing rate (after swap) = 5·5% - 0·46%	5·04%

Illustrative swap (not required)

Keshi borrows at	LIBOR + 0·4%
From swap Keshi receives	LIBOR
From swap Keshi pays	4·54%
Effective borrowing rate (as above)	4·54% + 0·4% + 0·10% = 5·04%

Discussion and recommendation

Under each choice the interest rate cost to Keshi will be as follows:

	Doing nothing	95·50 option	96·00 option	Swap
If rates increase by 0·5%	4·7% floating; 5·5% fixed	5·34%	5·08%	5·04%
If rates decrease by 0·5%	3·7% floating; 5·5% fixed	4·36%	4·60%	5·04%

Borrowing at the floating rate and undertaking a swap effectively fixes the rate of interest at 5·04% for the loan, which is significantly lower than the market fixed rate of 5·5%.

On the other hand, doing nothing and borrowing at the floating rate minimises the interest rate at 4·7%, against the next best choice which is the swap at 5·04% if interest rates increase by 0·5%. And should interest rates decrease by 0·5%, then doing nothing and borrowing at a floating rate of 3·7% minimises cost, compared to the next best choice which is the 95·50 option.

On the face of it, doing nothing and borrowing at a floating rate seems to be the better choice if interest rates increase or decrease by a small amount, but if interest rates increase substantially then this choice will no longer result in the lowest cost.

The swap minimises the variability of the borrowing rates, while doing nothing and borrowing at a floating rate maximises the variability. If Keshi wants to eliminate the risk of interest rate fluctuations completely, then it should borrow at the floating rate and swap it into a fixed rate.

(b) **Centralised vs decentralised treasury**

Free cash flows and therefore shareholder value are increased when corporate costs are reduced and/or income increased. Therefore, consideration should be given to how the centralised treasury department may reduce costs and increase income.

The centralised treasury department should be able to evaluate the financing requirements of Keshi's group as a whole and it may be able to negotiate better rates when borrowing in bulk. The department could operate as an internal bank and undertake matching of funds. Therefore it could transfer funds from subsidiaries which have spare cash resources to ones which need them, and thus avoid going into the costly external market to raise funds. The department may be able to undertake multilateral internal netting and thereby reduce costs related to hedging activity. Experts and resources within one location could reduce duplication costs.

The concentration of experts and resources within one central department may result in a more effective decision-making environment and higher quality risk monitoring and control. Further, having access to the Keshi group's entire cash funds may give the company access to larger and more diverse investment markets. These factors could result in increasing the company's cash inflows, as long as the benefits from such activity outweigh the costs.

Decentralising Keshi's treasury function to its subsidiary companies may be beneficial in several ways. Each subsidiary company may be better placed to take local regulations, custom and practice into consideration. An example of custom and practice is the case of Suisen's need to use Salam contracts instead of conventional derivative products which the centralised treasury department may use as a matter of course.

Giving subsidiary companies more autonomy on how they undertake their own fund management may result in increased motivation and effort from the subsidiary's senior management and thereby increase future income. Subsidiary companies which have access to their own funds may be able to respond to opportunities quicker and establish competitive advantage more effectively.

(c) **Salam**

Islamic principles stipulate the need to avoid uncertainty and speculation. In the case of Salam contracts, payment for the commodity is made at the start of the contract. The buyer and seller of the commodity know the price, the quality and the quantity of the commodity and the date of future delivery with certainty. Therefore, uncertainty and speculation are avoided.

On the other hand, futures contracts are marked-to-market daily and this could lead to uncertainty in the amounts received and paid every day. Furthermore, standardised futures contracts have fixed expiry dates and pre-determined contract sizes. This may mean that the underlying position is not hedged or covered completely, leading to limited speculative positions even where the futures contracts are used entirely for hedging purposes. Finally, only a few commodity futures contracts are offered to cover a range of different quality grades for a commodity, and therefore price movement of the futures market may not be completely in line with the price movement in the underlying asset.

Tutorial note: *Credit would be given for alternative, relevant discussion for parts (b) and (c).*

Answer 3 RIVIERE CO

(a)   **Free trade areas**

A free trade area like the European Union (EU) aims to remove barriers to trade and allow freedom of movement of production resources such as capital and labour. The EU also has an overarching common legal structure across all member countries and tries to limit any discriminatory practice against companies operating in these countries. Furthermore, the EU erects common external barriers to trade against countries which are not member states.

Riviere may benefit from operating within the EU in a number of ways as it currently trades within it. It should find that it is able to compete on equal terms with rival companies within the EU. Companies outside the EU may find it difficult to enter the EU markets due to barriers to trade. A common legal structure should ensure that the standards of food quality and packaging apply equally across all the member countries. Due diligence of logistic networks used to transport the food may be easier to undertake because of common compliance requirements. Having access to capital and labour within the EU may make it easier for the company to set up branches inside the EU, if it wants to. The company may also be able to access any grants which are available to companies based within the EU.

(b)   **Project Drugi**

Internal rate of return (IRR)

10% NPV: €2,293,000 (given)

Year	Current	1	2	3	4	5
Cash flows (€000s)	(11,840)	1,230	1,680	4,350	10,240	2,200
Try 20%		0·833	0·694	0·579	0·482	0·402
	(11,840)	1,025	1,166	2,519	4,936	884

NPV = €(1,310,000)

IRR = 10% + (2,293 ÷ (2,293 + 1,310) × 10%) = 16·4% approximately

Modified internal rate of return (MIRR)

Tutorial note: *MIRR is the annualised geometric cash return over a project's life under the assumption that the returns are reinvested at the firm's "hurdle rate"(assumed to be the cost of capital).*

Total PVs years 1 to 5 at 10% discount rate = €11,840,000 + €2,293,000 = €14,133,000

MIRR (using published formula) = $[(14{,}133 \div 11{,}840)^{1/5} \times 1\cdot10] - 1 = 14\%$

Alternatively:

Year	Cash flows €000	Multiplier	Re-invested amount €000
1	1,230	$1\cdot1^4$	1,801
2	1,680	$1\cdot1^3$	2,236
3	4,350	$1\cdot1^2$	5,264
4	10,240	$1\cdot1^1$	11,264
5	2,200	1	2,200

Total re-invested amount approx. = €22,765,000
MIRR = $(€22{,}765{,}000 \div €11{,}840{,}000)^{1/5} - 1 = 14\%$

Value at risk (VaR)

Based on a single tail test:

A 95% confidence level requires the annual present value VaR to be within approximately 1·645 standard deviations from the mean (using the published normal distribution tables).

A 90% confidence level requires annual present value VaR to be within approximately 1·282 standard deviations from the mean.

Tutorial note: *An approximation of standard deviations to two decimal places is acceptable.*

95%, five-year VaR = $400,000 × 1·645 × $5^{0.5}$ = approx. €1,471,000
90%, five-year VaR = $400,000 × 1·282 × $5^{0.5}$ = approx. €1,147,000

Tutorial note: *To convert annual standard deviation to five-year deviation it is necessary to multiply by the square root of five.*

	Privi	*Drugi*
Net present value (10%)	€2,054,000	€2,293,000
Internal rate of return	17·6%	16·4%
Modified internal rate of return	13·4%	14·0%
VaR (over the project's life)		
95% confidence level	€1,103,500	€1,471,000
90% confidence level	€860,000	€1,147,000

The net present value (NPV) and the modified internal rate of return (MIRR) both indicate that project Drugi would create more value for Riviere. However, the internal rate of return (IRR) for project Privi is higher. Where projects are mutually exclusive, the IRR can give an incorrect answer. This is because the IRR assumes that returns are re-invested at the internal rate of return, whereas net present value and the modified IRR assume that they are re-invested at the cost of capital (discount rate) which in this case is 10%. The cost of capital is a more realistic assumption as this is the minimum return required by investors in a company. Furthermore, the manner in which the cash flows occur will have a bearing on the IRR calculated. For example, with project Drugi, a high proportion of the cash flows occur in year four and these will be discounted more significantly by the higher IRR, thus reducing the value of the project faster. The IRR can give the incorrect answer in these circumstances. Therefore, based purely on cash flows, project Drugi should be accepted due to the higher net present value and modified IRR, as they give the theoretically correct answer of the value created.

The VaR provides an indication of the potential riskiness of a project. For example, if Riviere invests in project Drugi then it can be 95% confident that the present value will not fall by more than €1,471,000 over its life. Hence the project will still produce a positive net present value. However, there is a 5% chance that the loss could be greater than €1,471,000. With project Privi, the potential loss in value is smaller and therefore it is less risky. It should be noted that the VaR calculations indicate that the investments involve different risk. However, the cash flows are discounted at the same rate, which they should not be, since the risk differs between them.

Notwithstanding that, when risk is also taken into account, the choice between the projects is not clear cut and depends on Riviere's attitude to risk and return. Project Drugi gives the higher potential net present value but is riskier, whereas project Privi is less risky but gives a smaller net present value. This is before taking into account additional uncertainties such as trading in an area in which Riviere is not familiar. It is therefore recommended that Riviere should only proceed with project Drugi if it is willing to accept the higher risk and uncertainty.

(c) **Possible legal risks**

There are a number of possible legal risks which Riviere may face, for example:

- The countries where the product is sold may have different legal regulations on food preparation, quality and packaging. The company needs to ensure that the production processes and the transportation of the frozen foods comply with these regulations. It also needs to ensure that the promotional material on the packaging complies with regulations in relation to what is acceptable in each country.

- The legal regulations may be more lax in countries outside the EU but Riviere needs to be aware that complying only with the minimum standards may impact its image negatively overall, even if they are acceptable in the countries concerned.

- There may be import quotas in the countries concerned or the governments may give favourable terms and conditions to local companies, which may make it difficult for Riviere to compete.

- The legal system in some countries may not recognise the trademarks or production patents which the company holds on its packaging and production processes. This may enable competitors to copy the food and the packaging.

- Different countries may have different regulations regarding product liability from poorly prepared and/or stored food which cause harm to consumers. For example, Riviere may use other companies to transport its food and different supermarkets may sell its food. It needs to be aware of the potential legal claims on it and its supplier should the food prove harmful to the customers.

Possible mitigation strategies

- Riviere needs to undertake sufficient research of the countries' current laws and regulations to ensure that it complies with the standards required. It may even want to ensure that it exceeds the required standards to ensure that it maintains its reputation.

- Riviere needs to ensure that it also keeps abreast of potential changes in the law. It may also want to ensure that it complies with best practice, even if it is not the law yet. Often current best practices become enshrined in future legislation.

- Riviere needs to investigate the extent to which it may face difficulty in overcoming quota restrictions, less favourable trading conditions and lack of trademark and patent protection. If necessary, these should be factored into the financial analysis. It could be that Riviere has already taken these into account.

- Strict contracts need to be set up between Riviere and any agents it uses to transport and sell the food. These could be followed up by regular checks to ensure that the standards required are maintained.

- All the above will add extra costs and if these have not been included in the financial analysis, they need to be. These extra costs may mean that the project is no longer viable.

Tutorial note: *Credit would be given for alternative, relevant discussion for parts (a) and (c).*

JUNE 2015

Answer 1 IMONI CO

(a)   **Benefits of foreign direct investment as opposed to licensing**

Imoni may be able to benefit from setting up its own plant as opposed to licensing in a number of ways. Yilandwe wants to attract foreign investment and is willing to offer a number of financial concessions to foreign investors which may not be available to local companies. The company may be able to control the quality of the components more easily, and offer better and targeted training facilities if it has direct control of the labour resources. The company may also be able to maintain the confidentiality of its products, whereas assigning the assembly rights to another company may allow that company to imitate the products more easily.   Investing internationally may provide opportunities for risk diversification, especially if Imoni's shareholders are not well-diversified internationally themselves.   Finally, direct investment may provide Imoni with new opportunities in the future, such as follow-on options.

Drawbacks of foreign direct investment as opposed to licensing

Direct investment in a new plant will probably require higher, upfront costs from Imoni compared to licensing the assembly rights to a local manufacturer. It may be able to utilise these saved costs on other projects. Imoni will most likely be exposed to higher risks involved with international investment such as political risks, cultural risks and legal risks. With licensing these risks may be reduced somewhat. The licensee, because it would be a local company, may understand the operational systems of doing business in Yilandwe better. It will therefore be able to get off-the-ground quicker. Imoni, on the other hand, will need to become familiar with the local systems and culture, which may take time and make it less efficient initially. Similarly, investing directly in Yilandwe may mean that it costs Imoni more to train the staff and possibly require a steeper learning curve from them. However, the scenario does say that the country has a motivated and well-educated labour force and this may mitigate this issue somewhat.

Tutorial note: *Credit would be given for alternative, relevant suggestions.*

(b)   **Report on the proposed assembly plant in Yilandwe**

This report considers whether or not it would be beneficial for Imoni to set up a parts assembly plant in Yilandwe. It takes account of the financial projections, presented in detail in appendices 1 and 2, discusses the assumptions made in arriving at the projections and discusses other non-financial issues which should be considered. The report concludes by giving a reasoned recommendation on the acceptability of the project.

Assumptions made in producing the financial projections

It is assumed that all the estimates such as sales revenue, costs, royalties, initial investment costs, working capital, and costs of capital and inflation figures are accurate. There is considerable uncertainty surrounding the accuracy of these and a small change in them could change the forecasts of the project quite considerably. A number of projections using sensitivity and scenario analysis may aid in the decision making process.

It is assumed that no additional tax is payable in the USA for the profits made during the first two years of the project's life when the company will not pay tax in Yilandwe either. This is especially relevant to year 2 of the project.

1220

No details are provided on whether or not the project ends after four years. This is an assumption which is made, but the project may last beyond four years and therefore may yield additional positive net present value. Additionally, even if the project ceases after four years, no details are given about the sale of the land, buildings and machinery. The residual value of these non-current assets could have a considerable bearing on the outcome of the project.

It is assumed that the increase in the transfer price of the parts sent from the USA directly increases the contribution which Imoni earns from the transfer. This is probably not an unreasonable assumption. However, it is also assumed that the negotiations with Yilandwe's government will be successful with respect to increasing the transfer price and the royalty fee. Imoni needs to assess whether or not this assumption is realistic.

Tutorial note: *Increasing the transfer price and royalties will reduce taxable profits in Yilandwe in years 3-4 (after the tax holiday ends) but will lead to higher taxable profits in the USA in all years. Although tax is saved in Yilandwe at 40% this only occurs in two years whereas additional tax at 20% in the USA would be for four years – hence the overall effect of increasing the transfer price and royalties may be negligible.*

The basis for using a cost of capital of 12% is not clear and an explanation is not provided about whether or not this is an accurate or reasonable figure. The underpinning basis for how it is determined may need further investigation.

Although the scenario states that the project can start almost immediately, in reality this may not be possible and Imoni may need to factor in possible delays.

It is assumed that future exchange rates will reflect the differential in inflation rates between the respective countries. However, it is unlikely that the exchange rates will move fully in line with purchasing power parity.

Other risks and issues

Investing in Yilandwe may result in significant political risks. The scenario states that the current political party is not very popular in rural areas and that the population remains generally poor. Imoni needs to assess how likely it is that the government may change during the time it is operating in Yilandwe and the impact of the change. For example, a new government may renege on the current government's offers and/or bring in new restrictions. Imoni will need to decide what to do if this happens.

Imoni needs to assess the likelihood that it will be allowed to increase the transfer price of the parts and the royalty fee. The Yilandwe government may consider that agreeing to such demands from Imoni may make it obligated to other companies as well.

The financial projections are prepared on the basis that positive cash flows from Yilandwe can be remitted back to the USA. Imoni needs to establish that this is indeed the case and that it is likely to continue in the future.

Imoni needs to be careful about its ethical stance and the impact on its reputation, given that a school is being closed in order to provide it with the production facilities needed. Although the government is funding some of the transport costs for the children, the disruption this will cause to the children and the fact that after six months the transport costs become the parents' responsibility, may have a large, negative impact on the company's image and may be contrary to the ethical values which the company holds. The possibility of alternative venues should be explored.

Imoni needs to take account of cultural risks associated with setting up a business in Yilandwe. The way of doing business in Yilandwe may be very different and the employees may need substantial training. On the other hand, the fact that the population is well educated, motivated and keen may make this process easier to achieve.

Imoni also needs to consider fiscal and regulatory risks. The company will need to assess the likelihood of changes in tax rates, laws and regulations, and set up strategies to mitigate eventualities which can be predicted. In addition to these, Imoni should also consider and mitigate as far as possible, operational risks such as the quality of the components and maintenance of transport links.

Imoni should assess and value alternative real options which it may have. For example, it could consider whether licensing the production of the components to a local company may be more financially viable; it could consider alternative countries to Yilandwe, which may offer more benefits; it could consider whether the project can be abandoned if circumstances change against the company; entry into Yilandwe may provide Imoni with other business opportunities.

Recommendation

The result from the financial projections is that the project should be accepted because it results in a positive net present value. It is recommended that the financial projections should be considered in conjunction with the assumptions, the issues and risks, and the implications of these, before a final decision is made.

There is considerable scope for further investigation and analysis. It is recommended that sensitivity analysis and simulation modelling is undertaken. The value of any alternative real options should also be considered and incorporated into the decision.

Consideration must also be given to the issues, risks and factors beyond financial considerations, such as the impact on the ethical stance of the company and the impact on its image, if the school affected is closed.

Report compiled by:

Date:

Appendices

Appendix 1

(All amounts in YR millions)

Year	0	1	2	3	4
Sales revenue (W2)		18,191	66,775	111,493	60,360
Parts costs (W2)		(5,188)	(19,060)	(31,832)	(17,225)
Variable costs (W2)		(2,921)	(10,720)	(17,901)	(9,693)
Fixed costs		(5,612)	(6,437)	(7,068)	(7,760)
Royalty fee (W3)		(4,324)	(4,813)	(5,130)	(5,468)
Tax allowable depreciation		(4,500)	(4,500)	(4,500)	(4,500)
Taxable profits/(loss)		(4,354)	21,245	45,062	15,714
Tax loss carried forward				(4,354)	
				40,708	
Taxation (40%)		0	0	(16,283)	(6,286)
Add back loss carried fwd				4,354	
Add back depreciation		4,500	4,500	4,500	4,500
Cash flows after tax		146	25,745	33,279	13,928
Working capital	(9,600)	(2,112)	(1,722)	(1,316)	14,750
Land, buildings and machinery	(39,000)				
Cash flows (YR, millions)	(48,600)	(1,966)	24,023	31,963	28,678

(All amounts in $000s)

Year	0	1	2	3	4
Exchange rate	101·4	120·1	133·7	142·5	151·9
Remittable flows	(479,290)	(16,370)	179,678	224,302	188,795
Contribution (parts sales) ($120 + inflation per unit)		18,540	61,108	95,723	48,622
Royalty (W3)		36,000	36,000	36,000	36,000
Tax on contribution and royalty (20%)		(10,908)	(19,422)	(26,345)	(16,924)
Cash flows	(479,290)	27,262	257,364	329,680	256,493
Discount factors (12%)	1	0·893	0·797	0·712	0·636
Present values	(479,290)	24,345	205,119	234,732	163,130

NPV of the project before considering the impact of the lost contribution and redundancy is approximately $148 million.

The lost contribution and redundancy costs are small compared to the net present value and would therefore have a minimal impact of reducing the net present value by $0·1 million approximately.

Tutorial note: *In light of the year 2 profits it is arguable whether the tax loss in year 1 could be carried forward against year 3 profits.*

Appendix 2: WORKINGS

(1)   Unit prices and costs including inflation

Year	1	2	3	4
Selling price (€)	735	772	803	835
Parts ($)	288	297	306	315
Variable costs (YR)	19,471	22,333	24,522	26,925

(2)   Sales revenue and costs (in YR millions)

Year	1	2	3	4
Sales revenue	$150 \times 735 \times 165$	$480 \times 772 \times 180 \cdot 2$	$730 \times 803 \times 190 \cdot 2$	$360 \times 835 \times 200 \cdot 8$
	$= 18,191$	$= 66,775$	$= 111,493$	$= 60,360$
Parts costs	$150 \times 288 \times 120 \cdot 1$	$480 \times 297 \times 133 \cdot 7$	$730 \times 306 \times 142 \cdot 5$	$360 \times 315 \times 151 \cdot 9$
	$= 5,188$	$= 19,060$	$= 31,832$	$= 17,225$
Variable costs	$150 \times 19,471$	$480 \times 22,333$	$730 \times 24,522 \ 3$	$60 \times 26,925$
	$= 2,921$	$= 10,720$	$= 17,901$	$= 9,693$

(3)   Royalty fee

$20 million $\times 1 \cdot 8 = \$36$ million

This is then converted into YR at the YR/$ rate for each year: $120 \cdot 1$, $133 \cdot 7$, $142 \cdot 5$ and $151 \cdot 9$ for years 1 to 4 respectively.

Tutorial note: *Credit would be given for alternative, relevant approaches to the calculations, and to the discussion of the assumptions, risks and issues.*

Answer 2 CHAWAN CO

(a)   Dark pools

A "dark pool of liquidity" is a private network for trading shares in listed firms, as opposed to buying/selling the shares through the public stock exchange. Dark pools are mostly used by institutional investors.

A dark pool network allows shares to be traded anonymously, away from public scrutiny. No information on the order is revealed prior to the trade taking place. The price and size of the order are only revealed once the trade has taken place.

Two main reasons are given for dark pool networks: (i) they prevent the risk of other traders moving the share price up or down (ii) they often result in reduced costs because trades normally take place at the mid-price between the bid and offer prices and because stock exchange fees are avoided.

Chawan's holding in Oden is 27 million shares out of a total of 600 million shares, or 4·5%. If Chawan sold such a large holding through the stock exchange, the price of Oden shares may fall temporarily and significantly, and Chawan may not receive the value based on the current price. By utilising a dark pool network, Chawan may be able to keep the price of the share largely intact, and possibly save transaction costs.

Although the criticism against dark pool systems is that they prevent market efficiency by not revealing bid-offer prices before the trade, proponents argue that in fact market efficiency is maintained because a large sale of shares through a dark pool will not move the price down artificially and temporarily.

(b) **Evaluation of disposal of holding in Oden**

Focus on investor and profitability ratios

Oden	2014	2015	2016	2017
Operating profit/Sales revenue		16·2%	15·2%	10·4%
Operating profit/Capital employed		22·5%	20·4%	12·7%
Earnings per share		$0·27	$0·24	$0·12
Price to earnings ratio		9·3	10·0	18·3
Gearing ratio (debt ÷ (debt + equity))		37·6%	36·9%	37·1%
Interest cover				
(Operating profit/Finance costs)		9·5	7·5	3·5
Dividend yield	7·1%	7·2%	8·3%	6·8%
Travel and leisure (T&L) sector				
Price to earnings ratio	11·9	12·2	13·0	13·8
Dividend yield	6·6%	6·6%	6·7%	6·4%

Other calculations

Oden, sales revenue annual growth rate average between 2015 and 2017
= $\sqrt{(1{,}185 \div 1{,}342)} - 1 = -6·0\%$.

Between 2016 and 2017 = (1,185 – 1,335) ÷ 1,335 = –11·2%.

Oden, average financing cost

2015: 23 ÷ (365 + 88) = 5·1%
2016: 27 ÷ (368 + 90) = 5·9%
2017: 35 ÷ (360 + 98) = 7·6%

Share price changes	2014–2015	2015–2016	2016–2017
Oden	19·0%	–4·0%	–8·3%
T&L sector	15·8%	–2·3%	12·1%

Oden

Total Shareholder Return (TSR)	2015	2016	2017
Dividend yield	7·2%	8·3%	6·8%
Share price gain	19·0%	–4·0%	–8·3%
Total	26·2%	4·3%	–1·5%
Average: 9·7%			

Required return (based on capital asset pricing model (CAPM))	13·0%	13·6%	16·0%
Average: 14·2%			

T&L sector (TSR)	2015	2016	2017
Dividend yield	6·6%	6·7%	6·4%
Share price gain	15·8%	–2·3%	12·1%
Total	22·4%	4·4%	18·5%
Average: 15·1%			

Required return (based on CAPM)	12·4%	13·0%	13·6%
Average: 13·0%			

Tutorial note: *The averages for Oden, RTS and for the T&L sector, RTS are the simple averages of the three years: 2015 to 2017.*

Discussion

The following discussion compares the performance of Oden over time, to the T&L sector and against expectations, in terms of it being a solid investment. It also considers the wider aspects which Chawan should take account of and the further information which the company should consider before coming to a final decision.

In terms of Oden's performance between 2015 and 2017, it is clear from the calculations above, that the company is experiencing considerable financial difficulties. Profit margins have fallen and so has the earnings per share (EPS). Whereas the amount of gearing appears fairly stable, the interest cover has deteriorated. The reason for this is that borrowing costs have increased from an average of 5·1% to an average of 7·6% over the three years. The share price has decreased over the three years as well and in the last year so has the dividend yield. This would indicate that the company is unable to maintain adequate returns for its investors (please also see below).

Although Oden has tried to maintain a dividend yield which is higher than the sector average, its price to earnings (PE) ratio has been lower than the sector average between 2015 and 2016. It does increase significantly in 2017, but this is because of the large fall in the EPS, rather than an increase in the share price. This could be an indication that there is less confidence in the future prospects of Oden, compared to the rest of the T&L sector. This is further corroborated by the higher dividend yield which may indicate that the company has fewer value-creating projects planned in the future. Finally, whereas the T&L sector's average share price seems to have recovered strongly in 2017, following a small fall in 2016, Oden's share price has not followed suit and the decline has gathered pace in 2017. It would seem that Oden is a poor performer within its sector.

This view is further strengthened by comparing the actual returns to the required returns based on the capital asset pricing model (CAPM). Both the company and the T&L sector produced returns exceeding the required return in 2015 and Oden experienced a similar decline to the sector in 2016. However, in 2017, the T&L sector appears to have recovered but Oden's performance has worsened. This has resulted in Oden's actual average returns being significantly below the required returns between 2014 and 2017.

Taking the above into account, the initial recommendation is for Chawan to dispose of its investment in Oden. However, there are three important caveats which should be considered before the final decision is made:

(1)   Chawan should look at the balance of its portfolio of investments. A sale of $58 million worth of equity shares within a portfolio total of $360 million may cause the portfolio to become unbalanced, and for unsystematic risk to be introduced into the portfolio. Presumably, the purpose of maintaining a balanced portfolio is to virtually eliminate unsystematic risk by ensuring that it is well diversified. Chawan may want to re-invest the proceeds from the sale of Oden (if it decides to proceed with the disposal) in other equity shares within the same sector to ensure that the portfolio remains balanced and diversified.

Tutorial note: *The above caveat can be challenged as Chawan is itself a listed firm, in which case it would be reasonable to assume that most of its shareholders are institutional investors who would have themselves used portfolio diversification to remove unsystematic risk. Hence, even if Chawan disposes of its holding in Oden it is likely that Chawan's shareholders would still have their own direct holdings in the T&L sector.*

The second caveat is that Chawan may want to look into the rumours of a takeover bid of Oden and assess how realistic it is that this will happen. If there is a realistic chance that such a bid may happen soon, Chawan may want to hold onto its investment in Oden for the present time. This is because takeover bids are made at a premium and the return to Chawan may increase if Oden is sold during the takeover.

The third caveat is that Chawan may want to consider Oden's future prospects. The calculations above are based on past performance between 2014 and 2017 and indicate an increasingly poor performance. However, the economy is beginning to recover, albeit slowly and erratically. Chawan may want to consider how well placed Oden is to take advantage of the improving conditions compared to other companies in the same industrial sector.

If Chawan decides that none of the caveats materially affect Oden's poor performance and position, then it should dispose of its investment in Oden.

Tutorial note: *Chawan's stated policy of investing in equity shares until cash is needed for projects can itself be challenged. It may be more advisable to invest surplus cash in low-risk securities rather than speculate with shareholders' funds.*

Answer 3 OKAZU CO

(a) Management buy-out versus management buy-in

A management buy-out (MBO) involves the purchase of a business by the management team running that business. Hence, an MBO of Okazu would involve the takeover of that company from Bento by Okazu's current management team. However, a management buy-in (MBI) involves the purchase of a business by a management team brought in from outside the business.

The benefits of a MBO relative to a MBI for Okazu are that the existing management is likely to have detailed knowledge of the business and its operations. Therefore they will not need to learn about the business and its operations in a way which a new external management team may need to. It is also possible that a MBO will cause less disruption and resistance from the employees when compared to a MBI. If Bento wants to continue doing business with the new company after it has been disposed of, it may find it easier to work with the management team which it is more familiar with. The internal management team may be more focused and have better knowledge of where costs can be reduced and sales revenue increased, in order to increase the overall value of the company.

The drawbacks of a MBO relative to a MBI for Okazu may be that the existing management may lack new ideas to rejuvenate the business. A new management team, through their skills and experience acquired elsewhere, may bring fresh ideas into the business. It may be that the external management team already has the required level of finance in place to move quickly and more decisively, whereas the existing management team may not have the financial arrangements in place yet. It is also possible that the management of Bento and Okazu have had disagreements in the past and the two teams may not be able to work together in the future if they need to. It may be that a MBI is the only way forward for Okazu to succeed in the future.

(b) **Forecasting of future gearing levels**

Annuity (8%, 4 years) = 3·312

Annual repayment on 8% bond = $30,000,000 ÷ 3·312 = $9,057,971

Interest payable on convertible loan, per year = $20,000,000 × 6% = $1,200,000

Annual interest on 8% bond (all amounts in $000s)

Year end	1	2	3	4
Opening loan balance	30,000	23,342	16,151	8,385
Interest at 8%	2,400	1,867	1,292	671
Annuity	(9,058)	(9,058)	(9,058)	(9,058)
Closing loan balance	23,342	16,151	8,385	(2)*

*The loan outstanding in year 4 should be zero. The small negative figure is due to rounding.

Estimate of profit and retained earnings after MBO (all amounts in $000s)

Year end	1	2	3	4
Operating profit	13,542	15,032	16,686	18,521
Interest expense	3,600	3,067	2,492	1,871
Profit before tax	9,942	11,965	14,194	16,650
Taxation	1,988	2,393	2,839	3,330
Profit for the year	7,954	9,572	11,355	13,320
Dividends	1,989	2,393	2,839	3,330
Retained earnings	5,965	7,179	8,516	9,990

Estimate of gearing (all amounts in $000s)

Year end	1	2	3	4
Book value of equity	15,965	23,144	31,660	41,650
Book value of debt	43,342	36,151	28,385	20,000
Gearing	73%	61%	47%	32%
Covenant	75%	60%	50%	40%
Covenant breached?	No	Yes	No	No

Tutorial note: *The book value of equity consists of the sum of the 5,000,000 equity shares which Dofu and Okazu's senior management will each invest in the new company (total 10,000,000), issued at their nominal value of $1 each, and the retained earnings from year 1. In subsequent years the book value of equity is increased by the retained earnings from that year.*

The gearing covenant is forecast to be breached in the second year only, and by a marginal amount. It is forecast to be met in all the other years. It is unlikely that Dofu will be too concerned about the covenant breach.

(c) **Benefit of MBO for management team and Dofu**

Net asset valuation

Based on the net asset valuation method, the value of the new company is approximately:

$(1 \cdot 3 \times \$40,800,000) + \$12,300,000 - \$7,900,000$ approx. $= \$57,440,000$

Dividend valuation model

Year	Dividend	DF (12%)	PV
	$000		$000
1	1,989	0·893	1,776
2	2,393	0·797	1,907
3	2,839	0·712	2,021
4	3,330	0·636	2,118
Total			7,822

Annual dividend growth rate, years 1 to 4 $= (3,330 \div 1,989)^{1/3} - 1 = 18 \cdot 7\%$
Annual dividend growth rate after year 4 $= 40\% \times 18 \cdot 7\% = 7 \cdot 5\%$
Value of dividends after year 4 $= (\$3,330,000 \times 1 \cdot 075) \div (0 \cdot 12 - 0 \cdot 075) \times 0 \cdot 636 =$
$\$50,594,000$ approximately.

Based on the dividend valuation model, the value of new company is approximately:
$\$7,822,000 + \$50,594,000 = \$58,416,000$

The $60 million asked for by Bento is higher than the current value of the Okazu's net assets and higher than the value of the company based on the dividend valuation model. Although the dividend valuation model, rather than the current value of the net assets, is probably a better estimate of the potential of the company, the price of $60 million still seems excessive.

Nevertheless, both the management team and Dofu are expected to receive substantial dividends during the first four years and Dofu's 8% bond loan will be repaid within four years.

Furthermore, the dividend valuation model can produce a large variation in results if the model's variables are changed by even a small amount. Therefore, the basis for estimating the variables should be examined carefully to judge their reasonableness, and sensitivity analysis applied to the model to demonstrate the impact of the changes in the variables. The value of the future potential of the new company should also be estimated using alternative valuation methods including free cash flows and price-earnings methods.

It is therefore recommended that the MBO should not be rejected at the outset but should be considered further. It is also recommended that the management team and Dofu try to negotiate the sale price with Bento.

Tutorial note: *Credit would be given for alternative, relevant discussion for parts (a) and (c)).*

Answer 4 DAIKON CO

(a)   **Evaluation of alternative hedges**

Borrowing period is 6 months (11 months – 5 months)

Current borrowing cost = $34,000,000 \times \,^6/_{12} \times 4 \cdot 3\% = \$731,000$

Borrowing cost if interest rates increase by 80 basis points ($0 \cdot 8\%$) = $34,000,000 \times \,^6/_{12} \times 5 \cdot 1\% = \$867,000$

Additional cost = $136,000 [\$34,000,000 \times \,^6/_{12} \times 0 \cdot 8\%]$

Using futures to hedge

Need to hedge against a rise in interest rates, therefore go short in the futures market.

Tutorial note: *If interest rate rise the price of interest rate futures would fall. Therefore initially sell futures to gain from a falling price (a "short" position).*

Borrowing period is 6 months

No. of contracts needed = $\$34,000,000 \div \$1,000,000 \times \,^6/_3) = 68$ contracts.

Basis

Current LIBOR $3 \cdot 6\%$. Forward interest rate implied by futures price = $100 - 95 \cdot 84 = 4 \cdot 16\%$
Opening basis = $4 \cdot 16 - 3 \cdot 6 = 0 \cdot 56$
Unexpired basis (at beginning of November) = $^2/_7 \times 0 \cdot 56 = 0 \cdot 16$

Tutorial note: *From today (1 June) until the maturity date of the futures contacts (31 December) is 7 months. The hedge will be closed in 5 months from today (when the underlying loan commences) at which point 2 months' of basis will still be unexpired.*

Assume that interest rates increase by 0·8% (80 basis points) to 4·4%

Expected futures price = $100 - 4 \cdot 4 - 0 \cdot 16 = 95 \cdot 44$

Gain on the futures market = $(95 \cdot 84 - 95 \cdot 44) \times \$25 \times 68 =$	$68,000
Net additional cost = ($136,000 – $68,000)	$68,000

Using options on futures to hedge

Need to hedge against a rise in interest rates, therefore buy put options.

Tutorial note: *Rather than initially selling futures the firm acquires the right, but not the obligation, to sell futures. Acquiring put options achieves this and creates an interest rate "cap".*

68 put option contracts are needed ($\$34,000,000 \div \$1,000,000 \times \,^6/_3$).

Assume that interest rates increase by 0·8% (80 basis points) to 4·4%

Exercise price	95·50	96·00
Futures price	95·44	95·44
Exercise options?	Yes	Yes
Gain in basis points	6	56
Gain on options		
6 × $25 × 68	$10,200	
56 × $25 × 68		$95,200
Premium paid		
30·4 × $25 × 68	$51,680	
50·8 × $25 × 68		$86,360
Option benefit/(cost)	$(41,480)	$8,840
Net additional cost		
($136,000 + $41,480)	$177,480	
($136,000 – $8,840)		$127,160

Using an options collar to hedge

Buy put options at 95·50 for 0·304 and sell call at 96·00 for 0·223

Tutorial note: *An interest rate collar is a combination of a purchased cap and a written floor. Hence, simultaneously buy puts (pay a premium) and sell calls (receive a premium) to produce a relatively low-cost hedge that gives protection from rising LIBOR and (limited) participation if LIBOR falls. The cap should be above the floor (in terms of % interest rates) and hence buy puts at a 95·50 exercise price (to create a cap at 4·5%) and sell calls at 96·00 (to create a floor at 4%).*

Net premium payable = 0·081

Assume that interest rates increase by 0·8% (80 basis points) to 4·4%

	Buy put	Sell call
Exercise price	95·50	96·00
Futures price	95·44	95·44
Exercise options?	Yes	No

Tutorial note: *The put option would be exercised by Daikon, as by using the option it can sell futures at 95·50 instead of the market price of 95·44 and gain 6 basis points per contract. The call option would not be exercised by their holder who can buy the futures at a lower market price of 95·44.*

Gain on options	
6 × $25 × 68	$10,200
Premium payable	
8·1 × $25 × 68	$13,770
Net cost of the collar	$3,570
Net additional cost	
($136,000 + $3,570)	$139,570

Based on the assumption that interest rates increase by 80 basis points in the next five months, the futures hedge would lower the additional cost by the greatest amount and is significantly better than either of the options hedge or the collar hedge.

In addition to this, futures fix the amount which Daikon is likely to pay, assuming that there is no basis risk. The benefits accruing from the options are lower, with the 95·50 option and the collar option actually increasing the overall cost. In each case, this is due to the high premium costs.

However, if interest rates do not increase and actually reduce, then the options (and to some extent the collar) provide more flexibility because they do not have to be exercised when interest rates move in the company's favour. But the movement will need to be significant before the cost of the premium is covered.

On balance, it is recommended that hedging using futures is the best choice as they will probably provide the most benefit to Daikon.

However, it is recommended that the points made in part (b) are also considered before a final conclusion is made.

(b)   **Further issues**

Mark-to-market: Daily settlements

2 June: 8 basis points (95·76 – 95·84) × $25 × 50 contracts = $10,000 loss

3 June: 10 basis points (95·66 – 95·76) × $25 × 50 contracts + 5 basis points (95·61 – 95·66) × $25 × 30 contracts = $16,250 loss

[Alternatively: 15 basis points (95·61 – 95·76) × $25 × 30 contracts + 10 basis points (95·66 – 95·76) × $25 × 20 contracts = $16,250 loss]

4 June: 8 basis points (95·74 – 95·66) × $25 × 20 contracts = $4,000 profit

Both mark-to-market and margins are used by markets to reduce the risk of non-default by users of derivative products if prices move against them.

Each time a market-traded derivative product is opened, the purchaser (and seller) needs to deposit an "initial margin" with the broker, which consists of funds to be kept with the broker while the position is open.

The mark-to-market system closes all the open deals at the end of each day at that day's settlement price, and opens them again at the start of the following day. The notional profit or loss on the deals is then calculated and the margin account is adjusted accordingly on a daily basis.

The impact on Daikon is that if losses are made, then the company may have to deposit extra funds with its broker if the margin account falls below the "maintenance margin" level. This may affect the company's ability to plan adequately and limits funds for other activities. On the other hand, extra cash accruing from any notional profits can be withdrawn from the broker account if needed.

The value of an option prior to expiry consists of time value, and may also consist of intrinsic value if the option is in-the-money. If an option is exercised prior to expiry, Daikon will only receive the intrinsic value attached to the option but not the time value. If the option is sold instead, whether it is in-the-money or out-of-money, Daikon will receive a higher value for it due to the time value. Unless options have other features, like dividends attached to them, which are not reflected in the option value, they would not normally be exercised prior to expiry.

SEPTEMBER/DECEMBER 2015

Answer 1 CIGNO CO

(a)   **Sell-off versus management buy-in**

Both forms of unbundling involve disposing of the non-core parts of the company.

The divestment through a sell-off normally involves selling part of a company as an entity or as separate assets to a third party for an agreed amount of funds or value. This value may comprise of cash and non-cash based assets. The company can then utilise the funds gained in alternative, value-enhancing activities.

The management buy-in is a particular type of sell-off which involves selling a division or part of a company to an external management team, who will take up the running of the new business and have an equity stake in the business. A management buy-in is normally undertaken when it is thought that the division or part of the company can probably be run better by a different management team compared to the current one.

(b)   **Report to the board of directors (BoD), Cigno Co**

This report assesses the potential value of acquiring Anatra Co for the equity holders of Cigno Co, both with and without considering the benefits of the reduction in taxation and in employee costs. The possible issues raised by reduction in taxation and in employee costs are discussed in more detail below. The assessment also discusses the estimates made and the methods used.

Assessment of value created

Cigno estimates that the premium payable to acquire Anatra largely accounts for the benefits created from the acquisition and the divestment, before considering the benefits from the tax and employee costs' saving. As a result, before these savings are considered, the estimated benefit to Cigno's shareholders of $128 million (see appendix 3) is marginal. Given that there are numerous estimations made and the methods used make various assumptions, as discussed below, this benefit could be smaller or larger. It would appear that without considering the additional benefits of cost and tax reductions, the acquisition is probably too risky and would probably be of limited value to Cigno's shareholders.

If the benefits of the taxation and employee costs saved are taken into account, the value created for the shareholders is $5,609 million (see appendix 4), and therefore significant. This would make the acquisition much more financially beneficial. It should be noted that no details are provided on the additional pre-acquisition and post-acquisition costs or on any synergy benefits that Cigno may derive in addition to the cost savings discussed. These should be determined and incorporated into the calculations.

Basing corporate value on the price-earnings (PE) method for the sell-off, and on the free cash flow valuation method for the absorbed business, is theoretically sound. The PE method estimates the value of the company based on its earnings and on competitor performance. With the free cash flow method, the cost of capital takes account of the risk the investors want to be compensated for and the free cash flows are the funds which the business can afford to return to the investors, as long as they are estimated accurately.

However, in practice, the input factors used to calculate the organisation's value may not be accurate or it may be difficult to assess their accuracy. For example, for the free cash flow method, it is assumed that the sales growth rate, operating profit margin, the taxation rate and incremental capital investment can be determined accurately and remain constant. It is assumed that the cost of capital will remain unchanged and it is assumed that the asset beta, the cost of equity and cost of debt can be determined accurately.

It is also assumed that the length of the period of growth is accurate and that the company operates in perpetuity thereafter. With the PE model, the basis for using the average competitor figures needs to be assessed (e.g. have outliers been ignored); and the basis for the company's higher PE ratio needs to be justified as well. The uncertainties surrounding these estimates would suggest that the value is indicative, rather than definitive, and it would be more prudent to undertake sensitivity analysis and obtain a range of values.

Key factors to consider in relation to the redundancies and potential tax savings

It is suggested that the BoD should consider the impact of the cost-savings from redundancies and from the tax payable in relation to corporate reputation and ethical considerations.

At present, Cigno enjoys a good reputation and it is suggested that this may be because it has managed to avoid large scale redundancies. This reputation may now be under threat and its loss could affect Cigno negatively in terms of long-term loss in revenues, profits and value; and it may be difficult to measure the impact of this loss accurately.

Whilst minimising tax may be financially prudent, it may not be considered fair. For example, currently there is ongoing discussion and debate from a number of governments and other interested parties that companies should pay tax in the countries they operate and derive their profits, rather than where they are based. Whilst global political consensus in this area seems some way off, it is likely that the debate in this area will increase in the future. Companies that are seen to be operating unethically with regard to this, may damage their reputation and therefore their profits and value.

Nonetheless, given that Cigno is likely to derive substantial value from the acquisition, because of these savings, it should not merely disregard the potential savings. Instead it should consider public relations exercises it could undertake to minimise the loss of reputation, and perhaps meet with the government to discuss ways forward in terms of tax payments.

Conclusion

The potential value gained from acquiring and unbundling Anatra can be substantial if the potential cost savings are taken into account. However, given the assumptions that are made in computing the value, it is recommended that sensitivity analysis is undertaken and a range of values obtained. It is also recommended that Cigno should undertake public relations exercises to minimise the loss of reputation, but it should probably proceed with the acquisition, and undertake the cost saving exercise because it is likely that this will result in substantial additional value.

Report compiled by:

Date:

Appendix 1: Estimate of value created from the sell-off of the equipment manufacturing business

Average industry PE ratio ($2·40 ÷ $0·30)	= 8
Anatra's equipment manufacturing business PE ratio (8 × 1·2)	= 9·6

Share of pre-tax profit (30% × $2,490m)	= $747m
After tax profit ($747 million × (1 – 0·22))	= $582·7m
Value from sell-off ($582·7m × 9·6)	= $5,594m (approximately)

Appendix 2: Estimate of the combined company cost of capital

Anatra, asset beta = 0·68

Cigno, asset beta:
Equity beta = 1·10
Proportion of market value of debt = 40%; Proportion of market value of equity = 60%
Asset beta = 1·10 × 0·60 ÷ (0·60 + (0·40 × 0·78)) = 0·72

Combined company, asset beta
Market value of equity, Anatra = $3 × 7,000 million shares = $21,000m
Market value of equity, Cigno = 60% × $60,000 million = $36,000m
Asset beta = ((0·68 × 21,000) + (0·72 × 36,000)) ÷ (21,000 + 36,000) = 0·71 (approximately)

Combined company equity beta = 0·71 × ((0·6 + (0·4 × 0·78)) ÷ 0·6 = 1·08
Combined company, cost of equity = 4·3% + (1·08 × 7%) = 11·86%
Combined company, cost of capital = (11·86% × 0·6) + (6·00% × 0·78 × 0·4) = 8·99, say 9%

Tutorial note: *The calculations above follow the approach suggested by the directors. However, it could be argued that, as the discount rate will be used to value Anatra's cash flows (rather than the two companies' combined cash flows), Anatra's individual WACC should be used. As Anastra will be 100% involved in R&D following the acquisition, its WACC would be based on the asset beta of R&D (0·72) and Anastra's own capital structure. Any candidate who took this approach, and justified it, would be given full credit.*

Appendix 3: Estimate of the value created for Cigno Co's equity holders from the acquisition

Anatra Co, Medical R&D value estimate

Sales revenue growth rate	= 5%
Operating profit margin	= 17·25%
Tax rate	= 22%
Additional capital investment	= 40% of the change in sales revenue
Cost of capital	= 9% (Appendix 2)
Free cash flow growth rate after four years	= 3%
Current sales revenue (70% × $21,400m)	= $14,980m

Cash flows, years 1 to 4 ($m)

Year	1	2	3	4
Sales revenue	15,729	16,515	17,341	18,208
Profit before interest and tax	2,713	2,849	2,991	3,141
Tax	597	627	658	691
Additional capital investment	300	314	330	347
Free cash flow to the firm	1,816	1,908	2,003	2,103
Present value of cash flows (9% discount)	1,666	1,606	1,547	1,490

Value, years 1 to 4: $6,309m

Value, year 5 onwards: $(\$1,490 \times 1 \cdot 03) \div (0 \cdot 09 - 0 \cdot 03) = \$25,575m$

Total value of Anatra's medical R&D assets = $31,884m

Tutorial note: *Discounting free cash flow to the firm (pre-interest cash flows) at WACC gives the fair value of assets, not the value of equity.*

Total value of Anatra's assets following unbundling of equipment manufacturing business and continuing the medical R&D business: $5,594m (appendix 1) + $31,884m = $37,478m (approximately)

Anatra, current market value of debt = $9,000m

Value of Anastra's equity to Cigno = assets – liabilities = $37,478m - $9,000m = $28,478

Bid price (including premium) = $21,000m × 1.35 = $28,350m

Added value for Cigna's shareholders = $28,478 - $28,350m = $128m

Therefore the value attributable to Cigno's shareholders from the acquisition of Anatra before taking into account the cash benefits of potential tax savings and redundancies = $128m

Appendix 4: Estimate of the value created from savings in tax and employment costs following possible redundancies

Cash flows, years 1 to 4 ($m)

Year	1	2	3	4
Cash flows (4% increase p.a.)	1,600	1,664	1,731	1,800
Present value of cash flows (9%)	1,468	1,401	1,337	1,275

Total value = $5,481m

Value attributable to Cigno's shareholders from the acquisition of Anatra after taking into account the cash benefits of potential tax savings and redundancies = $5,481m + $128m = $5,609m

(c) **Anastra's defence strategy**

The feasibility of disposing of assets as a defence tool against a possible acquisition depends on the type of assets sold and how the funds generated from the sale are utilised.

If the type of assets is fundamental to the continuing business then this may be viewed as disposing of the corporation's "crown-jewels". Such action may be construed as being against protecting the rights of shareholders (similar to the conditions discussed in part (d) below). In order for key assets to be disposed of, the takeover regulatory framework may insist on the corporation obtaining permission from the shareholders first before carrying it out.

On the other hand, the assets may be viewed as not being fundamental to the core business and may be disposed of to generate extra funds through a sell-off (see part (a) above). This may make sense if the corporation is undertaking a programme of restructuring and re-organisation.

In addition to this, the company needs to consider what it intends to do with the funds raised from the sale of assets. If the funds are used to grow the core business and therefore enhancing value, then the shareholders would see this positively and the value of the corporation will probably increase. Alternatively, if there are no profitable alternatives, the funds could be returned to the shareholders through special dividends or share buy-backs. In these circumstances, disposing of assets may be a feasible defence tactic.

However, if the funds are retained but not put to value-enhancing use or returned to shareholders, then the share price may continue to be depressed. And the corporation may still be an attractive takeover target for corporations which are in need of liquid funds. In these circumstances, disposing of assets would not be a feasible defence tactic.

(d) **Regulatory devices**

Each of the three conditions aims to ensure that shareholders are treated fairly and equitably.

The mandatory-bid condition through sell out rights allows remaining shareholders to exit the company at a fair price once the bidder has accumulated a certain number of shares. The amount of shares accumulated before the rule applies varies between countries. The bidder must offer the shares at the highest share price, as a minimum, which had been paid by the bidder previously. The main purpose for this condition is to ensure that the acquirer does not exploit their position of power at the expense of minority shareholders.

The principle of equal treatment condition stipulates that all shareholder groups must be offered the same terms, and that no shareholder group's terms are more or less favourable than another group's terms. The main purpose of this condition is to ensure that minority shareholders are offered the same level of benefits, as the previous shareholders from whom the controlling stake in the target company was obtained.

The squeeze-out rights condition allows the bidder to force minority shareholders to sell their stake, at a fair price, once the bidder has acquired a specific percentage of the target company's equity. The percentage varies between countries but typically ranges between 80% and 95%. The main purpose of this condition is to enable the acquirer to gain 100% stake of the target company and prevent problems arising from minority shareholders at a later date.

Tutorial note: *Credit will be given for alternative, relevant approaches to the calculations, comments and suggestions/recommendations.*

Answer 2 ARMSTRONG GROUP

(a) Multilateral netting

(i) Transactions matrix

Owed by	Owed to	Local currency (m)	$m
Armstrong (USA)	Horan (South (Africa)	US $12·17	12·17
Horan (South Africa)	Massie (Europe)	SA R42·65	3·97
Giffen (Denmark)	Armstrong (USA)	D Kr21·29	3·88
Massie (Europe)	Armstrong (USA)	US $19·78	19·78
Armstrong (USA)	Massie (Europe)	€1·57	2·13
Horan (South Africa)	Giffen (Denmark)	D Kr16·35	2·98
Giffen (Denmark)	Massie (Europe)	€1·55	2·11

Owed to	Owed by				
	Giffen (De) $m	Armtg (US) $m	Horan (SA) $m	Massie (EU) $m	Total $m
Giffen (De)			2·98		2·98
Armtg (US)	3·88			19·78	23·66
Horan (SA)		12·17			12·17
Massie (EU)	2·11	2·13	3·97		8·21
Owed by	(5·99)	(14·30)	(6·95)	(19·78)	
Owed to	2·98	23·66	12·17	8·21	
Net	(3·01)	9·36	5·22	(11·57)	

Under the terms of the arrangement, Massie, as the company with the largest debt, will pay Horan $5·22m, as the company with the smallest amount owed. Then Massie will pay Armstrong $6·35m (11·57 - 5·22) and Giffen will pay Armstrong $3·01m.

(ii) Potential problems

The Armstrong Group may have problems if any of the governments of the countries where the subsidiaries are located object to multilateral netting. However, this may be unlikely here.

The new system may not be popular with the management of the subsidiaries because of the length of time before settlement (up to six months). Not only might this cause cash flow issues for the subsidiaries, but the length of time may mean that some of the subsidiaries face significant foreign exchange risks. The system may possibly have to allow for immediate settlement in certain circumstances (e.g. if transactions are above a certain size or if a subsidiary will have significant cash problems if amounts are not settled immediately).

(b) Hedging interest rate risk

Options on futures

Need to hedge against a fall in interest rate, therefore buy call options. Require 50 contracts $(25,000,000 \div 1,000,000) \times {}^6/_3$.

Tutorial note: *If interest rates fall, as feared by Massie, the price of interest rate futures (100 – rate) would rise. Therefore the firm needs to hold the right to buy futures and should purchase calls on futures to create an interest rate "floor". The underlying deposit to be hedged will be 25,000,000 for a period of 6 months, whereas settlement on the options is referenced to a sim of 1,000,000 for 3 months, therefore 50 options are required.*

As Massie plans make the underling deposit on 30 November the hedge will be closed on that date and therefore options on December futures should be used when opening hedge on 1 September.

Basis

LIBOR on 1 September = 3·6%. 100 - 3·6 = 96·4
Basis in December futures on 1 September = 96·4 – 95·76 = 0·64
There are 4 months between 1 September and the delivery date of December futures (31 December) but Massie plans to close its hedge on 30 November (i.e. 1 month before the delivery date).

Unexpired basis on 30 November = $\frac{1}{4} \times 0.64 = 0.16$

Option

Interest received on the underlying deposit will be $(LIBOR – 0.4\%) \times 25,000,000 \times \frac{6}{12}$

If interest rates increase by 0·5% to 4·1%

Expected futures price = $(100 – 4.1) – 0.16 = 95.74$

Exercise price	97·00	96·50
Futures price	95·74	95·74
Exercise option?	No	No
Gain in basis points	–	–
	€	€
Interest received		
($€25m \times \frac{6}{12} \times (4.1 – 0.4)\%$)	462,500	462,500
Gain on options	–	–
Premium		
($3.2 \times €25 \times 50$)	(4,000)	
($18.2 \times €25 \times 50$)		(22,750)
Net receipt	458,500	439,750
Effective interest rates	3·67%	3·52%

If interest rates fall by 0·5% to 3·1%

Expected futures price = $(100 – 3.1) – 0.16 = 96.74$

Exercise price	97·00	96·50
Futures price	96·74	96·74
Exercise option?	No	Yes
Gain in basis points	–	24
	€	€
Interest received		
($€25m \times \frac{6}{12} \times (3.1 – 0.4)\%$)	337,500	337,500
Gain on options		
(0 and $24 \times €25 \times 50$)	–	30,000
Premium		
($3.2 \times €25 \times 50$)	(4,000)	
($18.2 \times €25 \times 50$)		(22,750)
Net receipt	333,500	344,750
Effective interest rates	2·67%	2·76%

Using a collar

Tutorial note: *A collar will protect Massie against falling interest rates whilst allowing some participation in rising interest rates. The collar will be a "low-cost floor" involving a purchased floor (buy calls) and a written cap (sell puts). In terms of interest rates the floor must be below the cap.*

Buy December call at 97·00 (3% floor) for 0·032 and sell December put at 96·50 (3.5% cap) for 0·123. Net premium received = 0·091.

If interest rates increase to 4·1%

	Buy call	Sell put
Exercise price	97·00	96·50
Futures price	95·74	95·74
Exercise option?	No	Yes

	€
Interest received	462,500
Loss on exercise (76 × €25 × 50)	(95,000)
Premium (9·1 × €25 × 50)	11,375
Net receipt	378,875
Effective interest rate	3·03%

If interest rates fall to 3·1%

	Buy call	Sell put
Exercise price	97·00	96·50
Futures price	96·74	96·74
Exercise option?	No	No

	€
Interest received	337,500
Loss on exercise	–
Premium (9·1 × €25 × 50)	11,375
Net receipt	348,875
Effective interest rate	2·79%

Summary

	97·00	96·50	Collar
Interest rates rise to 4·1%	3·67%	3·52%	3·03%
Interest rates fall to 3·1%	2·67%	2·76%	2·79%

The option with the 97·00 exercise price has a higher average figure than the option with the 96·50 exercise price, and can be recommended on that basis, as its worst result is only marginally worse than the 96·50 option. There is not much to choose between them.

The collar gives a significantly worse result than either of the options if interest rates rise, because Massie cannot take full advantage of the increase. It is marginally the better choice if interest rates fall. The recommendation would be to choose the option with the 97·00 exercise price, unless interest rates are virtually certain to fall.

Answer 3 FLUFFTORT CO

(a)   **Projected financial statements**

Statements of financial position	(i)	(ii)
Assets	$m	$m
Non-current assets	69	125
Current assets excluding cash	18	42
Cash	–	5 (iii)
Total assets	87	172
Equity and liabilities		
Share capital	40	90
Retained earnings	5	5
Total equity	45	95
Long-term liabilities		
Bank loan	30	65
Loan note	5	–
Total long-term liabilities	35	65
Current liabilities	7	12
Total liabilities	42	77
Total equity and liabilities	87	172

Notes:

(i)   If Gupte VC's shares are repurchased and cancelled.
(ii)   If proposed refinancing and investment takes place.
(iii)   Balancing figure.

(iii)   Projected statement of profit or loss

	2019	2020
	$m	$m
Operating profit	20·0	25·0
Finance cost	(6·5)	(6·5)
Profit before tax	13·5	18·5
Taxation 20%	(2·7)	(3·7)
Profit after tax	10·8	14·8
Dividends	–	–
Retained earnings	10·8	14·8

(b)   **Current situation**

Initial product developments have not generated the revenues required to sustain growth. The new Easicushion chair appears to offer Flufftort much better prospects of commercial success. At present, however, Flufftort does not have the resources to make the investment required.

Purchase of Gupte VC's shares

In the worst case scenario, Gupte VC will demand repayment of its investment in a year's time. The calculations in (a) show the financial position in a year's time, assuming that there is no net investment in non-current assets or working capital, the purchase of shares is financed solely out of cash reserves and the shares are cancelled. Repayment by this method would mean that the limits set out in the covenant would be breached (45 ÷ 35 = 1·29) and the bank could demand immediate repayment of the loan.

The directors can avoid this by buying some of Gupte VC's shares themselves, but this represents money which is not being put into the business. In addition, the amount of shares which the directors would have to purchase would be greater if results, and therefore reserves, were worse than expected.

Financing the investment

The calculations in (a) show that the cash flows associated with the refinancing would be enough to finance the initial investment. The ratio of equity to non-current liabilities after the refinancing would be 1·46 (95 ÷ 65), in line with the current limits in the bank's covenant. However, financing for the subsequent investment required would have to come from surplus cash flows.

Shareholdings

The disposition of shareholdings will change as follows:

	Current shareholdings		Shareholdings after refinancing	
	Number in million	*%*	*Number in million*	*%*
Directors	27·5	55·0	42·5	47·2
Other family members	12·5	25·0	12·5	13·9
Gupte VC	10·0	20·0	30·0	33·3
Loan note holder	–	–	5·0	5·6
	50·0	100·0	90·0	100·0

Gupte VC's percentage shareholding will rise from 20% to 33·3%, enough possibly to give it extra rights over the company. The directors' percentage shareholding will fall from 55% to 47·2%, which means that collectively they no longer have control of the company. The percentage of shares held by family members who are not directors falls from 25% to around 19·5%, taking into account the conversion of the loan note. This will mean, however, that the directors can still maintain control if they can obtain the support of some of the rest of the family.

Position of finance providers

The refinancing has been agreed by the chief executive and finance director. At present, it is not clear what the views of the other directors are, or whether the $15 million contributed by directors will be raised from them in proportion to their current shareholdings. Some of the directors may not be able to, or wish to, make a significant additional investment in the company. On the other hand, if they do not, their shareholdings, and perhaps their influence within the company, will diminish. This may be a greater concern than the board collectively losing control over the company, since it may be unlikely that the other shareholders will combine to outvote the board.

The other family shareholders have not been actively involved in Flufftort's management out of choice, so a reduction in their percentage shareholdings may not be an issue for them. They may have welcomed the recent dividend payment as generating a return on their investment. However, as they appear to have invested for the longer term, the new investment appears to offer much better prospects in the form of a capital gain on listing or buy-out than an uncertain flow of dividends. The new investment appears only to have an upside for them in the sense that they are not being asked to contribute any extra funding towards it.

Rajiv Patel is unlikely to be happy with the proposed scheme. He is exchanging a guaranteed flow of income for an uncertain flow of future dividends sometime after 2020. On the other hand, his investment may be jeopardised by the realisation of the worst case scenario, since his debt is subordinated to the bank's debt.

The most important issue from Gupte VC's viewpoint is whether the extra investment required is likely to yield a better outcome than return of its initial investment in a year's time. The plan that no dividends would be paid until after 2020 is a disadvantage. On the other hand, the additional investment seems to offer the only prospect of realising a substantial gain either by Flufftort being listed or sold. The arrangement will mean that Gupte VC may be able to exercise greater influence over Flufftort, which may provide it with a greater sense of reassurance about how Flufftort is being run. The fact that Gupte VC has a director on Flufftort's board should also give it a clear idea of how successful the investment is likely to be.

The bank will be concerned about the possibility of Flufftort breaching the covenant limits and may be concerned whether Flufftort is ultimately able to repay the full amount without jeopardising its existence. The bank will be concerned if Flufftort tries to replace loan finance with overdraft finance. The refinancing provides reassurance to the bank about gearing levels and a higher rate of interest. The bank will also be pleased that the level of interest cover under the refinancing is higher and increasing (from $2 \cdot 0$ in 2018 to $3 \cdot 1$ in 2019 and $3 \cdot 8$ in 2020). However, it will be concerned about how Flufftort finances the additional investment required if cash flows from the new investment are lower than expected. In those circumstances Flufftort may seek to draw on its overdraft facility.

Conclusion

The key players in the refinancing are Gupte VC, the bank and the directors other than the chief executive and the finance director. If they can be persuaded, then the scheme has a good chance of being successful. However, Rajiv Patel could well raise objections. He may be pacified if he retains the loan note. This would marginally breach the current covenant limit ($90 \div 70 = 1 \cdot 29$), although the bank may be willing to overlook the breach as it is forecast to be temporary. Alternatively, the refinancing would mean that Flufftort just had enough spare cash initially to redeem the loan note, although it would be more dependent on cash surpluses after the refinancing to fund the additional investment required.

Answer 4 MOONSTAR CO

(a)   Securitisation

An annual cash flow account compares the estimated cash flows receivable from the property against the liabilities within the securitisation process. The swap introduces leverage into the arrangement.

Cash flow receivable	$m	Cash flow payable	$m
$200 million × 11%	22·00	A-rated loan notes;	
Less: Service charge	(0·20)	Pay $108 million (W1) × 11% (W2)	11·88
		B-rated loan notes:	
		Pay $27 million (W1) × 12%	3·24
		C-rated loan notes	
		Pay $27 million (W1) × 13%	3·51
	21·80		18·63
		Balance to the subordinated certificates	3·17

WORKINGS

(1)   Loan notes

		$m
A	$200m × 0·9 × 0·6	108
B	$200m × 0·9 × 0·15	27
C	$200m × 0·9 × 0·15	27

(2)   Swap

Pay fixed rate under swap	9·5%
Pay floating rate	LIBOR + 1·5%
Receive floating rate under swap	(LIBOR)
Net payment	11%

The holders of the certificates are expected to receive $3·17million on $18 million, giving them a return of 17·6%. If the cash flows are 5% lower than the non-executive director has predicted, annual revenue received will fall to $20·90 million, reducing the balance available for the subordinated certificates to $2·07 million, giving a return of 11·5% on the subordinated certificates, which is below the returns offered on the B and C-rated loan notes. The point at which the holders of the certificates will receive nothing and below which the holders of the C-rated loan notes will not receive their full income will be an annual income of $18·83 million (a return of 9·4%), which is 14·4% less than the income that the non-executive director has forecast.

(b)   **Benefits and risks of securitisation**

Benefits

The finance costs of the securitisation may be lower than the finance costs of ordinary loan capital. The cash flows from the commercial property development may be regarded as lower risk than Moonstar's other revenue streams. This will affect the rates that Moonstar is able to offer borrowers.

The securitisation matches the assets of the future cash flows to the liabilities to loan note holders. The non-executive director is assuming a steady stream of lease income over the next 10 years, with the development probably being close to being fully occupied over that period.

The securitisation means that Moonstar is no longer concerned with the risk that the level of earnings from the properties will be insufficient to pay the finance costs. Risks have effectively been transferred to the loan note holders.

Risks

Not all of the tranches may appeal to investors. The risk-return relationship on the subordinated certificates does not look very appealing, with the return quite likely to be below what is received on the C-rated loan notes. Even the C-rated loan note holders may question the relationship between the risk and return if there is continued uncertainty in the property sector.

If Moonstar seeks funding from other sources for other developments, transferring out a lower risk income stream means that the residual risks associated with the rest of Moonstar's portfolio will be higher. This may affect the availability and terms of other borrowing.

It appears that the size of the securitisation should be large enough for the costs to be bearable. However Moonstar may face unforeseen costs, possibly unexpected management or legal expenses.

(c)   **Islamic finance**

(i)   Sukuk

Sukuk finance could be appropriate for the securitisation of the leasing portfolio. An asset-backed Sukuk would be the same kind of arrangement as the securitisation, where assets are transferred to a special purpose vehicle and the returns and repayments are directly financed by the income from the assets. The Sukuk holders would bear the risks and returns of the relationship.

The other type of Sukuk would be more like a sale and leaseback of the development. Here the Sukuk holders would be guaranteed a rental, so it would seem less appropriate for Moonstar if there is significant uncertainty about the returns from the development.

The main issue with the asset-backed Sukuk finance is whether it would be as appealing as certainly the A-tranche of the securitisation arrangement which the non-executive director has proposed. The safer income that the securitisation offers A-tranche investors may be more appealing to investors than a marginally better return from the Sukuk. There will also be costs involved in establishing and gaining approval for the Sukuk, although these costs may be less than for the securitisation arrangement described above.

(ii)   *Mudaraba*

A Mudaraba contract would involve the bank providing capital for Moonstar to invest in the development. Moonstar would manage the investment which the capital funded. Profits from the investment would be shared with the bank, but losses would be solely borne by the bank. A Mudaraba contract is essentially an equity partnership, so Moonstar might not face the threat to its credit rating which it would if it obtained ordinary loan finance for the development. A Mudaraba contract would also represent a diversification of sources of finance. It would not require the commitment to pay interest that loan finance would involve.

Moonstar would maintain control over the running of the project. A Mudaraba contract would offer a method of obtaining equity funding without the dilution of control which an issue of shares to external shareholders would bring. This is likely to make it appealing to Moonstar's directors, given their desire to maintain a dominant influence over the business.

The bank would be concerned about the uncertainties regarding the rental income from the development. Although the lack of involvement by the bank might appeal to Moonstar's directors, the bank might not find it so attractive. The bank might be concerned about information asymmetry – that Moonstar's management might be reluctant to supply the bank with the information it needs to judge how well its investment is performing.

MARCH/JUNE 2016

Answer 1 LIRIO CO

(a)   Purchasing power parity and economic exposure

Purchasing power parity (PPP) predicts that the exchange rates between two currencies depend on the relative differences in the rates of inflation in each country. Therefore, if one country has a higher rate of inflation compared to another, then its currency is expected to depreciate over time. However, according to PPP the "law of one price" holds because any weakness in one currency will be compensated by the rate of inflation in the currency's country (or group of countries in the case of the euro).

Economic exposure refers to the degree by which a company's cash flows are affected by fluctuations in exchange rates. It may also affect companies which are not exposed to foreign exchange transactions, due to actions by international competitors.

If PPP holds, then companies may not be affected by exchange rate fluctuations, as lower currency value can be compensated by the ability to raise prices due to higher inflation levels. This depends on markets being efficient.

However, a permanent shift in exchange rates may occur, not because of relative inflation rate differentials, but because a country (or group of countries) lose their competitive positions. In this case the "law of one price" will not hold, and prices readjust to a new and long-term or even permanent rate. For example, the UK £ to USA $ rate declined in the 20th century, as the USA grew stronger economically and the UK grew weaker. The rate almost reached parity in 1985 before recovering. Since the financial crisis in 2009, it has fluctuated between roughly $1·5 to £1 and $1·7 to £1.

In such cases, where a company receives substantial amounts of revenue from companies based in countries with relatively weak economies, it may find that it is facing economic exposure and its cash flows decline over a long period of time.

(b)   **Discussion paper to the board of directors (BoD), Lirio Co**

Date: **Compiled by:**

Purpose of the discussion paper

The purpose of this discussion paper is:

(i)   To consider the implications of the BoD's proposal to use funds from the sale of its equity investment in the European company and from its cash flows generated from normal business activity over the next two years to finance a large project, instead of raising funds through equity and/or debt;

(ii)   To assess whether or not the project adds value for Lirio or not.

Background information

The funds needed for the project are estimated at $40,000,000 at the start of the project. $23,118,000 of this amount is estimated to be received from the sale of the equity investment (appendices 2 and 3). This leaves a balance of $16,882,000 (Appendix 3), which will be obtained from the free cash flows to equity (the dividend capacity) of $21,642,000 (Appendix 1) expected to be generated in the first year. However, this would leave only $4,760,000 available for dividend payments in the first year, meaning a cut in expected dividends from $0·27 per share to $0·0595 per share (Appendix 3). The same level of dividends will be paid in the second year as well.

Project assessment

Based on the dividend valuation model (DVM), Lirio's market capitalisation, and therefore its value, is expected to increase from approximately $360 million to approximately $403 million, or by just under 12% (Appendix 3). This would suggest that it would be beneficial for the project to be undertaken.

Possible issues

(1)   The DVM is based on a number of factors such as: an accurate estimation of the dividend growth rate, a non-changing cost of equity and a predictable future dividend stream growing in perpetuity. Also, it is expected that the sale of the investment will yield €20m but this amount could increase or reduce in the next three months. The DVM assumes that dividends and their growth rate are the sole drivers of corporate value, which is probably not accurate.

(2)   Although the dividend irrelevancy theory proposed by Modigliani and Miller suggests that corporate value should not be affected by a corporation's dividend policy, in practice changes in dividends do matter for two main reasons. First, dividends are used as a signalling device to the markets and unexpected changes in dividends paid and/or dividend growth rates are not generally viewed positively by them. Changes in dividends may signal that the company is not doing well and this may affect the share price negatively.

(3)   Second, corporate dividend policy attracts certain groups of shareholders or clientele. In the main this is due to personal tax reasons. For example, higher rate taxpayers may prefer low dividend payouts and lower rate taxpayers may prefer higher dividend payouts. A change in dividends may result in the clientele changing and this changeover may result in excessive and possibly negative share price volatility.

(4)   It is not clear why the BoD would rather not raise the required finance through equity and/or debt. The BoD may have considered increasing debt to be risky. However, given that the current level of debt is $70 million compared to an estimated market capitalisation of $360 million (Appendix 3), raising another $40 million through debt finance will probably not result in a significantly higher level of financial risk. The BoD may have been concerned that going into the markets to raise extra finance may result in negative agency type issues (e.g. having to make proprietary information public or being forced to give extra value to new equity owners or sending out negative signals to the markets).

Areas for further discussion by the BoD

Each of these issues should be considered and discussed further by the BoD. With reference to point 1, the BoD needs to discuss whether the estimates and the model used are reasonable in estimating corporate value or market capitalisation. With reference to points 2 and 3, the BoD needs to discuss the implications of such a significant change in the dividend policy and how to communicate Lirio's intention to the market so that any negative reaction is minimised. With reference to point 4, the BoD should discuss the reasons for any reluctance to raise finance through the markets and whether any negative impact of this is perhaps less than the negative impact of points 2 and 3.

Appendix 1: Expected dividend capacity prior to large project investment

	$000
Operating profit (15% × 1·08 × $300m)	48,600
Less interest (5% × $70m)	(3,500)
Less taxation (25% × ($48·6m – $3·5m))	(11,275)
Less investment in working capital ($0·10 × 0·08 × $300m)	(2,400)
Less investment in additional non-current assets ($0·20 × 0·08 × $300m)	(4,800)
Less investment in small projects	(8,000)
	———
Cash flows from domestic operations	18,625
Cash flows from Pontac's dividend remittances (Appendix 1·1)	3,297
Additional tax payable on Pontac's profits (5% × $5·6 million)	(280)
	———
Dividend capacity	21,642
	———

Tutorial note: *There is no need to add back depreciation as the scenario states that it equals the cash required to maintain the firm's existing capacity.*

Appendix 1.1: Dividend remittances expected from Pontac

	$000
Total contribution $24 × 400,000 units	9,600
Less fixed costs	(4,000)
Less taxation (20% × $5·6 million)	(1,120)
	———
Profit after tax	4,480
	———
Remitted to Lirio (80% × $4·48 million × 92%)	3,297
	———

Tutorial note: *Only 92% of the dividend will reach Lirio due to the 8% withholding tax*

Appendix 2: Euro (€) investment sale receipt hedge

Lirio can use one of forward contracts, futures contracts or option contracts to hedge the € receipt.

Forward contract

Since it is a € receipt, the 1·1559 rate will be used.
€20,000,000 × 1·1559 = $23,118,000

Futures contracts

"Go long" (buy futures) to protect against a weakening € and use the June contracts to hedge as the receipt is expected on 1 June (in three months' time).

Tutorial note: *Each futures contract is on the dollar (as the contract size is $125,000). Lirio needs to hedge against a rise in the dollar and on 1 March should establish the hedge by **buying** dollar futures (a "long" position makes gains if the underlying asset rises).*

Number of contracts bought = $23,121,387 ÷ $125,000 = approximately 185 contracts (resulting in a very small over-hedge and therefore not material).

Although the June contracts would expire on 30 June Lirio will close the hedge on 1 June – approximately one month before expiry. Linear interpolation between the price of March and June futures can estimate the "lock-in rate" for 1 June (i.e. the expected outcome from the hedge).

$0·8638 + (^2/_3 × (0·8656 – 0·8638)) = 0·8650$
Expected receipt = €20,000,000 ÷ 0·8650 = $23,121,387

Option contracts

Purchase the June call option to protect against a weakening € and because receipt is expected on 1 June.

Tutorial note: *Each option is on the dollar (as the contract size is $125,000). Lirio needs the right to buy dollars and therefore should acquire **call** options,*

> Exercise price is 0·86, therefore expected receipt is €20,000,000 ÷ 0·8600 = $23,255,814
> Contracts purchased = $23,255,814 ÷ $125,000 = 186·05, say 186
>
> Premium payable = 186 × 125,000 × 0·0290 = €674,250
> Premium in $ at spot = €674,250 × 1·1618 = $783,344
> Amount not hedged = €20,000,000 – (186 × 125,000 × 0·8600) = €5,000
> Use forward contracts to cover the €5,000 not hedged. €5,000 × 1·1559 = $5,780
>
> Total net receipt if options exercised = ($125,000 × 186) + $5,780 – $783,344 = $22,472,436

Advice and recommendation

Hedging using options will give the lowest receipt at $22,472,436 from the sale of the investment, while hedging using futures will give the highest receipt at $23,127,387, with the forward contracts giving a receipt of $23,118,000.

The lower receipt from the option contracts is due to the premium payable, which allows the option buyer to let the option lapse should the € strengthen. In this case, the option would be allowed to lapse and Lirio would convert the € into $ at the prevailing spot rate in three months' time. However, the € would need to strengthen significantly before the cost of the option is covered. Given market expectation of the weakness in the € continuing, this is not likely to be the case.

Although futures and forward contracts are legally binding and do not have the flexibility of option contracts, they both give higher receipts. Hedging using futures gives the higher receipt, but futures require margin payments to be made upfront and contracts are marked-to-market daily. In addition to this, the basis may not narrow in a linear fashion and therefore the amount received is not guaranteed. All these factors create uncertainty in terms of the exact amounts of receipts and payments resulting on a daily basis and the final receipt.

On the other hand, when using forward contracts to hedge the receipt exposure, Lirio knows the exact amount it will receive. It is therefore recommended that Lirio use the forward markets to hedge the expected receipt.

Tutorial note: *It could be argued that in spite of the issues when hedging with futures, the higher receipt obtained from using futures markets to hedge mean that they should be used. This is acceptable as well.*

Appendix 3: Estimate of Lirio's value based on the dividend valuation model

If the large project is not undertaken and dividend growth rate is maintained at the historic level.

Dividend history

Year to end of February	2015	2016	2017	2018
Number of $1 equity shares in issue (000)	60,000	60,000	80,000	80,000
Total dividends paid ($000)	12,832	13,602	19,224	20,377
Dividend per share	$0·214	$0·227	$0·240	$0·255

Average dividend growth rate = $(0·255 \div 0·214)^{1/3} - 1 = 1·0602$ (approx 6%)

Expected dividend in February 2019 = $0·255 × 1·06 = $0·270

Lirio, estimate of value if large project is not undertaken =
$0·270 $\div (0·12 - 0·06) = $4·50 per share or $360 million market capitalisation

If the large project is undertaken

Funds required for project	$40,000,000
Funds from sale of investment (Appendix 2)	($23,118,000)
Funds required from dividend capacity cash flows	$16,882,000

Dividend capacity funds before transfer to project (Appendix 1)	$21,642,000
Dividend capacity funds left after transfer (21,642,000 - 16,882,000)	$4,760,000
Dividend per share (4,760,000 ÷ 80,000)	$0·0595
Annual dividend (end of February 2019 and February 2020)	$0·0595
Dividend end of February 2021 (per scenario)	$0·3100
Subsequent growth rate	7%

Lirio, estimate of value if large project is undertaken =
$0·0595 × 1·12^{-1} + $0·0595 × 1·12^{-2} + $0·3100 × 1·12^{-3} + [$0·3100 × 1·07 $\div (0·12 - 0·07)$]
× 1·12^{-3} = $5·04 per share or $403 million market capitalisation

Tutorial note: *A discussion paper can take many formats. The answer provides one possible format. Credit will be given for alternative and sensible formats; and for relevant approaches to the calculations and commentary.*

Answer 2 LOUIEED CO

(a) **Advantages and disadvantages of the proposed acquisition**

Advantages of the acquisition

Louieed and Tidded appear to be a good strategic fit for a number of reasons. Louieed appears to have limited potential for further growth. Acquiring Tidded, a company with better recent growth, should hopefully give Louieed the impetus to grow more quickly.

Acquiring a company which has a specialism in the area of online testing will give Louieed capabilities quicker than developing this function in-house. If Louieed does not move quickly, it risks losing contracts to its competitors.

Acquiring Tidded will give Louieed access to the abilities of some of the directors who have led Tidded to becoming a successful company. They will provide continuity and hopefully will help integrate Tidded's operations successfully into Louieed. They may be able to lead the upgrading of Tidded's existing products or the development of new products which ensures that Louieed retains a competitive advantage.

It appears that Tidded's directors now want to either realise their investment or be part of a larger company, possibly because it will have more resources to back further product development. If Louieed does not pursue this opportunity, one of Louieed's competitors may purchase Tidded and acquire a competitive advantage itself.

There may also be other synergistic benefits, including savings in staff costs and other savings, when the two companies merge.

Disadvantages of the acquisition

It is not known what the costs of developing in-house capabilities will be. Although the process may be slower, the costs may be less and the process less disruptive to Louieed than suddenly adding on Tidded's operations.

It is not possible to tell which of Tidded's directors are primarily responsible for its success. Loss of the three directors may well represent a significant loss of its capability. This will be enhanced if the three directors join a competitor of Louieed or set up in competition themselves.

There is no guarantee that the directors who remain will fit into Louieed's culture. They are used to working in a less formal environment and may resent having Louieed's way of operating imposed upon them. This could result in departures after the acquisition, jeopardising the value which Tidded has brought.

Possibly Tidded's leadership in the online testing market may not last. If competitors do introduce major advances, this could mean that Tidded's current growth is not sustainable.

(b) **PE ratio**

Value of Louieed's share = $296m × 14 ÷ 340m = $12·19
Value of Tidded share per original bid = $12·19 × ($^5/_3$) = $20·32
Tidded earnings per share = $128m ÷ 90 = $1·42

Tidded PE ratio implied by:

Original bid = $20·32 ÷ $1·42 = 14·3
All Tidded's shareholders taking up the revised share offer = $12·19 × 2 ÷ $1·42 = 17·2
Mixed cash and share offer = ($22·75 × 0·4) + ($12·19 × 2 × 0·6) ÷ $1·42 = 16·7
All Tidded's shareholders taking up the cash offer = $22·75 ÷ $1·42 = 16·0

(c)   Funding of bid

No extra finance will be required if all Tidded's shareholders take up the share offer.

If all Tidded's shareholders take up cash offer:
Cash required = 90 million × $22·75 = $2,048m
Extra debt finance required = $2,048m – $220m – $64m = $1,764m

60% share-for-share offer, 40% cash offer:
Cash required = 40% × 90m × $22·75 = $819m
Extra debt finance required = $819m – $220m – $64m = $535m

Impact of bid on EPS

Louieed's EPS prior to acquisition = $296m ÷ 340 = $0·87

If all Tidded's shareholders take up share offer:
Number of shares after acquisition = 340m + (90m × 2) = 520m
EPS after acquisition = ($296m + $128m + $20m) ÷ 520m = $0·85

If all Tidded's shareholders take up cash offer:
Number of shares after acquisition = 340m
EPS after acquisition = ($296m + $128m + $20m – $11·36m – $105·84m) ÷ 340m = $0·96

$105·84m is the post-tax finance cost on the additional loan finding required of $1,764m.
Therefore $1,764m × 7·5% × 80% = $105·84m

$11·36m is the post-tax opportunity cost of interest foregone on the cash and cash equivalents surpluses of the two companies of $220m + $64m = $284m. Therefore $284m × 5% × 80% = $11·36m

60% share-for-share offer, 40% cash offer:
Number of shares after acquisition 340m + (90m × 2 × 0·6) = 448m
EPS after acquisition = ($296m + $128m + $20m – $11·36m – $32·1m) ÷ 448m = $0·89

$32·1m is the post-tax finance cost on the additional loan funding required of $535m.
Therefore $535m × 7·5% × 80% = $32·1m

Impact of bid on gearing (using market values)

Louieed's gearing using market values (Debt ÷ (Debt + equity)) prior to bid
= $540m ÷ ($540m + (340m × $12·19)) = 11·5%

If all Tidded's shareholders take up share offer:
Debt ÷ (Debt + equity) after bid = ($540m + $193m) ÷ ($540m + $193m + (520m × $0·85 × 14)) = 10·6%

If all Tidded's shareholders take up cash offer
Debt ÷ (Debt + equity) after bid = ($540m + $193m + $1,764m) ÷ ($540m + $193m + $1,764m + (340m × $0·96 × 14)) = 35·3%

60% share-for-share offer, 40% cash offer:
Debt ÷ (Debt + equity) after bid = ($540m + $193m + $535m)/($540m + $193m + $535m + (448m × $0·89 × 14)) = 18·5%

Comments

The calculations suggest that if Tidded's shares are acquired on a share-for-share exchange on the terms required by its shareholders, Louieed's shareholders will suffer a fall in earnings per share attributable to them from $0·87 to $0·85. This is because Tidded is being bought on a higher price-earnings ratio than Louieed and the synergies arising from the acquisition are insufficient to compensate for this.

Use of loan finance to back a cash offer will attract tax relief on interest. The cost of debt will be lower than the cost of equity.

Issuing extra shares will lead to a dilution of the power of Louieed's existing shareholders. If all of Tidded's shareholders take up the share-for-share offer, they will hold around a third of the shares of the combined company (180m ÷ 520m) and this may be unacceptable to Louieed's shareholders.

The benefits which Tidded's shareholders will gain will be fixed if they take up a cash offer and do not acquire shares in the combined company. If there are significant gains after the acquisition, these will mostly accrue to Louieed's existing shareholders if a significant proportion of Tidded's shareholders have taken a cash offer.

If the forecast for take up of the offer is correct, even by combining the cash flows of the two companies, the new company will have insufficient funds to be able to pay all the shareholders who are expected to take up the cash offer. Further finance will be required.

The alternative to loan finance is financing the bid by issuing shares. Depending on the method used, this may also result in dilution of existing shareholders' ownership and also there is no guarantee that the issue will be successful.

There is also no guarantee that the forecast of 40% of the shareholders taking up the cash offer is correct. If all five of the major shareholders decide to realise their investment rather than just two, this will increase the cash required by $512m (25% × $22·75 × 90m), for example.

Gearing will increase if loan finance is needed to finance the cash offer. If the mixed share and cash offer is taken up in the proportions stated, the gearing level of the combined company will increase from 11·5% to 18·5%. Current shareholders may not be particularly concerned about this. However, if all or most of the share capital is bought for cash, the gearing level of the combined company will be significantly greater, at maximum 35·3%, than Louieed's current gearing. This may be unacceptable to current shareholders and could mean an increase in the cost of equity, because of the increased risk, and also possibly an increase in the cost of debt, assuming in any case that debt finance at the maximum level required will be available. To guard against this risk, Louieed's board may want to limit the cash offer to a certain percentage of share value.

Answer 3 STAPLE GROUP

(a)   Evaluation of disposal options

Staple Local

Net assets valuation = 15 ÷ 18 × $66·6m = $55·5m.
It is assumed that the titles in this division are equal in size.

The division's pre-tax profits are $4·5m and post-tax cash flows $0·3m, with losses forecast for the next year. Therefore any valuation based on current or future expected earnings is likely to be lower than the net assets valuation.

Benefits of selling Staple Local

The local newspapers seem to have the poorest prospects of any part of the group. Further investment may not make a big difference if the market for local newspapers is in long-term decline.

The offer from Postway gives Staple Group the chance to gain cash immediately and to dispose of the papers. The alternative of selling the titles off piecemeal is an uncertain strategy, both in terms of the timescale required and the amounts which can be realised for individual titles. It is very likely that the titles with the best prospects would be sold first, leaving Staple Group with a remaining portfolio which is of very little value.

Drawbacks of selling Staple Local

The offer is not much more than a net asset valuation of the titles. The amount of cash from the sale to Postway will be insufficient for the level of investment required in the Daily Staple.

The digital platforms which will be developed for the Daily Staple could also be used to boost the local papers. Staff on the local titles could have an important role to play in providing content for the platforms.

Loss of the local titles may mean loss of economies of size. In particular, printing arrangements may be more economic if both national and local titles are printed at the same locations.

Staple View

Free cash flows to equity = $53·5m – $12·5m – $6·2m = $34·8m

Tutorial note: *It is debatable as to whether the $6·2m for working capital should be deducted as the $53·5m is a cash flow figure, not a profit figure, and should already have been adjusted for working capital.*

Free cash flow valuation to equity = $34·8m (1·04) ÷ (0·12 – 0·04) = $452·4m

The assumption of constant growth is most important in this valuation. It is possibly fairly conservative, but just as faster growth could be achieved by gaining the rights to broadcast more sporting events, results may be threatened if Staple View loses any of the rights which it currently has.

Benefits of selling Staple View

Present circumstances may be favourable for selling the television channels, given their current profitability. Staple Group may be able to obtain a better offer from a competitor than in the future, given recent acquisition activity in this sector.

Selling Staple View will certainly generate more cash than selling either of the smaller divisions. This will allow investment not only in the Daily Staple, but also investment in the other divisions, and possibly targeted strategic acquisitions.

Drawbacks of selling Staple View

The television channels have become a very important part of the Staple Group. Investors may believe that the group should be focusing on further investment in this division rather than investing in the Daily Staple, which may be in decline.

Selling the television channels removes an important opportunity for cross-selling. Newspaper coverage can be used to publicise important programmes on the television channels and the television channels can be used for advertising the newspaper.

Staple View is a bigger part of the group than the other two divisions and therefore selling it is likely to mean a bigger reduction in the group's borrowing capacity.

Staple Investor

The valuation made by the finance director is questionable as it is based on one year's profits, which may not be sustainable. There is no information about how the additional earnings have been calculated, whether the finance director has used a widely-accepted method of valuation or just used a best estimate. If a premium for additional earnings is justified, there is also no information about whether the benefit from staff's expertise and experience is assumed to be perpetual or just to last for a certain number of years.

Benefits of selling Staple Investor

This division appears to have great potential. Staple Group will be able to sell this division from a position of strength, rather than it being seen as a forced sale like selling the Staple Local division might be.

The division is in a specialist sector which is separate from the other areas in which Staple Group operates. It is not an integral part of the group in terms of the directors' current core strategy.

Drawbacks of selling Staple Investor

The division currently has the highest profit margin at 19·7% compared with Staple National 12·5%, Staple Local 3·0% and Staple View 14·8%. It seems likely to continue to deliver good results over the next few years. Investors may feel that it is the part of the group which offers the safest prospect of satisfactory returns.

Investors may be happy with the structure of the group as it is, as it offers them some diversification. Selling the Staple Investor division and focusing more on the newspaper parts of the group may result in investors seeking diversification by selling some of the shareholding in Staple Group and investing elsewhere.

Although Staple Group's management may believe that the valuation gives a good indication of the division's true value, they may not be able to sell the division for this amount now. If the division remains within the group, they may achieve a higher price in a few years' time. Even if Staple Investor could be sold for the $118·5 million valuation, this is less than the $150 million required for the planned investment.

Conclusion

Selling the Staple View division offers the directors the best chance to obtain the funds they require for their preferred strategy of investment in the Daily Staple. However, the directors are not considering the possibility of selling the Daily Staple, perhaps in conjunction with selling the local newspapers as well. Although this could be seen as selling off the part of the group which has previously been essential to its success, it would allow Staple Group to raise the funds for further investment in the television channels and the Staple Investor division. It could allow the directors to focus on the parts of the group which have been the most successful recently and offer the best prospects for future success.

(b) **Proposal to reduce staff costs**

Stakeholder conflicts

If Staple Group takes a simple view of the role of stakeholders, it will prioritise the interest of shareholders over other stakeholders, particularly employees here, and take whatever actions are required to maximise profitability. However, in Staple Group's position, there may be a complication because of the differing requirements of shareholders. Some may want high short-term profits and dividends, which may imply significant cost cutting in under-performing divisions. Other shareholders may wish to see profits maximised over the long term and may worry that short-term cost cutting may result in a reduction of investment and adversely affect staff performance at an important time.

Transformational change of the newspaper business is likely to require the co-operation of at least some current employees. Inevitably redundancy will create uncertainty and perhaps prompt some staff to leave voluntarily. Staple Group's management may want to identify some key current employees who can lead the change and try to retain them.

Also the policy of making employees who have not been with the group very long redundant is likely to make it difficult to recruit good new employees. The group will probably create new roles as a result of its digital investment, but people may be unwilling to join the group if it has a reputation for bad faith and not fulfilling promises to develop its staff.

Ethical issues

The significance of what the firm's annual report says about its treatment of employees may depend on how specific it is. A promise to treat employees fairly is rather vague and may not carry much weight, although it broadly commits the firm to the ethical principle of objectivity. If, however, the policy makes more specific statements about engaging with employees and goes in the statement beyond what is required by law, then Staple Group is arguably showing a lack of honesty if it does not fulfil the commitments it has made.

The suggestion that managers should ensure that employees who are perceived to be "troublemakers" should be first to be chosen for redundancy is dubious ethically. If managers do this, then they may be breaking the law, and would certainly be acting with a lack of honesty and transparency.

Answer 4 FURLION CO

(a)   **Project appraisal including the (call) option to expand**

Variables

Exercise price (P_e) = capital expenditure = $15m

Exercise date (t) = 3 years

Value of the underlying asset (P_a) = *today's* value of cash flows occurring after the exercise date. As the NPV on commencing the expansion = 0, the value of returns = $15m in year three terms. In today's terms = $15m × 0·712 = $10·68m (where 0·712 is a three-year discount rate at the cost of capital)

Volatility (s) = 30% = 0.30

Risk free rate (r) = 4% = 0.04

d_1 = [ln(10·68 ÷ 15) + (0·04 + 0·5 × 0·3^2)3] ÷ (0·3 × √3) = –0·1630
d_2 = –0·1630 – 0·3 × √3 = –0·6826

$N(d_1)$ = 0·5 – 0·0636 = 0·4364 (using -0·16 for d_1)
$N(d_2)$ = 0·5 – 0·2517 = 0·2483 (using -0·68 for d_2)

Value of call option = Pa × $N(d_1)$ – Pe × $N(d_2)$ × e^{-rt}
= (10·68 × 0·4364) – (15 × 0·2483 × $e^{-0·04 \times 3}$)
= 4·66 – 3·30 = $1·36 million

Overall value of the project including the option to expand = $1·36m – $1·01m = $0·35m

The investment has a positive net present value, so should be accepted on those grounds. Furlion should also consider the value of an abandonment option if results turn out to be worse than expected or a delay option if it wants to see how the reclamation programme is going to continue.

Assumptions made and other factors

Using real options for decision-making has limitations. Real options are built around uncertainties surrounding future cash flows, but real option theory is only useful if management can respond effectively to these uncertainties as they evolve. The Black-Scholes model for valuing real options has a number of assumptions which may not be true in practice. It assumes that there is an active market for the underlying asset and the volatility of returns on the underlying asset follows a normal distribution. The model also assumes perfect markets, a constant risk-free interest rate and constant volatility.

Furlion will also consider expectations about the future of the land reclamation programme. Has the programme been as quick and as effective as the Naswan government originally expected? Furlion will also want to consider how the programme will be affected by the amount of funding the government obtains and any conditions attached to that funding.

Furlion may also wish to consider whether its investment of this type will be looked on favourably by the Naswan government and whether tax or other concessions will be available. These may come with conditions, given the government's commitment to a sustainable economy (e.g. the way production facilities operate or the treatment of employees).

Given that this is a market which may expand in the future, Furlion should also consider the reaction of competitors. This may be a market where establishing a significant presence quickly may provide a significant barrier if competitors try to enter the market later.

As the investment is for the manufacture of specialist equipment, it is possible that there is insufficient skilled labour in the local labour pool in Naswa. As well as training local labour, supervision is likely to be required, at least initially, from staff based in other countries. This may involve cultural issues (e.g. different working practices).

(b) **Rho**

The sensitivity of the valuation of options to interest rate changes can be measured by the option's rho. The option's rho is the amount of change in the option's value for a 1% change in the risk-free interest rate. The rho is positive for calls as the holder of a call option benefits from being able to delay payment for the underlying asset.

However, interest rates tend to move quite slowly and the interest rate is often not a significant influence on the option's value, particularly for short-term options. However, many real options are longer term and will have higher rhos than short-term options. A change in interest rates will be more significant the longer the time until expiry of an option. For example if interest rates rise then the present value of Furlion's $15m capital expenditure could fall significantly, effectively reducing the cost of investment and increasing the value of the option.

Also, there are possible indirect economic effects of interest rate changes (e.g. on the return demanded by finance providers and hence on the cost of capital). Therefore the present value of project returns may also fall, potentially outweighing the benefit of the lower cost of investment.

(c) **Funding from the World Bank**

The World Bank provides loans, often direct to governments, on a commercial basis, for capital projects. Loans are generally for a long-term period, which may suit the Naswan government. However, the terms of the loan may be onerous, not just the finance costs but the other conditions imposed on the scope of the projects.

Given the circumstances of the investment, Naswa may be able to obtain assistance from the International Development Association, which is part of the World Bank. This provides loans on more generous terms to the poorest countries. However, it is designed for countries with very high credit risk which would struggle to obtain funding by other means, and Naswa may not be eligible.

Advanced Financial Management

September/December 2016 – Sample Questions

Time allowed: 3 hours 15 minutes

This question paper is divided into two sections:

Section A – This ONE question is compulsory and MUST be attempted

Section B – TWO questions ONLY to be attempted

Formulae and tables Not reproduced

Do NOT open this question paper until instructed by the supervisor.

This question paper must not be removed from the examination hall.

Think Ahead

**The Association of
Chartered Certified
Accountants**

Section A – This ONE question is compulsory and MUST be attempted

1   Morada Co is involved in offering bespoke travel services and maintenance services. In addition to owning a few hotels, it has built strong relationships with companies in the hospitality industry all over the world. It has a good reputation of offering unique, high quality holiday packages at reasonable costs for its clients. The strong relationships have also enabled it to offer repair and maintenance services to a number of hotel chains and cruise ship companies.

Following a long discussion at a meeting of the board of directors (BoD) about the future strategic direction which Morada Co should follow, three directors continued to discuss one particular issue over dinner. In the meeting, the BoD had expressed concern that Morada Co was exposed to excessive risk and therefore its cost of capital was too high. The BoD feared that several good projects had been rejected over the previous two years, because they did not meet Morada Co's high cost of capital threshold. Each director put forward a proposal, which they then discussed in turn. At the conclusion of the dinner, the directors decided to ask for a written report on the proposals put forward by the first director and the second director, before taking all three proposals to the BoD for further discussion.

First director's proposal
The first director is of the opinion that Morada Co should reduce its debt in order to mitigate its risk and therefore reduce its cost of capital. He proposes that the company should sell its repair and maintenance services business unit and focus just on offering bespoke travel services and hotel accommodation. In the sale, the book value of non-current assets will reduce by 30% and the book value of current liabilities will reduce by 10%. It is thought that the non-current assets can be sold for an after-tax profit of 15%.

The first director suggests that the funds arising from the sale of the repair and maintenance services business unit and cash resources should be used to pay off 80% of the long-term debt. It is estimated that as a result of this, Morada Co's credit rating will improve from Baa2 to A2.

Second director's proposal
The second director is of the opinion that risk diversification is the best way to reduce Morada Co's risk and therefore reduce its cost of capital. He proposes that the company raise additional funds using debt finance and then create a new strategic business unit. This business unit will focus on construction of new commercial properties.

The second director suggests that $70 million should be borrowed and used to invest in purchasing non-current assets for the construction business unit. The new debt will be issued in the form of four-year redeemable bonds paying an annual coupon of 6·2%. It is estimated that if this amount of debt is raised, then Morada Co's credit rating will worsen to Ca3 from Baa2. Current liabilities are estimated to increase to $28 million.

Third director's proposal
The third director is of the opinion that Morada Co does not need to undertake the proposals suggested by the first director and the second director just to reduce the company's risk profile. She feels that the above proposals require a fundamental change in corporate strategy and should be considered in terms of more than just tools to manage risk. Instead, she proposes that a risk management system should be set up to appraise Morada Co's current risk profile, considering each type of business risk and financial risk within the company, and taking appropriate action to manage the risk where it is deemed necessary.

Morada Co, extracts from the forecast financial position for the coming year

	$000
Non-current assets	280,000
Current assets	48,000
Total assets	**328,000**
Equity and liabilities	
Share capital (40c/share)	50,000
Retained earnings	137,000
Total equity	**187,000**
Non-current liabilities (6·2% redeemable bonds)	120,000
Current liabilities	21,000
Total liabilities	**141,000**
Total liabilities and equity capital	**328,000**

Other financial information

Morada Co's forecast after-tax earnings for the coming year are expected to be $28 million. It is estimated that the company will make a 9% return after-tax on any new investment in non-current assets, and will suffer a 9% decrease in after-tax earnings on any reduction in investment in non-current assets.

Morada Co's current share price is $2·88 per share. According to the company's finance division, it is very difficult to predict how the share price will react to either the proposal made by the first director or the proposal made by the second director. Therefore it has been assumed that the share price will not change following either proposal.

The finance division has further assumed that the proportion of the book value of non-current assets invested in each business unit gives a fair representation of the size of each business unit within Morada Co.

Morada Co's equity beta is estimated at 1·2, while the asset beta of the repairs and maintenance services business unit is estimated to be 0·65. The relevant equity beta for the new, larger company including the construction unit relevant to the second director's proposals has been estimated as 1·21.

The bonds are redeemable in four years' time at face value. For the purposes of estimating the cost of capital, it can be assumed that debt beta is zero. However, the four-year credit spread over the risk free rate of return is 60 basis points for A2 rated bonds, 90 basis points for Baa2 rated bonds and 240 basis points for Ca3 rated bonds.

A tax rate of 20% is applicable to all companies. The current risk free rate of return is estimated to be 3·8% and the market risk premium is estimated to be 7%.

Required:

(a) Explain how business risk and financial risk are related; and how risk mitigation and risk diversification can form part of a company's risk management strategy. (6 marks)

(b) Prepare a report for the board of directors of Morada Co which:

   (i) Estimates Morada Co's cost of equity and cost of capital, based on market value of equity and debt, before any changes and then after implementing the proposals put forward by the first and by the second directors; (17 marks)

   (ii) Estimates the impact of the first and second directors' proposals on Morada Co's forecast after-tax earnings and forecast financial position for the coming year; and (7 marks)

   (iii) Discusses the impact on Morada Co of the changes proposed by the first and second directors and recommends whether or not either proposal should be accepted. The discussion should include an explanation of any assumptions made in the estimates in (b)(i) and (b)(ii) above. (9 marks)

Professional marks will be awarded in part (b) for the format, structure and presentation of the report. (4 marks)

(c) Discuss the possible reasons for the third director's proposal that a risk management system should consider each risk, before taking appropriate action. (7 marks)

(50 marks)

2 Fernhurst Co is a manufacturer of mobile communications technology. It is about to launch a new communications device, the Milland, which its directors believe is both more technologically advanced and easier to use than devices currently offered by its rivals.

Investment in the Milland

The Milland will require a major investment in facilities. Fernhurst Co's directors believe that this can take place very quickly and production be started almost immediately.

Fernhurst Co expects to sell 132,500 units of the Milland in its first year. Sales volume is expected to increase by 20% in Year 2 and 30% in Year 3, and then be the same in Year 4 as Year 3, as the product reaches the end of its useful life. The initial selling price in Year 1 is expected to be $100 per unit, before increasing with the rate of inflation annually.

The variable cost of each unit is expected to be $43·68 in year 1, rising by the rate of inflation in subsequent years annually. Fixed costs are expected to be $900,000 in Year 1, rising by the rate of inflation in subsequent years annually.

The initial investment in non-current assets is expected to be $16,000,000. Fernhurst Co will also need to make an immediate investment of $1,025,000 in working capital. The working capital will be increased annually at the start of each of Years 2 to 4 by the inflation rate and is fully recoverable at the end of the project's life. Fernhurst Co will also incur one-off marketing expenditure of $1,500,000 post inflation after the launch of the Milland. The marketing expenditure can be assumed to be made at the end of Year 1 and be a tax allowable expense.

Fernhurst Co pays company tax on profits at an annual rate of 25%. Tax is payable in the year that the tax liability arises. Tax allowable depreciation is available at 20% on the investment in non-current assets on a reducing balance basis. A balancing adjustment will be available in Year 4. The realisable value of the investment at the end of Year 4 is expected to be zero.

The expected annual rate of inflation in the country in which Fernhurst Co is located is 4% in Year 1 and 5% in Years 2 to 4.

The applicable cost of capital for this investment appraisal is 11%.

Other calculations

Fernhurst Co's finance director has indicated that besides needing a net present value calculation based on this data for the next board meeting, he also needs to know the figure for the project's duration, to indicate to the board how returns from the project will be spread over time.

Failure of launch of the Milland

The finance director would also like some simple analysis based on the possibility that the marketing expenditure is not effective and the launch fails, as he feels that the product's price may be too high. He has suggested that there is a 15% chance that the Milland will have negative net cash flows for Year 1 of $1,000,000 or more. He would like to know by what percentage the selling price could be reduced or increased to result in the investment having a zero net present value, assuming demand remained the same.

Assessment of new products

Fernhurst Co's last board meeting discussed another possible new product, the Racton, and the finance director presented a range of financial data relating to this product, including the results of net present value and payback evaluations. One of the non-executive directors, who is not a qualified accountant, stated that he found it difficult to see the significance of the different items of financial data. His understanding was that Fernhurst Co merely had to ensure that the investment had a positive net present value and shareholders were bound to be satisfied with it, as it would maximise their wealth in the long term. The finance director commented that, in reality, some shareholders looked at the performance of the investments which Fernhurst Co made over the short term, whereas some were more concerned with the longer term. The financial data he presented to board meetings included both short and long-term measures.

Required:

(a) Evaluate the financial acceptability of the investment in the Milland and, calculate and comment on the investment's duration. (15 marks)

(b) Calculate the % change in the selling price required for the investment to have a zero net present value, and discuss the significance of your results. (5 marks)

(c) Discuss the non-executive director's understanding of net present value and explain the importance of other measures in providing data about an investment's short and long-term performance. (5 marks)

(25 marks)

3 Chithurst Co gained a stock exchange listing five years ago. At the time of the listing, members of the family who founded the company owned 75% of the shares, but now they only hold just over 50%. The number of shares in issue has remained unchanged since Chithurst Co was listed. Chithurst Co's directors have continued the policy of paying a constant dividend per share each year which the company had before it was listed. However, investors who are not family members have become increasingly critical of this policy, saying that there is no clear rationale for it. They would prefer to see steady dividend growth, reflecting the increase in profitability of Chithurst Co since its listing.

The finance director of Chithurst Co has provided its board with details of Chithurst Co's dividends and investment expenditure, compared with two other similar-sized companies in the same sector, Eartham Co and Iping Co. Each company has a 31 December year end.

	Chithurst Co			Eartham Co			Iping Co		
	Profit for year after interest and tax	Dividend paid	New investment expenditure	Profit for year after interest and tax	Dividend paid	New investment expenditure	Profit for year after interest and tax	Dividend paid	New investment expenditure
	$m	$m	$m	$m	$m	$m	$m	$m	$m
2012	77	33	18	95	38	30	75	35	37
2013	80	33	29	(10)	15	15	88	17	64
2014	94	33	23	110	44	42	118	39	75
2015	97	33	21	120	48	29	132	42	84

Other financial information relating to the three companies is as follows:

	Chithurst Co	Eartham Co	Iping Co
Cost of equity	11%	14%	12%
Market capitalisation $m	608	1,042	1,164
Increase in share price in last 12 months	1%	5%	10%

Chithurst Co's finance director has estimated the costs of equity for all three companies.

None of the three companies has taken out significant new debt finance since 2011.

Required:

(a) **Discuss the benefits and drawbacks of the dividend policies which the three companies appear to have adopted. Provide relevant calculations to support your discussion.**

Note: Up to 5 marks are available for the calculations. (15 marks)

(b) **Discuss how the market capitalisation of the three companies compares with your valuations calculated using the dividend valuation model. Use the data provided to calculate valuations based on growth rates for the most recent year and for the last three years.**

Note: Up to 5 marks are available for the calculations. (10 marks)

(25 marks)

4 Pault Co is currently undertaking a major programme of product development. Pault Co has made a significant investment in plant and machinery for this programme. Over the next couple of years, Pault Co has also budgeted for significant development and launch costs for a number of new products, although its finance director believes there is some uncertainty with these budgeted figures, as they will depend upon competitor activity amongst other matters.

Pault Co issued floating rate loan notes, with a face value of $400 million, to fund the investment in plant and machinery. The loan notes are redeemable in ten years' time. The interest on the loan notes is payable annually and is based on the spot yield curve, plus 50 basis points.

Pault Co's finance director has recently completed a review of the company's overall financing strategy. His review has highlighted expectations that interest rates will increase over the next few years, although the predictions of financial experts in the media differ significantly.

The finance director is concerned about the exposure Pault Co has to increases in interest rates through the loan notes. He has therefore discussed with Millbridge Bank the possibility of taking out a four-year interest rate swap. The proposed terms are that Pault Co would pay Millbridge Bank interest based on an equivalent fixed annual rate of 4·847%. In return, Pault Co would receive from Millbridge Bank a variable amount based on the forward rates calculated from the annual spot yield curve rate at the time of payment minus 20 basis points. Payments and receipts would be made annually, with the first one in a year's time. Millbridge Bank would charge an annual fee of 25 basis points if Pault Co enters the swap.

The current annual spot yield curve rates are as follows:

Year	One	Two	Three	Four
Rate	3·70%	4·25%	4·70%	5·10%

A number of concerns were raised at the recent board meeting when the swap arrangement was discussed.

– Pault Co's chairman wondered what the value of the swap arrangement to Pault Co was, and whether the value would change over time.

– One of Pault Co's non-executive directors objected to the arrangement, saying that in his opinion the interest rate which Pault Co would pay and the bank charges were too high. Pault Co ought to stick with its floating rate commitment. Investors would be critical if, at the end of four years, Pault Co had paid higher costs under the swap than it would have done had it left the loan unhedged.

Required:

(a) (i) Using the current annual spot yield curve rates as the basis for estimating forward rates, calculate the amounts Pault Co expects to pay or receive each year under the swap (excluding the fee of 25 basis points). *(6 marks)*

(ii) Calculate Pault Co's interest payment liability for Year 1 if the yield curve rate is 4·5% or 2·9%, and comment on your results. *(6 marks)*

(b) Advise the chairman on the current value of the swap to Pault Co and the factors which would change the value of the swap. *(4 marks)*

(c) Discuss the disadvantages and advantages to Pault Co of not undertaking a swap and being liable to pay interest at floating rates. *(9 marks)*

(25 marks)

Answers

1 **(a)** The owners or shareholders of a business will accept that it needs to engage in some risky activities in order to generate returns in excess of the risk free rate of return. A business will be exposed to differing amounts of business and financial risk depending on the decisions it makes. Business risk depends on the decisions a business makes with respect to the services and products it offers and consists of the variability in its profits. For example, it could be related to the demand for its products, the rate of innovation, actions of competitors, etc. Financial risk relates to the volatility of earnings due to the financial structure of the business and could be related to its gearing, the exchange rate risk it is exposed to, its credit risk, its liquidity risk, etc. A business exposed to high levels of business risk may not be able to take excessive financial risk, and vice versa, as the shareholders or owners may not want to bear risk beyond an acceptable level.

Risk management involves the process of risk identification, of assessing and measuring the risk through the process of predicting, analysing and quantifying it, and then making decisions on which risks to assume, which to avoid, which to retain and which to transfer. As stated above, a business will not aim to avoid all risks, as it will want to generate excess returns. Dependent on factors such as controllability, frequency and severity of the risk, it may decide to eliminate or reduce some risks from the business through risk transfer. Risk mitigation is the process of transferring risks out of a business through, for example, hedging or insurance, or avoiding certain risks altogether. Risk diversification is a process of risk reduction through spreading business activity into different products and services, different geographical areas and/or different industries to minimise being excessively exposed by focusing exclusively on one product/service.

(b) **Report to the board of directors (BoD), Morada Co**

This report provides a discussion on the estimates of the cost of equity and the cost of capital and the impact on the financial position and the earnings after tax, as a result of the proposals put forward by the first director and the second director. The main assumptions made in drawing up the estimates will also be explained. The report concludes by recommending which of the two directors' proposals, if any, should be adopted.

Discussion
The table below shows the revised figures of the cost of equity and the cost of capital (appendix 1), and the forecast earnings after tax for the coming year (appendix 2), following each proposal from the first and second directors. For comparison purposes, figures before any changes are given as well.

	Cost of equity *Appendix 1*	Cost of capital *Appendix 1*	Earnings after tax *Appendix 2*
Current position	12·2%	10·0%	$28·0 million
Following first director's proposal	11·6%	11·1%	$37·8 million
Following second director's proposal	12·3%	9·8%	$30·8 million

Under the first director's proposal, although the cost of equity falls due to the lower financial risk in Morada Co because of less debt, the cost of capital actually increases. This is because, even though the cost of debt has decreased, the benefit of the tax shield is reduced significantly due to the lower amount of debt borrowing. Added to this is the higher business risk, reflected by the asset beta, of Morada Co just operating in the travel services sector. This higher business risk and reduced tax shield more than override the lower cost of debt resulting in a higher cost of capital.

Under the second director's proposal, the cost of equity is almost unchanged. There has been a significant increase in the cost of debt from 4·7% to 6·2%. However, the cost of capital has not reduced significantly because the benefit of the tax shield is also almost eroded by the increase in the cost of debt.

If no changes are made, then the forecast earnings after tax as a percentage of non-current assets is 10% ($28m/$280m). Under the first director's proposal, this figure almost doubles to 19·3% ($37·8m/$196m), and even if the one-off profit from the sale of non-current assets is excluded, this figure is still higher at 12·9% ($25·2m/$196m). Under the second director's proposal, this figure falls to 8·8% ($30·8m/$350m).

Assumptions
1. It is assumed that the asset beta of Morada Co is a weighted average of the asset betas of the travel services and the maintenance services business units, using non-current assets invested in each business unit as a fair representation of the size of each business unit and therefore the proportion of the business risk which business unit represents within the company.

2. The assumption of the share price not changing after either proposal is not reasonable. It is likely that due to changes in the business and financial risk from implementing either proposal, the risk profile of the company will change. The changes in the risk profile will influence the cost of equity, which in turn will influence the share price.

3. In determining the financial position of Morada Co, it is assumed that the current assets will change due to changes in the profit after tax figure; therefore this is used as the balancing figure for each proposal.

Recommendation
It is recommended that neither the first director's proposal nor the second director's proposal should be adopted. The second director's proposal results in a lower return on investment and a virtually unchanged cost of capital. So there will not be a

meaningful benefit for Morada Co. The first director's proposal does increase the return on investment but results in a higher cost of capital. If the reason for adopting either proposal is to reduce risk, then this is not achieved. The main caveat here is that where the assumptions made in the calculations are not reasonable, they will reduce the usefulness of the analysis.

Report compiled by:

Date:

(Note: Credit will be given for alternative and relevant points)

Appendix 1: Estimates of cost of equity and cost of capital

Before either proposal is implemented

Cost of equity (Ke) = $3·8\% + 1·2 \times 7\% = 12·2\%$
Cost of debt (Kd) = $3·8\% + 0·9\% = 4·7\%$

Market value of equity (MV_e) = $\$2·88 \times 125$ million shares = $\$360m$

Market value of debt (MV_d)
Per $100 $6·20 \times 1·047^{-1} + \$6·20 \times 1·047^{-2} + \$6·20 \times 1·047^{-3} + \$106·20 \times 1·047^{-4} = \$105·36$
Total MV_d = $\$105·36/\$100 \times \$120m = \$126·4m$

Cost of capital = $(12·2\% \times \$360m + 4·7\% \times 0·8 \times \$126·4m)/\$486·4m = 10·0\%$

If the first director's proposal is implemented

MV_e = $\$360m$
BV_d = $\$120m \times 0·2 = \$24m$
Kd = $4·4\%$

MV_d per $100 $6·20 \times 1·044^{-1} + \$6·20 \times 1·044^{-2} + \$6·20 \times 1·044^{-3} + \$106·20 \times 1·044^{-4} = \$106·47$
Total MV_d = $106·47/\$100 \times \$24 = \$25·6m$

Morada Co, asset beta
$1·2 \times \$360m/(\$360m + \$126·4m \times 0·8) = 0·94$
Asset beta of travel services = $[0·94 - (0·65 \times 30\%)]/70\% = 1·06$
Equity beta of travel services = $1·06 \times (\$360m + \$25·6m \times 0·8)/\$360m = 1·12$

Ke = $3·8\% + 1·12 \times 7\% = 11·6\%$
Cost of capital = $(11·6\% \times \$360m + 4·4\% \times 0·8 \times \$25·6m)/\$385·6 = 11·1\%$

If the second director's proposal is implemented

MV_e = $\$360m$
The basis points for the Ca3 rated bond is 240 basis points higher than the risk free-free rate of interest, giving a cost of debt of 6·2%, therefore:
MV_d = $BV_d = \$190m$

Equity beta of the new, larger company = $1·21$

Ke = $3·8\% + 1·21 \times 7\% = 12·3\%$
Cost of capital = $(12·3\% \times \$360m + 6·2\% \times 0·8 \times \$190m)/\$550m = 9·8\%$

Appendix 2: Estimates of forecast after-tax earnings and forecast financial position

Morada Co, extracts from the forecast after-tax earnings for the coming year
(Amounts in $ 000s)

	Current forecast	Forecast: first director proposal	Forecast: second director proposal
Current forecast after-tax earnings	28,000	28,000	28,000
Interest saved due to lower borrowing ($96m x 6·2% x 0·8)		4,762	
Interest payable on additional borrowing ($70m x 6·2% x 0·8)			(3,472)
Reduction in earnings due to lower investment (9% x $84m)		(7,560)	
Additional earnings due to higher investment (9% x $70m)			6,300
Profit on sale of non-current assets (15% x $84m)		12,600	
Revised forecast after-tax earnings	28,000	37,802	30,828
Increase in after-tax earnings		9,802	2,828

Morada Co, extracts from the forecast financial position for the coming year
(Amounts in $ 000s)

	Current forecast	Forecast: first director proposal	Forecast: second director proposal
Non-current assets	280,000	196,000	350,000
Current assets (balancing figure)	48,000	43,702	57,828
Total assets	328,000	239,702	407,828
Equity and liabilities			
Share capital (40c/share)	50,000	50,000	50,000
Retained earnings**	137,000	146,802	139,828
Total equity	187,000	196,802	189,828
Non-current liabilities (6·2% redeemable bonds)	120,000	24,000	190,000
Current liabilities	21,000	18,900	28,000
Total liabilities	141,000	42,900	218,000
Total liabilities and capital	328,000	239,702	407,828

** **Note:** With the two directors' proposals, the retained earnings amount is adjusted to reflect the revised forecast after-tax earnings.

(c) [**Note:** *This is an open-ended question and a variety of relevant answers can be given by candidates depending on how the question requirement is interpreted. The following answer is just one possible approach which could be taken. Credit will be given for alternative, but valid, interpretations and answers therein.*]

According to the third director, risk management involves more than just risk mitigation or risk diversification as proposed by the first and second directors. The proposals suggested by the first and the second directors are likely to change the make-up of the company, and cause uncertainty amongst the company's owners or clientele. This in turn may cause unnecessary fluctuations in the share price. She suggests that these changes are fundamental and more than just risk management tools.

Instead, it seems that she is suggesting that Morada Co should follow the risk management process suggested in part (a) above, where risks should be identified, assessed and then mitigated according to the company's risk appetite.

The risk management process should be undertaken with a view to increasing shareholder wealth, and therefore the company should consider what drives this value and what are the risks associated with these drivers of value. Morada Co may assess that some of these risks are controllable and some not controllable. It may assess that some are severe and others less so, and it may assess some are likely to occur more frequently than others.

Morada Co may take the view that the non-controllable, severe and/or frequent risks should be eliminated (or not accepted). On the other hand, where Morada Co is of the opinion that it has a comparative advantage or superior knowledge of risks, and therefore is better able to manage them, it may come to the conclusion that it should accept these. For example, it may take the view that it is able to manage events such as flight delays or hotel standards, but would hedge against currency fluctuations and insure against natural disasters due to their severity or non-controllability.

Theory suggests that undertaking risk management may increase the value of a company if the benefits accruing from the risk management activity are more than the costs involved in managing the risks. For example, smoothing the volatility of profits may make it easier for Morada Co to plan and match long-term funding with future projects, it may make it easier for Morada Co to take advantage of market imperfections by reducing the amount of taxation payable, or it may reduce the costs involved with incidences of financial distress. In each case though, the benefits accrued should be assessed against the costs involved.

Therefore, a risk management process is more than just mitigating risk through reducing financial risk as the first director is suggesting or risk diversification as the second director is suggesting. Instead it is a process of risk analysis and then about judgement of which risks to hedge or mitigate, and finally, which risk-reduction mechanisms to employ, depending on the type of risk, the cost of the risk analysis and mitigation, and the benefits accruing from the mitigation.

2 (a)

	0 $000	1 $000	2 $000	3 $000	4 $000
Sales revenue (W1)		13,250	16,695	22,789	23,928
Variable costs (W2)		(5,788)	(7,292)	(9,954)	(10,452)
Contribution		7,462	9,403	12,835	13,476
Marketing expenditure		(1,500)			
Fixed costs		(900)	(945)	(992)	(1,042)
Tax-allowable depreciation (W3)		(3,200)	(2,560)	(2,048)	(8,192)
Taxable profits/(losses)		1,862	5,898	9,795	4,242
Taxation (25%)		(466)	(1,475)	(2,449)	(1,061)
Add back tax-allowable depreciation		3,200	2,560	2,048	8,192
Cash flows after tax		4,596	6,983	9,394	11,373
Initial investment	(16,000)				
Working capital	(1,025)	(41)	(53)	(56)	1,175
Cash flows	(17,025)	4,555	6,930	9,338	12,548
Discount factor	1·000	0·901	0·812	0·731	0·659
Present values	(17,025)	4,104	5,627	6,826	8,269
Net present value	7,801				

The NPV is positive, which indicates the project should be undertaken.

Workings

W1: Sales revenue

Year		$000
1	132,500 x 100	13,250
2	132,500 x 100 x 1·05 x 1·2	16,695
3	132,500 x 100 x 1·05^2 x 1·2 x 1·3	22,789
4	132,500 x 100 x 1·05^3 x 1·2 x 1·3	23,928

W2: Variable costs

Year		$m
1	132,500 x 43·68	5,788
2	132,500 x 43·68 x 1·05 x 1·2	7,292
3	132,500 x 43·68 x 1·05^2 x 1·2 x 1·3	9,954
4	132,500 x 43·68 x 1·05^3 x 1·2 x 1·3	10,452

W3: Tax allowable depreciation

Year		$000
		16,000
1	Tax-allowable depreciation	(3,200)
		12,800
2	Tax-allowable depreciation	(2,560)
		10,240
3	Tax-allowable depreciation	(2,048)
		8,192
4	Balancing allowance	(8,192)
		0

Duration

Year	1	2	3	4
Present value $000	4,104	5,627	6,826	8,269
Percentage of total PV	16·5%	22·7%	27·5%	33·3%

Duration = (1 x 0·165) + (2 x 0·227) + (3 x 0·275) + (4 x 0·333) = 2·78 years

The result indicates that it will take approximately 2·78 years to recover half the present value of the project. Duration considers the time value of money and all of the cash flows of a project.

(b) Reduction in selling price

Discounted revenue cash flows = (13,250 x 0·75 x 0·901) + (16,695 x 0·75 x 0·812) + (22,789 x 0·75 x 0·731) + (23,928 x 0·75 x 0·659) = $43,441,000

Reduction in selling price = 7,801/43,441 = 18·0%

Fernhurst Co would appear to have some scope to reduce the price in order to guarantee the success of the product launch. It would be useful to know whether the finance director's views on the success of the product would change if the product was launched at a lower price. There may be scope to launch at a price which is more than 18·0% lower than the planned launch price, and increase the sales price subsequently by more than the rate of inflation if the launch is a success.

If the directors are unwilling to reduce the price, then their decision will depend on whether they are willing to consider other ways of mitigating a failed launch or take a chance that the product will make a loss and be abandoned. They will take into account both the probability (15%) of the loss and the magnitude (at least $1,000,000 but possibly higher).

Presumably the finance director's assessment of the probability of a loss is based more on doubts about the demand level rather than the level of costs, as costs should be controllable. Possibly Fernhurst Co's directors may consider a smaller scale launch to test the market, but then Fernhurst Co would still be left with expensive facilities if the product were abandoned. The decision may therefore depend on what alternative uses could be made of the new facilities.

(c) The non-executive director has highlighted the importance of long-term maximisation of shareholders' wealth. The net present value is the most important indicator of whether an investment is likely to do that. However, the assessment of investments using net present value has to be modified if the company is undertaking a number of different investments and capital is rationed. It is not necessarily the case that the investments with the highest net present value will be chosen, as account has to be taken of the amount of capital invested as well.

However, investors are not necessarily concerned solely with the long term. They are also concerned about short-term indicators, such as the annual dividend which the company can sustain. They may be concerned if the company's investment portfolio is weighted towards projects which will produce good long-term returns, but limited returns in the near future.

Risk will also influence shareholders' views. They may prefer investments where a higher proportion of returns are made in the shorter term, if they feel that longer term returns are much more uncertain. The NPV calculation itself discounts longer term cash flows more than shorter term cash flows.

The payback method shows how long an investment will take to generate enough returns to pay back its investment. It favours investments which pay back quickly, although it fails to take into account longer term cash flows after the payback period. Duration is a better measure of the distribution of cash flows, although it may be less easy for shareholders to understand.

3 (a) Dividend payout ratio

	Chithurst Co	Eartham Co	Iping Co
	%	%	%
2012	42·9	40·0	46·7
2013	41·3	(150·0)	19·3
2014	35·1	40·0	33·1
2015	34·0	40·0	31·8

Residual profit (after-tax profit for the year – dividend – new investment)

	Chithurst Co	Eartham Co	Iping Co
	$m	$m	$m
2012	26	27	3
2013	18	(40)	7
2014	38	24	4
2015	43	43	6

Chithurst Co's policy

Benefits
Chithurst Co's policy provides shareholders with a stable, predictable income each year. As profits have grown consistently, dividend cover has increased, which suggests that, for now, dividend levels are sustainable. These are positive signals to the stock market.

Drawbacks
Chithurst Co's dividend policy is unpopular with some of its shareholders. They have indicated a preference for dividend levels to bear a greater relation to profit levels. Although they are still in a minority and cannot force the directors to pay more dividends, they are now possibly a significant minority. Ultimately, Chithurst Co's share price could fall significantly if enough shareholders sell their shares because they dislike the dividend policy.

The dividend policy may also have been established to meet the financial needs of the shareholders when Chithurst Co was unquoted. However, it is now difficult to see how it fits into Chithurst Co's overall financial strategy. The greater proportion of funds retained does not appear to be linked to the levels of investment Chithurst Co is undertaking. Chithurst Co's shareholders may be concerned that best use is not being made of the funds available. If there are profitable investments which Chithurst Co could be making but is not doing so, then Chithurst Co may find it more difficult in future to sustain the levels of profit growth. Alternatively, if profitable investments do not exist, some shareholders may prefer to have funds returned in the form of a special dividend or share repurchase.

Eartham Co

Benefits

For three out of four years, Eartham Co has been paying out dividends at a stable payout ratio. This may be attractive to some investors, who have expectations that the company's profits will keep increasing in the longer term and wish to share directly in increases in profitability.

The year when Eartham Co's dividend payout ratio differed from the others was 2013, when Eartham Co made a loss. A dividend of $15 million was paid in 2013, which may be a guaranteed minimum. This limits the downside risk of the dividend payout policy to shareholders, as they know they will receive this minimum amount in such a year.

Drawbacks

Although shareholders are guaranteed a minimum dividend each year, dividends have been variable. Eartham Co's shareholders may prefer dividends to increase at a steady rate which is sustainable over time, even if this rate is lower than the rate of increase in some years under the current policy.

If Eartham Co had another poor year of trading like 2013, shareholders' expectations that they will be paid a minimum dividend may mean that cash has to be earmarked to pay the minimum dividend, rather than for other, maybe better, uses in the business.

Having a 'normal' dividend policy results in expectations about what the level of dividend will be. Over time Eartham Co's managers may be reluctant to change to a lower payout ratio because they fear that this will give shareholders an adverse signal. Even if its directors maintain a constant ratio normally, shareholders may question whether the proportion of funds being retained is appropriate or whether a higher proportion could be paid out as dividends.

Eartham Co appears to be linking investment and dividend policy by its normal policy of allocating a constant proportion of funds for dividends and therefore a constant proportion of funds to invest. However, the actual level of new investments does not seem to bear much relation to the proportion of funds put aside for investment. When deciding on investments, the directors would also take into account the need to take advantage of opportunities as they arise and the overall amount of surplus funds built up over the years, together with the other sources of external finance available.

Iping Co

Benefits

Iping Co seems to have adopted a residual dividend policy, which links investment and dividend decisions. The strategy appears to be to make investments if they offer sufficient return to increase long-term company value and only pay dividends if there are no more profitable investments. They are assuming that internal funds are cheaper than external funds, or maybe Iping Co cannot raise the funds required from external sources.

The policy is likely to appeal to shareholders who are more concerned with capital growth than short-term income.

Drawbacks

Dividend payments are totally unpredictable, as they depend on the investment choices. Shareholders cannot rely on having any dividend income in a particular year.

Many shareholders may be prepared to sacrifice dividends for a while in order for funds to be available for investment for growth. However, at some point they may consider that Iping Co is well established enough to be able to maintain a consistent dividend policy as well as invest sufficiently for future growth.

(b) **Use of dividend valuation model**

Chithurst Co
Valuation = 33/0·11 = $300m

Chithurst Co's market capitalisation of $608m is considerably in excess of the valuation suggested by the dividend valuation model. This may suggest that investors have some positive expectations about the company and the lower cost of equity compared with the other two companies suggests it is regarded as a more stable investment. Investors could also be valuing the company using earnings growth rather than dividend growth. However, the lower market capitalisation compared with the other two companies and the smaller increase in share price suggest that investors have higher expectations of long-term growth from Eartham Co and Iping Co.

Eartham Co
One-year growth rate = $(48/44) - 1 = 9\cdot1\%$
Valuation using one-year growth rate = $48 (1 + 0\cdot091)/(0\cdot14 - 0\cdot091) = \$1,068\cdot7m$

Three-year growth rate = $\sqrt[3]{(48/38)} - 1 = 8\cdot1\%$
Valuation using three-year growth rate = $48 (1 + 0\cdot081)/(0\cdot14 - 0\cdot081) = \$879m$

Eartham Co's market capitalisation is closer to the valuation suggested by the dividend growth model using the one-year growth rate between 2014 and 2015 rather than the three-year growth rate between 2012 and 2015. This, together with the recent increase in share price, suggests that Eartham Co's shareholders have an optimistic view of its ability to sustain the profit growth and hence the dividend growth of the last two years, although its higher cost of equity than the other companies suggests that they are more wary about the risks of investing in Eartham Co. It indicates confidence in the directors' strategy, including the investments they have made.

Iping Co
One-year growth rate = (42/39) – 1 = 7·7%
Valuation using one-year growth rate = 42 (1 + 0·077)/(0·12 – 0·077) = \$1,052·0m

Three-year growth rate = $\sqrt[3]{(42/35)}$ – 1 = 6·3%
Valuation using three-year growth rate = 42 (1 + 0·063)/(0·12 – 0·063) = \$783·3m

The market capitalisation of Iping Co is higher than is suggested by the dividend valuation model, but the dividend valuation model may not provide a realistic valuation because dividends payable are dependent on investment opportunities.

The larger increase in share price compared with the other two companies suggests that Iping Co's investors expect its investments to produce high long-term returns and hence are presumably satisfied with its dividend policy.

4 (a) (i) Gross amount of annual interest paid by Pault Co to Millbridge Bank = 4·847% x \$400m = \$19·39m.

Gross amounts of annual interest receivable by Pault Co from Millbridge Bank, based on Year 1 spot rates and Years 2–4 forward rates:

Year
1   0·0350 x \$400m = \$14m
2   0·0460 x \$400m = \$18·4m
3   0·0541 x \$400m = \$21·64m
4   0·0611 x \$400m = \$24·44m

Working

Year 2 forward rate: $(1·0425^2/1·037)$ – 1 = 4·80%
Year 3 forward rate: $(1·0470^3/1·0425^2)$ – 1 = 5·61%
Year 4 forward rate: $(1·0510^4/1·0470^3)$ – 1 = 6·31%

Rates are reduced by 20 basis points in calculation.

At the start of the swap, Pault will expect to pay or receive the following net amounts at each of the next four years:

Year
1   \$14m – \$19·39m = \$(5·39m) payment
2   \$18·4m – \$19·39m = \$(0·99m) payment
3   \$21·64m – \$19·39m = \$2·25m receipt
4   \$24·44m – \$19·39m = \$5·05m receipt

(ii) Interest payment liability

	Impact %	Yield interest 2·9% \$m	Yield interest 4·5% \$m
Borrow at yield interest + 50 bp	(Yield + 0·5)	(13·60)	(20·00)
Receive yield – 20 bp	Yield – 0·2	10·80	17·20
Pay fixed 4·847%	(4·847)	(19·39)	(19·39)
Bank fee – 25 bp	(0·25)	(1·00)	(1·00)
	(5·797)	(23·19)	(23·19)

The interest payment liability will be \$23·19m, whatever the yield interest, as the receipt and payment are based on the yield curve net of interest rate fluctuations.

(b) At the start of the contract, the value of the swap will be zero. The terms offered by Millbridge Bank equate the discounted value of the fixed rate payments by Pault Co with the variable rate payments by Millbridge Bank.

However, the value of the swap will not remain at zero. If interest rates increase more than expected, Pault Co will benefit from having to pay a fixed rate and the value of the swap will increase. The value of the swap will also change as the swap approaches maturity, with fewer receipts and payments left.

(c) Disadvantages of swap arrangement
The swap represents a long-term commitment at a time when interest rates appear uncertain. It may be that interest rates rises are lower than expected. In this case, Pault Co will be committed to a higher interest rate and its finance costs may be higher than if it had not taken out the finance arrangements. Pault Co may not be able to take action to relieve this commitment if it becomes clear that the swap was unnecessary.

On the basis of the expected forward rates, Pault Co will not start benefiting from the swap until Year 3. Particularly during Year 1, the extra commitment to interest payments may be an important burden at a time when Pault Co will have significant development and launch costs.

Pault Co will be liable for an arrangement fee. However, other methods of hedging which could be used will have a cost built into them as well.

Advantages of swap arrangement

The swap means that the annual interest payment liability will be fixed at $23·19m over the next four years. This is a certain figure which can be used in budgeting. Having a fixed figure may help planning, particularly as a number of other costs associated with the investment are uncertain.

The directors will be concerned not just about the probability that floating rates will result in a higher commitment than under the swap, but also be concerned about how high this commitment could be. The directors may feel that rates may possibly rise to a level which would give Pault Co problems in meeting its commitments and regard that as unacceptable.

Any criticism after the end of the loan period will be based on hindsight. What appeared to be the cheapest choice at that stage may not have been what appeared most likely to be the cheapest choice when the loan was taken out. In addition, criticism of the directors for not choosing the cheapest option fails to consider risk. The cheapest option may be the most risky. The directors may reasonably take the view that the saving in cost is not worth the risks incurred.

The swap is for a shorter period than the loan and thus allows Pault Co to reconsider the position in four years' time. It may choose to take out another swap then on different terms, or let the arrangement lapse and pay floating rate interest on the loan, depending on the expectations at that time of future interest rates.

				Marks
1	**(a)**	Relationship between business and financial risk		3
		Risk mitigation and risk diversification as part of a company's risk management strategy		3
				6

			Marks
(b)	**(i)**	[Appendix 1]	
		Prior to implementation of any proposal	
		Cost of equity	1
		Cost of debt	1
		Market value of equity	1
		Market value of debt	2
		Cost of capital	1
		After implementing the first director's proposal	
		Market value of debt	2
		Morada Co, asset beta	1
		Asset beta of travel services only	1
		Equity beta of travel services only	1
		Cost of equity	1
		Cost of capital	1
		After implementing the second director's proposal	
		Market value of debt	2
		Cost of equity	1
		Cost of capital	1
			17

				Marks
	(ii)	[Appendix 2]		
		Adjusted earnings, first director's proposal		2
		Financial position, first director's proposal		2
		Adjusted earnings, second director's proposal		2
		Financial position, second director's proposal		1
				7

				Marks
	(iii)	Discussion		5–6
		Assumptions		2–3
		Reasoned recommendation		1–2
		(Note: Maximum 8 marks if no recommendation given)	Max	9

			Marks
Professional marks for part (b)			
Report format			1
Structure and presentation of the report			3
			4

				Marks
(c)	1–2 marks per point		Max	7
			Total	**50**

2 **(a)** Sales revenue 2
Variable costs 2
Fixed costs 1
Tax-allowable depreciation 2
Tax payable 1
Working capital 2
NPV of project 1
Comment on NPV 1
Duration calculation 2
Comment on duration 1
_____
15

(b) Reduction in selling price 3
Discussion 2–3
Max 5

(c) Significance of net present value 1–2
Shareholders' attitude to the longer and shorter term 2–3
Timeframe measures 1–2
Max 5
Total 25

3 **(a)** Benefits of dividend policy – 1–2 marks for each company Max 5
Drawbacks of dividend policy – 2–3 marks for each company Max 7
Calculations – Dividend payout ratios – 1 mark per company 3
Other calculations 2
Max 15

(b) Comments on valuation of each company, max 4 marks per company
(max 5 marks for valuation calculation(s)) Max 10
Total 25

4 **(a)** **(i)** Gross amount payable by Pault Co 1
Calculation of forward rates 3
Basis point reduction 1
Net amounts receivable or payable each year 1
_____
6

(ii) Yield interest calculations 5
Comment on interest payment liability 1
_____
6

(b) Up to 2 marks per point Max 4

(c) Advantages (up to 2 marks per relevant point) Max 5
Disadvantages (up to 2 marks per relevant point) Max 5
Max 9
Total 25

ABOUT BECKER PROFESSIONAL EDUCATION

Becker Professional Education provides a single solution for students and professionals looking to advance their careers and achieve success in:

- Accounting
- International Financial Reporting
- Project Management
- Continuing Professional Education
- Healthcare

For more information on how Becker Professional Education can support you in your career, visit www.becker.com/acca.